Introduction to Preaching

Scripture, Theology, and Sermon Preparation

Leah D. Schade, Jerry L. Sumney, and Emily Askew

ROWMAN & LITTLEFIELD
Lanham • Boulder • New York • London

Acquisitions Editor: Richard Brown
Acquisitions Assistant: Jaylene Perez
Sales and Marketing Inquiries: textbooks@rowman.com

Credits and acknowledgments for material borrowed from other sources, and reproduced with permission, appear on the appropriate pages within the text.

Published by Rowman & Littlefield
An imprint of The Rowman & Littlefield Publishing Group, Inc.
4501 Forbes Boulevard, Suite 200, Lanham, Maryland 20706
www.rowman.com

86-90 Paul Street, London EC2A 4NE

British Library Cataloguing in Publication Information available

Library of Congress Cataloging-in-Publication Data

978-1-5381-3859-5 (cloth)
978-1-5381-3860-1 (paperback)
978-1-5381-3861-8 (electronic)

∞™ The paper used in this publication meets the minimum requirements of American National Standard for Information Sciences—Permanence of Paper for Printed Library Materials, ANSI/NISO Z39.48-1992.

We dedicate this book to our past and future students
and pray that they will experience great joy, challenge,
and blessing as they follow the path of preaching.

Contents

List of Sermons

Guidance for the Instructor

This book is intended for readers from within the mainline Protestant spectrum of Christianity, though we believe that the method we offer here can be used by preachers within other traditions as well. As authors, we note that all three of us are white, able-bodied, and middle class, thus limiting our understanding of what it means to experience marginalization. Nevertheless, there are other diversity factors among us. Two of us are female. One is a lesbian. Two are located within the Disciples of Christ denomination; one of us is Lutheran (ELCA). What we share in common is a commitment to helping our students understand the complexities and intersectionalities of different forms of oppression. We share a common orientation to Progressive Christian values such as the ordination of women, LGBTQIA+ rights, racial and ethnic justice, attention to the marginalized, and care for God's Creation.

Breaking down the preaching process into discrete parts and laying them out in a particular order as we do in this book does run the risk of giving the impression that sermon preparation must always be done in a methodical, step-by-step process, when, in fact, creating a sermon is often much more fluid and nonlinear. It also may give the incorrect idea that biblical exegesis, theology, and the sermon-writing process are siloed into separate building blocks. In reality, the areas overlap and intersect with one another all along the way.

Our pedagogical philosophy is that by learning the different aspects of preaching piece by piece and step by step, we can focus on each component in its own right. This means that we focus on each part in turn, even while acknowledging that the process of preparing to preach is rarely so neatly categorized, nor does it always happen in this linear fashion. Nevertheless, we want students to see each aspect of sermon preparation as clearly and distinctly as possible in order to have a methodical foundation for learning how to preach. Once these areas are studied and understood, it is easy to see how they are interwoven and co-inform one another.

Some instructors may find this approach to be too formulaic, preferring a more intuitive, right-brain approach to creating a sermon. However, we have found that, similar to the way music students benefit from learning a step-by-step method for playing an instrument, beginning preachers have a good chance of building a skill set for preaching when using a more methodical approach.

Others may be concerned that adhering to such a methodical process could squelch the role of inspiration and the spontaneity of the Holy Spirit. So we want to be clear that this process is meant to serve as a scaffold for sermon preparation, not as a mechanical formula devoid of creativity. While some may find the process too restrictive or rigid, we have found that our students, many of whom are learning to preach for the first time, appreciate the step-by-step approach.

This is not to say that the elements of the book must be followed in lockstep. This textbook offers flexibility for use in different classroom settings and for different pedagogical configurations. The most obvious is to work through the chapters in chronological order. However, different chapters can be used as stand-alone readings in courses such as scriptural interpretation for preaching, theology and preaching, sermon preparation, the performative aspects of preaching, addressing social issues in preaching, or an entire sequence of the above courses. The exercises and appendices can be used as supplemental material in any preaching class.

Also, the chapters do not necessarily need to be followed in order. It is possible to start with identifying theological claims in Part II (chapters 8–11) then go back to Part I (chapters 1–7) for a course on exegesis for preaching. Instructors could also start with the "Central" chapters in Part III (chapters 12–17) and supplement with the previous chapters as needed for each step. Overall, we intend for this textbook to be a "one-stop-shop" with all the basic tools a preacher needs for preparing their sermons as well as preaching and delivering them effectively.

The process we are laying out in this book has been tested with our students over many years. Between the three of us, we have fifty years' worth of teaching experience, and we are grateful for the feedback our students have given us as we have tried new ideas, tweaked different approaches, and experimented with various learning exercises.

NOTE FOR HOMILETICS INSTRUCTORS: WHAT'S THE DIFFERENCE BETWEEN THE CENTRAL QUESTION, CENTRAL CLAIM, AND CENTRAL PURPOSE AND TOM LONG'S FOCUS AND FUNCTION STATEMENTS?

The first edition of Thomas G. Long's preaching textbook, *The Witness of Preaching*, was published in 1989 and has been a staple of homiletics classrooms for more than thirty years. One of the fundamentals to Long's method of teaching preaching was to have students write out focus and function statements for their sermons to help them move from the event of encountering a biblical text to making a claim about that text for preaching to the event of the sermon itself. "What the sermon aims to say can be called its 'focus,' and what the sermon aims to do can be called its 'function.'"[1]

This method has provided helpful guidance for preachers for three generations. Leah learned this method as a seminary student in the 1990s and has taught it to her students as a homiletics professor. However, what she found is that some students tend to get confused by what the terms "focus" and "function" mean, and this can lead to sermons that lack a clear theological claim, discernible direction, or solid coherence. This is not a fault of Long's method; rather, it has to do with students needing more basic direction and step-by-step instructions.

For example, Long states that "a focus statement is a concise description of the central, controlling, and unifying theme of the sermon. In short, this is what the whole sermon will be 'about.'"[2] Although he goes on to give examples that demonstrate how the claim from the text can manifest as the focus statement in the sermon, some students take the terminology and definition more literally and miss the point of the exercise. This leads students to write a statement only explaining what they are *focusing on* rather than clearly articulating the claim they are making in the sermon, as in: "This sermon will focus on forgiveness." Or "I will focus on why David needed to be held accountable when he ordered the death of Bathsheba's husband." In other words, students sometimes mistakenly take the focus statement to mean that they are only to talk *about* the general idea of the sermon rather than clearly articulate the point they want to make in the sermon that will make a difference in the lives of their hearers.

Students also have had trouble with the function statement by sometimes missing the point of that exercise as well. Long defines the function statement as "a description of what the preacher hopes the sermon will create or cause to happen for the hearers. Sermons make demands upon the hearers, which is another way of saying that they provoke change in the hearers (even if the change is a deepening of something already present). The function statement names the hoped-for change."[3] Again, the issue is not with Long's definition. Rather, the most common mistake students make is to write a second focus statement, such as "The function of this sermon is to explain that forgiveness is a vital spiritual discipline for Christians." Note that this sentence is really making a claim rather than stating what the sermon is supposed to do.

In response to this, Leah began experimenting with how to lead students through a process that more clearly explains the "why," "what," and "how" of developing a sermon. These became the Central Question, Central Claim, and Central Purpose. This method is intended to help students move step by step through the process of scriptural exegesis, theological analysis, interpretation of one's congregation and community, and delineation of the claim and purpose of the sermon.

NOTES

1. Thomas G. Long, *The Witness of Preaching*, third edition (Louisville, KY: Westminster John Knox, 2016), 126.
2. Ibid., 127.
3. Ibid.

Acknowledgments

We wish to thank Lexington Theological Seminary for the opportunity given to the three of us to teach in our respective disciplines and to collaborate in our pedagogy. We are grateful to our faculty colleagues who have encouraged us both individually and collectively over the years.

We especially thank O. Wesley Allen Jr., Lois Craddock Perkins Professor of Homiletics at Perkins School of Theology at Southern Methodist University, for the role he played in the original conception and design of a method to bring together biblical exegesis, theology, and preaching. As the associate professor of preaching and worship at Lexington Theological Seminary from 2003 to 2015, Wes worked with Emily Askew to help students think theologically about their preaching. He also worked with Jerry Sumney to develop what has become the Exegesis Guide Chart we use in this book. His creativity and scholarship contributed significantly to our work.

The team at Rowman & Littlefield has been a source of steadfast support and guidance for this project. We thank Rolf Janke, who originally approached us with the idea of creating a preaching textbook. We also thank our editor, Natalie Mandziuk, who shepherded the process to bring this book to fruition. Richard Brown helped to get us across the goal line, so to speak, and his expertise has been invaluable. And the behind-the-scenes work of Jaylene Perez and Elaine McGarraugh was essential. We are also grateful to the peer reviewers who provided crucial feedback and suggestions that significantly improved the manuscript.

Leah wishes to thank the congregations of Reformation Lutheran Church in Media, Pennsylvania; Spirit and Truth Worship Center in Yeadon, Pennsylvania; United in Christ Lutheran Church in Lewisburg, Pennsylvania; St. Thomas Lutheran Church in Richmond, Kentucky; and the many other congregations in which she has preached during the past twenty-five years.

Finally, we give thanks for the countless students we have taught over the decades. Leah wishes to especially acknowledge the students she taught at both Lexington Theological Seminary and the TEEM Certificate Program (Theological Education for Emerging Ministries) through Pacific Lutheran Seminary. Many of them read first drafts of these chapters as part of courses and noted areas that needed clarification or reorganization. Special thanks to Tanyce Addison, Dawn David, Wilma Garing, Charlie Martin, Robin Small, and Rebecca West-Estell, who gave us permission to use their Central Questions, Central Claims, and Central Purpose statements to illustrate the process. Thanks, also, to Erin Cash, who gave suggestions and feedback on Appendix N: Tips and Advice for Guest Preachers and Supply Preachers.

Introduction

The Who, What, Why, and How of Preaching

Can you remember a **sermon** you heard that touched your heart so deeply, you felt that the preacher was talking directly to you? Or how about the time when you heard a pastor preach and felt your mind open in a way that freed you to think differently? It just changed your whole perspective on things. Or perhaps you can recall a sermon that inspired you to live out your faith and respond to the call to follow Jesus Christ? It was a sermon that filled you with God's grace and compelled you to help build the Beloved Community of God in your own community.

Do you know what was happening in those sermons? The divine presence of God was communicating with you through the preacher, through the Scripture, and through the worshipping community around you. The Holy Spirit was working on you, inviting you into a new way of feeling, thinking, and acting. Isn't it amazing that God uses ordinary human words—ordinary human beings—to speak to us?

When we talk about "the Word of God," it refers to many different things. For one, it means the actual "word" that God spoke *in the beginning*. As we read in the first chapter of Genesis, God creates the cosmos, Earth, and all its inhabitants with just a word. "God said, 'Let there be light.' And there was light" (Gen. 1:3). Similarly, John's Gospel begins, "In the beginning was the Word, and the Word was with God, and the Word was God. He was in the beginning with God" (John 1:1-2). Thus, "the Word of God" is also Christ, the Word incarnate, made flesh among us. And more, "the Word" is also Scripture. In and through these words in the Bible, inspired by the work of the Holy Spirit and written by humans (as imperfect as they are), we can encounter God.

Preaching, too, is the Word of God. It is the living Word interpreted for this time and place by this particular preacher for this particular congregation. And when all the parts work together, preaching can be a means by which you encounter God. In the preaching event we see all aspects of the Word coalesce. God's Word in Scripture is incarnated once again in the interpretation of the preacher and in their relationship with the congregation, which is yet another manifestation of the Spirit of Christ. The church is God's Word because we were spoken into existence as a Christian community by the words of Baptism and Holy Communion. And when we gather around the font and table, and thus around words of Scripture, two things happen. We read them, but they also "read" us. They shape us as individuals and as a gathered people of God. These words in the Bible are not dead words of ancient times that have no meaning today. It's not a museum book. The Bible is meant to be the *living* Word of God. And it is through the ongoing, fresh, and contemporary work of preaching that the Word comes alive in the speaking and the hearing.

DEFINING PREACHING, SERMON, AND HOMILETICS

We'll be using three related terms throughout this book: preaching, sermon, and homiletics. While different people understand these terms in different ways, here's how we're defining them in this book.

PREACHING

Preach comes from the Latin word *praedicare*, which means to speak in front of or to announce. Generally speaking, to preach means to deliver a form of religious speech intended to persuade listeners to embrace certain beliefs and/or take actions in accordance with those beliefs. In this book, the term "preaching" refers to the proclamation of the good news of salvation in Jesus Christ with the recognition that this proclamation is informed by both the Hebrew and Christian Scriptures. Preaching can have many different purposes, including teaching, apologetics (justification of religious doctrine), comfort, challenge, inspiration, conversion, and exhortation, to name just a few. Kenyatta Gilbert notes that there are three "voices" in preaching: the Priestly voice, which has to do with Christian formation for morals and ethic; the Sagely voice, which conveys wisdom for vision and mission; and the Prophetic voice, which proclaims God's justice for all people and for God's Creation.[1]

SERMON

The word "sermon" comes from the Latin word *sermo*, which means speech or conversation. A sermon is a religious address or exhortation and refers to the written or oral event of preaching. John McClure points out that the word is also derived from the deeper Latin word *serere*, which means to link together. He notes that a sermon links together the four sources of authority for preaching: Scripture, Tradition, Experience, and Reason, what are commonly known as the Wesleyan Quadrilateral (more on that term in Chapter 1).[2] We specify that a sermon needs to say something about who God is, what God does, and what this means for individual believers, a congregation, a community, society, and God's Creation.

HOMILETICS

Homiletics is the study and art of preaching. The word comes from the term "homily," which is a short sermon. Those who study and teach preaching are called "homileticians."

NOTES

1. Kenyatta Gilbert, *The Journey and Promise of African American Preaching* (Minneapolis, MN: Fortress Press, 2011), 11.
2. John S. McClure, *Preaching Words: 144 Key Terms in Homiletics* (Louisville: Westminster John Knox, 2007), 125.

WHAT YOU'LL FIND IN *INTRODUCTION TO PREACHING*

This textbook is designed to provide you with the tools for crafting effective, engaging, and inspiring sermons so that your listeners will experience the living Word of God in their lives, their churches, and their communities. Co-written by a homiletician, a theologian, and a biblical scholar, *Introduction to Preaching* is a primer that provides the tools for interpreting Scripture, identifying and writing Theological Claims, and using a three-part schema—the Central Question, the Central Claim, and the Central Purpose—to provide the drive, direction, and destination for the sermon. We also offer ideas for activating "theological imagination" that spark creativity for writing sermons, along with different ways to structure your preaching using sermon forms. The last part of the book offers guidance on sermon delivery and performance, because how we use our voice and bodies for preaching is just as important as the content of our sermons. Our goal in this preaching textbook is to give you the tools for creating sermons that connect the Scripture to your listeners' context, connect Theological Claims to their lives, and help them experience the gospel in a way that clearly communicates God's love for them and for the world.

A BIBLICAL STORY ABOUT EFFECTIVE PREACHING

In Nehemiah Chapter 8, the people of Israel found out just how powerful the Word of God—and preaching—can be when they gathered to hear the Torah read to them for the first time in Jerusalem. They had been held captive in the Babylonian exile where practicing their faith was ridiculed. They didn't know who they were because they had no access to the ancient sources that helped them understand their identity as children of God. The temple was gone; the promised land was lost. The institutions that had taught God's law and the narratives of God's relationship with them were gone. So those who had returned didn't know God's law or the sacred words of worship for their liturgies.

But now they have returned to Jerusalem to reestablish their homes, their community, and their worship of God. So Ezra—a priest and scribe—gathers all the people together. All the men and women and children sit down in the gathering space, much like we do in worship services today, and they listen. They are hungry for the Word of God.

> *So they read from the book, from the law of God, with interpretation. They gave the sense, so that the people understood the reading.* (Nehemiah 8:8)

In other words, there was a sermon! In fact, there were many sermons, because Ezra appointed thirteen preachers to instruct the people about what the Scriptures meant for them, for their lives, and for how they were to live in community with one another.

But here's something curious. When the people heard the Scripture and listened to the sermon, *they cried.* It is likely that the people of Israel felt a mix of guilt, remorse, and hope when they heard the Word of God preached to them by the Water Gate. Did they realize they had not been treating one another as children of God? Did they have regrets about their behavior because of their lack of understanding? Is that why they wept and mourned?

Whatever the reason, we know that preaching moment had a tremendous effect on the gathering of the faithful. It prompted them to reexamine their lives and their faith. It spurred them to take action by rebuilding the temple. And it caused them to reflect on what it means to live in right relationship with God and one another.

EXERCISE

Share Your Memory of a Sermon That Impacted You

Have you ever listened to a sermon where you could feel yourself being broken open in a way you never had before? Something the preacher said, or something about your life at that moment, or something about the way the Holy Spirit worked on you just crumbled your defenses and laid you wide open to receive God's grace in a powerful way.

Write a paragraph about a sermon you recall from some time in your life. Do you remember the biblical text? The theme of the sermon? A story that the preacher told? Describe why the sermon had a significant impact on you and why it has stayed with you. With your preaching partner or in your preaching class, share your reflections with each other. Discuss the following questions:

1. What makes for an effective sermon? How do you know when you've heard a "good" sermon?
2. How do you understand the function of preaching? What does preaching do and who is preaching for?
3. How did you know you were called to preach? What were indications that you had the interest, skills, or talent for preaching?
4. What biblical passage encapsulates your call to preach? How do you experience God, Jesus Christ, or the Holy Spirit through that passage?

After you've shared your sermon memories with each other, read the reflections by Leah, Emily, and Jerry about their own memories of sermons that have formed their faith, touched their souls, and helped them connect with God and God's people.

LEAH SCHADE'S SERMON MEMORY

Leah is Associate Professor of Preaching and Worship at Lexington Theological Seminary. Here she shares a memory of a sermon that deeply impacted her life and her faith.

There have been many times when a sermon has moved me to tears. I'll share just one here. I was listening to Barbara Lundblad preach at the Festival of Homiletics many years ago. She was telling about an experience of being in a church that had a profound ministry of welcome for people with disabilities. She described a communion service where every single person was accommodated according to their needs. Those who were blind; those who were in wheelchairs; those with brain injuries—all manner of people who struggle to find a place at the table in the church were welcomed, given leadership roles, and elevated to their full human expression of God's grace.

As Barbara described this scene, I was overcome with tears because this sermon pierced my heart. One of my sisters was born with severe physical disabilities and was confined to a wheelchair all her life. My relationship with her was complicated and strained. I'm ashamed to admit that I often regarded her as a burden on our family. By the time she took her own life in her late twenties, we were not on speaking terms.

Barbara Lundblad did not know this, of course. But when she described this worship service of complete welcome and empowerment of all these people with disabilities, I was brought to my knees in a rush of guilt and remorse about my sister's life and our relationship. I had never thought of things in this way—a whole faith community working to restore the humanity to those deemed less than fully human. The way I saw the world, the way I saw my sister, the way I saw people with physical impairments—all of it shifted because of that sermon.

While I was weeping, however, Barbara's sermon also filled me with a sense of God's grace. This happened because she showed me a vision of the Realm of God where all children of all kinds are welcomed. That sermon rent the garment of my heart with both regret and remission of my sins. And it gave me hope for restoration through the church of Jesus Christ.

PREACHING IS ABOUT RELATIONSHIP

We can surmise that the preaching moment in Nehemiah was made possible because of the relationship between the preachers and the people. Over time, a preacher develops a relationship with his or her parishioners that should help them develop their relationship with God. Sometimes God's Word, spoken by and through the preacher, will make you squirm by holding a mirror up to you and our world to show you how things really are. That's what Martin Luther called "Law." But ultimately the purpose of preaching is to proclaim God's presence, the grace of Jesus Christ, and the power of the Holy Spirit working in our midst. You should hear Good News in just about every sermon. That's called "gospel," literally, *good news*. This good news is exactly what Ezra and Nehemiah proclaimed to the people of Israel:

> *"This day is holy to the Lord your God; do not mourn or weep." For all the people wept when they heard the words of the law. Then he said to them, "Go your way, eat the fat and drink sweet wine and send portions of them to those for whom nothing is prepared, for this day is holy to our Lord; and do not be grieved, for the joy of the Lord is your strength."* (Nehemiah 8:9-10)

God's future for the Israelites started on that day when the Word of God was read and preached. God's future for us started in the preaching, teaching, cross, and resurrection of Jesus. It is the promise of the resurrection that gives us the commission and power to preach.

Homiletician John McClure says that in the preacher's proclamation of grace "God's will and power are identified not with what *is* but with what *will be*."[1] This means that preaching engenders *hope* and cultivates *faith*, which is trust in God. God's Word in and through preaching helps us to imagine a new future and gives us the means and motivation to live as if that future is already happening now. As McClure says, "Anticipation of a new future grounded in faith in God conditions and motivates life. The Christian life is one of hope, consciousness-raising, learning from and suffering with the oppressed . . . hope for and involvement in the work of social transformation, and joy in the present, rooted in faith's hope for and vision of the future."[2]

We think it's no small thing that Ezra and Nehemiah encouraged the gathered congregation to share a meal after hearing the Word of God and the accompanying sermons. In fact, good preaching should feel like a good meal, like you've been fed. It should nourish your soul and your mind and your heart in some way.

EMILY ASKEW'S SERMON MEMORY

Emily Askew is Professor Emeritus of Theology at Lexington Theological Seminary. Here she recounts a sermon that spoke life to her in the midst of a tragic death.

Several years ago, a good friend of mine ended his life. He was a wonderful professor, mentor, historian, friend, father, and husband, and he lived with episodes of profound depression. It was during one such bleak period that he killed himself in despair. Complicating an already complicated scenario, his wife was the pastor of a big-steeple church in town, and he was a "non-traditional" believer at best. His God could not neatly fit in Scripture.

The day of his funeral, the church was filled with grieving family, graduate students, friends, and admirers. There was not a seat empty. I cannot tell you the name of the pastor who conducted his service, but I can tell you that it changed all of us there.

Too often suicide is at best never mentioned in a funeral homily or, at worst, considered a sin worthy of damnation. Not this time. In words of incredible comfort, this preacher dealt with suicide head-on, naming it as a symptom of a dangerous disease, depression, and not a mortal sin. He named my friend's struggle as the struggle of a chronic illness, de-stigmatizing depression at the same time that he elevated my friend's courage and good works in the world. His death was not a failure of resolve, or will, or character, but a symptom of a disease that often ends brilliant lives. We were comforted, loved, educated, relieved, and resolved by that single sermon in a very complicated time. He was a courageous, compassionate preacher, and I am so grateful for both of those qualities at such a hard time.

"FEED MY SHEEP." (JOHN 21:17): THE SUSTAINING WORD OF PREACHING

Sometimes in a sermon the preacher offers a taste of something the congregation has never tried before, or something that is a little hard to chew, a little on the sour side, or a little difficult to swallow. When this happens, hopefully the listeners will be able to trust that the preacher has the best intentions and their best interests—and the interest of the wider community—at heart. Not every sermon can be a feel-good dessert. We need protein and veggies, fiber, and vitamins. And sometimes, we need a dose of medicine for our sin-sick souls. It may not taste good, but it can help bring healing.

Good preaching over a period of time should offer a Word from God on many different topics, Bible passages, and theological themes. Not every sermon is going to be a gourmet meal or a bowl of ice cream. But if it's nourishing and has at least a little good flavoring, it will do wonders for the congregation's appetite for God's Word. Good preaching should keep the people of God coming back for more.

As one churchgoer said to another, "I may not remember every meal my spouse made over the years. But I know I was fed nourishing food that sustained me day to day. In the same way, I may not remember every sermon in detail. But I know I was fed on the nourishing Word of God that sustained me week to week." Thus, the goal of this preaching textbook is to teach you how to faithfully and deliberately study Scripture, discern who God is and what God does for the people of God and for the world, and proclaim that in the sermon in a way that connects with the listeners in their time and place. In this way, the people of God can be fed and nourished by God's Word.

JERRY SUMNEY'S SERMON MEMORY

Jerry Sumney is Professor of Biblical Studies at Lexington Theological Seminary. Here he tells about a sermon that was especially meaningful for him.

A number of years ago, Fred Craddock came to preach at the Lexington Theological Seminary chapel. His sermon was from Philippians, but I don't remember the precise text. The sermon went along as one might expect, but then at the end, there was an insight revealed about God's eschatological work that moved me deeply. When it was over, I turned to the person sitting next to me and said, "Wow!" It was not that I learned a new piece of information about who God is or about the blessings that we receive through Christ. But I experienced it in a different way through that sermon.

I had heard plenty of sermons and lessons that had taught me about these things and led me to believe them. I had also heard plenty of sermons that worked to evoke strong emotions about them. But this sermon had the mixture of theological depth and expression of its meaning for our life with God and one another that I was led to experience those blessings in a fuller and richer way than I had before. I felt the gift more profoundly that day than I had previously. That sermon changed the way I experienced the world. It led me to be able to lean more toward not just God's grace, but also toward what God wants for the world in the present. While the precise content of that sermon has faded over time, the experience it gave me continues to deepen my life of faith.

OVERVIEW OF *INTRODUCTION TO PREACHING*

This preaching textbook is divided into five sections that cover all the basics you need to know for learning how to preach. Part I begins with learning how to read and interpret Scripture. Using history, literary analysis, and perspective-explicit lenses, you'll learn how to go behind the text, within the text, and come from perspectives outside the text to gain a deeper and wider understanding of the Bible and what it means for preaching today. We'll also offer you a handy method for organizing the knowledge and insights you gain from consulting biblical commentaries in order to categorize them for application in a sermon. And we'll suggest ways to choose biblical passages for preaching based on lectionaries, topical preaching, or personal prayer and discernment. Part I closes out with a sermon exercise that pulls together everything you will have learned by that point so that you can see biblical interpretation in action for preaching.

Part II helps preachers think about the theological content of Scripture passages and their own sermons. We'll teach you how to identify and articulate an appropriate and coherent Theological Claim, and you'll learn how to identify Theological Claims in a biblical text and distinguish them from anthropological and ecclesiological claims. We'll also explain how to identify Theological Claims in a sermon and then to write your own, drawing from the exegetical tools in Part I. Part II concludes with a sermon exercise that draws together exegesis and theological analysis and has you practice analyzing a sermon using these skills.

In Part III, you will learn how to use a three-part schema—the Central Question, the Central Claim, and the Central Purpose—to provide the drive, direction, and destination for your sermons. This schema will be firmly grounded in the two primary disciplines that undergird preaching—theology and biblical interpretation. The Central Question brings together the biblical text and your preaching context in order to articulate the compelling inquiry driving the congregation to want to listen—and respond—to God's Word. The Central Claim brings together the Central Question and the Theological Claim in the biblical text to arrive at the primary assertion you want to make in the sermon. The Central Claim conveys both the message of the biblical passage and its implication for your preaching context. This leads to the Central Purpose. Informed by the Central Question and the Central Claim, the Central Purpose articulates what you want the sermon to do or accomplish in and for the listeners. The Central Purpose states what the sermon aims to do and why. Each set of chapters for the Central Question, Central Claim, and Central Purpose has an accompanying chapter with examples and exercises to practice writing them for your sermons.

Part IV focuses on cultivating creativity and structure for sermons. We will equip you to use descriptive language, imagery, and metaphors using exercises for cultivating "theological imagination." You'll learn how to use vibrant words, salient images, and evocative stories to help the sermon come alive. We'll also analyze two sermons that show how sermon illustrations work together with the Central Question, Central Claim, and Central Purpose to create salience, resonance, and coherence in a sermon. Part IV will also teach you how to integrate all of this—exegesis, theology, the Central Statements, and creativity—into different sermon forms. And you will learn strategies for starting a sermon, different ways to thread the different parts of the sermon together, and options for concluding the sermon in a way that has an impact and is most effective.

Part V begins with the importance of editing, formatting, and practicing your sermon and offers helpful tips for these practical aspects of preaching. Then we cover the basics of sermon delivery and performance, including methods of delivering the sermon, attending to the use of the voice and body, and some tips for how to handle nervousness. We will look at the use of space (online, on-site, and hybrid) and issues around preaching, media, and technology, as well as special concerns for preachers with historically marginalized bodies.

HOW TO USE THIS TEXTBOOK

The Central Question, Central Claim, Central Purpose method is designed to give preachers a way to organize their sermon preparation in a step-by-step process. The three of us—a homiletician, a biblical scholar, and a theologian—have taught at the same seminary and developed this method over many years in consultation and collaboration with one another for preparing students to preach. We hope that what we have modelled here in terms of a cooperative and collegial approach to teaching the art of preaching is something you will carry through in your own sermon preparation. To that end, in every chapter, you'll find exercises that you can do on your own, with a preaching partner, sermon prep group, preaching colleagues, or with your preaching mentor. These exercises are designed to give you practice in everything from biblical interpretation and theological analysis, to writing the Central Statements, to cultivating creativity and structuring your sermon, to delivering your sermon. Along the way, we give you guidance for using appropriate sermon forms, imagery, metaphors, and performance basics to deliver contextually relevant sermons using your body and voice with presence and authenticity.

We recommend that students start at the beginning of this textbook and work their way through each chapter, because each one builds on what came before. However, if there are specific aspects of preaching you want to review or improve, or if you are an experienced preacher and want to learn new approaches to augment your skills, each section and each chapter can serve as a stand-alone "lesson." Also, the appendices include a wealth of resources for preaching, including a list of recommended biblical commentaries (and how to use them); a description of theological categories; a worksheet for choosing biblical texts and planning to preach; names and metaphors for God; worksheets for the Central Question, Central Claim, and Central Purpose; a list of sermon forms; a worksheet for creativity exercises; and exercises for warming up your voice and body for preaching. The final appendix includes tips and advice for guest preachers and supply preachers. Along the way, you will see some words in bold print. You will find these terms defined in the glossary.

Of course, the Central Question, Central Claim, Central Purpose method is just one way that a preacher can use for sermon preparation; it is not *the* method for preaching. But it is a process we have used with our students that many of them have found helpful. Whether you are a lay preacher working on your own to learn how to write and deliver sermons, a seminary student in a formal classroom with an instructor, or an experienced preacher looking for new ideas, this textbook is designed to instruct you on the basics you need to know for creating sermons as well as to provide exercises, tools, examples, and inspiration for many aspects of preaching.

Even if you are an experienced preacher who learned other methods of sermon preparation, we hope you will find ideas and exercises in this textbook to add to your "homiletical toolbox." For example, you may find that you prefer to sit down and write out the draft of a sermon as the Spirit moves you. If that's your style, you can still use the Central Question, Central Purpose, and Central Claim to evaluate your draft to see if it holds together and accomplishes what you intend. Or you may prefer to start with *lectio divina* or some other "right brain" approach when first encountering a biblical text before engaging in deeper academic study. In this case, you can use the creativity exercises in Chapter 18 and then go back to Part I to guide your exegesis. In other words, there is no "right way" to engage in sermon preparation because it isn't always a linear task. Over time your process will change and evolve as you become more adept at preaching. We hope that the tools we provide in this textbook will serve you well as you develop your preaching skills throughout your ministry.

NOTES

1. John S. McClure, *Other-Wise Preaching: A Postmodern Ethic for Homiletics* (St. Louis, MO: Chalice Press, 2001), 137.
2. Ibid.

I

INTERPRETING SCRIPTURE FOR SERMONS

1

Interpreting Scripture for the Church

There are many reasons to read the Bible. Some read it to find a passage they want to meditate on; others go to Scripture seeking a word of comfort or assurance. Still others look for words to pray. All of these and more can be important and bring us closer to God. But these are not the kinds of readings we will talk about here. Instead of seeking these ways to experience God through individual and devotional readings, we want to talk about reading Scripture as a theological authority for the church. We want to think about reading Scripture as that collection of writings that guides what the church should believe and do. We do this because when we preach, we are responsible for interpreting the text so that listeners can understand and respond to the claim the text is making on our lives and on the church.

THE AUTHORITY OF SCRIPTURE FOR PREACHING

Some form of Scriptures has guided the church from its beginning. The earliest church looked to the Hebrew Scriptures, usually as they were read in the Septuagint (the Greek translation of the Hebrew Scriptures), as an authority that helped them interpret the life of Jesus and as a guide for how the church should live for God. Over time, various parts of the New Testament came to be seen as authoritative for the church. Even as the form of the New Testament was still incomplete, the majority recognized a significant body of texts (including Pauline letters, the four Gospels, and Acts) as authoritative for the church's beliefs and practices. Some form of this reliance on Scriptural texts has been a feature of the church's life ever since.

The Reformation emphasized the place of Scripture as an authority. Martin Luther's slogan *Sola Scriptura* (meaning "only Scripture"—as opposed to formulated church doctrines) epitomizes that emphasis. With that beginning, it has been a feature of the Protestant heritage to demand access to the Bible. But that access is meaningful only if we are able to understand what we find there and have ways to bring what we find into our historical and cultural situation.

Since Scripture is such an important authority for the church, we need to have clear ways of thinking about how to use it as a guide to our faith and action. That is, we need to think about how to figure out what Scripture has to say to us today. We have to have a method for finding and making good use of that authoritative word of Scripture in our time and place. It is as this authoritative guide to faith and practice that we want to talk about how to read Scripture.

THE IMPORTANCE OF INTERPRETATION FOR PREACHING

The first thing we should note is that all uses of Scripture are uses of *interpreted* Scripture. No one can read Scripture or say what is in Scripture without giving it an interpretation. This includes those who use **literalism** or say they read literalistically. (Literalists are people who believe in a literal interpretation of Scripture and say they follow the exact commands in the Bible.) However, they too have chosen an interpretive method. Given the various kinds of writings that appear in the Bible (psalms, narratives, oracles, etc.), choosing a literal reading of the text is by no means the obvious method of choice. Since we will choose some way to read Scripture, it is important for us to think about what methods are appropriate to both the text and the place in which we read, our own cultural setting. Unfortunately, this is not an easy task, as we can see from all the differing views that Christians have on so many issues.

The name of the study of how to go about interpreting things is **hermeneutics**. We engage in this art/science of interpretation all of the time; we just don't recognize we are doing it because we have been taught this skill our whole lives. We engage in the use of the tools and methods of hermeneutics every day. Every time we distinguish between one **genre** and another, we are exercising these skills. A genre is a type of writing with socially agreed-upon conventions developed over time. For example, we know the difference between a novel and a history text. We know that we should expect different things of each of them. If I were to pick up a novel about the Great Recession of 2008, I might find that the name given for the CEO of a financial institution was not the person who actually headed it or maybe that there was no financial institution with that name. If I were to say, this is a terrible novel, it has things in it that did not really happen, someone would need to explain to me that I had made a genre mistake. I was expecting the wrong thing from a novel. They might tell me that novelists are free to make up characters and events because that is the nature of fiction. If, however, I were reading a history textbook and discovered that it talked about a person of an institution that didn't actually exist at that time, I would have a valid complaint.

If we want to think about how easily and unconsciously we do this all the time, think about a newspaper. Whether it is online or on paper, we easily know the difference between the news on the front page and the comics. We have different expectations of those parts of the paper even though they appear in the same edition of the same publication. One more example will have to suffice. We know the difference between reading poetry and prose. We give more latitude to metaphor and simile in poetry than to other kinds of writings. Think of the Robert Burns poem where he says love is like "a red, red rose." If that were to appear in a biology textbook, we would have to say no, that is incorrect—we might say Burns was a bit mentally unstable. But in a poem, it can make perfect sense because there are ways that the beauty, delicacy, and softness of a rose may describe the loved one he is praising. We can think of the psalms here as well. The psalmist says, "God is my rock," and we think that makes perfect sense, because it is in a poem. We might have to ask what the psalmist means to fully understand what is being said, but we would not say that it is a ridiculous statement. On the other hand, if that sentence appeared in an article on geology or physics, we would say that it is completely wrong.

Again, notice that we don't really have to work at this. We do it naturally. Think of how quickly we change the way we hear something when it is from a campaign rally of a politician. Hearing that is nothing like listening to a lecture in an economics course on the current state of the economy. Of course, we know that some try to blur the edges between genres for political or economic gain. Think of the blurring of the line between the facts that a news reporter reports and giving an editorial that interprets pieces of the facts to support a political ideology. In other words, there are places where we must be more vigilant in recognizing the genre we are hearing.

As easy as it usually is for us to think about how to hear or read genres that we encounter regularly, it is more difficult to do this when we are reading ancient documents. It is more difficult because we don't know what the expectations were for various kinds of writings in the ancient world. We might expect some kinds of narratives to be historical, while they actually were designed to be read more poetically or metaphorically. What we expect of a biography or a history of a nation might be very different, indeed are very different, from what ancient people expected from those genres. This problem is made even worse by the nature of the materials in the Bible. The Bible consists of writings of several different genres. Present-day readers have to think about how each of those types of writings must be read differently. In this book we will talk about methods that will enable you to read various types as they were meant to be read, and we will look at some of them together.

HOW TO IDENTIFY DIFFERENT GENRES IN SCRIPTURE

Given our historical distance from the writing of the biblical books, it is often hard for us to identify what kind of text we are reading. The list below shows the general category for books of the Bible. These categories are broad, so more specific designations will often be important if we are working on a particular text. We should also remember that there can be more than one genre within any given book. For example, Genesis begins with poetic narrative and then moves to legend at Chapter 12. Similarly, the prophetic books have narrative, poetry, epiphanies, and more. A good Bible dictionary or commentary will help you determine the genre of the text under consideration. (See Appendix A for a list of recommended biblical commentary series.) The list below is also available for quick reference in Appendix B.

GENRES IN HEBREW SCRIPTURES

Primarily Legend and Sacred Stories

Genesis
Exodus
Numbers
Deuteronomy
Ruth
Esther
Parts of Daniel

Laws

Leviticus
Deuteronomy (parts of)

Theological Narratives/Histories

Joshua
Judges
1 and 2 Kings
1 and 2 Chronicles
Ezra
Nehemiah

Poetry

Psalms
Song of Solomon

Wisdom Literature

Job
Proverbs
Ecclesiastes

Prophetic Literature

Isaiah through Malachi

GENRES IN CHRISTIAN SCRIPTURES

Theological Ancient Biography

The Gospels

Theological Narrative/History

Acts of the Apostles

Letters

Romans through Jude

Apocalypse

Revelation

THE HISTORICAL CONTEXT OF THE BIBLE FOR PREACHING

Our problems with understanding the biblical texts have yet another dimension. All of the texts of the Bible were written in historical and cultural contexts that were very different from our historical and cultural contexts today. This means that some of the things they say or recommend seem to make no sense to us because we do not understand what those behaviors or actions meant in their world. The different meanings of various acts and customs between our time and that of the biblical writings suggests that we cannot assume that a particular command given to the church in the first century applies directly to the church today (that is, we cannot read as literalists). Take for example 2 Timothy 2:8-9. There the reader tells women in the church that they should not wear gold jewelry or braid their hair. When we read this, we wonder what could be unchristian about a woman braiding her hair. But if we take a moment to investigate the first-century context, this command makes plenty of sense.

In the first century, and particularly in the church, there were very few wealthy people. Only wealthy people would have had gold jewelry. In addition, women of the elite class gave a lot of attention to their hairstyle. The busts of women that survive from this era consistently show wealthy women with incredibly complex hairstyles. Some even had an enslaved woman as their personal beautician. Many of these hairstyles included the elaborate use of multiple braids. Such hairstyles were a way of demonstrating wealth and of distinguishing yourself from those in social classes below you. In this context we can see why it makes sense for 2 Timothy to tell women in the church not to wear gold and braid their hair. It is a way of telling them that they must not use their dress and appearance to distinguish themselves as better than other church members. It is putting into practice the baptism formula that proclaims that in Christ there is "neither Jew nor Greek, neither slave nor free, neither male and female" (Gal 3:28). With the command not to braid hair, 2 Timothy says that a person's social and economic status must not be taken into consideration within the church. In Christ, all have the same status and value.

Even those who claim to read the Bible very literally seldom take this command literally. Most would say that we must read that command in its social and cultural context. And that is exactly right. But if we should read this passage in 2 Timothy in its cultural context and so conclude that it does not apply literally and directly to our context, we must say that about the whole of 2 Timothy and, in fact, the whole of the Bible. We must be consistent in the method that we use to move from the message that the biblical text had for its original readers and the message it has for the church today. If we recognize the cultural differences only when we do not like what it says we should do, we have stopped having Scripture as an authority. We have made it so that Scripture cannot critique the beliefs and practices we hold. To have Scripture function as a real authority for the church, we must have a consistent method of moving from the ancient message to the message for the church of our time.

Our task as interpreters of Scripture for the church is to come to understand the commands, instructions, beliefs, and so on that we find in the ancient text. Then, we must think about how all of these can be translated into our culture so that the real message of the text shapes the church today. Think for a moment about this 2 Timothy text. If we just said that the passage tells us not to wear gold and not to braid hair, it would not say much to the church. Even if we did those things directly and literally, there is nothing there about wearing silver or platinum or expensive jewels. But if we think about the reason those commands were given, it could make a world of difference in our churches. What if we said that there must be no displays of wealth because they can lead to some people thinking that they have higher status in the Kingdom or at least in our congregation. We might think about what that has to say about putting names on rooms in the church or stained-glass windows. Or we might think about what it says about some who proclaim a "prosperity gospel" when they buy private jets or expensive cars. Think about how often we have heard of a large donor in the church leaving because he or she did not get their way on some issue. The problem that 2 Timothy addresses—ostentatiously displaying one's wealth—is alive and well. We just have to think about how to see it and how to have this text speak to it.

As we have already intimated, when it comes to the biblical text, the hermeneutical process has two steps. The first is to do **exegesis**. Here we try to determine what the text meant in its original context, what the specific instruction was and what that meant in the ears of the original recipients. We can ask what the presenting issue is and what cultural, political, and religious matters give rise to the text. Of course, we also want to see what the author's response was and what cultural, social, and religious ideas and beliefs supported that response.

The second task is to take what we find in that original setting and think about what it means for the church today. We have already noted that it is not really possible to be a consistent literalist. We should note here that this is not about picking on literalists. Just as literalists are really only part-time literalists, so most mainline church members, including preachers, are also part-time literalists—they just take different parts literally. Just think of how quickly mainline Christians are to quote the two greatest commandments when it seems they may have to question the ethical choices of some community either in their church or outside it. They may relativize other commands, saying they were for a different cultural setting, but not this one. Few people put this in the context of first-century Judaism or in the literary contexts of the Gospels in which it appears. We just use it as a command to be taken literally in all times and places. Don't misunderstand, those two commands certainly are of extreme importance. But we have to read them in their context and think about why Jesus said them where he did and why the Evangelists tell those stories as they do. Then we will be in a place to make a claim about what they say to us in particular situations.

The point is that it is simply hard to be consistent in the way that we bring the message of a biblical text into our contexts. So, we must give careful consideration to how we will make that move. As noted above, if we are inconsistent in the way we do this, then Scripture cannot really function as an authority for the church. Without a consistent method for bringing the ancient message into the present, our thoughts, inclinations, and prejudices replace Scripture as the arbiters of what the Word of God is. The result is that we become the arbiters of what the church should do and believe instead of the biblical text. It is not that everyone does that intentionally out of hubris (though that is sometimes the case); it is just the practical result of not having a consistent method.

Let's turn, then, to a way that we can legitimately bring the message of Scripture into our own church and world.

THE THEOLOGICAL AND HISTORICAL CONTEXT OF THE BIBLE FOR PREACHING

We remember that we start with exegesis, where we try to discover the original message of the text for its intended audience. We want to see more than the specifics of the commands, instructions, or even theological arguments. We want to find what in the Christian message (which includes what we come to know about God and God's will in the Hebrew Bible) led a particular writer to think that what he or she prescribed or recommended was the right thing to think or do in that particular setting. We want to get to the theological affirmation of this text that supports the specific instruction, or we want to see how the author develops a theological point so that it provides the reason for the practical advice the author gives. We begin this task by discerning a Theological Claim within its historical context.

It is only after we have come to our best understanding of the ancient situation, the author's practical response, and the author's theological reason for that response, that we turn to think about what the text might say to the church and the world today.[1] As we have noted, we must develop a hermeneutic that can be used consistently across the biblical texts, used with the instructions and ideas we like and those we instinctively do not. We have already noted that it is not possible to be a consistent literalist. We could cite many more examples of texts like that of 2 Tim 2:8-9 that we cited above. But we will let that example suffice here.

Nevertheless, we can bring the message of the biblical text to bear on our world in ways that are consistent with what those biblical authors wanted for their churches and that can significantly shape our lives. But remember that if we are not bringing *all* commands and instructions directly and literally into our world, we must not bring *any* of them into our context directly and literally. We need a consistent hermeneutic. When we see a command, we need to give thought to why that command was given. We need to ask what the theological basis is for that command. There may be cultural and social reasons for it as well, and we should take notice of them as we try to discern its theological basis. This hermeneutic provides a means for allowing the biblical texts to shape our attitudes and actions. It can mean that the whole of the Christian life can be shaped by Scripture.

AN EXAMPLE: PREACHING ON SEXUAL RELATIONSHIPS WITHIN A THEOLOGICAL AND HISTORICAL CONTEXT

We can take the command "Do not commit adultery" as an example. The hermeneutic we are suggesting says that preachers cannot take that command literally and directly into their context. Instead, we must think about the fundamental reasons for this command. One sociocultural reason was that men viewed women, in part, as property.

So if someone had sex with another man's wife, it was seen as a violation of the man's property. We should argue that this value is contrary to the gospel because it violates the basic understanding that all people are created in the image of God and that in Christ, gender does not grant privilege (Gal 3:26-28). Thus, this reason cannot support a direct application of this command in our time.

But the theological reasons for the command include the expectation that all of our relationships, including sexual relationships, should reflect the character of God. The characteristics of God that seem most relevant here are the love of God and the faithfulness of God (perhaps among other characteristics of God). These demand that all sexual relationships manifest the love and faithfulness of God. Further, this love demands that the good of the other person is also a constant in these relationships. This means that all kinds of casual sex violate what the commandment about adultery means in our world. The faithfulness of God demands that all sexual relationships reflect the commitment to and constant focus on the good of the other. Sex outside of committed relationships does not reflect these aspects of the character of God. This means that adultery is a sin in our context.

Beyond thinking of why the command not to commit adultery is a demand of our faith today, this hermeneutic allows us to think of matters beyond heterosexual relationships in new ways. If we see that what makes a sexual relationship Christian is that it reflects the character of God, then we are given a means of thinking about relationships that are not heterosexual. If we want to think about whether same-sex relationships are Christian, the command about adultery would have us ask whether they can reflect the love and faithfulness of God. If they do, then they should be seen as consistent with Christian values in the same way that heterosexual relationships that reflect those values are Christian.

When we say that no command from the Bible should be taken directly and applied to our context, it may sound like we are opening the door to any kind of behavior. But that is not the case. If we use this hermeneutic, we will end up examining all aspects of our lives through what we find in Scripture.

EXERCISE FOR OUR HERMENEUTICAL METHOD

Food Offered to Idols in 1 Corinthians 8-10

1. *Read 1 Corinthians Chapters 8-10.* Note Paul's instructions about food restrictions and what they mean for the faith community.
2. *Consider the historical and theological context.* Most of us don't have to worry about whether to have lunch in the temple of another god, but Paul's instructions about that problem in these chapters have a theological basis. Consult two or three commentaries to determine what is informing Paul's instructions about food offered to idols.
3. *Consider how to apply the biblical text today.* Once you have identified the theological basis for these instructions, think about how this should shape the way we understand the value of our fellow Christians and how that value should shape our treatment of them.
4. *Write down three possible ways this text could be applicable to our current context.*
5. *Go on to the next section,* "Understanding and Using Analogies for Preaching Biblical Texts," to compare your preliminary exegesis with what you find there. What did you miss? What did you learn?

UNDERSTANDING AND USING ANALOGIES FOR PREACHING BIBLICAL TEXTS

Implicit in what we have described thus far is that the way we find these connections between the biblical texts and the church's life is through the use of creative analogies. The correspondences of our questions will not always fit as easily as we were able to do above when thinking about sexual relationships. To bring Scripture to bear on today's questions and problems, we can look at what the biblical writers identify as the underlying cause of a problem they see. Then we seek the theological basis for the response they give. When we turn to think about application of that value or reflection of the character of God, we look for current manifestations of the same underlying cause. In the example from 1 Cor 8-10 where some people want to eat meals in the temple of another god, Paul sees the underlying problem to be that some church members are refusing to recognize their responsibility for the damage that their conduct may have on fellow church members. They were demanding their rights, seeing that as more important than considering the good of others.

This problem is not just an ancient problem. There are many places where the conflict between individual rights and the good of others shows itself today. What Paul has to say about this problem is relevant in all of these situations and should be one of the guides for what the church says about this matter.

Paul's solution is to say that those who are demanding their rights must think again about the value of their fellow church members. He tells them they are disregarding the good of persons so valuable that Christ died for them. If they are that valuable, no other Christian should be willing to do anything that would harm them. While we do not have to worry about whether to eat at a god's temple, we do have to think about whether our rights or the good of others is more important. With this hermeneutic, we have a Christian frame for talking about it.

Putting the good of others above our own rights is a countercultural value. It was in the first century, too. But Paul saw it as a part of the values of the Kingdom of God. And he shows that the example of Christ's willingness to die for others is the basis of that value. As we begin to think of how this value is lived out, it might start with how members behave toward one another in congregational meetings where contentious issues are discussed and debated. It might make a significant difference if someone were to say in the midst of a discussion in which each party wants their way, "You know, those people you are arguing with are so valuable that Christ was willing to die for them. What might that value and act of Christ call you to do in this discussion?" Living out this value in the church has implications for all kinds of settings. Such a passage might also give us a way to think about how we behave in the world of social and political policies.

This example helps us think about how to move from the biblical text to today's issues and questions. Granted, it puts a lot of responsibility on the interpreter and you as the preacher, but that is always the case. We have to be diligent and careful as we identify and use these analogies. But it will show how Scripture is relevant in the present.

USING THE WESLEYAN QUADRILATERAL FOR INTERPRETING AND PREACHING SCRIPTURE

We may also look beyond our own thinking to other sources of guidance as we seek to be sure that we are discerning the Word of God clearly. While Scripture is important, it is not the only source of revelation God has made available to us. John Wesley, the founder of the Methodist Church, identified three additional sources of revelation. They are Tradition, Reason, and Experience. These four sources of revelation have come to be known as the **Wesleyan Quadrilateral**. With these other sources of revelation, we can think about whether our interpretation of Scripture fits with the way the church before us understood the will of God. (See Chapter 8 for the ways in which the Wesleyan Quadrilateral can be used to make Theological Claims in a sermon.)

Here Tradition refers to what the church has said in creeds and other formal statements about the will of God. Some denominations and traditions have other resources that they rely on beyond these formal ecclesial statements. Some look to a tradition of hymns such as spirituals or to the writings of a founder. Such resources shape the ways preachers (and theologians) discern what they see as God's will for the church in the present.

But creeds and hymns, for example, are only a sort of snapshot of what the church was thinking in an earlier time. Wesley also saw God working in the church in the present. He was not thinking about personal experience by itself. Rather, experience here means the ways God is speaking to the community. It may start with a single person's experience, but that experience must be thought about and evaluated by the community as a whole to discern whether it is consistent with how they know God and how God has been revealed in Scripture and Tradition. This discernment might lead to leaving behind a particular earlier judgment of the church, but it will have taken that earlier decision seriously.

The fourth source of revelation Wesley identified was Reason. When he spoke of Reason, he meant that even without the benefit of Scripture or Tradition, humans can discern some things about God from the world around us. Here he was thinking about how the power and wisdom of God (among other things) may be seen in nature and even in relationships. Wesley also included the ideas that philosophers can discern through the use of logic as ways that Reason can help us understand God.

Whether we acknowledge that these other sources of revelation affect our reading or not, they do. Recognizing them can help us make sense of why we seem led to some of the decisions we lean toward. As we recognize them, we can also think explicitly about the relationships among them. We can think of which ones we give the most authority to and why, and then make sure that we use that decision to help us think about what the church should do and believe. We should note here that some churches have codified the relationship among these (e.g., the Roman Catholic Church and the Episcopal Church), but most have not acted quite as formally. In practice, however, there will probably be a relationship among them that is assumed, even if it is not articulated.

As an interpreter and as a preacher, you need to think about the relationship of these sources of revelation to one another. That can help you think about what Scripture says to the analogous situations to the biblical texts that you find in your world. If what you think a biblical text calls the church to do is in tension with some of these other sources of revelation, you can take a moment to see if the position that other source has taken should guide your reading of what Scripture says to this moment. You may still be right, but these resources have given you further ways to consider that decision. If what you advocate is consistent with what you find in these other sources, that can give you assurance that what you are thinking is supported by what other Christians have seen as the will and Word of God.

FINAL THOUGHT—STAY WITHIN THE TEXT

As you are using Scripture in sermons, you should be thinking about possible analogies to the underlying issue that sparked the author to write the text we are reading. You can probably recall sermons you've heard that take a word or a phrase in the text to talk about something that is not in that text at all. Though perhaps unintentional, this is a deceptive practice. The church reads the text as what authorizes and legitimates the Word of God that is proclaimed in the sermon. But if the sermon is not actually about something in the text, the preacher has falsely acted as though it does.

The topic and point of your sermon should be something that is actually in the text. The best practice is for preachers to make sure that their sermon is about the main point of the text that is read. But that may not be what is most needed in the context of a particular church at a particular time. So if you do not preach on the main point of your text, your sermon at least should be about some point that is in the text—even if it is to push back against or to expand on that point. Texts on one topic often make claims or demands in the midst of the argument about the main topic that are important in themselves. Those theological assertions can appropriately legitimate a sermon on those topics. If you discover that the topic you need to address in your sermon in the place your congregation finds itself is not in the text you originally chose (or that was given you by the lectionary), then you need to find a different text. You need to help the church see what biblical texts led you to hear the Word of God for that moment. That can help them begin to think about their own faith more clearly while demonstrating your integrity as an interpreter and proclaimer of God's Word.

With these thoughts about hermeneutics, we are ready to begin discussing methods used in exegesis. In the next chapter we will look at a number of different methods that together help us get to the meaning the text had for its original readers and to the theological affirmations and beliefs that supported the writers' responses.

KEY POINTS IN THIS CHAPTER

1. Because Scripture is a primary authority for the church, having a method for interpreting Scripture is imperative for preaching. All uses of Scripture are uses of *interpreted* Scripture; this applies even for those who claim to read the Bible *literally*.
2. Hermeneutics is the study of how we interpret texts and other things. Understanding the historical and cultural context of a biblical passage is important for finding the meaning of Scripture. This hermeneutical process of interpreting Scripture is called *exegesis*.
3. Having a consistent hermeneutic means that we take the theological and historical context of the Bible seriously in order to discern how it applies to our lives and communities today.
4. Analogies can help preachers bring Scripture to bear on today's questions and problems by discerning the underlying concerns and values of a biblical text and applying it to a modern-day situation.
5. The Wesleyan Quadrilateral is a helpful tool for discerning how to apply God's Word. In addition to Scripture, the revelation we find in Tradition, Reason, and Experience can guide the message of our preaching.
6. A sermon should be based on what is actually in the biblical text and address the main point or at least a supporting point of the text.

DISCUSSION QUESTIONS

1. How were you taught to read and interpret the Bible? Did your tradition emphasize a more literalistic interpretation? If so, how does this chapter challenge your understanding of a "literal" reading of Scripture? If not, how would you describe the interpretive lens of your faith community? How does this chapter challenge that view?
2. What is your understanding of Scripture as a theological authority for the church? How does the Bible function as an authority for your congregation? In terms of the Wesleyan Quadrilateral, how is the Bible weighted in your preaching context?
3. Ask a preaching colleague to share a sermon manuscript with you and analyze it using the Wesleyan Quadrilateral. Which of the four authorities—Scripture, Tradition, Reason, and Experience—do you detect in the sermon? Which one(s) seem to carry the most weight in the sermon?
4. Read the sermon "Jesus, Mother Hen" in Chapter 10 and notice how the preacher applies her exegesis of the text. In what way does she use the historical context of the passage to determine certain values that can be applied to today's context? How do you see the four authorities of the Wesleyan Quadrilateral in relation to one another in this sermon?

FOR FURTHER READING

Phyllis Bird. "Authority and Context in the Interpretation of Biblical Text." *Neotestamentica* 28 (1994): 323–37.

Michael J. Gorman, editor. *Scripture and Its Interpretation: A Global, Ecumenical Introduction to the Bible.* Grand Rapids: Baker Academic, 2017.

Joel B. Green. *Seized by the Truth: Reading the Bible as Scripture.* Nashville: Abingdon, 2007.

David Jasper. *A Short Introduction to Hermeneutics.* Louisville: Presbyterian Publishing, 2004.

NOTE

1. Note that some biblical texts do not have a solid or explicit theological foundation. Some responses may reflect more the cultural biases and values of the era than the character of God as we know God in the fuller or dominant voice of Scripture.

2

Using History to Understand the Text

In Chapter 1 we introduced the hermeneutical process. There we talked about it as a two-stage process in which the first part is exegesis and the second part is using the results of our exegesis to speak a word to today's church and world. We talked also about the second stage, that of using creative analogies to have the theological affirmations that undergird the instructions the biblical texts contain and address similar kinds of issues and circumstances today. But we did not say anything about how to arrive at a good understanding of the circumstance the biblical writers faced. Neither did we talk about methods of gaining a good understanding of how they addressed those questions and issues. In this chapter and the next, we will discuss the methods we use in historical-critical exegesis. At the end of the chapter, we'll look at a sermon that illustrates putting these exegetical tools to good use.

WHAT IS EXEGESIS?

Sometimes the name of this process is a bit off-putting when we first hear it. So let's begin by defining **historical-critical** exegesis. The term "exegesis" is sometimes initially a scary term, but it simply refers to the process of doing a careful interpretation of a text. It has been used since the nineteenth century to refer to the task of interpreting biblical texts. The word exegesis is a Greek word that means "explanation" or "interpretation." That Greek noun comes from a verb that means, most woodenly, "to lead out," and more generally "to describe" or "tell about." The point of exegesis is to draw out or describe the meaning that is in the text.

In exegesis we search the text as deeply as we can to discover what situation it addressed and how the writer responded to it. We try to hear clearly the explicit things that an author says and the things that author assumed or expected of the readers. In order to do this, we must investigate the social and cultural context of the author and the recipients of a text. We also need to come to as clear of an understanding as possible of the specific situation(s) that a text addresses. In addition, we need to identify what kind of literature a text is, that is, what genre it belongs to. As we noted in Chapter 1, the genre of a text tells us much about how to read it. In all of this, we are not really doing anything different from what interpreters of other ancient texts do when they study those texts carefully. Even though the term "exegesis" is usually used only for studying biblical texts, we would be using the same methods if we were reading Homer or Plato or any other writings from a time period and a culture that is not our own. We should note here that this is not the only way interpreters approach texts. Historical-critical exegesis tries to diminish as much as possible the perspective of the interpreter in order to hear or privilege the perspective of the text. As we will see in Chapter 4, other interpreters emphasize the experiences and perspectives of readers to help us think about the meanings of the texts.

If exegesis means drawing a meaning out of the text (as opposed to **eisegesis**, reading your own meaning into a text), the other two terms in "historical-critical exegesis" describe how we do that. Sometimes when people first hear the word "critical" used in connection with the Bible, they think it means talking about things that are wrong with it. But that is not the meaning here. We use the word "critical" with its meaning of "analytical." It has the meaning it has when we talk about a movie critic. The main job of a movie critic is not to tell you what is wrong with every movie the person sees, but to give you an analysis of it. The critic tells us what genre it belongs to, that is, whether it is a comedy or a drama, or whatever type. The critic will also tell us something about the content and perhaps the kind of cinematography it uses. Of course, the critic will also give us her or his opinion about the quality of the performances and the movie, but that is not her only or central task.

When we use the word "critical" to refer to our treatment of a biblical text, then, it means that we are analyzing it carefully. We use the methods we will talk about in this chapter and the next to give an analysis that allows us to hear what is in the text as clearly as possible. These kinds of analyses work to try to limit the biases we bring to our reading of the text so that we can hear more clearly what is really in the text. We noted in the previous chapter that it is also important to allow readers' perspectives to help them see and analyze aspects of the text. If we begin trying to let the texts speak on their own terms first, we will be in a better position to think about the presuppositions and assumptions their writers assume from their cultural contexts.

The term "historical" in "historical-critical exegesis" defines the kind of analysis we will use to interpret, to draw the meaning out of, our text. It means that we will analyze the text by setting it as clearly as possible in its own historical context. That means setting it in its own social, cultural, and political context. However much we may consider the biblical texts to be distinctive, the writers had to speak to people who lived in a world that was shaped by the things that other people believed, practiced, and experienced. As we noted above, we also want to uncover as much as we can about the specific circumstances that authors address. Setting the texts in their own historical context includes doing a careful **literary analysis** of them. This means that we learn about the expectations of various kinds of ancient writings and interpret the biblical texts with those expectations rather than with our expectations of various genres. Such analysis again helps us to listen for what the text wanted readers to hear.

TEXTUAL CRITICISM

With this understanding of what historical-critical exegesis is, we can turn to the methods that are used to accomplish its goals. If we want to understand the message that was given to the first readers of a text, we must first make sure we are reading the same words they read. So, the first method we will discuss is textual criticism.

The primary goal of textual criticism is to establish what the author(s) of a biblical book actually wrote. This may sound strange at first, but we have to remember that there was no printing press until the fifteenth century. Up to that time, all copies of the biblical text were copies made by hand. Your own experience at copying something can help you think about how difficult it is not to miss a word or letter or to write the wrong one or to leave something out. While many of the people who made copies of the biblical texts were professional copyists (scribes), they still made mistakes. There are no two copies of extensive parts of ancient biblical texts that are exactly alike. Textual critics' job is to work through and compare ancient manuscripts to try to identify what the original author wrote.

Before we talk about the methods of textual criticism, we need to think about the biblical texts that we read. Modern translations of the Bible into English work from what is known as a critical edition of the Hebrew Bible and the Greek New Testament. That critical edition is the result of the work of textual critics. For both the Hebrew Bible and the New Testament, the leading critical editions are produced by committees of textual critics so that the biases or theology of no one person or denomination dominates the decisions about which reading is more likely correct. Even when the decision is made to select one reading rather than others, these critical editions often put other relatively strong contenders in a footnote. There is no page of any of these critical editions that does not have multiple alternative readings. In these footnotes, the editors identify which ancient manuscripts (copies) contain the various readings. This allows other textual critics to think about the committee's decision on their own.

Unless you are doing your exegesis from the Hebrew or Greek text, you will not see most of these alternatives. The most important ones, however, will appear in the footnotes of some translations or in parentheses in the text with a note that will indicate that many manuscripts do not have the enclosed words. It is always important to look for these footnotes so that you are aware of the possibility that the wording of the original may be different from what you see in the translation. Where these alternatives are more important, you will find discussion of them in good critical commentaries.

We do not need to be alarmed at the idea that we are not always sure about what the original biblical authors wrote. Most text critics are confident that we have right about 95 percent of the biblical text. In some cases, the uncertainties are unimportant. It might be something as simple as whether the word should be "a" or "the." Of course, there are times when that might be important. There can be a significant difference between saying someone is "a son of God" and saying someone is "the son of God." We will talk about a real case of an important variant after we talk about the methods of textual criticism.

A Brief History of the Emergence of Biblical Texts

We don't know very much about how the text of the Hebrew Bible was passed down until about the year 1000 CE. It was at about that time that what is known as the Masoretic text took shape. The Masoretes were Jewish scholars of the sixth to tenth centuries CE who made it their life's work to preserve the texts of the Hebrew Bible. By the year 1000, the text had a set form, and it was revered in such a way that careful attention was given to its transmission. We are fortunate now to have the Dead Sea Scrolls. There are parts of the text of every book of the Hebrew Bible among them except for Esther. While there are some exceptions, the way the biblical texts appear in them and the way they appear in the Masoretic text are fairly congruent. That means that the text that was being used in the century just before the time of Jesus was preserved carefully.

The earliest copies of the works that became the books of the New Testament were written on papyrus. Papyrus is a form of paper that is made from reeds. Our earliest piece of the New Testament is a fragment of the Gospel of John, dated from about 125. Unfortunately, it is only about the size of a credit card. But we have most of the New Testament in the Chester Beatty Papyri. It contains twelve volumes that were produced around the year 200. This set gives us extremely valuable evidence for the early form of the text of the New Testament.

A significant development for ancient texts was the invention of the codex, which is a manuscript that is in the form of a book rather than a scroll. From the fourth century we have two important codices. Codex Vaticanus and Codex Sinaiticus are our earliest and most complete copies of the whole Bible. The text of the Hebrew Bible in these codices, however, has been translated into Greek. Still, these codices and the Chester Beatty Papyri give us our most substantial early evidence for what the authors of the New Testament wrote.

As we noted earlier, copyists make mistakes. Just as it happens when we copy things, there are some common errors. Sometimes we skip a word, or we write it twice when it should appear only once. If two consecutive lines end with the same word, we might even skip a whole line. There are examples of all of these kinds of errors and more in the biblical manuscripts. When more people began to want copies of the Bible, ways to copy the text expanded beyond one person copying one manuscript. Sometimes a room full of copyists would write as one person read the book they were reproducing. Some mistakes came from substituting a word that sounded the same but meant something different. An example from English is the word "there." If I say that word (rather than you reading it) you would have to decide whether I said "there," "their," or "they're." The only way to know which I meant is from the context. Sometimes these scribes who were listening to the text being read lost their concentration for a moment and wrote the wrong homonym.

But those are not the only kinds of changes that got into the text. At times, copyists corrected the grammar of a sentence or made it read more smoothly. Other times they corrected some spelling. Then, sometimes in the middle of theological arguments, copyists changed the text on purpose so that it matched what they thought or ruled out what the other side was asserting.

We are fortunate to have enough ancient copies of these texts to be able to recognize these differences and try to determine which is closest to what the original author wrote. But we also need systematic ways of evaluating and using the ancient copies. One way value is placed on a manuscript is to consider its age. In general, the older manuscripts are seen as more likely to preserve the original text. But age alone is not enough. Text critics also organize the manuscripts into groups or families. There are groups of manuscripts that seem to be related to the same early copy or to similar copies. You can tell that by the presence of a distinctive reading of a particular text that only they have or perhaps by following a form of certain books that is longer in some groups than in others. It is fortunate that the three manuscripts we talked about above belong to the same family, and it is the one usually seen as most reliable.

Of course, manuscripts within a family also have differences, so text critics have other rules that help them evaluate readings. One is that the shorter reading is usually correct. The logic is that copyists are more likely to expand a text to make it more clear than they are to leave things out. Another rule is that the text that is more different from a parallel text is more likely to be original. For example, if the same saying of Jesus appears in two different Gospels in a bit different form, the copyists sometimes made them match. That tendency means that the one that is more different from the parallel is more likely to be original.

Another rule of text critics is that the more difficult reading is preferred. The logic here is that copyists are more likely to make a text make better sense than to change it to be more difficult to understand. The final rule I will mention is that an unusual use of a word is more likely to be original because copyists are more likely to insert a word more commonly used to express an idea than to change the usual word for a less commonly used one.

Of the methods you will use in doing exegesis, you will spend the least time doing textual criticism. But it is important to know about how it works so that you can follow the arguments that interpreters make when there is a problem. This will sometimes be rather important for helping people understand what they find in their Bible. The exercise and example below illustrate the importance of textual criticism for preaching.

An Example: Jesus Defending the Woman Caught Committing Adultery (John 7:53–8:11)

An example of the importance of textual criticism is the well-loved story of the woman who was caught committing adultery that the religious leaders bring to Jesus to see if he will say she should be stoned. This whole story (7:53–8:11) was not originally a part of the Gospel of John. This is another text that does not appear until the fifth century. If you look in the *New Revised Standard Version* (NRSV), you will see that it is in the text, but it is set off from the rest of the text with double parentheses and a footnote appears at the end. That note says that the story does not appear in most ancient authorities and that it appears in other places in John in other manuscripts, something else that suggests it was an independent story that found its way into the text sometime after the Gospels were being read as Scripture. While this is a wonderful story that may go back to some early traditions about Jesus, we should be clear that it was not originally a part of John or any book of the Bible. We must, then, think about what that means about how we use it in the church.

A preacher who looks to Scripture as the authority for the message of a sermon will avoid using texts that do not seem to have been a part of the original text, texts such as our example and the exercise on Mark Chapter 16. While these are known and loved texts, they were not a part of the original texts and they were not part of the texts when they began to be read as Scripture. There may, however, be occasions on which you will need to teach lessons on these texts. Then it is important to be clear that these are not actually biblical texts. On the other hand, that does not mean that there are no good lessons to be learned from them. The material in these texts certainly was important to those who inserted them and to many who read them in subsequent centuries. Discussion of the values and beliefs that they reflect, then, can help today's church think about earlier Christians and how they understood the faith.

Hopefully, this brief introduction to textual criticism will help you be able to read the arguments in critical commentaries about these and other texts. The point of knowing this background is that it will help you be able to talk to others about these matters when questions arise and to preach sermons that are informed by this analysis.

EXERCISE

Analyzing the Ending of Mark

1. *Read Mark Chapter 16.* If you look at the NRSV, you will see three different endings. One version ends at v. 8, another adds just two sentences, and another ending goes through v. 16. The end of the Gospel of Mark is an example of a problematic text.
2. *Read the footnotes in the NRSV on the ending of Mark.* What general information do they give you about the various endings?
3. *Consult the biblical commentaries.* Refer to Appendix A for a list of recommended commentaries to help you understand the reasons for the different endings. What more do you learn about these divergent endings from biblical scholars?

4. *List reasons for concluding Mark with one of these three endings.* Think about the kinds of reasons for making this decision that we have talked about in our discussion of textual criticism.
5. *Think about how you might preach on this text.* What ending would you choose as the focus of the text? How would you explain your decision to focus on one ending over the others to those listening to your sermon?

The manuscripts that end this Gospel at v. 8 have Mark conclude it saying that the women leave the tomb and tell no one because they are afraid. For some copyists, that did not seem like a satisfactory conclusion, so they added other endings. The ending that has the next two sentences says they really did go tell the apostles, and the longer ending is the one found in the *King James Version* (KJV), which includes an appearance of the risen Jesus.

There are clear reasons to think that the original ending was at v. 8. The kind of information you will find in critical commentaries will give clear reasons for ending the book at v. 8. Among those reasons you will find that all of the earliest manuscripts end at v. 8. It is not until the fifth century that vv. 9-16 appear. Further, ending the book at v. 8 is the more difficult ending and it is the shortest. It can account for all the other endings. In fact, the evidence is so weak for the vv. 9-16 ending that it seems unlikely that it would be included in recent translations had it not been in the KJV. The KJV was completed at a time when textual criticism was not well developed. The manuscript tradition it depended on is not among the best. This is just one example of a place where the KJV relied upon inferior evidence and so made the wrong decision about what was originally written.

When preaching on this text, if you decide to stay with the original ending, which is, admittedly, not a "happy ending," you would want to think about how to approach this in a sermon. What might be the implications for a faith community of the women keeping silent about the resurrection? To see an example of how this challenging text might inform a sermon, see the sermon at the end of the chapter, "A COVID-19 Easter: Mark's Gospel Is Just What We Need."

HISTORICAL CRITICISM

An important initial step is locating our texts most broadly in their own cultural and historical settings. The biblical books were written in a number of different settings. At least the original forms of some books come from at least as early as the eighth century BCE, when prophets (or those around them) began writing their oracles. In the seventh century, after he is banned from the temple and the king's court, Jeremiah sends his secretary Baruch to read the oracle Jeremiah had dictated on behalf of God. At least parts of that scroll (really, it's a replacement because the king burned the original) are parts of the book of Jeremiah.

A number of the books of the Hebrew Bible took the form they have now in the sixth century BCE while the people of Judah were in exile in Babylon. Still other books reflect the time of the return from exile. The last of those to be put together seems to be the book of Daniel, which was written in the middle of the second century BCE. Then, the New Testament books were written from the mid-first century through about the first quarter of the second. Situating a work into its sociocultural setting is sometimes complicated by seeing that various parts of it come from different time frames. For example, the early parts of the book of Isaiah are from the eighth century, while the latest parts are from the sixth century. Each of those parts must be read in its own historical time frame. But we must also think about how the time and needs of the last person to add to or edit the book shaped the whole and so read each part in the context of the whole biblical book and the circumstances that last contributor and his or her community faced.

All of these are distinct cultural and political settings. How social systems worked in them differed. So did assumptions about how the world worked and how the gods related to it. They had different structures of governments and of legal systems. The religious beliefs of these various times and places also were different. That includes differing views about how to worship and what gods (including those beyond the God of Israel) want. What philosophers said about the world and the gods also differ across these settings. They will even have differences about how families and social relations should be structured. It would be nice if we could all be experts on all of these historical periods, but we cannot. However, we can turn to experts who have studied these periods to learn about these settings. Entries in good Bible dictionaries can help us understand these settings and the assumptions of those times and places. You can look up general periods and you can look up specific cultural practices. You can look up marriage practices or agricultural or commercial practices in these various places and times, for example. Good critical commentaries also will talk about those cultural and social expectations and point you to more detailed information about them.

Knowing this information helps us understand why an author writes what we find in a text. Sometimes what we see will be a rejection of the usual practices and sometimes it will reflect the cultural norms. We will see, then, how each writing reflects the concerns and beliefs of its time and how it seeks to stand apart from them or draw on them. This is the beginning of being sure that we do not assume that the way we see things is what the writers and readers of these texts thought of things.

SPECIFIC SITUATIONS AS THE CONTEXT FOR UNDERSTANDING TEXTS

Once we have this broad picture in view, we need to identify as specifically as possible the particular and immediate issues or topics that a book addresses. For the "historical books" of the Hebrew Bible, Genesis through 2 Chronicles, we have to set them in both the time of the action and in the time when they were written. In these books, the telling of the story from the past is used to speak to issues the community being addressed is facing in its present. So, if we were studying 1 and 2 Kings, we would want to think about how the king ruled in Judah in the ninth or eighth century BCE and how the author shapes that story to address the concerns of the sixth century BCE in Babylon, the time when the book was written.

The same is true for the Gospels. They do not tell their stories just to preserve stories and sayings of Jesus; they tell their stories as they do to address questions and concerns in their churches decades after the death of Jesus. This means we will ask about the ethnic composition of the recipients and what kinds of issues, questions, and problems the church was facing in the decades that the Gospels were penned. Some of those will be issues pressed on them from outside, and some will be questions that arise as they think about what they should believe and do as church members, as believers in Christ.

When looking at the Gospels and other books that tell of past events, some of what we can perceive about the problems and questions that the communities faced will remain unclear. Other kinds of writings allow us to discover more about their setting. Paul's letters often address very specific questions that churches have asked him or address problems that have arisen in his churches. In places, it is fairly easy to identify those historical circumstances but at other times, since he usually does not repeat the question, it is more difficult. But identifying this immediate exigence, this immediate thing that led him to say what he says in response, can be very important for understanding that response clearly.

Again, after reading the text carefully and thinking about it, an important place that we can begin to get this information is from a good Bible dictionary, looking up its section on the Occasion and Purpose of the book. Some dictionaries (usually multivolume dictionaries) are detailed enough to offer some of the reasons for identifying the problem in one way or another. Beyond a good dictionary, critical commentaries offer yet more detailed surveys and arguments for seeing the situation in a particular way. This information will be in both the introduction to the whole book and often in the commentary on the passage you are exegeting.

EXPLORING THE WORDING OF THE TEXT FOR PREACHING

One of the first things you will want to do as you start studying a passage is to read it in multiple translations. You can start with the NRSV, the *Revised Standard Version* (RSV), the *New International Version* (NIV), and perhaps the *Revised English Bible* (REB). These all fit within something of the same range of kinds of translations in the sense of where they fall between being wooden[1] in their translation and being paraphrastic.[2] Comparing these translations can give you a first look at what some of the interpretive issues may be. If they seem to have different emphases or seem to say something different, you can note that as something to give attention to as you begin to dig deeper into your text.

One way that you may want to dig more deeply into a text is to do word studies. In this work, you try to see what meanings a particular Greek or Hebrew word has in this context. A single word can have many different meanings. It is important to remember that the meaning of a word is determined to a large extent by the context in which it appears. This means that you cannot look at the range of meanings that a word has and just pick the one that you like. For an example, let's think about the English word "set." Think for a moment about how many meanings that word can have. It can talk about a group of dishes, a group of numerals, a segment of a tennis match, a piece of equipment that receives radio or television waves, the place where a play is performed, and many other things. And those are just its meanings as a noun. As a verb it can mean putting something down, styling wet hair, or something solidifying or gelling.

If you were talking about a tennis match and said that you saw a great set on center court, the meaning would not be that there was a display of a group of matching dishes. To insert that meaning would be absurd. Yet, when some readers first start to see the range of the meanings of biblical terms, they take this approach. They simply pick a meaning that they would like to find in the text. We must avoid that kind of misuse of what we discover about words by always thinking about what makes the best sense in the context. That is, we look at what the topic of the paragraph and the sentence is and how particular meanings of a term fit that topic and contribute to making a point about it that makes sense with the other things the author is saying.

Critical commentaries and good Bible dictionaries can help you think about the meanings of important terms that appear in your text and the important broader concepts that they may convey or point toward. You should allow yourself to be guided by those discussions. You may also want to use a concordance. A concordance is a book that lists the words that appear in the Bible. Under each word, it will show you every place that word appears. But you need to be careful here. You cannot rely on a concordance that works solely with English words. Often the same English word is used to translate several different Greek or Hebrew terms. Take for example the word "servant" in the NRSV or other translations. Many translations use that word to translate *doulos* (an enslaved person), *diakonos* (servant, without indicating whether the person is enslaved or free and sometimes used of government officials), and *pais* (a servant or a child). Each of these can have different nuances, depending on the context. You will, then, want to use a concordance that tells you what Greek or Hebrew word lies behind the English word in your passage.

Another caution is important here. Often a concordance that tells you which Greek or Hebrew term is found in the text will give you the English meaning of that term. But you should not take the concordance as an authority about that meaning. A concordance such as Strong's concordance will give you the meaning that the compiler thought was best for a particular verse, but the concordance will give no discussion of why that is the best rendering of the term in this or other passages. So, once you see where a term appears outside the passage you're reading, you will need to look to other resources for reasons to think one translation is more appropriate than another.

One of the most interesting things to observe in word studies is whether the author you are reading uses a term in a particular way. Sometimes authors use a word in a single way even when it has other meanings in other writings. Other times, an author will consistently give the term a particular nuance that is distinctive. These kinds of observations can help you move toward a clearer understanding of a passage.

We include word studies within historical methods rather than literary methods because we are trying to understand the terms in their historical context. We want to know what a word meant in the world of the author and readers of our texts and what it meant in this particular instance of its use.

An Example: Preaching with the Word "Redemption"

To see why it's important to understand the wording of a biblical text when preaching, let's consider Rom 3:24. You'll notice that one of the two words used for what the death of Christ accomplishes is "redemption." This presents a challenge for preachers today because we seldom use the word "redemption" or the verb "redeem." When we do, it is usually connected to using a coupon. That meaning of this English word has little to do with the meaning of the Greek word it represents (*apolytrōsis*).

The word *apolytrōsis* referred to paying a ransom for a person who had been kidnapped or taken captive in a war. It meant buying a person back from being entrapped or enslaved. This metaphor for salvation can help us broaden our understanding of biblical thought about the meaning of the work of Christ and render the word "redeemed" as something other than a vague religious word that we often think of as roughly synonymous with "saved"—yet another term that needs investigation in its ancient context.

Recognizing the meaning of this term shifts our understanding of what keeps us from being in proper relationship with God. Preaching about "redemption" gives an opportunity to think about sin as something that is bigger than just bad things we each do. This image for the gift the death of Christ brings implies that humans are trapped, taken hostage by sin. This gives us an image that helps us talk about systemic sin, about the ways that we are all required to live within systems that keep us from living out what God wants for the world. The metaphor of redemption says that we need to be rescued, not forgiven. As important as the idea of being forgiven is, talking about redemption gives us ways to think about sin and salvation that talking of forgiveness does not provide. In turn, that opens the door for us to preach about the church being called to fight against systemic sin because redemption frees us to oppose those systems that trap all people.

EXERCISE

Preaching about the Word "Sanctification"

1. *Read Romans 6:19-22.* The word "sanctification" appears twice in these verses.
2. *Think about the word "sanctification."* You'll notice that it is related to "righteousness." This presents a challenge for preachers today because we don't usually think of ourselves as righteous, and not all traditions use the word sanctification. These are often religious-sounding words given little significant explanation.
3. *Consult a Bible dictionary.* Look up the word "sanctification." You'll see that the Greek word for sanctification is *hagiamos*. What is the meaning of this term? What is the history of the use of this idea in the Hebrew Bible? How is it related to the word "holy"? How is it related to "righteousness"?
4. *Consider how you might preach about the word "sanctification."* This word can help us think about how Christians are to live and what living in that way means. How might you make the idea of becoming "holy" important, even attractive, to a congregation?
5. *Notice the other images in this text.* Consider how the ideas of being "enslaved to sin" and "enslaved to God" are related to sanctification. How might these metaphors help you talk about sanctification? How might you express the ideas in these images with metaphors that do not cause the kind of pain that talking of enslavement entails?

As you can see, paying close attention to the meanings of words in Scripture within their historical context can open important theological perspectives that will enrich our preaching. This attention to the meanings of words also alerts us to ways that we need to think about the literary forms and structures used by the authors of the biblical texts. We turn to those in our next chapter.

For now, let's look at a sermon that illustrates how textual criticism can inform the content and structure of a sermon. As you read this sermon, you'll see notes in italics highlighting the way exegesis has informed the sermon. Later when we learn about crafting the Central Question, we'll revisit this sermon to think about how one's preaching context intersects with biblical exegesis to shape the sermon.

SERMON EXAMPLE: "A COVID-19 EASTER: MARK'S GOSPEL IS JUST WHAT WE NEED"

Recall from this chapter the challenges posed by the alternate endings of Mark. In this sermon, you'll see an example of one way in which textual criticism can be utilized to inform a sermon that speaks to the existential crisis of a worldwide pandemic, as well as a family's crisis of illness and death. This sermon by Leah D. Schade was preached on Easter Sunday of 2020.

Text: Mark 16:1-8

"So they went out and fled from the tomb, for terror and amazement had seized them; and they said nothing to anyone, for they were afraid." (Mark 16:8)

1. That's it? That's how the Gospel of Mark ends? How unsatisfying. What a letdown. Where is the risen Jesus? Where are the stories of his appearances to Mary Magdalene, to the followers on the road to Emmaus, to the disciples on the fishing boat?
   Where's our happy ending?
2. The Gospel of Mark has none of this. That's why churches rarely read *this* Resurrection story on Easter morning. We want the angels. We want the faith-inspiring scene of Mary Magdalene hearing the risen Lord speak her name. We want to see Jesus!
3. But that's not what we get in the Gospel of Mark. We *do* get the women going to the tomb on the morning after the sabbath. We do get the heavy stone rolled away from the tomb. And we do see a mysterious figure dressed in white. We also hear the announcement that Jesus has been raised from the dead. So far, so good.
4. But when the young man in white gives the women instructions to tell the disciples that Jesus is going ahead to meet them in Galilee, what happens? The women run away in terror, amazement, and fear. And they tell nothing to anyone.
   What are we to do with this story?

(Notice that Leah chose to end the ***pericope*** *[a set of verses that forms one coherent unit or thought] at verse 8, the original ending of the text. This allowed her to ask questions in paragraphs 1–4 that capture the dissonance in the text and the jarring response of the listener.)*

5. It's disconcerting, because the women had been so faithful up to this point. They stayed with Jesus all through his ministry, supporting him financially. These women did not abandon him at the time of his crucifixion like the other disciples did. Yet when it comes time for them to really shine, to step into the role of apostles and announce the resurrection to the disciples, it appears that they fail in their assignment. How can this be? And if this is the case, what does it mean for us as followers of Jesus today?

(In paragraph 5, Leah wove in her exegesis of the text in which she pointed out the larger backstory of the narrative and the role of the women in Jesus's story. This led to a transition question that moves from exegesis to thinking about the meaning of the text for her listeners.)

6. I've been thinking a lot about Mark's Gospel in the midst of a fearful, COVID-19 Easter. In Chapter 15 that tells the crucifixion story, the curtain of the temple is torn in two. This symbolizes the ripping of the very fabric of the universe. The divide between the sacred and profane is ripped right down the middle.
7. In many ways, this virus pandemic has ripped through humanity, tearing asunder the very fabric of our society. Like the disciples after the crucifixion, we are huddled in our homes, afraid and isolated. Today does not *feel* like Easter. We are not in our churches filled with lilies, hearing soaring music, shouting and singing at the top of our lungs, "He is Risen! He Is Risen Indeed, Hallelujah!"
8. Instead this is a COVID-19 Easter. We are separated from each other and from our loved ones with whom we usually share this day. Many are out of work and are facing the end of their financial rope. Others have been working almost nonstop to try to find a treatment, test a vaccine. We see pictures of healthcare workers' faces after twelve-hour shifts, their skin marked with red lines from their face masks.
9. And on Good Friday, we watched with horror the video of the mass graves in New York's Hart Island off the coast of the Bronx. The families of tens of thousands of people across the globe are experiencing something more like a perpetual Good Friday than an Easter morning.
   The women ran from the tomb afraid. Words failed them. Maybe Mark's Gospel is exactly the story we need.

(In paragraphs 6–9, Leah weaves the crucifixion story with the lived experience of her congregation during the onset of the COVID-19 pandemic. Again, drawing on her exegesis, she is able to point out parallels between the biblical story and the contemporary situation that amplify the tension of feeling angst in the midst of what is supposed to be a joyous time.)

10. Later redactors and editors were so uncomfortable with the original ending that they felt the need to tack on not one, but two alternative endings to the Gospel of Mark. They're a mish-mash of post-resurrection material from other sources to give us the happy ending we so desire. Even Bible editors couldn't refrain from the Hollywood ending!
11. But if we are true to the text and really wrestle with what it means, I believe we will find the Good News that we need on this Easter morning. There are truths in Mark's story of the resurrection that we need to hear.

(Paragraphs 10 and 11 explicitly draw on textual criticism by pointing out the different endings of Mark. This allows the sermon to pivot into interpretation of the original ending for contemporary listeners.)

12. Sometimes we fail. And fail spectacularly. Sometimes we fail in the most important, key moments of life. How ironic that the women did not waver all during Jesus's life and during his death. But when faced with the good news of the resurrection, that's when they fled. I have to admit that I find myself alongside these women more often than I should. I often fail to understand the power of God and to trust that God is using that power for good.
13. Sometimes there are no words. The women had the best news to tell. And yet they told no one. They could not find their voice. I can relate to this. When being shown the resurrection in the midst of death, I often turn away inexplicably and find myself mute, unable to give voice to the good news that has been shown to me. And yet, there's another truth of Mark's Gospel: the story of the resurrection still comes to us.

(Notice in paragraphs 12 and 13, Leah returns to the characters of the women and humanizes them by relating to her own misgivings and failures. In Chapter 4, you'll learn about feminist interpretations of Scripture, one of the perspective-explicit perspectives that can inform our exegesis and preaching, which highlights the importance of women's voices and experiences in the Bible.)

14. The "unhappy ending" of Mark could lead us to despair. But here's the thing. We are still telling this story, aren't we? We do hold this Gospel in our hand. How is it that we have this story, if no one ever told the news?
15. Several years ago, I met with a young man in a previous congregation I served who wanted to be baptized. Let's call him Shawn. Shawn was not raised in the church. It just wasn't a part of his upbringing or experience. But he met and married a woman named Darlene who was a member of our church, along with her parents, Leonard and Charlotte. Leonard, Shawn's father-in-law, was diagnosed with a very aggressive disease that ravaged his body over a series of months. It was during this difficult time that Shawn and Darlene had their first child, little Fiona. This child's life and her relationship with Leonard, though all too brief, was such a blessing to him and to all of them.
16. I'll never forget when we all gathered at Leonard's bedside for a service of prayer and commendation, to bless him as he passed from this life. Fiona, only nine months old, was attentive, alert, and completely engaged in that prayer circle. She was fully present to that holy moment and to her grandfather.
17. After his funeral, it was only natural for them to have Fiona baptized in the church. And then Shawn said he wanted to be baptized as well.

(Paragraph 14 serves as a transition to the next section of the sermon. It names the tension that has been building in the first half of the sermon and then offers the glimmer of an "aha" moment by pointing out a possible way forward. The question asked at the end of the paragraph sets up the extended story that follows in paragraphs 15–17.)

18. This confluence of death and life had a profound effect on him. He had witnessed the care provided by the pastors and members of the congregation to their family. He realized the value of belonging to a church community. So he wanted to be baptized to help raise his daughter in the church.
19. We met for several sessions to talk and learn, to ask questions and reflect on answers. At one point, I talked with Shawn about how he might approach reading the Bible. We agreed that the book itself is so huge, it can be overwhelming. He needed a place to start. So after thinking about it he said, "Well, I really want to learn more about God. I want to get to know God better. And it seems that the best way to do that is to get to know Jesus. So I guess I want to start with the part about Jesus."

20. And I said, "Yes! You got it! If you want to know God, get to know Jesus. That's what Christianity is all about." So I pointed him to the Gospel of Mark, which is the earliest, shortest, and most basic Gospel. Let's read Mark, I said, because there you will encounter Jesus.
21. And then it hit me as we started reading the Gospel of Mark together. Just nine verses into Chapter 1, do you know what it says? "In those days Jesus came from Nazareth of *Galilee* and was baptized by John in the Jordan." Skip ahead to the last chapter. Where did the young man tell the women to meet Jesus? *In Galilee.*

(In paragraphs 18–21, Shawn's story and the Gospel story dovetail and converge. Note how textual criticism is utilized in paragraph 21 to highlight both the ending and the beginning of Mark's Gospel.)

22. Could it be that the author of Mark's Gospel had another reason for this strange ending? Is it possible that the message from the young man at the tomb was not just for the women and the disciples, but for Mark's own church, and for us as well? Maybe *we* are the ones who are supposed to meet Jesus in Galilee. Maybe we are being pointed back to the beginning of the story, to re-read the Gospel in light of what we know from the ending.
23. When we do that, we discover that this ending of Mark isn't really an ending at all! It's a beginning! It loops back around to the start. And it's telling us that even when we fail, even when we can't find the words, even when we are huddled in fear—this is not the end of the story. It's not the end of our discipleship.
24. Because here's the other truth of Mark's Gospel. The most important truth of all: Jesus is still risen, even if we can't recognize it yet.

(Paragraph 22 provides the answer to the question asked in paragraph 14. Notice how the listener is led to this answer in an organic way through the use of Shawn's story.)

25. This is what I told Shawn and Fiona on the Saturday Easter Vigil when they were baptized many years ago. No matter what they face, no matter how wrong the world is, this is not the end of the story. Jesus is still risen.
26. Even when Leonard's body failed him, that was not the end of the story. When little Fiona and her daddy, Shawn, eventually encounter their own failures, that will not be the end of the story. Jesus is still risen.
27. Even in the saddest, most painful moments of our lives, when the curtain of the temple is torn in two, when the fabric of our world is ripped to shreds—this is not the end of the story. Jesus is still risen.
28. Even on this COVID-19 Easter as we watch this virus overcome us, and our leaders fail us, and our voices are choked with grief, anger, and fear so that we cannot even speak—this is not the end of the story. Jesus is still risen.

(Paragraphs 25–28 each contain strong Theological Claims [which you will learn about in Chapters 8–10] and each end with a repeated refrain, "Jesus is still risen." This use of repetition is a rhetorical skill you'll learn about in Chapter 22 when we cover beginnings, transitions, and endings of sermons.)

29. Mark's Gospel points us back to the beginning. To the beginning of Earth's story when God created all things. The beginning of Israel's story in Egypt when God brought them out of slavery and oppression. The beginning of Jesus's story, in Galilee, entering our broken, violent, failing world to bring us out of our failure and into new relationship with God.
30. It brings us to the beginning of Fiona's story when her birth and infancy brought new hope to a dying man. And it brings us to Shawn's story when he learned that Jesus had already gone ahead of him to Galilee and was meeting him right here in the Bible, and in the church, and in the sacrament of Baptism.
31. Mark's Gospel calls us—even in the midst of our failure—to get up, turn around, and continue following Jesus. Back to Galilee. Back to the beginning, back to the basics.
32. In many ways, this coronavirus crisis has forced us to get back to the basics as well. We are rediscovering (or maybe learning for the first time) how vital it is to just have the essentials of life—our health, a safe home, food on the table, relationships with people who are important to us. And our faith.

(In paragraphs 29–32, Leah draws together the three different strands of the sermon—the biblical story, Shawn's story, and the congregation's experience living in a time of pandemic. Paragraph 31 articulates what you'll come to learn is the Central Claim of the sermon, which we'll cover in Chapters 14 and 15. Paragraph 32 draws implications of that claim for the listeners.)

33. The man in white at the tomb still calls to us: Do not be afraid; you are looking for Jesus of Nazareth, who was crucified. He has been raised; he is not here . . . He is going ahead of you to Galilee; there you will see him, just as he told you. God will meet us in the midst of this. Jesus is still risen and is already ahead of us in whatever we will face.
34. On this COVID-19 Easter, we are people who have died and risen with Christ. This is why we can live with hope in the midst of the unknown. It's why we will proclaim the resurrection even when the death counts rise and evil seems to surround us everywhere we turn.
    We will continue to proclaim with faith in the midst of fear:
    Christ is risen! He is risen indeed, Hallelujah!

(The final two paragraphs conclude the sermon with explicit theological claims unequivocally stating that Jesus is risen. The last paragraph reveals what the Central Purpose of this sermon is: to assure a fearful and weary congregation of Jesus's resurrection so that they can continue to proclaim the risen Christ with faith in the midst of fear. You'll learn about the Central Purpose in Chapters 16 and 17.)

KEY POINTS IN THIS CHAPTER

1. Exegesis means to draw out or describe the meaning that is in the text. Historical-critical exegesis is a method that analyzes Scripture in its own historical context in order to understand the social, cultural, economic, religious, and political concerns of the original text, author, and readers. This helps us discern what the text wanted readers to hear.
2. Textual criticism is a method of interpretation that focuses on what the author of a biblical book actually wrote. It helps us distinguish between the original form of the text and the accidental and intentional changes that copyists made throughout the centuries.
3. Biblical texts did not magically appear in toto. The books in the Bible emerged over thousands of years, beginning with oral tradition and then written transmission that depended on handwritten copies.
4. Reading and comparing a passage in multiple translations can reveal important words to study in order to see how different translations affect the meaning of the text.
5. Because the biblical books were written in a number of different settings over a period of thousands of years, we must read them in their own historical time frame, keeping in mind what their community faced that prompted the book to be written.
6. Bible dictionaries and critical commentaries are resources that every preacher should consult when exegeting a text in preparation of a sermon.

DISCUSSION QUESTIONS

1. Finding out that some of the texts in our Bibles were not what the authors originally wrote can be troubling. How would you help a church retain their confidence in the integrity and authority of the biblical text when this comes up? Perhaps talk with an experienced preacher about how they talk with their churches about this.

2. Do a textual comparison just on Genesis 1:1-2 looking at different translations of the text. What do you notice about the different words used in verse 2 for wind/spirit/breath? What do you notice about how each translation orders the syntax of the words? How might this inform a sermon about this text?
3. In Chapter 1 we talked about using creative analogies as a way to bring the meaning of the text into the present. How might the information you find about the situation a biblical book addresses help you do that in your preaching?
4. Commentators often disagree about the historical situation that a biblical book addresses. Sometimes these differences lead them to understand specific texts somewhat differently. When you find these differences, how do you decide which view of the situation is more likely to be correct? What kinds of reasons would lead you to think that one view was more likely to be correct? How would seeing the differences in interpreting a particular text influence the way you interpret it and the way you would preach from it?

FOR FURTHER READING

Gordon D. Fee. *New Testament Exegesis: A Handbook for Students and Pastors*, third edition. Louisville: Westminster John Knox, 2002.

Michael J. Gorman. *Elements of Biblical Exegesis: A Basic Guide for Students and Ministers*, third edition. Grand Rapids: Eerdmans, 2020.

John H. Hayes and Carl R. Holladay. *Biblical Exegesis: A Beginner's Handbook*, fourth edition. Louisville: Westminster John Knox, 2022.

Steven L. McKenzie and Stephen R. Haynes, editors. *To Each Its Own Meaning: An Introduction to Biblical Criticisms and Their Application*, revised edition. Louisville: Westminster John Knox, 1999.

NOTES

1. A wooden translation tries to stay as close to the wording of the original text as possible. But the word order in sentences is different in Hebrew and Greek than it is in English. If a more wooden translation tries to retain the original's word order (or other grammatical features), it may produce a sentence that makes no sense in English or is at least hard to understand.

2. A paraphrastic translation is one that concerns itself only with conveying the meaning that the translators see in the original into English. So they may change metaphors and produce sentences that are very different from the original language. This means that they insert more interpretation into the translation. That, in turn, means you do not have the opportunity to think about what it means on your own. They have made sure that readers understand the text in the way that the translator(s) understand(s) it.

3

Using Literary Analysis to Understand the Text

In the last chapter, we talked about how to set a biblical text in its historical context. In this chapter we will explore ways that methods of literary analysis can help us understand a text. As we do this, we are not turning in a completely new direction. Here, for example, we will think about how it is important to recognize the kinds of expectations readers had of different genres in the ancient world. Often these will be different from the expectations we have of similar genres. But we will also look at how more recent kinds of literary analysis can help us understand a text.

GENRE CRITICISM

We begin by drawing attention to the need to recognize the different kinds of writings (that is, genres) that appear in the Bible. In Chapter 1, we talked about biblical genres in a general way. Here we recognize that all types of material in the biblical texts have to be read in accordance with their genre. When we look at the Psalms, we know that they need to be read as poetry, for example. If we were to take the Psalms literally, much of what they say would be scientifically and factually false. Think of Psalm 19. It begins:

> The heavens are telling the glory of God
>   And the firmament proclaims his handiwork.
> Day to day pours forth speech
>   And night to night declares knowledge.

We all know that the stars and comets and moons do not actually say anything. But the psalmist uses that language to talk about how the glorious design and beauty of the cosmos is a demonstration of the power and amazing knowledge and wisdom of God. The psalmist even acknowledges in the next verses that the imagery just used is not factual in a literal sense. He notes that these elements do not actually speak, and yet their message is heard everywhere. The psalmist does not always remind the reader not to take the image literally—and does not need to. The writer assumes you know you are reading poetry and that you know what that means about how to understand images and metaphors.

EXERCISE

Using Genre Criticism to Examine Psalm 18

1. *Read Psalm 18:1-2.* Notice how metaphor is used in this passage.
2. *Determine the genre.* What does the way the psalm is printed in your Bible say about its genre? What does its style of language and use of imagery say about its genre?
3. *Identify the statement about God used at the beginning of v. 2.* Does the psalmist intend readers to take that statement literally? Is God really "a rock"? How does knowing the genre of this verse help you understand what it says about God? What does the writer intend to convey with this image?
4. *Consider how a sermon might point out the power of metaphor and the necessity of understanding genre in a biblical text.* Especially if there are listeners who insist on a "literal" reading of the Bible, how might a sermon on Psalm 18 help to explain the importance of understanding genres when reading and interpreting the Bible? (In Chapter 8, we'll further explore the importance of metaphor and theological language for preaching.)

Our genre analysis of Psalm 19 was fairly straightforward. Still, it shows how we must take genre into account when we read the psalms. It is just that important to pay attention to the genre of every biblical book, and often the various genres that appear within a single book. But we frequently have a more difficult time understanding the expectations and purposes of other kinds of literature and distinguishing those expectations from the expectations we have of similar genres of our own time. This can prohibit us from reading texts in ways that are fair to the genre.

Consider the genre of biography. When we read a biography, we expect specific, factual, and usually detailed and perhaps unknown information about the person. We want to know what kinds of things shaped the person to be the distinctive individual that she or he was. But this was not the expectation for ancient biographies. Ancient biographies commonly shaped the telling of the story of a person's life according to the pattern of a type of person. In this mode, a person often exemplified a particular kind of character. For example, a person might be presented as greedy. If so, all of the person's life would be presented as one episode after another that showed how greedy people act and what they would do in particular situations. Even from the telling of stories about the person's youth, he or she would act in greed. Such shaping of biographies is very evident in Plutarch's *Parallel Lives*. In the forty-eight extant biographies in this work, Plutarch sets out to teach moral lessons, often by comparing Greek and Roman leaders. There are contradictions within the tellings of the stories and any number of things that have little claim to being factual. But then, the facts were not the point. Seeing the lives of these people as examples of what to imitate and avoid was more important than the facts.

The same is true for the histories of various nations or ethnic groups that we find among ancient writers. They are more interested in telling readers what kinds of people these were, what their ethnic and cultural inclinations were, than in getting the facts of history correct. Historiographers even encouraged their fellow writers to make the "facts" fit the appropriate characteristics of the group they wrote about. We should be sure to keep these kinds of expectations and methods of writing in mind when we read books that tell stories of the lives of the Israelites, and even of the ancestors (Abraham, etc.) and Jesus. One of the first things we must do is think about what the authors of these kinds of writings saw as the most important thing to convey and how that is reflected in the biblical books.

Just as we must remember the methods and purposes of ancient biographies, we must do the same for all of the kinds of writings we find in the Bible. For the Hebrew Bible, we will need to think about the genres of wisdom literature, prophetic writings, national and ancestral narratives, and others. For the New Testament we will have to think about the genres of the Gospels, the origins of a kind of people (Acts), ancient letters and epistolary literature, and apocalyptic texts. Indeed, much harmful misinterpretation could have been avoided if interpreters had learned how to read books such as Revelation by looking at how that genre was composed and read in the 150 years before the biblical book and the decades and immediate centuries after it.[1]

AVOIDING HARMFUL STEREOTYPES

Preachers and other present-day readers need to keep in mind the historical categorizations of various nations and ethnic groups as they read biblical texts. If we forget that such writings intend to teach lessons by giving good and bad examples, we can perpetuate harmful stereotypes. For example, the Gospel of John has many harsh things to say about "the Jews." But the author does not think that those characterizations are factual in the sense that they describe all people who are Jewish. In fact, the author of this Gospel is Jewish and most people in the church he writes this Gospel for are Jewish. He has, however, adopted the term "Jews" (many think we should translate this word as "Judeans" here) to refer to the people who oppose the ministry of Jesus, particularly the authorities who are in charge in Jerusalem.

While it seems strange to us, John can say that "the Jews" are bad but that the descendants of Abraham (other Jewish people) are good. Unfortunately, throughout the centuries Christians have used the derogatory characterization of those enemies of Jesus (and of John's church) to promote anti-Semitism. If preachers recognize both the methods of the genre John adopts and the limited way John uses the name "Jews," we can avoid unwittingly continuing to support anti-Semitism.

While it is often overlooked, then, the first step in exegeting (i.e., giving a careful interpretation of) a biblical passage is determining the genre of the work in which it appears. Good critical commentaries will give careful attention to these matters and help you think about how to identify a book's genre and so think about reading it. (See Appendix A for a list of reliable biblical commentaries.) As we noted earlier, there are also multiple genres within some books. Prophetic books often move from narrative to poetry (the prophet's oracle) and back to narrative. Other biblical books insert selections of known material of a different genre into their text. Paul often inserts a known liturgy or hymn or confession into his letters. It is important for us to recognize this as we go about interpreting his letters and analyzing the ways he tries to convince his readers to believe or do certain things. We will say more about this in connection with form criticism.

FORM CRITICISM

Form criticism works to identify the appearance, use, and function of smaller literary units within a larger work. Here we look for things such as differing kinds of prophetic discourses, parables, hymns, liturgical pieces (confessions, etc.), birth narratives, healing stories, various types of psalms, and other known types of literary units. We are trying to identify places where an author takes material that is already in some set oral or written form and inserts it in the text we are reading. Identifying such literary units in a work helps us understand that particular unit and the section in which it appears, as we see the use the author makes of that preformed material. Given the range of writings that we have from the ancient world outside the Bible, we are often able to compare kinds of material in the Bible with what appears elsewhere. Outside the biblical accounts we have creation stories, law codes, and even religious interpretations of the victories of a particular nation over others. For New Testament materials there are extra-biblical hymns to gods, parables, miracle stories, exorcism stories, and stories of visions of heavenly beings.

By comparing the biblical examples of these kinds of materials with those outside it, we are able to see how the biblical materials follow the usual patterns and how they differ from them. When making such comparisons we might note that the biblical creation story has a single god create the cosmos, while other Ancient Near Eastern creation stories have multiple gods come together to form the world. In such stories we might note that the process of creation in Genesis seems to emphasize the power of God by not having stories about the struggles with forces of chaos that the gods engage in parallel stories. Or if we look to exorcism stories in the New Testament, we could note how they have the same elements or steps in the form of the story as exorcism stories outside the Bible. But at the same time, Jesus seems to wield significantly more power and so have an easier time of exorcising demons. Knowing of these patterns and parallels helps us hear the stories more like the original hearers heard them. This helps us get closer to understanding the message the text conveyed to those hearers.

In the early years of the development of form criticism, it drew significantly on the anthropological roots of the method. Anthropologists had used this method to make cross-cultural comparisons. They noted that the same kinds of stories, with the same structures, often appeared in parallel cultural situations—including in places where there had been no cultural contacts. This led them to hypothesize that certain kinds of cultural and social experiences lead humans to create certain kinds of stories that have the same literary patterns. For example, the mining communities of Appalachia in the United States have the story of "Big John," the strong miner who holds up the roof beam of a collapsing mine while his fellow miners escape. When he lets go, the mine caves in on him and he dies a hero. When we look for parallels, it seems that mining communities in Russia had much the same story, told in much the same way.

It seemed, then, that parallel cultural and social experiences led to the creation of parallels stories, parallel not just in plot, but also in literary form. This led many biblical practitioners of form criticism to think they could work back from the literary form to understanding the experience of the community that produced a story and its form. They placed the type of story in its *Sitz im Leben*, its situation in life. They thought they could determine whether a particular piece originated in a worship setting or in a polemical situation or some other setting within the life of the church. This allowed them to talk about not just the meaning of the piece in the biblical book at hand, but also to say something about the experience of the church that first formulated the smaller unit.

Form critics are generally more reluctant now to make the leap to identifying the circumstances that produced a liturgy or miracle story or whatever kind of unit appears than they once were. But this kind of analysis still helps us see the parallels and contrasts that the authors of the original piece and the authors of our texts wanted the readers to note and think about. Noting that authors include such preformed material also helps us trace how they try to convince the readers to believe and do the things the authors recommend. Good critical commentaries will identify the various smaller genres that appear in a biblical book. They will discuss how they are structured and how this knowledge helps us interpret the passage at hand.

TRADITION CRITICISM AND SOURCE CRITICISM

Tradition criticism and source criticism are closely related endeavors. Both seek to identify sources that a biblical author drew from or simply inserted into a text. The distinction lies in the kinds of sources they deal with. Tradition criticism tries to identify oral sources that are incorporated into a text, while source criticism looks more toward identifying written sources the author used. Both try to understand the biblical text by identifying the preexisting materials that made their way into the biblical text. Both identify and try to reconstruct those preexisting materials. And they try to date them as a means to consider how the biblical writers took up and developed the ideas contained in them.

Among the oral traditions may be stories about or oracles from prophets. But some of these were passed down in written form as well. Similarly, most interpreters are convinced that the first five books of the Bible are drawn from a number of prior sources that began as oral traditions and then at least in part took written form. If we look to the New Testament, we see Paul cite traditions such as his account of the institution of the Lord's Supper in 1 Cor 11:23-26. He even identifies it as a tradition that was passed on to him. Matthew and Luke seem to rely on both Mark and a written account known as "Q." While no copies of Q are extant, most scholars give the name "Q" to what they reconstruct as a written document that contained sayings of Jesus. In addition to Mark, Matthew and Luke may also rely on oral traditions about what Jesus did and said. We do not know which of those oral traditions were written down before these Evangelists (authors of the Gospels) wrote their accounts of Jesus's life. The not uncommon process of oral traditions becoming written sources shows how closely related tradition criticism and source criticism are. They are distinguished more by whether they investigate oral or written sources more than by the methods they use.

Investigations into the sources the biblical writers use can help us see how these writers adopt the views of their communities and how they challenge them. They also give us a broader context in which to understand the biblical text we are reading.

REDACTION CRITICISM

The next sort of literary criticism we need to consider is redaction criticism. As a first step toward understanding this kind of analysis we should note that the word "redaction" comes from the French word for editing. Redaction criticism analyzes how an author takes a preformed piece and changes it, edits it, to fit what that author wants it to mean. Different writers can take up the same parable or story or confession and change a word or two to make it mean something rather different from what the original meant or from what another writer might make it mean. You might think of someone you know who has a favorite story. Somehow, that person manages to get the story to be relevant to a wide range of topics. It only takes telling a different detail or two or perhaps shifting the description of the location at which it happened to make it fit yet another conversation.

Redaction criticism works hand in hand with form criticism and source/tradition criticism. While form criticism identifies the usual form and tradition/source criticism identifies the content of material an author uses, redaction criticism identifies where a particular text departs from that form or content and attempts to explain why. The reasons are related to what the author intended to accomplish by citing this source or perhaps to the author's theological tendencies. Most interpreters are confident, for example, that Paul is quoting a liturgy or hymn that someone else wrote in Phil 2:6-11. Form critics are nearly unanimous in this judgment. Redaction critics note that v. 8 seems to include a part that does not fit the literary structure as well as most of the rest of the piece. The phrase "even death on a cross" in this verse seems to interrupt the flow of the poetic rhythm. Since many see the cross as a special emphasis of Pauline theology, many redaction critics argue that Paul inserted that phrase because it gives fuller expression to his understanding of the work of Christ.

EXERCISE

Using Redaction Criticism to Examine the Beatitudes

The Beatitudes provide a good example of how useful redaction criticism can be to understanding and preaching on a text. We more commonly read and recite these sayings as they appear in Matthew's Sermon on the Mount. But many of them also appear in Luke's Sermon on the Plain. Comparing just a few of them helps us see how the authors shape the sayings of Jesus to support their understanding of the message of Jesus.

1. *Read Matthew 5:1-11 and Luke 6:20-26.* Notice the differences in how each Gospel presents the teaching of Jesus. What is the location where Jesus proclaims the Beatitudes? How are the blessings and woes different between Matthew and Luke?
2. *Compare the first Beatitude in Matthew 5:3 with Luke's version of it in Luke 6:20.* What difference do you observe? What does that difference suggest about what each Gospel writer wanted to say?
3. *Compare Matthew's fourth Beatitude in 5:6 with Luke's version of it in Luke 6:21.* What difference do you observe? What does that difference suggest about what each Gospel writer wanted to say? What does seeing these two differences together suggest about these writers? What do these differences suggest about the ways these Gospel writers edited and presented the sayings of Jesus?
4. *Consult the introductions to the two Gospels in critical commentaries.* What do you learn about Matthew's audience as compared to Luke's? How might this be shaping their presentation of Jesus's teaching? How does this shape their understandings of the ministry of Jesus?
5. *Consider how a sermon might highlight these differences and particularities.* Think about the context in which a sermon about the Beatitudes is preached. Is the congregation struggling with poverty issues or are they financially comfortable? Are they dealing with police brutality or relatively safe in their community? Do they engage in prophetic protest against injustice or do they look askance at those who engage in this kind of witness? How might any of this affect the way you construct and preach a sermon about the Beatitudes?

Perhaps the most extensive example of redaction that we can follow comes from 1 and 2 Chronicles. These books take up the material in 1 and 2 Samuel and 1 and 2 Kings and give some of it a different interpretation, an interpretation that conforms even more closely to the Deuteronomic expectation that national faithfulness brings God's blessings and national unfaithfulness brings national disaster. A clear example of this redactional work is the story of King Josiah. In both 2 Kings and 2 Chronicles, Josiah institutes momentous reforms that lead to proper worship of God in Judah. But after all of that good work, Josiah is killed in battle before the completion of the ideal forty years as king. The story in 2 Kings gives no explanation for how this could happen. It seems to violate the promise of Deuteronomy. The authors of 2 Chronicles fix this problem. They add to the story that Josiah refused to allow an Egyptian king to pass through Judah on the way to a war elsewhere. The pharaoh explained that God had told him to do this and that if Josiah did not get out of the way he would be opposing the will of God. But Josiah did not listen. Thus, Josiah dies because he did not obey the word of the Lord that came through the Egyptian king (2 Chron. 35:21-23). This addition lets the story conform to the Deuteronomistic pattern. Trouble comes when Josiah fails to obey God's Word. Of course, we might ask how Josiah is supposed to know that God has actually spoken to this Egyptian king. But the authors of Chronicles were less worried about such questions than they were concerned about preserving the pattern Deuteronomy sets out.

For the New Testament, redaction criticism is used most extensively in the study of the Gospels. There we can see how authors have taken the same material and made different uses of it. There are many places in the Gospels where commentators see the Evangelists shaping the material they have inherited from various sources about the life and teaching of Jesus. Sometimes we see Matthew and Luke reshaping what they find in Mark, and other times (as in the above example) we see them shape material that they find in Q or some other written and oral sources. The comparisons of these changes that redaction criticism observes help us understand how these writers understood Jesus and his ministry and message, as well as a particular passage.

RHETORICAL CRITICISM

Another tool of literary analysis that helps us understand the biblical texts is rhetorical criticism. While some interpreters draw largely on modern rhetorical theory, more biblical scholars look to ancient advice about how to construct persuasive arguments to help them understand the text. Ancient rhetoricians gave most of their attention to how to compose speeches, but they also saw that advice as relevant for written materials. In addition, we should remember that the biblical writings were heard, not read, by most people. Few people in the ancient world could read. This meant that the educated and often the religious experts read the texts while others listened. This suggests that the biblical writers would have paid careful attention to how their writings sounded, perhaps even more than to how they came across as things that were read.

We know much more about the conventions of rhetoric for the Greek and Roman world than about the world of the Hebrew Bible. Much of what we can say about the rhetorical techniques of the Ancient Near East come from comparing extant works with one another and observing common patterns. But we have explicit advice about how to construct and deliver persuasive speeches in Greek and Roman rhetoricians. Aristotle provides us with one of the earliest extant handbooks on rhetoric. He and the teachers of rhetoric that came later give advice on what kinds of arguments to make in particular settings, how to arrange those arguments, and what style to use, in both language and delivery.

These rhetoricians identified three broad categories of arguments. They identified them as arguments from ethos, pathos, and logos. Arguments from ethos rely on character. If you are speaking for someone else, you show what a virtuous person he or she is. It is also important for the speaker, even if speaking for another person, to show that he (as was the case in Greco-Roman settings) was virtuous and had the best interest of the audience at heart. This was often one of the most important things to establish. If the speaker is reliable, then you can trust that what he tells you is the truth. Authors usually do not do this for themselves today. But we still put significant stock in a speaker's ethos. That is why an advertisement for a lecture or a speech will tell where the speaker went to school, what she has written, or what positions she has held. Then at the time of the speech itself, someone will repeat some of this and perhaps add what awards the person has won or relate an anecdote to help the audience know and trust the speaker. All of this is working to establish the ethos of the speaker.

Ancient authors, however, were expected to do this for themselves. Paul uses this technique in Gal 1-2. Most of the material in those chapters is designed to show that he is the person who has always stood up for the recipients of the letter and that he will continue to do that. Since he is so reliable, they should trust that what he tells them about how to live for God is correct. That may not sound like a good argument to us, but it was common and persuasive in the first century. (And given the usual introductions of speakers today, perhaps it remains more persuasive than we would like to think.)

EXERCISE

Using Rhetorical Criticism to Establish Paul's Ethos

Ancient authors were expected to establish their character, their ethos, for themselves when they spoke or wrote. We can see how Paul uses this technique in Galatians Chapters 1–2.

1. *Read Galatians Chapters 1 and 2.* Notice how Paul establishes his credentials.
2. *Read 1:1.* How does this beginning of the greeting serve to establish Paul's ethos?
3. *Read 1:11-12, 15-17, and 2:1-5.* How do the claims and the narrative about Paul's vision and his early days as a missionary serve to establish Paul's ethos?
4. *Consult commentaries that focus on rhetorical criticism.* How do they help you think about the function of the verses you have read? What do they say about why Paul is taking so much time at the beginning of this letter to the Galatians to talk about himself? How does this introduction function for the community to which he is writing?
5. *Consider how a sermon could use ethos.* How might a preacher use self-disclosure to establish their credibility with their listeners? Note that Paul does not hold back on disclosing the truth about his former persecution of Christians (1:13, 23), but uses that detail to establish the truth and power of God to change him into a champion of the faith. While there is debate among homileticians about how much self-disclosure and vulnerability is appropriate in the pulpit, these chapters in Galatians demonstrate that telling one's story is sometimes necessary to point to the power of God while also establishing credibility with one's listeners.

The second kind of argument, pathos, was an appeal to the emotions. The speaker might make the audience feel sorry for him or admire him or come to like him or the person he represented as a way to get the hearers to do what he wanted them to do. On the other hand, it was also seen as effective and legitimate to make the other people in the argument look bad, as bad as you could make them look. Aristotle was a big believer in logic as the most important basis for making decisions, but even he acknowledged that pathos was almost always more successful than logic.

The third kind of argument was from logos, that is, logic. It was important to include arguments in a speech that made logical sense. These are the kinds of arguments we would prefer, but they are not always the arguments that we find in the biblical texts. Still, rhetoricians gave advice about how to construct and present logical arguments.

Biblical writers used all of these kinds of arguments to try to persuade their readers/listeners to take their advice about what to do and believe. Some commentaries are focused on helping readers see how the arguments within the biblical texts follow the advice of rhetoricians. They can be useful in helping us understand why the writers thought certain kinds of proofs and certain ways of arranging them would move the audience in the direction they wanted them to go.

It may seem surprising to hear that biblical writers used known techniques for getting their readers to think and act in certain ways and not others. But we should remember that all of the biblical texts are written to persuade people to believe certain things and to reject other beliefs. That is as true for the telling of the creation story as it is for the prophets who explicitly tell people to change their ways. Similarly, the Gospels don't just tell stories about Jesus so that people will remember them, but so that readers will believe certain things about Jesus and what his ministry, death, and resurrection accomplish. The Gospel of John tells you this explicitly in 20:30-31. There the author says that he has written this book so that readers will believe the right things about Jesus. That means that his arrangement and telling of the stories is an argument that is designed to convince the readers to believe certain things. While not all biblical writings say this explicitly, it is the purpose of them all.

Fewer critical commentaries have given explicit attention to rhetorical criticism than to the other kinds of analyses we have talked about. But the end of the twentieth century and the beginning of the twenty-first have seen an increase in attention to rhetorical criticism. Some commentary series explicitly emphasize this type of criticism, but many others now give attention to how biblical authors drew on well-known rhetorical forms and techniques. Tracing how the biblical works try to make their arguments persuasive can help us understand the messages of the texts more clearly.

FLOW OF THE ARGUMENT

As we think about how to understand the message of biblical texts as clearly as possible, we need to give careful attention to how their authors structured them. Rhetorical criticism can be of help here as we remember what rhetoricians advise about how to construct a persuasive **argument**. But we must also look beyond such advice. We need to look for the outline of whole books to see how authors have given an overall structure to their material. We need to look at how various sections fit with those that are around them. (Of course, rhetorical criticism can be of significant help with these things as well.)

Often a series of paragraphs will be on the same topic. Interpreters need to note this and try to determine how those paragraphs work together to make the author's larger point. Perhaps one paragraph introduces the topic, the next begins to give reasons for thinking a particular way about it, and then a third states the conclusion(s) that the author wants the readers to accept. It may be that a further paragraph draws out implications of that conclusion. There is no one way that such sections are organized. It may be that the first paragraph, or even sentence, sets out the basic thesis and then the next several paragraphs give reasons for believing that the thesis is correct. Or the following paragraphs may all draw out implications. Alternatively, all the arguments for the basic thesis may come before it, so that it serves as the conclusion to the larger section. Only a careful reading of the larger whole and the various sections can help us identify how the argument is structured.

Philippians 2:1-18 shows us how multiple sections can fit together to make an emphatic point. Verses 1-5 are composed of various exhortations about how to treat one another within the church. It includes stringent demands such as, "think of others as better than yourself," and, "put the good of others above your own good." This section,

EXERCISE

Analyzing the Flow of Argument in Colossians 1:12-23

1. *Read Colossians 1:12-23.* Note what topic the writer seems to set out in vv. 12-14. Note the change in genre in vv. 15-20 and the shift back to regular prose in vv. 21-23.
2. *Consider the function of 1:15-20.* How do these verses support the assertions in vv. 12-14? How do the assertions of vv. 21-23 draw out the consequences of vv. 15-20?
3. *Consult commentaries.* What is the point Paul is making in this passage? How are the claims about forgiveness related to the poetic liturgy in vv. 15-20? How does one section flow to the next and develop Paul's argument?
4. *Consider how a sermon on Colossians 1 could mirror this flow of argument.* When preaching on this text, the sermon could follow the same flow of argument that Paul uses. The preacher could begin with assurances of forgiveness and relationship with God, quote a familiar hymn that illustrates those promises, and draw out implications that can be applied in the believers' lives and current context.

or subsection, ends by exhorting the readers to adopt the same way of thinking that Christ had. Then, vv. 6-11 are a liturgy about the incarnation of Christ and how he gave up so much for the good of others. This liturgy is not there to provide teaching about Christology, but to give the example that believers are to follow. They are to give up what is good for themselves, as Christ did for them. That is what following the example of Christ means here. So, the liturgy is the basis for the preceding exhortation. Then, vv. 12-18 draw out further ways that the readers are to live out following the example of Christ. These are three discrete sections (vv. 1-5, 6-11, 12-18), but they all fit together to support the central point about how to live together as the church. Of course, there are additional important points made along the way. And it is certainly permissible to use Phil 2:6-11 to discuss Christology. But we first need to see how this material functions in its context so that we get to the central point the author wants to make.

Examining Paragraphs within the Biblical Text

Beyond this examination of the broader structure, we must also pay attention to how the parts within a paragraph (more often called a pericope in biblical studies) work together to make a point. Remember that a good paragraph usually has a central point that other things in the paragraph either support or draw implications from. To understand the main point a text makes, we must see how the parts of paragraphs fit together. This is the close-up work of reading each sentence in its literary context.

It is also important to determine where a paragraph ends and begins. To help us determine this we can look to transition language, perhaps a "therefore," that starts a new section that draws a conclusion from the previous paragraph (though not all uses of "therefore" begin a new paragraph). Sometimes there is a shift in style or even in the terms that are repeated. In places there will be a change of kinds of literature. In the Gospels such changes can be signaled by the arrival or departure of characters or moving to a new location. Those kinds of changes also appear in the prophets and in the narratives of the Pentateuch and the Deuteronomistic histories.

Identifying where a paragraph begins is particularly important when the first sentence is the topic sentence. How we decide where a paragraph begins and ends can dramatically change how we understand it. An examination of Ephesians Chapter 5 illustrates this.

EXERCISE

Preaching about the Boundaries of Ephesians Chapter 5

Once we have determined where the exhortations begin in Ephesians 5, we can think about how to help our church understand this text.

1. *Read different translations of Ephesians Chapter 5.* Note the differences in where the subheadings and paragraph breaks are placed.
2. *Consult commentaries.* What do scholars say about how the sentences should be arranged in vv. 21-33? What difference does it make in how we interpret the meaning of the text? Note the differences in how older and more recent commentaries deal with this text. What does that suggest about the presuppositions commentators bring to their study of texts?
3. *Consider how a sermon on Ephesians 5:21-33 could address these differences in sentence placement.* How does the historical and cultural context help us understand what is happening in this text? In what ways has this text been used to reinforce patriarchy? How might the placement of just one sentence shift our understanding and application of this text?

Throughout the last few centuries of biblical interpretation, interpreters have often begun a new paragraph at Eph 5:22. It begins, "Wives, be subject to your husbands." That expectation of submission then determines how wives and children and enslaved people are to relate to those above them. But the paragraph actually begins at v. 21, "Be subject to one another out of reverence for Christ." In fact, vv. 21 and 22 are part of the same sentence in Greek. The only verb in the sentence appears in v. 21. It is, in fact, the verb "submit." Thus, a translation that more nearly reflects the grammar of the sentence is: "Be subject to one another out of reverence for Christ, wives to your husbands." Note the significant change in the meaning of the sentence and the paragraph. The topic sentence of the paragraph has as its primary exhortation that all members of the church be subject to one another. Wives are just the first example of how that is to be done. We may think that the instructions that follow are inconsistent with that initial exhortation that all people be subject to one another, but the cultural context of the author of Ephesians seems to have led him to think the instructions make good sense together. In any case, the basic assertion of the text changes significantly when we begin the paragraph in the right place. This is just one of many places that such decisions make a big difference.

NARRATIVE CRITICISM

Some of the kinds of analyses we looked at in this chapter break the text up into units to discover what we can about the author's concerns, community, and message. Narrative criticism focuses on reading the biblical book as a whole. It has been used mostly on books that are primarily narratives (e.g., Exodus, Numbers, the Gospels), but it is also used to analyze the story that is presupposed by other kinds of writings. This criticism looks at how individual parts contribute to our understanding of the whole text. Rather than looking through the text to see what is happening in the writer's community, narrative criticism looks to the world that the text creates. Through the stories that it tells, a text expresses certain values and ideas that are developed and clarified as the story moves forward.

Narrative criticism explores how characters are developed through the course of a narrative. It looks for ways that an author's ideas and theology come to expression through that character development. In addition, narrative criticism explores how settings convey meaning. It uses both character development and analysis of settings to help us understand how the progress of the book's plot develops. This method also looks at the role of the narrator in conveying the message of the book. Narrative critics ask how the narrator clarifies issues or has knowledge that the characters in the story don't have and how that shapes the telling of the story and its meaning. Narrative critics also give careful attention to the literary devices the author uses to identify the work's concerns and emphases. It notes how devices such as repetition or figures of speech or even irony function in the telling of the story.

As narrative critics use these techniques, they develop an image of both an "implied author" and an "implied audience." These can be separated from the actual author and audience. The implied author is the person who embodies the implicit values and beliefs that come to expression in the narrative. The "implied audience" or "implied reader" is the imaginary person who is the ideal reader that the text was intended to reach. To read with this implied audience, we must think about what that reader was expected to know and what that reader did not know. For example, the implied reader of Luke does not know the stories about Jesus in John or even the story line of the life of Jesus as that is given in John. The story will, then, be crafted so that the reader does not need to know what is in John. Narrative criticism, then, tries to help us hear the story in the ways that its expected readers would have heard it.

CONCLUSION

All of these kinds of literary analysis help us read the texts more carefully. They help us look at both the details and the whole. The purpose of historical-critical exegesis is always to help us move beyond an initial impression that is shaped solely by our own social and cultural expectations. It helps us understand the texts on their own terms. This requires us to dig into the details of what kinds of genres authors use, how they use materials that are passed to them, and how they construct their books in detail and as wholes. We will talk more about how the various criticisms work together in the next chapter.

KEY POINTS IN THIS CHAPTER

1. When we recognize the genre of a biblical text, we know to read it in an appropriate way, depending on whether that genre is poetry, history, a letter, or apocalyptic, for example. Genre criticism helps us understand what the writer was trying to convey and how we can interpret the text for contemporary application. Preachers need to be aware of genres and the different types of literary criticism to accurately interpret the text, discern its meaning, and construct sermons based on those texts.
2. Form criticism is a method for identifying the appearance, use, and function of smaller literary units within a larger work. Form criticism helps us compare different biblical materials to identify patterns and parallels that original hearers would have recognized so that we can understand the message of the text for the intended recipients.
3. Traditional criticism and source criticism seek to identify sources that biblical authors drew from when writing their texts. This is how we understand the development of ideas among and between biblical authors in both the Hebrew and Christian Scriptures.
4. Redaction criticism analyzes how an author takes a preformed piece and changes or edits it to fit what that author wants it to mean. Using this method to analyze biblical texts helps us recognize different meanings or emphases intended by biblical writers.
5. Rhetorical criticism focuses on how ancient writers and orators constructed persuasive arguments for their audiences. This method is especially useful when examining Christian texts because we know the authors of that time would have been familiar with well-known concepts of ethos (character), pathos (emotion), and logos (logic) for making their case to an audience.
6. Narrative criticism focuses on reading the biblical book as a whole. By looking at the way the individual parts contribute to our understanding of the whole text, we can be more certain of the central values and ideas the author was trying to express.
7. Attending to the ways in which the authors of biblical texts structured their message helps us understand the flow of their argument. This, in turn, helps us identify the central point they were trying to make.

DISCUSSION QUESTIONS

1. Meet with an experienced preacher and talk with them about how they use literary criticism to read, interpret, and preach a text. Of the methods explained in this chapter, which ones do they tend to rely on most? Examine together one of their sermons that illustrates how literary criticism either informed or was explicitly mentioned in their preaching.
2. The section on narrative criticism explains that this method helps us understand how a character and plot is developed throughout a story. Read the book of Ruth using narrative criticism to trace the development of Ruth's and Naomi's character. How are the women introduced in the text? How does the author use Ruth's and Naomi's actions to tell us something about who God is and what God does for God's people? How does the plot of the story make a point about being faithful to God and trusting God's goodness?
3. Ask a preaching colleague to share a sermon with you and examine it using rhetorical criticism. Which of the three categories of argument—ethos, pathos, or logos—are most prominent in the sermon? In other words, how does the preacher use character, emotion, and/or logic to construct their argument in the sermon? Talk with your colleague about the strengths and risks with using each approach in preaching.

FOR FURTHER READING

Ronald J. Allen. "Form Criticism." In *New Interpreter's Handbook of Preaching*, edited by Paul Scott Wilson. Nashville: Abingdon Press, 2008.

Yaira Amit. *Reading Biblical Narratives: Literary Criticism and the Hebrew Bible.* Minneapolis: Fortress, 2001.
Joel B. Green, editor. *Hearing the New Testament: Strategies for Interpretation,* second edition. Grand Rapids: Eerdmans, 2010.
George A. Kennedy. *New Testament Interpretation through Rhetorical Criticism.* Chapel Hill: University of North Carolina Press, 1984.
Thomas G. Long. *Preaching and the Literary Forms of the Bible.* Philadelphia: Fortress Press, 1989.
Steven L. McKenzie. "What Is Source Criticism?" n.p. [cited October 1, 2021]. https://www.bibleodyssey.org:443/tools/bible-basics/what-is-source-criticism-mckenzie.
James L. Resseguie. *Narrative Criticism of the New Testament.* Grand Rapids, MI: Eerdmans, 2005.
John M. Rottman. "Introduction: Literary Forms." In *New Interpreter's Handbook of Preaching,* edited by Paul Scott Wilson. Nashville: Abingdon Press, 2008.

NOTE

1. For an introduction to reading and preaching from apocalyptic literature, see Leah D. Schade and Jerry L. Sumney, *Apocalypse When? A Guide to Interpreting and Preaching Apocalyptic Texts* (Eugene, OR: Cascade, 2020).

4

Using Explicit Perspectives to Understand the Text

One of the goals of historical-critical exegesis is to focus attention on the text itself and to try to eliminate the influence of the interpreter's identity on interpretation. This goal is in line with the goals of the Enlightenment's outlook. But it has become increasingly clear in the sciences as well as in the study of texts that we cannot attain complete objectivity. In a sense, biblical exegetes acknowledged this by establishing journals of biblical study where authors exchanged ideas and critiqued the observations and interpretations of other interpreters. These exchanges often pointed out how the perspectives and presuppositions of other scholars clouded their vision of what was actually in the text. This is a way that scholars try to move all readers closer to an "objective" interpretation of a text. While we can acknowledge that an identity-free or objective reading of a text is not fully possible, we can still recognize the importance of trying to hear a text on its own terms. Without this beginning, we will not be able to speak clearly about the text. While we see this as the starting point for further kinds of analysis and examination, other kinds of readings are also crucial.

Perspective-explicit interpretations recognize, highlight, and take advantage of the observations and reactions that come when readers listen from other various social locations, identities, and ideologies. Beginning in the twentieth century, a growing number of interpreters argued that it was important, indeed absolutely necessary, to listen to texts from varying perspectives, particularly those perspectives that had not been represented in traditional historical-critical exegesis.

Reading explicitly from a particular perspective has significant benefits. First, it helps us understand the text more clearly. Trying to read without taking one's perspective into account leads us to miss things that are in the text. Readings from, for example, a feminist perspective have helped interpreters understand the early church more clearly and see things in the biblical texts that other readings had missed. In addition, explicitly reading from varying perspectives helps us see how each text is shaped by the author's unconscious and sometimes problematic presuppositions. For example, biblical writers nearly always assume that God is male. Thus, all the pronouns and most of the images of God in the Bible are male. But a moment of theological reflection lets us realize that the essence of the creator of all that is (male and female) must be beyond being male or female. Recognizing this can allow us to understand God more fully and truly. It opens the way for us to think of God's care and love in ways that transcend our cultural constructs of masculine and feminine.

We can acknowledge that this means we claim to see something about God that the authors of biblical texts often missed. This does not need to mean that we no longer see Scripture as an authority (though it could mean that). Neither does it mean that reading from any perspective (e.g., that of a white supremacist) is valid. Some who read from an explicit perspective do decenter Scripture as an authority, making their ideological viewpoint more authoritative than Scripture. We take a different approach. We think it is important to take numerous perspectives and critiques of the ideologies/viewpoints that are expressed and presupposed by biblical texts into full account. We evaluate those critiques with what we see as the dominant message of Scripture. At the same time, that dominant message is made clearer as we listen to these varying perspectives. But Scripture's message remains a significant touchstone for discerning God's will in the present.

We will discuss here some important representatives of perspective-explicit interpretations. This is, of course, an incomplete list, and the short definitions below cannot reflect the breadth of the diversity within even the perspectives that are mentioned. We are distilling ways of reading that are complex and multifaceted, as further reading about and use of them will demonstrate. All of these hermeneutical approaches are rich in what they can show readers about the biblical texts, the traditional interpretations given the texts, and the salvific possibilities they unearth. We hope these descriptions will alert readers to the range of perspectives that are represented in these readings and provide a glimpse into what they contribute to interpreting and preaching biblical texts for the church today, as well as move you to explore them further.

SOME REPRESENTATIVES OF PERSPECTIVE-EXPLICIT INTERPRETATIONS

Latin American Liberation Readings

In many ways, Latin American liberation reading is the parent of the other perspective-explicit interpretations. It was the first kind of reading to take context seriously as a conversation partner for reading the biblical text. It points to how both aspects of the biblical texts and the dominant readings of them support the social and economic oppression of people who are economically and socially disadvantaged. It seeks to hear biblical texts in the ways they are heard by people who are marginalized and oppressed in various ways. This reading aims to support social change by emphasizing the biblical values that support the liberation of people who are oppressed. Since this kind of reading was developed, the definition of who is considered oppressed and in what ways these groups are marginalized has changed over time.

Feminist Readings

Feminist readings focus on the political, social, and economic experiences and rights of women. They expose the ways that texts have incorporated values that oppress and demean women. At the same time, they search for ways that the biblical texts also contain elements that support the liberation of women. Among the ways these readings accomplish these goals is to find ways to reclaim the voices of women whose presence has been obscured by the text and its readers.

African American Readings

African American readings interpret the biblical texts through the experience of being black in America, which includes the history of slavery, Jim Crow laws, segregation, and police violence, to name just a few ways in which blacks have experienced oppression in the United States. This reading focuses attention on stories that highlight the liberatory purposes of God (especially prominent have been the exodus and the ministry of Jesus), even as they draw on resources from African American experience, such as slave narratives. These readings also give careful attention to how interpretations of the biblical text have been used to enslave and oppress African Americans and provide alternative readings and critiques of the values in the texts.

Womanist Readings

Womanist readings give a sharper focus to the insights of African American and feminist readings by focusing on the experience of being a woman of color, often more specifically on African American women. They read from the experience of being oppressed by both their ethnic identity and their gender, a combination that seemed to receive too little attention in feminist and African American readings. Womanist readings, then, uses the interlocking and multidimensional nature of various kinds of oppression and marginalization that women of color experience as its lens for analyzing texts and interpretations.

Mujerista Readings

Mujerista readings reflect the experiences and reading methods of Latina women. They read the Bible to investigate how it promotes the liberation of Latinas. This reading intends to reveal how the texts have been used to oppress and emphasizes the biblical stories of women who survived oppression as resources to support Latinas who now struggle against oppression.

Post-colonial Readings

Post-colonial readings look to the coping strategies used by those who were colonized by European powers in the nineteenth and twentieth century to formulate methods of interpreting the biblical texts. These interpreters read from the perspective of the people who were colonized, noting how the dominant interpreters imposed the colonizers' values on the text. Of course, colonialism remains present in both its earlier form and the transnational capitalism that oppresses individuals, communities, and cultures. They also note how biblical writers support and oppose the values of the empire under which they lived, often observing how the biblical writers used coping mechanisms similar to those found among the colonized in later eras. Seeing these coping mechanisms in the text helps readers recognize that the Bible contains texts that reflect the perspectives of those who are colonized, even as it also has texts that reflect the perspectives of those who colonized others.

Asian American Readings

Asian American (as distinct from Asian) readings interpret biblical texts through the lens of both elements of Asian culture and the experience of discrimination against Asian Americans. Some of these readings have worked to identify Asian American experience of exclusion with stories in the Bible about those outside the political, social, ethnic, and religious structures (e.g., the Ethiopian eunuch). Others read the text more broadly through Asian American experience to see what new light is shed on the text. Many such interpretations use post-colonial reading methods and many draw on Asian concepts (e.g., ancestry, wisdom, yin-yang) to interpret biblical ideas. Because of the diversity within Asian cultures, Asian American readings often give rigorous attention to being very specific about their social location.

Queer Readings

Queer readings emphasize the extent to which sexual orientation is a part of one's identity, perspective, and social location when interpreting biblical texts. They reject heteronormativity as the lens through which to understand human existence and critique interpretations of Scripture that perpetuate harmful gender stereotypes. This reading highlights the ways the assumptions of heterosexuality and of definitions of gender shape the biblical texts and the interpretations they usually receive.

Ecological Readings

Ecological readings point to how biblical texts have been used to justify ecologically unsustainable practices. They further show how biblical texts have resources that support promoting care for the planet, including matters that are broader than the welfare (or salvation) of humans. They emphasize the intrinsic worth of the Earth and the interconnectedness of all of Creation.[1] These readings highlight the goodness of Creation, God's care for it, and the divine command that humans care for the environment.

Disability Readings

Disability readings look to the ways biblical texts and interpretations of them present people who are disabled as inferior. These readings locate disabled people among the marginalized and oppressed because of cultural perceptions of them. But these readings emphasize that the different experiences of disabled people are an essential part of human diversity. These readings often call for new understandings of texts such as healing stories, as they note the ableist assumptions of many of them.

EXERCISE

Reading Genesis 41:53–42:5 with Different Perspective-Explicit Approaches

1. *Read Genesis 41:53–42:5 with a historical-critical lens.* How does the story function in the context of Genesis and the story of the Israelites? What themes does the author want readers to focus on?
2. *Read the text again using a post-colonial lens.* What insight might we gain about this text? How does the experience of migration undergird this story? What are examples of migration in our own time that might find resonance with the story of Jacob and his family?
3. *Read the text again, this time using an ecological lens.* How is the land itself a character in this story? What is the relationship between the land and Jacob? Between the land and Joseph? What are examples of regional drought in our own time for which this story might have insight?
4. *Read the text a fourth time using a Latin American liberation lens.* In what ways do you see economic oppression hinted at in the text? How does this story convey the saga of a marginalized people and their struggle for survival? In what ways might those seeking economic and social liberation for oppressed peoples today draw on this text to raise awareness about the intersecting factors that contribute to their oppression?
5. *Read the sermon at the end of this chapter.* Notice how the sermon weaves together all three of these perspective-explicit approaches (post-colonial, ecological, Latin American liberation) to glean insight from the biblical text and apply it to the contemporary issue of climate migration.

RECEIVING PERSPECTIVE-EXPLICIT READINGS

Thinking about how these perspectival readings bring new approaches to the biblical text can lead to a number of reactions. Some will be relieved and gratified as their experiences and understandings of the world and the faith are given expressions. Some, particularly from majority cultures, will find it painful to hear how their interpretations and outlooks have inflicted pain and supported oppression. Perhaps we all must admit that while confession may be good for the soul, it is painful. It is helpful to see all of these perspective-explicit interpretations as ways of pointing to various aspects of systemic sin. Each looks to a way that the text has been interpreted and has supported the oppression of various groups by dominant cultural systems.

When we talk about **systemic sin**, we mean the values and practices that manifest in the economic, social, and political systems of the world that violate the will of God. Biblical texts talk about this in various ways. A clear example appears in Rom 5:12-21, where Paul speaks of how the world is ruled by the "powers" of sin and death. He speaks of sin and death entering through Adam and taking control of the world. These "powers" are Paul's metaphors for the injustices that are built into our economic and social systems. Before going forward, we need to note that we are all trapped in, participate in supporting, and benefit from these systems, though in differing ways and to differing degrees. Those who read from an explicit perspective and those who do not are participants in systemic sin and can see only with limited perspectives.

Those who read from explicit perspectives are not surprised to hear that the systems we live in are unjust and oppressive. But those from majority cultures often find acknowledging and confronting systemic sin to be painful, particularly when we did not recognize that we were involved in and supported unjust systems. However, it is important for all of us to recognize our complicity in the systems that give some people advantages and some disadvantages. It is certainly hard to acknowledge complicity in sin when we see ourselves as good people who work to do what is right. Importantly, the tension between these two realities does not make either one of them false. We can struggle to be good people even while failing to see some types of sin that we perpetuate. Recognizing the reach of systemic sin that we cannot fully escape can help us strive for yet clearer ways to seek and do God's will.

It is also important to recognize, as good perspective-explicit interpreters do, that no one of these perspectives has cornered the market on truth. Further, interpreters who read from one of these perspectives sometimes ignore or do not fully recognize the truths seen in other perspectives. It is hard, actually impossible, for limited, sinful human beings to always keep in view all ways of perceiving God's will most fully. So, we sometimes single out one group as the sinners and others as the saints. All readers and preachers need to hear from a wide range of interpretive perspectives constantly and intentionally so they can more clearly perceive cultural realities and the Word of God.

SPACES FOR DISCERNMENT

As some of us find these readings difficult because we recognize ways that we have been a part of the problem, we may want to react as people who are being falsely accused. At the least, many of us will have hurt feelings. It is in these places that the preacher must seek to interpret the Bible and the will of God for the church. Having heard from these explicit interpretive perspectives, we may ask how we can seek the will of God in the midst of these revelations and hurt feelings.

We have suggested that such readings can help us all discern the will of God as we seek to hear the dominant message of Scripture more clearly with these perspectives. This can also lead us to ask how we might honorably and legitimately use these methods and insights when we are not members of the groups that read from those perspectives. Preachers will need to consider carefully how they can honor the experiences and perspectives of those who are different. This means learning how to hear and use methods and ideas from other social locations and perspectives without co-opting the experience as their own. This does not mean that a person outside a particular group cannot use the methods and perspectives of a perspective-explicit interpretation. For example, there are many male scholars who have adopted a feminist hermeneutic. But as they do so, they recognize that the experience that they privilege is not their own. It is the constant work of interpreters to retain their own identity while honoring and learning from the methods and perspectives of other interpretive stances.

All readers must also recognize **intersectionality**. By intersectionality we mean the ways that each of us have multiple kinds of identities that intersect, impinge upon, complexify, and co-inform each other. Because this is the case, the same person may have some characteristics that bring them privilege and some that bring disadvantage or oppression. For example, a white woman is privileged by being white. She will receive cultural and social advantages because of her whiteness. At the same time, she is disadvantaged because she is a woman in a patriarchal culture. And things get yet more complicated. Economic status will either privilege or disadvantage the same person. We are all (as Paul would say) trapped, kidnapped into, a world that both gives us privilege and oppresses us. Of course, some have more factors that bring oppression and others less. But we can see that we are all trapped in systems of sin.

After reading the accompanying example, "Using Intersectionality and Discernment for Ephesians 6:10-19," you'll see that our point is that all of us are both oppressors and the oppressed to some degree. This does not relieve us of the responsibility of working for more justice in the world, but it should help us to see the situation that traps us all. These readings, then, lead us to ask where we are the oppressor and where we are being liberated. They reveal how we each benefit from and participate in the oppression that is part of our world. At the same time, they ask us to see how God is working to free each of us from this oppression.

One of the things that perspective-explicit interpretations can do is to help us ask who we might identify with in a text. We might ask whether our congregation is the Israelites or the Egyptians when we read the Exodus story. It is tempting to want to identify with the Israelites, even when one's more dominant social and economic position might locate them more with the Egyptians. Perspective-explicit interpretations help us ask texts new questions and unmask some kinds of perspectives in them that have made us too comfortable as the good people whenever we read a biblical text. At times our churches may need to focus on the ways they oppress others and at other times on how they are harmed by sin.

AN EXAMPLE OF USING INTERSECTIONALITY AND DISCERNMENT FOR EPHESIANS 6:10-19

In Ephesians 6:12, Paul says, "For our struggle is not against enemies of blood and flesh, but against the rulers, against the authorities, against the cosmic powers of this present darkness, against the spiritual forces of evil in the heavenly places" (NRSV). This is theological language for systemic sin, but when preaching about this concept, it is helpful to have an illustration so that listeners can grasp how "the powers" manifest themselves in today's world. Here's an example to illustrate the reality that each of us are trapped in systems of sin, either as the oppressed, the oppressor, the beneficiary of systemic sin, its victim, or as an accomplice—and nearly always a person or community will occupy different roles simultaneously.

We all need to wear clothes. The clothes that we wear are all (or nearly so) made by people who work for wages that we would consider unjust for ourselves and people in our families. They are often made by children in dangerous conditions. We almost never think about this. It is only when some tragedy, such as a fire in a sweatshop, kills dozens of people that we gasp about the terrible conditions people have to work under. But we forget about that the next time we need a shirt.

Some of us are ignorant of these conditions; others of us choose not to think about them. Some of us (but not many) may have enough money to purchase some of our clothes from sources that do not unjustly exploit workers. But others have no choice but to buy clothes that are the cheapest they can find. Others of us just want nice clothes that seem to be what all people in our social groups seem to wear (which seems to justify them as not extravagant). But none of us have a choice about buying clothes, and every time we do, we support the system that oppresses those workers who suffer from those unjustly low wages and inexcusably dangerous conditions. People of all social classes, genders, and ethnic groups have no choice but to support this injustice. Both the people who are privileged and the people who are oppressed because of their ethnicity, gender, or economic class often have no choice but to support the system of injustice that produces clothing. All of us support the system of injustice that produces clothing. We are all trapped by systemic sin, the "spiritual forces of evil" that manifest themselves in our economic systems.

In vv. 13-17, Paul goes on to use another metaphor to explain how the faithful can defend themselves against the powers—that of the "armor of God." He encourages believers to put on a "belt of truth," shoes that will enable them to proclaim the "gospel of peace," lift up a "shield of faith," don the "helmet of salvation," and take up the "sword of the Spirit, which is the word of God" (vv. 14-17). Note that this is not a call to take up physical weaponry, but to surround oneself with the spiritual resources that enable resistance to the powers—even as it uses militaristic and colonizing imagery.

So a sermon on Ephesians 6:10-19 would also want to include an illustration of the "armor of God" that listeners may want to put on in addressing the intersecting injustices of the clothing industry. For example, the anti-sweatshop movement that began in the 1990s was begun by young people who "put on the belt of truth" by raising awareness about the deplorable working conditions of textile workers. A preacher might encourage their congregation to learn about how they can support socially responsible companies and lace up their shoes to proclaim the "gospel of peace" by advocating for workers' rights.

FINAL THOUGHTS ON READING WITH PERSPECTIVE-EXPLICIT INTERPRETATIONS

These critiques of presuppositions in the text may make us nervous. But perhaps we can take some solace in knowing that the texts sometimes do this to themselves. Consider the stories of the ancestors of Israel. They recognize and at least accept a system in which women are so much the property of men that men can have multiple wives—and have sexual access to those women's enslaved women. But if we read these stories carefully, we will note that all of those polygynous families are dysfunctional. Never does that system produce a family in which love and harmony prevail. As the system continues sporadically in the narratives, we may see Solomon with his one thousand wives and concubines as the perfect example of the sinful nature of the system. Not only does it not bring peace, but the text blames them (a move that grows out of misogyny) for the unfaithfulness of Solomon and the nation. While the critique has its own problems, the writers of the narratives of the life of the Israelites implicitly unmask the injustice of the polygynous system.

Seeing that the biblical texts themselves sometimes undermine some of the things that leading characters and even the leading story line seem to accept can give us reason to ask hard questions about the presuppositions in the texts. For preachers, the point of asking these questions and thinking about the text from multiple perspectives and experiences is to discern the Word and will of God for the church. Paying attention to all of these perspectives is one of the ways we strive to hear what is in the text rather than allowing our perspectives and presuppositions to be the sole determinant of what the text says to the church today.

SERMON EXAMPLE: "CLIMATE MIGRATION— HOW SHOULD THE CHURCH RESPOND?"

This sermon demonstrates how a preacher might weave together different perspective-explicit readings for a sermon. To address the issue of climate migration, Leah Schade drew from Genesis 41:53–42:5 (Jacob sends his sons to Egypt to buy grain during a famine) and Luke 9:51-58 (Jesus laments that "the Son of Man has no place to lay his head"). Notice how the perspectives of post-colonial, ecological, and Latin American liberation inform her reading of the texts and how they are integrated into the sermon. This sermon was preached in April of 2021 for a congregation wanting to do more with their Earth Care ministry.

1. The old man kneels down onto the hard, crumbling soil beneath his feet. His bony fingers caress a stalk that should be green and full of grain but instead snaps and frays into brittle, brown sinews. His knees creak as he stands up, his eyes scanning the withered fields around him. Feelings of failure and despair well up in his chest.
2. What has caused the land to do this? Did they not find favor with God? Were they being punished? It felt like there were forces much bigger than him and his family that were pushing them away from this land.
3. He had tried so hard for so many years to make this work. But the drought just would not relent. He would need to send his family away from this land that they loved.
4. He heard that there was a country far away where there was plenty of food. This is where they would go. But what would they face on the journey? Would they even survive? Would they be welcomed when they arrive in that new land?
5. He reaches down and picks up a handful of the dry, dusty dirt. He weeps a prayer as the wind whips at his teary face, scattering the dirt from his hands.
6. Are you wondering who this man is? His name could be Jacob, and his story could be as old as Genesis. This could be a scene from the saga about Joseph and his brothers and their father Jacob in the lands of Canaan and Egypt. That is a story where a massive drought drove the desperate migration of people away from their land seeking survival in a foreign country.

(Notice how the first five paragraphs of the story contain deliberate ambiguity—the name of the man is not specified, nor is the location. Note, as well, the use of descriptive language to draw the listener into the scene. Paragraph 6 introduces the possibility that this story could be about Jacob and describes the scenario using the term "migration.")

7. But the man in this story is one we will call "Rodrigo," and his story is happening now. This is one scene in the saga of climate failure in hot zones across the world that is driving millions of desperate people to leave their homelands seeking some way to survive.
8. According to a *New York Times Magazine* article by Abrahm Lustgarten, Guatemala, the country where Rodrigo lives, is expected to see a decrease in rainfall "by 60 percent in some parts of the country, and the amount of water replenishing streams and keeping soil moist will drop by as much as 83 percent." Researchers project that by 2070, yields of some staple crops in the state where Rodrigo lives will decline by nearly a third. Like so many other countries in Central America, "Half the children are chronically hungry, and many are short for their age, with weak bones and bloated bellies."[2]
9. For his part, Rodrigo pawned his last four goats for money so that his son Jorge and his seven-year-old grandson could pay the coyote to take them north to America. Jorge's wife stayed behind with their two younger children, not knowing what the future will hold for them or for her husband and oldest son.

(Paragraph 7 reveals that this is a contemporary story, but the listener has already been primed to see the parallels with the biblical story of Jacob because of the setup in paragraph 6. Paragraphs 7–9 provide context for Rodrigo's situation and begin to flesh out his story.)

10. If this *was* Jacob's story, we would know the outcome. His sons make the perilous journey to Egypt to purchase grain so that their tribe will not die of starvation. There is a chapters-long drama recounting their brother, Joseph, testing the men to see if they had changed from their earlier days when they had sold him into slavery. In a God-guided turn of events, Joseph rises from wrongful imprisonment to become the head of Egypt's economy. Years later, in the midst of a drought that devastates the land, he eventually reconciles with his brothers and allows their whole tribe to migrate to Egypt and resettle there.

(Paragraph 10 weaves the biblical story from Genesis back into the sermon. You will notice that this weaving happens several times through the course of the sermon where Leah moves back and forth between Jacob's and Jorge's story.)

11. But Jorge and his son will likely face a far different outcome. There is no guarantee that they will survive the journey across wilderness landscapes with very little access to food, water, places to rest, or medical care for any injuries. They will face threats from violent assaults along the way. And when they finally reach the border where they hope to find "Egypt's bread," they will not be welcomed. This will not be a nation where a benevolent political leader or government official will set aside land for them to live and rebuild their lives.
12. No, in this country, they will be put into detention centers and treated like criminals, possibly separating father from son. They will not be able to apply for asylum due to climate disasters because that is not recognized as a reason for seeking protected status. So there is a chance they will be turned away.
13. Even if they are allowed to enter this country, they will need to go through a complicated process of seeking a sponsor who will help them find somewhere to live, a job, a place for the boy to go to school. They will have to learn a new language. And they will likely face hostility from the people in the town where they will eventually settle.

(Paragraph 11 delineates the contrasts between Jacob's and Jorge's story, and the listener is given an ethical framework based on the biblical story with which to hear Jorge's story. In this way, Leah is using both a post-colonial and a Latin American liberation theological perspective to inform this aspect of the sermon.)

14. Maybe it will be your town or city. Maybe your own neighbors will look at Jorge with suspicion and complain that he doesn't speak English. Maybe your own children or grandchildren will pass Jorge's son in the hallway at school where their peers call him names and shove him against the cold metal lockers.
15. Maybe you yourself will have difficulty getting the nasty epithets out of your mind when you watch Jorge ring up your cup of coffee at the Quikmart. Coffee that would have come from his own land back in Guatemala if the drought had not ravaged his crops. And the hurricane before that. And the flood before that.
16. Or maybe you will never see Jorge at all because he works nights at the meatpacking plant making less money than you pay your kids' babysitter. Or because he works in the orchard fields of an agro-conglomerate that does not supply him with protective equipment when it sprays pesticides and herbicides. And when he stands in these fields, his skin and lungs burn as he thinks about his father Rodrigo picking the few kernels from shriveled cobs of their own fields back home.

(Paragraphs 14–16 bring the story to the personal level by using the second-person singular to address the listeners. Suddenly, this is no longer a distant story but is as close as the Quikmart coffee in their hand.)

17. Or maybe . . . when you see Jorge you will remember that you are a Christian. And you will recall the words of the man Jesus Christ whom you worship. Jesus said, "Foxes have holes, and birds of the air have nests; but the Son of Man has nowhere to lay his head." Just like Jorge and his son, who made the perilous journey over weeks, perhaps even months, and found nowhere to safely lay their heads. In that single sentence, Jesus aligns himself with those who have no home, no safety, no rest for their weary bodies. Jesus, whose parents fled with him when he was just a baby seeking refuge in a foreign land—Egypt. Just like their ancestor Jacob and his tribe had sought safety in Egypt generations before.

(Paragraph 17 shifts the tone of the sermon in that the listener, made uncomfortable by the description of the treatment of Jorge and his son, experiences a different way to regard them—through the lens of Jesus's alignment with those who have no homes and those who migrate. Again, the post-colonial and Latin American liberation perspective influence the sermon.)

18. Jacob may have asked the very same questions that Jorge and his father, Rodrigo, asked. What has caused their land to fail? Did they not find favor with God? Were they being punished? It felt like there were forces much bigger than them pushing their family away from this land.
19. But here is where Jacob's story and Rodrigo and Jorge's story diverge. Those forces driving them from their land are not because of God's punishing hand. Ironically, those forces originate in the very country where they are now seeking refuge. This country—the United States of America—which has burned so much fossil fuel over the last two hundred years that, together with other developed nations, has blanketed the earth's atmosphere with heat-trapping greenhouse gases. This is resulting in hot zones along the equator, making them unlivable for millions of people.

(Paragraph 18 weaves Jacob's story back into the sermon but is followed by another shift in paragraph 19 where the lens of ecological theology converges with both the biblical story and the contemporary story of migration.)

20. You see, climate change is what's known as a "threat multiplier." Cameron Ramey, writing for the Yale Program on Climate Change Communication, explains that in Central America, "Since 2014, a series of droughts have wrecked the region's harvest, forcing almost one-third of its people into food insecurity. In Honduras, the changing climate likely contributed to the 2018 drought that wiped out over 80 percent of maize and bean crops. Failing harvests and increasingly destructive weather events have exacerbated migration in this region by escalating hunger, poverty, and violence."[3]
21. But this is not what most of us think about when we hear that a "migrant caravan" is coming up through Mexico to our southern border. Most of us hear voices from screens warning us that these are lazy, no-good criminals and job stealers who will take what is ours and suck off our economy. Never mind that it is our economy that is both exploiting and destroying the countries from which these people are coming in the first place.

(Paragraph 20 provides just enough information about the intersection between climate change and the plight of those living in Central America to allow the listener to connect the dots. This prepares them for paragraph 21, where they hear the prophetic critique of the rhetoric being used by many in the United States to disparage those from Latin America. The influence of post-colonialism on this paragraph is evident.)

22. So we return to Rodrigo's weeping prayer carried on the wind that scatters the parched soil in his hand. We must ask, how can we as Christians, as churches, be part of God's answer to that prayer?
23. What is our role in this story? This saga unwittingly finds us as not the heroes, but as the antagonists. We are the ones who have contributed to the conditions that drive Jorge and millions like him to our borders. We have benefited from the burning of fossil fuels while largely avoiding the costs. What is the church's response to this?
24. Several of our denominations and many people of faith are already thinking about how best to prepare for the immigrants who will be seeking refuge in this country this year and in the decades to come. They are sharing stories of people like Rodrigo and Jorge that "give a human face to one of the most tangible consequences of unmitigated climate change that we face today."[4]
25. As your church is thinking about next steps for your Creation-care ministry, I want to challenge you to go even deeper and broader by expanding your ministry to advocate for climate migrants who are suffering the effects of multiple environmental, economic, and societal crises. You can do this by helping to educate people about the urgency that is driving families to our communities from these climate-ravaged countries. And why it's necessary that they must leave their home countries, even when they want nothing more than to stay. And why it's necessary to change our immigration system so that climate is factored into their legal ability to seek asylum.

26. As *PBS Newshour* writer Miranda Cady Hallett explains, "In the absence of coordinated action on the part of the global community to mitigate ecological instability and recognize the plight of displaced people, there's a risk of what some have called 'climate apartheid.' In this scenario—climate change combined with closed borders and few migration pathways—millions of people would be forced to choose between increasingly insecure livelihoods and the perils of unauthorized migration."[5]
27. Organizations like Faithful America and some denominations have programs to help Christians and congregations become sponsors of these immigrants, which vastly increases their chance of being allowed entrance into the country. Even more important is providing support when they arrive, helping them find employment, helping them learn English, helping them feel welcome in their new communities.

(Paragraphs 22 and 23 move the listeners to the "so what" of the sermon [which will be discussed at length in Chapters 16 and 17 about the Central Purpose]. Paragraphs 24–27 offer suggestions for how individuals and congregations can respond to the climate migration crisis as a matter of faith.)

28. I want to stress that this is not about Christian charity. We need to understand the part we, in this industrialized nation, have played in the inequality, injustice, and climate pollution that has contributed to the conditions that require people to have to emigrate from their lands. Certainly, our participation in this domination system is unwitting and unintentional. But while these immigrants have no choice in what has happened to them, we have a plethora of choices about how we can respond to the needs of others we helped create.
29. So these efforts aren't about charity or even solidarity. They are part of our efforts of repentance, restoration, and reparations. Our Christian responsibility is to help to right these wrongs, especially when we have played a part in creating them. We as Christians and as congregations have a chance to reshape Rodrigo and Jorge's story. We can't make it a happy ending. But we can help make their story a little less painful, to ease the suffering to which we ourselves have contributed. We have a chance to make amends. To help the trajectory of this story bend toward justice instead of snapping and fraying into brittle, brown sinews of empty stalks in empty fields.

(Anticipating the unspoken assumption that caring for climate refugees is an act of charity or solidarity, Leah reframes such actions as acts of "repentance, restoration, and reparations" and uses the image of the empty stalks to help recalibrate listeners' assumptions.)

30. We can help lift up Rodrigo and point north to where his son and grandson have found a community that welcomes them. Where congregations like yours are doing everything they can to help mitigate the climate crisis and actively engage environmental justice issues. Where Jorge has found work that enables him to send home money for his family left behind.
31. So that maybe the feelings that well up in Rodrigo's chest are not just failure and despair, but relief and hope. Hope that comes from the God of Jacob, Joseph, and his brothers to reconcile over bread in a foreign land. Hope that comes from a Savior who knew what it meant to sojourn in a wilderness, to seek refuge from violence, to have no home to lay his head.
    We can cup our hands to catch those tear-stained prayers carried on the dusty wind.
    Amen.

(Paragraphs 30 and 31 cast a positive vision for Rodrigo and his family based on the anticipation of the congregation's response to what they have heard. This enables a final sermonic claim that blends the call for response with the strong theological proclamation of what God has done in the past and how Jesus aligns with those who migrate to create hope for a better future.)

KEY POINTS IN THIS CHAPTER

1. While trying to hear a biblical text objectively on its own terms is important in exegesis, it is not actually possible to remove one's identity and social location when interpreting a text. For this reason, there are perspective-explicit interpretations that unapologetically claim their social locations, identities, and ideologies when reading Scripture. In fact, these perspectives are important correctives because they have been historically underrepresented in historical-critical exegesis.
2. Reading explicitly from particular perspectives helps us understand the Bible more clearly and allows us to see things we might have otherwise missed. However, we must evaluate all approaches in light of the dominant message of Scripture. This helps to safeguard against attempts to co-opt the Bible in ways that run counter to God's will as discerned from the entirety of Scripture.
3. Latin American liberation readings can be considered the progenitor of many other perspective-explicit readings such as feminist, African American, womanist, Mujerista, post-colonial, queer, ecological, and disability standpoints.
4. Perspective-explicit interpretations look to the ways that the Bible has been interpreted and has supported the oppression of various groups by dominant cultural systems. Such perspectives can lead some readers to feel relieved to have their viewpoint represented, but others to feel defensive or guilty when they realize their outlooks have inflicted pain and supported oppression. This gives us the opportunity to talk about systemic sin and how the biblical texts address this in various ways.
5. Readers of the Bible must recognize the intersectionality of different perspectives and how they impinge on and co-inform each other. The Bible itself alludes to this idea using the language and rhetoric of ancient times to describe the ways in which systems of sin overlap and entangle individuals and groups of people.
6. In the midst of our discomfort with approaching the Bible from these perspective-explicit viewpoints, we can think about how they also help us to discern the Word and will of God for the church, and specifically how our sermons can reveal and speak to God's vision for dismantling systems of oppression.

DISCUSSION QUESTIONS

1. Of the ten perspective-explicit approaches to reading the Bible outlined in this chapter, which one(s) most closely align with your own standpoint? Which ones are very different from your social location? Which ones would you want to explore to help you gain more insight for interpreting biblical texts?
2. This chapter gave examples of how systemic sin is recognized and talked about in Scripture and how it can be explained using contemporary illustrations. As another example, how might buying groceries be thought of as an experience that involves us in systemic sin? What are other examples of systemic sin that might benefit from an intersectional reading of the Bible? What are stories in Scripture that help us to understand what systemic sin looked like for ancient peoples and how we might gain insight to address injustices today?
3. What are the injustices in our world today that need to be unmasked? Perhaps systemic racism or ableism? Maybe xenophobia or the modern sex slave industry? Pick two or three and discuss with a colleague how each of the perspective-explicit approaches might give us tools for uncovering the systemic sin that undergirds these evils. What are biblical texts that might be read from one of the perspective-explicit lenses to inform a sermon about these issues?

FOR FURTHER READING

Efrain Agosto. "Latino/a Hermeneutics." In *Hearing the New Testament: Strategies for Interpretation*, second edition, edited by Joel B. Green. Grand Rapids, MI: Eerdmans, 2010.

Ronald J. Allen, ed. *Preaching the Manifold Grace of God, Volume 2: Theologies of Preaching in the Early Twenty-First Century.* Eugene, OR: Cascade, 2022.

Richard Bauckham. *Bible and Ecology: Rediscovering the Community of Creation.* Waco, TX: Baylor University Press, 2010.

Mark Corner and Christopher Rowland. *Liberating Exegesis: The Challenge of Liberation Theology to Biblical Studies.* Louisville: Westminster John Knox, 1989.

Elizabeth Schüssler Fiorenza. *But She Said: Feminist Practices of Biblical Interpretation.* Boston: Beacon, 1992.

Norman Habel. "Introducing Ecological Hermeneutics." *Lutheran Theological Journal* 46 (2012): 97–105.

Holly E. Hearon. "Lesbian Interpretation." *New Interpreter's Dictionary of the Bible*, vol. 3, edited by Katherine Doob Sakenfeld. Nashville: Abingdon, 2006–2009, 637–38.

Robert Jewett. Introduction: "Practical Realism and Historical-Critical Methods." *Romans: A Commentary*. Hermeneia, Minneapolis: Fortress, 2007, 1–3.

Pablo A. Jiménez. "Liberation Criticism." *New Interpreter's Handbook of Preaching*, edited by Paul Scott Wilson. Nashville: Abingdon Press, 2008.

Tat-siong Benny Liew. *What Is Asian American Biblical Hermeneutics? Reading the New Testament.* Honolulu: University of Hawaii Press, 2008.

Esau McCaulley. *Reading While Black: African American Interpretation as an Exercise in Hope.* Grand Rapids, MI: IVP Academic, 2020.

Steven L. McKenzie, editor. *Oxford Encyclopedia of Biblical Interpretation.* Oxford: Oxford University Press, 2013.

Candida R. Moss. "Disability Criticism." *Oxford Encyclopedia of Biblical Interpretation.* Oxford: Oxford University Press, 2013.

Deborah A. Organ. "Cultural Hermeneutics." *New Interpreter's Handbook of Preaching*, edited by Paul Scott Wilson. Nashville: Abingdon Press, 2008.

Emerson B. Powery. "African American Interpretation." In *Hearing the New Testament: Strategies for Interpretation*, second edition, edited by Joel B. Green. Grand Rapids, MI: Eerdmans, 2010.

Anna Runesson. *Exegesis in the Making: Postcolonialism and the New Testament.* Leiden: Brill, 2011.

Fernando F. Segovia. *Decolonizing Biblical Studies: A View from the Margins.* Maryknoll, NY: Orbis, 2000.

Ken Stone. "Gay Interpretation." *New Interpreter's Dictionary of the Bible*, vol. 2, edited by Katherine Doob Sakenfeld. Nashville: Abingdon, 2006–2009, 526–27.

R. S. Sugirtharajah. *Postcolonial Reconfigurations: An Alternative Way of Reading the Bible and Doing Theology.* St. Louis: Chalice, 2003.

NOTES

1. Authors' note: We capitalize the word "Creation" throughout the book so as to denote the level of respect we afford the other-than-human world as subject rather than object. We do the same with the term "Earth" when addressing it as an entity (as opposed to lowercase earth, a synonym of soil).

2. Abrahm Lustgarten, "The Great Climate Migration," *New York Times Magazine*, July 23, 2020, accessed April 28, 2021, https://www.nytimes.com/interactive/2020/07/23/magazine/climate-migration.html.

3. Cameron Ramey, "Climate Migration Needs Personal Stories," Yale Program on Climate Change Communication Blog, January 5, 2021, accessed April 28, 2021, https://climatecommunication.yale.edu/news-events/climate-migration-needs-personal-stories/.

4. Ibid.

5. Miranda Cady Hallett, "How Climate Change Is Driving Emigration from Central America," PBS.org, September 8, 2010, accessed April 28, 2021, https://www.pbs.org/newshour/world/how-climate-change-is-driving-emigration-from-central-america.

5

Practical Use of Exegesis

A NOTE FOR INSTRUCTORS

For those who are using this text to teach students, you may find it helpful to know how we teach exegesis. We begin by providing a general introduction to a biblical book and its broader context. Then we send students to use the commentaries to do individual research on the text. After that, we have them work in groups to compare what they found and share insights with one another. Finally, we have them fill out the chart you will find later in the chapter (also available in Appendix C) and share what they learned with the class. In that final step, we have them compare and justify their results. We have found this method works well for having students work both independently and with small groups as they are learning to exegete texts for preaching.

In this chapter we will think about how to use together all of the methods we have talked about in Chapters 3 and 4 to come to a good interpretation of a biblical text. Then we will explore how to bring that text's message into the present. We have described a number of discrete ways of analyzing texts. Using just any one of them will lead us to miss the fuller interpretation that using all of them that are appropriate for a particular text can offer. For example, if we were to use only form criticism on a text, we might do an excellent job of identifying a narrative about one of Jesus's healings as a miracle story and see how it conforms to and deviates from the standard pattern of telling such stories. But to get the fuller meaning of this pericope and its contribution to our understanding of the whole of a Gospel, we will need to use at least redaction criticism and think about how it fits into the flow of the section's thought progression. Or if we were reading the prophet Amos, we might notice how the oracles against the nations, and then against Israel, follow the pattern of messages that diplomats representing the ruler of an empire would deliver to vassal states that had violated the terms of peace. Then we would need to think of how these fit into the flow of thought in Amos, how he uses this form to get his message across to the nation of Israel. This chapter, then, will describe a way of bringing the various kinds of criticism together to get that fuller meaning.

All of the tools that we have talked about in the previous two chapters are designed to help you develop detailed interpretations of biblical texts. That detailed interpretation is our ultimate goal. But as we begin our use of these tools and methods, we will aim for a more limited goal. In the work we will do in this chapter, we will use those methods to identify the main point(s) that biblical texts try to make for their original readers. In essence, this is the first step you would take in moving toward a more detailed exegesis of a text. In addition to delineating a way to reach this initial goal, we will identify many of the things you would need to study to complete a more comprehensive exegesis of a particular passage.

GETTING STARTED

The place to begin exegesis is always with a careful reading of the text itself. Identify things that stand out to you and things that you have questions about. Think about what ideas and terms seem important. At this early stage, hold all of these things lightly because they may change as you begin to examine the text more thoroughly. After some preliminary work, you will come back to another "initial" reading of the text.

To understand any pericope or paragraph in a text clearly, we must begin with some understanding of the book in which it appears. We can begin to gain this broad knowledge using Bible dictionaries and the critical introductions that appear at the beginnings of commentaries. In these sources we find the leading hypotheses about when a book was written, who wrote it, who its original audience was, what circumstances that original audience faced, what overall the author wanted to accomplish, and often the main theological themes of the book. These introductions will also often provide an outline of the whole book. This is also where we identify the genre of the whole book.

It is important not to rely on study Bibles for this information. Many of them, the majority it seems, do not reflect the work of biblical scholars over the last hundred years or more. The introductions and notes are often written by editors at the publisher who are not experts in the field and are tasked with simply repeating the traditional views of conservative churches. This makes these books acceptable to a broad range of readers (so they sell a lot of them), but they are not helpful in coming to an interpretation of a passage that rests on the best scholarship (both liberal and conservative) of the last century. There are, of course, exceptions to this. Among them are the *HarperCollins Study Bible* (NRSV or NRSVue [updated edition]), the *New Interpreter's Study Bible* (NRSV), and the *Common English Bible Study Bible* (CEB). The authors of the introductions to the biblical books and the notes on the text in these study Bibles are scholars in the field and do rely on good current research. Part of what can help you identify such sources as more reliable is that they identify who the author of each part is. That makes the volume more accountable to the standards of scholarship. Still, even these study Bibles can at best give you the conclusions the scholars reach. For the work of exegesis, you need more than those conclusions; you need the reasons that support those conclusions.

Beginning with study of a biblical book as a whole helps us set the particular part of it that we are studying in both its historical and literary context. You will notice, however, that good interpreters may disagree about some of these introductory matters. When that is the case, you will want to weigh the reasons given for each view and come to your own conclusions about which seems to be more probable. You may also want to note which is the more widely accepted view. The majority view is not always right, but you should be able to acknowledge what that view is. Then if you disagree with it, say why your view fits the evidence better.

DON'T BE AFRAID TO DISAGREE!

When students begin to do exegesis, they are often reticent to disagree with a commentator or other scholar. They are often unwilling to weigh the evidence for themselves and come to their own conclusions because they know that the person who wrote the commentary or article is more experienced at exegesis and knows more about the field of biblical studies than they do. But you should not allow yourself to be intimidated in this way.

Yes, those writers do know more about the book as a whole and about the biblical world. They also know more about what others say about a particular book and specific passage. But you have the advantage of reading what that expert has written. You get to compare it with other interpreters (equally knowledgeable) who both agree and disagree. You get to stand on the shoulders of those interpreters who have come before you. That can embolden you to take up the arguments that are given for multiple understandings of a text, a phrase, or a word, and think about how those arguments support one of the positions interpreters take or lead you to propose a view that those you have read did not adopt. Whether you agree with an earlier position someone has taken or set out a distinctive one, you always need to give reasons for thinking that the position you take is correct or at least the better option among the various possibilities.

After learning about the setting of the biblical book as a whole, we can begin to think about how our particular text fits into the larger outline of a book. This helps us see what larger topics or concerns our passage is related to. It will also help us see where our passage fits into the flow of the argument in its immediate surroundings. At this point we are beginning to use some of the tools of literary criticism as we are analyzing the flow of thought in the section our passage is a part of.

After studying these broader questions about the biblical book as a whole and its outline, it is time to read your text carefully again. See if any new themes, ideas, or questions emerge in light of what you now know about the book as a whole. We then move forward by determining what the boundaries of our passage are, where it begins and ends. If we are working with a pericope in a book that is a narrative, we will look for a new scene or character or discussion. At the same time, we will need to use form criticism to help us determine if the author is using a known literary form to tell the story. If so, we will notice how the author has followed the form and how she or he has deviated from it. When possible, we will also do a redactional analysis, looking for ways that the author has conformed the story to his or her own theological outlook and made it fit into his or her flow of the narrative. If our passage is not in a narrative work, we will look for other signs that a new paragraph has begun and ended. We may look to changes in topics or shifts in emphases. We will also watch for transition words (e.g., therefore) that signal a beginning of a new section or expressions that indicate that a thought unit is complete.

AN EXEGESIS GUIDE CHART

As we set out this way of initially approaching a text and using various exegetical methods, we'll be referring to the chart in Table 1 (also available in Appendix C). This chart is designed to help you begin to organize the information you need to arrive at your interpretation of a biblical text. It does this by asking you to think about the text from distinctive angles. The chart has spaces that ask for the Primary Exigence and Primary Response for four different aspects of the text: Occasional, Literary, Theological, and Contemporary. By **exigence**, we mean the need, desire, condition, or concern that led the author to write about what a particular text contains. We are asking what happened that made the author think that he or she needed to write about the text's topic or to bring up an idea. When we talk about the Response, we are referring to how the author addressed the issue or question in relation to the Occasional, Literary, and Theological aspects of the text. The Contemporary Exigence and Response is where you'll think about the current situation your congregation is facing and how this text might help them think or respond.

For texts that address situations directly, such as the oracles of prophets in the Hebrew Scriptures and Paul's letters in the Christian Scriptures, we recommend starting with the Occasional Exigence and Response to determine what concerns of the community the author is addressing. That leads to the Literary Exigence and Response, where we look at the overall structure of the document and this pericope's place in the flow of the argument.

For genres such as narratives, histories, wisdom literature, poetry, and apocalyptic literature, it's best to start with Literary Exigence and Response to see how the pericope fits into the text as a whole. Then move to Occasional Exigence and Response to determine what historical factors might be informing the author's intent in writing the story or historical narrative, for example.

Primary Occasional Exigence and Response

For writings such as letters and others that directly address the issues and questions raised in a community, the first exigence we address is the Occasional Exigence. The word "occasional" here does not mean happening from time to time. We are using the word in its meaning of being a factor that gives rise to or causes something. When we ask about the Occasional Exigence, we are inquiring about the specific historical things that are going on for believers at that time that are being addressed. We are asking what is happening "on the ground" that our passage discusses. That is, we are asking what is occurring in the community that the work addresses that leads the writer to take up the topic of our passage. Some New Testament letters and other kinds of texts may provide fairly straightforward clues about what is happening among the recipients of the text that leads the author to address the topics that are raised. For example, in 1 Cor 6:1-11 Paul tells the Corinthians not to sue each other over business matters. The Primary Exigence is that members of the Corinthian church are in fact suing each other. That fact on the ground in Corinth is the "Occasional Exigence" of that text.

Table 1. Exegesis Guide Chart

	Primary Exigence	Primary Response
Occasional Historically, what's happening "on the ground"? What specific things were going on for believers at the time?		
Literary Within the text itself, what has happened in the flow of the written document that leads to this passage? How does this pericope fit with and function within the rest of the document?		
Theological What is the theological category (see Appendix D)? What is the theological question or issue that the occasional problem or issue raised? What aspect of faith is being addressed? How does the author think the reader should think or act in response to this issue?		
Contemporary What are creative analogies between the ancient situations the texts addressed and the world we live in? What kinds of present-day issues or situations might be parallel to the Theological Exigence that the passage raises?		

Even in writings that address the situation of the recipients fairly directly, identifying the Occasional Exigence is not always so straightforward for us. The text may respond directly to what is happening in a community, but readers today may still have a difficult time figuring out what that issue was. That is the case in part because the authors assume that the recipients know what the issues and problems are. Thus, they do not need to state the question; they can just start with the response. This often leaves us later readers at a loss, especially at the beginning of our study. An example can help us see this.

The most general exigence for the book of Haggai is that the prophet thinks there needs to be more diligence in completing the construction of the temple now that Judah has returned from exile. The discussion of what makes things clean or unclean in 2:10-19, then, has the Occasional Exigence of the need to be ready to enter the temple when it is finished. The readers of Haggai seem to be saying they do not need to complete work on the temple because they are unclean and so not permitted to enter it even if it were running. These verses in Haggai take up this issue of who will be eligible to worship in the temple in the face of these questions. Those questions are the Occasional Exigence of this passage. But Haggai did not tell us this directly, even though he is addressing that issue directly.

The Occasional Response is how the author reacts to that exigence. What way of thinking about the exigence does the text offer to think about this matter or what way of acting does it recommend? The primary Occasional Response is what the author tells the readers they should do or believe in the specific circumstance in which they find themselves. In Haggai, the response to noting that the people are unclean is that God blesses them and makes them clean so that they will be able to worship, now that the building of the temple has begun. In the case of 1 Cor 6, the Occasional Response is that Paul tells them they must not sue one another in civil court. So again, the primary Occasional Response consists of what the writer tells the readers they should do or think in response to the primary Occasional Exigence.

A COMPLICATED CASE FOR OCCASIONAL EXIGENCE

2 Corinthians

2 Corinthians is another text that presents difficulties when determining the Occasional Exigence. It is clear that all of this work (and the multiple letters in it[1]) are about the legitimacy of Paul's apostleship. Some at Corinth have called it into question, and so he must defend it. In Chapter 3 he compares his ministry with the ministry of Moses. Interpreters are sharply divided over why Paul makes this comparison.

Some interpreters contend that some teachers at Corinth are pointing to Moses and in some way the Mosaic covenant as important for the life of this church that is composed mostly of Gentiles. Others argue that Paul is the one who brings up Moses because he thinks that the comparison will help him make the case for the legitimacy of his apostleship by elevating his ministry above the ministry of Moses. This dispute among interpreters means that the Occasional Exigence of this passage is difficult to discern. How you resolve the question may well change what you hear as the central message of the text. In such cases, attention to the Literary Exigence and Response may need to precede our identification of the Occasional Exigence and Response. That may help us clarify the situation the text tries to address.

NOTE

1. Most interpreters are convinced that the 2 Corinthians in our Bible is composed of at least two (and maybe as many as six) letters that have been put together to form this one book.

Primary Literary Exigence and Response

The Literary Exigence asks what has happened in the flow of the written document that leads to the discussion in our passage. From our 1 Cor 6 example, Paul has started in Chapter 5 addressing a series of issues that he has heard about that are causing problems in Corinth. He has been told that believers are suing each other. The primary Literary Exigence of this text, then, is that Paul is addressing problems he has been told about and now turns to discuss the issue of them suing one another that is among the issues he has heard about. For genres that directly address the readers (such as letters), the Occasional and the Literary Exigencies will often be substantively the same or very close. That is the case for 1 Cor 6, where the Occasional Exigence is that the problem is happening in Corinth and the Literary Exigence is that Paul is moved to write about that problem because he has heard about it. Still, it can be important to distinguish the two exigences in many cases.

PASSAGE SELECTION AND LITERARY EXIGENCE

We might note that one of the general Occasional Exigencies of Philippians is that there is a dispute between some leaders in the congregation. It seems that 2:1-18 as a whole addresses this problem. However, if our passage was 2:6-11, the Literary Exigence would be Paul telling them why they should follow his instructions about how people relate to fellow church members. Paul talks about this largely because of the problem with the leaders, but we need to see the function of the liturgy of 2:6-11 in its literary context, seeing it as a reason to follow his instructions, as well as the occasional or congregation-specific historical context.

For works in a genre that speaks directly to the situation they address, we usually identify the Occasional before identifying the Literary Exigence. But for works in a narrative genre, seeking the Occasional Exigence comes after we set the pericope in the context that the narrative creates. It is only after we see how the passage functions in its narrative context that we can discern what kinds of issues it addresses in the readers' lives. We begin by setting our pericope in the narrative world that the author constructs. Once we understand it in that setting, we can look for what the author wants the story to say to the community for whom the work is written.

When working with a narrative, the Literary Exigence may be that a new character arrives on the scene or in the Gospels that Jesus goes to a new place where he encounters a newly introduced person or situation and perhaps at a particular time. The same is the case for narratives in the Hebrew Bible. The Literary Exigence may be that Abraham goes to a new place or that some new characters arrive at his camp. The same holds true for stories about the Israelites' wilderness wandering (and the rest of the narratives through 2 Chronicles). There they move to a new place that starts a new story or a new crisis emerges. It is the flow of the stories that presents us with new situations and so new questions.

For example, in Gen 18 the Lord appears to Abraham at the oaks of Mamre. There the primary Literary Exigence would be that the Lord appears to Abraham and Sarah because they still do not have the child of promise, even though God has just sealed a covenant with Abraham (ch. 17, in which there are comments about Ishmael). The tension between the covenant promise and the lack of a child is what the story intends to address.

Again, how we proceed with our study will be determined in part by the genre of the document we are reading. Reading works that directly address things happening among the recipients need to be treated differently than narratives. This is because narratives tell stories of other times and places. Still, those stories are intended to address issues, questions, and problems in the communities they were written for. But since they do not address those matters by giving direct instructions to the readers (as Paul's letters do), we have to work from the stories they tell to try to determine what the issues in that recipient community are. Even when Jesus interprets a parable or some other saying or act, he is interpreting it first for the characters in the scene in the Gospel. That may well be the point that the author wants the readers to get, but they get it by listening to what Jesus tells the people in the story. This means that instead of beginning with the Occasional Exigence, we must begin with the Literary Exigence when reading a narrative.

The primary **Literary Response** addresses the matter that the Literary Exigence raises. In a genre such as a letter, that response may be fairly straightforward, even as it will often broaden the response so that it is not just about the immediate issue but also about the character of God or the character of the community or some other theological affirmation.

In narratives, the response will be the way that the main character (or others who may carry the scene) responds to the challenge or problem or question that the narrative situation presents. Our access to the situation in the community is more clouded when reading a narrative than when reading a work that directly addresses the community's questions or issues. In a narrative, we have to discover what issue the particular story raises to think about what is happening in the addressed community. We should not expect a direct correspondence, but there will be a relationship between the issue the story raises and issues in the community that is being told the story. For example, the creation stories in Genesis do more than get the story of the world started. In the face of other creation stories from surrounding nations about other gods creating the world, these stories provide readers ways to reject those other accounts and embrace the worship of the one God. Of course, they also address more specific issues, but perhaps this can serve as a broad example.

We can look to the Gospel narratives for a more specific example of primary Literary Exigence and Response. The story in Matt 9:2-8 has Jesus forgive a person's sins and then heal that person. Here the Literary Exigence is that people bring a person who is paralyzed to Jesus to be healed. The Literary Response is that Jesus first forgives the man's sins and then heals him. The point of this response is that when the healing comes after Jesus claims to forgive his sins, it serves as evidence that Jesus does have authority to forgive sins. Such a story seems to respond to questions about who has authority to forgive sins. If we remember that Matthew is written for a predominantly Jewish church, it is probable that fellow Jews who are not church members have raised questions about whether Jesus can provide forgiveness—perhaps this is an even more urgent question following the fall of the temple. Seeing the point of the story as demonstrating that Jesus can forgive sins is supported by the direct discussion about the authority to forgive that appears in the story. This story, then, provides Matthew's church with evidence that Jesus does indeed have the authority or power to forgive their sins. Thus, the Occasional Exigence is the dispute about who can forgive sins or perhaps more specifically whether Jesus can. The Occasional Response is that Jesus can forgive sins. We can get to this information about what is happening in Matthew's church only through our analysis of the Literary Exigence and Response of the episode.

DISTINGUISHING BETWEEN THE LITERARY EXIGENCE AND THE OCCASIONAL EXIGENCE

Jeremiah 36 presents us with another setting for a narrative. It has the prophet send his secretary to the temple to read a scroll that condemns the polytheistic practices of the elites in Jerusalem. Here a narrative is embedded into a work of the prophetic genre. In the narrative, King Jehoiakim burns that scroll but Jeremiah re-dictates it, and some of it becomes part of the book of Jeremiah. The primary Literary Exigence is that the king hears that this oracle was read at the temple and calls for it to be read to him. The primary Occasional Exigence of the original reading of that material (and so here the literary setting of the story) is the unfaithfulness of the seventh-century temple and royal court in Jerusalem.

But when the material is included in the book of Jeremiah, which was compiled later during the period of the Babylonian captivity, it intends to address the situation that those later readers face. So, we would need to search for what ideas and/or practices would lead the later compilers of that book to think that this specific material should be included in this way for the readers/listeners of their own time. This issue in the lives of those the book is written for would be the Occasional Exigence of this passage in Jeremiah.

Primary Theological Exigence and Response

Once we have identified the Occasional and Literary Exigence and Response, we can turn to identifying the theological message of the text by attending to the **Theological Exigence and Response** part of the chart. For the sake of preaching, this is getting us to the reason that we are studying these texts in a detailed and systematic manner. But we cannot get to the Theological Exigence and Response until we have done our work on the Literary and Occasional Exigence and Response. The Theological Exigence is the theological question or issue that the occasional problem or issue raised. Here we should remember that the authors of these texts purposefully frame the issues in particular ways. They tell a story or raise a question about a practice in the way they do so that the readers will see how it relates to some specific aspect of the faith. That is, the author wants the readers to shape their thinking about the issue around a particular belief that the community holds. The author may discuss the issue or tell the story so that it points to an aspect of the character of God or so that it relates, for example, to how they understand the community (ecclesiology) or some other theological framework.

Think of our example from 1 Cor 6. The Occasional Exigence is that church members are suing one another. The Occasional Response is telling them they must not do this. The Theological Exigence looks for the reason Paul thinks this is what church members must not do. As Paul talks about this issue, he makes it be about the identity of church members and about the ethical expectations for church membership. Our central Theological Exigence, then, might be who church members are or what kinds of behavior church membership requires.

The Theological Response is what the author says that this theological framing shows about why the readers should act in a particular way or what they should believe in the face of the issue(s) raised. Most of the time, biblical writers do not just give orders to the readers. They make arguments by giving reasons why the readers should do the things they tell them to do. It is those theological reasons that are of central value when preaching.

Let's return to our example of 1 Cor 6. If we identify the Theological Exigence in one of the ways we have suggested, the Theological Response would be that God has given church members the ability to make just judgments or that God requires church members to adhere to certain kinds of ethical behavior. Notice that the Theological Exigence and Response are broader matters than the specifics of the Corinthians' situation. The question that the problem in Corinth raises is broader than the specifics of the situation. The way Paul responds to that immediate problem makes it a question of Christian identity and of the expectations that church membership imposes. Note that what we see here is the way that the author chooses to frame the question. The author makes the practical problem a manifestation of a theological issue. When we get to this theological issue, we are getting to what this text can say in our context.

Having said that the Theological Response in this Corinthian text is that God makes ethical demands for church membership and/or God gives the church the ability to discern what is just, we should note that those demands include how church members conduct their professional and personal lives. (Doing a more detailed exegesis will lead us to examine the nature of these expectations more specifically.) Notice again that the Theological Response is no longer about the specifics of the Corinthian situation; instead, it is about the broader theological issue that the specific problem raises. This broader setting and response give us a theological assertion to bring to bear on our situation and on the issues that our churches face.

It will also be helpful at this point to identify the theological category in which the assertion in the Theological Response belongs. See the list below as well as Appendix D. This helps us focus our attention on the message of the text. Giving attention to the assertion's theological category can help us see the message of the text rather than falling back onto moralistic advice or general exhortations about being good people. It helps us remember that these texts are doing serious theological work.

In the case of our 1 Cor 6 passage, the theological category is ecclesiology or perhaps ecclesiological ethics. Its assertion is about the nature of the church and what is required of church membership. These are topics that are seldom the main themes of sermons in mainline churches, but this text should move the preacher to address these matters.

THEOLOGICAL CATEGORIES

(See Appendix D for a full explanation of each category.)

Christology
Discipleship
Ecclesiology
Eschatology
Ethics, Theological/Ecclesiological
Hermeneutics
Pneumatology
Revelation
Sacraments/ordinances, Theology of
Soteriology
Theological Anthropology
Theology
Worship, Theology of

Primary Contemporary Exigence and Response

Finally, the Contemporary Exigence moves beyond exegesis. In Chapter 1 we talked about how to bring the message of the text into the present without treating it in a literalistic manner. There we said that a way to take the text seriously (and as an authority) without being literalists is to seek creative analogies between the ancient situations the texts addressed and the world that we live in. When we turn to the Contemporary Exigence of our text, we are asking what kind(s) of present-day issue(s) or situation(s) might be parallel to the Theological Exigence that the passage raises. We are looking for those analogies we talked about in Chapter 1. We are not looking for the very same problem or question, but rather matters in our churches that seem to grow out of the same theological assertions and occasional (on the ground, practical) quandaries.

We can think about how that might work in relation to our 1 Cor 6 passage. There the problem was that some believers are cheating others in business deals and the matter is going to court. We have said that we do not look to that particular situation, but to what issues the author sees being raised by this situation. We have seen that the theological issue involves the meaning of and ethical requirements for church membership. By analogy, we might say that the primary Contemporary Exigence is the question of whether or what kinds of ethical expectations there are for church membership. If we think that the emphasis of the passage is more on the ability of the church to discern what is just (which seems less likely to be the main point), then the Contemporary Exigence would be about how the church exercises that discernment. We can narrow the first of those Contemporary Exigencies by asking about what church membership demands of believers in particular arenas: what does living by God's ethical standards for church members require in business life, political life, church life?

The Contemporary Response, then, looks to how preachers can draw on the Theological Response (that is shaped by the Occasional and Literary Response) to address those analogous issues in their churches. It asks how the understanding of the faith that shaped the specific response in the ancient situation can speak to and shape what the church today does and believes.

The Theological Response in the case of 1 Cor 6 requires the preacher to assert that there are, indeed, ethical expectations for church membership. This may be a difficult message. It opposes the inclination to let people who behave in any way they want to be members just because we are so desperate for members or are reticent to say that some behaviors violate God's will. Such a message challenges us to overcome our reticence to claim that some things are, in fact, incompatible with being a member of the church that this text says has been "made holy." We do not get all the specifics about how we should act as church members, but the text gives us ways to think about contemporary issues. Its expectations require us to do the work of discerning how to live out the demands it sets forth.

CONCLUSION

When we have gone through these steps, we have completed an initial interpretation of a text. We have come to understand its primary reason for being written and how the author addresses that exigence. We have also seen how the author frames that issue and what theological affirmations the author thinks readers should employ to think about this matter. In addition, we have identified analogies in our contemporary world and seen how this text calls the church to think about them. This will prepare you to proclaim a basic meaning of this text for the church today.

At the same time, our work on the chart is only an initial interpretation of a text. After we complete this work, we are ready to turn to a more detailed investigation of our text. Now we are ready to begin to investigate more fully what particular phrases and terms mean. Now we are ready to investigate further the specifics of some cultural phenomena and how they may be manifesting themselves in the community the text addresses. Now we are ready to examine more closely the progression of the logic of the text's argument. These more detailed studies will either confirm or cause us to adjust our initial reading of the text as it is seen in our chart. The more detailed treatment of each word, phrase, and idea in the text will be required for your exegesis work that pushes beyond your initial reading. That more detailed study is also what you will need to do to prepare for a sermon, and especially a more detailed Bible study, in your church. There you need to be able to help your church understand the text, including not just asking them to take your word for what it means. You need to be able to give them solid reasons for the interpretation that you give a text. This reasoned interpretation of the ancient setting and message will give them confidence that you are able to make good use of the text for the present.

The primary Contemporary Exigence moves beyond exegesis to application. This is where the preacher can determine what situations in our churches reflect issues that are analogous to the issues raised by the Occasional and Theological Exigencies. The Contemporary Response addresses the analogous issues in their churches and makes a claim in light of the Theological Response.

In Chapter 7, you will see two examples of texts analyzed using the Exegesis Guide Chart. But first, we will discuss how to choose biblical texts for preaching and worship in the next chapter.

KEY POINTS IN THIS CHAPTER

1. In performing exegesis for preaching, we must use as full a complement of all the critical methods of interpreting a scriptural passage as possible to get its meaning.
2. Using the Exegesis Guide Chart is a way to organize a preacher's examination and analysis of a passage. The chart has spaces that ask for the primary exigence (what issue or subject is raised in a particular text) and primary response for four different aspects of the text: Occasional, Literary, Theological, and Contemporary.
3. The primary Occasional Exigence and Response are the specific historical things that are going on in the church being addressed that prompt the author to write this passage, how the author reacts to that situation, and what they want the readers to do or think.
4. The primary Literary Exigence looks at the flow of the written document and, especially in a narrative, the world that the author constructs. The primary Literary Response addresses the matter that the Literary Exigence raises, whether that is in a narrative (where the characters respond) or a direct situation, such as in a letter.
5. The Theological Exigence is the theological question or issue that the Occasional Exigence raised. The Theological Response is what the author says the theological framing shows about why the readers should act in a certain way or what they should believe in light of the issue.
6. The Contemporary Exigence seeks to bring the message of the text into the present by asking what kind(s) of present-day issue(s) or situation(s) might be parallel to the Theological Exigence that the passage raises. Through the use of creative analogies between the ancient situations that the texts addressed and the world in which we live, the Contemporary Response elucidates matters in our churches that seem to grow out of the same theological assertions and occasional (on the ground, practical) quandaries of the original hearers.

DISCUSSION QUESTIONS

1. In our discussion of Matt 9:2-8 above, we talked about how the story reveals something about the Occasional Exigence and the Response this text provides. In Chapter 1 we identified creative analogies as a good way to bring the meaning of a text into the present. How might you use a creative analogy about the situation Matthew's community faced to relate this story to the present? Thinking about the Theological Response that this story gives, what message could a sermon proclaim that addresses the analogous situation you identified?
2. Throughout this chapter we used 1 Corinthians 6 as an example, concluding that its theological assertion is that there are ethical demands for church membership. How might you use its Occasional Exigence and its Theological Response to write a sermon that addresses the church today? What kinds of analogies would you draw? What kinds would you avoid?
3. We have talked about how studying the Literary and Occasional Exigence and Response of texts can help you discern the Theological Exigence and Response. How do you see the relationship between the Literary and Occasional Exigence and Response, on the one hand, and the Theological Exigence and Response, on the other? How do you see the relationship between the Theological Response in a text and its contemporary message?

FOR FURTHER READING

Gordon D. Fee. *New Testament Exegesis: A Handbook for Students and Pastors*, third edition. Louisville: Westminster John Knox, 2002.

Mark Allan Powell. "How Do Biblical Scholars Study the New Testament?" n.p. [cited October 1, 2021], https://www.bibleodyssey.org:443/tools/bible-basics/how-do-biblical-scholars-study-the-new-testament.

Sarah Shectman. "How Do Biblical Scholars Read the Hebrew Bible?" n.p. [cited October 1, 2021], https://www.bibleodyssey.oQrg:443/tools/bible-basics/how-do-biblical-scholars-read-the-hebrew-bible.

6

Choosing Biblical Texts for Preaching

So far, you've learned the basics for interpreting Scripture, using history and literature for understanding the text, and how to chart the exegesis of your chosen passage to help you craft the claims for your sermon. But we haven't yet talked about how to choose the biblical passage itself. Different traditions have various ways of deciding what texts will be the basis of the worship service and the sermon. Some preachers use lectionaries; some plan out sermon series based on themes; others preach sequentially through an entire book; and some rely on a regular practice of prayer and discernment to choose their text for preaching each week. Many preachers use different methods at different times for choosing their texts depending on their denomination, the season of the liturgical year, or what is happening in the congregation, community, nation, or on a planetary scale that needs sermonic attention.

In this chapter, we will examine these methods for choosing a text for preaching, weighing the benefits and drawbacks of each. We'll also discuss how to choose a pericope from any given biblical text so that it is manageable for preaching. And we'll talk about best practices for integrating texts in the sermon and the liturgy. In Appendix E, you'll find a worksheet to help you plan a sermon that takes all these variables into account.

UNDERSTANDING THE LITURGICAL YEAR

One thing that can influence the way preachers decide what text will be the basis of their sermon is the season of the liturgical year. The chart in Figure 1 shows the cycle of seasons and major holy days built around the birth, life, ministry, crucifixion, resurrection, and ascension of Jesus Christ. Notice that there is a Christmas cycle and an Easter cycle within the larger yearly cycle. We begin at Advent, which heralds the birth of Jesus, followed by Christmas and then Epiphany. After Ash Wednesday there is Lent, followed by Easter and the day of Pentecost, which begins a very long season lasting for nearly half the year until we come back around to Advent again. There are other important days to note within this cycle, but for our purposes, you just need to know the basic sequence of the seasons.

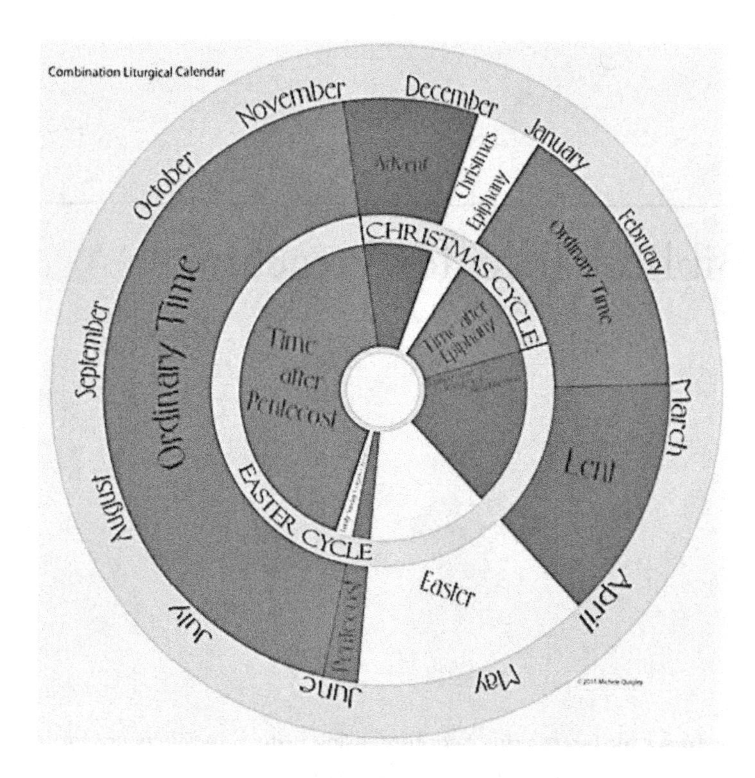

Figure 1. The Liturgical Year. This image is copyright by Michele Quigley. Used with permission.

Below is a list of the primary holy days within the liturgical year. We begin with the four weeks of Advent followed by two Sundays of Christmas. Epiphany is both a holy day and a season that lasts until the Sunday of the Transfiguration and Ash Wednesday, which leads into the forty days of Lent. That season concludes with Palm Sunday which leads into Holy Week—Maundy Thursday, Good Friday, and Saturday Vigil, culminating with the Sunday of the Resurrection of Jesus Christ also known as Easter Sunday. This begins a fifty-day season of Easter that ends on the day of Pentecost (when we remember the gift of the Holy Spirit given to the disciples), which marked the beginning of the Christian church. Then we have several months in the season of Pentecost until we return to Christ the King Sunday, which is like the liturgical "New Year's Eve" of the coming year.

HOLY DAYS AND SEASONS IN THE LITURGICAL YEAR

(Note: Seasons are listed in all caps.)

ADVENT (season)
CHRISTMAS (day and season)
EPIPHANY (day and season)
Transfiguration (day)
Ash Wednesday (day)
LENT (season)
Holy Week: Palm Sunday, Maundy Thursday, Good Friday, Holy Saturday
EASTER (day and season)
Pentecost (day)
SEASON OF PENTECOST (season, sometimes called "Ordinary Time")
Christ the King Sunday (day)

While not all Christian traditions or denominations mark every part of the liturgical year, all major Christian denominations celebrate both Christmas and Easter. So, all preachers must take into consideration these poles of the liturgical year when they are choosing their biblical texts for sermons. For preachers in traditions that mark the fuller spectrum of the liturgical year, they may choose to use a resource called the *Revised Common Lectionary* to help them decide on the texts they want to be the basis of the worship service and their sermon. In this next part, we'll learn what a lectionary is and how it's used for preaching and worship.

THE ORIGINS AND USE OF LECTIONARIES

Let's begin by looking at the way lectionaries came into being and how they're tied to the liturgical year. Then we'll discuss the pros and cons of using a **lectionary** for preaching and worship.

"Lection" comes from the Latin word *legere*, which means "to choose." In Christian parlance, the lection refers to a "scripture lesson." A collection of these lessons is called a *lectionary*. And the person who reads the lessons in the worship service is called a *lector*.

A related term is "pericope." You may hear clergy talk about going to a "pericope study" with their colleagues. Pericope literally means "cutting around" in Greek and refers to a set of verses from a book of the Bible that forms one coherent unit or thought. It's important to note that a lection may include different parts of a pericope. A lection may start or end in the middle of a thought unit or may omit material in the middle. This is why it is important to engage in literary analysis of a lectionary reading to see what comes before and after the selected passage and what might be missing from the middle.

THE *REVISED COMMON LECTIONARY*

The lectionary many churches use is called the *Revised Common Lectionary* (RCL). The origins of the RCL arose from Vatican II, the Second Vatican Council that happened in the 1960s when Pope John XXIII gathered an assembly of Roman Catholic religious leaders to settle doctrinal issues and, more importantly, renew the spirit of the church. One of the results of this renewal was bringing together not just Catholics, but also Protestants and Jews, to prepare a lectionary that could be shared throughout Christendom. In the ensuing years, this collection of readings went through several iterations, the most current one having been released in 1994.

In the RCL, each Sunday includes a reading from the Hebrew Scriptures, a Psalm, an Epistle, and a reading from a Gospel. These readings are divided into a three-year cycle:

Year A—Matthew
Year B—Mark
Year C—Luke

Readings from the Gospel of John are woven throughout the three years.

The creators of the RCL designed the readings so that on most Sundays, the Hebrew Scripture reading, Psalm, and Gospel pericopes contain a similar theme and relate to one another in ways that reinforce a particular story, character, or theological concept. The Epistle reading may or may not relate to one of the other readings and is usually a sequence of pericopes from one of the letters of the New Testament. As you can see, a preacher has several possibilities to choose from when using the RCL as the basis of their sermon. This does not mean, however, that a preacher is required to mention *all four readings* in their sermon. In fact, it's usually best *not* to try to address all the day's lessons in one sermon. You may find a point of resonance between, say, the Epistle and the Gospel, or the Hebrew Scripture reading and the Psalm that you want to highlight in some way, and that is perfectly fine. But if you try to weave together three or four lessons, you may find your sermon trying to do too much.

How do these lessons jibe with the liturgical year? The lessons are chosen to correspond with the seasons. For example, at the beginning of the church year, which starts in Advent, the Gospel readings focus on the disruption of the status quo and the preparation for the coming of the Christ child. Christmas, of course, contains the birth narratives, but in Year A, it also includes the heartbreaking story in the Gospel of Matthew of Herod's slaughter of the innocents in his efforts to kill the newborn Messiah.

The season of Epiphany focuses on stories of the gospel being encountered by those in the Gentile world to demonstrate that the "light of Christ" has far-reaching global implications. Lent, with its focus on repentance and contemplation in preparation for Holy Week, contains stories that highlight Jesus's journey to Jerusalem. Easter, of course, has the stories about Jesus's resurrection. During the fifty days that follow Easter, the readings focus on Jesus Christ's appearances to his disciples before his ascension. You'll also notice that during the season of Easter, the first lesson comes from the book of Acts rather than the Hebrew Scriptures. The season of Easter ends with the day of Pentecost, which marks the "birthday" of the church when the Holy Spirit was given to the disciples to carry the gospel of Jesus Christ to all the nations. The time after Pentecost is when the lectionary looks at the parables of Jesus and focuses on his teachings, miracles, healings, and encounters with all sorts of characters during his travels.

There are also special days within the liturgical year, such as the Baptism of Jesus, Ash Wednesday, the Day of Ascension, Holy Trinity Sunday, and All Saints Day, that have their own sets of readings specific to that occasion. Usually those readings are the same each year.

Benefits and Drawbacks of Using the *Revised Common Lectionary*

There are many positives to using the *Revised Common Lectionary*, but there are some downsides as well. Let's start with the benefits. When we use the RCL, we are united with Christians around the world in reading the same Scripture passages each week. This enhances ecumenism, the spirit of working together across denominational lines and finding a common purpose. Adhering to the RCL also cultivates a discipline of preaching on texts you might not normally choose and removes some of the temptation to preach only on texts that are "easy" or that you enjoy.

Another benefit is that there are many published and online resources available for planning worship. Denominations often provide these for their clergy and worship leaders. Also, the *Feasting on the Word* series by Westminster John Knox Press provides four perspectives of the RCL scripture for each week (exegetical, theological, homiletical, and pastoral). The publishers have also created worship companions that offer various options for worship, readings, hymns, and so on.[1] They even have Children's Moment guides and Sunday School curriculum. All together, these resources can be helpful for worship-planning teams. Especially in larger churches that involve many different persons in the planning and execution of the worship service, having everyone on the same schedule is helpful and even necessary.

A church following the RCL would find plenty of resources for planning of worship and education each week with appropriate hymns, choir anthems, and ideas for sermons. It makes for efficient planning. Some resources even have ready-made liturgical prayers, communion liturgies, bulletin covers, liturgical art (such as banners and graphics), and inserts based on the season of the year and the assigned readings for the day. With these resources, preachers can spend more time developing the sermon instead of choosing the readings and hymns and developing the liturgy each week.

But there are also drawbacks to using the RCL. Because the RCL tends to emphasize smaller pericopes, it can be easy to disregard the fact that they are tied to larger texts. In order not to lose perspective, it's important to perform literary exegesis, as described in Chapter 3. Another quirk with the RCL is that a preacher may find that the thematic connection between the different readings of the day seems a bit arbitrary, and the harmonization between the lessons can appear forced. While the creators of the RCL were diligent and faithful in their work, it's important to recognize that the decisions were made by a committee, and all committees are fallible. So there are times when the connections don't always seem apparent. Other times, it appears that some stories and themes receive an inordinate amount of attention (for example, there are many pericopes about John the Baptist, and a great deal of attention is given to the "bread" passages in the Gospels during the season after Pentecost), while other themes, stories, and characters are ignored altogether. For example, there are very few stories in the RCL about female figures in the Bible. As Wilda C. Gafney observes, "The scriptures are androcentric, male-focused, as are the lectionaries dependent on them."[2] In her experience as a priest and congregant, she says, "Those lectionaries are not simply *as* androcentric as are the scriptures, women are even less well represented in them than they are in the biblical text."[3]

Speaking of leaving things out, while it's true that the RCL provides a comprehensive method for reading through the content of the Bible over the course of three years, and that a section of nearly every book of the Bible makes an appearance over the course of the cycle, much of the Bible is not covered. For example, there is only one passage from Judges, one from Song of Solomon, very little from Daniel, and large portions of the Minor Prophets are left out. There are even some parables of Jesus that don't make it into the RCL. In fact, only about 25 to 30 percent of the Bible is covered over the course of the three years in the RCL. This means that if you read only from the RCL, your congregation is missing out on about three-quarters of the Bible. So a preacher may want to consider other methods for choosing biblical texts for preaching.

ALTERNATIVE LECTIONARIES

Narrative Lectionary

The *Narrative Lectionary* (NL) is a four-year cycle of readings for use in congregational worship and preaching. The goal is to preach annually through the biblical narrative in order to center the lives of believers in God's story. Each week, two texts are assigned—a preaching text and an accompanying text. Preachers and congregations have the benefit of working through a sequence of readings to get a sense of how the book of the Bible fits within the larger scope of the story of God and God's people. The website Working Preacher has both the RCL and NL and contains links for sermon ideas.[4]

Women's Lectionaries

As mentioned earlier, the *Revised Common Lectionary* does not adequately represent the presence of the Bible's women in its pericopes. In 2021, two resources were published to fill the "gender gap" in the RCL. One is *The Women's Lectionary: Preaching the Women of the Bible Throughout the Year* by Ashley M. Wilcox. This single volume provides an entire year's worth of readings focused on women in the Bible for each Sunday and on holy days. Each of the sixty-five sets of readings pairs a pericope from the Hebrew Scriptures with one from the New Testament and provides commentary as well as discussion questions. The other is a series called *A Women's Lectionary for the Whole Church* with years A, B, C, and W (a multi-Gospel, single-year lectionary) by Wilda C. Gafney. In each volume, there are eighty-nine readings, including three different options for both Christmas and Easter and additional readings for each day of Holy Week and Easter Week as well as other holy days. Gafney's volumes follow the traditional four-fold model with a first lesson from the Hebrew Bible, a Psalm, a Christian Testament lesson, and a Gospel. Each set of readings is accompanied by textual notes for exegesis as well as preaching prompts. Both authors offer a much-needed corrective to the androcentrism of existing lectionaries by focusing on women's stories, female images for the Divine, and the complex and often disturbing ways in which the Bible (and our contemporary society) renders the personhood of females. The aim of each of these authors is to enable preachers and congregations to more fully understand and reflect on humanity made in the image of God, especially the women and girls who are often relegated to silence, namelessness, and subservience.

The African American Lectionary

A collaborative project of the African American Pulpit and American Baptist College of Nashville, the African American Lectionary is an online resource (http://www.theafricanamericanlectionary.org/) that highlights the African American ecclesial traditions and moments that creatively express the joy, freedom, and challenges of being both African American and Christian (e.g., Watch Night, African Heritage Sunday, Usher's Day, and Women's Day). The site also recognizes days on the liturgical calendar that are celebrated across a variety of ecclesial traditions (e.g., Advent, Christmas, Lent, Easter, and Pentecost). By incorporating both the moments of significance across many African American ecclesial traditions and some of the traditional moments of any lectionary cycle, the *African American Online Lectionary* allows users to select from a vast array of material that will fit their congregation's needs and expectations. The Lilly Foundation–funded project began in 2008 and concluded in 2013. The website contains a link on liturgical colors specific to African American contexts as well as ideas for sermon illustrations and essays on Black preaching.

Season of Creation

The *Season of Creation* works on the three-year cycle that focuses on the theme of celebrating, lamenting, and protecting God's Creation. Each cycle contains four Sundays that focus on a theme in nature, such as oceans, animals, forests, or plants. The lectionary is designed to start on the first Sunday in September and culminate on the first Sunday in October, which is the feast day for St. Francis of Assisi. However, the four Sundays can be used at other times of the year, such as after Easter or after the day of Pentecost. They can also be spread out over the course of four months, with a Sunday each month dedicated to Creation. The website (http://seasonofcreation.com/) contains resources to connect congregations with the vibrant parts of Creation that sustain us and all living things. There are resources for music, children's messages, visual aids, and sermons, as well as other worship helps. Preachers have the benefit of a published resource specifically for the *Season of Creation, The Season of Creation: A Preaching Commentary* by Norman C. Habel, David Rhoads, and H. Paul Santmire.

Fourth-Year Lectionaries

There are also lectionaries that offer supplements to the RCL so that preachers and worshippers can encounter a fuller scope of the Bible. One is *Beyond the Lectionary: A Year of Alternatives to the Revised Common Lectionary* by David Ackerman. The pericopes are chosen for both continuity (progressing in order through the Bible) as well as complementarity (mutually relating to each other in a way that enhances the individual readings). The resource also offers commentaries and prayers.

Another option is *Year D: A Quadrennial Supplement to the Revised Common Lectionary* by Timothy Matthew Slemmons. This book supplements the *Revised Common Lectionary* with a fourth year of lections and arranges many previously excluded biblical texts in an orderly, one-year preaching plan. It helps to expand a preacher's (and their congregation's) encounter with Scripture to include a fuller range of voices and stories missing from the RCL.

CHOOSING PERICOPES INDEPENDENT OF LECTIONARIES

Not all denominations and not all congregations use a lectionary for the basis of their worship services. Likewise, not all preachers use a lectionary when choosing texts for their sermons. Even if their church uses the lectionary on a regular basis, a preacher may choose to go off-lectionary for a sermon for any number of reasons.

Topical Preaching and Sermon Series

Sometimes a preacher may want to address a particular topic, create a sermon series built around a theme, or address a crisis either in the congregation or community. When this happens the assigned lectionary texts simply may not provide the biblical basis for addressing the topic or issue.[5] In any case, choosing texts based on a subject is called "topical preaching," and there are both advantages and disadvantages to this type of sermon.

There are two main risks with topical preaching. One is the temptation toward eisegesis, which is reading one's own meaning into the text or imposing an interpretation that is driven by an ideological agenda or bias. For example, a preacher may feel called to speak on a particular contemporary issue or news item, but if they cherry-pick passages that support their partisan position, this may result in a sermon that sacrifices theological and scriptural integrity for the sake of their political agenda.

The other risk with topical preaching is doing very little exegetical work and just skimming the surface of the text. For instance, a preacher may want to do a sermon series on "Superheroes in the Bible," but in their effort to paint heroic portraits of, say, Abraham and David, they may overlook the very real sins committed by both men (such as Abraham casting out Hagar and Ishmael and David committing both adultery and murder).

Yet there are times when a topical sermon can be both appropriate and helpful. In his book *Preaching the Topical Sermon*, Ronald J. Allen explains that topical sermons can be biblically sound and demonstrate exegetical integrity. The key is to ask, "'How does [Scripture] lead us to understand the topic?'"[6] He notes that there may be times and occasions that call for a temporary pause in following the lectionary in order to address a topic that "can be better addressed from the standpoint of the gospel itself than from the standpoint of the exposition of a particular passage (or passages from the Bible)."[7] In other words, a preacher can draw from a wide range of texts that speak to a topic, and as long as this is done without abusing the passages themselves, the sermon can shed light on important topics using insights from the study of Scripture.

Another advantage to topical sermons or sermon series is being able to develop a theme or address an issue over several Sundays. Not only does this allow the preacher to examine the different layers and approaches to a topic or theme, it can help listeners gain a more comprehensive view on a subject (say, for example, rivers or mountains in the Bible, or the theme of forgiveness). This kind of preaching also has the pedagogical advantage of building on ideas in a sequential way so that listeners can assimilate the knowledge the preacher imparts each week, knowing that it is building toward a climax or conclusion. For example, in her book *Preaching in the Purple Zone: Ministry in the Red-Blue Divide*, Leah has developed an approach to preaching on social issues called the sermon-dialogue-sermon method. In this process which takes place over several weeks, the topic is first introduced in a nonpartisan sermon called the "prophetic invitation to dialogue" that invites the congregation to engage the topic. This sermon is followed by a deliberative dialogue on the issue, after which a second sermon, the "communal prophetic proclamation," is preached integrating the wisdom and insights that arose from the dialogue on the topic.[8]

Choosing Scripture through Personal Prayer and Discernment

Some preachers prefer to engage in a regular practice of prayer and discernment to choose their texts for each sermon. This may result in topical sermons or series as described above. Or it may be directed more by what some may call "the movement of the Spirit." The advantages to preaching untethered by a lectionary are that a preacher can be nimble in responding to the needs of the congregation, community, or current events. Also, their discipline of daily Scripture reading, prayer, and meditation may result in new insights or allow for discernment that is informed by pastoral-care needs, cultural events (such as holidays, festivals, deaths of national figures, etc.), issues that arise in congregational Bible study, and even the spontaneous questions about faith that come from children, youth, and adults.

Preaching this way does have downsides, however. A preacher may choose only passages or books of the Bible they are partial to, thus ignoring other parts of the Bible or intentionally avoiding more challenging pericopes. This approach also runs the risk of what James F. White calls "reshaping scripture in the preacher's own image."[9] In other words, if a preacher has a certain bias or ideology (conscious or unconscious), they may choose texts that either implicitly or explicitly contribute to or reinforce this stance.[10] Congregations may also notice a lack of discipline from preachers who do not address biblical texts in a methodical manner. Whim may usurp consistency.

To minimize these risks, here are some suggested practices for choosing Scriptures and topics for preaching that can ensure you hold yourself accountable and maintain a high level of integrity in your treatment of biblical texts. These practices can be useful for both lectionary and non-lectionary preachers.

SUGGESTED PRACTICES FOR CHOOSING SCRIPTURES AND TOPICS FOR PREACHING

- Create a spreadsheet that lists the books of the Bible. Over the course of a year, mark each time you preach from a book, including chapter and verses. Note how often you preach from certain books of the Bible and even certain passages. Make it a point to address books or stories that are more challenging to you or that you would rather avoid.
- On this spreadsheet, make a category for the types of sermons you preached, such as expository, topical, social issues, personal morality, doctrinal, or theological theme, for example. Track how often you preach certain types of sermons and make it a point to vary your types of sermons and subject matter.
- Also on this spreadsheet, make a category for how often you preach from a text that mentions female characters in the Bible. Be intentional about preaching sermons that feature women from Scripture.[1]

- Experiment with following a lectionary for a year (or following a different one than you usually use). What changes do you notice in terms of your worship planning, sermon preparation, and how the congregation receives the sermon?
- Consult with clergy colleagues and discuss how you choose texts for preaching. Covenant with each other to either broaden, deepen, or change your approaches to biblical texts and reflect on how this furthers your development as a preacher.

NOTE

1. Religion professor Lynn Japinga has written several books that are very helpful for preachers wanting to craft sermons that include women from the Bible. See "For Further Reading" at the end of the chapter for a list of these books.

CONCLUDING THOUGHTS ON CHOOSING BIBLICAL TEXTS

No matter how you choose your texts for preaching, it's always good to meet with other clergy for text study, be part of interfaith study groups, and/or engage in study of the texts with those who will listen to the sermon. Studying the text with parishioners as part of one's sermon preparation can be fruitful on many levels. In his book *The Roundtable Pulpit,* John McClure describes a process of having a group of people from the congregation meet with the pastor over several weeks to look at the scripture passages that will be used in the sermon and discuss what they read, what resonates with them, what troubles them, and where they see God at work in the passage, in the world, and in their lives.[11] The sermon then incorporates what was shared at the "roundtable." Not only does the preacher gain insights from the congregation through this process, but it also affirms input of the congregation as co-creators of the sermon. This practice also increases the congregation's biblical literacy. McClure advises that the pastor should start a new group every few months so that different voices and perspectives are heard.

For early-career preachers just starting out, we recommend following the three-year cycle of the *Revised Common Lectionary* at least once. This establishes a good habit of discipline and ensures a fairly broad coverage of biblical content. We also recommend that preachers have their congregations read from more than just the New Testament during the worship service. The temptation may be to include only one or two lessons for the sake of time. But for many parishioners, Sunday morning is the only time they will hear or read the Bible during the week. Christians need to encounter *more* of the Bible, not less.

This means that preachers themselves need to engage in a regular discipline of reading through the whole Bible. A simple internet search will turn up many different programs for reading through the entire canon in a year. As we encounter these texts year in and year out, we will be a different person each time we spiral back around to them, and our congregation will be different from when we previously read these lessons. We will be bringing different experiences, losses, new members, new children, new contemporary issues to the text each time we come around to them. So there is always the opportunity for digging deeper, digging from a different angle, digging with a different tool, and unearthing new insights from the Word of God. This will help both the preacher and the listeners to grow and flourish in their faith journey.

KEY POINTS IN THIS CHAPTER

1. The season of the liturgical year can play a significant role in determining what biblical text will be used for a sermon. In the traditional liturgical calendar, Advent begins the church year in December, followed by Christmas and then Epiphany, Lent, Easter, and the very long season of Pentecost, which concludes at the end of November.

2. Lectionaries are collections of lessons (sometimes called pericopes) arranged in accordance with the seasons of the liturgical year. Many lectionaries follow a cycle of readings that rotate every few years.
3. The most popular lectionary is the *Revised Common Lectionary* (RCL), a three-year cycle that includes four lessons for each Sunday (a reading from the Hebrew Scriptures, a Psalm, an Epistle, and a reading from a Gospel). Other alternative lectionaries include the *Narrative Lectionary*, the *African American Online Lectionary*, the *Season of Creation*, women's lectionaries, and fourth-year lectionaries that supplement the RCL.
4. Another way that preachers choose texts is through topical preaching, where Scripture passages are chosen to support a theme, a series, or a certain occasion. Still another way to choose Scripture is through personal prayer and discernment.
5. All methods of choosing Scripture for preaching have benefits and drawbacks. Preachers should be sensitive to the needs of their congregation, avoid the trap of preaching only the texts with which they are comfortable, and be sure to preach on texts that mention women in the Bible, since most lectionaries are lacking in this area.
6. All preachers should engage in a regular discipline of prayerfully reading through the Bible and engaging in text studies with clergy colleagues as well as with parishioners.

DISCUSSION QUESTIONS

1. How closely is the liturgical year followed in your congregation? If they observe the seasons and holy days, how much does that influence your preaching? If not, what are the main factors that influence how you might choose biblical texts to preach?
2. Talk with an experienced preacher about how they choose Scripture readings for worship services and sermons. Do they use a lectionary, and if so, why and which one(s)? And if not, why not? Based on your conversation, list what you think are the pros and cons of using a lectionary.
3. Talk with a group of preaching colleagues about alternative lectionaries (lectionaries other than the *Revised Common Lectionary*). Which ones have they used? What were the benefits and drawbacks of using them? Would any of your colleagues be willing to partner with you in trying one of the alternative lectionaries for a season or a year and engage in joint text study and sermon preparation?

FOR FURTHER READING

Ronald J. Allen. *Preaching the Topical Sermon*. Louisville, KY: Westminster John Knox, 1992.

Feasting on the Word is a series of commentaries and resources published by Westminster John Knox Press and offers commentaries on the readings from the *Revised Common Lectionary*.

James F. Kay. *Seasons of Grace: Reflections from the Christian Year*. Grand Rapids, MI: Eerdmans, 1994.

John S. McClure. *The Roundtable Pulpit: Where Leadership and Preaching Meet*. Nashville, TN: Abingdon Press, 1995.

Steve Thorngate. "'What's the Text': Alternatives to the Common Lectionary." *Christian Century*. October 16, 2013. http://www.christiancentury.org/article/2013-10/what-s-text.

Melinda Quivik. *Serving the Word: Preaching in Worship*. In Elements of Preaching Series. O. Wesley Allen Jr., series editor. Minneapolis, MN: Fortress Press, 2009.

Books by Lynn Japinga on preaching about women of the Bible:

Preaching the Women of the Old Testament. Louisville, KY: Westminster John Knox, 2017.

From Widows to Warriors: Women's Stories from the Old Testament. Louisville, KY: Westminster John Knox, 2020.

From Daughters to Disciples: Women's Stories from the New Testament. Louisville, KY: Westminster John Knox, 2021.

NOTES

1. See https://www.wjkbooks.com/Products/CategoryCenter/FOTW/Feasting_on_the_Word.aspx.

2. Wilda C. Gafney, *A Women's Lectionary for the Whole Church* (New York: Church Publishing, 2021), xxi.

3. Ibid.

4. See https://www.workingpreacher.org/narrative-faq.

5. Also, topical sermons are often used in the case of weddings and funerals so that the preacher can tailor the message to the specific occasion of the marriage of two people or to the themes that arise around a person's life and faith. See Thomas G. Long, *Accompany Them with Singing: The Christian Funeral* (Louisville, KY: Westminster John Knox Press, 2009); Scott M. Gibson, *Preaching for Special Services* (Grand Rapids, MI: Baker Books, 2001); Barbara G. Schmitz, *The Life of Christ and the Death of a Loved One: Crafting the Funeral Sermon* (Lima, OH: CSS Publishing Company, 1995).

6. Ronald J. Allen, *Preaching the Topical Sermon* (Louisville, KY: Westminster John Knox Press, 1992), 5.

7. Ibid., 3.

8. Leah D. Schade, *Preaching in the Purple Zone: Ministry in the Red-Blue Divide* (Lanham, MD: Rowman & Littlefield, 2019).

9. James F. White, *Introduction to Worship*, third edition (Nashville, TN: Abingdon, 2001), 75.

10. Note that bias and ideology are different from perspective-explicit interpretations that we discuss in Chapter 4. The difference is that those writing from perspective-explicit interpretations consistently hold themselves accountable to at least two poles of the Wesleyan Quadrilateral, whereas those whose positions are merely informed by bias or ideology may eschew accountability to Tradition, Reason, others' Experience, or in-depth exegesis.

11. John S. McClure, *The Roundtable Pulpit: Where Leadership and Preaching Meet* (Nashville, TN: Abingdon Press, 1995).

7

Sermon Exercise

"A House with Many Rooms: The 'Living Stones' of a Seminary"

The sermon we will examine in this chapter was preached by Leah Schade at Lexington Theological Seminary (LTS). LTS is a primarily online seminary where students are only on campus for intensive terms twice a year. This sermon was preached at one of the daily worship services during the January 2017 intensives where the seminary celebrated Leah's installation as assistant professor of preaching and worship.

For this sermon, we will walk you through the exegetical steps Leah took in putting together her ideas. First, you will see how she chose her texts for this sermon and the worship service, drawing on what we discussed in the previous chapter about choosing biblical texts for preaching. Then we will give you some exercises for exegeting the texts on your own and comparing them with the exegesis Leah performed in preparation for the sermon. Finally, we will look at the sermon manuscript along with explanatory notes to show how Leah incorporated her exegesis and applied it to this occasion.

CHOOSING BIBLICAL TEXTS FOR THE SERMON "A HOUSE WITH MANY ROOMS: THE 'LIVING STONES' OF A SEMINARY"

For this sermon, Leah chose to follow the path of topical preaching. As we discussed in the previous chapter, for a topical sermon, the preacher chooses the biblical text(s) based on a particular subject, theme, or occasion. She decided upon 1 Peter 2:4-10 and John 14:1-7 (also assigned readings for the Fifth Sunday of Easter in Year A of the *Revised Common Lectionary*) because the imagery of "living stones" and "house of many rooms," respectively, occurred to her as she was considering the spirit of the moment (installing a new professor), the larger seminary community and its relationship to the church, and the community in Creation.

In the two sections that follow, you will practice using the Exegesis Guide Chart for each passage and compare that with the summaries from Leah's exegetical work. Then we will explain how Leah made her choices for what to emphasize from her exegesis in the sermon she preached.

EXERCISE

Exegesis for 1 Peter 2:4-10

Here is the passage for 1 Peter 2:4-10.

> Come to him, a living stone, though rejected by mortals yet chosen and precious in God's sight, and [5]like living stones, let yourselves be built into a spiritual house, to be a holy priesthood, to offer spiritual sacrifices acceptable to God through Jesus Christ. [6]For it stands in scripture:
> 'See, I am laying in Zion a stone,
> a cornerstone chosen and precious;
> and whoever believes in him will not be put to shame.'
> [7]To you then who believe, he is precious; but for those who do not believe,
> 'The stone that the builders rejected
> has become the very head of the corner,'
> [8]and
> 'A stone that makes them stumble,
> and a rock that makes them fall.'
> They stumble because they disobey the word, as they were destined to do.
> [9] But you are a chosen race, a royal priesthood, a holy nation, God's own people, in order that you may proclaim the mighty acts of him who called you out of darkness into his marvelous light.
> [10] Once you were not a people,
> but now you are God's people;
> once you had not received mercy,
> but now you have received mercy.

1. Use the Exegesis Guide Chart to collect what you learn from engaging commentaries on 1 Peter 2:4-10. (See Appendix C.)
2. Note that this passage is an epistle, so begin with Occasional Exigence and Response. What was going on for the congregations that received this letter? What was happening in history? What was happening in the early church at that time? Why did the author of this letter think it necessary to address the congregation in this way, using these particular images and references to the Hebrew Scripture?
3. Next consider the Literary Exigence and Response. Where does this passage fall in the sequence of the entire letter? What is the significance of where it is placed? What comes right before this passage? What follows immediately after?
4. Now determine the Theological category, Exigence, and Response. What are the theological questions or issues raised by this part of the letter? Refer to the list of categories in Appendix D.

Once you have filled out your Exegesis Guide Chart, discuss your findings with a partner or a small group. Then read on to see how Leah summarized the findings from her exegesis.

EXEGESIS FOR 1 PETER 2:4-10

Scholars doubt that Peter is the true author of these letters and believe they were written after his death. However, writing a letter in the name of a respected person to represent their views and concerns was a practice sometimes used to gain a hearing in ancient times. Because the letter refers to sufferings that Christians were enduring, the letter is believed to have been written sometime after 80 CE when persecution of Christians began to be widespread. The salutation in v. 1 says that the letter is addressed to exiles in Roman provinces in what is now the country of Turkey.

Occasional Exigence and Response

Why does the author of 1 Peter write these verses that encourage believers to come to God as a "living stone" and to be built into a "spiritual house"? What was happening in the early church at that time that would necessitate these words? We turn to the Occasional Exigence to think about how this part of the letter addresses something important to the Christians in these Roman provinces.

By the end of the first century, the church had rapidly expanded into Asia Minor and was wrestling with how to understand its identity and mission in the face of suffering at the hands of the Roman Empire. Believers were being rejected by their families and communities, and the authorities were persecuting them because of their faith in Jesus Christ. Churches facing this kind of stress and pressure are tempted to give up their faith, abandon the gospel, and succumb to the forces that are causing them to suffer.

In response to this situation, then, the author stresses that Jesus's own suffering, death, and resurrection will sustain them in their distress and will provide hope and new life. In these verses, the author uses vivid imagery to convey God's action of building up this community and sending them to proclaim this message of faith in the midst of persecution. This part of the letter emphasizes the importance of living their faith not just as individuals but as part of a community of fellow believers.

Literary Exigence and Response

Now that we have established the reason for the letter and for this section under consideration, we turn to the Literary Exigence and Response. This passage comes after 1 Peter Chapter 1 in which the author uses the metaphor of "new birth" (v. 3) to describe what life is like for someone who has recently become a Christian. There is a strangeness and unfamiliarity that can be disconcerting, and this new identity can elicit animosity from others who do not share their calling. Nevertheless, this new identity gives them access to a community that they did not have before—fellow believers who can share in their suffering as well as their joy, not to mention the salvation that comes through Christ. This means that they must live lives that reflect a call to holy living as a reflection of their faith in God who is holy. Following 2:4-10 are instructions on how to live as servants of God, how to follow the example of Christ's suffering, how to live in marital relationships, and how the leaders are to tend the church as a shepherd does the flock.

In 2:4-10, the metaphors of "living stone" and "spiritual house" are directly related to Jesus Christ as a "cornerstone" that had been rejected (just as they are experiencing rejection). They are a new people who must live in community with a distinct identity and mission, which is to proclaim God's mighty acts. Verses 9-10 are meant to encourage a beleaguered people by assuring them that they are "a chosen race, a royal priesthood, a holy nation, God's own people."

Theological Exigence and Response

With our Occasional and Literary Exigences and Responses in place, we can discern the theological questions that are being raised and addressed in this part of 1 Peter. There are two possible theological categories in this passage, and we will need to determine which one is more prominent. One is Christological. These verses imply that Christ is the living stone because he is risen from the dead; he is the cornerstone for those who build their lives on trust in him. Thus, they share his risen life, no matter what rejection they face in their present circumstances. Readers will also note that vv. 6-8 quote Isaiah 28:16, "therefore thus says the Lord God, See, I am laying in Zion a foundation stone, a tested stone, a previous cornerstone, a sure foundation: 'One who trusts will not panic.'" Other New Testament writers used this same imagery of the cornerstone to describe Jesus Christ (Matt. 21:42, Acts 4:11). So, a significant Theological Claim in this text is that despite being rejected, God has made Jesus Christ the cornerstone of a new people in faith.

However, the Christological claim actually undergirds the larger theological category of this passage—the ecclesiological one. As a theological category, ecclesiology is about the church's relationship with God and with one another. There is an internal and external quality to these relationships that are to reflect the character of God and the values of God. We can tell that this passage is primarily ecclesiological because it is addressed to the believers and calling them into relationship with one another as the church and with Jesus Christ as their cornerstone. This passage answers the question: who will we be and what will we do as a church given the persecution we are enduring? The answer given in this part of the letter is that they should not cower or run away, but rather enter all the more into the spiritual house as "living stones" and a "holy priesthood" (v. 5).

Contemporary Exigence and Response

Now that we understand the historical situation behind 1 Peter 2:4-10, as well as the literary and theological issues that shape its meaning, we can turn to the Contemporary Exigence and Response. This will allow us to apply our exegesis to a present-day situation, in this case, a professor's installation in 2017 at a seminary that is primarily online but has gathered for this occasion of teaching, worship, and fellowship. What kinds of contemporary issues or situations might have parallels with what Christians faced in the early church? How might the theological category of ecclesiology as illustrated in the metaphorical language of vv. 4-10 apply to this seminary community?

Leah began to formulate the idea for this sermon after seeing a bulletin board in a hallway at the seminary that displayed all the students' pictures and the states where they lived. She felt it would be important to convey the connectedness they experienced as a seminary community, even though they were usually separated by long distances. Even more expansively, she wanted to integrate her commitment to being inclusive of all God's Creation in her preaching and underscore that LTS's mission extends into God's realm in myriad ways.

What especially intrigued Leah about this passage was the imagery of the "living stone," in Greek, *zonta lithos*. What does it mean to be a living stone? How can stones, which are not living beings, be alive? Obviously, the passage is communicating that the Christian community is not meant to be passive, yet a building is often viewed as stationary and immobile. So what image could convey that Christians are to be active in their Christian life and yet solidly built into a "spiritual house"?

As Leah pondered these questions for the sermon, she also considered the Gospel reading that she chose for the worship service, John 14:1-7. In the next section, you will try your hand at exegeting this passage and then see how it compares with Leah's work.

EXERCISE

Using the Exegesis Guide Chart for John 14:1-7

Here is the passage for John 14:1-7:

> [Jesus spoke to his disciples, saying:] 'Do not let your hearts be troubled. Believe in God, believe also in me. [2]In my Father's house there are many dwelling-places. If it were not so, would I have told you that I go to prepare a place for you? [3]And if I go and prepare a place for you, I will come again and will take you to myself, so that where I am, there you may be also. [4]And you know the way to the place where I am going.' [5]Thomas said to him, 'Lord, we do not know where you are going. How can we know the way?' [6]Jesus said to him, 'I am the way, and the truth, and the life. No one comes to the Father except through me. [7]If you know me, you will know my Father also. From now on you do know him and have seen him.'

1. Use the Exegesis Guide Chart to collect what you learn from engaging commentaries on John 14:1-7 (see Appendix C).
2. Note that this passage is a narrative, so begin with determining the Literary Exigence and Response. Where does this passage fall in the sequence of John's Gospel? What is the significance of where it is placed in the larger narrative? What comes right before this passage? What follows immediately after?
3. Next, examine the Occasional Exigence and Response. What was going on for John's community at the time this was written? What was happening in history? What was happening in the early church? Why did John think it was necessary to include this speech from Jesus in his Gospel?

4. Now determine the Theological category, Exigence, and Response. What are the theological questions or issues raised by this passage? Refer to the list of categories in Appendix D.
5. Finally, think about the Contemporary Exigence and Response. What are present-day issues or situations that might parallel the Theological Exigence that the passage addresses? Can you think of analogies between the quandaries faced by the original hearers of this text and those we face today? How might you address those in your sermon?

Once you have filled out your Exegesis Guide Chart, discuss your findings with a partner or in a small group. Then see the next section for how Leah summarized her exegetical findings for this sermon.

EXEGESIS FOR JOHN 14:1-7

The Gospel of John was the last of the Gospels written and differs in many ways from the synoptic Gospels (Matthew, Mark, and Luke), which all drew from much of the same source material. In contrast, John has stories and themes not found in the first three, including the section that includes this pericope that is part of Jesus's extended farewell discourse on the eve of his betrayal. Biblical scholars believe that this Gospel was written around 90–110 CE for Jewish Christians who were at odds with the Jewish religious hierarchy for their beliefs, as well as with the Roman authorities.

John's Gospel has a very strong Christological emphasis highlighting Jesus Christ as the "Word" of God incarnate. John's purpose is to establish the identity of Jesus Christ as one with God, and thus irrefutably divine. The passage we are studying, 14:1-7, draws out implications of this relationship between Jesus Christ and God as it pertains to those who follow Jesus—his disciples. These implications, in turn, mean something for the faith of the Johannine church and for believers today as well.

Literary Exigence and Response

This passage is part of the second half of the Gospel which focuses on Jesus's last meal with his disciples, his arrest and crucifixion, his resurrection, and his post-resurrection appearances to his followers. Our passage, 14:1-7, is part of a section that readers of that time would have recognized as a "farewell discourse" in the tradition of Moses and other faith leaders within the tradition. The section begins with Jesus washing the disciples' feet in the upper room and contains an extended discourse where Jesus talks with his disciples about what to expect, what to remember, and what will sustain them as he is taken from them for crucifixion. It is an intimate discussion with his closest companions to prepare them for the grief and trauma they are about to endure.

These verses follow a rather disturbing exchange where Peter offers to lay down his life for Jesus. But Jesus responds by predicting Peter's betrayal. Yet he immediately follows with these words: "Do not let your hearts be troubled. Believe in God. Believe also in me" (v. 1). In other words, Jesus is not mincing any words about the reality they will face, but he also urges them to be reassured by their belief in God and in himself.

Occasional Exigence and Response

What's going on historically that John sees fit to include these words from Jesus in this farewell discourse? The Johannine church is struggling against enemies that are persecuting them. Similarly, in the text, the disciples are struggling with anticipatory grief because they are about to be separated from their rabbi because of enemies that will torture and kill him. As Gail O'Day and Susan Hylen put it:

> It is as if time stands still for a moment, so that Jesus can prepare those he loves for the life they will lead during and after the events of his hour. Jesus explains the significance of his death and departure to his disciples before the events happen, so that when they occur, the disciples will be able to interpret the events through the eyes of faith and not despair.[1]

John has Jesus speak these words, then, not just to address the disciples' concerns, but to speak words of encouragement and instruction to those who will read these words in the future. They are to rely on their faith in God and in Jesus, trusting that even though chaos and evil seem to reign, their presence within God's abode is assured. Further, the imagery of a "dwelling place" is a metaphor for their relationship with Jesus and thus with God. In fact, paradoxically, Jesus's departure is what enables a new kind of relationship to be possible, one in which this room in which they have experienced this ritual of foot washing is a kind of prototype for the loving service they are to extend to one another.

Theological Exigence and Response

Now that we have established the Literary and Occasional Exigence and Response, we can determine the theological questions that impel this speech. It may be natural to assume the theological category of this text is eschatological because it appears to refer to a time in the future when the disciples will dwell with God and Jesus. However, O'Day and Hylen urge us not to jump to this interpretation. "Reading verses 1–4 primarily as a reference to believers' future place in heaven limits what Jesus is saying here," they explain. "Jesus' hour [of his impending death] creates new possibilities for relationship with God in the present life of the believer."[2]

We might say, then, that this passage has an ecclesiological theme as well, in that believers are instructed about how to respond to persecution and how to understand what is happening in a larger theological sense. We see this in the exchange between Thomas and Jesus, where Thomas asks a question and Jesus explains in a way that expands his limited thinking. Similar to Jesus's interchanges with Nicodemus (Ch. 3) and the Syrophoenician woman (Ch. 4), Thomas's questions implicitly speak for all believers and open a space for Jesus to move them from misunderstanding to a new, life-giving comprehension. The church, then, is to learn from these exchanges and follow Jesus, whose life and teachings are "the way, and the truth, and the life" (v. 6). It follows, then, that there is also a Christological theme in this passage since this statement echoes the identity of Jesus as the Word, which John has taken pains to establish from the very beginning of his Gospel. Saying that he is "the way, and the truth, and the life" also points to his identity as savior.

Contemporary Exigence and Response

We are now ready to make some interpretive moves to apply what we learned in our exegesis for a contemporary situation. If our two primary theological categories are eschatological and ecclesiological, what are contemporary issues or situations that might draw wisdom or solace from John 14:1-7?

As Leah pondered this question, she recalled the recent history of LTS, that they had entered financial exigency six years prior, sold their original campus building, and transitioned into being an online/in-person hybrid seminary. Thus, there had been a great deal of anxiety within the LTS community about whether or not the institution would survive. However, this occasion of installing a new professor was evidence that the seminary was not only surviving but thriving, thus giving evidence of God's continued presence and guidance of their mission.

Leah also considered the political situation that loomed over this celebratory service of installation—the election of Donald Trump to the presidency just two months earlier and his impending inauguration. The election season had been filled with hateful rhetoric, symbols, and actions against people of color, foreigners, immigrants, refugees, those with disabilities, the LGBTQIA+ community, and women by Trump supporters and the candidate himself. After the election, a significant portion of the country was experiencing alarm and legitimate fear about their physical and emotional safety, or for their family members, friends, fellow students, and co-workers. Many were desperately worried about their safety and health as the new administration came into power.

Recognizing the parallels between persecution of Christians in the first century and the fear of persecution of those who were not straight, white Christians in the United States, Leah wanted to convey the importance of the church—and this seminary—providing sanctuary and support for those in danger. Since we know that the word "house" is a metaphor that refers to the domain of God rather than a literal domestic abode, how might this word frame the theological understanding of a seminary community preparing students for ministry in a hostile world? As you read the sermon, you'll see how Leah attempted to answer that question.

A WORD OF EXPLANATION—AND CAUTION—ABOUT HARMONIZING BIBLICAL TEXTS

For the sermon "A House with Many Rooms: The 'Living Stones' of a Seminary," two metaphors from the biblical passages of 1 Peter 2:4-10 and John 14:1-7 are chosen as the foundational images—"living stones" and "house with many rooms," respectively. It is important to recognize that the preacher is making an interpretive move by conjoining these images from two separate passages that are not inherently related.

While there is nothing intrinsically wrong with bringing two texts into conversation with each other, preachers do need to be cautious about the danger of eisegesis, which is reading one's own meaning into the text instead of drawing meaning from the text from study and research (see Chapter 2). By using two different metaphors in a sermon, preachers risk confusing their listeners or forcing a point that doesn't exist in either text. However, if the images are complementary and mutually reinforcing of an Occasional or Theological Response in both texts, the sermon can be enhanced by using both images.

Another thing to keep in mind is that one of the risks with topical preaching is imposing an interpretation on the text that is driven by an ideological agenda or bias, as we discussed in the previous chapter. This can be the case if two texts are chosen that seem to support the preacher's agenda rather than what is true to the individual texts themselves. This can happen with texts in lectionaries as well. As we noted in the previous chapter, those who create lectionaries are already exercising certain hermeneutical liberties on the texts by choosing the ones they want to be read side by side in a worship service. Lectionaries implicitly impose an interpretation on the texts by putting them together the way that they do.

So, what are steps a preacher can take when attempting to "harmonize" two biblical passages or two metaphors from two different biblical authors so that they neither violate the integrity of the passage nor conjoin them in a way that is forced and unnatural? Here is a list of guidelines for addressing two different biblical texts in a sermon.

GUIDELINES FOR ADDRESSING TWO DIFFERENT BIBLICAL TEXTS IN A SERMON

1. If you are an early-career preacher, it is usually best to focus on just one biblical text for your sermons as you are learning how to preach. Exegeting one passage is already plenty of work for a preacher to do. Trying to do two not only requires twice the amount of research, it also requires more work when writing the sermon itself. Give yourself enough time to gain facility with exegeting and writing a sermon on just one text before you attempt to address two passages in a sermon.
2. If you are an experienced preacher, don't feel obligated to address more than one text in a sermon, even if two or more are listed in a set of lectionary readings for a worship service. At the same time, if you see a natural connection between two texts (for instance, if a New Testament author quotes something from the Hebrew Scriptures), there may be an opportunity to develop these texts in tandem with each other during your sermon preparation and in the sermon itself.
3. If you do decide to address two different texts in a sermon, do equal exegesis on both of them. Don't short-change either of them; give them both the same exegetical attention. You may decide that one text will be the primary basis of the sermon and the other will serve in a supporting role, but they will both need to be researched if you address them in the sermon.
4. Avoid forcing an incongruous match. There's no need to perform preaching acrobatics and contort a sermon in order to connect two disparate texts, concepts, ideas, or metaphors. Even if you think you see a tenuous thread of connection, if you have to work too hard to build it out or have it make sense, your listeners may end up feeling confused or even manipulated for the sake of an agenda.

5. Be clear with your listeners about the distinctions of both texts. Don't assume that your listeners will recognize that these passages and metaphors are from different parts of the Bible. In your sermon, note that they are written by two different authors at two different times for two different communities. Be transparent about the fact that you see a natural connection between them that you think is worth exploring and developing.
6. Use the knowledge that you gain from your exegesis to draw parallels between the two texts. Just as you identify analogies between the situation an original author and faith community faced and a contemporary situation faced by believers today, you can do the same between the circumstances of two different biblical authors and their faith communities. This can provide the listener with a strong lattice to understand the theme you are developing while also reinforcing the message you are trying to convey in the sermon.

INTRODUCTION TO THE SERMON "A HOUSE WITH MANY ROOMS: THE 'LIVING STONES' OF A SEMINARY"

As worshipers entered the room before the service began, each was handed a small piece of coral. Leah chose coral as a tangible illustration of "living stones" for this sermon, which gave listeners something to hold onto and take with them as a reminder of key points in the sermon. In this way, you can see how she connected the biblical image with an image from nature to illustrate the implications of being "living stones" built into a "house of many rooms."

As you read the sermon below, here are things to look for that demonstrate that Leah followed the guidelines above when it comes to addressing two different texts in a sermon.

- She has done her homework. As seen in the sections above, Leah gave equal exegetical attention to both 1 Peter 2:4-10 and John 14:1-7. The insights from her exegesis of both texts are brought into conversation with each other and integrated throughout the sermon. (See paragraphs 2, 3, 5, 7, 16, 20, 24–27.)
- She included brief explanations about the historical background of each text so that listeners would know that these images are from two different authors addressing two different communities. At the same time, she pointed out the similarities in their circumstances (both were addressed to persecuted communities of early Christians) so that listeners would see the parallels. (See paragraphs 3 and 7.)
- As a result of her exegesis, she saw a natural connection between the metaphors of "living stones" and "house of many rooms" and developed that throughout the sermon. Both are images that help the faith community understand itself as the church as well as the nature of Jesus Christ and his relationship with God. She applied this to her audience of a seminary community gathered for worship and how their work supports the mission of the larger church. (See paragraphs 3–5, 7, 15, 16, 20, 24, 26–27.)
- This sermon has a strong ecclesiological theme that both passages support since they each address this theological category as well. (See paragraphs 5, 9, 11, 14–16, 19, 23, 25–27.) This ecclesiological theme is applied to the context of Lexington Theological Seminary to frame the community's understanding of itself as a "spiritual house" and as part of the larger "ecosystem of faith." (See paragraphs 8, 20, 24.)
- The parallels from the two persecuted communities of 1 Peter and John are extended to the contemporary situation of this congregation watching the gathering clouds of an incoming presidential administration poised to persecute many different groups of people deemed "other" and thus enemies of white, heterosexual, Christian Americans. (See paragraphs 21–22.)
- The sermon is developed in the form of a lattice that weaves together several different but interrelated strands: the passages of 1 Peter 2:4-10 and John 14:1-7, the imagery of the coral reef, the contemporary ecclesial issues of the church, and the seminary community. Note that attempting this kind of complexity is not something we recommend for early-career preachers. Nevertheless, this gives you an example of how the exegesis of two biblical texts can be integrated into a sermon and applied to a contemporary situation, resulting in a strong proclamation about the nature and actions of God for the sake of the church and the world.

SERMON EXAMPLE: "A HOUSE WITH MANY ROOMS— THE 'LIVING STONES' OF A SEMINARY"

Texts: 1 Peter 2:4-10 and John 14:1-7

1. In the months since I've begun here at Lexington Theological Seminary, and especially this last week when I've had the pleasure of meeting students in person, I have been struck by the reach of this seminary across this country. When I first interviewed here nearly a year ago, I remember seeing the bulletin board right out here in the hall with the pictures of the students and where they are located on the map. Taken together, we might say that LTS is like a vast coral reef network. It might not be immediately visible if you're just looking out over the surface of the water, but LTS is a vital part of the ecosystem of the Christian church.
2. You may have noticed the piece of coral handed out to each of you before the service. This coral used to be part of a reef on the ocean floor. What you hold in your hand are pieces that were collected from beaches where bits of coral washed up on the sand. You can't tell it now, because it only looks like a piece of rock or stone, but this used to be a living organism. We might say that coral is like a "living stone."
3. In the letter of 1 Peter, we read: "Come to [Jesus], a living stone, though rejected by mortals yet chosen and precious in God's sight, and like living stones, let yourselves be built into a spiritual house" (1 Peter 2:4). The author of 1 Peter was writing to Christians in Asia Minor who were being persecuted by the Roman Empire and were in need of encouragement. He uses this intriguing imagery of a "living stone" to metaphorically describe what it's like to be part of the church that has Christ as its cornerstone.
   What does it mean to be a living stone? How can a stone be alive?
4. Take a look at this piece of coral in your hand. Coral offers us a surprising example of what a "living stone" looks like in nature. "Corals are tiny invertebrates that [live] in symbiosis with tiny, microscopic algae called zooxanthellae, which live inside the coral's tissue. (The zooxanthellae provide food to the coral by converting sunlight into energy.) Corals build up hard exoskeletons made of layers of secreted calcium carbonate, which form the reef."[3] The structure is sturdy yet porous, allowing water to flow through it, absorbing nutrients and housing microscopic life-forms.
5. If you look closely at your piece of coral, you can see the pattern of the calcium carbonate of the coral's tissue that housed all those zooxanthellae. We might say that the church of Jesus Christ is like a coral reef—a spiritual house of living stones. We each are nurtured by this community, this ecosystem of faith, and we each help to build God's kingdom that welcomes all people.
6. Coral reefs provide habitat, food, and spawning grounds for countless species of fish and ocean plants. About one-third of everything that lives in the ocean lives in a coral reef. "In a healthy reef, you can see everything from tiny seahorses to big sharks swimming amid a network of coral as intricate as a medieval cathedral."[4]
7. It reminds me of our reading from John's Gospel: "In my Father's house there are many dwelling places" (John 14:2). Like the Christians in Asia Minor, John's church also faced persecution. They needed to hear reassurance that God's grace was open to them not just in the future, but right now through their relationship with Jesus Christ.
8. We might say that God's Realm[5] is like a coral reef because there are many dwelling places for all that live in the reef. So the structure of teaching we provide here at LTS is like being connected to the network of coral reefs—with students and pastors tucked into those niches all across the country, the world even—all of us supporting the life of countless churches, ministries, and faith-based organizations and agencies.
9. And the significance of the coral reef is not just for the church. God's coral reef is a vital support for the secular world as well. There are innumerable fish that swim in the waters of our coral reef, benefiting from the lives and work of our parishioners living out their vocation in the secular world. Each person has different gifts and talents, and we all contribute to God's plan to make this a thriving, colorful ecosystem of human community.
10. But like the coral reefs in our planet's oceans, church ecosystems are sensitive to systemic and environmental conditions. *Time* magazine featured an article a few years ago by Bryan Walsh called "Ocean View" about a global effort to study and photo-document coral reefs using state-of-the-art technology.[6] What they've found is that coral reefs are suffering from destruction and a process called "bleaching," where the zooxanthellae die, and the coral loses its color. The article listed several reasons why coral reefs are dying—overfishing, coastal

pollution and development, global warming, and ocean acidification are all having detrimental effects on our oceans' coral reefs. Seventy-five percent of the world's reefs are threatened. In some locations coral cover has dropped from 80 to 13 percent over the course of the last twenty-five years.

11. A parallel can be seen in the state of our churches as well. The ecosystems of faith that used to thrive in our societies are now finding the conditions around us to be increasingly hostile to the life of the church. And as with the coral reefs, there is a complex interplay of reasons for the diminishment of our churches. Our society has become more secularized, which means that it has less respect for the sacred.
12. We might say that the "pollution" of commerce is littering our Sabbath time. Sunday is a prime shopping day and there are probably more people in stores than there are in churches on Sunday mornings these days. Not to mention the 24-hour, 7-day a week availability of social media.
13. There is also the growth of "the nones"—folks who indicate adherence to "no religion" in surveys. We're in a time where two and three generations have never set foot inside a house of worship, except for maybe a funeral or wedding. Churches are perceived as irrelevant by a growing number of people.
14. What many do not realize, however, is just how valuable the church is to society, like the way coral reefs are often not recognized for just how much they contribute to our food supply, our economies, and even our medical treatments. There are foods and medicines that we receive from coral reefs that we can't get any other way. Similarly, the church throughout history right up to the present day has been responsible for much good that most people take for granted and would likely not have been able to access any other way.
15. Consider, for example, charity toward widows and orphans—that is a repeated command throughout the Bible. Or the establishment of hospitals, public health, and education—those were church-based initiatives. Then there's the abolition of slavery and the Civil Rights Movement of the 1950s and 1960s, both of which were powered by churches. Not to mention the role of the church in raising of children with strong moral and ethical values. All of these have their origins in churches and other houses of worship and have had a profoundly positive impact on human society. For centuries, Christians have been building themselves as "living stones" into God's house of many rooms.
16. This is not to say that the church has not had its problems. We must, of course, recognize the ways in which the church has abused its power and caused incredible harm over the centuries and even today. But when Christians follow the call to become God's people and build their work on the cornerstone of Christ, who is "the way, the truth, and the life," churches contribute much to their communities and society by assisting the poor and prophetically addressing the causes of poverty. Congregations and denominations respond to natural disasters, provide relief to refugees, advocate for society's most vulnerable citizens, provide counseling and spiritual direction, distribute food and clothing, and provide leadership and resources for addressing justice issues. Not to mention, some of the greatest leaders who have lifted up and inspired humanity's highest ideals have arisen from the church.
17. The *Time* article noted that public attention to the plight of coral reefs has suffered because the reefs are not easy to see. Very few people ever swim amid coral reefs. And there hasn't been much photo-documentation of these fragile ecosystems. The good work of churches, too, sometimes goes unnoticed and underappreciated. Less and less people are coming into our churches, swimming amid our coral reefs, so to speak.
18. But now there are 360-degree cameras they are using to photograph the ocean floor (similarly to the way Google Earth has shown us the surface of our planet in astounding ways). People who study coral reefs know something important: we will not save what we do not love. And oceanographers want us to fall in love with our coral reefs, these houses with many rooms, so that as a human species we will take steps to preserve what is left.
19. As church leaders, we want people to fall in love with our churches, these houses with many rooms, so that they will see the church as a vital institution for a community. People will not save what they do not love. That's why it's so important to tell people what goes on in our churches and faith communities, what great work we do in serving those in need and upholding the values that keep a society healthy.
20. That's why, here at LTS, we put so much effort into creating our courses and training you, our students, to be the vital leaders the church needs. LTS is a "spiritual house" and you are a "royal priesthood" called to serve your churches and communities in the name of Jesus Christ. We need to shout from the rooftops (or, in this case, the "reef-tops") what we do as a seminary, and what your church does, and why we're here. It's about documenting and making a case for the validity and value of our faith within the larger ecosystem in which we are located. Not only that, but we are modelling for people what it means to be "living stones" built into Christ as a spiritual house.

21. It is especially important because the waters in which we swim are becoming increasingly toxic. It's not just from the rhetoric of hatred but because of the actions, decrees, and legislation of some who would actually be quite happy with a bleached-white coral reef—emphasis on the word "white." There are many who have been very clear that they would much prefer a coral reef where the variety of colors and shapes and sizes and religions and sexual orientations would simply be reduced to a few select pedigree fish floating across a homogenous pale landscape devoid of any diversity.
22. Of course, we know such a world is what would result from what they are intending to create, the walls they want to erect, the climate-change cancer they want to see metastasize, the genitalia they want to grab and use and control. We know that world is one that leads to death. A bleached coral reef is a dead coral reef. We know that. But for some, the fear, hatred, and anger have distorted hearts and minds to such a degree that the water has become too hot, too toxic for life to survive.
23. Some of you here know what it's like to wonder and worry if what you love, who you love, is going to survive. Some of you are wondering and worrying if your church is going to survive. From what I've been told, there was a time when people weren't even sure if this seminary was going to survive.
24. But like the scientists and environmental activists who are not giving up, even when all signs seem to point to despair, this seminary did not give up. Because God does not give up! You have saved what you love because you knew this was a place worth saving. The coral reef of LTS looks much different than it did six years ago, but the fish are still schooling in, aren't they? LTS is a house with many rooms where our students, faculty, and staff can find a spiritual dwelling place and have their diverse gifts and talents valued. A place where they can encounter the welcoming presence of God. A place where they can be empowered to protect and preserve the vulnerable ones within the reef, even the reef itself.
25. The Realm of God is like a strong coral reef that hosts a dazzling array of life-forms. And just like the fish that swim around the coral reef, we are nurtured and protected by God through the church that gives us a spiritual home.
26. What a thriving, bustling coral reef we are! And that's the way churches should be—like a house with many rooms welcoming all people in a symbiotic relationship of mutual care and service. We must be activists for the coral reefs of faith, even as we work to preserve and protect the actual coral reefs in God's Creation. Because they are "precious in God's sight."
27. I want you to remember that every time you look at your piece of coral. You are an important part of God's ecosystem of faith. God provides you with protection and guidance and unconditional love. You help to build the coral reef by adding yourself as a living stone. Come to God, a living stone. It doesn't matter what your income level is, where you work, what gender you love, what age you are, what pigment your coral is, what accomplishments you've achieved, or what mistakes you've made. You are chosen and precious in God's sight. And like living stones, let yourselves be built into the spiritual house of many rooms—God's coral reef of faith. Amen!

KEY POINTS IN THIS CHAPTER

1. Preachers can choose to address more than one biblical text in a sermon; however, they should take care to honor the integrity of both texts by giving equal attention to exegesis for each of them. Harmonizing should not do harm to either text.
2. When using two different metaphors in a sermon, the preacher should be sure that they have a natural and obvious connection so that listeners are not confused and the sermon doesn't feel disjointed or manipulative toward a certain agenda.
3. Early-career preachers should stick with addressing just one biblical text in a sermon until they become adept with exegesis and sermon preparation.
4. The advantages to including two texts in a sermon are that the message can be reinforced, the imagery can be complementary, and the theme can be jointly applied to the context of the preacher's listeners.

DISCUSSION QUESTIONS

1. If you were to preach a sermon based only on 1 Peter 2:4-10, what aspects of your exegesis would you incorporate into your sermon? Would you relate it to the congregation you serve? Or to the community in which your church is located? Would you focus on the imagery of "living stones," "cornerstone," or some other metaphor in the passage?
2. Another way to integrate two texts into a sermon on 1 Peter 2:4-10 is to exegete Isaiah 28, which contains the reference to the cornerstone. Consider researching this passage and using the guidelines for addressing two texts in a sermon. What parallels do you see between Isaiah's listeners and 1 Peter's? What are differences between them? What themes do they share that you could apply to your own context in a sermon?
3. John 14:1-7 is part of Jesus's "farewell discourse" to his disciples. Yet, Leah chose to use this passage as the basis of a kind of "inaugural discourse" to her seminary community. Discuss with a partner or group the risks and opportunities for using biblical texts in ways the author had not originally intended. How can preachers gauge if they are doing a disservice to the intention of the text? At the same time, how can they (and the congregation) trust that the sermon is creatively interpreting or applying a biblical text for the purpose of proclaiming the Gospel in a fresh and new way? How might the Wesleyan Quadrilateral be used to navigate the tensions between Scripture, Tradition, Reason, and Experience when thinking about these questions?
4. In this sermon, Leah chose to focus on the ecclesiological category of the texts rather than the eschatological. If you were to write a sermon that focused on the eschatological, how might you approach it? What aspects of Christ's imagery of a "house with many rooms" could speak to the future hope of a congregation living in the midst of trials and difficulties?

NOTES

1. Gail R. O'Day and Susan E. Hylen, "John," in *Westminster Bible Companion* (Louisville, KY: Westminster John Knox, 2006), 143.
2. Ibid., 145.
3. Bryan Walsh, "Ocean View," *Time*, April 14, 2014, 43.
4. Ibid.
5. Authors' note: Throughout this book, we often use the term "Realm of God" in place of the traditional term "Kingdom of God" in order to avoid a strictly patriarchal metaphor and to be more inclusive and expansive in our imagery for God.
6. Walsh, 43.

II

IDENTIFYING THEOLOGICAL CLAIMS FOR SERMONS

8

Theology and Theological Claims

In the previous chapters, we learned the techniques for exegeting a biblical text. We looked at methods for understanding what a biblical passage meant in its original setting as well as methods that recognize various social locations, identities, and ideologies that can help us understand the text better and reveal unconscious (and problematic) presuppositions that may lead to harmful interpretations. We also began to think about how to read Scripture for its theological content as part of our overall work of discerning the message of a text and how we might prepare a sermon based on that message.

In this section, we will concentrate specifically on theology and sermons, including how to identify and articulate an appropriate and coherent Theological Claim, how to analyze a biblical text and draw a Theological Claim from it, and how to analyze sermons for their theological content. All of this will prepare us for making Theological Claims from a biblical text that we can use to guide the theological content of our preaching.

NOTE FOR INSTRUCTORS

Theology *within* Sermons versus Theology *of* Preaching

This chapter deals with theology *within the content of sermons*, not the theology *of preaching*. Our decision not to address the theology of proclamation is because there are many different theological traditions that inform both how preachers define the Word of God and understand the authority of the preacher, and these questions are beyond the scope of our project. This is not to say that the theological foundations and purposes of Christian preaching are not important; in fact, we believe it is vital for students to understand their theological stance concerning preaching. However, we leave that to you, the instructor, to help your students engage the many different theological elements that inform the task of defining Christian proclamation and develop a sound, coherent theological stance thereto.

Here is a list of questions that can be used for sparking conversation with students about their theology of preaching.

- What is the role of God in preaching? Where is God in the inspiration, crafting, act of preaching, and reception of the sermon by the listeners?
- In what way is the Holy Spirit active in the preacher's preparation and delivery of the sermon and/or in the congregation's reception of the sermon? How do we gauge the presence and activity of the Holy Spirit?
- What authority do preachers have? What is the basis of their authority? Who grants the authority? What are signs of their authority (how is the authority manifest)? What are the limits to the preacher's authority? In what ways can authority be abused in preaching?
- What is the relationship between preaching and the whole of worship (e.g., prayers, music, Baptism, Holy Communion, etc.)?

At the end of the chapter, we list some resources that can be used for guiding students in the exploration and articulation of their theology of preaching.

WHAT IS "THEOLOGY"?

Let's start with some basic information. The word **theology** is made up of two Greek words, *theos* (God) + *logos* (study of or words about), so theology is simply the study of God or "God talk." The word "theology" is used in two ways. It stands for a whole field of thought, including thinking about the church, how and why we were created, and what happens at the end of history. And the word refers to a specific doctrine that considers the nature and actions of God. The ideas we are starting with in this chapter apply to both uses of the word. When we get to the process of making statements about God, we will be using the word in the narrower, doctrinal sense.

First, all Christians are already theologians to some degree whether we know it or not. That is, every time we think or say something about God, what God wants us to do, the nature of the church, or how we are supposed to live, we are doing theology by thinking and speaking about our Christian life of faith with God. We often forget, though, that this "God talk" is some of the most powerful language we have. For many of us, when we put the word "God" into a sentence, we have just added the most powerful name we have to whatever we are speaking about.

So, it is fair to say that many of us find ourselves using this powerful language uncritically and unconsciously in ways that might unintentionally belittle God or use God's name for purposes of injustice. For example, consider a claim like "God was on our side in that game tonight." Uncritically, we have not only invoked the name of God into a sports game, but we have said that God was *not* on the side of the losers. In this case we need to ask if we really believe this: does God choose winners and losers in a game? If we do not believe this, then, as people of faith, we need to change how we use the most powerful name we have.

Second, using this powerful God talk uncritically can do more damage than simply reducing God to a referee. Many women, Black, Indigenous, Asian, Latiné, people of color, migrants, members of the LGBTQIA+ community, and maybe even you reading this book have been terribly hurt by ministers, family, and friends making uncritical statements about who God is and what God wants from human beings. Hopefully, you will see that we are teaching you ways to think theologically that help you critically consider what you are saying in order to do the justice God calls us to for all members of God's Beloved Community, including justice for Creation itself. As preachers, then, thinking clearly and critically about what we say about God is not only good homiletics, but it contributes to the pastoral care of your congregation and serves to build the values of the Realm of God.

Finally, theology both as a whole field and as a doctrine has gotten a bad reputation as being boring and difficult and done only by old, heterosexual, White men. That reputation is deserved in some ways (though many of us who are not old, heterosexual, White, and male have been inspired by theologians who are). Theology has sometimes been written in ways that exclude lay people—it seems to be written to "insiders" with specialized vocabulary and knowledge. And theology does come with its own specific elements of language that are helpful to learn. Remember, though, that you have already been "baptized" into the role of being a theologian simply by virtue of making faith claims about God. Now it is time to give you your pastoral and professional skill set for theology. Also, we are going to draw from a wide array of theologians and homileticians in our examples and exercises so you can see and hear the amazingly creative, diverse, and inviting enterprise that thinking theologically can be.

WHAT ARE "THEOLOGICAL CLAIMS"?

Before we explain what a Theological Claim is, let's define what we mean by the word "claim." A **claim** is an assertion that one posits as true, accurate, and genuine. A claim says something about the ontological nature of the subject, its being, its essence. A claim is more than a mere observation or description, which are pieces of evidence or statements about something that is or has happened. For example, "Then the church throughout Judea, Galilee and Samaria enjoyed a time of peace and was strengthened" (Acts 9:31) is merely descriptive of what happened during this period of the early church. It's not making a claim about the church. However, a claim *can be* descriptive. For example, "God is compassionate and merciful" is an assertion that uses descriptive language.

A claim is also different from an opinion, which is a personal belief or point of view that can't be proven as fact. And a claim is different from a fact, which is incontrovertible and provable or disprovable. So, when we are seeking to identify claims in Scripture or in sermons, we are looking for statements that contend, assert, declare, or proclaim something.

Speaking now about theology in its narrow sense—as the doctrine of God—we can say that ***Theological Claims in Scripture and sermons are assertions about the nature of God and God's work in the world.*** Further, assertions about the nature and work of Jesus Christ and the nature and work of the Holy Spirit are also Theological Claims.[1] Theological Claims in sermons will name God (or Jesus Christ or the Holy Spirit) as the subject of the sentence and then name an attribute or action of God in the predicate of the sentence. For example, "In the beginning, God created the heavens and the earth" (Gen 1:1). The subject is God, and God's action is creating heaven and earth. We will be looking at numerous Theological Claims in the exercises of this chapter and throughout the book. In Appendix F you can find a brief review of the grammar of sentence structure, which will help you find Theological Claims in Scripture and to identify them in sermons.

USING THE WESLEYAN QUADRILATERAL TO MAKE THEOLOGICAL CLAIMS

Theological Claims do not come out of thin air; they are not just made up. This is the case because we can't just say anything we want about God and deem it true simply because we thought it or felt it. Claims of God as an oppressor or as demonic stand in stark opposition to the God revealed to us in Scripture and in God's revelation in the life and ministry of Jesus Christ. Thus, there are limits on what we can and *should* say about God. That being said, *informed* **theological imagination** should be involved in crafting good Theological Claims, and we will see this informed imagination at work when we consider two powerful metaphors for God below.

In Chapter 1, we learned about the Wesleyan Quadrilateral (WQ) as a framework for interpreting Scripture. In this chapter, we will use the WQ to craft and evaluate Theological Claims in our preaching. The WQ is one tool to help us make strong and appropriate Theological Claims in sermons, and while there are other ways to analyze such claims, we have found that this framework allows for consistency across the disciplines of biblical studies, theology, and homiletics.

In order to make strong and appropriate Theological Claims, we suggest that what we say theologically in sermons about who God is and what God does should be informed by using the Wesleyan Quadrilateral. To be clear, what we are offering in this book is our adaptation of the WQ as a tool for bringing the biblical text into a larger conversation with other elements that inform the Christian faith. First named by Charles Wesley's brother John, this device (never imagined by him as an actual geometric form) served as a way to validate Christian claims according to elements of the existing tradition, the power of logic and reason, and the experiences of the faith community. In our adaptation, the WQ serves as a conversation partner for preachers in crafting strong, appropriate Theological Claims.

The conversation partners, poised on each side of our imaginary quadrilateral, are: Scripture, Tradition, Reason, and Experience. All four sources should be considered when doing good theological thinking, but as we will make clear below, theologians and homileticians will not always give equal authority to each source. For example, you may find three out of four of them explicitly involved in a Theological Claim in a sermon, but that does not mean that the fourth element has been ignored; it simply may not be explicit. In the text box, you'll see some reminders about how we understand each source—Scripture, Tradition, Reason, and Experience.

It is important to note that each interpreter will *enter* the Wesleyan Quadrilateral starting at different places. Consciously or unconsciously, these starting places may be informed by the theology of the preacher's denomination or the theological school to which they adhere. If you are an early-career preacher, you might not yet know the theological school that will inform your preaching. However, you can still make decisions about how to enter the WQ based on the experience and tradition you already have as you use this book to help craft sermonic claims. So, for instance, some theologians and homileticians may begin with Scripture and then move to tradition and experience with less emphasis on reason. Others may begin from the experience of God in the midst of the believing community as it reflects the biblical text and reason, giving less emphasis to tradition. In the examples below we will see how two well-known theologians include these sources in their crafting of theologically sound but critically imaginative metaphors for God. Before we look at these, we need to say a few words about metaphor and the Bible.

THE FOUR SOURCES OF AUTHORITY IN THE WESLEYAN QUADRILATERAL

SCRIPTURE

Clearly, Scripture needs to inform how we think and speak about God. In Chapters 1–6, you learned about how to work with Scripture to hear its Theological Claims in its own culture and history. Also, since Scripture is always interpreted by people, we need to make sure that we are doing critical and just interpretations of Scripture when crafting Theological Claims. The perspective-explicit approaches described in Chapter 4 can help with this.

TRADITION

A second source of authority is Tradition. Of this conversation partner we ask: "What resources from the history of my denomination or the larger Christian church help inform my thinking about a potential Theological Claim?" Some denominations will have more structured resources from the Tradition than others, such as catechisms, creeds, letters, and sermons from church leaders. But Tradition can also include such things as spirituals, hymns, artwork, and writings of forefathers and foremothers in the faith.

REASON

A third side of the Wesleyan Quadrilateral, Reason, comes with the question: "How does the world of science, social science, and branches of philosophy (Logic) inform my theological thinking?" Notice here the pole of Reason does *not* refer to individual assessments of "reasonableness." You are not asking a question of yourself as to whether you think it is sensible. (Remember that human beings are easily deluded by their own thoughts!) Reason refers to elements in the secular worlds of science, social science, and some branches of philosophy that help us understand who God is and what God is doing. For instance, if you are preaching on Creation, can you only discuss Genesis literally, that is, that God created the world in six days and, thus, conclude that evolution is untrue? Or is there something to learn from planetary science that helps us make sense of Creation in Genesis for contemporary hearers? The pole of Reason argues for the latter. In this chapter, we will look at an example of a Theological Claim in conversation with planetary science.

EXPERIENCE

Finally, we need to ask about how potential Theological Claims reflect the experience of the community of believers. We can ask, "Does this claim ring true to our experience of God in the midst of my community?" Note that "Experience" here is not private (what I feel about God) but rather how God is known to me in my community of faith. How do *we experience* God? This communal aspect of experience is important because, as we have learned throughout Christian history, our finite, individual minds are often misled into believing we are hearing the voice of God when it is actually the voice of our own biases and prejudices. Bringing experience into the realm of the communal lessens the likelihood that we are proposing something discriminatory and unjust. While community theological discernment can sometimes go astray in harmful ways, communal experience as a source of theological discernment can also be expansive and liberating. For example, below we will look at a powerful Theological Claim made by the African American theologian James Cone. He says, "God is Black." To help craft this claim, he relies on the experience of the African American community in the United States as it has experienced life under White racism. The collective experience of his community rather than just his individual experience serves as an important conversation partner. Note, too, that it's important for those who do not share the experience of a particular community to listen to and test their assumptions and biases against this community's discernment as well. This is where perspective-explicit interpretations can be helpful (see Chapter 4).

THE USE OF METAPHOR IN THEOLOGY

Another helpful resource for crafting Theological Claims comes in understanding the power of **metaphor** in biblical and theological language. In Chapters 2 and 3, you were introduced to the importance of metaphor in determining the genre of a biblical text. You learned that the Bible is filled with metaphors that attempt to say something about the ultimately inexpressible nature of God. All of these metaphors for God experienced and expressed by our ancestors in the faith have a purpose—they keep us from making God an idol with our words for God. As theologian Sallie McFague explained, "Thinking metaphorically means spotting a thread of similarity between two dissimilar objects, events or whatever, one of which is better known than the other and using the better-known one as a way of speaking about the lesser known."[2]

Metaphors tell us that yes, God is something like this, but no, God is not this entirely. All of these metaphors remind us that no single name or attribute of God should be used to define God. All the biblical metaphors together and even more are needed to say something about who God is. This is why we hold all language for God "loosely," remembering that it is human speech attempting to point toward the ultimately inexpressible nature of God. Some of these metaphors are easier for us to recognize than others, and, as you'll see in the exercise below, we need to think about the ramifications of using metaphorical language in our sermons.

EXERCISE

Comparing and Contrasting Metaphors for God

1. *Read Psalm 23.* Notice that "the Lord is my Shepherd" in v. 1 uses the metaphor of a shepherd tending her sheep.
   a. *How does the metaphor function?* We know that God can engage the world in ways similar to that of a good shepherd caring for her sheep. What are the qualities held in common by both a shepherd and God? At the same time, we know that God is not *literally* a shepherd, and we are not *literal* sheep. So if someone would take offense at being referred to as a "sheep" if you preached on this imagery, how might you respond? (See Chapter 19 for an example of a sermon about Psalm 23 using this imagery of the shepherd.)

2. *Read Isaiah 64:8.* Notice that this verse contains the metaphor, "We are the clay and you our potter," which tells us something about God's role in our creation.
   a. *How does the metaphor function?* What are the qualities held in common by both a potter and God? However, is God a literal potter? Of course not, so how would you handle this metaphor in a sermon? How are human beings like clay, and at what point does the metaphorical comparison break down?

3. *Read John 6:25-40.* In v. 35, Jesus says, "I am the bread of life." This metaphor tells us about Jesus's ability to feed our spiritual hunger.
   a. *How does the metaphor function?* What are qualities about bread that describe Jesus and his teaching? Of course, Jesus is not actually a loaf of bread, so how might you preach about the religious leaders' response to his metaphor that John describes in vv. 41-59? What is the nature of their dispute, and how does their debate around bread and manna inform our understanding about Jesus Christ today?

As our examples show, metaphors for God or Jesus Christ or the Holy Spirit advance our thinking and expand what we know about God, but they are never literal descriptions of God. We remember that no word or name alone is sufficient to describe the immensity of God. God is beyond every name. But metaphors can certainly function as Theological Claims. Consider this from Psalm 18:2:

> The LORD is my rock, my fortress, and my deliverer, my God, my rock in whom I take refuge, my shield, and the horn of my salvation, my stronghold.

This verse is filled to bursting with metaphors to describe the nature of God as strong and protective. God is not literally any of these things but shares attributes with some things in the material world that we understand. These are very clearly metaphors at work. And all of these together make an explicit Theological Claim—they tell us something about who God is. Now let's look at some metaphors that are harder to discern because we have repeated them so many times that they seem to literally name God.

Deconstructing Familiar Metaphors for God

Returning to Psalm 23, which we examined in the exercise, there is another "hidden" metaphor in the verse, "The Lord is my Shepherd; I shall not want." The metaphor is in the name "Lord." It suggests that God is a lord. But remember that while the title "Lord" designates that God is sovereign over us, God is not a literal "Lord." Lord is a metaphor for God, but we have used it so often that it has become almost synonymous with the name God. How often do prayers begin with the metaphor "Lord" as opposed to other metaphors, such as "Potter" (Isaiah 64:8) and "Mother Hen" (Luke 13:34)?

Let's also take a second look at Isaiah 64:8:

> Yet, O Lord, you are our Father;
> we are the clay, and you are our potter;
> we are all the work of your hand.

Here we see another hidden metaphor: "Father." For many people, the language of God the Father has become so comfortable that they cannot pray without it. But when we drill down, is God really, literally a father? Or does God have characteristics of what we believe a good parent has, such as patience, wisdom, love, forgiveness? Likely, we would say that it is the latter.

Notice that when we literalize metaphors for God, such as father and lord, and fail to recognize them as simply two among many descriptive names for God, we begin to do injustice not only to God but to God's people. Consider what it might feel like for a woman who has been sexually assaulted by her human father to have to call God "Father" rather than parent or mother or some of the hundreds of other potential names and qualities for God the Bible offers us (see Appendix G). The language we use for God has real-world consequences that we need to take into consideration when we are crafting our Theological Claims.

In Appendix G, we have given you many other biblical metaphors to use beyond "Father" and "Lord." These can keep preachers from making an idol of our metaphors for God or for insisting on language that has unintended but still damaging consequences. With these resources at the ready, let's look at two contemporary metaphors that utilize sources in the WQ along with an informed theological imagination to address contemporary problems.

AN EXAMPLE OF METAPHOR IN THEOLOGY: GOD IS BLACK

In his groundbreaking African American liberation theology, theologian James Cone makes the claim that God is Black, an assertion that is both biblically accurate and contextually important.[3] First, Cone clearly understands that language for God is metaphorical, thus the word "Black" here has both a similarity and a dissimilarity inherent in it. No, God is not the color black, but yes, God, as a poor, brown, Jewish infant, born of a teenaged mother, living and working on the margins of society, embodies the conditions that characterize the lives and history of Black people in the United States. "Black" here is the metaphor for the conditions of social and cultural oppression faced by African Americans. God, in coming into the world in human form in Jesus, chose to take on the conditions of what it means to be Black. Cone, like all liberation theologians, knows that throughout the Bible God has committed Godself to liberating the oppressed. For Cone, that includes African Americans. Thus, he is reading the biblical text in conversation with the communal experience of Black people in the United States.

Further, Cone uses his reading of the biblical text through the lens of the community of African American believers (the experiencing community) to answer the urgent question "what has the gospel of Jesus Christ to do with the Black struggle for justice in the United States?"[4] To understand the depth and contours of this struggle, Cone engages resources from the movement for civil rights and Black power movements from the 1960s. Thus history, as a form of reason, animates and drives his theology. Notice that reason and faith work in concert here and are not diametrically opposed, as some would have it.

Finally, his claim demonstrates prophetic imagination. The simple statement "God is Black" challenges everything about the blonde-haired, blue-eyed Jesus who has become the default image for most White Christians. "God is Black" takes the resources of Scripture, Tradition, Reason, and Experience and confronts the evils of racism in ways that open our eyes to the nature of God in new ways. "God is Black" also draws on the tradition of Christianity within the slave church as it articulated a liberating God through spirituals, the sermons of Black preachers, and the eventual development of denominational bodies that created their own ecclesial structures apart from the dominant White church in America.

From these sources he crafts a metaphorical claim that both shocks and comforts. Thus, context matters in the effects of this metaphor for God. In a predominantly White church, the metaphor of "God is Black" might be unsettling and even offensive because it unearths some White Christians' almost unconscious assumptions of who God is—a Big White Man in the sky. But consider how this same metaphor might impact parishioners in an African American ecclesial context. In this setting, God is talked about as taking on the conditions that African Americans experience every day by living within structures of racism and White supremacy. It might be profoundly liberating and empowering to believe that God has chosen to be embodied within those conditions.

ANOTHER EXAMPLE OF METAPHOR IN THEOLOGY: THE EARTH IS GOD'S BODY

Here is a second example of a powerful contemporary metaphor crafted to address injustice. It comes from the environmental theology of Sallie McFague in her book *The Body of God: An Ecological Theology*.[5] Here, she makes the claim that the Earth should be considered as God's body. This is a powerful metaphor that engages predominantly Scripture, theological Tradition, and planetary science (Reason) through prophetic imagination to address the ways we are destroying the Earth.

Scripturally she notes, against the great Western dualism that has shaped and distorted Christianity since Augustine, that Christianity is inherently corporeal—that is, it is centered around embodiment. God takes on a body in Jesus Christ; Jesus suffers and dies in a body; Jesus tends to the needs of bodies, feeding them, healing them, bringing them back into community. Thus, she can say from her examination of Scripture that embodiment matters to God. God is not a spirit separate from the world but is deeply, intimately connected to all bodies and to the Earth as our collective body.

From her study of planetary science (Reason) and her concerns for humans' desecration of the Earth (environmental science), she uses theology—God talk—to call attention to the plight of the Earth. How would we behave if we believed that the Earth was God's body? Would we trample and pollute the Divine body that envelops yet also transcends the boundaries of the Earth? Her argument is that we would not violate something as sacred as the body of God if this is what we truly believed. In terms of tradition, McFague relies on historical theological influences as conversation partners to make the case that God should be considered as more than disembodied Spirit. Her lifelong experiences as part of the environmental community help her argue with this metaphor that Christians, in particular, need to reorient themselves away from obsessing about the afterlife and toward the needs of this life—the needs of the planet that she loves and believes God loves as well. "The Earth as God's body" offers us a provocative, imaginative, faithful Theological Claim that opens up dimensions of God we have not seen before with a metaphor that is surprising, but also firmly rooted in the WQ. Again, as with "God is Black," the impact of this metaphor relies on the context in which it is preached. For those Christians who are concerned about the life of the planet under increasingly dire conditions, the idea of God as literally embodied in the Earth we love, and that God created, is profoundly meaningful. But for those who see a stark separation between the fallen material world and the pristine spiritual realm that God is said to inhabit, this metaphor is offensive and even heretical. Thus, in assessing the power of using metaphors in preaching, consider the context in which the claim is being made. Will it shock or reassure—or both? What does a congregation need to hear about the nature of God at this time in this specific place?

These two examples from James Cone and Sallie McFague are substantive Theological Claims that are metaphors. To various degrees, they each engage the poles of the WQ in order to make use of the already metaphorical nature of all language for God. Each incorporates an informed and prophetic imagination. Each in its own ways uses the resources of the WQ in the service of needs in the contemporary world to make the Good News relevant to this time and place. So, we invite you to embrace both the power of metaphor in thinking about language for God and the importance of the conversation partners of Scripture, Tradition, Reason, and Experience in crafting your own theologically substantive claims.

Before we go on, let's address some attitudes of preachers that might keep their Theological Claim from being as strong and appropriate as can be. In what ways might we unintentionally undermine our own best Theological Claims?

PREACH WHAT YOU BELIEVE: AVOIDING CLICHÉS AND APHORISMS

In his book *Preaching: An Essential Guide*, Ron Allen makes the following statement.

> I am still surprised by the number of preachers who say things that they do not truly believe. This phenomenon usually takes place because preachers simply do not pay attention to contradictions between what they say (sloppy thinking), or because preachers use familiar language from the tradition that the preacher has not studied carefully and thus does not express what the preacher truly believes.[6]

Allen brings forward two problems that plague preachers when they attempt to make Theological Claims: saying things they don't believe and using clichéd language simply because it is familiar.

As to the first, the preacher must pay attention to the message of the text and its coherence with the beliefs of the community who will hear the message. For instance, let's think about this passage from Exodus 22:24: "My wrath will burn, and I will kill you with the sword, and your wives shall become widows and your children orphans" (NRSV). In this passage the author tells us that not only will God kill, but God doesn't seem to care about the collateral damage: God intends to leave wives widowed and children orphaned. The Theological Claim here is that God destroys people and leaves families bereft. This is what the passage says. Does that mean that the preacher and the congregation must accept it and believe it? Allen argues that there are cases like this that contradict what we know about the nature of God and the work of grace. Preachers should not preach this as if they believed it or were advocating that it should be believed. Think about what you are saying. Listen to it. Do not use language unconsciously. Biblical language should be listened to and critiqued. In other words, there are times when we may need to preach *against* the text.

Also, remember that we must conduct a thorough exegesis of the text. In this case, we need to read the passage within its fuller context instead of plucking it out as an example of a wrathful God. Given that God is described as "compassionate" a few verses later, we need to think about why the author thought it necessary to use this kind of violent language to describe God's actions in v. 24. The fuller text is this: "You shall not wrong or oppress a resident alien, for you were aliens in the land of Egypt. You shall not abuse any widow or orphan. If you do abuse them, when they cry out to me, I will surely heed their cry" (vv. 21-23). That is the reason God threatens to kill—it is a warning to those who abuse their power, exploit foreigners living among them, and harm those most vulnerable in society. Preachers can help people think about what to do with problematic passages like this that seem to contradict God's love and grace by helping them see the bigger picture.

More often, however, preachers preach clichés or aphorisms that they assume mean something but which, in fact, are void of meaning. An aphorism is a short phrase or adage that is meant to convey a truth. A cliché is a trite phrase or expression. While clichés or aphorisms may be familiar and popular, they can be hollow and unhelpful at best, harmful at worst.

Consider the aphorism "God is love." We repeat and hear that sentence frequently. But what does it really mean? Now consider theologian Clark Williamson's unpacking of that statement: "God graciously and freely offers the divine love to each and all . . . and this God who loves all creatures therefore *commands* that justice be done to them."[7] In Williamson's claim we see God freely acting on a love that is not disembodied but *concrete*—this love commands justice. There is no love without justice. This is how we are called to live. This tells us something substantial about the nature of God and by extension the nature of ourselves. When we preach, then, we want to avoid clichés—unless we are intentionally unpacking or deconstructing them as such in the sermon. Now let's practice evaluating Theological Claims.

EXERCISE

Evaluating Theological Claims

Consider the following claims:

1. Let go and let God.
2. God's justice is God's love, and God's love is God's justice.
3. Jesus died for our sins.

For each of the Theological Claims, choose whether it is:

A. Problematic
B. Possible, but weak
C. Strong and appropriate

Then write a paragraph to justify your answer. After you have written your paragraph, compare your answer to what we have explained below.

Let go and let God.

Not only is this not a claim (because it does not make an explicit assertion about God), this is a cliché and is problematic. This sentence has been associated with twelve-step recovery groups and has become part of the cultural lexicon of the twenty-first century. It has certainly been viewed as a helpful statement by some who struggle with addictions. But in terms of using it as the Theological Claim for a sermon, it is not sufficient. The essence of this statement is that we need to let go of our own will and turn over trust to God to lead our lives. This is an important idea when you are used to having a lot of social or political capital in your life, when you have had a lot of control and seen your will dominate in many ways, sometimes destructively and sometimes effectively. The call of this statement, then, is to remove your ego from the mix if your life is out of control and figure out what God's will is for you. In this case, letting go of some of that ego will be liberative and life-giving.

However, there are some interesting insights into this statement from feminist critiques of the traditional twelve steps. What does this say about agency when you have never been in a social or political position to actually assert your own desires? How can you give up something you have never had? For women, Black, Indigenous, people of color, and LGBTQIA+ folks who have never felt real agency to effect change in their own cultures and maybe even their own lives, the call needs to be to *increase* our agency and not give away something that doesn't exist. This, then, is not just a cliché; for some, it can lead to further disempowerment.

God's justice is God's love and God's love is God's justice.

Some may hesitate with this statement at first because of differing definitions of the word "justice." One sense of this word has to do with punishment and may bring to mind the image of a harsh and punitive judge. However, as we explained above, justice in the biblical sense has to do with fairness, equity, restoration, protection of the vulnerable, and accountability for those who abuse, exploit, and oppress. Therefore, we would suggest that this is a strong and appropriate Theological Claim in much the same way as the example we gave above from Clark Williamson amplifying the claim "God is love." Here we are able to say that wherever acts of justice take place, that is an expression of God's love.

God's love, then, is not a warm and fuzzy emotion limited to our hearts, but an expansive, active power that frees us from exploitation and oppression. It means that while humans may try to thwart God's intentions, the intentions of God for justice (and thus love, and vice versa) do not change, especially for the exploited, abused, and oppressed. Further, it means that when we humans engage in acts of justice, we are exemplifying God's love here and now.

But does this claim mean that where there is no justice there is no divine love? Consider the example of a woman living in domestic violence. She may not have experienced justice in her situation. Her partner has never been arrested or removed from the home. Does this mean that God does not love her? No, it means that God's love is working through her to help both her (and all of us) find her voice, her strength, and her agency. God's love looks like the increase in empowerment for all God's beloved children to do the justice work (the love work) that will create the Realm of God in the present.

We can also note that this claim would meet all four corners of the Wesleyan Quadrilateral. Scripturally, justice and love are mutually connected as we see from the frequent pairing of *mishpat* (justice) and *tsĕdaqah* (righteousness) throughout the Hebrew Scriptures. Passages such as Jeremiah 22:3, Psalm 112, and Isaiah 1:17 speak of God's justice as restoring blessedness to those who have been treated with inequity. History tells us that the greatest movements of justice are founded in love—the kind of love based on nonviolence and *agape* for the neighbor, even one's enemy. An examination of the work of people such as Gandhi and the Rev. Dr. Martin Luther King Jr. would verify that. Reason helps us understand that God's justice and love cannot be separated. As Dietrich Bonhoeffer explained in *The Cost of Discipleship*, justice without love is merely punitive, not restorative.[8] Love without justice is "cheap grace."[9] Finally, experience can also verify this claim. For example, when those who perpetrated the system of injustice in South Africa were held to account through the Truth and Reconciliation Commission (which was founded on the biblical principles of both love and justice), the process yielded healing rather than simply vengeance and retaliation. Those who went through this process (both victims and perpetrators) experienced God's justice through love.

Jesus died for our sins.

Some of you will have found this claim to be strong and appropriate, but we want to suggest that the statement has come to be a shorthand for personal and individual salvation and thus does not go far enough as a substantive Theological Claim. Therefore, this is an aphorism, so we would assess this statement as possible, but weak, because it has lost whatever deeper meaning it might have once had, and because it has been assumed as self-explanatory.

In fact, this may even be a problematic statement because there are assumptions in this common truism that have troubling implications. We can unearth some of those assumptions by asking probing questions. Some of those questions have to do with the implications of violence and divinity. For example, *why* did Christ allow people to kill him? What were contextual conditions surrounding his acquiescence to death? If he died as a passive response to violence, what does that passivity mean for us today in the face of violence? Does his passive acceptance of death mean one thing if a person is participating in a Black Lives Matter protest and another when a woman faces a violent partner?

Other questions have to do with the ramifications regarding sin and salvation. Did Jesus only die so that I (or the people who believe as I do) can go to heaven? Are we off the hook from our sins because Jesus "paid the price"? Am I supposed to feel something in response to this statement, such as gratitude or guilt? Am I required to do something (perhaps get others to believe so they can get to heaven too)? Or is it about more than me? Does Christ's decision to practice radical hospitality, forgiveness, justice, and reconciliation to his dying breath make a difference in the world now? If so, how do we live into that new reality he was and is creating?

As we wrestle with these and other questions, we realize that if we are to use a statement like this in our preaching, at the very least it must be accompanied by serious engagement with whatever assumptions people bring to it. Asking these kinds of questions helps us to expand on the meaning of his death and the meaning of human sin so that we move away from a hollow, formulaic axiom and toward a deeper, more robust, and more ethical engagement with the death and resurrection of Jesus Christ.

Now that you have worked through this exercise, here is a list of other Theological Claims that are clichés and thus have no real meaning but which you may have heard frequently:

- This is all part of God's plan; or, God is in control.
- Love the sinner, hate the sin.
- There but for the grace of God go I (or us).
- What would Jesus do?
- God helps those who help themselves.[10]

As you unpack each of these, think about reasons why they are so often repeated but why they may be weak or even problematic. This does not mean you cannot address them in a sermon; but it does mean that in such a sermon you will need to explore that piece of conventional wisdom, challenge it, deconstruct it, and reconstruct a stronger Theological Claim in a biblically and theologically sound way.

KEY POINTS IN THIS CHAPTER

1. Theological Claims name God (or Jesus Christ, or the Holy Spirit), and God's nature or actions.
2. Theological Claims are created in conversation with Scripture, Tradition, Reason, and Experience.
3. All Theological Claims, including sermonic claims, are necessarily metaphorical, not literal. Our human language for God simply cannot contain the immensity and otherness of God.
4. Theological Claims should be consistent with what the preacher believes to be the core of the gospel and the nature of God. Preachers must stand behind what they say.
5. Theological Claims must be substantial. Clichés or aphorisms, simply because they are familiar, do not tell the hearer anything and may actually do harm.

DISCUSSION QUESTIONS

1. The next time you are interacting with people at your congregation, at your family gathering, in your community, or on social media, notice the ways in which they use "God talk," that is, theological language. Do you hear it in meetings of the governing board? In the kitchen as people are preparing meals? In Sunday School lessons? In social media posts? In a sermon, how might you highlight the everyday theology expressed by people, and in what ways can you affirm or push back against the implications of the theological language we encounter?
2. Find a preaching partner and trade sermon manuscripts to evaluate each one using the Wesleyan Quadrilateral. Which of the four poles—Scripture, Tradition, Reason, Experience—do you see explicitly in the sermon? Of the poles that are more implicit, how might the sermon be approached in a way that makes them more obvious?
3. With that same sermon, examine it for how the preacher uses metaphor(s) for God. What are images, illustrations, or comparisons used in the sermon to help listeners understand the nature and actions of God, people, communities, or human society? How do the metaphors function? What is the tension between the "yes" and "no" that the metaphors convey?
4. Gather with a group of preaching colleagues to discuss how they handle theological clichés and aphorisms that they hear from parishioners. How have they used sermons to unpack or challenge empty or problematic theological sayings?

FOR FURTHER READING

Richard Lischer. *A Theology of Preaching: The Dynamics of the Gospel*, revised edition. Eugene, OR: Wipf and Stock, 2001.
Sallie McFague. *Metaphorical Theology: Models of God in Religious Language.* Philadelphia: Fortress Press, 1982.
John S. McClure. "Theology and Preaching." In *Preaching Words: 144 Key Terms in Homilets.* Louisville, KY: John Knox Press, 2007, 136.
Donald McKim. *The Westminster Dictionary of Theological Terms*, second edition. Louisville, KY: Westminster John Knox Press, 2014.
Dorothee Soelle. *Thinking about God: An Introduction to Theology.* Eugene, OR: Wipf & Stock, 2016.
Howard Stone and James Duke. *How to Think Theologically.* Minneapolis: Fortress Press, 2013.
Articles under "Theology" in *The New Interpreter's Handbook of Preaching*, edited by Paul Scott Wilson. Nashville: Abingdon, 2008:
"Anthropology." Amy Plantinga Pauw
"Christology." Bryan Chapell
"Ecclesiology." William H. Willimon
"Theology in the Sermon." James R. Nieman

Resources for exploring a theology of preaching:

Ronald J. Allen. *Thinking Theologically: The Preacher as Theologian.* In Elements of Preaching Series. O. Wesley Allen Jr., series editor. Minneapolis, MN: Fortress Press, 2008.
Ronald J. Allen, ed. *Preaching the Manifold Grace of God, Volume 1: Theologies of Preaching in Historical Theological Families.* Eugene, OR: Cascade, 2022.
Ronald J. Allen, ed. *Preaching the Manifold Grace of God, Volume 2: Theologies of Preaching in the Early Twenty-First Century.* Eugene, OR: Cascade, 2022.
Selections from *The New Interpreter's Handbook of Preaching*, edited by Paul Scott Wilson. Nashville: Abingdon, 2008:
"Call," David Greenhaw; "Holy Spirit and Preaching," Cheryl Bridges Johns; "Theology of Proclamation," James Kay; "Authority (Theology)," Thomas G. Long; "Authority of the Preacher," Charles Rice; "Sermon as Proclamation," David Lose.
James F. Kay. *Preaching and Theology.* St. Louis, MO: Chalice Press, 2007.
John S. McClure. "Theology of Preaching." In *Preaching Words: 144 Key Terms in Homiletics.* Louisville, KY: John Knox Press, 2007, 137–39.

NOTES

1. In discussing theology as a broad discipline, the nature, works, and person of Jesus Christ and the Holy Spirit each have their own individual doctrines that theologians think about; these are called Christology and Pneumatology respectively. For our purposes in this chapter and the next, we are thinking about theology in the narrow sense as only the doctrine of God. Because part of understanding the nature of God is God in three persons, we include statements about Jesus Christ and the Holy Spirit as Theological Claims. Just know that there are many more questions to ask about Jesus Christ and the Holy Spirit, but these are accomplished in doctrines we are not including here. In the next chapter we will be discussing other kinds of claims in Scripture—statements about human beings (anthropological claims) and statements about the nature and work of the church (ecclesiological claims). We will say more about how these relate to the nature of God in that chapter. But for now, we are just thinking about who God is and what God does.
2. Sallie McFague, *Metaphorical Theology: Models of God in Religious Language* (Philadelphia: Fortress Press, 1982), 15.
3. James Cone, *A Black Theology of Liberation* (Maryknoll: Orbis, 1986), Chapter 4.
4. Ibid., preface to the 1986 edition, xv.
5. Sallie McFague, *The Body of God: An Ecological Theology* (Minneapolis: Fortress Press, 1993).
6. Ronald Allen, *Preaching: An Essential Guide* (Nashville: Abingdon Press, 2002), 53.
7. Clark Williamson, quoted in Ron Allen's *Preaching: An Essential Guide*, 51.
8. Dietrich Bonhoeffer, *The Cost of Discipleship* (New York: Touchstone, 1995. Previously published: New York: Macmillan, 1959).
9. Ibid., Chapter 1.
10. Here is an article with a list of these maxims and explanations as to why they are not helpful in sermons, in pastoral care, or anywhere: "Adages," *Living Lutheran*, June 24, 2015. Accessed May 13, 2021. https://www.livinglutheran.org/2015/06/adages/.

9

Identifying Theological Claims in a Biblical Text

Before we turn to finding Theological Claims in the biblical text and crafting a Theological Claim from the text for the sermon, we need to do a little more refining of what is and is not a Theological Claim. First, we need to distinguish the differences between *theological*, *anthropological*, and *ecclesiological claims*.

THEOLOGICAL, ANTHROPOLOGICAL, AND ECCLESIOLOGICAL CLAIMS

Theological Claims have as the subject of the sentence either God, Jesus Christ, or the Holy Spirit. They make an assertion about who God is or what God does. Below we will discuss why statements made by God or Jesus are not always self-evidently Theological Claims. But here is one of the first explicit Theological Claims we encounter in Scripture: "In the beginning, God created the heavens and the earth" (Gen 1:1). God is the subject of the sentence and "created" is the action of God.

Anthropological claims have as their subject us (human beings). These are sentences that make claims about who human beings are as creations of God and, as such, what we are to believe or do. Below we will discuss some of the challenges to identifying anthropological claims, but here is a clear example: "For now we see in a mirror, dimly, but then we will see face to face. Now I know only in part; then I will know fully, even as I have been fully known" (1 Cor 13:12). In the first sentence of this verse, "we" is the subject; in the second sentence, "I" is the subject. Both are making anthropological claims about the limitations of human understanding in this life. They are also making *implicit Theological Claims* that God will enable our full understanding when we are ultimately united with the Divine Presence, and that God fully knows us. One thing to note is that anthropological claims can be about a single individual, a group, or humanity in general; this is something you'll need to determine when exegeting a biblical text.

Ecclesiological claims have as their subject the church and are usually related to the growth or nature of the church as it instantiates the body of Christ. You may wonder, what is the difference between an anthropological claim about a group of people and an ecclesiological claim? Ecclesiological claims make reference to the worshipping assembly or the community of Christ believers. (While there are claims about the identity of the people of God in the Hebrew Bible, only in the Christian Scriptures is the term *ekklesia* used. Therefore, for our purposes, we are using the term ecclesiology to refer to the Christian church.)

An example of an ecclesiological claim would be: "For as in one body we have many members, and not all the members have the same function, so we, who are many, are one body in Christ, and individually we are members one of another" (Rom 12:4-5). An ecclesiological claim will also clearly be addressing a group of Christian believers who identify themselves as the church. In the Romans passage above, for example, it is clear that Paul is addressing the church in Rome and making a claim about who they are and how they are to function and relate to one another as members of the church of Christ.

Why is it important to know the difference between theological, anthropological, and ecclesiological claims? Because they are everywhere in Scripture and sermons, so knowing the difference between them will allow you to identify and then write *explicit Theological Claims*. This is not to say that anthropological and ecclesiological claims aren't important, because, of course, they are essential to both Scripture and preaching. And we know that statements about us and statements about the church are always related to and derived from the nature and character of God. For instance, saying anything about who we are and what we should do is derived by first understanding that we are beloved creatures made by God in God's image. Likewise, the church understands its existence and mission to live out the qualities of God expressed in the countercultural values of the Realm of God. Given these realities, we are simply arguing that a sermon needs to clearly state who God is and what God does as its primary function; the anthropological and ecclesiological claims are in response to the explicit Theological Claim in the text and the sermon.

We must also note that deciding on the category a claim falls into may seem easier when we discuss it in this chapter than it might actually be when you confront it in a text. Consider this Theological Claim from Acts 10:42: "He commanded us to preach to the people and to testify that he is the one ordained by God to judge the living and the dead." Though it is a statement about who Jesus Christ is (judge) and what he wants us to do (preach and testify), it is also a claim about the Second Coming of Jesus Christ at the eschaton—the end of human history. Jesus Christ will return to judge the living and the dead. If you look in Appendix D, you will see that there is a whole theological category that deals with the eschaton called "eschatology." Though this is a Theological Claim about Jesus Christ, it is also what the future will be like when Christ returns. Familiarizing yourself with the different theological categories will help you discern other kinds of influences that are entailed in a Theological Claim.

EXPLICIT AND IMPLICIT THEOLOGICAL CLAIMS

Now that we have distinguished between theological, anthropological, and ecclesiological claims, we need to differentiate between an explicit and an implicit Theological Claim. For our purposes in this chapter and in general for crafting sermons, we want you to know how to identify **explicit Theological Claims** and distinguish them from **implicit Theological Claims**.

Explicit Theological Claims clearly name the nature or actions of God, Jesus Christ, or the Holy Spirit. God, Jesus Christ, or the Holy Spirit is the subject of the sentence.[1] Explicit claims are plainly expressed and direct. For instance, the following examples are all explicit Theological Claims.

a. God has a preferential option for the poor.
b. Jesus calls us to love our enemies.
c. The Holy Spirit inspires people to acts of justice.

All of these statements name one member of the Divine life and clearly tell you something about each one's nature or actions.

Implicit Theological Claims suggest something about God, Jesus Christ, or the Holy Spirit but have as their primary focus a different subject for the sentence. Implicit Theological Claims usually are derived from either anthropological or ecclesiological claims. Implicit claims are indirect and the Theological Claim must be inferred. This can be a bit confusing, so let's look at some examples of implicit Theological Claims.

1. *"Christians put love into action as a response to God's love for us."* What is the subject of this sentence? The subject is "Christians." It is not directly about God, Jesus Christ, or the Holy Spirit, so it is not an explicit Theological Claim. It tells us something about *us* and what we are supposed to do; therefore, this is an anthropological claim telling us that we are supposed to put love into action. An anthropological claim has humans as the subject. While the name "God" does appear in the sentence, God is not the subject. However, the sentence implicitly says something about God. The implicit Theological Claim is that God loves us. If we were going to make this an explicit Theological Claim, it would look like this: "God loves us and calls Christians to respond to that love by putting faith into action." The subject here is God and tells us something about God's love and what God does (calls Christians to respond). But the sentence in the example only *implies* something about God's nature and actions, and we must infer the implicit Theological Claim therein.

2. *"The church proclaims the Good News of Jesus Christ."* As with the first example, we do see Jesus Christ mentioned in the sentence. But he is in the predicate, so this is not an explicit Theological Claim. This sentence is an example of an ecclesiological claim because the church is the subject. This sentence tells us what the church is supposed to do (proclaim the Good News). However, it also has an implied Theological Claim: "Jesus Christ is the Good News." If we were going to turn this implied claim into an explicit Theological Claim, it would be, "Jesus Christ is the Good News, which the church is called to proclaim." But the example above is an ecclesiological claim.

EXERCISE

Distinguishing between Explicit and Implicit Theological Claims

1. Consider this sentence from Luke 13:34: Jesus says: "How often have I desired to gather your children together as a hen gathers her brood under her wings, and you were not willing!" Is this an explicit or implicit Theological Claim? Explain your answer.
2. Consider a different sentence from Luke 13, this one in verse 35: Jesus says: "And I tell you, you will not see me until the time comes when you say, 'Blessed is the one who comes in the name of the Lord.'" Is this an explicit or implicit Theological Claim? Explain your answer.

If you had said that Luke 13:34 is an explicit Theological Claim, you would be correct. Why? Because Jesus is making a claim about himself, that he desired to gather the people of Jerusalem to him as a hen gathers her chicks. Notice that he is using metaphor to make this claim by comparing himself to a mother hen.

If you had said that verse 35 was an implicit Theological Claim, you would be correct. Why? Because this verse is actually an anthropological claim, which is that the people will not see Jesus until they publicly recognize him for who he is. You might have been thrown off by the opening clause, "And I tell you," but remember, this is just the clause. The subject of the sentence is "you." So what might the implicit Theological Claim be for this verse? As you will see when we analyze this passage more thoroughly in Chapter 11, the implicit Theological Claim is that Jesus can foretell that there will be public acclamation when he arrives in Jerusalem. This ability to see what is to come confirms his divine power.

Statements by God or Jesus

Statements made by God or Jesus in Scripture might be confusing as you are thinking about finding explicit Theological Claims. Just because it is said by God does not mean that it tells us something about God's nature or actions. Consider this example from Matthew 25:13. Jesus says, "Woe to you scribes and Pharisees, hypocrites. For you lock people out of the kingdom of heaven." Though it is said by Jesus, does it explicitly say something about his nature or actions? No. It is about the actions of the scribes and Pharisees.

What about this foundational statement by God in the creation of the world: "Let there be light!" God says it, but is God the subject of the sentence? No. Is there an implicit Theological Claim here? Yes. The implicit claim is that God created the light, but it is not an explicit Theological Claim.

Here is another example that is built on a metaphor. In John 15:5 Jesus says, "I am the vine, and you are the branches." Is this an explicit Theological Claim? Yes, and notice how it uses metaphor to make its claim. Jesus's nature and actions are like that of a vine on which we, the branches, are dependent.

What about this statement from God in the Gospel of Mark, when John the Baptist baptizes Jesus: "You are my Son, the Beloved" (Mark 1:11)? Yes, this is an explicit Theological Claim. This tells us something about the nature of Jesus—he is God's beloved. So, when you consider statements by God or Jesus Christ, you need to ask yourselves if they are saying something about themselves. If so, it is an explicit Theological Claim; if not, it is simply a statement *by* them but not *about* them.

Commands

If you look at the review of grammar in Appendix F, you'll see that we cover what kinds of sentences commands are. When you are looking for explicit Theological Claims in Scripture, you will come across many things that God and Jesus say via commands, such as "Seek God's face!" or "Repent and believe in the Gospel." But just because God or Jesus says them, it does not make them Theological Claims. In commands, the subject of the sentence is "you." Remember that sentences need a noun or pronoun as a subject. The subject of commands is actually the hearer(s) of the command, so it is most often an implied "you."

So if it were spelled out, these two commands would be "You, seek God's face," and "You, repent and believe." This makes these and most commands anthropological claims, because their subject is really us (human beings) and what we are supposed to do (or not do). To be explicit Theological Claims, the subject needs to be a statement about God, Jesus Christ, or the Holy Spirit saying something about their nature or actions.

Passages with No Explicit Theological Claims

Let's look at a passage that has *no* explicit Theological Claims, but only implicit claims. What should a preacher do in that case?

Psalm 34:1-6

I will bless the LORD at all times;
his praise shall continually be in my mouth.
[2] My soul makes its boast in the LORD;
let the humble hear and be glad.
[3] O magnify the LORD with me,
and let us exalt his name together.
[4] I sought the LORD, and he answered me,
and delivered me from all my fears.
[5] Look to him and be radiant;
so your faces shall never be ashamed.
[6] This poor soul cried, and was heard by the LORD,
and was saved from every trouble.

Here the psalmist has said nothing *explicit* about the nature of God, but implicitly we learn much about who God is. For instance, we learn that God is in relationship to those who praise and worship God ("I sought the Lord and he answered me"). We also learn that God will answer the prayers of those who cry out to God and free them from fear ("This poor soul cried and was heard by the Lord and was saved from every trouble"). Thus, we can say that we learn that God is good, God listens, and God saves those with whom God is in relationship. In a passage with no explicit Theological Claim, ask yourself what the strongest *implicit* Theological Claim is and use that as your sermonic claim.

With these differentiations in mind, let's turn to a passage of Scripture to locate explicit and implicit Theological Claims.

EXERCISE

Identifying Theological and Anthropological Claims in Psalm 24

1. *Read Psalm 24.* In this psalm you will find two claims: theological and anthropological. See if you can identify which one is which.
2. *Analyze the text.* After you complete your analysis, see how it compares with what we explain below.

[1] The earth is the LORD's and all that is in it,
the world, and those who live in it;

Verse 1 is a statement about Creation and contains an implicit Theological Claim that God has ownership of all the Earth.

[2] for he has founded it on the seas,
and established it on the rivers.

Verse 2 is an explicit Theological Claim because it tells us what God has done: founded the earth on the seas and established it on the rivers.

[3] Who shall ascend the hill of the LORD?
And who shall stand in his holy place?
[4] Those who have clean hands and pure hearts,
who do not lift up their souls to what is false,
and do not swear deceitfully.
[5] They will receive blessing from the LORD,
and vindication from the God of their salvation.

Verse 3 is not a claim, but a question. However, it gives us a clue that verse 4 is an anthropological claim. That verse has "those" as its subject and tells us what is required for the ones who desire to ascend to God's holy place. In the same way, verse 5 is also an anthropological claim because it tells us what will happen to those who engage in right conduct before God.

[6] Such is the company of those who seek him,
who seek the face of the God of Jacob.

Verse 6 is an anthropological claim because it refers to "the company of those who seek" God—meaning the entire assembly.

[7] Lift up your heads, O gates!
and be lifted up, O ancient doors!
that the King of glory may come in.
[8] Who is the King of glory?
The LORD, strong and mighty,
the LORD, mighty in battle.
[9] Lift up your heads, O gates!
and be lifted up, O ancient doors!
that the King of glory may come in.
[10] Who is this King of glory?
The LORD of hosts,
he is the King of glory.

Verses 7 and 9 are tricky because they are a command addressed to the gates and ancient doors of the worship place. But we can infer that these are anthropological claims because they are implicitly addressed to the worshipping assembly. They are a command to open the way to God.

Verses 8 and 10 are Theological Claims because God is the subject and they describe characteristics of God (strong and mighty in battle, Lord of hosts, King of glory).

EXAMPLE

Identifying Claims in 2 Timothy 1:3-7

Here is a passage from 2 Timothy 1:3-7. Begin by underlining the verses that mention God, Jesus Christ, or the Holy Spirit, so that it looks like this:

> [3]I am grateful to God—whom I worship with a clear conscience, as my ancestors did—when I remember you constantly in my prayers night and day. [4]Recalling your tears, I long to see you so that I may be filled with joy. [5]I am reminded of your sincere faith, a faith that lived first in your grandmother Lois and your mother Eunice and now, I am sure, lives in you. [6]For this reason I remind you to rekindle the gift of God that is within you through the laying on of my hands; [7]for God did not give us a spirit of cowardice, but rather a spirit of power and of love and of self-discipline.

Next, mark what you think are the implicit and explicit Theological Claims in this passage.
Let's work through this together.

1. *Is v. 3 an explicit Theological Claim?* No. Remember that just because a verse or sentence mentions God, this does not necessarily make it a Theological Claim. This verse is about Paul's gratitude. The subject of the sentence is Paul.
2. *Is v. 4 an explicit Theological Claim?* No. There is no mention of God, Jesus Christ, or the Holy Spirit in this sentence.
3. *Is v. 5 an explicit Theological Claim?* No. God is not mentioned at all. It is an anthropological claim because it is about Timothy's faith. But is there an implicit Theological Claim here? Yes. The implicit Theological Claim is that God passes faith through the generations. And in this passage, we can infer that God deems women worthy to be keepers of the faith.
4. *Is v. 6 an explicit Theological Claim?* This is tricky, but it is actually a form of command by Paul to Timothy, which is "rekindle the gift of God that is within you." So, we remember that commands are most often anthropological claims with an implied "you" in it. Here that "you" is Timothy. But there is an implicit Theological Claim here as well, which is, "God gives gifts through the laying on of hands." You might also name as an implicit Theological Claim that God uses specific rituals (here it is the laying on of hands) to bestow gifts on people.
5. *Is v. 7 an explicit Theological Claim?* Yes. It says something clear and direct about God's nature and actions. God is the subject in this verse, and we learn what God does and does not do: "God does not give us a spirit of cowardice, but rather a spirit of power and of love and of self-discipline."

In summary, then, the implicit Theological Claims in this passage are:

- Faith in God is passed down through the generations.
- God deems women worthy and appropriate for passing on the faith to others.
- God gives gifts through the laying on of hands.
- God uses religious rites, such as the laying on of hands, to convey gifts.

The only explicit Theological Claim in this passage is:

- God does not give a spirit of cowardice but of power, love, and self-discipline.

MAKING A SERMONIC CLAIM FROM AN EXPLICIT THEOLOGICAL CLAIM IN A SCRIPTURE PASSAGE

Now that we've learned how to distinguish between explicit and implicit Theological Claims in a Scripture passage, we can think about how we would use this information as the basis for making a claim in a sermon. In preaching, we want to be sure that our sermons contain strong, clear claims about who God, Jesus Christ, and/or the Holy

Spirit is based on the explicit Theological Claims we see in the text. This is what distinguishes a sermon from other types of speech. Sermons are not just moral pep talks (though they often contain aspects of morality), nor are they merely didactic lectures (though they often have some educational aspect), nor are they simply motivational speeches for making the world a better place (though they often inspire people to do good in the world). *No matter what their theme or style, all sermons must be firmly rooted in Scripture and theology and tell us something about the character and/or nature and/or actions of God and what the implications are for individuals, the church, and the world.* It is the Theological Claims within preaching that make a sermon distinct from other types of speeches.

Let's look at an example from the sermon "Climate Migration—How Should the Church Respond?" found in Chapter 4. One of the biblical passages for that sermon was Luke 9:51-58 and focused specifically on v. 58: "And Jesus said to him, 'Foxes have holes, and birds of the air have nests; but the Son of Man has nowhere to lay his head.'" In this verse, Jesus is making an explicit Theological Claim about himself in response to someone piping up that they will follow Jesus wherever he goes. He warns them that there will be no comfortable bed waiting for them at the end of each day's ministry. Theirs will be a life of wandering with no home base to provide comfort and familiarity.

In the sermon, Leah took that explicit Theological Claim in the text and made the following sermonic claim: "Jesus aligns himself with those who have no home, no safety, no rest for their weary bodies." Notice that not only does this connect to the verse in the text but also goes a step further by making a prophetic statement about Jesus's solidarity with those who must emigrate from their homes. Later at the end of the sermon, she recapitulates this same idea by saying that hope comes "from a Savior who knew what it meant to sojourn in a wilderness, to seek refuge from violence, to have no home to lay his head."

In the next exercise, we return to 2 Timothy 1:3-7, which we discussed earlier in this chapter, and see how we might derive a sermonic Theological Claim from the explicit Theological Claim in the passage.

EXERCISE

Making a Sermonic Claim from 2 Timothy 1:3-7

1. Recall the explicit Theological Claim from this passage that is in v. 7: "for God did not give us a spirit of cowardice, but rather a spirit of power and of love and of self-discipline." Write down three possible sermonic claims you might make from this passage.
2. Work with a preaching partner to evaluate each other's claims. Do they make a statement about the nature of God and/or God's actions? Are they consistent with the Theological Claim in the passage?
3. Consider these possible claims and decide which one is stronger:
   a. God does not want us to be fearful cowards.
   b. God gives the gifts of power, love, and self-discipline.
4. If you chose "b," you would be correct. If "God does not want us to be fearful cowards" was the sole Theological Claim you made in your sermon, it would be insufficient because you are simply talking about the *absence* of qualities. It would make for a very thin premise. You would certainly want to name that God does not desire for us to be cowards, but you can't end there because the passage goes on to name the positive gifts God does give us. "God gives the gifts of power, love, and self-discipline" would be a stronger sermonic claim from the passage for a sermon because it clearly states what God does—gives us power, love, and self-discipline.

DEVELOPING IDEAS FOR A SERMON FROM THE THEOLOGICAL CLAIM

Now let's think about how we might take a sermonic claim based on an explicit Theological Claim in a biblical text and build sermon ideas around it. At this point, we are just at the germination phase; we will more fully explain this process in ensuing chapters. But for now, we can begin to imagine different approaches to a sermon on 2 Timothy 1:3-7.

Here are some possibilities for a sermon based on the claim "God gives the gifts of power, love, and self-discipline." Notice that these ideas would go hand in hand with the exegetical work you would do on this passage.

- You could compare and contrast the spirit of cowardice with the gifts of power, love, and self-discipline.
  - You could begin by asking: "What did the spirit of power, love, and self-discipline look like for Paul and Timothy in their context?"
  - And then ask: "What does power, love, and self-discipline look like in our day and in our own community?"
  - Your comparison and contrast, then, would be twofold. It would compare the different kinds of qualities and the different forms in which they appear both in Paul's time and faith community and in our own.
- You could ask: "How do we rekindle the gifts of power, love, and self-discipline?"
  - You can look at the rest of Paul's letter for clues. For example, in Chapter 4 he states: "Proclaim the message; be persistent whether the time is favorable or unfavorable; convince, rebuke, and encourage with the utmost patience in teaching. . . . Always be sober, endure suffering, do the work of an evangelist, carry out your ministry fully" (vv. 2, 5).
  - After you have explained how to rekindle these gifts, you could ask: "In what ways do we do this in our families and in our lives? In the church? In society?"

You may wonder, could you preach a sermon that focuses only on the fact that God gives the gift of power? Or just love? Or just self-discipline? No, you can't separate these. This is the case because power alone is easily abused; love without power and self-discipline has neither muscle nor determination; and self-discipline without power and love is too narrow and rigid. What this means, then, is that God's gifts, as named here, are a "package deal"—one cannot come without the other two. This sermonic claim—God's gifts come as a package deal—could be an interesting centerpiece for a sermon.

Now let's examine another biblical passage, this time from the Hebrew Scriptures, Genesis 32:22-32. This is the story of Jacob wrestling with the mysterious stranger at the Jabbok River.

ANALYZING GENESIS 32:22-32, JACOB WRESTLING AT THE JABBOK

We begin by underlining the verses that mention God, Jesus Christ, or the Holy Spirit, so that it looks like this:

> The same night [Jacob] got up and took his two wives, his two maids, and his eleven children, and crossed the ford of the Jabbok. [23]He took them and sent them across the stream, and likewise everything that he had. [24]Jacob was left alone; and a man wrestled with him until daybreak. [25]When the man saw that he did not prevail against Jacob, he struck him on the hip socket; and Jacob's hip was put out of joint as he wrestled with him. [26]Then he said, 'Let me go, for the day is breaking.' But Jacob said, 'I will not let you go, unless you bless me.' [27]So he said to him, 'What is your name?' And he said, 'Jacob.' [28]Then the man said, 'You shall no longer be called Jacob, but Israel, for you have striven with God and with humans, and have prevailed.' [29]Then Jacob asked him, 'Please tell me your name.' But he said, 'Why is it that you ask my name?' And there he blessed him. [30]So Jacob called the place Peniel, saying, 'For I have seen God face to face, and yet my life is preserved.' [31]The sun rose upon him as he passed Penuel, limping because of his hip. [32]Therefore to this day the Israelites do not eat the thigh muscle that is on the hip socket, because he struck Jacob on the hip socket at the thigh muscle.

Analyzing the Text

Unlike the passage in 2 Timothy, identifying the strongest Theological Claim is not so cut and dry for this passage. In Genesis 32:22-32 there are only three verses that mention God—vv. 28, 29b, and 30. But none of these is an explicit theological statement. This sometimes happens in Scripture. There are passages where neither God, nor the Holy Spirit, nor Jesus Christ are mentioned. (In fact, there are two whole books that never mention God: Esther and Song of Solomon.) This means you'll need to derive your theological statement using the implicit claims in the text. In these cases, especially with narratives or parables, you have to take the story as a whole to determine what Theological Claim it is making. This is the case with the story of Jacob's wrestling match.

In verse 28, the implicit Theological Claim might be stated this way:
God strove with Jacob, allowed him to prevail, and changed his name.

Verse 29a is tricky because the identity of the mysterious stranger is deliberately ambiguous. Scholars conjecture that Jacob could be wrestling with an angel, wrestling with himself, or perhaps wrestling with Esau, his twin brother. But it's also possible that the stranger is actually God. If your exegesis leads you to this conclusion, then you could make the case that 29b is an explicit Theological Claim:
God blessed Jacob.

In verse 30, the implicit Theological Claim could be written like this:
God met Jacob face to face and preserved his life even in the midst of the struggle.

Making the Sermonic Claim

After having analyzed the theological content of the passage, we are challenged to craft a Theological Claim that will capture the spirit of the passage and what this story conveys about God. Here's one option:
God sometimes struggles with humans, and that struggle often changes them.

While this is certainly a true statement and alludes to the story, it's not clear that this statement is based on this particular passage.

A second possibility might be this:
God preserves Jacob's life even after struggling with him.

This statement gets us closer to the story, but it's a bit thin in its development.

Here's a third possibility:
God's wrestling with Jacob resulted in both pain and blessing, transforming him in the process, as symbolized by his new name—Israel.

This claim is clearly based on the biblical passage, which becomes evident to us through good exegetical work and gives us a substantive understanding of what God does with Jacob—wrestling, transforming, and renaming him.

IDEAS FOR DEVELOPING A SERMON ON GENESIS 32:22-32 BASED ON THE THEOLOGICAL CLAIM

With this claim, we would next employ our Exegesis Guide Chart to help us more deeply engage this text and, in turn, think about the sermon we might want to develop. We might recount the circumstances in Jacob's life prior to this midnight wrestling match—his usurping of his brother's birthright, his encounter with the "stairway to heaven" at Bethel after fleeing his brother's rage, and his struggles with Laban, the father-in-law of his two wives, Leah and Rachel. The sermon might invite listeners to consider the ways in which God keeps coming back to us—even after we have ruined relationships—so that we might be restored.

Or we might read this text from the perspective of someone who is physically disabled, just as Israel's hip was permanently damaged. How do those with physical challenges "wrestle with God"?

Another option is to consider what this means not just on an individual level, but for a community. For example, what does it mean to come face-to-face with the "holy other," the divine stranger who strives against us, yet also blesses us in the midst of the pain. What does Peniel look like for a church in the midst of a community that is changing demographically, for instance? As you can see, in all of this, the way our sermon takes shape will depend on the context in which we are preaching this passage.

EXERCISE

Theological Analysis Using a Text of Your Own Choosing

In Chapter 6, you learned about how to choose a biblical text for preaching (lectionary-based, topical, prayerful discernment). Choose a pericope you would like to preach on so that you can practice doing a theological analysis. The passage needs to be more than a single verse but not more than a typical reading in a worship service (approximately five to ten verses).

1. Underline the verses that mention God, Jesus Christ, or the Holy Spirit.
2. Mark what you think are the implicit and explicit Theological Claims in this passage. Explain why it is implicit or explicit.
3. Star the strongest explicit Theological Claim in the passage. Explain why you think this is the strongest explicit Theological Claim.
4. Write one claim based on this passage that could be used for the basis of a sermon.

KEY POINTS IN THIS CHAPTER

1. When analyzing the theological content of Scripture, it's important to distinguish between theological, anthropological, and ecclesiological claims.
2. It's also necessary to distinguish between explicit and implicit Theological Claims in Scripture.
3. *Explicit* Theological Claims clearly name the nature or actions of God, Jesus Christ, or the Holy Spirit. In an explicit Theological Claim, God, Jesus Christ, or the Holy Spirit is the subject of the sentence. An explicit Theological Claim is plainly expressed and direct.
4. *Implicit* Theological Claims suggest something about God, Jesus Christ, or the Holy Spirit but have as their primary focus a different subject for the sentence. Implicit Theological Claims usually are derived from either anthropological or ecclesiological claims. Implicit claims are indirect, so the Theological Claim must be inferred.
5. Sermons should contain strong, clear claims about who God, Jesus Christ, and/or the Holy Spirit is based on the explicit Theological Claims we see in the text.

DISCUSSION QUESTIONS

1. Re-read the sermon "A COVID-19 Easter: Mark's Gospel Is Just What We Need" in Chapter 2. What is the Theological Claim in the text that the sermon is based upon? Go through the sermon and see if you can find the sermonic claims. Notice how they are consistent with the claim in the biblical text and are applied to the congregation's context.
2. Ask an experienced preaching colleague to share one of their sermon manuscripts with you. Analyze the biblical text on which the sermon is based to determine the explicit Theological Claim in the text. Then read the sermon to find the sermonic claims. Talk with your colleague about their process for coming up with ideas for this sermon based on the text.

3. As mentioned in this chapter, the book of Esther does not explicitly mention God anywhere in the story. But you could make sermonic claims based on the implicit Theological Claim of the story. Talk with a preaching partner about possible implicit Theological Claims you could craft from that story. Then discuss ideas for a sermon based on those claims.

FOR FURTHER READING

Ronald J. Allen. *Preaching: An Essential Guide.* Nashville, TN: Abingdon, 2002.
 Chapter 2 ("Does the Sermon Honor the Integrity of the Bible or the Topic?")
 Chapter 3 ("Is the Sermon Theologically Adequate?")
Thomas G. Long. *The Witness of Preaching,* third edition. Louisville, KY: Westminster John Knox, 2016.
 Chapter 2 ("The Biblical Witness in Preaching") and Chapter 3 ("Biblical Exegesis in Preaching")

NOTE

1. Need a refresher on subjects and predicates? See Appendix F for a review of grammar that will help you in identifying explicit and implicit Theological Claims.

10

Identifying Theological Claims in a Sermon

In the last two chapters, you learned how to identify and articulate an appropriate and coherent Theological Claim and how to analyze a biblical text and draw a Theological Claim from it. In this chapter, we'll talk about how to identify Theological Claims in a sermon, as well as ecclesiological and anthropological claims. We'll do this by analyzing sample sermons for their Theological Claims. You may be wondering, what's the point in simply identifying how *other* preachers use claims in their sermons? Why not just teach us how to make Theological Claims in a sermon and then let us do it right away? Our rationale is that by first seeing the use of these claims modelled for you in others' sermons, this will help you to work through the process using "training wheels," if you will. Later, we'll take off those training wheels and you'll practice riding on your own.

For now, we'll begin by reading a biblical text and doing some preliminary exegetical work using the tools you learned in previous chapters. Then we'll focus on identifying the different types of claims in the text. This will help us to point out the claims in a sermon. We'll do this by reading a sermon and identifying the "God sentences"—the ones that explicitly mention God, Jesus Christ, or the Holy Spirit, as well as those that make claims about how we are to be or act in response to God either as individual believers or as a church (anthropological or ecclesiological, respectively).

THE IMPORTANCE OF BASING SERMONS ON A THEOLOGICAL CLAIM

You may be wondering, is it imperative that all sermons be based on a Theological Claim? We would argue in the affirmative, and here's why. In the previous chapter, we explained that sermons are distinguished from other types of speech precisely because they are rooted in biblical and Theological Claims that say something about who God is or what God does, as well as what that means for who we are and what we do as people of faith today. This is not to say that a sermon can't take its starting point from a contemporary situation or question, but it must always make some kind of claim that is clearly theological and biblical (even if it means preaching *against* the text, such as the example of Exodus 22:24 discussed in Chapter 8, where the divine call for violence is not something a preacher should echo).

As an example, we may recall that during the onset of the COVID-19 pandemic in 2020–2021, people were urged to wear masks to help stop the spread of the virus. So a preacher might have decided to preach a message advocating for the wearing of masks in church. But that message needs to be clearly connected to biblical principles (such as, "Love your neighbor as you would love yourself") or theological precepts (God desires for the vulnerable to be protected and kept safe, which means wearing a mask during worship services during this time of pandemic). A speech made from a pulpit that encourages people to wear a mask but does not find its grounding in biblical or theological principles is, well, merely a speech. It might be a good and compelling speech with important things to say. But it wouldn't be a sermon.

In other words, the premise of a sermon must be biblically and theologically based, and its argument must be as well. A sermon about the importance of wearing masks could be based on biblical principles such as "As you do for the least of these, you do for me" and would make the argument that wearing a mask is a way to live out one's Christian calling to do right by one's neighbors and those most vulnerable.

This is not to say that a sermon can't incorporate science, or the experiences of the congregation, or their history as a faith community. As our discussions about the Wesleyan Quadrilateral have shown, they absolutely should. But a sermon's primary purpose is to proclaim the Word of God in the midst of a faith community and/or the public square. A sermon needs to be in service of bringing about the Realm of God, however we see that manifesting for the particular time, place, and people to whom we are preaching.

"BLESSED IN *LA LUCHA*," ADA MARÍA ISASI-DÍAZ

To practice learning to identify sermonic claims, we will examine a sermon delivered by Ada María Isasi-Díaz at the Colgate University baccalaureate in 2006. Isasi-Díaz was a Cuban American educator, theologian, and innovator of Latiné theology. She is noted for developing Mujerista theology, feminist theology from a Hispanic women's perspective. The sermon we are considering for this exercise is titled "Blessed in *La Lucha*" and is based on Jeremiah 1:4-10.[1] *La luche* means "the struggle" in Spanish, which Isasi-Díaz explains in her sermon. We'll start with using our Exegesis Guide Chart to understand the historical background of the passage and what it might mean for us today. Then we'll analyze the text of Jeremiah 1:4-10 for its theological content. Finally, we'll discuss Isasi-Díaz's sermon and the choices she made for integrating theology and exegesis in her preaching.

Exegesis for Jeremiah 1:4-10

By consulting basic commentaries about the book of Jeremiah, we learn that Jeremiah was one of the major prophets in the Hebrew tradition and is believed to have written in a period between 650 and 570 BCE. He witnessed horrendous events in the history of Israel, including military invasion of his country, desecration of their holy places, idol worship, and even the sacrifice of children. The author of the text interpreted this to be a consequence of their unfaithfulness to God.

In terms of genre, the book of Jeremiah is a prophetic oracle that addresses the unfaithfulness of the seventh-century temple leaders and royal court in Jerusalem. Using literary criticism, we learn that the first chapter describes when Jeremiah received his initial call to speak on behalf of God against the sins of the leaders and the people—when he was "only a boy." Yet, as we will discuss, God assures Jeremiah that because this call was foreordained, God will give him the words to speak. Once God makes God's case that Jeremiah has been called and commissioned to prophesy, the following chapters lay out God's complaint against Israel and the plea to return to faithfulness.

Let's turn to the Exegesis Guide Chart to learn more about this prophetic oracle.

Occasional Exigence and Response

The Occasional Exigence is twofold. Historically, the problem is that the people, and especially the leaders, have been unfaithful to God's covenant. The Occasional Response is that God decides to appoint someone (Jeremiah) to be God's spokesperson and warn the people to repent and return to God. But there is a more personal exigence for Jeremiah—his hesitance to accept his prophetic call due to his young age. God responds to this concern as well, assuring Jeremiah that he will be given the right words to say and divine deliverance from those who would oppose him.

Literary Exigence and Response

The Literary Exigence positions this passage right after the first three verses that state who has written this book (Jeremiah), his lineage (son of Hilkiah), what kings were in power at what time during his prophetic acts (a span of forty years during the reign of King Josiah, followed by King Jehoiakim, and finally King Zedekiah), and what marked the end of his prophetic work (the captivity of Jerusalem). We will also note that Jeremiah is actually made up of different prophetic books that were written and put together after the death of the prophet. Whoever the author of this particular section was, it was important for them to present this as coming from Jeremiah in order to establish the authority of the oracle.

The Literary Response follows in verse 4 with God addressing Jeremiah directly, telling him that before he was even born, God knew him. So, just as the author situates readers in Israel's history in the first three verses, verse 4 situates them in Jeremiah's personal history and relationship with God.

Theological Exigence and Response

In terms of the Theological Exigence and Response, we can again see a twofold issue. In the larger view of God's relationship with Israel, we ask the question, what is God doing to respond to the people's and the leaders' unfaithfulness? On a more personal level, Jeremiah wondered why God would call "only a boy" and entrust him with such a monumental task of being "prophet to the nations." The Theological Response also works on two levels. God announces judgment against Judah in response to their sin. At the same time, however, God tells Jeremiah to "gird up your loins" (v. 15) and prepare himself to announce God's judgment in hopes that his words may turn them away from their sin. God also assures Jeremiah that even when the leaders oppose him, they will not prevail because God is with him (vv. 17-19).

More broadly, the theological assertion of this passage is that God cares about how the community's leaders conduct themselves, how they govern, and what they model in terms of right relationship with God and others. When leaders refuse to follow God's commands, the consequence is that the whole community suffers, as evidenced by what happens during Jeremiah's tenure. More specifically, when God calls someone to serve as a prophet, God equips them with the words they will need and protects them for the work they must do. As we will see, this Theological Claim will inform Isasi-Díaz's sermon. We can say, then, that the theological categories for this passage would be theological anthropology and theological ethics.

Contemporary Exigence and Response

Turning to the Contemporary Exigence, we can think about what sorts of present-day situations the Jeremiah passage might address. Since this passage is about God calling a prophet to confront the leaders for being unfaithful to the ethical requirements of God, we might imagine a situation in our own time of young prophets being called to address today's leaders—be they in the realms of religion, business, government, military, or institutions—who are acting or creating policy that harms the community or certain populations within that community. As we will see in Dr. Isasi-Díaz's sermon, her context is addressing college graduates, and so her preaching encourages them to take up the prophetic work of listening to those most vulnerable and advocating for their needs.

Having completed this exegesis, we can now dig into the more detailed work of analyzing Jeremiah 1:4-10 for its theological content, just as we learned to do in the previous chapter. This, in turn, will enable us to examine the sermon by Dr. Isasi-Díaz to see how she developed her sermon.

EXERCISE

Analyze Jeremiah 1:4-10

Begin by underlining any verse that includes God, Jesus Christ, or the Holy Spirit. Then mark the ones that you believe contain explicit Theological Claims—claims that tell us about who God is or what God does. Finally, star the one that you believe contains the strongest explicit Theological Claim. Here is the passage.

[4] Now the word of the LORD came to me saying,
[5] 'Before I formed you in the womb I knew you,
and before you were born I consecrated you;
I appointed you a prophet to the nations.'
[6]Then I said, 'Ah, Lord GOD! Truly I do not know how to speak, for I am only a boy.' [7]But the LORD said to me,
'Do not say, "I am only a boy";
for you shall go to all to whom I send you,
and you shall speak whatever I command you.
[8] Do not be afraid of them,
for I am with you to deliver you, says the LORD.'
[9]Then the LORD put out his hand and touched my mouth; and the LORD said to me,
'Now I have put my words in your mouth.
[10] See, today I appoint you over nations and over kingdoms,
to pluck up and to pull down,
to destroy and to overthrow,
to build and to plant.'

Now that you've analyzed the text, see if it matches our explanation. You'll see that we've included explanatory notes as well.

THEOLOGICAL ANALYSIS OF JEREMIAH 1:4-10

[4]Now the word of the Lord came to me saying,

[Even though this sentence contains the word "Lord," it's not a Theological Claim in and of itself because it's simply stating that God spoke to Jeremiah. However, this signals that what comes next may, in fact, be a Theological Claim if it tells us something about who God is or what God does.]

[5] 'Before I formed you in the womb I knew you,
and before you were born I consecrated you;
I appointed you a prophet to the nations.'

[Verse 5 is an explicit Theological Claim because it tells us what God did. God knew Jeremiah before he was even conceived. Before he was even born, God consecrated and appointed him to be a prophet to the nations.]

[6]Then I said, 'Ah, Lord God! Truly I do not know how to speak, for I am only a boy.'

[Even though it addresses God, this is not a Theological Claim since it's not saying anything about God. It is an anthropological statement because it's about Jeremiah himself.]

[7]But the Lord said to me,
'Do not say, "I am only a boy";
for you shall go to all to whom I send you,
and you shall speak whatever I command you.

[Though God is making a statement here, this is an anthropological claim because "you" (Jeremiah) is the subject of the sentence. However, there is an implicit Theological Claim, which is that God sends prophets, even those of a young age, to speak what God commands.]

[8]Do not be afraid of them,
for I am with you to deliver you, says the Lord.'

[This verse has both a command and a promise. So 8a is anthropological and 8b would be an explicit Theological Claim, which is that God is with Jeremiah to deliver him.]

[9]Then the Lord put out his hand and touched my mouth; and the Lord said to me,
'Now I have put my words in your mouth.

[This verse is an explicit Theological Claim because it tells us about God's action—reaching out to Jeremiah and giving him words to speak.]

[10] See, today I appoint you over nations and over kingdoms, to pluck up and to pull down,
to destroy and to overthrow, to build and to plant.'

[This is also an explicit Theological Claim telling us that God appointed Jeremiah as a prophet over the nations. Note also that Jeremiah's work requires deconstruction (pluck up and pull down, destroy and overthrow) before there can be reconstruction (build and plant).]

Determining the Primary Theological Claim for Jeremiah 1:4-10

From the analysis above, we see that we have four explicit Theological Claims to choose from in this passage: vv. 5, 8b, 9, and 10. Now we must decide what we think is the *primary* Theological Claim in this text. Remember that this is not an exact science. But we can start by process of elimination. Even though 8b is a strong claim ("I am with you to deliver you"), it's not as strong as the other claims in this text because it's too narrowly focused when we consider the larger context of Jeremiah's call. Verse 9 is also more narrowly focused because it only names that God gave words to Jeremiah. This is important, of course, but there's more to this passage than just receiving the prophetic words.

This leaves us with two possible claims, 5 and 10. In this situation, a case could be made for either one of these to be the primary Theological Claim. We might say that verse 5, "Before I formed you in the womb I knew you, and before you were born I consecrated you; I appointed you a prophet to the nations," is the primary Theological Claim because it tells us about God's relationship with Jeremiah (an intimate knowing before even being conceived in the womb) and God's decision to consecrate Jeremiah as a prophet before he was even born. The rest of the text flows from this initial claim and expounds on it. So a preacher could choose verse 5 as the primary Theological Claim.

Or you might decide that verse 10 is the primary Theological Claim, "See, today I appoint you over nations and over kingdoms, to pluck up and to pull down, to destroy and to overthrow, to build and to plant." In this verse, God gives the reason *why* Jeremiah is to prophesy. This is the outcome of the foreordained consecration and prophetic appointment. All the previous verses bring us to this hard-hitting claim, so a sermon could certainly be based on this verse as well.

Now that we've done our exegesis of Jeremiah 1:4-10, conducted our theological analysis, and determined the primary Theological Claims, we will look at the way Ada María Isasi-Díaz constructs her sermon.

ANALYSIS OF "BLESSED IN *LA LUCHA*"

Isasi-Díaz begins her sermon by acknowledging the reluctance she feels, paralleling Jeremiah's hesitancy, to "unveil the word of God." Yet, she follows Jeremiah's lead in praying for a clean heart and purified lips as she follows the command to speak the Word of God. She echoes the theme of being called, noting that it is God's hand that has brought her to stand before this assembly on this occasion, the baccalaureate for the graduating class of Colgate University. But just like Jeremiah, she is aware that she is being held to the highest standard of living up to what she preaches—and that she often fails. Nevertheless, she continues to engage in the struggle by standing up again and again. This struggle, *la lucha*, represents the work of Latiné women to continue to stand in the face of opposing forces.

From this struggle, she offers the graduates two valuable lessons. One is to learn how to stand up—not how to avoid falling. The second is that in getting up, one must be open to being converted to whom God is calling us to be (which is one of her anthropological claims in the sermon). She tells her listeners that the reading from Jeremiah presents three understandings that can help in this struggle, which she explains throughout the rest of the sermon.

The first understanding is also her first Theological Claim: "First, God knows us. God knows us in a most intimate way. God knows us in such a way that we cannot hide from God." We can see that she is drawing directly from Jeremiah 1:5 for this claim. This is the first understanding that Jeremiah offers for us in the struggle and reminds us that we can rely on God to know us and lead us where we need to go. This leads to her second point, which is to assure the graduates that being afraid at times is normal, but because God knows us, we are encouraged to stand up each time we fall. We can see that she is drawing from verse 8b for this point. Her third point is that God calls us to the prophetic task. Here she draws on both verses 5 and 10. She admonishes the graduates that they are responsible for advocating for those in need, "the poor, the oppressed, the marginalized, the exploited, the abused." The second half of the sermon is spent explaining what this prophetic work will look like.

She uses the image of the banquet—a frequent theme in the Gospels—to make her case that God invites all to the banquet of life. We will note that this is an interpretive move on her part and not immediately obvious in the Jeremiah text. She is drawing on multiple ideas from other biblical texts as well when she proclaims, "God's banquet is set; the party is all ready—just like this one of your graduation. Invitations have gone out, food has been readied, the house has been cleaned, the table is set. This is God's banquet of life to which we are all invited." This is another strong Theological Claim in her sermon. It's a direct statement about what God has done and is doing. Here you can notice a connection to Jeremiah 1:10; the charge to "build and plant" results in a house cleaned and a table ready for God's welcoming feast.

The image of a banquet is one that the students would be familiar with because of their graduation parties. So she is incorporating the context of her audience into her sermon, building a Theological Claim around both the biblical text and her listeners' experience. Thus, she moves from the feelings of anguish, self-doubt, and hesitancy at the beginning of Jeremiah (and in her sermon, as well as what the graduates themselves might be feeling) to the assurance of God's prophetic call and God's abiding presence in the midst of that call. In this way, the preacher is incorporating two of the four poles of the Wesleyan Quadrilateral—Scripture and Experience.

We might say that this Theological Claim—God's banquet is set—is the centerpiece of this sermon. It is the theme around which the whole sermon revolves. Isasi-Díaz took Jeremiah's theological premise of God knowing the prophet, equipping him (and us) for the struggle, and sending him (and us). She applied this premise to doing the prophetic work of inviting all people—especially the marginalized and oppressed—to God's banquet of life.

This is just one example of how one preacher took a particular text and developed its Theological Claims into a sermon. In the next chapter, we'll work with a text from the New Testament, perform the exegesis, analyze the theological content of the text, and examine a sermon in full for its theological, anthropological, and ecclesiological claims.

KEY POINTS IN THIS CHAPTER

1. A sermon's primary purpose is to proclaim the Word of God in the midst of a faith community and/or the public square. The sermon needs to be in service of bringing about the Realm of God, however we see that manifesting for the particular time, place, and people to whom we are preaching.
2. A sermon must have a theological premise that is connected in some way to Scripture (even if it means preaching *against* the text).
3. Theological Claims can be used anywhere in the sermon, depending on how the preacher chooses to construct the flow of the message.
4. Just as with identifying Theological Claims in a scriptural passage, we must locate (and write) Theological Claims in a sermon because they say something about who God is or what God does.

DISCUSSION QUESTIONS

1. In analyzing Jeremiah 1:4-10, we determined that there were two strong Theological Claims, one in v. 5 and one in v. 10. Ada María Isasi-Díaz chose to focus on v. 5 for her sermon, "Blessed in *La Lucha*," but v. 10 could work for a different sermon. If you were to sketch a sermon based on this verse ("See, today I appoint you over nations and over kingdoms, to pluck up and to pull down, to destroy and to overthrow, to build and to plant"), what would be the primary claim you would want to make about who God is and what God does based on this verse and the larger passage?
2. Knowing that the audience for her sermon was college students about to graduate, Isasi-Díaz chose to focus on God equipping those whom God calls to serve as a prophet, even (and especially) when they are in the struggle, *la lucha*. We know from our exegesis that the broader context for this passage is God announcing judgment

against Judah in response to their sin, specifically those charged with leading the people. If you were to craft a sermon that addressed the corruption of leaders that was hurting a community, how might you use God's words to Jeremiah to create your theological message?

3. If you were asked to deliver a baccalaureate sermon for graduates of a nearby college and chose to use Jeremiah 1:4-10 as your primary text, in what ways would you contemporize the Theological Claim that God sometimes calls young prophets to speak truth to power? Who are examples of young leaders today that exemplify the kind of prophetic voice that Jeremiah exercised? What is the sermonic claim you would want to make sure your listeners hear in your sermon?

FOR FURTHER READING

Ada María Isasi-Díaz. *Mujerista Theology: A Theology for the Twenty-first Century*. Maryknoll, NY: Orbis, 1996.

Ada María Isasi-Díaz. *En La Lucha/In the Struggle: Elaborating a Mujerista Theology*. Minneapolis: Fortress Press, 2004.

NOTE

1. See the full text for this sermon here: Ada María Isasi-Díaz, "Blessed in 'La Lucha,'" in "Ada María Isasi-Díaz Delivers Baccalaureate Address for 185th Commencement," Colgate College, May 21, 2006, https://www.colgate.edu/news/stories/ada-maria-isasi-diaz-delivers-baccalaureate-address-185th-commencement.

11

Sermon Exercise on Luke 13:31-35—"Jesus, Mother Hen"

Exegesis, Theological Analysis, Sermon Analysis

In the previous chapter, we examined a passage from the Hebrew Scriptures (Jeremiah 4:1-10) and a sermon by Ada María Isasi-Díaz based on the primary Theological Claim in the text. In this chapter, we will synthesize everything we've learned in Parts I and II, exegesis and theology, by working with a passage from the Christian Scriptures, Luke 13:31-35, and seeing how Leah developed a sermon entitled "Jesus, Mother Hen—This Is the God I Want to Worship." We'll start with the Exegesis Guide Chart to engage in historical and literary criticism of the passage. Then we'll analyze it to identify the claims in the text. Finally, we'll look at the sermon to identify its claims and how they grow out of her exegesis and theological analysis of the passage.

EXERCISE

Using the Exegesis Guide Chart for Luke 13:31-35

1. Use the Exegesis Guide Chart to collect what you learn from engaging commentaries on Luke 13:31-35 (see Appendix C).
2. Note that this passage is a narrative, so begin with determining the primary exigence and primary response for the literary aspects of the text. Where does this passage fall in the sequence of Luke's Gospel? What is the significance of where it is placed? What comes right before this passage? What follows immediately after?
3. Next, examine the Occasional Exigence and Response. What was going on for Luke's readers at the time this was written? What was happening in history? What was happening in their faith community? Why did Luke think it was necessary to include this particular narrative in his Gospel?
4. Now determine the Theological category, Exigence, and Response. What are the theological questions or issues raised by this story? Refer to the list of categories in Appendix D.
5. Finally, think about the Contemporary Exigence and Response. What are present-day issues or situations that might be parallel to the Theological Exigence that the passage raises? Can you think of analogies between the quandaries faced by the original hearers of this text and those we face today? How might you address those in your sermon?

Once you have filled out your Exegesis Guide Chart, discuss your findings with a partner. Then read on to see how Leah used the insights from her exegesis in the sermon.

EXEGESIS FOR LUKE 13:31-35

The Gospel of Luke was likely written in the late first century CE after having been passed down in oral form for decades. The tension between Jerusalem (the site of the temple for the Jewish people) and Rome (the empire that threatened and ultimately destroyed the temple) is apparent throughout Luke's Gospel. There are political ramifications in Jesus's story that weave themselves throughout Luke, including the scene in Chapter 13 where Jesus laments over the holy city Jerusalem in light of the power struggle between Herod, the Pharisees, and himself—all under the shadow of the Roman imperial occupation.

The genre of Luke is a gospel and is thus a narrative. Using the tool of literary criticism, we see that the passage under consideration is within the sequence of stories that tell of Jesus's teachings, healings, and miracles as he encounters both friends and foes on his way to Jerusalem to face the religious and imperial power structures head-on.

Now let's see how your notes about the passage compare with our exegetical work.

Literary Exigence and Response

We begin with examining the Literary Exigence of the text. Our passage in Chapter 13 comes just after Jesus has warned that those who think they have an instant "in" with God will be surprised to find themselves thrown out of God's kingdom while those who are presumably beyond the reach of God's mercy will be welcomed. Just as Jesus says this, some Pharisees approach him with the news that Herod is seeking his life, so he'd better escape while he still can.

The Literary Response is that Jesus instructs them to tell Herod, whom he calls a "fox," that he will not be deterred from his mission of healing and casting out demons since he is on his way to meet his prophetic destiny in Jerusalem. He follows this with a poignant lament about the city and its people that stones and kills prophets instead of heeding their words. Jesus then describes himself using the metaphor of a hen (a notable contrast to Herod's "fox") wanting to protect her brood. The passage ends with a foreshadowing of his entrance into Jerusalem, predicting that they will say, "Blessed is the one who comes in the name of the Lord," when he arrives. Indeed, this is what happens six chapters later when the crowds call out these very words as Jesus rides a colt into the city. Further, his words prefigure an eschatological event of his return on the day of judgment. We might also note that Jesus again laments over Jerusalem in 19:41-44 just after his triumphal entry amidst waving palm branches and an enthusiastic crowd.

Occasional Exigence and Response

Why does Luke include this story in his Gospel? We turn to the Occasional Exigence to think about how this story demonstrates something important to Luke's original audience. At the time when Luke's Gospel was written—forty years after Jesus's death and resurrection—his readers have witnessed the destruction of Jerusalem and the temple. They know that not only is the fulfillment of the promises of God delayed, but the evidence also seems to point to the obstruction or even obliteration of these promises.

The Occasional Response then, is having Jesus utter this doleful lament. His words about Jerusalem not only demonstrate that he foresaw what was to come, but also signals that the fall of the temple was neither unexpected by Jesus nor an indication that something has gone wrong with God's intention for God's people. The smashing hand of Rome's forces—aided and abetted by traitors within Jesus's own people (Herod and the religious leaders)—comes as no surprise to Jesus. Yet his response is not to run, but to continue in his mission, even as his heart breaks for his people. In other words, Jesus will fulfill his mission because of his love for his people and because of his courage in the face of murderous threats.

Theological Exigence and Response

Turning to the Theological Exigence, we need to articulate what theological questions or issues are raised by this story. For this text, there are several theological dynamics in play. In the broadest terms, Luke's readers might have asked, how can we reconcile our faith in God against the reality of Jerusalem's destruction? This question would be along the lines of theodicy, wrestling with the seemingly incompatible premises that God is all-knowing, all-powerful, and all good, yet evil persists. A related question is a Christological one: who is Jesus, and what will he do in the face of the colluding powers of Rome and Israel seeking his death? A third theological question is eschatological—what is the relationship between catastrophic events and the final judgment of God?

The Theological Response to the theodicy issue in this passage is directly related to the Christological issue. This story insists that Jesus is, in fact, all-knowing because he foresees the destruction of Jerusalem. Yet his power does not come from pitting might against might in the traditional authoritarian sense. Rather, Jesus's power comes from love—the love that he describes using the surprising metaphor of a mother hen caring for her chicks. As the story continues, we see that love manifest as a willingness to sacrifice his life for the sake of those he loves—even the "foxes" themselves. Thus, we come to understand that this kind of power is greater than that of Herod. In fact, it is even greater than the holy city of Jerusalem that stones and kills the prophets. This understanding of the theodicy and Christological implications of this passage, in turn, helps us arrive at a response to the eschatological issue. We can say that even in the face of destruction, persecution, and catastrophe, we can be assured of Jesus's power and love and so entrust our future to him.

Contemporary Exigence and Response

Turning to the Contemporary Exigence, we can move from our exegesis to posit some initial thoughts about how we might apply what we've learned to a present-day situation. What kinds of contemporary issues or situations might find resonance with the Theological Exigence of theodicy, Christology, and eschatology in this text? We could think about present-day circumstances of God's prophets facing death threats and what this passage might say to them. Or we might address the tension between church and state when it comes to the oppression of the marginalized and note that Jesus's response is one of courage and persistence. This passage could also speak a word to a faith community that has witnessed and endured destruction of its sacred spaces, persecution and oppression of its people, and the murder of its prophets.

So, what will Leah choose for the primary theological category to craft this sermon: theodicy, Christology, or eschatology? Recall from Chapter 4 that we can also bring perspective-explicit interpretations to bear on a biblical passage. In the sermon below, you'll see that Leah utilizes a feminist lens to focus specifically on Jesus's metaphor to describe himself—mother hen—and makes a case for how we can regard the nature of God in the face of various situations that may threaten our faith. Thus, she chooses the Christological response.

EXERCISE

Theological Analysis of Luke 13:31-35

1. Begin by underlining any verse that includes God, Jesus Christ, or the Holy Spirit.
2. Determine whether these verses are explicit or implicit Theological Claims.
3. Mark the verses that you believe contain explicit Theological Claims and note why you think they are explicit; in other words, what do they directly tell us either about who God is or what God does?
4. Star the verse that you believe contains the strongest explicit Theological Claim. Explain why you think this is the strongest.
5. Write down one sermonic claim you could make based on this text and its strongest Theological Claim that could be the basis for a sermon. Here is the text:

At that very hour some Pharisees came and said to [Jesus], "Get away from here, for Herod wants to kill you." [32]He said to them, "Go and tell that fox for me, 'Listen, I am casting out demons and performing cures today and tomorrow, and on the third day I finish my work. [33]Yet today, tomorrow, and the next day I must be on my way, because it is impossible for a prophet to be killed outside of Jerusalem.' [34]Jerusalem, Jerusalem, the city that kills the prophets and stones those who are sent to it! How often have I desired to gather your children together as a hen gathers her brood under her wings, and you were not willing! [35]See, your house is left to you. And I tell you, you will not see me until the time comes when you say, 'Blessed is the one who comes in the name of the Lord.'"

Now that you've analyzed the text, look at our example and compare it with your analysis. What did you miss? What did you see differently?

THEOLOGICAL ANALYSIS OF LUKE 13:31-35 WITH EXPLANATORY NOTES

[31]At that very hour some Pharisees came and said to [Jesus], "Get away from here, for Herod wants to kill you."
[Even though the passage is talking about the Pharisees coming to Jesus, it's not making any claims; this is just setting the scene.]
[32]He said to them, "Go and tell that fox for me, 'Listen, I am casting out demons and performing cures today and tomorrow, and on the third day I finish my work.
[This is an explicit Theological Claim. Jesus is saying what he is doing—casting out demons and performing cures, finishing on the "third day."]
[33]Yet today, tomorrow, and the next day I must be on my way, because it is impossible for a prophet to be killed outside of Jerusalem.'
[This is also an explicit Theological Claim because Jesus is again saying what he is doing—he is setting his sights on Jerusalem and will not be deterred from his mission as a prophet, even unto death.]
[34]Jerusalem, Jerusalem, the city that kills the prophets and stones those who are sent to it! How often have I desired to gather your children together as a hen gathers her brood under her wings, and you were not willing!
[The second half of this verse is an explicit Theological Claim because Jesus is not only describing himself using the metaphor of a mother hen, he is also describing his desire to protect those he cares for, even when they refuse that care. Jesus's use of metaphor in this verse reiterates what we learned in Chapter 8, that there are lots of metaphors for God and Jesus in the biblical text. Also, recall that explicit Theological Claims can rely on nonliteral (metaphorical) language.]
[35]See, your house is left to you. And I tell you, you will not see me until the time comes when you say, 'Blessed is the one who comes in the name of the Lord.'"
[Even though Jesus is speaking, this is an anthropological claim because the subject is "you." There is an implicit Theological Claim here, which is that Jesus can foretell what is to come when he finally enters Jerusalem. Thus, he is able to foresee the future, a gift that confirms his divine power. There is also an eschatological claim because it alludes to the future coming of Jesus.]

Determining the Primary Theological Claim for Luke 13:31-35

Our exercise above shows us that we have three explicit Theological Claims in this passage: 32, 33, and 34b. All of them have the potential to be primary Theological Claims in this passage. In this case, it would make sense to see verses 32 and 33 as one complete Theological Claim since they both tell us what Jesus is doing, the work he intends to perform on his way to meet his fate in Jerusalem, and his determination to fulfill his mission as a prophet, even if it means his death. 34b is another possible primary claim. There is a definite change of tone between 32/33 and 34, moving from boldness in the face of death to sadness in the face of his people's betrayal and coming destruction. This claim sets up a contrast between Herod's power as a predator (fox) and Jesus's power as a maternal protector (hen). This, in turn, has implications for how we think about the "mothering" nature of Jesus in the face of the myriad "predators" that threaten people of faith.

As you can see, there are two equally compelling theological directions one could take in this sermon: Jesus's courage and determination as a prophet and Jesus's mothering heart breaking for his "brood" in the city of Jerusalem. Having exegeted this passage and engaged in theological analysis, we can now see how Leah develops her sermon.

Introduction of "Jesus, Mother Hen—This Is the God I Want to Worship"

This is a sermon that Leah wrote for a Lutheran congregation she served in central Pennsylvania in 2013. She begins the sermon noting that most images and nearly all pronouns used to refer to God are decidedly masculine, such as king and father. She describes the pushback and looks of askance she sometimes receives when praying in a public place using female pronouns for God. She then goes straight to the passage in Luke to note the metaphor Jesus uses to describe himself: "a hen who gathers her brood under her wings" (v. 34). And she observes that this mother hen is facing some vicious foxes in the form of Herod and the religious leaders who are seeking his life. Not only are they angry with his insistence on outsiders being allowed into the Kingdom of God (a nod to the story leading up to this passage), now he has the nerve to call himself a "mother hen"! It's downright offensive!

"Nobody likes a mother hen," she observes. "Mother hens are overprotective, interfering, overbearing. They cluck and pick and watch constantly. Nobody likes a mother hen." But then she makes an abrupt move to contradict this statement:

> Unless . . . you are a vulnerable chick in need of protection. Unless all your life you've been deprived of a mother's care. Unless all you've known is the feeling of being abandoned, left to your own devices, stranded to face the fox all by yourself. Then maybe having a mother hen would not be so bad after all.

The rest of the sermon proceeds using the form of David Buttrick's "moving pictures" with short vignettes that illustrate the positive qualities of a mother hen (we'll talk more about sermon forms in Chapters 20 and 21). Each segment includes a brief story that captures these qualities, and all of the vignettes (four in all) are linked by the refrain, "I think those are qualities I want in the God I worship." The sermon concludes by describing Jesus at the crucifixion, "Like a mother bird, wings pinned to the cross, still sheltering us from evil." She ends by noting that "Today, I'm opting for the Mother-Hen-God. The God who welcomes all her children under her wings, no matter how they behave, or how they look, or what annoying and inappropriate things they do. The God who opens her heart of healing."

Let's look at the full sermon. Notice that there are certain sections that are underlined. These sections contain either implicit or explicit Theological Claims.

SERMON: "JESUS, MOTHER HEN—THIS IS THE GOD I WANT TO WORSHIP"

Section 1: Introduction

"How often I have longed to gather your children together, as a hen gathers her brood under her wings." (Luke 13:34)

1. Mother hen? It seems odd that Jesus would refer to himself this way, doesn't it? We're used to the image of the king and warrior. "Our Father who art in heaven." We're not used to hearing feminine images when thinking about God. In fact, some people get quite angry if you dare use a female pronoun to refer to God. "God is great, God is good, and we thank Her for our food. Amen."

(Notice the implicit claim in paragraph 1, that God can be imaged as both male and female.)

2. Does that ever give people pause and raise eyebrows when my children and I pray that prayer at restaurants or in the presence of other family members or friends! "God is not a woman. God would never be a female. It's just not possible. It's not natural. It's not right."

Section 2: Move to the Biblical Text

3. And yet . . . here is Jesus referring to himself as a hen, a mother bird. And this mother bird is facing some very vicious foxes.
4. Herod and the Pharisees are seeking to have Jesus killed for the way he is causing trouble throughout Galilee. He is filling people with thoughts about God as accepting all people, loving the unlovable, the unclean, the contaminated, the annoying. It's not enough that Jesus is saying that all these undesirable individuals should be allowed into our churches, into God's Kingdom. Now Jesus has to go and call himself a mother hen. That's downright offensive.
5. Nobody likes a mother hen. Mother hens are overprotective, interfering, overbearing. They cluck and pick and watch constantly. Nobody likes a mother hen.
6. Unless . . . you are a vulnerable chick in need of protection. Unless all your life you've been deprived of a mother's care. Unless all you've known is the feeling of being abandoned, left to your own devices, stranded to face the fox all by yourself. Then maybe having a mother hen would not be so bad.

Section 3: First Picture

7. Some years ago, I read a story about Margaret Cundall, a retiree who offers sick children from Chernobyl an incredible gift—the chance to boost their health. The nine- and ten-year-old children, from Belarus which

suffered 70 percent of the fallout from the nuclear disaster in 1986, take to Margaret like chicks running to a mother hen when she welcomes them in the summer. She is caring, physically demonstrative, and exudes warmth that draws the children to her.[1]

8. When your life is filled with suffering and pain, it's nice to have a mother hen. Caring, welcoming, warm. I think those are qualities I would like in the God I worship.

(Paragraph 8 is also an implicit claim. We can infer from this that God is caring, welcoming, and warm.)

Section 4: Second Picture

9. Did you know that mother hens have the ability to feel their chicks' pain? This is a quality called empathy, an ability that was once thought to be uniquely human. But recent studies suggest that animals may also experience empathy. "A new study has uncovered, for the first time, that mother hens are such attentive, caring parents that they 'feel' their chicks' pain. In experiments, female chickens showed clear signs of anxiety when their young were in distress. [They] found that adult female birds possess at least one of the essential underpinning attributes of empathy—the ability to be affected by, and share, the emotional state of another."[2]
10. Empathy. The ability to feel my pain. Being moved to protect me from pain. I think those are qualities I would like in the God I worship.

(Paragraph 10 is another implicit claim, that God empathizes with us, feels our pain, and protects us.)

Section 5: Third Picture

11. Delmer Chilton, a Lutheran pastor and writer, tells the story of going to get eggs from his grandmother's chicken yard one evening and hearing a racket. "A sudden raising of dust, flurry of feathers and scattering of hens and chickens, much screeching and squawking, and then, just as suddenly, things calmed down and an old gray hen emerged from the bushes with a large black snake in her mouth."[3]
12. Strength. Courage. No-nonsense. A bold female risking all to protect her chicks. I think those are qualities I would like in the God I worship.

(Paragraph 12 is yet another implicit claim about God's strength, courage, and no-nonsense. Note, too, the metaphor implies that God is like a bold hen unafraid to protect her chicks. Also, notice the pattern here and the repetition of "I think those are qualities I would like in the God I worship.")

Section 6: Return to the Biblical Text

13. Like that old gray hen, Jesus is not afraid of a fox like King Herod. Jesus is not afraid of dying, and he sends a message back with Pharisees that Herod doesn't even have to come after Jesus. Jesus will go to him, right to Jerusalem. Because that's what a prophet does—goes bravely into the spaces of danger to confront evil.
14. But when he mentions Jerusalem, suddenly the tone of Jesus's words shifts. They turn to words of sadness. He laments that the people of Jerusalem are like chicks that refuse to be cared for, looked after, or protected. "You were not willing. Your house is left to you."

(The underlined sentences in paragraphs 13 and 14 are all explicit Theological Claims because they are directly telling us about the characteristics of Jesus [compared to the old gray hen, brave, and direct] and what Jesus does [goes to Jerusalem to confront those who want to hurt him; laments about the people of Jerusalem]).

15. Says Chilton: "All too often, we have failed to understand or respond to God's love. All too often, we have turned God's word of love into a life of hate; all too often, we have turned God's call to repentance into pointing fingers and a call to arms. The sly fox of the world turns us away from that which is good and eternal and pulls us in the direction of those things that satisfy now but do not linger and live with us for an eternity with God."[4]

Section 7: Fourth Picture

16. The mother hen sat crying in my office. She was sharing with me the pain she felt knowing that she could not protect her daughter from the drugs and alcohol that had taken over her life. Her tears flowed as she recounted the many times she tried to bring her daughter back into the loving embrace of her family, away from the fox of addiction. But every time, the daughter made choices that pulled her further and further away. Instead of having the protection of those holy wings, the daughter served time in jail, wasted away in strangers' homes, and wandered the streets of the city.
17. But this mother looked me in the eye and said, "Pastor, I know God understands that I have done everything I can. I have to let her make her own decisions. I am at peace."

(In paragraph 17 the explicit claim comes from the mother in this story, that God understands her efforts to help her daughter.)

18. Knowing what it's like to love someone who doesn't want protection. Knowing the pain that comes in realizing that you can't save them, you can't make them change, you can't make them choose a different path. Knowing a mother's pain and yet giving her peace. I think those are qualities I want in the God I worship. After a moment, the mother added these words. "No matter what happens, my daughter knows my arms are always open to her."

(Here in paragraph 18, the refrain of the implicit claims about God reaches its climax.)

Section 8: Conclusion

19. Arms open. Heart exposed. Wings spread. Feathered breast exposed.
The mother hen, like the mother bird who fluttered over the nest egg of the world in Genesis . . .
Like the dove that fluttered away from Noah's hand over the receding flood waters . . .
Like the dove fluttering from heaven, hovering around Jesus as he emerged from the baptismal waters . . .
Like a mother bird, wings pinned to the cross, still sheltering us from evil.

(All of these sentences are explicit claims about God. Remember that explicit claims can be metaphors or similes, which is what all of these sentences contain in their descriptions of who God is and what God does.)

20. You can have your king-god. You can have your warrior-god. You can have your father-god. Today, I'm opting for the Mother-Hen-God. The God who welcomes all her children under her wings, no matter how they behave, or how they look, or what annoying and inappropriate things they do. The God who opens her heart of healing.
21. This is the God I want to worship. The God who feels what I feel, who validates me as a mother, who assures me that when I have made mistakes, when I have wandered from the right path, and when I have been overwhelmed by the foxes, those holy wings are still spread over me, protecting me, sheltering me, keeping me safe, loving me. Loving us all. Amen.

(The final part of the sermon draws together the various aspects of the image of the mother hen in a culmination of explicit Theological Claims that directly state who God is and what God does.)

COMMENTARY ON THE SERMON

Did you notice that sections 3, 4, 5, and 7 all had the ending of the section underlined? These are implicit Theological Claims. Rather than directly stating that God has these qualities, Leah merely states that these are qualities she wants in the God she worships. She is building her theological case for the character of Jesus as a mother hen through the use of stories and illustrations.

Section 6 paragraph 13 has the first explicit Theological Claims of the sermon:

> Like that old gray hen, Jesus is not afraid of that fox, King Herod. Jesus is not afraid of dying, and he sends a message back with Pharisees that Herod doesn't even have to come after Jesus. Jesus will go to him, right to Jerusalem. Because that's what a prophet does—goes bravely into the spaces of danger to confront evil.

You can see how Leah is drawing on her exegetical work to make a specific claim about Jesus and his characteristics, which are his fearlessness in the face of the powers intent on killing him and his self-understanding as a prophet.

In section 7, her story about the mother lamenting about her daughter contains another Theological Claim, one uttered by the woman herself: "God understands that I have done everything I can." Thus, a connection is made between the suffering of this mother and the lament of Jesus, who understands her pain. From there, Leah references other images of the Divine Feminine in the Bible (the bird-like spirit of God over the face of the waters of Creation, Noah's dove winging across the waters, and the Spirit as a dove descending on Jesus at his baptism), thus reinforcing her claim about Jesus as a mother hen.

The sermon's conclusion draws together the three parts of the Wesleyan Quadrilateral that support this sermon—Scripture, Reason, and Experience. You can also detect Tradition in this sermon, but in this case, she pushes back against the patriarchal tradition of the church that images God exclusively with male metaphors. The authority of Scripture guides the Theological Claim asserting the validity of imaging Jesus and God using other-than-male pronouns and images. Reason comes through the use of science in explaining the qualities of hens and the relationships between hens and their chicks. Experience is affirmed through the four vignettes that witness to the power of maternal love as a valid metaphor for God's love. In sum, these three poles actually push *against* the Tradition pole asserting that only male images and pronouns for God are valid. Instead, this sermon makes the case that Jesus's own self-reference, as well as his prophetic courage, enables us to expand our ideas about and metaphors for God that are liberating, comforting, validating of women's experience, and open to all in need of God's protective love and care.

KEY POINTS IN THIS CHAPTER

1. Exegeting a biblical text to learn its historical background provides important context for the interpretation of the text and the message of the sermon.
2. Discerning the Literary Exigence and Response of a text reveals important clues about the author's intent for the passage within the overall scope of the passage.
3. Uncovering the Occasional Exigence and Response of a text helps the preacher understand what was at stake for the original audience.
4. Determining Theological Exigence and Response guides the preacher to make appropriate Theological Claims based on the theological questions or issues raised by the text.
5. Perceiving the Contemporary Exigence and Response allows the preacher to begin to apply what they have learned in their exegesis to their present-day context and to bring a theological framework to the questions that are on the hearts and minds of today's listeners.
6. Performing a theological analysis of a biblical text enables the preacher to distinguish between the theological, anthropological, and ecclesiological claims of a passage and, in turn, to determine the strongest explicit Theological Claim of the text to use in a sermon.

DISCUSSION QUESTIONS

1. We saw from working on the Exegesis Guide Chart that there were three possible theological categories for Luke 13:31-35—theodicy, Christology, and eschatology. Leah chose to focus on the Christological aspect of the passage, but there are many other directions a preacher might choose. If you were to sketch out ideas for a

sermon on this passage based on the eschatological category, what contemporary situation might you address for which Jesus's words would be an assurance of hope? For example, in what ways are people experiencing persecution today? What are catastrophes that have occurred where people need a reassuring word that destruction is not the final chapter?

2. Leah chose to focus on v. 34 for her sermon. But as we noted above, vv. 32-33 are equally compelling Theological Claims in this passage: *'Listen, I am casting out demons and performing cures today and tomorrow, and on the third day I finish my work.* [33] *Yet today, tomorrow, and the next day I must be on my way, because it is impossible for a prophet to be killed outside of Jerusalem.'* If you were to write a sermon based on these verses, what is the Theological Claim you would want to make? What is Jesus saying about himself, what he is doing, and what is it he intends to do? Why would this be important for your listeners to hear? How might Jesus's prophetic courage inspire those who are facing "foxes" who seek to undermine, silence, or harm them for their Christian witness and work?
3. As you read the sermon, you saw that Leah used four illustrations to make her case that referring to Jesus using female imagery and metaphors was not only appropriate to the biblical text, it also has the potential to bring comfort, hope, and inspiration to those seeking expansive ways to think about God. How did you personally respond to the sermon? How do you think your congregation might respond to this sermon? If you were to use the structure of this sermon but substitute different stories that illustrate Jesus as a "mother hen," what examples would you use?

NOTES

1. Mark Welford, "She's Like a Mother Hen; Nominated for Caring Nature," *Evening Gazette* (Middlesbrough, England), August 15, 2009, accessed February 23, 2013, http://www.thefreelibrary.com/She%27s+like+a+mother+hen%3b+Nominated+for+caring+nature-a0205904357.
2. Asian News International (ANI)—All Rights Reserved. Provided by Syndigate.info, an Albawaba.com company, 2011, accessed February 23, 2013, http://www.thefreelibrary.com/Mother+hens+'can+feel+their+chicks'+pain'.-a0251104710.
3. Delmer Chilton, "The Fox in Our Henhouse," *Living Lutheran*, 2013, accessed February 23, 2013, http://www.livinglutheran.com/blog/2013/02/the-fox-in-our-hen-house.html#.USk5ZqUsmSo.
4. Ibid.

III

CENTRAL QUESTION, CENTRAL CLAIM, CENTRAL PURPOSE

12

The Central Question

Context, Congregation, and Community

In the first half of this book on preaching, we laid the groundwork for sermon preparation. Beginning with a deep dive into Scripture, we learned how to perform exegesis—ways to interpret the text within its historical and cultural context to determine the underlying issues, values, and theological categories that can have relevance for listeners today. We also explored other ways to critically read the texts that can show us the ideologies, assumptions, biases, and social locations that shaped not only the original text, but also traditional ways of interpreting it. Then in Chapters 8 through 11, we learned a method to analyze Scripture for identifying the Theological Claims within a biblical passage so that we can, in turn, craft a Theological Claim in a sermon. Not only did we distinguish between strong and appropriate Theological Claims and those that are problematic or weak, we also saw examples of using solid Theological Claims in sermons.

Now it's time move into the next steps of sermon-writing. In these next six chapters you'll learn the process for crafting the Central Question, Central Claim, and Central Purpose. Beginning with the Central Question, you'll think about the people to whom you will preach, what's important to them, what needs to be brought to their attention, and how the Word of God might speak to them at this particular time within the theological commitments of their tradition. In a sense, you will take the exegesis skills you learned for interpreting a biblical text and use them for "interpreting" the congregation and community in which you will be preaching the sermon. In other words, you will determine the underlying concerns, values, and theological assumptions of the people who will hear the sermon, the culture in which they will engage God's Word, and the larger social issues that are shaping our interpretations of the Bible.

Thinking about the context in which you preach will allow us to determine the Central Question for your sermon, the compelling inquiry that is driving the congregation to want to listen and the reason they should want to respond to the sermon. In turn, we will bring the Central Question and Theological Claim of the text together into what we will call the Central Claim of the sermon, the main point you are making that should mean something for our listeners' lives, for our neighbors near and far, and for all in God's Creation. After that, we will determine what this sermon intends to do and what it will accomplish—the sermon's Central Purpose. We might think of the Central Claim as the "so what" of the sermon and the Central Purpose as the "so that." In Chapters 14 through 17 we will focus on the Central Claim and Central Purpose, respectively. In this chapter, we begin with the Central Question.

THE CENTRAL QUESTION

The **Central Question** is the compelling inquiry for the sermon. In *one* sentence, it asks the question that is at the heart of our biblical exegesis of a passage and one's preaching context. This question captures the "existential oomph" for why you are crafting this sermon. Informing the Central Question is the basic inquiry: "Why does this matter?" In other words, why did the biblical writer think it was important to put stylus to parchment and write these words? Similarly, why should anyone today care about this text? And why should your listeners want to hear you preach about it?

Crafting the Central Question gives us the compelling reason for preaching the sermon. We might think of the Central Question as the "engine" of the sermon. It is what propels you to preach about this text at this time for this particular congregation. It contains the intellectual, emotional, and spiritual energy of the sermon. So how do we write a Central Question? It begins with understanding our preaching context.

CONTEXT—PREACHING DOESN'T HAPPEN IN A VACUUM

As we have discussed throughout this book, preaching is always done for a specific time and a specific place for a specific group of people—what is known as **context**. We must be thinking about our scriptural exegesis and Theological Claims while having our context always in view, in earshot, and in our hearts and minds. In this way, we will be integrating the four aspects of the Wesleyan Quadrilateral because we will be bringing Experience and Reason into conversation with Scripture and Tradition. Context is important because the lived experiences of each congregation are unique, and they change as time progresses. So does human knowledge change over time due to developments in science and technology, medicine and health, psychology, and many other fields that may intersect with our Christian ethics. These changes require a fresh interpretation every time we approach a biblical text.

As an example, a preacher who follows the *Revised Common Lectionary* (RCL) will have different approaches each year to a sermon on the second Sunday of Advent depending on what is happening in their congregation, in their community, or in current events. In this chapter and the next, we'll compare scenarios for two Gospel readings for Advent 2 in the RCL: one for Luke 3:1-6 in Year C and Mark 1:1-8 for Year A. We'll start with Luke 3:1-6. As you read this text, think about what is happening in your own time and congregation and how it might affect their reception of this passage.

> Luke 3:1-6
> [1]In the fifteenth year of the reign of Emperor Tiberius, when Pontius Pilate was governor of Judea, and Herod was ruler of Galilee, and his brother Philip ruler of the region of Ituraea and Trachonitis, and Lysanias ruler of Abilene, [2]during the high-priesthood of Annas and Caiaphas, the word of God came to John son of Zechariah in the wilderness. [3]He went into all the region around the Jordan, proclaiming a baptism of repentance for the forgiveness of sins, [4]as it is written in the book of the words of the prophet Isaiah,
> 'The voice of one crying out in the wilderness:
> "Prepare the way of the Lord,
> make his paths straight.
> [5] Every valley shall be filled,
> and every mountain and hill shall be made low,
> and the crooked shall be made straight,
> and the rough ways made smooth;
> [6] and all flesh shall see the salvation of God."'

In light of the season of Advent, a preacher may choose to focus on the theme of *waiting* or *expectation*. But how one preaches on that theme will look different from year to year in a congregation. Perhaps one year finds the church in a period of hopeful expectation as they are launching a new ministry initiative or a building expansion. But in another context, the waiting may be filled with dread and foreboding if the nation is preparing for war. In still another time, the church may find it difficult to juxtapose the hopeful expectancy of the birth of Jesus with the fact that a beloved church member is dying of cancer. All of this is to say that when we are thinking about biblical texts and how we preach them, we must take into consideration the circumstances of the listeners who will engage the sermon.

As we ascertain the context for our sermon, this will allow us to formulate a Central Question. In our exegetical work, we study the Scripture in its original context to identify the primary question of the author and their first hearers. We need to do the same thing to determine a primary question of our preaching context that can be addressed in this sermon. Our goal is to craft a single concise sentence, the Central Question, that speaks to the exigency of both the Scripture passage and that of the present-day situation in which we will preach.

EXEGETING THE BIBLICAL TEXT AND ONE'S PREACHING CONTEXT

Recall from Part I that we asked several questions to help us learn about the historical and cultural setting for a biblical text. Those questions included:

- Who was the original author and audience for the text?
- What is the genre of the passage?
- In what time period was it written?
- What was going on in history at that time?
- What political, cultural, and social dynamics were at play either within the text or in the background?
- What were the theological concerns of the author and what purpose did it serve to write this text at this particular time for this particular community?

In addition, we learned to draw on perspective-explicit interpretations to help us ask other crucial questions, such as:

- What would a liberationist reading of the text tell us about those who are marginalized and oppressed?
- From a feminist perspective, how is the text liberating or suppressing the witness of biblical women?
- What might an African American perspective help us understand about the experience of slavery, police brutality, and segregation?
- How could womanist and Mujerista readings shed light on the text from the perspective of African American or Latina women?
- What would a post-colonial perspective bring to the text in terms of understanding the dynamics of empire and those who resist hegemonic colonizing?
- How might Asian American concepts of ancestry, wisdom, and yin-yang intersect with the passage that could yield new insights?
- From a Queer perspective, what needs to be interrogated in the text about heteronormativity, or might the text itself be "queering" binary assumptions of its own time (as well as ours)?
- How could we read this text through an ecological lens to discern wisdom for the relationships between God's people and the rest of God's Creation?
- What does a disability reading of the text invite us to consider about the ableist assumptions on the part of the author and community, as well as in our own time?

In considering these perspective-explicit questions, you will want to focus on just one, maybe two at the most, in preparing the sermon so as not to overwhelm yourself or your listeners. However, if you take time to consider these perspectives each time you encounter a text, it is likely that you will bring to light insights and liberative readings that will enhance your preaching. In turn, your congregation will benefit from what you have learned, have their horizons expanded, and encounter a fresh interpretation of these ancient texts.

As you perform your biblical exegesis, you will also assess the context of the people who will hear this sermon, in a sense, "exegeting" the congregation. Not only will the questions above help you gain a fuller understanding of the text, they can also be brought into conversation with the questions you ask of your own preaching context. To do this, we recommend using Five Questions for Exegeting a Preaching Context.

FIVE QUESTIONS FOR EXEGETING A PREACHING CONTEXT

1. *What is happening in the world or society that is on people's minds (or that they need to pay attention to)?* This may be an actual event (like an election), an ongoing issue (such as climate change), or a more general theme (such as conflict and/or peace). These larger issues can have a direct impact on the congregation or simply be in the background.
2. *What is happening in the local community?* Again, this may be an actual event (perhaps conflict over the proposed siting of a landfill in the region), an ongoing issue (such as an increase in gun violence), or a more general theme (how to be welcoming to immigrants). Just as with global or national issues, local concerns can directly affect members of the church or simply be a backdrop against which they hear the sermon.
3. *What is happening in the congregation as a whole?* Perhaps they are in the midst of cottage meetings to discern the direction of the ministry for the next five years. Or maybe there have been a number of deaths in the congregation that are weighing heavily on people's hearts and minds. Whatever the situation may be, this question allows the preacher to think about their congregation as a faith community living, working, worshipping, creating, struggling, praying, and discerning together.
4. *What are individual congregation members dealing with?* Through pastoral conversations we come to know the day-to-day and year-to-year challenges and celebrations of those who will hear our sermons. For example, we become familiar with the struggles parents face when raising children, or the unexpected joys of visiting folks in a retirement home. We recognize the rage of those experiencing racial injustice, or the grief and lament of selling the family farm. While preachers must always protect confidences and ask permission if they want to share personal information about others to help illustrate a sermon, they can still speak in a general way about themes that come up in the lives of parishioners.
5. *What are the political, cultural, and social dynamics that shape our hearing and interpreting of the text today?* This question requires preachers to interrogate issues around privilege and oppression in all its forms, such as White supremacy, misogyny, heteronormativity, ableism, economic injustice, and so on. As with the perspective-explicit questions, we can ask, what are the assumptions and lenses that may distort a congregation's (or a preacher's) hearing and interpretation of the text? For instance, how a White, wealthy congregation may initially interpret a text could be skewed by their racial privilege, economic comfort, and being conditioned to center themselves rather than the voices of those who have been historically marginalized. Such lenses would need to be revealed and deconstructed by a preacher using perspective-explicit interpretations (see Chapter 4).

We might think of these questions using a chiastic frame (an X-shape) going from global to local to individual at the center, then widening out to get a broader scope of larger dynamics (see Figure 2).

These questions for exegeting your preaching context can be used to guide your interpretation of any scriptural passage for any congregation. For example, what questions does the expectant mother bring to Psalm 139 as her body "hems in" the child in her womb (v. 5)? What does the elected official in your congregation need to hear from James 3:26 about "bridling the tongue" when it comes to their words in the political arena and on social media? What similarities are there between the Israelites gathering manna in the wilderness (Exodus 16) and the guests who visit the church's food pantry each week? How might the immigrant farm worker respond to the story in Genesis 41:37-57 of Joseph pushing massive agricultural production to prepare for the impending famine?

As you can see, the possible angles for the Central Question are numerous. As you're preparing to formulate the Central Question, the ideas may spark quickly, or they may take time to percolate. But you won't need to, nor should you, incorporate all the different angles into one sermon. As you begin to bring the biblical text and your preaching context together, you should be able to discern one unifying question that can both undergird and provide the impetus for your sermon.

Five Questions for Exegeting a Preaching Context

What is happening in the world or society?

What is happening in the local community?

What is happening in the congregation?

What are individual congregation members dealing with?

What are the political, cultural, and social dynamics that shape our hearing and interpreting of the text today?

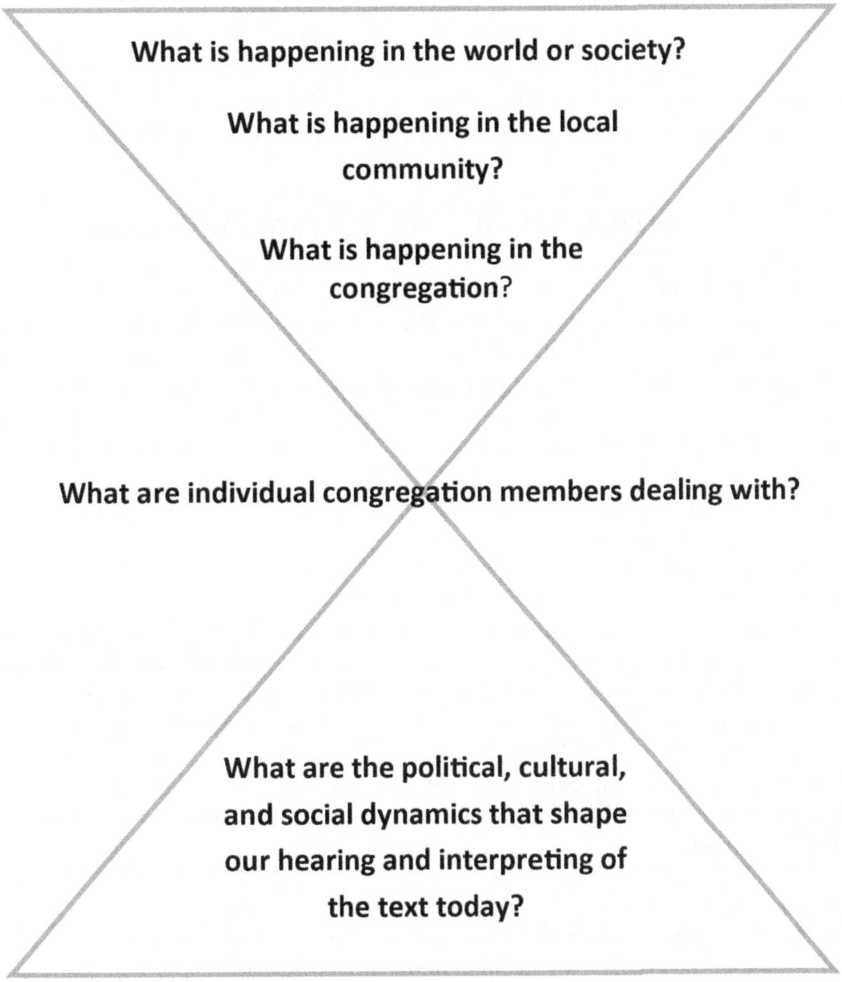

Figure 2

WHAT IF YOU DON'T KNOW THE CONTEXT IN WHICH YOU'LL BE PREACHING?

There may be times when you serve as a guest preacher or supply preacher for a congregation and won't have the kind of knowledge of the congregation that a settled pastor has. You won't know what individual congregants are dealing with. And you won't have more than a cursory understanding of what is happening in the local community or the congregation as a whole. However, in these cases, you can still use two of the five questions for exegeting a preaching context: *What is happening in the world or society that is on people's minds (or that they need to pay attention to)? What are the political, cultural, and social dynamics that shape our hearing and interpreting of the text today?* There are also ways to find out as much about the local context and congregation as you can when preparing to preach in a church you're not familiar with. See Appendix N, where you will find some tips and advice for guest preachers and supply preachers to help you prepare for sermons in these unique circumstances.

WRITING THE CENTRAL QUESTION

As we ponder the biblical exigencies alongside our contemporary context, we need to give space for them to meet and converse so that we can write the Central Question. We recommend a five-step process for this. You'll notice that for steps #1, 3, and 5, we suggest that you write three questions for each. This is to give you different options as you're refining your thinking about the sermon. Later, you may find that you only need to write two or just one as you become more adept with the process and your thinking becomes more streamlined.

STEPS FOR WRITING THE CENTRAL QUESTION

1. *List the questions the text/author is asking.* Based on your consultation with biblical commentaries and your Exegesis Guide Chart, write down three questions that you hear the biblical author or community asking that articulates what was happening in the world behind the text that makes this passage necessary. Or what was happening in the faith community that this passage addressed? Or what was on the hearts and minds of the author and/or listeners that necessitated this passage? As you continue to engage in your exegesis, you may change these questions, but this is a place to start.
2. *Answer the Five Questions for Exegeting a Preaching Context.*
   - What is happening in the world or society that is on people's minds (or that they need to pay attention to)?
   - What is happening in the local community?
   - What is happening in the congregation as a whole?
   - What are individual congregation members dealing with?
   - What are the political, cultural, and social dynamics that shape our hearing and interpreting of the text today?
3. *List the questions the congregation or community is asking.* Based on your answers to the Five Questions, write down three questions that you or your congregation are asking (explicitly or implicitly). Circle the one that seems most compelling. This may change as you work on your sermon, but it's a place to start.
4. *Write three possible Central Questions.* Write down three possible sentences in the form of a question that connect the biblical and contextual questions in a coherent and compelling way. Circle the one that seems to capture the most energy for your preaching about this passage at this time for these people. This is the Central Question for the sermon.

Note that a preacher can begin with the Five Questions for Exegeting a Preaching Context followed by the list of the questions the text is asking. In other words, you may decide that you want to ruminate about the situation with your congregation *first,* then contemplate the question of the biblical passage. Either way is fine as long as both the text and your context get sufficient attention.

It's also important to realize that you may need to revise your Central Question as you continue in your sermon preparation process. But don't completely discard the drafts of the other questions you wrote. These questions may find a place elsewhere in the sermon, perhaps as an opening "hook" or as a transition point.

GUIDELINES FOR WRITING THE CENTRAL QUESTION

As you are crafting the Central Question, here are things to keep in mind.

- The Central Question should be *one sentence* that concisely articulates the question of the biblical text and its relationship to the question of your congregation.
- It shouldn't be just a "yes" or "no" question. Ask it in a way that challenges you as the preacher to delve deeper into nuance and different layers of the biblical passage and your preaching context.
- Incorporate "question words" and phrases such as:
  a. Who, what, when, where, why, how?
  b. If . . . then?
  c. What does it mean?
  d. What can we learn?

e. How can we respond?
f. Who is God?
g. What is God doing?

EXAMPLES OF CENTRAL QUESTIONS

To give you an idea of what a Central Question can look like, let's examine some examples for two different biblical texts.

Central Questions for Genesis 15:1-18

The first set of examples we'll look at are based on Genesis 15:1-18, the story of God making the covenant with Abram. Here are three Central Questions from students who brought together their exegesis of the biblical text and their exegesis of their context.

Example 1: Why were God's promises of descendants and land important to Abram—and the Israelites in exile—and how do we trust those same promises as we are discerning our future?

Explanation: Notice that this preacher not only thought about the story itself (God's making promises of descendants to Abram) but also considered the context in which this story was originally written down (the Babylonian exile). Thus she used both Literary Exigence and Occasional Exigence when crafting her Central Question. Then the preacher drew on her Contemporary Exigence to create a parallel with her own context of a congregation grappling with an uncertain future.

Example 2: As God reassured Abram in his doubts, how will we, in times of pandemic and estrangement, remember God's promises and receive reassurance when we are in doubt?

Explanation: Notice the parallels between two words: *doubts* and *reassurance*. This preacher homed in on Abram's doubts about God's promise of land and descendants and applied it to their context of a congregation emerging from the COVID-19 lock-down period and feeling estranged from one another.

Example 3: How did God instill faith in Abram in his later years when all hope seemed lost, and how does that same faith come to us today in the midst of our anxiety about an aging and diminishing congregation?

Explanation: This preacher picked up on the detail of Abram's advanced years and thought about their own congregation made up of older members trying to sustain a diminishing congregation. For this Central Question, the word *faith* ties together both the question about the biblical text and the preacher's context.

Central Questions for Luke 4:1-13

The next examples we'll look at are based on Luke 4:1-13, the story of Jesus being tempted by the devil in the wilderness. Here are three Central Questions from students who brought together their exegesis of the biblical text and their exegesis of their context.

Example 1: What do the devil's temptations of Jesus mean within Luke's Gospel as well as for Luke's church; and how do we grapple with the temptations of materialism, power, and security that draw us away from God's Spirit and Word?

Explanation: This preacher used both a Literary Exigence (what do the temptations mean in Luke's Gospel) and Occasional Exigence (what do they mean to Luke's church) to arrive at the first part of their Central Question. Then she applied this to the parallels of materialism, power, and security in her own context, thus drawing on her Contemporary Exigence.

Example 2: How did Luke's church maintain their faith in Christ and know him as God while dealing with the temptations to abandon their faith; and how can we trust the Spirit to guide us by resisting the temptation to abandon our faith?

Explanation: Notice the parallel between the first and second part of this Central Question: *abandon their faith* and *abandon our faith*. This preacher thought about the ways in which the Lukan church was tempted by the many gods of the Roman Empire and drew comparisons to the many "gods" that tempt us today and draw us away from God. He also picked up on the theme of the Spirit guiding both Jesus and, consequently, us as well.

Example 3: How did Luke use the story of Jesus resisting the devil's temptation to strengthen the faith of his church; and how can our church use the Word of God to speak to our community that is tempted to give up hope in the face of horrific violence?

Explanation: This preacher was ministering in a context overwhelmed by gun violence and police brutality against Black Americans. So she delved into the context of Luke's church and why this story of Jesus's temptation was necessary for them to hear in the midst of persecution. Then she applied that to her own community weighed down by helplessness and despair. Thus, she drew primarily from her Occasional Exigence and Contemporary Exigence for this Central Question.

EXERCISE 1

Writing the Central Question for Luke 3:1-6

Try your hand at writing the Central Question for Luke 3:1-6. As you complete this exercise, have in mind a particular congregation who might hear this sermon.

1. *List the questions the text/author is asking.* Based on your consultation with biblical commentaries and your Exegesis Guide Chart, write down three questions that you hear Luke or his congregation asking that articulate what was happening in the world behind the text that makes this passage necessary. What was happening in the faith community that this passage addressed? What was on the hearts and minds of Luke and his original readers that necessitated this passage? What do you learn from the commentaries that can help you refine or redirect your questions? Is there a perspective-explicit interpretation that you could bring to bear on this text as well?
2. *Answer the Five Questions for Exegeting a Preaching Context.*
   - What is happening in the world or society that is on people's minds (or that they need to pay attention to)?
   - What is happening in the local community?
   - What is happening in the congregation as a whole?
   - What are individual congregation members dealing with?
   - What are the political, cultural, and social dynamics that shape our hearing and interpreting of the text today?
3. *List the questions the congregation or community is asking.* Based on these answers, write down three questions that you or your congregation is asking (explicitly or implicitly). Circle the one that seems most compelling. This may change as you work on your sermon, but it's a place to start.
4. *Write three possible Central Questions.* Write down three sentences that connect the biblical and contextual questions in a coherent and compelling way. Circle the one that seems to capture the most energy for your preaching about this passage at this time for these people. This is the Central Question for the sermon.

As you are formulating your Central Question, you might talk with parishioners, lay leaders, people within the community, judicatory leadership, or clergy colleagues to help in this discernment process. They may have insights to help you find the most compelling aspects of the question in the text and the question of your community, and how the two intersect. Write three drafts of your question and then pick the one that most closely captures the compelling inquiry for this sermon.

Once you have finished this exercise, you'll see in the next chapter how your work compares with what Leah did for her sermon.

EXEGESIS OF BIBLICAL TEXT + EXEGESIS OF CONTEXT = CENTRAL QUESTION

WHAT THE CENTRAL QUESTION IS AND IS NOT

It can be tempting to ask only surface-level questions when crafting the Central Question. These are initial questions that might come up during an initial reading of the text, such as what a certain word means, why a character does something in a story, or general inquiries about the theme or certain concepts in the text. Or we might ask initial questions about our context such as whether or not we are following the biblical teaching or what a concept might mean in a very general way for our time. While these questions can spark our curiosity and give us clues for pursuing our exegesis and thinking about our congregational context, they are not what we're looking for in the Central Question.

Instead, when it comes to the biblical passage, the Central Question needs to keep in mind what the original author and hearers of the text were living through, wrestling with, or troubled by that necessitated the story or letter or parable being written down in the first place. In other words, draw on your historical-critical and literary exegesis to help you dig deeper into the background of the text in order to unearth the question that was driving them. Use your Exegesis Guide Chart for this. What was the Occasional Exigence for the passage? The Literary Exigence? What is the theological category that undergirds this text and why was it important to this author and their audience?

In the same way, the "exegesis" of your preaching context needs to think pointedly about what your listeners are living through, wrestling with, or troubled by that this story or letter or parable could speak to in some way. That is to say, draw on your Five Questions for Exegeting a Preaching Context in order to help you dig deeper into the fundamental concerns that are driving the global, local, cultural, and personal conversations happening in front of this biblical passage. Use the last part of your Exegesis Guide Chart for this. What is the Contemporary Exigence for your time and place that this Scripture passage can speak to?

Here are examples of Central Questions that miss the mark.

Example 1: Have we repented for the forgiveness of our sins?

Problem: While this is an important question, it is vague and gives no indication that the preacher has completed the Five Questions for Exegeting a Preaching Context. Nor does it show that the preacher has engaged in exegesis of the text. It is also a yes-or-no question, which we want to avoid.

Revision: Why did John call for a baptism of repentance for the forgiveness of sins, and does his proclamation prepare us to hear a truth about ourselves we may not be ready to hear?

Explanation: This sentence demonstrates that the preacher is thinking about approaching the text using historical exegesis. It also indicates that the preacher has begun to think more concretely about the Contemporary Exigence in a more specific way. This is a Central Question that will be ideal for the preacher to address when working on the Central Claim, which you'll learn about in Chapter 14.

Example 2: What does it mean that "the crooked shall be made straight and the rough ways made smooth"?

Problem: This is merely an initial question that would come up in a first reading of the text. That doesn't mean it's an unimportant question. But it does not concisely articulate the question of the biblical text and its relationship to the preacher's congregation. It also gives no evidence of what the preacher has learned from their exegesis of the passage or their exegesis of their congregation.

Revision: What was the significance of Isaiah's prophetic "crooked and rough" imagery for Luke's congregation, and how might this shape our understanding of Baptism and what it means for our faith community?

Explanation: In the revision, we can see that the preacher is keeping in mind the larger scope of Luke's Gospel and what the images symbolize for his congregation. In turn, the preacher is thinking ahead to what the significance of these images could do for deepening the congregation's understanding of Baptism. When the preacher begins working on their Central Claim, this Central Question will prompt deeper thinking about sacramental theology and its relationship to faith formation for the baptized community.

Example 3: Why does John cry out in the wilderness and who is crying out today?

Problem: This is an example of surface-level questions for both the biblical text and the preaching context. They are too general and do not give evidence of exegeting either the biblical text or the preacher's context. This sentence needs more depth in its development.

Revision: What is the significance of quoting Isaiah's prophecy about "the wilderness" for Luke's congregation, and how can this ancient wisdom speak to us in our "wilderness" of grief at this time?

Explanation: In this Central Question, the preacher is making the connection between the Lukan text and the reference from Isaiah. Obviously, the preacher has been reading commentaries that indicate there was a reason why Luke referenced this specific prophet in regards to the figure of John the Baptist. The Central Claim will be able to speak to this historical and intertextual conversation. Also, this sentence shows that the preacher is aware of something going on in the congregation that needs attention—grief. In the Central Claim, the preacher will be able to draw implications from their exegesis and apply it to the context of their congregation's grief.

WHAT IS THE ROLE OF THE CENTRAL QUESTION IN THE ACTUAL SERMON?

You may be wondering, is it necessary for the Central Question to be incorporated into the sermon itself? The answer is that no, it is not necessary; however, you may find that it works well to articulate the Central Question directly in the sermon. For example, it may be that the Central Question used near the beginning of the sermon can capture people's attention and set the stage for the message you will develop. Or you may find that the Central Question serves as a helpful transition between the introduction and a section where you delve into the background on the biblical text. The Central Question may also serve as a kind of refrain if you use a sermon form in which you approach your topic from different angles, each time coming back to the Central Question.

However, it is often the case that the Central Question is never actually articulated in the sermon itself, which is fine. Its main purpose is to give you intellectual, emotional, and spiritual energy as you are writing the sermon. Even if the Central Question remains behind the scenes, it can still be detected in the way that it undergirds and empowers your sermon.

In the sermon excerpt in the next chapter based on Luke 3:1-6, you can see how the Central Question provided the existential energy for Leah's proclamation. She brought together her exegesis of the biblical text with her exegesis of the congregation to create a sermon that juxtaposed the context of the Scripture passage with the context of her congregation. For now, let's review what we learned about the Central Question.

KEY POINTS IN THIS CHAPTER

1. Understanding the context of the congregation in which we will preach our sermon is vital to the sermon preparation process. We need to think about the people to whom we will preach, what's important to them, what needs to be brought to their attention, and how the Word of God might speak to them at this particular time.
2. Just as we exegete a biblical text to get a sense of the historical setting in which the passage was originally written and received, we can also "exegete" our congregation and community. Likewise, we can ask questions from perspective-explicit readings to give us important insight. This enables us to determine the underlying concerns, values, and theological assumptions of the people who will hear the sermon, the culture in which they will engage God's Word, and the larger social issues that are shaping their (and our) interpretation of the Bible.
3. Thinking about context for the Central Question helps the preacher to integrate the four parts of the Wesleyan Quadrilateral—Scripture, Tradition, Reason, and Experience.
4. The Central Question is the compelling inquiry for the sermon. In *one* sentence, it asks the question that is at the heart of the biblical exegesis and one's preaching context.

5. Use the Five Questions for Exegeting a Preaching Context to help you exegete your congregation and community:
   a. What is happening in the world or society that is on people's minds (or that they need to pay attention to)?
   b. What is happening in the church's local community?
   c. What is happening in the congregation as a whole?
   d. What are individual congregation members dealing with?
   e. What are the political, cultural, and social dynamics that shape our hearing and interpreting of the text today?
6. Use this process to write the Central Question:
   a. List the question the text/author is asking based on your Exegesis Chart.
   b. Answer the Five Questions for Exegeting a Preaching Context.
   c. List the questions the congregation or community is asking either implicitly or explicitly.
   d. Write a sentence that connects the biblical and contextual questions in a coherent and compelling way. This is the Central Question for the sermon.

DISCUSSION QUESTIONS

1. Look back at the sermon in Chapter 11, "Jesus, Mother Hen." Use the Five Questions for Exegeting a Preaching Context to think about preaching on Luke 13:31-35 in your own context. Then use the process you learned in this chapter to write a Central Question you could use for such a sermon. How would the direction of your sermon be different from the one Leah took for her sermon?
2. For the sermon "A House with Many Rooms: The 'Living Stones' of a Seminary," in Chapter 7, there were two texts that required exegesis (1 Peter 2:4-10 and John 14:1-7). How did Leah bring the exegesis of the texts together with the exegesis of her context? Reread the section "Contemporary Exigence and Response" in that chapter and see if you can answer the Five Questions for Exegeting a Preaching Context based on what was described about the seminary community and what was going on in the larger society at that time.
3. Gather a group of preaching colleagues and practice using the Five Questions for Exegeting a Preaching Context. Choose an upcoming lectionary reading or some other biblical passage to think about preaching in different contexts. How do the congregational dynamics and concerns influence the direction each of you chooses for the sermon?
4. Using this same pericope, use the process to arrive at a Central Question for the sermon. Work individually and then share how you arrived at your Central Question. Talk through your thought process and explain how you chose the primary question for the text, for the preaching context, and how you fused them together for the Central Question.

FOR FURTHER READING

Sally A. Brown and Luke A. Powery. *Ways of the Word: Learning to Preach for Your Time and Place.* Minneapolis: Fortress Press, 2016.

Lisa Cressman. *Backstory Preaching: Integrating Life, Spirituality, and Craft.* Collegeville, MN: Liturgical Press, 2018.

Eunjoo Mary Kim. Ch. 7, "Preaching and Worship as Reflective Practical Theology." In *Christian Preaching and Worship in Multicultural Contexts: A Practical Theological Approach.* Collegeville, MN: Liturgical Press, 2017.

Thomas G. Long. "Biblical Exegesis for Preaching." In *The Witness of Preaching,* third edition. Louisville, KY: Westminster John Knox, 2016.

13

Two Examples of Developing the Central Question

In the last chapter, you learned the basics for developing the Central Question for a sermon:

EXEGESIS OF BIBLICAL TEXT +
EXEGESIS OF CONTEXT = CENTRAL QUESTION

Then you practiced this process with a passage from Luke. In this chapter you can compare your work with what Leah did for her sermon. Then we'll look at a text for a different second Sunday in Advent, this one in Year B—Mark 1:1-8. To be clear, what you write for these exercises will certainly differ from what you see in these examples because your context will be different than Leah's. But you'll be able to see the process for how she crafted her Central Question so that you can compare and contrast it with your own.

BRIEF EXEGESIS ON LUKE 3:1-6

While we won't take time to go through the entire Exegesis Guide Chart for this passage, we can say that after consulting commentaries, Leah learned that Luke's Gospel was written after the Romans destroyed the Jewish temple in Jerusalem in 70 CE. In the face of persecution, Luke wrote to encourage and strengthen his congregation. He also challenged them to live lives that were faithful to Jesus's teachings and to act in ways that align with the eschatological hope that comes through Christ.

Further, she learned that this passage announces the good news of Jesus Christ and sets the stage for John as the herald of Christ's coming. Luke situates the story of Jesus Christ within a wider historical and secular perspective by naming the rulers in power at the time of Jesus's birth. He also connects John's ministry and the future of God's reign in Jesus Christ to the prophet Isaiah's words, indicating that what is to come emerges directly from what God has done within Israel's past. Further, Jesus's ministry (and thus John's proclamation) is an eschatological fulfillment of Isaiah's prophecy. This means that when Luke's church first heard these verses, they would have recognized that not only was Jesus's ministry an explicit critique of the Roman Empire and its claim that Caesar was divine, but that the qualities of Jesus's reign align with that which was foretold by the prophets, and thus is legitimate and authentic.

EXAMPLE 1

The Central Question Process in Action: Luke 3:1-6

For a sermon Leah prepared to preach on Luke 3:1-6 at United in Christ Lutheran Church in Lewisburg, Pennsylvania, in 2012, she followed the steps to create her Central Question in the following way. For this sermon, she began with the biblical text and then thought about her preaching context.

List the Questions the Text/Author Is Asking

Based on her consultation with biblical commentaries and the Exegesis Guide Chart for Luke 3:1-6, Leah wrote down three questions that she discerned Luke and his community asking. These questions articulate what was happening in the world behind the text that made this passage necessary.

a. What is the significance of Luke including the names of the rulers, and what did it mean for his listeners?
b. When Isaiah wrote the words that Luke is quoting, who was the "messenger" he was referring to and what similarities and differences are there when considering the figure of John the Baptist in this text?
c. Why does God send the messenger into the wilderness and what does this signify for the Lukan church?

Answer the Five Questions for Exegeting a Preaching Context

Leah answered the context questions as follows. Note, however, that not every one of these questions is necessary or relevant for every sermon; this is simply a way to collect your thoughts and observations about your context:

- *What is happening in the world or society that is on people's minds (or that they need to pay attention to)?* Leah thought it would be interesting to substitute the list of political and religious leaders' names in this text with the equivalents of the current time. This would help people understand that they are situated in God's story, just as John and Jesus were situated within a particular time in history.
- *What is happening in the church's local community?* Just as Luke's text lists the rulers and religious leaders from the regional level down to the local, Leah decided she could do the same in this sermon. Naming these local leaders would hint at the local concerns of the community.
- *What is happening in the congregation as a whole?* This congregation was mourning the deaths of several pillars of the church in the past year. This was a "family" congregation made up of members who came from generations of families who worshipped in the church for more than 150 years. Leah discerned that this grief might influence how they would hear this text.
- *What are individual congregation members dealing with?* Watching beloved members of the older generation die had been difficult for everyone, especially the grandchildren. Leah knew this because the youth had shared their grief in conversations during youth group. She decided to ask permission of one of the youth to share her story in the sermon.
- *What are the political, cultural, and social dynamics that shape our hearing and interpreting of the text today?* There is a cultural tendency to push people to "get over" their grief and "move on." The tension between the commercialized happiness of the Christmas season and the grief felt by many in the congregation is something that Leah believed she should name and attend to theologically.

List the Questions the Congregation or Community Is Asking

Based on these answers, Leah wrote down the questions that were on the hearts and minds of her church members. There are many angles she could have used to approach these questions, but she picked just a few that had both specificity and general interest. Remember that for this church at that time, many congregants were in mourning even while dealing with the rush and flurry of the Advent season. Here are the questions.

a. In what ways does God meet us in the midst of our pain and grief?
b. How will we get through this "wilderness" when the culture around us doesn't seem to care about our grief, what we are feeling, or how we are coping?
c. What can the church do to help those who are mourning the loss of loved ones?

Write Three Possible Central Questions

Next, Leah overlayed the questions of the text and the questions of her congregation in order to craft the Central Question for the sermon. She wrote three possible Central Questions for Luke 3:1-6 that connected the biblical and contextual questions in a coherent and compelling way.

A. What did the wilderness mean for Luke's listeners, and how do we experience the wilderness today?
B. How did Luke situate Jesus and John within their larger context, and how might God be situating us in this story within our own contemporary context so that we can encounter grace in the wilderness?
C. What is the role of John the Baptist in preparing the people to meet Jesus Christ in the wilderness, and how might the church help those who are grieving prepare for Jesus Christ's coming today?

As we recall the Guidelines for Writing the Central Question (see Chapter 12), notice that each of these is *one sentence* that concisely articulates the question of the biblical text and its relationship to the question of her congregation. Also, none of these is a "yes" or "no" question; all three are open-ended, inviting reflection on some aspect of the biblical passage as well as her preaching context. Note, as well, the "question words" used in these sentences: *what* and *how* for A, *how* in B, and *what* and *how* for C.

As you'll see in the sermon below, Leah integrated elements of all three possible questions, but she settled on B.

Central Question for Luke 3:1-6: How did Luke situate Jesus and John within their larger context, and how might God be situating us in this story within our own contemporary context so that we might encounter grace in the wilderness?

With this question in mind, read the first half of the sermon with commentary. See if you can discern how the Central Question helped to "power the engine" of this sermon.

SERMON EXCERPT, PART ONE: JESUS MEETS US IN THE WILDERNESS OF GRIEF

Text: Luke 3:1-6
Second Sunday of Advent, Year B, 2012

1. When we read this list of names, did it make you wonder: who are these people and why should we care? Listen again: "In the fifteenth year of the reign of Emperor Tiberius, when Pontius Pilate was governor of Judea, and Herod was ruler of Galilee, and his brother Philip ruler of the region of Ituraea and Trachonitis, and Lysanias ruler of Abilene, during the high-priesthood of Annas and Caiaphas, the word of God came to John son of Zechariah in the wilderness."
2. Whew, that's quite a Who's Who, isn't it? At the time this was written, these names meant something to people. But when we read them now, they are just a list of long-forgotten rulers and political and religious figures. So why are they in this Gospel reading?

(Paragraphs 1 and 2 contain questions that come directly from the Central Question and are asked in a way that invites the listener into the historical backstory of the passage.)

3. Well, Luke is very concerned about placing his Gospel narrative very firmly in the context of history. The other Gospel writers are not so interested in such mundane historical details; they just launch right into the story of Jesus. But Luke takes time to tell us what was going on in the world when these holy stories were

unfolding. This is because he knew that the story of Jesus cannot be separated from the everyday goings-on of life. And notice that he goes from the most famous names down to the least famous names: emperor—governor—priests—John.

(In paragraphs 1–3, notice how Leah draws on her exegesis to address the implicit question people might ask as they are listening to the text: who cares about all these names we don't recognize? Here she is drawing on the Occasional Exigence and Response aspect of the Exegesis Guide Chart because she is noting the way the author of the Gospel is situating the scene in its historical context. Also notice that she makes a Theological Claim in paragraph 3: "the story of Jesus cannot be separated from the everyday goings-on of life.")

4. This is particularly of interest to us, as we are in the midst of this Advent season. Because it means that we, too, can place God's story in the context of our own story, and at the same time, frame our specific place and time within the workings of God's holy time. So . . . let it be heard among you, church! Hear ye, hear ye:
5. "In the fourth year of the reign of President Barak Obama, when Tom Corbett was governor of Pennsylvania, and Bob Casey and Patrick Toomey were the senators from Pennsylvania, and Tom Marino was the representative from Union County; at the time when Mark Hanson was bishop of the Evangelical Lutheran Church of America, and Robert Driesen was bishop of the Upper Susquehanna Synod, and The Rev. Leah Schade was preaching . . . the Word of God came to the people of United in Christ Lutheran Church in Lewisburg, Pennsylvania."
6. Now . . . where do you fit into this story? Again, we've gone from the big names to the little names: president to governor and local representatives, bishops and congregation.

(In paragraph 5, Leah immediately pivots to the contemporary context of the congregation by substituting the names from the text with equivalent names of secular and religious leaders of that time and place. Her question "where do you fit into this story?" invites the listener to situate themselves within the narrative. In this way, she is touching on both Scripture and Experience from the Wesleyan Quadrilateral.)

7. When the Word of God came to John, where was he? In the wilderness. I would propose that we, like John, are a wilderness people. Now I'm not saying we're all living out in the woods wearing animal furs and eating bugs for lunch. We live in a different kind of wilderness. Not necessarily a physical one—but a mental, emotional, and spiritual wilderness. Last week we talked about the unpredictable nature of our world—the threats of terrorism, violence, disease, and death, all menacing our sense of safety and peace. Each of our little lives is affected by the bigger forces, just as it was for the people who first listened to Luke's Gospel. These are wilderness times we live in.
8. You see, the wilderness is a place of harsh and difficult existence. And it is felt most keenly when death takes away someone we love. Someone who helped us live in this cold, dark wilderness and invited us to sit at their campfire with them, giving us warmth and tenderness, feeding our bodies and souls, nurturing our minds and spirits. And when we watch that person's life snuffed out before our very eyes, we find ourselves out in that wilderness feeling more alone, disoriented, and sadder than we've ever felt before.

(In keeping with the wilderness theme in her Central Question, Leah makes an interpretive move in paragraphs 7 and 8 to frame the wilderness of the biblical text not just as a physical place, but as a symbol for the precariousness of life driving the need for companionship, love, and sustenance.)

9. Having talked with many of you over the past year and conducted several funerals in this congregation, I'm guessing that's where some of you find yourself in this story—in the wilderness. Just last night I was talking with Carrie, who shared with me how much she and her family are missing her grandmother, Esther. As you know, Esther died this past summer, and it's been a time of mourning for both their family and our congregation. Carrie told me (and has given me permission to share) that on Thanksgiving it was so difficult not to see her grandmother at the head of the table. But Carrie's little nephew insisted that a place be set with Esther's name and a little pilgrim hat he had made.

10. As Carrie shared this with me, I was reminded how much I still miss my husband's grandmother, whom we called Mam Mam, who passed away in 2005. She was one of the purest souls I have ever met. Her house and garden was a place of refuge in the wilderness. Her food was cooked from scratch and fed us in ways that made us crave the taste long after the meal was over. And her unconditional love for us sustained us like that well-tended campfire, always available, always open, always providing warmth and light in a hostile world.
11. But since she has died, her absence has overshadowed all of our holidays. Thanksgiving will never be the same without her, always tinged with sadness. Christmas will now carry with it an empty space and a shadow where there wasn't one before. As Carrie and her family can testify, it is a bittersweet shadow, full of memories and tender yearning for her grandmother's presence.
12. So if a Gospel story were to be written specifically for you, Carrie, it might begin something like this: "In the year of the death of Esther, when Carrie was in her first year of college, the Word of God came to her and her family in the wilderness."

(In paragraphs 9–12, you can see Leah narrow her focus to specifically name a family in mourning. With permission from Carrie, Leah shared the touching story of what her grandmother meant to the family. She also related her memories of a grandmother in her own life. Leah then situates a family's personal story within God's story. Note another theological claim that emerges from this recapitulation: "the Word of God came to her and her family in the wilderness.")

13. As I said before, Luke is very interested in how the hand of God touches people in the very real places of their existence. What this passage says to me is that a voice calls out in the wilderness: "Prepare the way of the Lord, make his paths straight. Every valley shall be filled, and every mountain and hill shall be made low, and the crooked shall be made straight, and the rough ways made smooth; and all flesh shall see the salvation of God."
14. Of course, when you're deep in the wilderness, the temptation is to resist this voice and put off the preparation, saying, "Once I get out of the wilderness, then I can prepare the way of the Lord." After we get out of this war; after we get through this round of chemo; after the divorce is final, after, after, after . . .
15. No, says the voice—right now, right here in the wilderness. Even in that place that feels so hopeless and so helpless, we need to prepare the way. So what would it look like for us to prepare a way for God in the midst of this wilderness?

(Having made the case that 1) we in our contemporary context are situated in God's story, just as Jesus and John were situated in their contemporary context; and 2) the context for our congregation is one of a grief-filled wilderness, Leah is now transitioning for the second half of the sermon that will provide an answer to second part of the Central Question: how might God be situating us in this story within our own contemporary context so that we can encounter grace in the wilderness? *We'll come back to the second half of this sermon in Chapter 15 to see how Leah answers this question, as well as how the Central Question informs the Central Claim of this sermon.)*

EXAMPLE 2

The Central Question Process in Action: Mark 1:1-8

To demonstrate how a different context will alter one's approach to a theme, let's look at a biblical passage for a sermon Leah preached on another Second Sunday in Advent, this one for a different congregation eight years later using Mark 1:1-8, the Gospel reading for Advent 2, Year B. We'll begin by having you work on writing the Central Question based on your own context. Then you'll see how Leah developed the Central Question for her congregation.

EXERCISE

Writing the Central Question for Mark 1:1-8

To see the contrast of discerning the Central Question between different contexts, work with a partner on the questions below for Mark 1:1-8. Here is the passage.

Mark 1:1-8
The beginning of the good news of Jesus Christ, the Son of God.
[2] As it is written in the prophet Isaiah,
'See, I am sending my messenger ahead of you,
who will prepare your way;
[3] the voice of one crying out in the wilderness:
"Prepare the way of the Lord,
make his paths straight."'
[4]John the baptizer appeared in the wilderness, proclaiming a baptism of repentance for the forgiveness of sins. [5]And people from the whole Judean countryside and all the people of Jerusalem were going out to him, and were baptized by him in the river Jordan, confessing their sins. [6]Now John was clothed with camel's hair, with a leather belt around his waist, and he ate locusts and wild honey. [7]He proclaimed, 'The one who is more powerful than I is coming after me; I am not worthy to stoop down and untie the thong of his sandals. [8]I have baptized you with water; but he will baptize you with the Holy Spirit.'

1. Each person consult a different commentary on Mark 1:1-8 and then both fill out the Exegesis Guide Chart together. Compare your findings.
2. Work together to write three possible questions you hear in the foreground or background of the text.
3. Using the Five Questions for Exegeting a Preaching Context, interview each other about your congregations.
4. Each person write three different questions you think your partner's congregation might be asking implicitly or explicitly.
5. Each person craft three possible Central Questions that join Mark 1:1-8 with the concerns of your partner's congregation. Discuss the process together. Does your partner resonate with the Central Questions you drafted, and do you resonate with one or two they wrote for you? Is one more compelling than the others? Where might you go in the sermon with these questions?

After you have completed this exercise, read Example 2 to see how Leah constructed a Central Question for Mark 1:1-8 for her own congregational context.

Brief Exegesis on Mark 1:1-8

In Year A, the *Revised Common Lectionary* includes Mark's version of the "prepare ye" passage for Advent 2. Mark's Gospel was written around 70 CE, sometime just before or just after the Romans destroyed the Jewish temple in Jerusalem. We can't read Mark without understanding just how much this event traumatized the members of his church.

Like Luke, Mark quotes Isaiah's words, "the voice of one crying out in the wilderness: 'Prepare the way of the Lord, make his paths straight'" (Isa. 40:3). But Mark does not list the rulers at the time. He also does not include the verses about the valleys being filled and the mountains made low, as Luke does. Instead, a shorter segment of Isaiah's prophecy is used as the inaugural announcement for Mark's Gospel. Also, his description of John the Baptist is more condensed than what we find in Luke.

The preacher will also need to be aware that Luke and Mark have different nuances in their pictures of John. Though they are both drawing from similar source material, there are important differences between the presentations of John in Mark and Luke. For example, whereas Luke has John be a cousin of Jesus and sets his ministry more clearly against the rulers of the Roman Empire, Mark's description of John intends readers to identify him with Elijah. It was believed that the Hebrew prophet would return to mark the beginning of the messianic era, so it makes sense for Mark to begin his Gospel with John's pronouncement. Despite these differences, the themes of waiting and preparation for Christ's coming, sojourning in a wilderness, and heeding John's prophetic ministry are common to both Gospels.

You'll see that when Leah worked on the Central Question this time, she started with the Five Questions for Exegeting a Preaching Context, switching the order of the steps. As we noted in the previous chapter, flipping them is perfectly acceptable as long as all steps receive sufficient treatment.

Answer the Five Questions for Exegeting a Preaching Context

In December of 2020, Leah considered the themes of waiting and preparation in a very different context from when she preached on the Lukan version of the story eight years earlier. This time the congregation was St. Thomas Lutheran Church in Richmond, Kentucky, and the Sunday of this sermon was during the interregnum (the period between the election and inauguration) following the contentious 2020 presidential election. Notice that her answers to the Five Questions are very different from when she considered them in 2012.

1. *What is happening in the world or society that is on people's minds (or that they need to pay attention to)?* That Second Sunday of Advent in 2020 followed the most conflicted and politically divisive election in recent US history. As the nation awaited the final results of the election process, there was turmoil due to false claims about election cheating. The fallout was rippling across the nation on every level, including households, workplaces, and even churches.
2. *What is happening in the local community?* St. Thomas is a mostly White moderate-to-progressive church located in a conservative county of Kentucky. Members felt the political tension with their neighbors, with their co-workers, and within the local community.
3. *What is happening in the congregation as a whole?* This congregation had not met in person since March of 2020 due to the COVID-19 pandemic. They were meeting via Zoom and had maintained steady worship attendance, though they were missing one another and feeling the strain of pandemic restrictions.
4. *What are individual congregation members dealing with?* Congregation members had expressed their frustration about family, friends, and acquaintances who had been repeating talking points from conspiracy theories and disinformation campaigns regarding both the election and the pandemic. This put a strain on their relationships with their loved ones, those they worked with, and people in their communities.
5. *What are the political, cultural, and social dynamics that shape our hearing and interpreting of the text today?* The voices competing for legitimacy and political clout in the midst of the election season and pandemic created a tumultuous and fractured social environment. It was hard to know who to trust, who to believe, and how to respond with integrity and confidence.

List the Questions the Congregation or Community Is Asking

Remember that for this sermon in 2020, Leah was preaching in a context where people were experiencing polarization due to political divisiveness. Here are some questions she heard them asking both implicitly and explicitly:

a. How can we hold our community and our nation together when we are being torn apart by people who have such opposing political positions and conflicts are disrupting the functioning of our society?
b. What will it take to address the divisiveness in our culture, our community, and our congregation in a way that honors different perspectives without allowing harmful rhetoric to further polarize us?
c. Where is God in the midst of our fractured society and in our own congregation?

Rather than choosing a single question right away as the basis of the sermon, Leah tried a "mix-and-match" approach with the questions and came up with three possible Central Questions for the sermon, which you'll see further on. Later, you'll see how she narrowed down her focus with these questions.

List the Questions the Text Is Asking

Here are three questions Leah wrote that arose from her exegesis of Mark 1:1-8.

a. What is the significance of Mark beginning his Gospel by using the term "good news" and the title "Son of God" for Jesus Christ?
b. Who is the "messenger" Isaiah referred to in his original text, and what similarities and differences are there when considering John the Baptist in Mark?
c. Why does God send the messenger into the wilderness, and what does it mean to prepare a "straight path" for the Lord?

Instead of choosing the most compelling question right away, Leah simply let these three questions marinate as she considered the questions the congregation was asking either implicitly or explicitly.

Write Three Possible Central Questions

Next, Leah overlayed the questions of the text and the questions of the congregation in order to craft the Central Question for the sermon. Here are three possible Central Questions that Leah wrote after contemplating the significance of Mark 1:1-8 for a congregation waiting on many levels—waiting for the election process to resolve, waiting out the pandemic, and waiting for the coming of Christ during the Advent season:

A. As our congregation is in the midst of political divisiveness, who are God's messengers today, and how can we listen for their voices calling to us?
B. What does John's "straight path" look like for our community and our congregation, and how might we guide people to that path as we wait in this Advent season?
C. Who can we trust as we sojourn in the wilderness, and how can John's prophetic message help us prepare the way for Jesus Christ?

Which Central Question did she choose? In the next chapter, we'll not only see which of these three options she chose but also how she used the Central Question to inform the Central Claim, which then led to the Central Purpose. In the meantime, see Appendix H for a worksheet to develop the Central Question.

KEY POINTS IN THIS CHAPTER

1. The Central Question for your sermon is derived from your exegesis of the biblical text and the exegesis of your preaching context.
2. The Central Question is informed by determining the questions that the biblical author and their community are asking given what was happening in the world behind the text. Ask: what was happening when this was being written that makes this passage necessary?
3. When answering the Five Questions for Exegeting a Preaching Context, note that not every question will be necessary or relevant for the sermon; this is simply a way to collect your thoughts and observations about your context.
4. Listing the questions that the congregation or community is either explicitly or implicitly asking helps the preacher discern what is on people's hearts and minds that the sermon may be able to address.
5. Writing three possible Central Questions gives the preacher different options for connecting the biblical and contextual questions. Choose the one that best captures the energy that will drive the sermon.

DISCUSSION QUESTIONS

1. Before turning to the next chapter and seeing which of the Central Questions Leah chose for a sermon on Mark 1:1-8, which one of these three do you think would resonate most strongly in your preaching context and why? What is going on in your church or community that would lend itself to that particular Central Question?
2. Did you notice how Leah began the sermon on Luke 3:1-6? She stated the obvious question that might be on the minds of listeners as they first encounter the text. This is one technique for starting a sermon—raising the question that will be answered at some point in the sermon. What are other ways she might have begun this sermon? In Chapter 22, you'll learn other ways to start and end sermons.
3. If you could write the second half of the sermon on Luke 3:1-6, where would you go next? What would you want to say to your congregation knowing that you would want to answer this part of the question, "how might God be situating us in this story within our own contemporary context so that we can encounter grace in the wilderness?"

FOR FURTHER READING

Lisa Cressman. Ch. 4, "The Preacher as Trusted Guide." In *The Gospel People Don't Want to Hear: Preaching Challenging Messages*. Minneapolis, MN: Fortress Press, 2020.

Karoline M. Lewis. Ch. 3, "A Faithful Sermon is Contextual." In *A Lay Preacher's Guide: How to Craft a Faithful Sermon*. Minneapolis, MN: Fortress Press, 2020.

Thomas H. Troeger and Leonora Tubbs Tisdale. Ch. 8, "Exegeting the Congregation for Preaching." In *A Sermon Workbook: Exercises in the Art and Craft of Preaching*. Nashville, TN: Abingdon Press, 2013.

14

The Central Claim

Integrating Scripture, Theology, and Context

In the previous two chapters, we learned how to assess the context in which we preach our sermons just as we exegete the biblical texts from which we preach. This enables us to write the Central Question for our sermon, the driving inquiry that compels our engagement with the biblical text and with the congregation who will hear the sermon. In this chapter we begin by reviewing the process for determining the strongest explicit Theological Claim in a biblical text for the sermon so that we can bring the Central Question and Theological Claim together into the Central Claim of the sermon. The **Central Claim** is the main point you are making in the sermon that should mean something for the congregation, the community, and/or God's Creation. Having the Central Question and Central Claim will then lead into the Central Purpose—what the sermon intends to do and what it will accomplish, which we will cover in Chapters 16 and 17.

The Central Claim is the primary assertion of the sermon—in *one* sentence. Think of it as writing a one-sentence sermon to convey the essence of your message. This may seem daunting or even unreasonable at first. How can a sermon be boiled down to one sentence? However, we have found that engaging in this process of writing the Central Claim helps to keep the sermon succinct, on track, and coherent.

As you are learning to write the Central Claim, you'll see that it is informed by two things: 1) the Central Question that you derived from exegeting the biblical passage and your preaching context and 2) the Theological Claim that you derived from analyzing the Scripture passage. Together, the Theological Claim and Central Question are connected so that you can make a singular Central Claim that conveys both the message of the biblical passage and its implication for your preaching context. In this way, the Central Claim gives evidence of incorporating at least two parts of the Wesleyan Quadrilateral—Scripture and Experience.

REVIEW

What Is a Claim?

Let's review what we learned in Chapter 8 about the word "claim" and what we mean when we use this term. "Claim" comes from the Latin word *clamare,* which means to cry out or shout. It is related to the Latin verb *calare,* meaning "to call." Thus, a claim is a statement that asks for, calls for, or even requires a response. When a biblical text is making a claim about who God is and what God does, there are implications and ramifications for believers. Similarly, when a sermon makes a claim, it should mean something for the hearers and have an impact on their identity as Christians and as a church in and for the world.

PREPARING FOR THE CENTRAL CLAIM: STARTING WITH THE CENTRAL QUESTION AND THEOLOGICAL CLAIM

As we prepare to develop the Central Claim for the sermon, let's review what we learned about the two components that will inform the Central Claim: the Theological Claim and the Central Question. Recall that in Chapter 9, you learned the keys for analyzing a biblical passage to determine its strongest explicit Theological Claim:

1. Distinguish between theological, anthropological, and ecclesiological claims.
2. Distinguish between explicit and implicit Theological Claims in Scripture.
3. Explicit Theological Claims clearly name the nature or actions of God, Jesus Christ, or the Holy Spirit.
4. Implicit Theological Claims suggest something about God, Jesus Christ, or the Holy Spirit but have as their primary focus a different subject for the sentence. Implicit Theological Claims usually are derived from either anthropological or ecclesiological claims. Implicit claims are indirect and the Theological Claim must be inferred.
5. Though there may be several strong explicit Theological Claims to choose from in a biblical passage, pick the strongest explicit Theological Claim for the sermon that will speak to this particular congregation at this time.
6. If there is no explicit Theological Claim in the text, choose the strongest implicit Theological Claim for the basis of your sermon.

Then in Chapters 12 and 13, we learned the steps for writing the Central Question:

1. *List the questions the text is asking.* Based on your consultation with biblical commentaries and your Exegesis Guide Chart, write down three questions that you hear the biblical author or community asking that articulates what was happening in the world behind the text that makes this passage necessary. Or what was happening in the faith community that this passage addressed. Or what was on the hearts and minds of the author and/or listeners that necessitated this passage. As you engage in your exegesis, you may change these, but this is a place to start.
2. *Answer the Five Questions for Exegeting a Preaching Context.*
   - What is happening in the world or society that is on people's minds (or that they need to pay attention to)?
   - What is happening in the local community?
   - What is happening in the congregation as a whole?
   - What are individual congregation members dealing with?
   - What are the political, cultural, and social dynamics that shape our hearing and interpreting of the text today?
3. *List the questions the congregation or community is asking.* Based on your answer to the Five Questions, write down three questions that you or your congregation are asking (explicitly or implicitly). Circle the one that seems most compelling. This may change as you work on your sermon, but it's a place to start.
4. *Write three possible Central Questions.* Write down three sentences that connect the biblical and contextual questions in a coherent and compelling way. Circle the one that seems to capture the most energy for your preaching about this passage at this time for these people. This is the Central Question for the sermon.

Now you are ready to begin writing your Central Claim for the sermon. You will do this by bringing the Central Question into conversation with the Theological Claim. Remember, the Central Claim combines the Theological Claim you've chosen to be most relevant for your congregation with the Central Question we are asking in this sermon. Taken together, they inform the Central Claim, which is the primary assertion of the sermon crafted in *one* sentence.

KEYS TO WRITING THE CENTRAL CLAIM

There are two major requirements for the Central Claim. First, it needs to mention God, Jesus Christ, and/or the Holy Spirit and say something substantive about their nature, character, or actions. Second, it needs to make an explicit connection between the content of the biblical text and the preaching context, thus connecting Scripture and Experience in the Wesleyan Quadrilateral. (A sermon certainly can reference Tradition and Reason as well, but Scripture and Experience are a must.) Let's look at these requirements in detail.

1) *The Central Claim needs to mention God, Jesus Christ, and/or the Holy Spirit and say something substantive about their nature, character, or actions.* If there is no mention of who God is or what God does in your Central Claim, this means there is no theological content. A sermon needs to say something about the character, nature, or actions of God, Jesus Christ, or the Holy Spirit. Therefore, the Central Claim needs to do this as well.
2) *The Central Claim needs to make an explicit connection between the content of the biblical text and the preaching context.* If there is no biblical connection in the Central Claim, this means that there is no obvious scriptural basis for what you are saying. At the same time, if there is no connection to the preaching context, then the sermon will be too abstract. We might think of the Central Claim as the answer to the Central Question. Because the Central Question contains the compelling inquiry about the Bible and one's context, the Central Claim needs to make an assertion that responds to this question.

What the Central Claim Is *Not*

Before we go further, let's pause to clarify what the Central Claim is not. This will help avoid confusion and keep our focus clear.

- *The Central Claim is not a statement about the theme of the sermon.* The sentence cannot be merely a general statement regarding what the sermon is about. It must make an assertion about who God is or what God does and what this means for the listeners, the church, the community, society, or God's Creation.
- *The Central Claim is not a lengthy excurses describing the sermon.* It is not an outline or a paragraph. It is *one sentence* that contains the major contention or argument about the nature or actions of God and what it means for us today.
- *The Central Claim is not a sermon title.* Sermon titles are like teasers to catch the listener's attention. Or they can be brief summaries of the theme. But a Central Claim is different from a title; it must be a complete sentence with much more substance.

Further on, we will look at examples of Central Claims that do not measure up to the criteria we have set forth here. In the meantime, here are the steps for writing the Central Claim.

STEPS FOR WRITING THE CENTRAL CLAIM

1. Follow the steps for writing the Central Question. (List the questions the text is asking, answer the Five Questions for Exegeting a Preaching Context, list the questions the congregation or community is asking, write three possible Central Questions.)
2. Analyze the biblical passage to determine the strongest explicit Theological Claim you want to use for this sermon.
3. Write a first draft of the Central Claim drawing on the Central Question and Theological Claim. This should be the primary assertion of the sermon—in *one* sentence. Be sure that the Central Claim is derived from the biblical passage and your Theological Claim and that it provides an answer to your Central Question. The Central Claim should convey both the message of the biblical passage and its implication for your preaching context.

Note that steps 1 and 2 can be switched. As long as both steps are followed, the order is interchangeable. Also, know that as you work on the sermon, you may revise the Central Claim. But you'll want to make sure that the final version of your sermon aligns with the Central Claim so that your sermon is consistent with your intention.

THEOLOGICAL CLAIM + CENTRAL QUESTION = CENTRAL CLAIM

RHETORICAL FRAMEWORKS FOR THE CENTRAL CLAIM

While there is no exact formula for writing the Central Claim, there are rhetorical frameworks that can be helpful as you're drafting the primary assertion for the sermon. Here are some suggestions.

- Because [state the situation in the biblical text], God/Jesus Christ/Holy Spirit [state what they do], which means [implications for today].
- Since God/Jesus Christ/Holy Spirit [state some aspect of their nature or actions based on the text], we know that [implications for today].
- In the past [what happened in the biblical text], and God/Jesus Christ/Holy Spirit [action or response], which tells us that [ramifications for listeners].
- If [situation today], we can be assured that God/Jesus Christ/Holy Spirit [action or response] because [what the Scripture passage shows us].
- Because [what God/Jesus Christ/Holy Spirit] has done [based on biblical passage], today we are called to [how the congregation should respond].
- As we are facing [challenge today], we can turn to [biblical passage], which tells us [something about God/Jesus Christ/Holy Spirit], which means that [the meaning, or how we might respond].

These are just a few examples of how a Central Claim might be structured; there are plenty of other ways as well. We'll come back to structuring the Central Claim when we get to Chapters 20 and 21 and learn about different sermon forms. In the meantime, notice that all of these rhetorical frameworks mention God, Jesus Christ, or the Holy Spirit, they reference the biblical text and draw on the Theological Claim, and they suggest implications that may result from this claim.

EXAMPLES OF CENTRAL CLAIMS

To give you an idea of what a Central Claim can look like, let's examine some examples for two different biblical texts. These are building from the examples of students' Central Questions in Chapter 12.

Central Claims for Genesis 15:1-18

The first set of examples we'll look at are based on Genesis 15:1-18, the story of God making the covenant with Abram. Here are three Central Claims from students who brought together their Theological Claim (drawn from their analysis of the biblical text) and their Central Question (based on their exegesis of the text and their preaching context).

Example 1: God promised Abram—and, by extension, the Israelites in exile—a community, an identity, and a legacy, and God promises that our congregation's legacy transcends our limitations and expectations of what seems possible.

> Explanation: In analyzing Genesis 15:1-18, this preacher chose v. 18 as the strongest explicit Theological Claim ("On that day the Lord made a covenant with Abram, saying, 'To your descendants I give this land, from the river of Egypt to the great river, the river Euphrates'"). She brought that into conversation with her Central Question ("Why were God's promises of descendants and land important to Abram—and the Israelites in exile—and how do we trust those same promises as we are discerning our future?"). Notice that her Central Claim tells us what God did (promised Abram, as well as the Israelites in exile) and applied that to her own congregation's struggle in the face of an uncertain future.

Example 2: Just as God's promise reassured Abram, God's Word today gives us hope in the midst of our own doubts and feelings of isolation and separation.

Explanation: This preacher's Central Question was, "As God reassured Abram in his doubts, how will we, in times of pandemic and estrangement, remember God's promises and receive reassurance when we are in doubt?" So she chose a different part of the passage as the strongest Theological Claim than the one in Example 1. For her, v. 1 was the explicit Theological Claim she wanted to highlight ("After these things the word of the Lord came to Abram in a vision, 'Do not be afraid, Abram, I am your shield; your reward shall be very great'"). Abram's doubts paralleled her congregation's doubts and led her to write a Central Claim about reassurance in the midst of doubts and feelings of isolation and separation. Notice that the claim tells us two things about God: God's promise reassured Abram and God's Word gives us hope.

Example 3: God promised to be with Abram and bless him in his journey to a new land, so God will continue to accompany and guide us as we discern our future in a "new land."

Explanation: Recall that this preacher was in a congregation made up of older members trying to sustain their diminishing congregation. Her Central Question was "How did God instill faith in Abram in his later years when all hope seemed lost, and how does that same faith come to us today in the midst of our anxiety about an aging and diminishing congregation?" So, for her, v. 7 was the strongest explicit Theological Claim of the passage ("Then God said to Abram, 'I am the Lord who brought you from Ur of the Chaldeans, to give you this land to possess'"). The reason she chose this verse was because she believed that her congregation was also being called to a "new land," in a metaphorical sense, and wanted to pick up on that detail in her sermon.

Central Claims for Luke 4:1-13

The next examples we'll look at are based on Luke 4:1-13, the story of Jesus being tempted by the devil in the wilderness. Here are three Central Claims from students who brought together the Theological Claim they identified from the passage and their Central Question.

Example 1: Because Jesus resisted the devil's temptation, we are called to do the same, trusting in the Spirit and God's Word when we are tempted with the empty promises of materialism, power, and security.

Explanation: This preacher's Central Question was, "What do the devil's temptations of Jesus mean within Luke's Gospel as well as for Luke's church; and how do we grapple with the temptations of materialism, power, and security that draw us away from God's Spirit and Word?" But figuring out the strongest Theological Claim in Luke 4:1-13 was a challenge because there is only one explicit claim in the passage, which is v. 1, "Jesus, full of the Holy Spirit, returned from the Jordan and was led by the Spirit in the wilderness." This tells us something about Jesus (that he was full of the Holy Spirit) and what the Spirit did (led him into the wilderness). So she knew she would have to draw on the implicit Theological Claims in the text based on what she could infer from Jesus's quotations of Scripture in the three temptations. This led her to focus on how Jesus resisted the lures of materialism, power, and security. Then she used that to make a claim that meant something for her congregation as well, that they should also trust the Spirit and God's Word.

Example 2: God does not promise that we will avoid the forces of evil and temptation but does give us the Spirit and the Scriptures that speak to us and help us resist.

Explanation: Unlike the previous example, this preacher did choose v. 1 as the strongest Theological Claim, "Jesus, full of the Holy Spirit, returned from the Jordan and was led by the Spirit in the wilderness." He was intrigued by the fact that it was the *Spirit* that led Jesus into the wilderness where he was tempted. In his exegesis of the passage and thinking what the story meant for the people in Luke's church, he wrote this Central Question: "How did Luke's church maintain their faith in Christ and know him as God while dealing with the temptations to abandon their faith; and how can we trust the Spirit to guide us by resisting the temptation to abandon our faith?" This led him to write a Central Claim that stated very succinctly what God does when we are faced with temptation, which is to give us the Spirit and the Scriptures to help us resist.

Example 3: Just as Jesus turned to God's Word during the Devil's temptation, empowered by the Holy Spirit, we can turn to God's Word when violence and oppression threaten to separate us from God and weaken our faith.

Explanation: Recall that this preacher was ministering in a church that was dealing with gun violence and police brutality against Black Americans. Her concern led her to write this Central Question: "How did Luke use the story of Jesus resisting the devil's temptation to strengthen the faith of his church; and how can our church use the Word of God to speak to our community that is tempted to give up hope in the face of horrific violence?" Like the preacher in Example 1, she drew on the implicit Theological Claim about Jesus's ability to resist the Devil's temptation, and thus giving them strength to resist temptation and bolster their faith.

WHAT IS THE ROLE OF THE CENTRAL CLAIM IN THE ACTUAL SERMON?

You may be wondering, is it necessary for the Central Claim to be incorporated into the sermon itself? As with the Central Question, it's not required to put the Central Claim word for word in the sermon. But there may be times when stating the Central Claim within the sermon is useful. For example, if you are creating a deductive sermon where you state your thesis near the beginning of the sermon, the Central Claim might be the singular opening and controlling refrain for the sermon. Conversely, if you are using an inductive sermon form, you may wait until closer to the end of the sermon to reveal the Central Claim. (Note: We will explain the difference between deductive and inductive sermon forms in Chapter 20.) You may also find that you include only a portion of the Central Claim in the sermon (which you'll see illustrated in the sermon on Luke 3:1-6 further on).

Yet, the Central Claim does not necessarily have to be explicitly stated in the sermon. You may find that the Theological Claim you wrote leading up to the Central Claim is more apt for the sermon. Or the sermon may be supported by the Theological Claim, Central Question, and Central Claim without any of them making an explicit appearance in the sermon. Remember that the Central Claim's purpose is to provide the *direction* for your sermon. The biblical and theological aspects of this statement are like the two rails of a train track. If those rails aren't solid and aligned, your sermon is likely to go off track. So even if the Central Claim isn't obvious within the sermon itself, its guidance should still be apparent.

EXERCISE

Writing a Central Claim for Mark 1:1-8

In the previous chapter, you experimented with writing the Central Question for Mark 1:1-8 by working with a partner to think about each other's preaching contexts. Now it's time to practice writing the Central Claim for this passage. Follow the steps below to write a Central Claim for a possible sermon. You may draw from the work you did with your partner from the previous exercise in Chapter 13 for steps 1–4. Here is the passage.

> Mark 1:1-8
> The beginning of the good news of Jesus Christ, the Son of God.
> [2] As it is written in the prophet Isaiah,
> 'See, I am sending my messenger ahead of you,
> who will prepare your way;
> [3] the voice of one crying out in the wilderness:
> "Prepare the way of the Lord,
> make his paths straight."'
> [4]John the baptizer appeared in the wilderness, proclaiming a baptism of repentance for the forgiveness of sins. [5]And people from the whole Judean countryside and all the people of Jerusalem were going out to him, and were baptized by him in the river Jordan, confessing their sins. [6]Now John was clothed with camel's hair, with a leather belt around his waist, and he ate locusts and wild honey. [7]He proclaimed, 'The one who is more powerful than I is coming after me; I am not worthy to stoop down and untie the thong of his sandals. [8]I have baptized you with water; but he will baptize you with the Holy Spirit.'

1. *List the questions the text is asking.* Based on your consultation with biblical commentaries and your Exegesis Guide Chart on Mark 1:1-8, write down three questions that you hear Mark or his community asking that articulate what was happening in the world behind the text that makes this passage necessary. Or what was happening in the faith community that this passage addressed. Or what was on the hearts and minds of the author and/or listeners that necessitated this passage.

2. *Answer the Five Questions for Exegeting a Preaching Context*:

   - What is happening in the world or society that is on people's minds (or that they need to pay attention to)?
   - What is happening in the local community?
   - What is happening in the congregation as a whole?
   - What are individual congregation members dealing with?
   - What are the political, cultural, and social dynamics that shape our hearing and interpreting of the text today?

3. *List the questions the congregation or community is asking.* Based on your answers to the Five Questions, write down three questions that you or your congregation are asking (explicitly or implicitly). Circle the one that seems most compelling. This may change as you work on your sermon, but it's a place to start.
4. *Write three possible Central Questions.* Write down three sentences that connect the biblical and contextual questions in a coherent and compelling way. Circle the one that seems to capture the most energy for your preaching about this passage at this time for these people. This is the Central Question for the sermon.
5. *Analyze Mark 1:1-8 to determine the strongest explicit Theological Claim you want to use for this sermon.*
6. *Write a first draft of the Central Claim for Mark 1:1-8 drawing on the Theological Claim and Central Question.* This should be the primary assertion of the sermon—in *one* sentence. Be sure that the Central Claim is derived from the biblical passage and your Theological Claim and that it provides an answer to your Central Question. The Central Claim should convey both the message of the biblical passage and its implication for your preaching context.

Once you and your partner have finished this exercise, share your work with each other and discuss the process. Then look at the example below to see how it compares with what Leah did in writing the Central Claim for a sermon on Mark 1:1-8.

EXAMPLE OF THE CENTRAL CLAIM IN ACTION: MARK 1:1-8

In Chapter 13, we saw how Leah worked on the Central Question for the context of a sermon to be preached on Mark 1:1-8 on the Second Sunday of Advent in 2020. This was a time of disinformation about the presidential election and the COVID-19 pandemic. There were three possible Central Questions she wrote:

A. As our congregation is in the wilderness of political divisiveness, who are God's messengers today, and how can we listen for their voices calling to us?
B. What does John's "straight path" look like for our community and our congregation, and how might we guide people to that path as we wait in this tumultuous Advent season?
C. Who can we trust as we sojourn in the wilderness, and how can John's prophetic message help us prepare the way for Jesus Christ?

Before choosing which one she wanted for this sermon, she went back to the text to perform a theological analysis and determine the strongest Theological Claim she wanted to use for this sermon. Below is the text. You'll see that she underlined every verse that mentioned God or Jesus Christ. Then she determined whether these were implicit or explicit Theological Claims.

Mark 1:1-8
The beginning of the good news of Jesus Christ, the Son of God.
[2] As it is written in the prophet Isaiah,
'See, I am sending my messenger ahead of you,

who will prepare your way;
[3] the voice of one crying out in the wilderness:
"Prepare the way of the Lord,
make his paths straight."'
[4]John the baptizer appeared in the wilderness, proclaiming a baptism of repentance for the forgiveness of sins. [5]And people from the whole Judean countryside and all the people of Jerusalem were going out to him, and were baptized by him in the river Jordan, confessing their sins. [6]Now John was clothed with camel's hair, with a leather belt around his waist, and he ate locusts and wild honey. [7]He proclaimed, 'The one who is more powerful than I is coming after me; I am not worthy to stoop down and untie the thong of his sandals. [8]I have baptized you with water; but he will baptize you with the Holy Spirit.'

Theological Analysis of Mark 1:1-8

V. 1 is an explicit Theological Claim. Though it is not a complete sentence in English, it is an announcement that everything that follows is about Jesus Christ. This verse also claims that Jesus Christ is the Son of God, which describes who he is.

V. 2b is an explicit Theological Claim, because the "I" of the sentence is God, so the sentence is telling us what God has done, which was to send a messenger to prepare for the coming of God.[1]

V. 3 is an anthropological claim because the subject of the sentence is *you*. The implicit Theological Claim is that the one sent from God is coming and expects believers to prepare by "making his paths straight."

V. 7 is an explicit Theological Claim because John is telling us something about Jesus (that he is more powerful than him and will follow him).

V. 8b is an explicit Theological Claim, telling us what Jesus will do (baptize us with the Holy Spirit).

For this passage, Leah determined that v. 2b was the strongest Theological Claim of the passage because of its connection to Isaiah and because it sets up everything else that follows in the passage. Note that an argument could also be made for either v. 7 or v. 8 to be the primary Theological Claim of this passage since they make a strong Christological claim. However, keeping in mind her context, v. 2b was the direction she chose.

Here is the Theological Claim she crafted:

To prepare God's people for receiving the Messiah, God sent John to call for making a direct path so that we may encounter Jesus Christ.

As a reminder, the Theological Claim you crafted is likely different from Leah's due to how you thought about your own context as well as the theological family or denomination within which you are situated. Recall that in Chapter 8, we briefly discussed the fact that preachers make Theological Claims in connection with their ecclesial and doctrinal commitments and identities. Preachers are influenced by the theological worldview with which they identify, whether that is neo-Orthodox, liberal, evangelical, post-liberal, feminist, post-colonial, and so on. Also, their Theological Claims will be shaped by their doctrinal views on things such as sanctification or sin or the sacraments, to name a few. For example, Leah locates herself within a progressive Christian Lutheran theological framework with a strong commitment to feminism, ecological theology, and social justice. This constellation will influence and shape her Theological Claim and thus her Central Claim. But a preacher in another denomination embedded within a different theological family will likely have a different approach.

In any case, once she wrote her Theological Claim, Leah was able to determine which of the Central Questions was most appropriate for the direction taking shape for this sermon.

She chose B: *What does John's "straight path" look like for our community and our congregation, and how might we guide people to that path as we wait in this Advent season?* Even though A and C didn't make the cut, as you'll see in the sermon in Chapter 17, these two possible Central Questions ended up having supporting roles in the sermon.

WRITING THE CENTRAL CLAIM FOR MARK 1:1-8

Taking the Theological Claim and the Central Question together, Leah came up with the Central Claim below. Notice that this sentence also references v. 1 in order to situate its Christological claim more clearly and firmly:

Because Jesus Christ is the Messiah, the Son of God, we must maintain our commitment to the faithful witness of John and follow the straight path of truth in a politically polarized society.

Let's analyze this Central Claim using our criteria from above.

- Does the Central Claim mention God, Jesus Christ, or the Holy Spirit and say something substantive about their nature, character, or actions? *Yes. Jesus is described as the Messiah, the Son of God.*
- Does the Central Claim make an explicit connection between the content of the biblical text and the preaching context? *Yes. The sentence references John the Baptist and the straight path. The mention of a polarized society indicates the preaching context. The thing to note about this claim is the phrase "straight path of truth," which gives us a clue about how she will be framing this biblical image for this particular time when conspiracy theories and deliberate disinformation are rampant.*
- One other thing to note about this Central Claim is its rhetorical form. You might recognize it from the list above: *Because [what God/Jesus Christ/Holy Spirit] has done [based on biblical passage], today we are called to [how the congregation should respond].*

We'll return to Mark 1:1-8 in Chapter 17 when we build on the Central Question and Central Claim to arrive at the Central Purpose. In that chapter we will also see the sermon that developed from the whole process.

In the meantime, the next chapter will give us an opportunity look at two more examples of crafting a Central Claim for a sermon. We'll begin with a short passage from Exodus and apply the process to that text. Then we'll return to Luke 3:1-6, building on the work we did in the previous chapter. For now, we'll summarize the key points about the Central Claim. Also, see Appendix I for the Central Claim Worksheet.

KEY POINTS IN THIS CHAPTER

1. The Central Claim is the primary assertion of the sermon—in *one* sentence. Think of it as writing a one-sentence sermon to convey the essence of your message.
2. The Central Claim is informed by two things: 1) the Central Question that you derived from exegeting the biblical passage and your preaching context and 2) the strongest explicit Theological Claim that you derived from analyzing the Scripture passage that you discern would be appropriate for a sermon for this congregation at this time. Together, the Theological Claim and Central Question are connected so that you can make a singular Central Claim that conveys both the message of the biblical passage and its implication for your preaching context.
3. The Central Claim needs to mention God, Jesus Christ, and/or the Holy Spirit and say something substantive about their nature, character, or actions. If there is no mention of who God is or what God does, this means there is no theological content. Because a sermon needs to say something about the character, nature, or actions of God, Jesus Christ, or the Holy Spirit, the Central Claim needs to do this as well.
4. The Central Claim needs to make an explicit connection between the content of the biblical text and the preaching context. Because the Central Question contains the compelling inquiry about the Bible and one's context, the Central Claim needs to make an assertion that responds to this question.
5. The Central Claim is not a statement about the *theme* of the sermon. Nor is it a lengthy excurses describing the sermon. It's also not a sermon title. The Central Claim should substantively convey both the message of the biblical passage and its implication for your preaching context.

DISCUSSION QUESTIONS

1. We mentioned that distilling a sermon's message down to one sentence can seem daunting at first, so it may help to practice. Revisit the sermon "Jesus, Mother Hen" in Chapter 11. If you were to write the Central Claim for this sermon, what would it be? Try this exercise with your preaching partner and compare notes.
2. Ask a preaching colleague or mentor to share the manuscript of one of their sermons with you. After reading through the sermon, try writing what you think is the Central Claim for the sermon. Or maybe you can identify a Central Claim in the sermon itself. Does the preacher agree with what you discern to be the primary assertion and what it means for their preaching context? If not, what did you miss? Or, alternatively, was there something in their sermon that made it difficult to discern their Central Claim?
3. In this chapter, we clarified that the Central Claim is not a sermon title. Discuss with your preaching colleagues the topic of sermon titles. Are they necessary? Do they accomplish what we intend? Does your congregation expect to see a sermon title in the bulletin? What if you submit a title for your sermon but then want to change it at the last minute? Talk about the pros and cons of titling sermons.

FOR FURTHER READING

Ronald J. Allen. *Preaching: An Essential Guide.* Nashville: Abingdon Press, 2002. Chapters 1, 2, and 3.

Casey Barton. "The Big Idea." In *New Interpreter's Handbook of Preaching*, edited by Paul Scott Wilson. Nashville: Abingdon Press, 2008.

Paul Scott Wilson. "The Gospel and the Theme Sentence." In *The Practice of Preaching*, revised edition. Nashville: Abingdon Press, 1995.

NOTE

1. Just a reminder that not everything God says is an explicit Theological Claim. In this case, because God is saying something about what God has done, it counts as an explicit Theological Claim.

15

Two Exercises and Examples of Developing the Central Claim

Now that you have learned the basics of writing the Central Claim in the previous chapter, it's time to practice and see this process in action. We'll start with thinking about a sermon on one of the commandments from Exodus Chapter 20. Then we'll revisit Luke 3:1-6, which we worked on in Chapters 13 and 14.

EXAMPLE 1: DEVELOPING THE CENTRAL CLAIM FOR EXODUS 20:1-6

Suppose you would like to do a sermon series on the Ten Commandments starting with the first commandment in Exodus 20:1-6, the commandment to have no other gods. We'll move fairly quickly through the preparatory steps in order to concentrate on the process of writing the Central Claim. Here is the passage:

> *Exodus 20:1-6*
> *[1]Then God spoke all these words: [2]I am the LORD your God, who brought you out of the land of Egypt, out of the house of slavery; [3]you shall have no other gods before me. [4]You shall not make for yourself an idol, whether in the form of anything that is in heaven above, or that is on the earth beneath, or that is in the water under the earth. [5]You shall not bow down to them or worship them; for I the LORD your God am a jealous God, punishing children for the iniquity of parents, to the third and the fourth generation of those who reject me, [6]but showing steadfast love to the thousandth generation of those who love me and keep my commandments.*

Brief Exegesis of Exodus 20:1-6 and Questions the Text Is Asking

We'll summarize our exegetical work by noting that most scholars believe that even though the *story* about the emergence of the Hebrew people from slavery in Egypt took place in a period around 1250 BCE, the *book* was probably composed around 600 BCE when the Israelites were living in exile in Babylon. While scholars dispute the historicity of the text and count it mostly as a sacred story rather than historical fact, the story functioned as an important repository of community identity during the time of exile and as an explanation of the need for ethical behavior. That is to say, if God had the power to extract a beleaguered population from an enslaving nation such as Egypt, surely God can and will act to return the Israelites from exile and restore them to their promised land. In the meantime, the people must recall the mighty acts of Yahweh, who will brook no injustice against or within the community of God's people. Living in covenant, then, entails following God's commands for right relationship with God and with the community of faith.

EXERCISE

Writing the Central Claim for Exodus 20:1-6

1. Follow the Steps for Writing the Central Question for Exodus 20:1-6.

   - *Answer the Five Questions for Exegeting a Preaching Context*:
     a. What is happening in the world or society that is on people's minds (or that they need to pay attention to)?
     b. What is happening in the local community?
     c. What is happening in the congregation as a whole?
     d. What are individual congregation members dealing with?
     e. What are the political, cultural, and social dynamics that shape our hearing and interpreting of the text today?
   - *List the questions the text is asking*. Based on your consultation with biblical commentaries and your Exegesis Guide Chart, write down three questions that you hear the biblical author or community asking that articulates what was happening in the world behind the text that makes this passage necessary. Or what was happening in the faith community that this passage addressed. Or what was on the hearts and minds of the author and/or listeners that necessitated this passage. As you engage in your exegesis, you may change these, but this is a place to start.
   - *List the questions the congregation or community is asking*. Based on your answers to the Five Questions, write down three questions that you or your congregation are asking (explicitly or implicitly). Circle the one that seems most compelling. This may change as you work on your sermon, but it's a place to start.
   - *Write three possible Central Questions*. Write down three sentences that connect the biblical and contextual questions in a coherent and compelling way. Circle the one that seems to capture the most energy for your preaching about this passage at this time for these people. This is the Central Question for the sermon.

2. Analyze Exodus 20:1-6 to determine the explicit Theological Claim of the passage you want to use for this sermon.
3. Write a first draft of the Central Claim for Exodus 20:1-6. Remember, this is the primary assertion of the sermon—in *one* sentence. Be sure that the Central Claim is derived from the biblical passage and your Theological Claim and that it provides an answer to your Central Question. The Central Claim should convey both the message of the biblical passage and its implication for your preaching context. You may revise the Central Claim later as you're working on the sermon, but this at least gives you a start.

Just a reminder that steps 1 and 2 can be switched; as long as both steps are followed, the order is interchangeable. Once you have completed this exercise, read on to see how a preacher might work through the process.

In this first of what has come to be known as the Ten Commandments, God insists that the Israelites worship no other gods and make no idols that symbolize these false deities. The first commandment implies that other gods existed in other cultures outside of Israel, especially those that conquered the tiny nation. This command is in direct defiance of the nation of Egypt (and Babylon), which encouraged polytheism and demanded worship of the ruler. The Israelites are not to make any physical representations of the Divine in any form, because this will draw them away from the one true God.

To save time, we'll list just one question that Leah saw emerging from the list of questions the text is asking:

Why did God insist that the Israelites have no other gods, and what did this mean as they had just escaped captivity in Egypt?

Brief Exegesis of Preaching Context and Question the Congregation or Community Is Asking

Now let's consider a context in which a sermon about Exodus 20:1-6 might be preached. We'll imagine a church where the American flag is prominently displayed at the front of the sanctuary, clearly visible in the nave. There are military veterans and others in the congregation who feel that the flag is a necessary fixture in the church because it represents the country that protects the congregation's freedom of religion and honors those who sacrificed their lives for this freedom. But there also are people for whom the flag represents colonialism, oppression, and state-sanctioned violence. At the very least, from a theological and biblical perspective, the placement of the flag in the worship space alongside the sacred symbol of the cross certainly raises questions. Could the flag in the worship space be idolatrous? Could it be proclaiming allegiance to a god other than the God of Israel?

Thus, our initial question for this preaching context might be:

How can the first commandment and the ministry of the church counter the spirit of nationalism that could become a false god?

Central Question for Exodus 20:1-6

Taken together, the primary question for the biblical text and the primary question for the preaching context gives us this Central Question for the sermon:

> *Central Question for Exodus 20:1-6: What does it mean to worship the God of Israel in a culture that deifies its national identity, and how will the church witness to the God of liberation in this community?*

Notice that the sentence combines both the primary question for the biblical text and the primary question for the preaching context. This question also has the potential to connect three corners of the Wesleyan Quadrilateral. Scripture and Experience will be tethered by the parallels drawn between the commandment in Exodus to worship no other gods and the contemporary situation of a church resisting the god of nationalism worshipped within the culture. A preacher could also draw on Tradition in this sermon if they note the ways in which the Christian church in America was one of the architects of slavery and White supremacy from its beginning, which were part and parcel to the founding of this country.[1] In this case, Tradition would be critiqued and the case made that Christians today have a moral obligation to dismantle the idolatry that undergirds the symbolism of the flag.

Developing the Theological Claim for Exodus 20:1-6

Recall from Chapter 9 the process for analyzing a biblical text for its Theological Claims. Here's how we analyzed Exodus 20:1-6, first by underlining the parts that mention God, then identifying the explicit and implicit Theological Claims in the paragraphs that follow.

> *[1]Then God spoke all these words: [2]I am the LORD your God, who brought you out of the land of Egypt, out of the house of slavery; [3]you shall have no other gods before me. [4]You shall not make for yourself an idol, whether in the form of anything that is in heaven above, or that is on the earth beneath, or that is in the water under the earth. [5]You shall not bow down to them or worship them; for I the LORD your God am a jealous God, punishing children for the iniquity of parents, to the third and the fourth generation of those who reject me, [6]but showing steadfast love to the thousandth generation of those who love me and keep my commandments.*

In this passage, vv. 1 and 2 are an explicit Theological Claim. They are making an assertion that God exists, that God has declared the Israelites to be God's own people, and that God liberated them from slavery in Egypt.

V. 3, "You shall have no other gods before me," is an anthropological claim because it is a command *not* to have other gods (remember that the subject of a command is "you"). But v. 3 contains an implicit Theological Claim as well. At a fundamental level, the passage is saying that because of who God is (sovereign over all Creation) and what God has done (liberated the Israelites from slavery), no other gods are necessary. In fact, worshipping other gods is an attempt to negate who God is and what God does. Thus, idolatry must be forbidden. Further, because the word "shall" conveys both a sense of what will inevitably happen in the future as well as a command for the people to follow, the claim tells us a truth about what it looks like to worship the God of Israel; it is both an expectation and a promise. In short, we will know we are truly acknowledging the sovereignty of God when we have turned away from all idolatries. Having no other gods is a clear indication that the individual and the community is truly trusting God and God alone.

Vv. 5b and 6 are Theological Claims stating the nature of God ("jealous," i.e., intolerant of other gods) and how God will respond both to those who worship other gods (punishing) as well as to those who remain faithful (showing steadfast love). It is interesting that the length of time for God's love (the thousandth generation) is significantly longer than the punishment for deviance (third or fourth generation). We might say that God's anger is only .004 percent of God's relationship to us when we stray.

Although there are several explicit Theological Claims in this text, a case could be made for the strongest Theological Claim being vv. 1-2 or 5-6, depending on what the preacher wanted to emphasize in the sermon. In this case, Leah wrote two possibilities for a Theological Claim.

> Option 1, based on vv. 1-2: *God's sovereignty and liberation require trust and faith that no other gods are necessary.*
> Option 2, based on vv. 5-6: *God has claimed the Israelites as God's own and liberated them from slavery, so that the worship of other gods is both unnecessary and blasphemous.*

Notice how both statements specifically incorporate the message of the text and draw implications from it. Below, we'll see which one Leah picked as the basis for her Central Claim.

Writing the Central Claim for a Sermon on Exodus 20:1-6

Thus far, we have our Central Question (*What does it mean to worship the God of Israel in a culture that deifies its national identity, and how will the church witness to the God of liberation in this community?*). And we suggested two options for the Theological Claim based on either vv. 1-2 or vv. 5-6. For this sermon, Leah chose option 2 because it is more direct with a stronger tone: *God has claimed the Israelites as God's own and liberated them from slavery, so that the worship of other gods is both unnecessary and blasphemous.*

With our Central Question and Theological Claim in place, we are ready to write our Central Claim. Remember, the Central Claim combines the Theological Claim of the Scripture passage we have chosen for this sermon with the Central Question we are asking in this sermon. Taken together, they inform the Central Claim, the primary assertion of the sermon crafted in *one* sentence.

THEOLOGICAL CLAIM + CENTRAL QUESTION = CENTRAL CLAIM

Here is one possible Central Claim we might make for this sermon:

> *Because the God of Israel commanded believers to have no other gods, our congregation must engage in a serious discussion about the appropriateness of having the American flag, an engraved image of nationalism, within our worship space.*

Notice that this claim has the two key components: it mentions God in a substantive way by stating what God has done in the past, and it draws out implications for the congregation in response to what God expects for believers today.

Central Claims for Exodus 20:1-6 That Fall Short

As you look at the first draft of your statement, you'll want to do so with a critical eye to see if it falls short in any way. You may want to do this examination with a partner and critique each other's drafts, remembering the criteria for a strong Central Claim. Below are some examples of Central Claims for Exodus 20:1-6 that do not meet the criteria.

Example A: The Central Claim in this sermon is about being called to denounce nationalism.

Critique: This is merely a statement of the general theme or content of the sermon. This statement has neither a Theological Claim nor a reference to the biblical content of the passage for this sermon. So this would not work for a Central Claim.

Example B: American Idol: The Flag and the First Commandment.

Critique: While this is catchy, it is not a Central Claim; it's a sermon title. Remember, the Central Claim makes an assertion about who God is and/or what God does, it references the Scripture passage on which the sermon is based, and it states what this means for listeners today.

Example C: In this sermon, I will talk about how nationalism is like an idol and violates the commandment not to worship other gods. I will point to the American flag as an example of how a symbol like this can pull us away from worshipping the one, true God, and that we need to concentrate on the cross of Jesus Christ as the focal point of our worship and devotion.

Critique: One reason this is not a Central Claim is that it is too long; it has two sentences. This means that it's trying to say too much. Another reason Example C would not work is because it only describes what the preacher intends to do in the sermon; it does not make an assertion about who God is or what God does and what it means for us today.

Example D: The Israelites were an oppressed people in need of liberation, so Christians should work for the liberation of oppressed people.

Critique: There is no mention of God in this sentence, so it would not be considered a Central Claim. Here is how the sentence might be rewritten so that it becomes a Central Claim with explicit theological content:

> Example D Revised: *God freed the people of Israel from the false gods of Egypt who enslaved them; therefore, we who worship the sovereign God of liberation are called to renounce and dismantle the idol of nationalism.*

See the difference? In this revision, God is clearly named as the reason for Christians to work for liberation. This claim tells us what God has done and draws out implications of the claim for this congregation.

Here's an example of a Central Claim about Exodus 20:1-6 that is missing biblical content:

Example E: American nationalism is a false idol in our community, which God is calling us to reject.

Critique: While there is theological language in this sentence (God is calling us to reject American nationalism as a false idol), there is no reference to anything from Exodus 20 in this claim. Thus, it's missing the specificity of this particular scriptural text. It's a statement that could be drawn from any number of biblical passages that mention idols.

Here is how the sentence could be rewritten so that it becomes a Central Claim with solid biblical content based on this specific passage:

> Example E Revised: *Because the God of Israel is sovereign and requires followers to turn away from idols, the church must denounce American nationalism as a false god, repent of this sin, and proclaim the true God of liberation.*

In this claim you see three connections to Exodus 20: 1) the claim that God is sovereign; 2) the claim that God requires followers not to practice idolatry; 3) the claim that God liberates.

In Chapter 17, we'll return to Exodus 20:1-6 to see how the Central Question and Central Claim come together to make the Central Purpose. For now, let's circle back to the work we have been doing on Luke 3:1-6.

EXAMPLE 2: DEVELOPING THE CENTRAL CLAIM FOR LUKE 3:1-6

In Chapters 13 and 14, you completed an exercise where you developed a Central Question for Luke 3:1-6. Now it's time to build on that work and develop a Central Claim.

EXERCISE

Writing the Central Claim for Luke 3:1-6

Analyze Luke 3:1-6 for its Theological Claims to determine the strongest explicit Theological Claim in the passage.

1. Write a Theological Claim based on Luke 3:1-6 that could be the seed for a sermon.
2. Bring the Theological Claim and the Central Question together to create a Central Claim for a sermon in your preaching context. What is the theological assertion that you want to make for this congregation at this time? How is it connected to the passage? How does it relate to the people of this congregation, to current events, or to issues of public concern?

After you have written your first draft, see how your work compares with what Leah did for her sermon.

The Central Claim Process in Action: Luke 3:1-6

In Chapter 14, we saw how Leah developed the Central Question for Luke 3:1-6 on the Second Sunday of Advent in 2012 preaching for a congregation that was experiencing grief in the midst of the holiday season. After exegeting the text and her congregation, she arrived at this Central Question: *How did Luke situate Jesus and John within their larger context, and how might God be situating us in this story within our own contemporary context so that we might encounter divine grace in the wilderness?* Now let's look at how she analyzed Luke 3:1-6 to arrive at the strongest Theological Claim for this congregation at this time.

Theological Claim for Luke 3:1-6

Recall that for this process, we underline any sentence that mentions God, and then we determine which ones are theological, anthropological, or ecclesiological claims. After that, we choose the strongest explicit Theological Claim in the text and write a Theological Claim that we could make in a sermon based on that text. Here is Leah's analysis of the passage:

Luke 3:1-6
[1]In the fifteenth year of the reign of Emperor Tiberius, when Pontius Pilate was governor of Judea, and Herod was ruler of Galilee, and his brother Philip ruler of the region of Ituraea and Trachonitis, and Lysanias ruler of Abilene, [2]during the high-priesthood of Annas and Caiaphas, the word of God came to John son of Zechariah in the wilderness. [3]He went into all the region around the Jordan, proclaiming a baptism of repentance for the forgiveness of sins, [4]as it is written in the book of the words of the prophet Isaiah,
'The voice of one crying out in the wilderness:
"Prepare the way of the Lord,
make his paths straight.
[5] Every valley shall be filled,
and every mountain and hill shall be made low,
and the crooked shall be made straight,
and the rough ways made smooth;
[6] and all flesh shall see the salvation of God."'

V. 1 has a very long list of names before getting to "the word of God came to John son of Zechariah in the wilderness." This is an explicit Theological Claim because it tells what God did (send God's word to John in the wilderness). Recall that in the first part of the sermon from the previous chapter, Leah substituted names of leaders with those of that particular time. This was to demonstrate that the word of God still comes to us in the wilderness, which, for this sermon, Leah used as a metaphor for the experience of grief.

V. 4 is a quote from the prophet Isaiah. Although this sentence mentions the Lord, this is an anthropological claim because it is a command addressed to an unspecified "you." The implicit Theological Claim we might draw from this is that God expects believers to prepare for God's presence by making a clear and straight path.

V. 5 is trickier because it's not clear who is leveling the valleys and mountains. Is it the people of God? Or is God doing this work? A sermon could explore this ambiguity.

V. 6 mentions God, but this is an anthropological claim because "all flesh," meaning all living things, is the subject of the sentence. However, the implicit Theological Claim is that God makes sure that every creature will witness the saving power of God. This has a strong eschatological meaning when used to frame the ministry of John, and, subsequently, Jesus Christ. While Isaiah's community was reassured of God's presence in the midst of exile, Luke uses this passage to demonstrate that John's and Jesus's ministry is a fulfillment of what Isaiah had foretold. But it happens in an unexpected way that Isaiah could not have known—the coming of Jesus Christ as the messiah.

The only explicit Theological Claim in this passage, then, is v. 1, "The word of God came to John son of Zechariah in the wilderness." The verses that follow describe what John does in response to receiving that word. And they establish that his proclamation recapitulates the ancient prophet's promise that God's presence is coming, so we are to prepare appropriately. Luke also implies that we can expect huge shifts in the landscape, so to speak, as we prepare for the coming of God.

Based on this explicit claim in the text, Leah wrote a Theological Claim that could become a seed for the sermon:

God's word comes to prophets in wilderness places who call us to prepare for the arrival of Christ in our midst.

Then she drew on the Central Question and Theological Claim to write a Central Claim:

Just as the Word of God came to John in the wilderness to prepare the way of the Lord, so Jesus still comes to us in the wilderness today, even when the paths are still crooked, the valleys are still deep, and the mountains seem insurmountable.

This Central Claim meets the criteria of being based on both the biblical passage and the Theological Claim she chose for this sermon. It also attends to the Central Question: *How did Luke situate Jesus and John within their larger context, and how might God be situating us in this story within our own contemporary context so that we might encounter divine grace in the wilderness?*

Recall that the first half of the sermon specifically referenced the historical situation of the biblical text and reframed it for the contemporary situation. Then Leah addressed the way the congregation experienced grief using "wilderness" as a metaphor to describe the feelings of loss, loneliness, and mourning. Now we will see the second half of the sermon and take note of the way in which the Central Claim undergirds and guides the direction of the sermon. You'll also see the Theological Claims underlined in the sermon.

SERMON EXCERPT, PART TWO: JESUS MEETS US IN THE WILDERNESS OF GRIEF

Text: Luke 3:1-6
Second Sunday of Advent, Year B, 2012
(Note: the paragraph numbering picks up from Chapter 13.)

15. So what would it look like for us to prepare a way for Jesus Christ in the midst of this wilderness? For those who are in a time of grief, Luke's image of the wilderness really captures what that place of mourning can be like—lonely, barren, and devoid of hope. Yet Luke is proclaiming that God is filling in the valleys, leveling the rocky terrain, and straightening the crooked paths. So what could this mean for us?
16. When it comes to grief and loss, the most important step in preparing the way for God in the wilderness is to start by being honest about the wilderness you're in. Make a straight path to the truth about your experiences. John, in his wilderness, was a truth-teller. Of course, John was not a grief counselor. However, we can learn something about the importance of being forthright with God and others as part of our faith. So I encourage you to give yourself permission to be honest about your grief during this holiday season. <u>Christ has promised to meet you on that path in the wilderness.</u>
17. Death brings profound changes in everyone's roles, in the traditions and rituals, in the boundaries, and in the meaning of these special days. That is simply the reality of the wilderness. What I have learned is that it's important to try and find the words for loss, and to say them out loud, even if it makes other people uncomfortable. It's also important to find someone who can hear your words, listen to your story, and sit with you as you process through the memories and feelings.
18. When you live through a death or significant loss, you find that the fabric of your world has been torn and needs mending. And it takes a tremendous amount of time for this mending to happen. Contrary to what our culture expects, you don't just "get over" grief. It takes a long time to realize the impact of this loss on your life and how it affects birthdays, holidays, anniversaries, and whole seasons. The relationship you had with that person never goes away, even after the person dies. But it does change. It is constantly unfolding and refolding itself in different ways. Like an origami of grief.
19. So we need to realize that while God is, indeed, working in our lives during the times of grieving, it does not mean that things will return to "normal" any time soon. Remember, we're told that "Every valley shall be filled, and every mountain and hill shall be made low." <u>This means that</u> <u>even as the entire landscape is being altered around you, God finds you in the midst of the upheaval</u>. It's very disorienting, and you have every right to experience the entire spectrum of emotions that accompany this grief process. But be assured that, as promised, "all flesh shall see the salvation of God." This includes you.

(Leah draws on the imagery of the wilderness in the biblical text to shape this part of the sermon by addressing those who find themselves in the midst of grief. She discerned that there were thematic and theological points that Luke's use of the wilderness imagery may well have been intended to evoke. So, while Luke was not addressing grief directly, Leah used the language of the text to speak to the exigence of her congregation. That exigence is met with the "straight path," which, as Leah frames the imagery, is the way of honesty where they will meet God. In this way, the valleys filled and mountains laid low are not signs of God's absence, but of God's presence.)

20. It may be that you know someone who has experienced a loss or is in mourning at this time. If this is the case, then you have a unique opportunity to accompany those who are on this path in the wilderness. Take the time to slow down from your holiday rush and talk to this person. Ask them, "How are you feeling, really?" Then wait for them to share with you. Don't be afraid to ask them how they are hurting and how you can be helpful. Just hearing your voice offering to listen to them may be the greatest gift you could give them.
21. Receiving their story, bearing witness to their pain—just listening—is a way for God to fill in the valleys and smooth out the rough places. Often, listening rather than trying to offer words is the most powerful way to accompany people in the wilderness of grief. Too often we feel that we should have something to say to make the person feel better. When we feel this pressure, we may say things that minimize or distort someone's experience of grief. When in doubt, simply listen and respond with a word of thanks for them sharing their thoughts and feelings with you.
22. And then, help them get re-oriented in their wilderness by offering a little light along the way. *[Take taper and light a candle. Hold up candle for all to see.]* Invite them to sit at your campfire for a while to get warm and find a place of safety and comfort. Help them think of ways they can cope with the holidays and remember the significance of their loved one. Offer to help create an ornament to hang on the tree, or to help make a memory book with them of their loved one. Some in our congregation can even make a prayer shawl to drape over the shoulders of a wilderness traveler.
23. Whatever you do, <u>God can use your expression of support to remind them that the love of Christ is still with them, even in the wilderness.</u> Again, Luke is very interested in how the hand of God touches people in the very real places of their lives. And by walking with someone along that path in the wilderness, you can help them see where they are in relation to the bigger picture, no matter who is president or governor or bishop.

(The sermon shifts from encouraging those in grief to be honest about their feelings to encouraging others to receive those feelings and accompany them along the wilderness road. The Theological Claim in this part of the sermon states that God can use them as a channel for the bereaved to experience Christ's love in the wilderness. Thus, the Central Question is answered, and the Central Claim is given a concrete illustration. In the worship service, a table of candles was arranged at the front of the sanctuary so that congregants could light a votive in memory of a person they would be missing during the holiday season. So this section leads into the candle-lighting ritual with a rhetorical introduction of the light and a reference to the campfire from earlier in the sermon.)

24. There are all kinds of important, famous people in that list. But we are in that list, too, including Esther and Carrie, you and me. <u>And you may be the very person God uses to remind someone that they, too, shall see the salvation of God.</u>
25. Finally, no matter where we find ourselves in the wilderness, each of us can offer to share the light with someone. Pray with them, invite them to coffee, invite them to church. Our presence with one another is a reminder that we are not alone in this wilderness. God's light shines through us as part of this faith community even when the paths are still crooked, the valleys are still deep, and the mountains seem insurmountable.

John's proclamation is as true and powerful as it was two thousand years ago. The Word of God is still breaking into the wilderness places of our lives, lighting the way with this Divine Love. Amen.

(The sermon concludes by referencing back to the list of people in Luke's Gospel and in the contextual list for that time and place, reinforcing the idea that our story is situated in God's story. You can see a fragment of the Central Claim, "even when the paths are still crooked, the valleys are still deep, and the mountains seem insurmountable," make an appearance in the final paragraph.)

KEY POINTS IN THIS CHAPTER

1. The Central Claim for your sermon is derived from the Theological Claim that you discerned from analyzing the text along with the Central Question that came from exegeting both the Scripture passage and your preaching context.
2. The Central Claim addresses the Central Question by bringing the Theological Claim to bear upon the questions that the biblical author/community and your own community are asking.
3. Analyzing a biblical text for its theological, anthropological, and ecclesiological claims will help you discern the explicit Theological Claim you want to make in your Central Claim, especially as it relates to your context.
4. A Central Claim can fall short for any number of reasons: if it is merely a statement of the general theme or content of the sermon; if it's really only a sermon title; if it's too long and tries to say too much; if it doesn't make an assertion about the character or actions of God; or if it does not reference the biblical text with enough specificity. So be sure to craft your Central Claim with a critical eye.

DISCUSSION QUESTIONS

1. For the sermon on Exodus 20:1-6, Leah had written two possible Theological Claims: option 1) *God's sovereignty and liberation require trust and faith that no other gods are necessary;* and option 2) *God has claimed the Israelites as God's own and liberated them from slavery, so that the worship of other gods is both unnecessary and blasphemous.* She chose option 2 as the basis for her Central Claim. But what if she had chosen option 1? How would that Theological Claim influence the Central Claim? Which of the two would you be more apt to include in a sermon in your preaching context?
2. In the section "Central Claims for Exodus 20:1-6 That Fall Short," Leah suggested another possible Central Claim for Exodus 20:1-6: "Because the God of Israel is sovereign and requires followers to turn away from idols, the church must denounce American nationalism as a false god, repent of this sin, and proclaim the true God of liberation." Take five minutes to brainstorm five different ways you could begin such a sermon. What are images, stories, examples, questions, or statements you could use to hook your listener and get them interested in what you are about to preach? (In Chapter 22, you'll learn about how to create a strong beginning for a sermon.)
3. For the second half of the sermon on Luke 3:1-6, Leah chose to use the imagery of the wilderness as a metaphor for grief, though that was not the original intent of the passage. Discuss with your preaching partner or

mentor when it is appropriate to stretch the text in ways beyond its original intent, and when it's not. How far can a preacher push a text beyond its historical context to suit a particular contemporary need? At what point does this become eisegesis, forcing the text to mean what you want, and thus misusing the text?

FOR FURTHER READING

Ronald J. Allen. *Preaching: An Essential Guide*. Nashville: Abingdon Press, 2002. Chapters 4 and 5.

Karoline M. Lewis. Ch. 1, "A Faithful Sermon Is Biblical." In *A Lay Preacher's Guide: How to Craft a Faithful Sermon*. Minneapolis: Fortress Press, 2020.

Marvin A. McMickle. *Shaping the Claim: Moving from Text to Sermon*. In Elements of Preaching Series, O. Wesley Allen Jr., series editor. Minneapolis: Fortress Press, 2008.

NOTE

1. See: Robert P. Jones, *White Too Long: The Legacy of White Supremacy in American Christianity* (New York: Simon & Shuster, 2020).

16

The Central Purpose

Integrating Context, Claim, and Intention

In Chapters 12 through 15, we learned about the Central Question and the Central Claim. We might think of these as two of the "legs" of the three-legged stool supporting our sermon preparation. In this chapter, we will learn about the third leg of that metaphorical stool, the **Central Purpose**, which articulates what you want a sermon to do or accomplish in and for the listeners. The Central Purpose helps us gauge the effectiveness of the sermon and determine if it does what you want it to do.

In addition to the three-legged stool image, the other way we can think about this method of sermon preparation is by imagining a train with an engine to power it (the Central Question), the track on which to travel (the Central Claim), and a destination (the Central Purpose). The Central Question is like the "engine" of the sermon providing the intellectual, emotional, and spiritual energy. The Central Claim is like the "rails" guiding the sermon where you want it to go. The biblical and theological aspects of the Central Claim keep the sermon from going in the wrong direction due to unrelated tangents, stories, illustrations, or ideas that do not relate to or support the overall assertion of the sermon.

The Central Purpose, then, is the destination of the sermon. It tells us where you want the sermon—and the congregation—to arrive *and* why you want them to be there. The Central Purpose is the primary goal of the sermon—stated in *one* sentence. The Central Purpose succinctly states what you want the sermon to do or accomplish in and for the listeners as well as the reason for, or outcome of, this intention. The Central Purpose is informed by two things:

1) the Central Question that you derived from exegeting the text and your preaching context
2) the Central Claim that contains the primary assertion of the sermon

Together, the Central Question and the Central Claim inform the Central Purpose so that you can state in *one* sentence what the sermon aims to do and why.

CENTRAL QUESTION + CENTRAL CLAIM =
CENTRAL PURPOSE

PREPARING FOR THE CENTRAL PURPOSE: BRINGING TOGETHER THE CENTRAL QUESTION AND CENTRAL CLAIM

As we prepare to craft the Central Purpose for the sermon, let's review the components that inform this sermon preparation process. In the previous chapters, you learned that the Central Question is brought together with the Theological Claim from the biblical text that you chose for this sermon to help you write the Central Claim, the primary assertion of the sermon stated in a single sentence. We stressed that the Central Claim needs to mention God, Jesus Christ, and/or the Holy Spirit and say something substantive about who God is and what God does. Also, the Central Claim needs to make an explicit connection between the content of the biblical text and the preaching context, thus connecting at least two parts of the Wesleyan Quadrilateral—Scripture and Experience. As a reminder, the steps for writing the Central Claim are as follows:

1. Follow the Steps for Writing the Central Question. (List the questions the text is asking, answer the Five Questions for Exegeting a Preaching Context; list the questions the congregation or community is asking; write three possible Central Questions.)
2. Analyze the biblical passage to determine the strongest explicit Theological Claim you want to use for this sermon.
3. Write the Central Claim drawing on the Central Question and Theological Claim. This should be the primary assertion of the sermon—in *one* sentence. Be sure that the Central Claim is derived from the biblical passage and your Theological Claim and that it provides an answer to your Central Question. The Central Claim should convey both the message of the biblical passage and its implication for your preaching context.

After you have articulated the Central Question and Central Claim, you are ready to craft the Central Purpose. The Central Purpose says very succinctly in *one* sentence what you want this sermon to do or accomplish and the reason this goal is important. Or it states the result you hope to see in your listeners and the reason why.

QUESTIONS TO PREPARE FOR THE CENTRAL PURPOSE

Here are some questions to help you think about the Central Purpose for the sermon. Answering these can help your Central Purpose articulate the means by which you will both answer your Central Question and gain traction for the Central Claim in the sermon.

- Who is your intended audience for this sermon? What is important *to* them and *for* them in terms of this biblical passage?
- If the Central Claim was an answer to the Central Question, what is your intention for your listeners upon hearing that answer? What do you want them to do or how would you hope they respond? What would you like to see changed in their lives, in the congregation, in the community, or in God's Creation?
- How do you want the listeners to feel by the end of this sermon?
- What is the aim of the sermon? What might be indicators that your listeners are heading in the right direction toward this goal?

KEYS TO WRITING THE CENTRAL PURPOSE

If the Central Question is the "why" of the sermon, and the Central Claim is the "who" and "what," then the Central Purpose is the "how." In other words, the Central Purpose indicates the means by which the Central Question will be answered as well as the way in which the Central Claim will be made real in the lives of the hearers. This means that we will want to think about the action verb(s) that best conveys the intent of the sermon. This is because we answer a "how" question with a verb, as we'll see in the examples below.

RHETORICAL FORMS FOR THE CENTRAL PURPOSE

We recommend writing the Central Purpose like this:
The Central Purpose of this sermon is to [VERB] [OBJECT] so that [VERB] [OBJECT].
Or
This sermon will [VERB] [OBJECT] in order to [VERB] [OBJECT].
You can also use the present tense:
This sermon [PRESENT TENSE VERB] [OBJECT] resulting in [NOUNS].

Let's look at two examples of Central Purpose statements that give a sense of different ways they can be written. As you read them, underline the verbs you find in the sentence.

- For the sermon "Jesus, Mother Hen" (see Chapter 11), here is the Central Purpose:
  The Central Purpose of this sermon is to break open our limited conceptions of a "male" God so that we may embrace the "female" images of the Divine and expand the ways we encounter grace.
  Notice the verbs in the sentence: *break open, embrace, expand*, and *encounter*. The verbs tell us what the sermon intends to do and how the preacher hopes the listener will respond to the sermon. Take a look at that sermon in Chapter 11 again and see if the Central Purpose accurately describes the way you experienced it. Did you find yourself becoming more open to depictions of the Divine using female images? Did you experience grace in an expanded way through the sermon? If so, then it's likely that the sermon accomplished what it set out to do. If not, then there may be incongruity somewhere between the intention and the execution of the sermon, and we would need to think about why that is.
- For the sermon "Jesus Meets Us in the Wilderness of Grief" (see Chapters 12, 13, and 15), here is the Central Purpose:
  This sermon invites listeners to experience their wilderness journey within the larger scope of God's story, which will result in comfort for those who are bereaved and faith in Christ's presence.
  The verbs in this sentence are: *invites* and *experience.* As you think back to that sermon, do these verbs capture the spirit of what you encountered in the sermon? Did you feel invited to see your wilderness experience in a new way? Did you experience comfort or feel your faith in Christ strengthened? If not, then the sermon may have missed the mark. But if this describes your experience of the sermon, then it's likely that the sermon was effective because it did what the preacher intended it to do.

In both cases, you can see that the *verbs* are the key to Central Purpose statements. You'll also notice that there is a so that either explicitly stated or implied somewhere in the Central Purpose. We'll look at both of these components in turn, starting with the significance of verbs, both for the Central Purpose and for the sermon itself.

VIGOROUS VERBS MAKE THE CENTRAL PURPOSE— AND THE SERMON—COME ALIVE

In his book *Let the Whole Church Say Amen: A Guide for Those Who Pray in Public,* Laurence Hull Stookey encouraged the use of "**vigorous verbs**" for public prayers. "A good story, well told, marches along on sturdy verbs. So also does a good prayer," he said.[1] And, we would add, so does a good sermon need vigorous and sturdy verbs. This means that the Central Purpose needs vigorous and sturdy verbs as well. Vigorous verbs are active and energetic. Using robust and dynamic verbs can do wonders for both praying and preaching.

To understand what counts as a "vigorous verb," it helps to define its opposite, what Stookey called "**anemic verbs**." These are verbs that are vague, weak, or flaccid.[2] Just as Stookey encouraged worship leaders to pray with confidence, we want to encourage you to *preach* with confidence. Using vigorous verbs in your Central Purpose will help you do this.

So, as you are crafting your Central Purpose, use the action verb(s) that best suits what you want the sermon to accomplish in and for the listener. Build the Central Purpose around those verbs. Remember, the Central Purpose is what applies the Central Claim and helps to answer the Central Question. It identifies what you hope the result of the sermon will be and what will compel the listeners to feel or act in a certain way in response to hearing the Word of God preached in their midst.

VIGOROUS VERBS TO USE AND ANEMIC VERBS TO AVOID IN THE CENTRAL PURPOSE

Here are some suggested "vigorous verbs" that could serve well in a Central Purpose. (There are others, of course, but this gives you a start.)

accompany
advocate
beckon
build
challenge
comfort
compel
create
direct
disrupt
encounter
encourage
establish
guide
initiate
inspire
instruct
invite
lead
model
open
persuade
prepare
proclaim
reconcile
reshape
restore
reveal
strengthen
support
surprise
teach
transform
unite
urge

At the same time, we want to avoid "anemic verbs" that are merely about understanding or intellectual knowledge. Remember, the Central Purpose is not just another Central Claim. The Central Claim tells us the assertion of the sermon—it is describing what you hope the listener will come to *understand.* In contrast, the Central Purpose tells us what this sermon is setting out to *do.* We want verbs that do more than elicit a head nod or mere intellectual assent. So as a rule of thumb, we wouldn't want these kinds of words for our Central Purpose:

clarify
communicate
convey
explain
express
help people understand that
make the case that
reflect on
share
suggest
tell

THE CENTRAL PURPOSE NEEDS A "SO THAT"

One of the reasons some sermons fall flat in their proclamation of God's Word or fall short of inspiring a response is because the preacher has not thoroughly thought through the reason for the sermon in the first place. The Central Question is designed to assist you in that thought process by helping you articulate the compelling inquiry within the biblical text as well as the existential need driving the congregation. Then the Central Claim answers that question by asserting how God, Jesus Christ, or the Holy Spirit responds to the needs of the people, society, and Creation, and what it means today. The third part of the process, the Central Purpose, completes the progression by stating what the sermon will accomplish, and just as importantly, *why* or *what might result.*

QUESTIONS FOR DEVELOPING THE "SO THAT" OF THE CENTRAL PURPOSE

Here are some questions to ask yourself as you are thinking about the "so that" for the Central Purpose (and as you're writing the sermon as well).

- Why does your congregation need to hear this sermon about this text at this particular time?
- Who will care that this sermon has been preached? What difference will this sermon make in the lives of your listeners, the church as a whole, those who are vulnerable, God's Creation, or the community?
- Why does the Central Claim matter? How do you hope your listeners will respond to the Central Claim?
- How do you envision things being different as a result of this sermon?

Including the "so that" within the Central Purpose will state the hoped-for response or result of the sermon. This will increase the likelihood that your sermon will be effective in accomplishing the goal you have set for it. And it will help to ensure that the congregation is inspired to respond in the way you intend rather than simply nod in passive agreement without any meaningful engagement.

REMEMBER: THE CENTRAL PURPOSE IS NOT ANOTHER CENTRAL CLAIM

A common mistake students make with the Central Purpose is to make it another Central Claim. A clue that you have done this is if you use anemic verbs that call only for intellectual assent to a statement that you are making. For example, this would not be correct:

The Central Purpose of this sermon is to help people understand that Jesus calls us.

This is a Central Claim masquerading as Central Purpose. The first clue is that the sentence is using the anemic verbal phrase *help people understand.* Then it merely restates a claim that the preacher wants the congregation to understand, "Jesus calls us." Also, it does not include what the sermon is accomplishing, what the hoped-for response would be.

To avoid writing a second Central Claim, ask yourself:

- Am I using vigorous verbs?
- Is this sentence asking only for intellectual assent? Will people only nod their heads in agreement but not feel compelled to respond in any way?
- Is there a "so that" in this Central Purpose? Am I clearly stating what I hope this sermon will do and how people will respond?

A revised version of the Central Purpose above might look like this:

The Central Purpose of this sermon is to prepare the congregation for responding to Jesus's call so that they can participate in a life of discipleship.

Notice that this sentence has three vigorous verbs: *prepare, responding,* and *participate.* It also provides the reason for this purpose, "so that they can participate in a life of discipleship."

EXAMPLES OF CENTRAL PURPOSE STATEMENTS

To give you an idea of what a Central Purpose can look like, let's examine some examples for two different biblical texts. These are building on the students' Central Questions in Chapter 12 and Central Claims in Chapter 14.

Central Purpose for Genesis 15:1-18

Example 1: The Central Purpose of this sermon is to inspire engagement with the community, stepping out in faith just as Abram did, so that the congregation can envision a new direction guided by God's promises.

Explanation: This preacher's Central Question was, "Why were God's promises of descendants and land important to Abram—and the Israelites in exile—and how do we trust those same promises as we are discerning our future?" Her Central Claim was: "God promised Abram—and, by extension, the Israelites in exile—a community, an identity, and a legacy, and God promises that our congregation's legacy transcends our limitations and expectations of what seems possible." Notice that her Central Purpose builds on both the Central Question and the Central Claim and uses several vigorous verbs: *inspire, stepping out, envision*, and *guided*. It also includes a "so that" articulating the hoped-for response: "envision a new direction guided by God's promises."

Example 2: This sermon invites listeners to use the story of God's promise to Abram to transform their doubt and actively discern their future together.

Explanation: This preacher's Central Question was, "As God reassured Abram in his doubts, how will we, in times of pandemic and estrangement, remember God's promises and receive reassurance when we are in doubt?" Her Central Claim was, "Just as God's promise reassured Abram, God's Word today gives us hope in the midst of our own doubts and feelings of isolation and separation." We can see three vigorous verbs in her Central Purpose: *invites, transform*, and *actively discern*. The "so that" is indicated by the simple word "to" in the middle of the sentence, which indicates the result she hopes the sermon will accomplish: "transform their doubt and actively discern their future together."

Example 3: This sermon will encourage the congregation to trust in God's power to fulfill the covenant so that they will be open to journeying to a "new land" and discovering a new future with their ministry.

Explanation: This preacher's Central Question was, "How did God instill faith in Abram in his later years when all hope seemed lost, and how does that same faith come to us today in the midst of our anxiety about an aging and diminishing congregation?" Her Central Claim was, "God promised to be with Abram and bless him in his journey to a new land, so God will continue to accompany and guide us as we discern our future in a 'new land.'" Recall that this preacher was in a congregation made up of older members trying to sustain their diminishing congregation. So, in her Central Purpose she used several vigorous verbs: *encourage, trust, be open to journeying*, and *discovering*. Notice that she used the theme of discovering and journeying to a "new land" in both her Central Claim and Central Purpose, which provides cohesion between the two while also tying into the biblical story.

Central Purpose for Luke 4:1-13

The next examples we'll look at are based on Luke 4:1-13, the story of Jesus being tempted by the devil in the wilderness. Here are three Central Purpose statements building from the examples of students' Central Questions in Chapter 12 and Central Claims in Chapter 14.

Example 1: This sermon will challenge the temptations of materialism, power, and security, so that we will stay hungry for God's Word and rely on the Spirit to deepen our faith and mission in the community.

Explanation: This preacher's Central Question was, "What do the devil's temptations of Jesus mean within Luke's Gospel as well as for Luke's church; and how do we grapple with the temptations of materialism, power, and security that draw us away from God's Spirit and Word?" Her Central Claim was, "Because Jesus resisted the devil's temptation, we are called to do the same, trusting in the Spirit and God's Word when we are tempted with the empty promises of materialism, power, and security." She used three vigorous verbs for her Central Purpose: *challenge, stay hungry*, and *rely*. She cleverly referenced the temptation to turn stones into bread in the "so that" part of her Central Purpose, "so that we will stay hungry for God's Word and rely on the Spirit to deepen our faith and mission in the community."

Example 2: The Central Purpose of this sermon will be to equip the congregation to confront the truth about temptation's power, resist the forces of evil, and trust the power of the Holy Spirit as revealed in Scripture.

Explanation: The preacher's Central Question was, "How did Luke's church maintain their faith in Christ and know him as God while dealing with the temptations to abandon their faith; and how can we trust the Spirit to guide us by resisting the temptation to abandon our faith?" His Central Claim was, "God does not promise that we will avoid the forces of evil and temptation but gives us the Spirit and the Scriptures that speak to us and help us resist." In his Central Purpose the four vigorous verbs are seamlessly woven together to provide the "so that" of the statement: *equip, confront, resist*, and *trust*. Notice, too, that the Holy Spirit shows up in all three statements, indicating the emphasis he will place on the Spirit's work in this biblical passage and in the lives of his listeners.

Example 3: This sermon will compel the congregation to follow the example of Jesus so that instead of giving into helplessness when faced with oppression, they will trust God's Word and the Holy Spirit as they reshape our community from one of violence to safety.

Explanation: This preacher's Central Question was, "How did Luke use the story of Jesus resisting the devil's temptation to strengthen the faith of his church; and how can our church use the Word of God to speak to our community that is tempted to give up hope in the face of horrific violence?" Her Central Claim was, "Just as Jesus turned to God's Word during the Devil's temptation, empowered by the Holy Spirit, we can turn to God's Word when violence and oppression threaten to separate us from God and weaken our faith." Recall that this preacher was ministering in a church that was dealing with gun violence and police brutality against Black Americans. So she chose the following vigorous verbs for her Central Purpose: *compel, follow, trust,* and *reshape.* Notice that in her "so that," she defined what she wanted to direct her congregation away *from* (giving into helplessness) and *toward* (trust God's Word and the Holy Spirit).

EXERCISE: TRADING ANEMIC VERBS FOR VIGOROUS VERBS

Circle the weak or anemic verbs that you find in the Central Purpose statements below. Think about what vigorous verbs from the list above could more powerfully convey the Central Purpose. Then look at the explanation about why the original was problematic, followed by the revision, and how it corrects the problems.

Example 1. This sermon reminds the congregation that the role of the church is to lead people into reconciliation through Christ.

Problems: This Central Purpose statement uses the anemic verb *reminds.* Such a verb is not likely to bring about any change because it is only about garnering agreement from the listener. Also, there is no "so that" for this statement, further reducing the likelihood that the sermon will have any impact once the preacher sits down.

Revision: This sermon transforms our thinking about the church from that of a social club to an agent of Christ's reconciliation so that our community might experience healing.

Explanation: By using the verb *transforms,* the preacher is articulating that the sermon itself has a role to play in changing the way people view the church. There is also a clear goal that the preacher is working toward, which is moving the congregation to think of themselves as an active participant in the reconciling work of Christ right in their own community.

Example 2. The Central Purpose of this sermon will be to share a powerful story of the Holy Spirit changing lives.

Problems: The verb *to share* is not as strong as it could be for the intention of this sermon. This sentence is also lacking a "so that," which means that there is no clearly articulated goal for the sermon.

Revision: The Central Purpose of this sermon will be to disrupt the malaise of the listeners with a powerful story of the Holy Spirit changing lives in order to inspire a renewed sense of purpose.

Explanation: The verb *disrupt* may seem jarring at first. But suppose this is a congregation that has been beaten down by oppression that is resulting in a kind of collective depression. In this case, a jolt of prophetic preaching may be just what is needed. This revision also includes a clear "so that," which is to *inspire a renewed sense of purpose.*

Example 3. The Central Purpose of this sermon is to help listeners understand that because Jesus welcomed all people, LGBTQIA+ people should be welcomed as well.

Problems: Not only does this sermon have the anemic *to help listeners understand,* it is also restating a claim that, at best, will elicit only nods of agreement. Further, the claim is written using the passive verb, "should be welcomed." This results in there being no clearly stated outcome for this sermon, no hoped-for response from the listeners. Using an active verb would help make the Central Claim less vague and wishy-washy and more direct and concrete.

Revision: The Central Purpose of this sermon is to urge the listeners to boldly proclaim their faith in the risen Christ by voting to become a congregation that welcomes LGBTQIA+ individuals and their families.

Explanation: Some sermons have a very specific intention because of the occasion. In this case, the sermon will precede a vote to embrace LGBTQIA+ folks as part of the congregation's understanding of welcoming all people in Christ's name. In these situations, the preacher should not be shy about what they intend to do through the sermon for the occasion, and the Central Purpose should reflect that. In this example, the congregation had undergone years of study, education, and training to decide if they were ready to publicly proclaim their willingness to embrace LGBTQIA+ folks. So the sermon's Central Purpose should be clear about its intention for this occasion and not hide behind vague euphemisms or jargon.

To be clear, not every Central Purpose needs to be this precise. And, indeed, not all sermons would have such a specific goal. Preaching is not about checking off outcomes each week. But preaching should result in some kind of substantive response from listeners, whether that is expressed outwardly through words or behavior or experienced inwardly through changed hearts and minds. Therefore, the Central Purpose should contain active verbs and a stated intention but also leave room for the Holy Spirit to work on listeners' responses to the sermon in whatever way is appropriate.

MUST THE CENTRAL PURPOSE BE WRITTEN *AFTER* THE CENTRAL QUESTION AND CENTRAL CLAIM?

At this point, you may be wondering about the order of the Central Statements. Is it possible to start with the Central Purpose and then write the Central Claim? Or could a preacher start with a Central Question and jump straight to the Central Purpose? Certainly, it's possible that a preacher may want to do this. However, we recommend this specific order of Central Question, Claim, and Purpose because it is important to be grounded in Scripture and theology *first*. If you jump to what you want this sermon to do, you may end up trying to impose *your will* on the congregation rather than inviting them to experience and respond to *God's will* for this congregation at this time. In other words, the order of the process is intentional because it disciplines the preacher to prioritize exegesis of the biblical text and one's context (Central Question), discernment of the Theological Claim, proclamation of the Central Claim, and *then* invitation to respond with the Central Purpose.

This is not to say that you can't be taking notes about all three Central Statements along the way. You'll see in the worksheets in the appendix that there is room for jotting notes so that you can capture ideas as the inspiration strikes you. But, by doing this process in the order we have presented here, we believe you are more likely to have a biblically and theologically sound sermon that is coherent, cohesive, and compelling.

EXERCISE 2: PRACTICE REVISING CENTRAL PURPOSE STATEMENTS

In this exercise there are drafts of three Central Purpose statements for you to practice revising. This will prepare you for the next chapter, where you will have a chance to craft your own Central Purpose statements.

For each of these statements, circle the verbs and note whether they are vigorous or anemic. Underline what you think is the "so that" of the statement (if there is one). After you have completed all three, turn to page 182 to see how we revised the drafts so that you can compare your answers.

1. The Central Purpose of this sermon is to awaken listeners to recognize God's presence in the midst of their daily lives and hear God's call to join the God of our ancestors and all generations to build God's kingdom so all of God's children and Creation will thrive.

Problems you should notice: There are multiple verbs here—*awaken, recognize, hear, join, build, thrive*. That's too many verbs for one sermon (four is usually the maximum), and the sentence itself is too long. You can revise it by choosing the two verbs that you think are most important for accomplishing the goal of this sermon. Or you can choose different (but fewer) verbs and write a more condensed sentence. Also, what did you underline for the "so that" of the statement? Was it clear and concise?

Write your revision:

____

2. The Central Purpose of this sermon is to remind listeners to reflect on whether they are just showing up at church to be seen or if they truly understand the call of God.

Problems you should notice: This Central Purpose uses anemic verbs that lead only to intellectual assent. Also, there is no clear "so that" to this statement.

Write your revision:

____

3. This sermon will tell the congregation about the parable of the wedding banquet in Matthew 22:1-14 and explain why we should put on robes of righteousness and join God's banquet.

Problems you should notice: The verbs in this Central Purpose are not vigorous. *Tell* and *explain* are clues that this sentence is talking only about what the sermon will address, not what it will do in and for the listener, the church, or beyond. Also, there is no "so that" in this statement.

Write your revision:

____

Turn the page to see how we revised these Central Purpose statements.

REVISIONS OF CENTRAL PURPOSE STATEMENTS IN EXERCISE 2

On the previous pages, you practiced revising three different Central Purpose statements that had several problems, including issues with anemic verbs, lack of a clear "so that," and general wording issues. Below you can see how we revised these Central Purpose statements. Undoubtedly, they will be different from what you wrote, and that is perfectly fine. But this gives you an idea of ways we can reword and strengthen the Central Purpose, which will help to ensure a stronger sermon.

> #1 Revised: The Central Purpose of this sermon is to invite listeners to join with each other and with God in the work of the kingdom so that they may experience the blessings of serving together.

Explanation: In this revision, we used the verbs *invite, join*, and *experience*. There is also a clear "so that," which is *experience the blessings of serving together*. This sentence is much more focused than the original and is more likely to help the preacher achieve the goal of the sermon.

> #2 Revised: The Central Purpose of this sermon is to challenge listeners to actively live into the call of God, inviting others to join them in this response of joyful service.

Explanation: In this revision, we replaced the anemic verbs with vigorous verbs: *challenge, actively live*, and *invite to join*. Even though the words "so that" are not explicitly used in this Central Purpose, it is clear what the outcome of the sermon is to be: *invite others to join them in this response of joyful service.*

> #3 Revised: This sermon will beckon the congregation to put on robes of righteousness and join God's banquet so that we establish priorities of discipleship.

Explanation: The verbs in this revision are *beckon, put on, join*, and *establish*. The statement indicates that the preacher is inviting the congregation to rethink their priorities and how they use their resources in light of the parable of the wedding banquet in Matthew 22:1-14.

WHAT IS THE ROLE OF THE CENTRAL PURPOSE IN THE ACTUAL SERMON?

As with the Central Question and Central Claim, you may be wondering what role the Central Purpose has within the sermon itself. It is less likely that you'll want to use the Central Purpose word for word in the sermon. This part of the process is more behind the scenes because, generally, you won't want to reveal the purpose so directly.

This is not to say that you couldn't state right up front what the purpose is for the sermon. In fact, some preachers prefer to do this, especially if they are using a deductive sermon form where they state right at the beginning the claim of the sermon and what the sermon intends to do. (You will learn about the deductive sermon form in Chapter 20.) Then they would spend the rest of the sermon making the case for the claim and explaining why the purpose is necessary with a recapitulation of the claim and purpose at the end.

But for the most part, the Central Purpose need not be stated outright. With all three Central Statements, we might think of a duck on a pond. Its webbed feet are busy paddling beneath the water, but all we see on top is the duck smoothly gliding along the surface. Similarly, all your parishioners need to see is your sermon gliding along smoothly; they don't need to see the paddling feet below.

In the next chapter, we'll look at the process for creating a Central Purpose using two biblical texts we've discussed in the previous chapters. For now, remember that the Central Question, Central Claim, and Central Purpose statements are to help you be as strong and effective a preacher as you can be. It will serve your congregation to have a preacher who is solid in their inspiration, message, and intention for the sermon, so these Central Statements will provide the structure for effective preaching. See Appendix J for the Central Purpose Worksheet.

KEY POINTS IN THIS CHAPTER

1. The Central Question is like the "engine" of your sermon, driving it with intellectual, emotional, and spiritual energy. The Central Claim is like the theological and biblical "tracks" that provide direction for the sermon. The Central Purpose is the destination of the sermon. It tells us where you want the sermon—and the congregation—to arrive as well as the reason for getting there.
2. The Central Question is the "why" of the sermon; the Central Claim is the "who" and "what"; and the Central Purpose is the "how." In other words, the Central Purpose indicates the means by which the Central Question will be answered and how the Central Claim will be made real in the lives of the hearers.
3. The Central Purpose articulates what you want a sermon to do or accomplish in and for the listeners in *one* sentence. The Central Purpose helps us gauge the effectiveness of the sermon and determine if it does what the preacher intends it to do.
4. The Central Purpose is informed by 1) the Central Question that you derived from exegeting the text and your preaching context and 2) the Central Claim that contains the primary assertion of the sermon.
5. The Central Purpose should contain a "so that"—the *why* or *what might result* from the sermon.
6. When writing the Central Purpose, be sure to use "vigorous verbs" and avoid "anemic verbs."

DISCUSSION QUESTIONS

1. Trade sermon manuscripts with a preaching partner. Each of you write what you think is the Central Purpose of your partner's sermon, then discuss. If what you intended does not align with what you actually did, then there is a disjuncture, and you'll need to think about why that is.
2. With this same sermon from your preaching partner, focus on the "so that" of the Central Purpose. Discuss what actions might result from a congregation hearing this sermon. What difference could this sermon make in the lives of those who hear the sermon, the church as a whole, those who are vulnerable, God's Creation, or the community?
3. Talk with an experienced preacher about the concept of "vigorous verbs." Ask them to share a sermon manuscript with you and analyze the verbs in it. Reflecting on the sermon together, were there other verbs that could have been used that would have been more evocative or active and less "anemic"?

FOR FURTHER READING

Thomas G. Long. Ch. 4, "The Focus and Function of the Sermon." In *The Witness of Preaching*, third edition. Louisville, KY: Westminster John Knox, 2016.

Richard W. Voelz. *Preaching to Teach: Inspire People to Think and Act.* Nashville: Abingdon Press, 2019.

Paul Scott Wilson. Ch. 11, "Composing to Persuade." In *The Practice of Preaching*, revised edition. Nashville: Abingdon Press, 2007.

NOTES

1. Laurence Hull Stookey, *Let the Whole Church Say Amen: A Guide for Those Who Pray in Public* (Nashville: Abingdon Press, 2001), 27–34.

2. In terms of prayer, Stookey points to one verb that is particularly anemic: "Chief among these is the very popular *be with* petition. Not only is this weak because it says little, but it contravenes the promises of the Christ" who has already promised to be with us (27).

17

Two Exercises and Examples of Developing the Central Purpose

Now that you have learned the basics for developing the Central Purpose for a sermon and practiced revising samples in Chapter 16, it's time to try your hand at writing some for some sample texts. First, we'll return to Exodus 20:1-6, for which you have already developed a Central Question and Central Claim (see Chapter 15). We'll develop a Central Purpose statement that could be used for a sermon on the First Commandment. Then we'll come back to Mark 1:1-8, the assigned Gospel for the Second Sunday in Advent, Year A. You will practice writing a Central Purpose for that text and see how it compares to what Leah wrote for a sermon she preached. You'll also see the sermon that resulted from the entire Central Statements process for Mark 1:1-8. To be clear, what you write for the exercises will differ from what you see in these examples because your context will be different from Leah's. But you'll be able to see the process for how she crafted her Central Purpose so that you can compare and contrast it with your own.

CENTRAL QUESTION + CENTRAL CLAIM = CENTRAL PURPOSE

REVIEWING THE CENTRAL PURPOSE

As a review, here are the questions to prepare for the Central Purpose that were introduced in the previous chapter:

- Who is your intended audience for this sermon? What is important to them and for them in terms of this biblical passage?
- If the Central Claim was an answer to the Central Question, what is your intention for your listeners upon hearing that answer? What do you want them to do or how would you hope they would respond? What would you like to see changed in their lives, in the congregation, in the community, or in God's Creation?
- How do you want listeners to feel by the end of this sermon?
- What is the aim of the sermon? What might be indicators that your listeners are heading in the right direction?

Also, recall these questions for developing the "so that" of the Central Purpose:

- Why does your congregation need to hear this sermon about this text at this particular time?
- Who will care that this sermon has been preached? What difference will this sermon make in the lives of your listeners, the church as a whole, those who are vulnerable, God's Creation, or the community?
- Why does the Central Claim matter? How do you hope your listeners will respond to the Central Claim?
- How do you envision things being different as a result of this sermon?

As you are writing the Central Purpose, remember that this is a single sentence that articulates what you want a sermon to do or accomplish in and for the listeners and why it is important. The Central Purpose is informed by 1) the Central Question that you derived from exegeting the text and your preaching context and 2) the Central Claim that contains the primary assertion of the sermon.

EXERCISE 1: DEVELOPING A CENTRAL PURPOSE FOR EXODUS 20:1-6

In Chapter 15, you practiced developing the Central Claim for Exodus 20:1-6. First, you analyzed the text to determine the strongest explicit Theological Claim of the passage that you want to use for the sermon. Then you followed the five steps for writing the Central Question. This led to writing the Central Claim. Referring to your notes on that first part of the process, pick one of the sentence outlines below to write a first draft of a Central Purpose for a sermon on Exodus 20:1-6.

1. The Central Purpose of this sermon is to [VERB] [OBJECT] so that [VERB] [OBJECT].
2. This sermon will [VERB] [OBJECT] in order to [VERB] [OBJECT].
3. This sermon [PRESENT-TENSE VERB] [OBJECT] resulting in [NOUNS].

After you have completed your first draft, trade with your preaching partner and discuss what you each wrote. Is your partner's Central Purpose written as a single sentence that articulates what the preacher wants the sermon to do or accomplish in and for the listeners? Does the Central Purpose use "vigorous verbs"? Is the sentence truly a Central Purpose, or is it really a Central Claim in disguise? Is the "so that" detectable in the Central Purpose?

Once you have discussed each other's Central Purpose sentences and revised them accordingly, continue to the example below to see other ways that a Central Purpose on Exodus 20:1-6 could be constructed.

EXAMPLE OF THE CENTRAL PURPOSE IN ACTION: EXODUS 20:1-6

Recall from the example in Chapter 15 that our Theological Claim for Exodus 20:1-6 was this:

God has claimed the Israelites as God's own and liberated them from slavery so that the worship of other gods is both unnecessary and blasphemous.

Also recall that we imagined a church context where the American flag is clearly visible at the front of the worship space. This raises questions about what the congregation truly worships and whether the nation's flag in the sacred space is a form of idolatry. Yet, the congregation is comprised of people who want to keep the flag in the sanctuary as well as those who think it is inappropriate. So, after exegeting both the biblical text and the church's context, our Central Question was this:

What does it mean to worship the God of Israel in a culture that deifies its national identity, and how will the church witness to the God of liberation in this community?

This led us to craft the following Central Claim:

Because the God of Israel commanded believers to have no other gods, our congregation must engage in a serious discussion about the appropriateness of having the American flag, an engraved image of nationalism, within our worship space.

Now we can experiment with possible Central Purpose statements. Below are three options. As you read them, underline the verbs and consider how they each set a different tone for the sermon.

1. The Central Purpose of this sermon is to compel the congregation to confront nationalism, name it as idolatry, and worship only the God of liberation.
2. This sermon will challenge listeners to question their loyalties to those things that are not of God, including nationalism and the display of the American flag in the church sanctuary, so that we can worship the true God of freedom.
3. This sermon initiates a conversation about what it means to worship the God of Israel so that we can speak honestly about fulfilling the commandment not to worship other gods.

Notice that the verbs in options #1 and 2 are more direct in their language while option #3 is more invitational. Also note that each option is specific in its goals. Option #1 not only has the vigorous verb *compel*, telling us what the sermon will do, but also utilizes active verbs to describe what the preacher wants the congregation to do: *confront, name,* and *worship*. Option #2 also has two vigorous verbs for what the congregation should do upon hearing this sermon: *question their loyalties* and *worship the true God of freedom*. The verbs in option #3 are softer but also specific: *initiates, worship, speak honestly,* and *fulfilling the commandment*.

Finally, let's consider the "so that" of these statements. Option #1 does not have an explicit "so that," but it could be inferred from the last part of the sentence, "worship only the God of liberation." The "so that" for option #2 is very clear; the preacher wants them to "worship the true God of freedom." And in option #3, while the intention is to invite the congregation into a conversation about what idolatry is, there is no specific naming of the American flag as an example of a graven image and a symbol of idolatry. The Central Purpose for option #3 might lead to a sermon that only mentions the idolatry of the national flag as one of several examples of worshiping other gods in our contemporary society. It would not be as direct as option #1 or 2. But depending on the preacher's context, the length of time they have served their congregation, the trust level between the congregation and the preacher, and their tolerance for engaging social issues, option #3 might be the most prudent Central Purpose.[1] In Chapter 20, we'll look at possible sermon forms that could be designed around these three different Central Purposes.

EXERCISE 2: DEVELOPING A CENTRAL PURPOSE FOR MARK 1:1-8

In Chapter 14, you worked on the process for writing the Central Question and Central Claim for Mark 1:1-8, the passage about making a "straight path" in the wilderness for the coming of Christ. First, you followed the five steps for writing the Central Question. Then you analyzed the text to determine the strongest explicit Theological Claim of the passage for this congregation at this time. This led to writing the Central Claim. Referring to your notes on that first part of the process, pick one of these sentence outlines to write a first draft of a Central Purpose for a sermon on Mark 1:1-8:

1. The Central Purpose of this sermon is to [VERB] [OBJECT] so that [VERB] [OBJECT].
2. This sermon will [VERB] [OBJECT] in order to [VERB] [OBJECT].
3. This sermon [PRESENT-TENSE VERB] [OBJECT] resulting in [NOUNS].

After you have completed your first draft, trade with your preaching partner and discuss what you each wrote. Is your partner's Central Purpose written as a single sentence that articulates what they want the sermon to do or accomplish in and for the listeners? Does the Central Purpose use "vigorous verbs"? Is the sentence truly a Central Purpose, or is it really a Central Claim in disguise? Is the "so that" detectable in the Central Purpose?

Once you have discussed each other's Central Purpose sentences and revised them accordingly, continue with Example 2 to see how Leah constructed a Central Purpose for Mark 1:1-8.

EXAMPLE OF THE CENTRAL PURPOSE IN ACTION: MARK 1:1-8

In Chapters 13 and 14, we saw Leah's process of developing the Central Question and Central Claim for a sermon on Mark 1:1-8 that she preached on the Second Sunday in Advent, December 2020. Recall from Chapter 14 the Theological Claim she discerned from the text:

To prepare God's people for receiving the Messiah, God sent John to call for making a direct path so that we may encounter Jesus Christ.

This was paired with her Central Question:

What does John's "straight path" look like for our community and our congregation, and how might we guide people to that path as we wait in this Advent season?

She then took the Theological Claim and Central Question to craft the Central Claim for her sermon:

Because Jesus is the Messiah, the Son of God, we must maintain our commitment to the faithful witness of John and follow the straight path of truth in the wilderness of a politically polarized society.

Now we will see how she worked on the Central Purpose for the sermon. First, let's take a look at how she answered the questions to prepare for the Central Purpose.

- Who is your intended audience for this sermon? What is important to them and for them in terms of this biblical passage?
    - *This sermon is for the congregation at St. Thomas Lutheran Church in Richmond, Kentucky, a small moderate-to-progressive church in a conservative county. This congregation believes it is important to discern how they can faithfully follow the "straight path" in a divided society.*

- If the Central Claim was an answer to the Central Question, what is your intention for your listeners upon hearing that answer? What do you want them to do or how would you want them to respond? What would you like to see changed?
    - *My intention is to give the congregation theological language for understanding what is happening in our country at this time so that they are equipped to discern truth, avoid conspiracy theories, and feel bolstered in their Christian witness.*

- If the Central Claim was an answer to the Central Question, what is your intention for your listeners upon hearing that answer? What do you want them to do or how would you hope they would respond? What would you like to see changed in their lives, in the congregation, in the community, or in God's Creation?
    - *I will draw parallels between our current political situation and the historical situation for the writer of Mark 1:1-8 to show that this is not the first time God's people have been divided by political forces. I will encourage the listeners to look to John as a faithful witness to the truth that comes through Christ.*

- How do you want the listeners to feel by the end of this sermon?
    - *I want the listeners to feel that they have a path to follow (or help to create) as they are in this season of waiting in the wilderness of political divisiveness and conspiracy theories. I also want them to feel affirmed in their faith in Jesus Christ.*

- What is the aim of the sermon? What might be indicators that your listeners are heading in the right direction toward the goal?
    - *The aim of this sermon is to give people an "aha" moment so that they can recognize the truth and trustworthiness of Jesus Christ and be strengthened in their faith. Since worshippers usually stay on Zoom after the service to engage in fellowship, hear announcements, and sometimes discuss the sermon, I will be listening for comments and conversations about the sermon's content after the service. I'll know if the sermon hit the mark if they follow some of the suggestions I make in the sermon for engaging in education to discern truth. Or I may see ideas sprout at a later time from the seeds planted by this sermon.*

This is how she answered the questions for developing the "so that" of the Central Purpose.

- Why does your congregation need to hear this sermon about this text at this particular time?
    - *This sermon is taking place several weeks after the 2020 election. As we're awaiting the final count of the votes, lies and conspiracy theories are propagating about the election, the COVID-19 pandemic, and other social issues that have become politicized. They need to hear a word from God about why John's testimony is reliable and why they should trust Jesus.*

- Who will care that this sermon has been preached? What difference will this sermon make in the lives of your listeners, the church as a whole, those who are vulnerable, God's Creation, or the community?
    - *Parishioners have been commenting about how frustrated they are with friends, family members, co-workers, and members of the community who follow conspiracy theories, disbelieve science, and accept disinformation as truth. This sermon will encourage them to stay true to the values of honesty, integrity, and truth.*

- Why does the Central Claim matter? How do you hope your listeners will respond to the Central Claim?
  - o *The Central Claim matters because it's possible that some members might be drawn to QAnon or other sources of disinformation, or they may be dealing with others who have succumbed to cult-like groups and they need encouragement to both stay on the "straight path" and help create it for others.*

- How do you envision things being different as a result of this sermon?
  - o *I believe it is important for the church to engage these kinds of public issues so that Christians can have the biblical and theological tools to make sense of what is happening and how their values as followers of Christ should guide their actions. My hope is that parishioners will see their church as a place where they can talk about and be equipped to discern these issues.*

With this preparatory work completed, Leah wrote three possible options for her Central Purpose. As you read them, underline the verbs and think about how each one would set a different tone and direction for the sermon.

1. The Central Purpose of this sermon is to guide the congregation through the "wilderness" of political divisiveness by proclaiming the truth of Jesus Christ so that they will trust in him and seek out the straight path.
2. This sermon will strengthen the resolve of congregants to follow the straight path of John the Baptist and be bold in speaking Christ's truth in the midst of a wilderness of lies, conspiracy theories, and cultish behavior.
3. This sermon prepares the congregation for a ministry of truth-telling and education so that during this Advent season of anxious waiting, they can help forge the straight path of Christ for people to follow.

Let's analyze these three options to see how Leah chose the one she would use for the sermon on Mark 1:1-8. Each of them is a single sentence that articulates what she wants to do or accomplish in and for the listeners, thus that criteria is met. Also, each of these Central Purpose statements incorporates images and concepts from the biblical text, speaks to the context of the congregation, and shows what the results of the Central Claim will be.

Now let's look at the "vigorous verbs" and the "so that" for each sentence.

- In option #1, the verbs for the sermon are *guide, proclaiming, trust,* and *seek out.* The sentence clearly states the hoped-for result, that listeners will trust Jesus and seek out the straight path.
- In option #2, the verbs are *strengthen, follow,* and *be bold in speaking.* These are stronger verbs than those in option #1 and indicate a more active role for the congregation in the "so that" part of the statement.
- In option #3, the verbs are *prepare* and *help forge the straight path.* These verbs more closely mirror the biblical text. The results of this sermon would have more to do with educating and equipping the congregation. There is also more of an emphasis on the theme of waiting and, because it specifically mentions Advent, it is more contextualized within the liturgical season.

Any one of these Central Purpose statements could work for a sermon. It all depends on what the preacher discerns is the most appropriate for this congregation at this time. Which would you choose if you were preaching this kind of sermon in your congregation? Would your congregation resonate more with *guiding* in option #1, *being bold* in option #2, or *preparing to forge the straight path* in option #3?

As you read the sermon below, you'll see in the comments how Leah constructed the sermon and the influence of the Central Question, Central Claim, and Central Purpose. You'll also learn which Central Purpose she ultimately chose for this sermon. As you read, underline the Theological Claims you see in the sermon. Each paragraph is numbered to facilitate quick reference for discussion.

SERMON: "FINDING OUR WAY IN THE WILDERNESS OF CONSPIRACY THEORIES: WHAT IS THE 'STRAIGHT PATH'?"

Text: Mark 1:1-8

1. Guess what Tuesday is? It's Safe Harbor Day! What, you've never heard of Safe Harbor Day? Well, before this year's election, I hadn't heard of it either. Safe Harbor Day is when states finalize their vote counts and

certify their electors that will be meeting to cast their votes for president. Normally, this day passes with little notice. But this year is different because one of the candidates is insisting that there was voter fraud, and his supporters are echoing his cries to "stop the steal."

2. I don't know about you, but the waiting of these past few weeks has been nerve-wracking and anxiety-producing. There are many competing claims of authority. Who should we believe? Who can we trust? Many people are worried that the lies about the election process may lead to violence. Some are even concerned that we're in the midst of a "soft coup." We're in a season of waiting and we don't know how things are going to turn out.

(By naming what is happening with the interregnum period between the election and inauguration, the sermon begins with contextualizing itself in current events. Paragraph 2 introduces the idea of waiting in a time of uncertainty, which will be a primary theme of the sermon.)

3. Interestingly, this also happens to be the season of waiting for us as Christians. Advent is a time of introspection and preparation for the coming of Christ, Emmanuel, God with us. But this is a difficult time to feel joyous about the coming Christmas season. The COVID-19 pandemic has ravaged our world, stopping us in our tracks. We're in a prolonged season of waiting with the coronavirus: waiting for the vaccine to be developed, waiting for the pandemic to end. What makes the waiting even more difficult is the way the coronavirus has become politicized and the deliberate disinformation that is causing people to doubt the science. Between the conspiracy theories, misinformation, and propaganda, it can feel like we're in a wilderness with no way out.

(Paragraph 3 continues contextualizing by speaking about Advent and the COVID-19 pandemic. The theme of waiting in a time of uncertainty is further developed. The last sentence mentions the word "wilderness," *which serves as a transition to the biblical text for the sermon.)*

4. And yet, Mark's Gospel begins with a voice crying out to us: "Make straight the way of the Lord!" Mark announces that what he is sharing is the good news of Jesus Christ and that Jesus is the Son of God. He quotes the Hebrew prophet Isaiah's words, "See I am sending my messenger ahead of you, who will prepare your way." Then John the Baptist appears in the wilderness announcing that this path leads right through the waters of baptism there at the Jordan River.
5. What does this mean, prepare the way of the Lord, make his paths straight? Why should we believe John the Baptist when there are so many others who claim to have "the truth"? Who is John anyway? Isn't he just another guy with a platform? Why should we believe him? Why should we trust him?

(Paragraph 5 consists of a series of questions the preacher asks on behalf of the listeners. You may recognize the influence of one of the options for the Central Question from Chapter 13: Who can we trust as we sojourn in the wilderness, and how can John's prophetic message help us prepare the way for Jesus Christ? *As we mentioned earlier, even the drafts of Central Questions, Claims, and Purposes that we don't ultimately use can be repurposed as openings, supporting material, transitions, or endings in the sermon.)*

6. The people coming from the Judean countryside might have asked these very questions when they came down to the Jordan River to see this strange man wearing a camel's hair tunic and eating bugs for lunch. Remember that there were lots of other voices vying for attention in those days. John was not the only prophet and certainly not the only voice claiming to speak for God. There were also other religious leaders competing for legitimacy and authority as well.
7. You see, this tug-and-pull isn't just within the story itself; it was also something that Mark's congregation experienced as well. There were many sources that claimed to have authority and insisted people listen to them, including the Roman Emperor, the religious leaders, and itinerate prophets galore. Who should they believe? Who should they trust? Who's telling the truth? Who will they follow?

(Paragraphs 6 and 7 draw directly from the work Leah did in her exegesis of this passage. Not only did she reference the primary Literary Exigence of the passage [competing voices of authority vying for the people's attention], but also the

Occasional Exigence of what the original recipients of Mark's Gospel faced [competing voices of authority vying for their attention].)

8. Just like that crowd at the riverside, we, too, are trying to figure out who to trust and who to believe. When it comes to COVID-19, we hear some voices telling us to wear masks and social distance. Others say that the coronavirus isn't even real, and that people aren't really dying from it. Who should we believe?
9. When it comes to the election, we hear some voices telling us that the process was rigged and that the results we see aren't real. Others insist that voting proceeded just as it should, and that we can trust the democratic process. Who's telling the truth?
10. In fact, there are millions of people who follow certain sources of information that insist we can't believe anything we see or what science has shown us. We can't believe that the climate is in crisis. We can't believe that racism is real. We can't believe that Holocaust happened, or that the Earth is round, or that the universe is billions of years old.
11. On the contrary, they insist that we *should* believe Barack Obama is not an American citizen (which is a lie), that vaccines are dangerous (which the evidence refutes), and that there was a pedophile ring in the basement of a pizza shop in Washington, DC (which, incidentally, has no basement). Between the internet, social media, and certain politicians, it's hard to know what's real, what's questionable, and what's an outright lie.

(Paragraphs 8 through 11 return to the exigence of the congregation, drawing parallels with both Mark's congregation and the crowd gathering around John at the Jordan River. The sermon is building dramatic tension here by continuing to ask questions about who we should believe, who's telling the truth, how to know what's real and what's a lie. Throughout this section, you can see the influence of Reason from the Wesleyan Quadrilateral.)

12. You might wonder, what is God's role in all of this? The Gospel is very clear that God sends John to prepare the way and "make his paths straight." People are to believe John's testimony. Why? Because it is true, it's trustworthy, and it is trust-producing.
13. This is the straight path. It's not some winding, erratic, illogical obstacle course that forces you to engage in mental acrobatics to figure out what's true. The prophet's path is straightforward.
14. It follows, then, that John's testimony is intended to prepare the way for Jesus Christ, who is himself true, trustworthy, and trust-producing because he is the Son of God. This is exactly the voice we need to listen to and the path we need to follow as we are in this Advent wilderness.

(Paragraph 12 is a pivot point in the sermon because it makes a turn toward explicit Theological Claims, beginning with, "The Gospel is very clear that God sends John to prepare the way and 'make his paths straight'" *(which you should have underlined as a Theological Claim). The next two paragraphs explain what the straight path means, how it connects to Christ, and the way it situates us within the wilderness of Advent. Again, these paragraphs draw on Reason in that they are appealing to logic and truth as a way to encounter God. The first sentence in paragraph 14 is another one you should have underlined because it makes a strong Christological claim that Jesus Christ is "true, trustworthy, and trust-producing because he is the Son of God." Here you can see the influence of the Central Claim. This will become a refrain for the rest of the sermon.)*

15. However, just because the path is straight does not mean that it's going to be easy. The crowd at the river, and we today, need to come to terms with the fact that following Jesus Christ means going to the wilderness places. It means squaring off against those whose intention is to pull people in different directions precisely to create confusion, sow division, and unravel the very fabric of society.
16. Discerning what is the straight path is especially critical in our current wilderness where voices are trying to undermine truth. They're trying to get us to question reality. They want to lead us into dangerous fantasies of conspiracy and intrigue.
17. Tiny viruses of doubt have exploded into a pandemic of propaganda. They are attacking truth, science, and reality itself. Lies, half-truths, and manipulative spin are spun out of so-called news organizations like Fox, NewsMax, and OANN. Bloated media personalities, including the one in the Oval Office, bullhorn their

hate-filled falsehoods to millions of followers. Social media networks profit from the propagation of propaganda. Not to mention the shadowy QAnon cult that draws in millions of followers with its siren song of conspiracy theories.

(The word "however" at the beginning of paragraph 15 clues us that we have come to another pivot. In this paragraph, the sermon again references its Central Claim, which is: Because Jesus is the Messiah, the Son of God, we must maintain our commitment to the faithful witness of John and follow the straight path of truth in the wilderness of a politically polarized society. *Paragraphs 16 and 17 name organizations that are the sources of lies, divisiveness, and conspiracy theories. In some churches, being this specific would be a risky move; however, Leah knows that the members of this congregation have already bemoaned this reality in informal conversations. So while this is a bold statement, it wouldn't be controversial in her preaching context.)*

18. So, how can we be the church in this wilderness? In the midst of this bizarro, upside-down world where fact is made fiction and lies become truth, what is the role of the church?
19. Just like that crowd at the river, and just like Mark's congregation, we're going to have to make choices. Are we going to follow those who deliberately undermine truth and the gospel of Jesus? Or will we follow John's straight path?

(Paragraph 18 makes still another pivot, this time to the implications of the Central Claim for the congregation. The questions in this paragraph are a way to lead the listeners to think about the "so what" of the sermon. Paragraph 19 alerts them to the choices they will have to make, just as the people in the story and the people in Mark's church had to make choices. Here you can see the three corners of Experience, Reason, and Scripture coming together.)

20. John defiantly refused to participate in a system that traffics in half-truths, lies, gaslighting, conspiracy, and manipulation. His ministry was about prophetic truth-telling. "Make straight the path of the Lord!" None of this curvy, conspiracy theory, connect-the-dots kind of path.
21. We must maintain our commitment to the faithful witness of John and the truth that is Jesus Christ because Jesus himself is true, trustworthy, and trust-producing. This means we have to come to terms with the fact that the straight path runs right through the wilderness. Our focus *must* be on creating and following the straight path. We must join John in testifying to the light of Jesus. In turn, *we* have to be true, trustworthy, and trust-producing.

(Paragraphs 20 and 21 further explain the importance of John's ministry and reiterate the Theological Claim that Jesus Christ is "true, trustworthy, and trust-producing." Paragraph 21 is also the first clue as to what Leah chose for her Central Purpose—option #3, "This sermon prepares the congregation for a ministry of truth-telling and education so that during this Advent season of anxious waiting, they can help forge the straight path of Christ for people to follow." *You may have seen the influence of option #2 on this sermon as well, because the sermon encourages people to "speak Christ's truth in the midst of a wilderness of lies, conspiracy theories, and cultish behavior." However, the next several paragraphs show that Leah wanted the congregation to think about how they could play an active role in creating the "straight path" of truth. So option #3 became the Central Purpose.)*

22. What are ways that we as the church can create that path of truth and teach our members how to recognize what is true, trustworthy, and trust-producing? How might the church create this straight path in the wilderness, especially as we are in this anxious season of waiting?
23. Well, it's time to get back to the basics. The church needs to help people learn how to distinguish what is true from what is not. We're going to have to brush off that Eighth Commandment, "You shall not bear false witness." This is a direct command from God not to lie or spread falsehoods.
24. We're going to have to confront the brutal dishonesty of our communications industry and hold them accountable for the consequences of their lies. We're going to have to tell the truth about the systems of race, wealth, and privilege that benefit from lies, gaslighting, and manipulation through fear.

25. The church is going to have to engage in the difficult but necessary conversations about what it means to live in a twisted moral paradigm that rewards and profits from lying, disinformation, and undermining truth. We're going to have to have real talk about what this toxic environment of deceitfulness means for our society, for our children and communities, and for the church. Most importantly, we have to be clear that these efforts to deceive are not the will of God. God desires only what is true, trustworthy, and trust-producing.

(Paragraphs 22 through 25 are exhortations for the congregation to put their faith into action based on their values and ethical commitments as followers of Christ. Notice that paragraph 25 has two strong theological statements that you should have underlined: "these efforts to deceive are not the will of God. God desires only what is true, trustworthy, and trust-producing." *Leah felt it was important to clearly state the nature of God and what God wants for us and our communities. Recapitulating the phrase* true, trustworthy, and trust-producing *solidifies this Theological Claim.)*

26. So we'll have to do some education. We can hold forums for teens and adults about how to figure out what is "true" and real on the internet. We have educators in our congregation who can help us! They can give us a refresher course on the scientific method, how it works, and why it's necessary for a functioning society. We can offer a forum on critical thinking skills to equip people for staying grounded in reality and discerning what is true.
27. Above all during this season of waiting, we need to preach and teach the gospel of Jesus Christ, the one who was true, trustworthy, and trust-producing, precisely because he is the Son of God. We need to model honesty, basic decency, and compassion so that our friends, family, and neighbors will know that this is who we are as Christians. In the midst of a dishonest, corrupt, and abusive wilderness, we need to care for the vulnerable, honor our neighbors, and protect the weak.

(In paragraphs 26 and 27, Leah gives specific suggestions for how the congregation might respond and put their faith into action. Her suggestions are further evidence that option #3 was the Central Purpose she chose for this sermon because it focused on education.)

28. Ultimately, Mark's Gospel proclaims that there is a power that is greater and longer-lasting than lies. It is the power of truth, honesty, and discernment. It's the power of advocating for and protecting the vulnerable. And it's the power of casting a vision for the Realm of God through the coming of Jesus Christ.
29. This is the truth to which John testified. This is what Jesus's ministry, life, death, and resurrection were about. This is who God is, what God does, and what God wants the church to be about. Prepare and make straight the way of the Lord. Seek out the path of truth. Listen to John. Follow Jesus. Amen.

(You probably underlined every sentence in paragraphs 28 and 29, because these last two paragraphs conclude the sermon with strong Theological Claims and reiterate the biblical injunctions to prepare, make the straight paths, listen, *and* follow.*)*

REFLECTION ON THE SERMON

How did the congregation respond to this sermon? Recall that Leah had said that she would be on the lookout for comments about the sermon after the service as the congregation engaged in conversation during the Zoom fellowship time. While there were a few comments and words of appreciation for naming what was happening, there was not an immediate jump to act on any of the suggestions from the sermon. However, one month later the nation watched an actual coup attempt on January 6, 2021, the day when Congress counted the votes of the Electoral College and certified the results of the election. So, there was plenty of conversation the next Sunday recalling this sermon. In the months that followed, the congregation planned and carried out a series of anti-racism book studies and prepared for next steps to be a witness of truth-telling within their community.

KEY POINTS IN THIS CHAPTER

1. The Central Purpose for your sermon is derived from the Central Question and the Central Claim.
2. Use the questions to prepare for the Central Purpose to determine your audience and what's important to them, your intention for your listeners upon hearing this sermon, and how you want the listeners to feel. Think about what might be indicators that your congregation is heading in the right direction based on your aim for the sermon.
3. Use the questions for developing the "so that" of the Central Purpose to determine why your congregation needs to hear this sermon about this text at this particular time, who will care that this sermon has been preached and the difference it will make, why the Central Claim matters, and how you envision things being different as a result of this sermon.
4. There are some basic sentence structures that can be used to formulate the Central Purpose. The key is to use "vigorous verbs" that articulate what the preacher wants the sermon to do or accomplish in and for the listeners.
5. Avoid making the Central Purpose just another version of the Central Claim. One way to do this is to steer clear of "anemic verbs" that only lead to intellectual assent rather than an inspired response.
6. Think about how certain verbs set the tone for the sermon. Carefully consider what action words will best convey the intent of the sermon as well as the "so that," the hoped-for result.

DISCUSSION QUESTIONS

1. One aspect of the text that got only a brief mention in the sermon was the role of baptism in Mark 1:1-8. If you were to rewrite this sermon with an emphasis on that aspect of the text, what would you change? What would you add, take away, or shift so that baptism could become more of a focal point of the sermon?
2. This sermon pulled together three aspects of the Wesleyan Quadrilateral—Scripture, Experience, and Reason. If you were to bring in Tradition, how might you do that? What could you reference from church history that would speak to divisiveness, disinformation, and conspiracies? Or what aspect of your denomination's history could you reference for this sermon?
3. In the reflection on the sermon about Mark 1:1-8, it was noted that sometimes the seeds from a sermon don't sprout until later. Can you recall a time when a sermon you heard planted seeds for you that needed time to germinate? Looking back, how was the Holy Spirit working on you through that sermon in ways that weren't immediately apparent?

FOR FURTHER READING

Jared E. Alcántara. Ch. 2, "Preach Convictionally." In *The Practices of Christian Preaching: Essentials for Effective Proclamation.* Grand Rapids, MI: Baker Academic, 2019.

Karoline M. Lewis. Ch. 7, "A Faithful Sermon Is Inspirational." In *A Lay Preacher's Guide: How to Craft a Faithful Sermon.* Minneapolis, MN: Fortress Press, 2020.

Robert Stephen Reid. Ch. 9 Introduction, "Seeking a Response." In *New Interpreter's Handbook of Preaching,* edited by Paul Scott Wilson. Nashville: Abingdon Press, 2008.

NOTE

1. To learn more about developing sermons on challenging social issues in politically divided congregations, see *Preaching in the Purple Zone: Ministry in the Red-Blue Divide* by Leah D. Schade (Rowman & Littlefield, 2019).

IV

CREATIVITY AND STRUCTURES FOR SERMONS

18

Activating Theological Imagination in Sermons with Salience, Resonance, Coherence, and Creativity

Up to this point in our work on sermon preparation, we've given you step-by-step instructions for exegeting a biblical text and your community, theologically analyzing a scriptural passage, and crafting the Central Question, Central Claim, and Central Purpose statements. Another important task of preaching is to cultivate what we have called "theological imagination" to make the biblical text come alive for preachers and their congregations. Recall that in Chapter 8, you learned about *theological imagination* and the power of metaphor to craft appropriate Theological Claims. In that chapter we spotlighted the metaphors of the Earth as God's body (drawing on Sallie McFague) and God is Black (drawing on James Cone). Both images expanded traditional White patriarchal notions of God and challenged the oppressive systems that use harmful theology to justify slavery and destroying God's Creation.

In this chapter, we will build a "theological imagination toolbox" for preaching that will equip you to use descriptive language, imagery, metaphors, and creativity in developing your preaching. We will identify various rhetorical and creative techniques for crafting engaging sermons, and we will introduce some exercises for sparking creativity in your preaching, including (but not limited to) drawing on the arts, music, comedy, poetry, and storytelling. This chapter will teach you to utilize techniques such as "mind-mapping" and "writing off the page" while considering the context of your listeners to create points of salience and resonance. Using these techniques for preaching will help you engage your listeners, create a powerful experience of God's justice and grace, and invite the congregation to live out the gospel in the world.

ACTIVATING THEOLOGICAL IMAGINATION WITH SALIENCE AND RESONANCE

As you worked through the process for your Central Question, Central Claim, and Central Purpose, you probably noticed that ideas began to emerge for how you might illustrate your sermon with creative images, metaphors, analogies, stories, or descriptive language. Or your ideas might have come during your initial reading of the biblical text and during your exegesis. At other times, flashes of inspiration for a sermon might come to you through a conversation with a pastoral colleague, or while listening to a piece of music, taking a walk, taking a shower, or taking out the trash. Sermon ideas can come through songs on the radio, when you're watching a movie or television show, visiting a parishioner in an assisted living facility, scrolling news headlines, reading a gripping novel, or simply while standing in line at the grocery store. No matter how or when the inspiration comes, all preachers must choose which **illustrations** will be most effective for helping their sermons connect with their congregation. They also have to decide what illustrations will best support their Central Statements.

Karyn Wiseman says, "Preaching needs creativity and imagination almost more than anything else to avoid the chance of being boring or uninspiring."[1] She acknowledges that preaching a sermon certainly requires "deliberate exegesis, contextual study, personal prayer, meticulous preparation, careful analysis, presentation practice, and other necessary elements." However, she also notes that "for preaching to ignite the fires in the belly of those hearing the sermon there often needs to be something to catch their imagination, to spark their creative thoughts, and to push their minds to see where the word, the sermon, and the preacher are going. This type of creativity invites people to see a text with new eyes, to hear a story in an innovative and creative way."[2]

Imagination is the capacity to form concepts or images in one's mind that are not immediately present. This mental faculty enables us to create pictures in our minds, solve problems, and create art, music, poetry, and, yes, sermons. In Chapter 8, we spoke of *theological imagination*, the capacity to be inspired and guided by God's mysterious Spirit, which gives us the capacity to envision God's Realm and how we might be partners in co-creating it. Theological imagination is how the "magic" happens when a preacher gains sudden insight into the biblical text and then communicates that in a way that makes their listeners perk up with heightened attention to what God is doing in their lives and in the world. Linda Clader describes the process of engaging the imagination for preaching this way:

> We may have been pouring over erudite commentaries, aware only of our most rational function, and—bam!—we feel the truth of the scriptural story in our hearts and in our bones. Neurologists tell us that our limbic system, our "emotional brain," behaves "something like a valve, deciding what will grab our attention and what will not." They call this phenomenon "salience"—that which jumps out at you.[3]

Salience is when something springs up or juts out to demand our attention. Salience in a sermon might be experienced through a story that speaks to one's heart, an analogy that helps create understanding, or an image from Scripture that is explored in depth. Whatever its form, a salient illustration will stand out for the listeners and give them something to hold onto as they are listening to you preach. For example, you may recall the "coral reef" illustration from Chapter 7 and the "mother hen" imagery from the sermon in Chapter 11. We'll analyze these and other salient images in the next chapter.

In addition to salience, another important part of theological imagination is **resonance**, which, in physics, describes the phenomenon where an object vibrates in sync with a nearby sound. For example, Leah is a harpist, and she has noticed that when she plucks one string on the instrument, the other strings around it will vibrate as well, enhancing the overall sound. However, if she puts her hand on the surrounding strings to dampen them, the sound of the single string quickly fades. Applied to preaching, sermon illustrations should resonate with the listener by activating something in their hearts and minds and connecting with sights, sounds, smells, textures, tastes, and emotions that "reverberate" for them. Part of our work in this chapter is to remove any "dampeners" that may hinder that resonance in your preaching so that your sermon rings true with authenticity, connects "head and heart" (intellect and emotion), and facilitates an experience of the gospel.

HOW TO TEST YOUR THEOLOGICAL IMAGINATION TO ENSURE IT IS "OF THE SPIRIT"

In Chapter 8, we noted that Theological Claims do not come out of thin air; they are not just made up. We can't just say anything we want about God and deem it true just because we think it or feel it. Because we are finite and easily misled, we might come up with some demonic ideas about God that do damage by authorizing oppression, abuse, neglect, or violence. Thus, there are limits on what we can and *should* say about God.

So how can we test our theological imagination to ensure that it is "of the Spirit," that is, in alignment with the God revealed to us in Scripture and in God's revelation in the life and ministry of Jesus Christ? Here are some guidelines and questions for using theological imagination as you are crafting your sermons.

1. Test your theological imagination against the Wesleyan Quadrilateral. Are your images and metaphors based on a critical and justice-oriented interpretation of Scripture? Are they informed by your theological Tradition? Does the world of science, social science, and branches of philosophy (i.e., Reason) inform your theological imagination? Does this image or metaphor ring true to the community's discernment about their experience of God (i.e., Experience)?

2. Speaking of community, test your theological imagination by sharing your ideas with others. You can do this with a preaching mentor, with a group of preaching colleagues, with parishioners, or with people outside of your congregation who can offer a different perspective. Ask them to help you discern if your insights, hunches, and inspiration are "of the Spirit."
3. Does your theological imagination expand the Realm of God to others who are often silenced, shamed, diminished, oppressed, feared, or hated in society? Or does it reinforce harmful stereotypes, uphold heteronormative White patriarchal notions about God. Alternatively, does it "domesticate" God, Jesus Christ, or the Holy Spirit? In other words, does it diminish or restrict the Divine?
4. Is your theological imagination prophetic without being punishing? In other words, do the words, images, metaphors, and stories you use call power structures to account while also extending justice and mercy to listeners?
5. Are your words, images, metaphors, and stories connecting with people's emotions without sentimentality or manipulation? As the philosopher Mary Midgley has said, emotion is the "powerhouse" of ethics.[4] But preachers need to avoid sentimentality, which is indulging in feeling and emotion for its own sake. And they must be careful not to use the sermon to manipulate people's emotions, which will raise doubts about one's authenticity and trustworthiness.

COHERENCE: DEVELOPING YOUR THEOLOGICAL IMAGINATION FOR—AND FROM—THE CENTRAL STATEMENTS

Another important aspect of utilizing theological imagination in a sermon is that it must have **coherence** with the biblical text, with one's Theological Claim, and with the Central Question, Central Claim, and Central Purpose. When something *coheres*, it holds together. A coherent sermon illustration will hold together with one's exegesis, will accurately demonstrate or elucidate the theological concept being conveyed, and will be intelligible in one's context. In short, we need illustrations that make sense and logically communicate what the preacher is trying to convey. One way to increase the chances that your illustration is coherent with your exegesis and Theological Claim is to think about how theological imagination grows out of, as well as informs, the Central Question, Central Claim, and Central Purpose.

Theological Imagination and the Central Question

Theological imagination can inform a preacher's Central Question because it allows for developing empathy with those who are in pain, seeing beneath the surface to the underlying dynamics of a biblical passage, and perceiving the emotional drive behind an author's intent. Alyce McKenzie calls this "a knack for noticing," which means to be "attentive to life within us and around us."[5] She explains, "We need to pay attention to our inner life (inscape), life around us (landscape), and the life of the biblical text (textscape)."[6] The Central Question, then, can activate that theological imagination as well as capture the energy that flows from the text and the community to address the exigencies of life.

Theological Imagination and the Central Claim

Theological imagination also informs, and is informed by, the Central Claim. As HyeRan Kim-Cragg describes it, imagination "is what the preacher uses to help the congregation conjure a new world in their minds and hearts."[7] Theological imagination has a vital role in helping a congregation see something different from what presently exists, especially when it comes to systemic injustice, colonialism, fear of people of diverse sexual orientations who identify outside the gender binary, and White supremacy, for example. Through theological imagination, preachers can help a congregation "move beyond present realities into something that has yet to be fully grasped."[8] In this way, the Central Claim, which is the primary assertion of the sermon, draws on theological imagination to help listeners to both see the world as it is and envision the Realm that God seeks to bring to fulfillment.

Theological Imagination and the Central Purpose

The Central Purpose, too, has a lot to do with theological imagination. We can use theological imagination to foresee how the text might be relevant for our congregation's lives and then invite them to respond accordingly. Lisa L. Thompson notes that "the engagement of lived experience is the subtle yet poignant bridge between what is familiar and what is unfamiliar in preaching. A preacher must carve out a place for the reception of her message when helping a community imagine new possibilities."[9] Thompson explains that this happens "by determining ways to use that which the community already knows to forge something new."[10] The preacher, then, can use imagination to draw out the implications of the Central Claim in order to derive the Central Purpose for the sermon. In this way, the congregation can enact that which they and the preacher have imagined together.

SPARKING AND CULTIVATING THEOLOGICAL IMAGINATION

So how does a preacher cultivate their theological imagination? There are many ways we can describe what it's like to develop the "knack for noticing" and the skill of crafting sermon illustrations with salience, resonance, and coherence. For some, it's like opening a Wi-Fi connection or tuning a radio dial to be able to pick up the signals of the Holy Spirit. For others, developing the theological imagination is like working on one's athletic skills by practicing and working the muscles that allow them to play the game with prowess and responsiveness. For still others, cultivating theological imagination is what some art teachers describe as "learning how to see." This is not necessarily seeing in the physical sense, because even those who have sight impairment can create art, play a sport, and preach a sermon. Rather, it's about developing the capacity to *perceive with clarity*. This, in turns, helps us to generate and receive inspiration.

In other words, we can develop *habits of creativity*. Such habits of creativity take discipline, practice, and intentionality. As Wiseman explains:

> We have to discover connections to our creative selves. Ways to do this include avoiding perfectionism to allow your creative spirit the much needed room to stretch and grow; taking risks to let your creative self "play" within whatever medium you are working at the time; taking jealousy of others' talents or skills out of the equation; and finding a sacred space in which to work, a space that connects you to your creative self, to your best self, and to God.[11]

Below, we'll experiment with several exercises that can help you develop some habits of creativity and build your theological imagination. (See also Appendix K for a quick reference guide to the exercises.)

CAUTIONS REGARDING THE USE OF THEOLOGICAL IMAGINATION

While enriching one's theological imagination is important work, this aspect of preaching is not meant to replace or circumvent the deeper biblical and theological engagement with the text and topic. In other words, the exercises below must coincide with serious and responsible historical, literary, rhetorical, and theological criticism.

Preachers must also be sure to expand their theological imagination beyond their own point of view. This will help them to avoid being limited or biased by their positionality in terms of gender, race, sexual orientation, geographic region, physical ability, socioeconomic position, and language. At the same time, preachers must also guard against universalizing or overgeneralizing their own experience or observations. It's best to avoid sentences such as, "Everyone knows what it's like to . . ." or "Surely, all of us have had this experience . . ." Undoubtedly, there will be at least one person who is an exception to your assumption and will feel left out. Instead, use qualifying language such as, "Maybe some of you have had this experience . . ." or, "While we all have different experiences, here's just one example . . ."

Another thing to note is that when it comes to using theological imagination, a preacher is not expected to use all of these exercises for every sermon. Nor should they try to stuff too much into one sermon. When it comes to sermon preparation, don't get overwhelmed by the number of possible ways to engage imaginatively when doing your sermon preparation. We suggest that a preacher try just one of these for a sermon and experiment with a different technique each week. And when it comes to using the words, images, and stories that result from these exercises, be selective about the one or two that will buttress your Central Statements rather than overwhelm the congregation with imagination overload.

LECTIO: APPROACHING THE BIBLE WITH "BEGINNER'S MIND"

In her book *Backstory Preaching*, Lisa Cressman recommends that preachers begin their sermon preparation through a process called *lectio*, a Latin word that can mean both "a reading" and "selection." Some may be familiar with the practice of ***lectio divina***, which means "divine reading" in Latin. Lectio is a method of engaging Scripture through prayer and meditation without going immediately to meaning-making or exegesis. Of course, this practice doesn't replace exegesis and interpretation by any means. But it is a practice that can be used to cultivate the "knack for noticing" about the text itself. In this way, we approach the text with what Buddhists call "beginner's mind," putting aside our preconceived notions, assumptions, and biases to make room for what the Spirit might reveal.

Cressman describes the lectio process this way:

> [R]ead the passage several times. Read out loud. Read in different tones of voice. Read with an accent. Read as a child who wouldn't understand half the words. Take note of who is in the story, where it happens, the time, the season, the objects mentioned, the materials, and the building. In your imagination, stand still and turn around 360 degrees. What do you see, hear, smell, taste, and feel? Pastorally, what do you sense?

This exercise can help to guide the formulation of your Central Question because it can alert you to the "splinter" in the text that draws our attention. Then when you do your exegetical work, you may discover insights about this question, or you might find other points of interest that will help you and your congregation better understand the text.

EXERCISE 1

Lectio with a Biblical Text

This is an exercise that Leah does with her students in class, with a different person reading the text each time. If practicing this alone, simply adapt the instructions for a single reader.

Things you'll need:

- A Bible open to the passage you've chosen for the basis of your sermon.
- A notebook and pen or pencil.
- (Optional) A recording device, such as a voice recording app on your phone.

1. Begin with centering prayer asking for the Spirit to open your heart and mind to receive the Word of God.
2. Have someone read the text out loud and simply listen.
3. Sit in contemplative silence for sixty seconds. Take deep cleansing breaths.
4. Have someone else read the text (perhaps from a different translation) and record it for future listening. Notice one word that jumps out for you. Write down that word.
5. Sit in contemplative silence for sixty seconds. Take deep cleansing breaths.
6. Have a third person read the text and each person write down their questions, observations, "gaps," or "splinters."
7. Sit in contemplative silence for sixty seconds. Take deep cleansing breaths.
8. Share and discuss what has come up for you that might guide your Central Question.
9. Conclude with prayer thanking God for the insights, wisdom, and questions that have been shared through this reading.

CAPTURING YOUR IDEAS: MIND-MAPPING, WRITING OFF THE PAGE, AND SENSORY NET

One of the most important, but sometimes overlooked, parts of sermon preparation is *collection*—finding a way to generate and capture good ideas for sermon illustrations. Jennifer L. Lord's book, *Finding Language and Imagery*, includes a chapter on "Weekly Word Work" that helps preachers attend to the words and imagery both in the biblical text and in the sermon itself. She suggests a process to accompany one's exegesis in which you study the words and imagery in the text: keep notes about important words; write down images that come to mind; note words, sentences, or sentence fragments the come to mind; and categorize the words and images.[12]

Lord offers several exercises that we have found useful with our students. One of them is called "mind-mapping," where a word is written in the center of a page (or a dry erase board) and related words are written around it. Free association like this can often reveal themes or related concepts not immediately apparent on a first encounter with a biblical text. A second one is called "writing off the page," which is a concentrated, short burst of stream-of-conscious exercise. In this exercise, you write nonstop for five minutes about a word, sentence, or sentence fragment from the biblical text.[13] This can provide fodder for developing sermon ideas and illustrations.

A third exercise that Leah has developed for her students is called the "sensory net." In this exercise, you write down sights, sounds, tastes, touch, smells, as well as emotions, that the biblical text evokes. Such a practice can activate theological imagination and put flesh on the bones of our preaching. As Lord states, "sense language is one way of making abstract ideas become tangible."[14]

All of these exercises can intersect with your theological engagement with the text and the sermon. For example, recall the importance of *metaphor* for both the biblical text and your sermon. A metaphor is a figure of speech that brings two unrelated ideas together to illustrate a comparison or an abstract concept. The Bible uses metaphorical language to convey theological ideas; sermons can and should do the same. Mind-mapping, writing off the page, and the sensory net are ways to tap into metaphorical thinking by opening our minds to new connections, alternative perspectives, and engagement with the senses that can illuminate theological concepts and truths.

EXERCISE 2

Mind-mapping

Things you'll need:

- Bible open to the passage you've chosen for the basis of your sermon.
- Large piece of paper and pen/pencil. Also works with large notepad on an easel or dry erase board for large groups.

1. Begin with centering prayer and then read the text out loud. Choose one word you think is central to the text (either a concept or a thing/person/place/verb).
2. Write down the word in the center of the page.
3. Without discussion or judgment, write down all the words that come to your mind about the center word. Don't stop to assess what you've written—that comes later. Simply write other words and phrases all over the paper surrounding that word.
4. Circle five things that resonate for you.
5. In a "wheel-and-spokes" fashion, draw lines connecting those five words with one another and how they relate to the center word.
6. Think about or discuss with others how these ideas might inform the Central Question, Central Claim, or Central Purpose.

EXERCISE 3

Writing off the Page

Things you'll need:

- Bible open to the passage you've chosen for the basis of your sermon.
- Journal or piece of paper and pen/pencil.
- Timer.

1. Begin with centering prayer and then read the text. Underline one word, phrase, or image that calls to you.
2. Set your timer for five minutes.
3. Write the word, sentence, or image at the top of the page and then start the timer.
4. Using stream-of-consciousness, write down your thoughts about the word without stopping for five minutes. Even if it's gibberish, just keep writing and don't stop until the five minutes are up.
5. Go back through and underline the ideas that seem salient or resonant for you.
6. Think about or discuss with others how these ideas might inform the Central Question, Central Claim, or Central Purpose.

EXERCISE 4

Sensory Net

Things you'll need:

- Pen/pencil.
- One piece of paper oriented horizontally. Make six columns with the following headings:
  a. I see . . .
  b. I taste . . .
  c. I smell . . .
  d. I touch . . .
  e. I hear . . .
  f. I feel . . .
- An audio recording of the biblical text you will use for the basis of your sermon.

1. Begin with centering prayer. Then, using a recording app on your phone, record yourself (or someone else) reading the biblical text *slowly*. (Alternatively, you can use one of the many audio recordings of the Bible available on the internet or in an audiobook.)
2. Listen to a recording of the text and write down the sights, tastes, smells, textures, sounds, and emotions that come to you as you listen.
3. For "I feel," imagine the emotions of each character in the story—including the other-than-human beings and even objects.[1]
4. Think about (or discuss with a group) how you might use this sensory information to inform your Central Question, Central Claim, or Central Purpose.
5. Begin jotting notes for how you might use what you've collected in this Sensory Net to create evocative images and illustrations for your sermon and to connect head and heart in your preaching.

NOTE

1. A wonderful source of ideas for thinking about the "experience" of objects is the podcast *Everything Is Alive*, an interview show in which all the subjects are inanimate objects (https://www.everythingisalive.com/). In each episode, the object tells its life story with surprising poignancy, humor, cleverness, and insight into the human condition. A preacher might creatively imagine the "life story" of certain significant biblical objects such as Miriam's tambourine (Exodus 15:20), the stones along the road when Jesus enters Jerusalem (Luke 19:40), or the jail cell holding Paul and Silas (Acts 16:22-34).

PREACHING OFF THE PAGE: EXPERIMENTING WITH EXTEMPORANEOUS PREACHING

An exercise related to writing off the page is one Leah developed called "preaching off the page." This exercise challenges a preacher to speak off-the-cuff for three minutes about a biblical passage without any preparation. The exercise is inspired by the Table Topics challenge used by Toastmasters International, an organization that teaches public speaking and leadership skills through a worldwide network of clubs. In a Table Topic challenge, speakers are given a topic that is not revealed until they step to the podium. For three minutes they must give an impromptu speech about the topic. The exercise trains members to be able to think on their feet, organize their thoughts on the fly, and gain confidence with public speaking.[15]

In Leah's sermon classes, she has students pull out a short biblical passage at random from a basket, read it out loud, take thirty seconds to center their thoughts, and then "preach" about the passage for three minutes. Even students who are nervous about speaking are often surprised at how easily they are able to conjure up an idea on the spur of the moment. They also find that the rush of adrenaline often leads them to talk about a story, an image, or an idea that they wouldn't have had access to if they had only stayed curled up on the couch with their Bible and a warm beverage.

The "preaching off the page" exercise can also be done in the privacy of one's home or office to help a preacher generate ideas for their sermon. In some ways, it is similar to the stream-of-consciousness exercise of "writing off the page." However, brain researchers have discovered that our abilities to speak and write are each controlled in two separate (though related) parts of the brain. So, speaking off-the-cuff uses a different part of the brain than writing off-the-cuff, which is slower and more thoughtful. A preacher could try this exercise by themselves or with a group of colleagues.

EXERCISE 5

Preaching Off the Page

Things you'll need:

- Bible open to the passage you've chosen for the basis of your sermon. Do not read it silently ahead of time because that will defeat the purpose of the exercise.
- Timer.
- Recording device such as a video camera or audio recording app. You don't want to lose any nifty ideas that might come to you in this exercise!

1. Begin with centering prayer and then set your timer for three minutes.
2. Hit the "record" button.
3. Read the text out loud.
4. Pause for thirty seconds to breathe, calm your mind, and gather your thoughts.
   a. Ideas and questions to get you started:
      i. Does this passage remind you of a story?
      ii. Can you talk about an image or a word in the text and what it brings up for you?
      iii. What were you taught or what did you think about this passage growing up? What do you think about it now?
      iv. Who does this passage remind you of?
      v. When was a time you faced something like this in your life?
      vi. How does this passage make you feel?
      vii. What are the sights, smells, sounds, textures, and tastes that come to you as you read this passage?
5. Begin the timer.
6. If in a group, be sure to look at the people in the room. If alone, look in the camera or pretend that you're looking at a group of people, talking to them.
7. Remember that you don't have to have a complete "sermon." Your conclusion of this impromptu speech might be that you have hit upon the question you want to address in the rest of the sermon. Or that you see a clue about what your Central Claim might be for this sermon.
8. When the timer stops, finish your sentence and then stop the recorder.
9. Watch the recording and think about or discuss with others how these ideas might inform the Central Question, Central Claim, or Central Purpose.

PREACHING PREP WITH PLAY-DOH

Even though preaching is all about *words*, which involve mostly the brain, eyes, and ears, it's also important to invite different parts of the body to experience the biblical text. Some preaching professors get out crayons and invite their students to draw or color what they see or hear in a Scripture passage. Karyn Wiseman uses an exercise with her preaching students that includes Play-Doh or modelling clay. Once a text is read, the students are invited to mold something that came to their mind as they listened. "Many of the passages have included clear images of trees, boats, bread, and other obvious concrete and visual items—but not all. Some students molded items that were not as obvious, many of which sparked wonderful conversation within the gathered group," she explains.[16]

In Leah's adaptation of the exercise below, you'll see instructions for this as a group activity. But it's also possible to do this on your own by listening to recordings of someone (or yourself) reading the text while you sculpt.

EXERCISE 6

Play-Doh-ing with the Bible

Things you'll need:

- Bible open to the passage you've chosen for the basis of your sermon.
- Containers of Play-Doh or modelling clay. (Note: a pile of pipe cleaners can also be used; just substitute the instructions accordingly.)
- Dry erase board (for larger groups).

1. Choose one container of Play-Doh and then begin with centering prayer.
2. One person reads the Scripture passage out loud—slowly, so that people have time to knead the dough and allow their fingers and hands to work. Repeat the reading if people need more time to finish.
3. As the passage is read, work the dough into an image or something that represents how you feel when you hear the words read. It can be something concrete or more abstract, like a design.
4. A second person reads the Scripture passage. This time, everyone walks around and looks at the different sculptures as they listen to the text.
5. Reflect on the sculptures. Each person shares one word about what they saw expressed in others' sculptures. Write these on the board.
6. Circle the words in one color that have a negative connotation. Circle the words in a different color that have a positive connotation. (Dotted-line circles for uncertain connotations.)
7. Invite each person to share why they sculpted what they did.
8. Discuss—Where are the "heart" places of this passage? What are the "pain points"? Where is hope or growth? Where is the struggle? Where is God?
9. Discuss how these ideas might be worked into your Central Question, Central Claim, or Central Purpose.

EMBODYING THE TEXT: GROUP-SCULPTING THE SCRIPTURE AND GROUP IMPROVISATION

Christians, along with Jews and Muslims, are considered "People of the Book," meaning that our faith both springs from and finds its grounding in holy writ. Words are *very* important for us—both those written in Scripture and preached in sermons. But there is also a physicality and incarnational aspect of our faith and our Scriptures that we sometimes overlook, ignore, or even suppress. So it can be helpful to engage in creative activities that put us back into our own bodies in relation to the text. Two exercises that you can try are called "story sculpting" and group improvisation. These are activities that can be done with a group of at least three to five people.

Group-Sculpting the Scripture

Sculpting the Scripture is based on a technique devised by family therapists called "family sculpting." In this exercise, one member of the family physically arranges the other members in relationship to one another. Like mannequins arranged in a display, the members of the group are placed by the sculptor to show how they wish to represent a certain scenario. For example, a teenager may be prompted to create a sculpture of what it's like when their family members are fighting. She may put her parents with their backs to each other, arms folded. Then she may put her younger sibling hiding in a corner, while she stands with her hands pleading. Afterward, the therapist talks with the family members to learn how they experienced their relationships relative to one another. Often, emotions surface through this wordless but physical activity that cannot be accessed by classic talk therapy.

When applied to a biblical text, story sculpting can be a creative way to gain a new perspective on a passage. For example, a group sculpting Jeremiah 11:18-20 might put one participant on their hands and knees being led to a person with a knife (to represent a lamb being led to the slaughter), while another person might be placed as a tree with two others pretending to hold axes ready to chop it down. Yet another person might be designated as the figure of God in the passage standing with their arms outstretched to stop the slaughter and the axe. After freezing in this tableau, participants would discuss what it was like for them in these different roles. This might elicit ideas for the Central Question such as, "How does it feel to be vulnerable in the face of threats, and what is God's role in defending the weak?" Or the exercise might inform the Central Claim: "God reveals the intentions of those preying on the vulnerable and works through the church to stay the hand of evildoers." Similarly, an insight from the exercise might influence the Central Purpose: "The purpose of this sermon is to encourage congregants to enact their faith in our protecting God by assisting with a community initiative to draw attention to domestic violence and help keep families safe."

This exercise could be done before starting the exegesis on a text in order to capture the immediate impressions and feelings. Or it could be done after reading commentaries on the text to find out the historical context, which could add a different perspective on the sculpting exercise. When this exercise is done as a before-and-after exercise with exegesis, this could yield important insights for preaching. Note that sculpting exercises even of the Bible can elicit strong emotions. The Bible has words, images, and stories that could have a powerful impact on people, so be pastorally prepared.

EXERCISE 7

Group-Sculpting the Scripture

Things you'll need:

- Bible open to the passage you've chosen for the basis of your sermon.
- At least three to five participants—one to serve as the "sculptor" and the others as the participants in the sculpture. This can be done with fellow preachers or with youth and/or adults in one's congregation.
- A few chairs to serve as props or to enable sitting.

1. Begin with centering prayer and then read the passage out loud.
2. Invite the sculptor to place participants in positions that they feel represent some aspect or aspects of the text (and/or the historical situation, if some exegesis has been done).
3. After freezing in the position, invite the sculptor to explain their choices for placement.
4. Ask each participant to share how it felt to be in their posed position.
5. Discuss the experience and how the insights might inform the Central Question, Central Claim, or Central Purpose.

Group Improvisation

The word "improvise" comes from the Latin word *improvisus*, which means "not provided" or "not foreseen." When we improvise, we create something without any preparation or forethought. It is spontaneous and in the moment. Improvisation classes are often used in the fields of music and drama where participants can draw on skills they have learned to create a scene or a musical offering on the spur of the moment without prior rehearsal. As Kirk Byron Jones describes the process among musicians, "To play improvisationally is to play with trusting openness, to go wherever the music wants to go in the moment."[17] The key word here is *play*, not just in the sense of playing a musical instrument, but to be playful, as in the way of children. To play is to enact the creative potential of any moment, object, idea, or, in this case, a biblical text.

Improvisation is similar to the Table Topics exercise above, but in this activity, a group works together to act out a biblical passage. Usually, a narrative works best for this exercise. For example, Leah once had her preaching students do an improvisation on the feeding of the five thousand as told in John 6:1-14. She assigned each student a part: one person was Jesus, one was the boy with the loaves and fishes, others were disciples, and still others were part of the crowd who were fed. First, she read the text and had them simply pantomime what they heard. In the discussion, everyone remarked how the person playing Jesus held her arms in the orans position (arms outstretched) and then lifted up the bread as if she were presiding at Communion. This liturgical aspect of the passage was something many of them missed in prior readings of the text.

Leah reassigned the parts and had them act out the passage again, but this time *without hearing it read.* This challenged them to recall what they remembered from the first round and to fully embody the text without benefit of the written words. This time they noticed how much the people in the crowd pointed to their mouths and empty stomachs to indicate how hungry they were. This brought up a possible angle for a Central Question: "How does hunger manifest in our world today, and what is the role of the church in filling that hunger in Jesus's name?"

Finally, she reassigned the parts yet again and told the students that not only would the text be read aloud, but that they were permitted to talk this time. An astonishing thing happened. When she got to vv. 8 and 9 where the disciple Andrew brings the boy with the loaves and fishes to Jesus, the student playing the little boy pulled away. "No, you can't have these," she said, her lip quivering. "My mommy said I was to bring these right home. If you take them, I can't feed my family." The student playing Jesus looked the boy in the eye and said, "I promise that you'll have more than enough to feed your family. Can I please have these?" The student playing the little boy whispered, "But I'll get in trouble if I give them to you." The room fell silent. No one had ever considered this story from the little boy's perspective. The student who played Jesus said, "I'll tell you what. How about we hold them together and say a prayer, and let's see what happens." All the students gathered around the little boy as Jesus prayed. When the prayer was done, the little boy shouted, "Wow! Look at all this food!" The whole group erupted into peals of joyful laughter and set about munching and sharing the food. At the end, they sent the boy off with a basket of food so full, he could barely carry it.

In the discussion, there were several ideas generated for the Central Claim, such as: "When the church gathers around those most in need, Jesus can provide an abundance of blessings." Several of them decided to do this activity during the reading of the Gospel itself in a worship service so that the congregation could experience their own Spirit-led spontaneity with the text. Others decided to write a script based on the powerful third exercise and invite their youth to act it out for the congregation.

EXERCISE 8

Improv with the Biblical Text

Things you'll need:

- Bible open to the passage you've chosen for the basis of your sermon.
- At least four participants—one to serve as reader, and the others to do the improvisation. This can be done with fellow preachers or with youth and/or adults in one's congregation.

1. Begin with centering prayer and then choose a narrator and assign parts in the story to the participants.
   a. Don't overlook the silent characters in the story when assigning parts. This includes the other-than-human characters as well. For example, in Jesus's parable about the birds of the air and the flowers of the field, assign someone each of those roles so that God's Creation can be represented as well. This can result in perspectives and insights coming to light that are often overlooked in an anthropocentric reading. (See "Ecological Readings" in Chapter 4.)
2. In the first round, have the narrator read the story out loud, slowly and with dramatic inflection. Participants act out what they hear but *without talking.*
3. Discuss the experience.
4. In the second round, assign participants to different roles. Have them act out the story without words *and* without the Scripture being read.
5. Discuss the experience. Notice what things people remembered and carried with them from the first improvisation. What new aspects were added this time, and what things changed?
6. In round three, have participants change roles again. The narrator reads the story out loud, but this time participants act out the story and are allowed to speak—even to the narrator if they wish!
7. Discuss the experience. What differences did they notice between acting without words compared with being allowed to speak? What insights from the exercise might inform the Central Question, Central Claim, and Central Purpose?

OTHER SOURCES OF INSPIRATION FOR YOUR SERMONS

So far, we have discussed many ways in which preachers can activate theological imagination for their preaching, including exercises with lectio, mind-mapping, writing off the page, sensory net, preaching off the page, improvisation, and Play-Doh. Before we close this chapter, here are a few more ideas drawn from Sunggu A. Yang's *Arts and Preaching* and Kirk Byron Jones's *The Jazz of Preaching* for cultivating creativity and getting the imagination juices flowing.

Yang encourages preachers to see an intersectionality between preaching and the aesthetics of art forms such as painting, architecture, fashion, film, and drama. Not only does this encourage a dynamic spiritual formation of the preacher, it allows the preacher and congregation to experience the Bible in a fresh and innovative way.

Using the unique music form of jazz to frame his approach to sermons, Jones helps preachers to improve their preaching by drawing on concepts such as rhythm, tone, call and response, melody, harmony, and dissonance. He encourages preachers to draw on many sources of inspiration for their sermons, often in unconventional ways. His book provides many opportunities for engaging both the aural and emotional qualities of the Bible—from celebration to lament—with suggestions for integrating the insights that emerge from our encounter with God's Word that will enliven our preaching.

Encounter Art Work and Architecture

Encountering art and architecture can teach us important lessons about perspective and spirituality. Study a painting in an art museum or gallery and notice how the artist uses light and shadow, color, space, and framing to capture their subject and convey a message that transcends words. The same elements can be explored in architecture as well, but with the added component of dimension. "Architecture conveys human stories, feelings, philosophies, and cultural histories, and interacts with viewers, occupants, artists, and surrounding communities through them," Yang says.[18] A preacher can creatively apply these concepts when encountering a biblical text and when composing a sermon.

Analyze Film

Yang makes a compelling case that both preaching and film share two essential theological qualities—communication and communion[19]—and encourages preachers to engage cinema as "a critical cultural, spiritual, revelatory conversation partner."[20] This is done not just by including popular movie references in a sermon for illustrative purposes, but to conceive and deliver the sermon the way a movie director shoots a film. In other words, the preacher thinks about the visuals, actions, sounds, and emotional qualities of the sermon. Another way is to design a sermon's literary flow so that it tracks with the narrative structure from an actual movie. This challenges the preacher to study the overall story arc of a film and think creatively about how the structure of one's sermon can utilize these same elements.[21]

Imagine a Soundtrack

If you listen closely, you can hear the Bible sing. Sometimes it is the blues of Lamentations. Other times it is the heraldic trumpets of Psalm 24. And if you bend down beneath the palms waving overhead, you can hear the songs of stones as Jesus enters Jerusalem in Luke 19. One way to think imaginatively about Scripture is to bring to mind the "soundscape" that might accompany a passage. Similarly, what music would you play behind your sermon? ACDC? Rihanna? Vivaldi? B. B. King? John Coltrane? Jones describes the ways in which jazz, like good preaching, can capture the deepest melancholy blues and also riff on the most invigorating joy.[22] Experiment with the "sound palette" of your sermon. Is it a soundscape of resistance? Empowerment? Comfort? Lament? Praise?

Read Poetry

As Jones says, "Poets can teach preachers much about precision, about listening longer in preparation and during the preaching act for the right word or phrase to emerge."[23] Poetry makes use of metaphor, descriptive language, similes, analogies, and imagery, all of which are necessary for powerful preaching. We'll explore these aspects of writing and language in the next chapter.

Study Comedians

This may seem an odd piece of advice. Why would a preacher want to watch a comedian? What can they teach us about preaching? Good comedians are expert observers of the world and of the things that are incongruous and, thus, funny. They have a knack for taking two different ideas and putting them together in unexpected and hilarious ways. Some of them also have the ability to be quite prophetic, in the sense that they are able to convey the truth about injustice, but are able to deliver it couched in humor, like a "spoonful of sugar" with the medicine. "Comedians can teach us much about inflection, nuance, and pacing," says Jones. "They know that a great joke can be ruined by poor timing, or saying the right word in the wrong way. [They] can teach us about pausing, the unsung essential of effective verbal communication. As there is not music without rests, there is no preaching without pauses."[24]

FORM A "SERMON CREATIVITY TEAM"

As you have seen in this chapter, there are myriad ways to spark ideas and exercises for expanding one's theological imagination. Another way to stretch your creativity even further is by working with a group of people who covenant with you as a preacher to practice these exercises together. Some pastors prefer to sequester themselves in their office, a library, or at the local coffee shop to develop the ideas for their sermon. However, you might consider putting together a Sermon Creativity Team to broaden your preaching horizons. Working with a team of people from your congregation to help you think creatively about the sermon can be a way to not only multiply your sources of inspiration but also expand the "roundtable pulpit" of those who have input on your sermon.[25]

Who might be three or four individuals either in your own congregation or from the community who can work with you on creating a sermon experience that will engage the senses of the congregation? Suggestions might include your music director or musicians, artists, actors or individuals with theatre experience. Youth and young adults can also be incredible sources of inspiration and innovation.

Once you have invited these individuals, schedule a time to read the biblical text together well in advance of when you will preach the sermon, at least six to seven days prior, or even a week or month before. This will give you time to integrate the ideas from the team. Set aside an hour to meet with them and to experiment with one or two of the creativity exercises in this chapter.

As you work through these exercises, you may find the group commenting about how much more deeply they are engaging the biblical text than they would with a single hearing on a Sunday morning. This is another benefit of working with the Sermon Creativity Team—they often gain as much from this deep dive into the Bible as the preacher does! This, in turn, enables them to engage the Word of God in ways that provide a fresh perspective. When Leah has worked with students who have used a Sermon Creativity Team for their preaching assignments, they often report that the process results in deeper sharing and is actually fun for everyone because of the invitation to "play" with the text.

Try working with this team once a month for a season. Then invite a new group of individuals to serve as your Sermon Creativity Team for the next season. This will allow for diverse voices to have input and avoids the exercises becoming stale for the participants.

Even if you have difficulty putting together a Sermon Creativity Team on a regular basis, it's important to seek out diverse voices and perspectives to cultivate your theological imagination. As Jared Alcántara asks, "When it comes to preaching, do you read, listen to, or bounce ideas off people who look just like you and believe the exact same things as you, or do you expose yourself to diverse voices and perspectives?"[26] By incorporating different perspectives, we un-stunt our creative growth, expand our theological imagination, and encounter the freshness of the Holy Spirit.

KEY POINTS IN THIS CHAPTER

1. *Imagination* is the capacity to form concepts or images in one's mind that are not immediately present. *Theological imagination* is inspired by God's mysterious Spirit and guides us toward proclaiming God's Realm in creative and innovative ways. Theological imagination is how the "magic" happens when a preacher gains sudden insight into the biblical text and then communicates that in a way that makes their listeners perk up with heightened attention to what God is doing in their lives and in the world.
2. *Salience* in a sermon happens when an image, story, analogy, metaphor, or any kind of illustration stands out and gives the listener some "hand holds" for what the preacher is trying to convey.
3. *Resonance* is when a sermon illustration "vibrates" with an experience of recognition, realization, or emotional response for the listeners.
4. *Coherence* is necessary for sermon illustrations so that they "hold together" with the biblical text, with the Theological Claim, and with the Central Question, Central Claim, and Central Purpose. Sermon illustrations that make sense and logically communicate what the preacher is trying to convey will help the sermon hold together for the listener as well.
5. Creativity can be developed, strengthened, and expanded by engaging in a regular practice of exercises that help the mind and body "play" with the biblical text. In this chapter, we experimented with lectio, mind-mapping, writing off the page, sensory net, preaching off the page, Play-Doh-ing ideas and feelings, sculpting the Scripture, and group improvisation.
6. Music, poetry, artists, and comedians can be sources of inspiration for sermons and preaching. Also, forming a Sermon Creativity Team in your congregation can enhance the experience of engaging everyone's theological imagination.

DISCUSSION QUESTIONS

1. In this chapter, we discussed the importance of *play* for activating one's theological imagination. What did you use to love to play when you were a child? What kinds of make-believe or "let's pretend" did you enjoy? How might you recapture some of that wonder and joy in your preaching?

2. We discussed the importance of having ways to generate and collect ideas for sermon illustrations. Talk with colleagues about what they use to capture their creative thoughts. Do they keep a journal? Collect images and stories in files? Use a computer app to store their ideas?
3. What are other ways that you activate your theological imagination that have not been mentioned in this chapter? Do you view art and photography for inspiration? Have you tried doodling, drawing, or painting when contemplating a biblical text? Does your church have a liturgical dance troupe that could work with you to convey the reading of a biblical text or provide a dance background to your preaching?

FOR FURTHER READING

Lisa Cressman. *Backstory Preaching: Integrating Life, Spirituality, and Craft*. Collegeville, MN: Liturgical Press, 2018.
Kirk Byron Jones. *The Jazz of Preaching: How to Preach with Great Freedom and Joy*. Nashville: Abingdon Press, 2004.
HyeRan Kim-Cragg. *Postcolonial Preaching: Creating a Ripple Effect*. Lanham, MD: Lexington Books, 2021.
Jennifer L. Lord. *Finding Language and Imagery*. Minneapolis, MN: Fortress Press, 2010.
Jacob D. Myers. *Stand-Up Preaching: Homiletical Insights from Contemporary Comedians*. Eugene, OR: Cascade Books, 2022.
Karyn L. Wiseman. *I Refuse to Preach a Boring Sermon! Engaging the 21st Century Listener*. Cleveland, OH: Pilgrim Press, 2013.
Sunggu A. Yang. *Arts and Preaching: An Aesthetic Homiletic for the Twenty-first Century*. Eugene, OR: Cascade Books, 2021.

NOTES

1. Karyn Wiseman, *I Refuse to Preach a Boring Sermon: Engaging the 21st Century Listener* (Cleveland, OH: Pilgrim Press, 2013), 47.
2. Ibid.
3. Linda L. Clader, *Voicing the Vision: Imagination and Prophetic Preaching* (Harrisburg, PA: Morehouse, 2003), 85.
4. Mary Midgley, "Emotion, Emotiveness, and Sentimentality," in *The Essential Mary Midgley*, edited by David Midgley (New York: Routledge, 2005), 112.
5. Alyce McKenzie, *Novel Preaching: Tips from Top Writers on Crafting Creative Sermons* (Louisville, KY: Westminster John Knox, 2010), 11, 12.
6. Ibid., 17.
7. HyeRan Kim-Cragg, *Postcolonial Preaching: Creating a Ripple Effect* (Lanham, MD: Lexington Books, 2021), 5.
8. Ibid., 31.
9. Lisa L. Thompson, *Ingenuity: Preaching as an Outsider* (Nashville: Abingdon Press, 2018), 39.
10. Ibid.
11. Wiseman, 49.
12. Jennifer Lord, *Finding Language and Imagery*. In Elements of Preaching Series, edited by O. Wesley Allen Jr. (Minneapolis, MN: Fortress Press, 2010), 29–37.
13. Ibid., 38.
14. Ibid., 39.
15. See Maureen Zappala, "A Table Topics Workout: The Power-packed Exercise for Stretching Your Brain," *Toastmaster* magazine, February 2016, accessed September 15, 2021, https://www.toastmasters.org/Magazine/Articles/Table-Topics-Workout.
16. Wiseman, 76.
17. Kirk Byron Jones, *The Jazz of Preaching: How to Preach with Great Freedom and Joy* (Nashville: Abingdon Press, 2004), 80.
18. Sunggu A. Yang, *Arts and Preaching: An Aesthetic Homiletic for the Twenty-first Century* (Eugene, OR: Cascade Books, 2021), 21.
19. Ibid., 157–59.
20. Ibid., 161.
21. See Chapter 5 of Yang's *Arts and Preaching* for a more detailed explanation of this process.
22. Jones, 11–24.
23. Ibid., 32–33.
24. Ibid., 33.
25. For an explanation of the "roundtable pulpit," see John S. McClure, *The Roundtable Pulpit: Where Leadership and Preaching Meet* (Nashville: Abingdon Press, 1995).
26. Jared E. Alcántara, *The Practices of Christian Preaching: Essentials for Effective Proclamation* (Grand Rapids, MI: Baker Academic, 2019), 177.

19

Vibrant Words, Vivid Images, and Evocative Stories

Sermon Illustration Examples and Exercises

In the previous chapter, you learned about the importance of cultivating "theological imagination" for preaching in order to create sermon illustrations with salience, resonance, coherence, and creativity. You also experimented with several exercises to activate your imagination and begin to develop "habits of creativity." In this chapter, we will look at three different types of sermon illustrations that we have found to be most accessible and "user-friendly" for early-career preachers—vibrant words, vivid images, and evocative stories. We will give you exercises to practice with these types of illustrations. We'll also look at two sermons that utilize sermon illustrations to see how they work together with the Central Question, Central Claim, and Central Purpose to create salience, resonance, and coherence.

THE MEANING OF ILLUSTRATION AND WHY IT IS IMPORTANT FOR PREACHING

The word "illustrate" comes from the Latin word *illustrare*. In that word you can see the root *lustre*, which means "radiant or luminous brightness." Something with luster shines by reflecting light, like a polished piece of metal or the soft sheen of satin fabric. *Illustrare*, then, means "to illuminate" or "to make clear." Both of these senses of the word apply to sermon illustrations. With vibrant words, salient images, and resonant stories, a sermon can illuminate and make clear the biblical text and the theological concepts the preacher wants to convey. At the same time, illustrations add luster to the sermon itself, making it radiant by reflecting the light of the gospel message.

There is a third meaning to illustrate that also deserves our attention, and that is "give glory to." This is an important aspect of sermon illustrations as well—they must ultimately serve the purpose of giving glory to God. This is not to say that every image must be *about* God in a sermon. Rather, every sermon illustration's job is to serve the larger purpose of the sermon, which is to bring together the biblical text, the Theological Claim, and the context of our listeners in order to aid in the proclamation of who God is and/or what God does and what this means for us today.

USING THE "GLORY STANDARD" TO ASSESS SERMON ILLUSTRATIONS

The "**glory standard**"—that which gives glory to God or illustrates something about who God is or what God does—is good to keep in mind when you are deciding what words, images, and stories to use in your preaching. To determine whether an illustration meets the "glory standard," we can ask the following questions:

- Does this illustration contribute to an understanding of the biblical text or the context of the listeners?
- Does this illustration illuminate some aspect of who God is or what God does?
- Am I using this illustration in a way that supports or makes clear the Central Question, Central Claim, or Central Purpose?
- Does the illustration have salience, resonance, and coherence for this sermon?

If the answer is "no" to any of these questions, then you may have to rethink the illustration or replace it with something that serves the sermon better. For example, if you tell a story to give an analogy about a biblical text but it doesn't make sense or causes confusion for your listeners, you may need to set it aside and choose one that is clearer and more accessible. Or, if your choice of metaphors to describe God are always based on male imagery, you would want to consider using images that draw on the many other ways to illustrate God's nature in all its diversity (see Appendix G, Names and Metaphors for God from the Bible).

With vibrant words, vivid images, and evocative stories, the sermon can come to life, the listener can be engaged, and the Word of God can truly inspire. Let's look at these three types of illustrations, see examples of them in sermons we have included in this book, and practice using them in your own sermon preparation. Then we will look at two different sermons and analyze the way they use illustrations to serve the Central Question, Central Claim, and Central Purpose, ultimately proclaiming the Word of God for the people of God.

VIBRANT WORDS: USING DESCRIPTIVE LANGUAGE, THE SENSES, AND METAPHOR

Jared E. Alcántara describes why creativity is so important for engaging listeners with the biblical text:

> Creative preaching leads listeners into the biblical story so that what mattered then will matter now. It enrolls them in the world of the text. Too many sermons sound like historical reports on data from the past. Preachers bring worlds together: the world of the biblical text and the world in which people live their lives. Preachers show how this world relates to that one, and they also involve people who live in this world in the stories of people who lived in that world.[1]

One of the ways preachers can enroll listeners in the world of the text is by using vibrant words. "Good preachers play words well," writes Kirk Byron Jones in his book *The Jazz of Preaching*. "They know that how a word sounds is as important as what it means, that the sounding of words can work wonders with their meaning," he says.[2] Adds Alcántara, "Devote yourself to crafting sermonic language known for its care, precision, and artfulness. Words are more powerful than we realize."[3] In fact, as we learn from Genesis Chapter 1, words matter so much that God used them to speak the world into existence!

Vibrant, Descriptive Language

"Vibrant" means pulsating with life. It can also describe the quality of a resonant sound or a bright color. So when we speak of vibrant words, we mean those that come alive and *do something* to our brains by making us experience something in our imaginations. For instance, recall the conclusion of the sermon "Jesus, Mother Hen" in Chapter 11 based on Luke 13:31-35:

> *Arms open. Heart exposed. Wings spread. Feathered breast exposed.*
> *The mother hen, like the mother bird who fluttered over the nest egg of the world in Genesis . . .*
> *Like the dove that fluttered away from Noah's hand over the receding flood waters . . .*
> *Like the dove fluttering from heaven, hovering around Jesus as he emerged from the baptismal waters . . .*
> *Like a mother bird, wings pinned to the cross, still sheltering us from evil.*

With these words, we can see Jesus on the cross with his arms spread wide and chest exposed. But the overlay of the mother hen imagery is a metaphor that adds a different dimension for our conception of Jesus. The word "fluttered" connects the biblical imagery from the creation story in Genesis to Noah's story and then to Jesus's story. The transposition comes full circle to the cross with the description of a mother bird, wings pinned, but still protecting her vulnerable chicks.

Not only does our use of language connect us with the world of the Bible, it also enables us to name and expose the sin that results in the brokenness and pain of our world. And it connects us to those who have borne the brunt of that sin, those whom society has shunned, ignored, exploited, silenced, abused, or violated. Consider, for example, the words used in the sermon, "Climate Migration—How Should the Church Respond?" in Chapter 4 to describe the scene of Rodrigo in his field in Guatemala:

> *The old man kneels down onto the hard, crumbling soil beneath his feet. His bony fingers caress a stalk that should be green and full of grain but instead snaps and frays into brittle, brown sinews. His knees creak as he stands up, his eyes scanning the withered fields around him. Feelings of failure and despair well up in his chest.*

Notice the descriptive adjectives and nouns: hard, crumbling soil; bony fingers; brittle, brown sinews; withered fields. Note, too, the "vigorous verbs": caress, snaps, frays, creak, well up. What senses are invoked by these words and images? We can see and touch the soil and stalk. We can feel knees creaking. And the emotions of failure and despair are palpable. In other words, this paragraph creates empathy for the man in the story—a man who would otherwise only be a statistic or regarded as a potential menace.

But our vivid sermonic language does not leave us in those broken and abused places. It also "seeks to advance God's vision for shalom in the world through Christ followers who act justly, love mercy, and walk humbly with God (Mic. 6:8)," says Alcántara.[4] For example, after explaining the causes and effects of climate change that exacerbate the refugee crisis and making the case that the church must respond as an act of faith as well as moral obligation, the sermon concludes by returning to Rodrigo:

> *We have a chance to make amends. To help the trajectory of this story bend toward justice instead of snapping and fraying into brittle, brown sinews of empty stalks in empty fields.*
>
> *We can help lift up Rodrigo and point north to where his son and grandson have found a community that welcomes them. Where congregations like yours are doing everything they can to help mitigate the climate crisis and actively engage environmental justice issues. Where Jorge has found work that enables him to send home money for their family left behind.*
>
> *So that maybe the feelings that well up in Rodrigo's chest are not just failure and despair, but relief and hope. Hope that comes from the God of Jacob, Joseph, and his brothers to reconcile over bread in a foreign land. Hope that comes from a Savior who knew what it meant to sojourn in a wilderness, to seek refuge from violence, to have no home to lay his head.*
>
> *We can cup our hands to catch those tear-stained prayers carried on the dusty wind.*

Here, the sermon "bookends" with the images from the beginning of the sermon but modulates them with a new vision of possibility (we'll cover "bookends" in Chapter 22). The listeners are invited into the scene by lifting up Rodrigo and pointing north, pointing to hope, pointing to their own congregation doing the work of Christ. As Thomas H. Troeger and Leonora Tubbs Tisdale put it, "Preachers, then, cultivate the imagination for three primary reasons: to empathize, integrate, and envision. The practice of imaginative thinking enriches our ability to touch the depths of the human soul with holy wonder and grace."[5]

EXERCISE 1

Playing with Descriptive Language and Sensory Words

1. Read the parable of the barren fig tree in Luke 13:6-9.
2. Using the Sensory Net exercise from Chapter 18, make six columns with the following headings across the top of the page (one for each column):
   a. I see . . .
   b. I taste . . .
   c. I smell . . .
   d. I touch . . .
   e. I hear . . .
   f. I feel . . .

3. For each of the physical senses, consider the parable from the perspective of that sense. For example, what did the vineyard owner smell like? Expensive cologne? Rich leather? Fermenting grapes? Conversely, what did the gardener smell like? Sweat? Soil? Rotting compost?
4. For "I feel," imagine the emotions of each character in the story—including the fig tree, the ground, and even the manure!
5. Share what you wrote with your preaching partner. As you read or listen to each other share, what pulsated with life for you? What activated your imagination? Highlight those for possible use in a sermon on this parable.
6. Read the sermon "Composting Our Anger and Grief" in Chapter 26 and note the descriptive language. Did it match anything you or your partner came up with?

Expansive Metaphors for God and Theological Concepts

Recall from Chapter 8 our discussion of metaphors in theology and the importance of using expansive ways to conceive of the character of God beyond traditional masculine imagery. The sermon "Jesus, Mother Hen" explored several different ways to conceive of God using both feminine and masculine images. Later in this chapter in the sermon "When Psalm 23 Shepherded Me," you'll see an image of God tenderly applying baby lotion, "smoothing out the rough spots." Later in Chapter 21, you'll see someone describe God as Toto from the movie *The Wizard of Oz*, the tenacious little dog that pulled away the curtain to reveal the mere man behind the image of "the great and powerful Oz." In part A of the exercise below, try your hand at describing God, Jesus Christ, and the Holy Spirit using the suggested biblical metaphors (keeping in mind that there is both the "yes" and the "no" in each metaphor that is both descriptive but also limited).

You might also remember the discussion about avoiding clichés and aphorisms when it comes to making Theological Claims. Oftentimes, we use formulaic phrases and insider language without fully unpacking their meaning. As Troeger and Tisdale note, this especially can be the case with "large abstract theological concepts such as sin, salvation, or grace," which are very challenging to "incarnate" through words.[6] "One of the greatest temptations ministers will face is either using these words and concepts in sermons without defining them at all—an especially problematic practice in a day when so many of the people sitting in our pews did not grow up attending church or being schooled in the faith—or, alternatively, falling prey to cliché," they warn.[7] To help preachers "find ways to bring the great words of faith alive so that people grasp the redeeming truth to which they point," Troeger and Tisdale offer an exercise in sensory descriptions of theological concepts that we have adapted in part B below.[8]

EXERCISE 2

Experiment with Expansive Metaphors for God and Theological Concepts

PART A: EXPANSIVE METAPHORS FOR GOD, JESUS CHRIST, AND THE HOLY SPIRIT

1. Write a short paragraph beginning with one of the following sentence starters. Use descriptive language that engages the senses and evokes emotions.
   a. God is a like a mother bear robbed of her cubs. (Hosea 13:8)
   b. Jesus Christ is a writer, authoring our salvation and our faith. (Hebrews 5:9 and 12:2)
   c. The Holy Spirit is a gentle whisper. (1 Kings 19:12)
2. Share your paragraph with your preaching partner. Note how each of you used vibrant words. Do you see other possibilities for giving even more precise and detailed descriptions?

PART B: METAPHORS FOR THEOLOGICAL CONCEPTS

1. Take one of the following theological terms and write a sentence beginning with one of the starters below. Use descriptive language that engages the senses and evokes emotions.
   Faith
   Grace
   Holy
   Justice
   Redemption
   Salvation
   Sin
   a. {Term} smells like . . .
   b. {Term} When I think of {term}, I see . . .
   c. {Term} The sound of {term} is what you hear when . . .
   d. {Term} When I touch {term}, my skin feels . . .
   e. {Term} reminds me of the taste of . . .
2. Share your paragraph with your preaching partner. Note how each of you used vibrant words. Do you see other possibilities for giving even more precise and detailed descriptions? Also, as you "test the Spirit" of these words (see Chapter 18) and apply the "glory standard," do you see any harmful language about God or others that needs to be removed or corrected?

VIVID IMAGES: CONCRETIZING OUR FAITH

In the previous section, we examined the smallest unit of language in a sermon—words—and thought about how to make them as vibrant, scintillating, and imagination-activating as possible. In this section, we move to a larger unit—the image. An **image** is a picture, either tangible or in one's mind, that is the likeness or representation of something. The first time we hear about an image in Scripture is when Genesis tells us that human beings were created in God's image, *imago Dei* in Latin (Genesis 1:27). The Bible is replete with imagery—word pictures that help listeners conceive of the character and nature of God, the stories of God's people, and the vision of how we are called to live in the world in light of our faith.

Many church sanctuaries contain images that are inspired by Scripture—the cross, the dove, fire, water, to name just a few. These are **symbols**—physical objects or visual representations that take on meaning beyond their immediate properties and point to something beyond themselves. For example, the cross is just two beams of wood that were used to execute criminals in the Roman Empire. But because Christians believe that this instrument of death is what led to the resurrection of Christ and the salvation of the world, these two pieces of wood have become a symbol of eternal life and are thus infused with sacred significance.

When preachers use images in a sermon, they can help concretize and illustrate the point they are trying to make or, as we said in the previous chapter, give the listener "hand holds" for grabbing onto the sermon. Just as religious symbols are infused with sacred significance because they point to something beyond themselves, so, too, images in sermons should point to something beyond themselves. They should meet the "glory standard" of 1) contributing to an understanding of the biblical text or the context of the listeners, 2) illuminating some aspect of who God is or what God does, and 3) supporting or making clear the Central Question, Central Claim, or Central Purpose.

Imagery also must have salience for the sermon. Recall from the previous chapter that salience is when something springs up or juts out to demand our attention. An image that is salient will stand out for the listeners and give them something to hold on to as they are listening to you preach. This can be done by using vibrant words and sometimes by bringing a visual representation or even a physical object into the sermon itself.

Consider, for example, Leah's use of the coral reef as an image in Chapter 7's sermon, "A House with Many Rooms," to illustrate the idea of the "living stones." Not only did she display colorful pictures of coral reefs during the sermon, she also handed out pieces of coral for people to hold in their hand and examine as she preached. This use of the coral met the requirements for the "glory standard" in the following ways:

- The image of the coral illustrated both biblical texts (1 Peter 2:4-10 and John 14:1-7) as well as the context of the listeners (the seminary community).
- The image of the coral illuminated the "living stone" aspect of Jesus Christ and the vast hospitality of God's Realm.
- The image of the coral supported the Central Question (*What does it mean that Jesus Christ is a "living stone" and how does that impact our identity as an online seminary community stretched across the country?*), Central Claim (*The Realm of God is like a strong coral reef that hosts a dazzling array of life-forms; and just like the fish that swim around the coral reef, we are nurtured and protected by God through the church that gives us a spiritual home*), and Central Purpose (*This sermon will inspire the seminary community to continue in their ministry of education to support the mission of the larger church).*
- The image of the coral had salience both visually and as a tactile object. She also used vibrant words to describe both the coral reef and the church ("see the pattern of the calcium carbonate," "students and pastors tucked into those niches," "fall in love with our churches," "a homogenous pale landscape devoid of any diversity," "What a thriving, bustling coral reef we are!").

CAUTIONS WHEN USING IMAGES

Because images are so powerful, they must be handled with care in a sermon. Be sure that the image actually "works" for the sermon. Even though the analogy makes sense to you, it might not make sense to your listeners. So, consider discussing your use of it in a sermon with a trusted colleague.

Also, preachers need to think about the push-and-pull of images. On the one hand, we want the image to be one that our listeners will understand and relate to (the pull). On the other, we want to avoid using an image that, while it may be familiar, may also reinscribe harmful stereotypes around gender, race, culture, body size, disability, and socioeconomic status (the push).

Take, for instance, images of heteronormativity and how they can unwittingly reinforce prejudices against LGBTQIA+ individuals. When we use the familiar phrase "brothers and sisters in Christ" the "pull" is that it is intended to describe our fellowship as a church community. The "push," however, is that this phrase perpetuates a gender binary instead of recognizing the spectrum of genders. An alternative is to use the phrase "siblings in Christ" as an image that is more inclusive.

As Emily Askew and O. Wesley Allen note in their book, *Beyond Heterosexism in the Pulpit*, we need to be aware that our words and images will be heard by both straight and LGBTQIA+ listeners. "Sermons that assume or never question heteronormativity may just seem 'normal' to straight people, but homosexuals may feel excluded when they are never named—or worse, when they are stereotyped. Conversely, when heterosexism is appropriately exposed, homosexuals in the pews will feel affirmed while heterosexuals may feel uncomfortable, guilty, resistant, or angry."[9] To begin normalizing LGBTQIA+ people, a preacher can mention gay relationships in the context of other relationships but without tokenizing or singling out that one trait. "We need to use gay people in our sermons as representative of *humans* instead of only as representative of *homosexuals*," Askew and Allen explain.[10]

Preachers in monolingual and culturally homogenous congregations also risk using images that perpetuate bias and prejudice. This can happen in obvious ways, such as using stereotypical tropes to describe people of certain racial or ethnic groups. But it also can happen simply by ignoring the vast diversity that exists just beyond the church doors. By failing to include stories and images from people of other cultures in our sermons, we put blinders on our congregation and limit the full scope of God's interactions with people who are different from us.

This is why HyeRan Kim-Cragg encourages preachers to employ a post-colonial homiletic in their sermons. Her strategy "allows preachers to zoom in on the colonial experiences of people otherwise hidden and unspoken in the Bible" as well as in our pulpits.[11] One creative way to do this is simply by learning about the language of another people and how the nuances of their words can open up a new way of understanding traditional images and ideas. Take, for instance, the East Asian character for "home," *ka*. It is made up of two ideograms, one meaning "roof" and one meaning "pig." "The idea is that if we have a roof and an animal together, then we have a home for a human,"

Kim-Cragg explains.[12] Imagine using that image to preach about the place where Jesus was born—a stable that was home to both animals and the Son of God on that night. Further, she says, "This idea of home communicates the important notion of a symbiotic relationship between humans and animals. It shows how interdependent and interconnected we are."[13] Thus, *ka* has global implications as we consider an Earth-care ethic when preaching about Genesis and other passages about God's Creation.

In the exercises below, you can experiment with image-fashioning that is both imaginative and descriptive as well as paradigm-shifting to allow new insights and understandings for both the biblical text and our contemporary times.

EXERCISE 3

Experiment with Vivid Images for Preaching

PART A: FLESHING OUT A BIBLICAL IMAGE

1. Read Psalm 23. Choose one of the following images in vv. 1-2 for this exercise: shepherd, sheep, green pastures, still waters.
2. Use the mind-mapping exercise you learned in Chapter 18. Put the word at the center of a large piece of paper and write down all the things that come to your mind about this image.
3. Use the sensory net exercise to capture as much descriptive language about the image as you can. What do you see, hear, taste, touch, smell, or feel emotionally about this image?
4. Write one paragraph about this image based on these exercises.
5. Exchange paragraphs with your preaching partner or group. What sparks your imagination about each other's image-building? How could you use this in a sermon?

PART B: FLESHING OUT A THEOLOGICAL CONCEPT

1. Return to the sentence you wrote for a theological concept in Exercise 2, Part B.
2. For this exercise, choose either the Play-Doh or group sculpting experiment that you learned about in Chapter 18.
3. Play-Doh: Sculpt an image of the theological concept you chose, either faith, grace, holy, justice, redemption, salvation, or sin. Feel the tactileness of the material, malleable and soft in your hand. Work the dough into an image that, for you, represents this idea. How does this build on the descriptive language you used in the previous exercise? Show your creation to your preaching partner and explain to them what this image means to you. How might this three-dimensional exercise inspire image-making for a sermon?
4. Group sculpting: Use the members of the group to form a "living sculpture" of the image you chose, either faith, grace, holy, justice, redemption, salvation, or sin. How will you place each person in the tableau? What will you have them do? Will they be interacting or separate? How does this build on the descriptive language you used in the previous exercise? Discuss your sculpture with the group. How did it affect each of them as they were positioned in the sculpture? What emotions did you feel as you finished the living sculpture? How might this three-dimensional exercise inspire image-making for a sermon?

EVOCATIVE STORIES: BRINGING THE BIBLE AND THE SERMON TO LIFE

To say something is *evocative* means that it elicits a response, usually in an emotional way. To evoke means to draw forth or call to mind, such as evoking a memory or conjuring an image in one's imagination. The word "evocative" can also mean "suggestive," in the sense that a room might be decorated in a way that is evocative of a certain historical period.

So, when we talk about using evocative stories in sermons, we mean that the story should be told in a way that enables the hearers to imagine it in their minds and feel it in their emotions. A story told well can help listeners enter the world of the biblical text. It can also allow them to conceive of how the text applies in a different time and place, especially their own. Just as vivid images use vibrant words, evocative stories use both vibrant words and vivid images to come alive in people's imaginations. As Graham Johnston says, the idea is to "paint the mental picture that is necessary in order for the listener to identify with the story."[14]

Where can a preacher find good stories to illustrate their sermons? There are many places to look, including news stories, blogs, books, journals, and magazines. Podcasts that feature short stories are another great place to find compelling narratives.

How about movies, television, or video shorts? On the one hand, they can have cultural relevance and provide instant recognition for listeners who have seen them. On the other hand, if listeners have not seen the show or movie, it might not make sense or might take too long to explain. Also, listeners may get sidetracked thinking about the movie instead of focusing on the message of the sermon. So, if you plan to use this kind of media as the source of a story, be sure to keep the illustration tightly focused and rein it in to serve one of the Central Statements so that it doesn't gallop away with your listeners.

Criteria for Effective Stories and the Effective Use of Stories

Karyn Wiseman suggests three criteria we can use for evaluating the effectiveness of a story: "Making sure our stories *make sense, flow naturally*, and *have an emotional connection* is vital to avoid boring sermons and to keep the attention of the listeners" (emphasis added).[15] She also advises, "Do not pick a story that is complicated or needs several side stories to give enough context for those present to grasp the flow of the story. Use a story that makes sense for your people."[16]

There are many ways that a story can be used in preaching, and there are several examples used in sermons throughout this book. Sometimes a story can be a brief "case-in-point" to illustrate an argument being made in the sermon. You saw a series of these stories in the sermon "Jesus, Mother Hen," in Chapter 11. And you will see an example of a brief illustrative story in the sermon further on, "When Psalm 23 Shepherded Me." A sermon can also tell the biblical story so that it is fleshed out with details that enable listeners to vividly imagine the scene or narrative. You'll see an example of this in the sermon "Jesus Sighed: Being Open in Mark 7:24-37" in Chapter 23.

A sermon story can also be longer and used to flesh out a theme or an idea, such as Chapter 2's sermon, "A COVID-19 Easter: Mark's Gospel Is Just What We Need," which told about Shawn and Fiona, a father and his infant daughter being baptized after an encounter with the Gospel of Mark. Other times a story can be woven throughout the sermon with accompanying theological interpretation. You'll see an example of this in Chapter 21, with the sermon "Pastor Tom, Gladys, and a Flag with Legs." There are also times when a story can be braided into the sermon by paralleling a biblical story with a similar theme. Chapter 4's sermon, "Climate Migration—How Should the Church Respond?" is an example of this, with the story of Rodrigo and Jorge interwoven with the story of Jacob, both of which involve migration due to drought and environmental devastation. And there are times when the entire sermon is the telling of a story, which you'll see in Chapter 21's sermon, "The Big Red, White, and Blue in the Room." In the exercise below, you'll practice writing a story that could be used in a sermon about Psalm 23.

GUIDANCE FOR USING PERSONAL STORIES IN A SERMON

Homileticians have different opinions about whether or not a preacher should use a story from their own life as a sermon illustration. Some believe that using one's own story puts the spotlight on them instead of on God and should thus be avoided. However, others insist that unless a preacher can testify about how God has worked in their own life, their witness won't be as strong or authentic.

Our recommendation is that personal stories can *occasionally* be used in the sermon, *if* they meet the following criteria:

- The personal story should not make the preacher look like the hero. Instead, sharing a story of a moral or ethical struggle, or an "aha" moment can be a way to model the process of discernment or spiritual growth for others.
- A preacher must not use the pulpit as a form of personal therapy or to gain sympathy. Seek a counselor to work through your "stuff" instead of working it out in a sermon.
- The story must serve one of the Central Statements and not be an end unto itself.
- The story must point beyond itself to God instead of making the preacher the focal point of the sermon.

There are also criteria to keep in mind when considering using *other's* stories in a sermon, especially if they involve people you know or stories that are not public:

- If wanting to use the story of a family member or friend, ask their permission first. This is especially important for spouses and children of preachers. Don't reduce them to mere sermon illustrations.
- If wanting to share the story about a parishioner, ask their permission first. Otherwise, you may be violating their trust and the boundaries of confidentiality.
- Be wary of using "overcoming" stories too often, as in stories that illustrate a protagonist overcoming a great trial or obstacle with the help of God so that "they all lived happily ever after." While such stories can be inspirational, "sometimes we need to trust our listeners more and let them see that things do not always work out for the best, but God is present in those situations just as much as God is present in the overcoming stories we so often tell," Wiseman advises.[17]

EXERCISE 4

Telling Your Story about Psalm 23

Almost everyone can think of a time when they heard the Twenty-third Psalm. Maybe it was at a funeral. Maybe you learned it as a child in a Sunday School class or church camp. Perhaps an adult in your life helped you to memorize it. In this exercise you'll use the *lectio* practice you learned about in the previous chapter to help you write your own story about Psalm 23.

1. Begin with centering prayer asking for the Spirit to open your heart and mind to receive the Word of God.
2. Read Psalm 23 out loud and simply take it in.
3. Sit in contemplative silence for sixty seconds. Take deep cleansing breaths.
4. Read Psalm 23 again. This time, notice one word that jumps out for you. Write down that word.
5. Sit in contemplative silence for sixty seconds. Take deep cleansing breaths.
6. Read Psalm 23 a third time and think about a memorable time when you heard this passage. Put yourself back in that situation. Using vibrant words, write down the story. What did you see, hear, smell, taste, touch, or feel emotionally? What did Psalm 23 mean for you? What did it do for you?
7. Sit in contemplative silence for sixty seconds. Take deep cleansing breaths.
8. Share and discuss what you wrote with your preaching partner or group. How might you incorporate this story into a sermon about Psalm 23?
9. Conclude with prayer thanking God for the insights, wisdom, and questions that have been shared through this reading.

SERMON ANALYSIS EXERCISE FOR PSALM 23

Below is an example of a sermon based on a form called Expository, or Puritan Plain Style, that you will learn about in Chapters 20 and 21. In this sermonic form, the preacher gives an introduction then moves through the biblical text verse by verse giving commentary and offering theological reflection. Then the preacher applies the theological insights to a contemporary situation so that the listener can understand the relevance of the passage for their lives and our world. As you analyze this sermon, here are the Central Statements:

Central Question: How can the Twenty-third Psalm be framed for contemporary listeners so that they go deeper in their relationship with God's Word and in their faith?

Central Claim: God gives us Psalm 23 to help us learn to rely on God, so committing its words to our hearts and minds is one way to experience the Psalm as a steadfast companion.

Central Purpose: This sermon takes listeners on a "guided tour" of Psalm 23 so that, by the end, listeners will experience it as a faithful companion for life's journey and want to learn it by heart as well as teach it to others.

As you read through the sermon, see if you can detect the influence of the Central Statements at different points in the sermon.

1. Where you see evidence of the Central Question, write in the initials CQ.
2. Where you detect the Central Claim, write in the initials CC.
3. At the point where you notice the Central Purpose, write the initials CP.

Also, analyze the sermon for its use of illustrations.

1. Circle the vibrant words. How do they appeal to the senses and emotions in order to pulsate with life?
2. Underline the vivid images. In what way do they create a picture in your mind's eye? How do they help to concretize the message?
3. Bracket the evocative story. Does it make sense, flow naturally, and have an emotional impact? Does it serve the larger purpose of the sermon, pointing beyond itself to the Central Claim?

SERMON: "WHEN PSALM 23 SHEPHERDED ME"

Introduction

1. "The Lord is my shepherd." I only have to say those first five words, and, almost everyone to whom I give pastoral care can join with me in reciting this precious psalm. This is, of course, the most famous of all the psalms. We hear it most often at funerals. But Psalm 23 has such poignant imagery, it could be used in many more varied contexts. Today I want to explore that imagery and talk about why this psalm is so significant for our lives today.

(The sermon begins with the familiar words of Psalm 23, which are evocative right from the start because the psalm is so familiar. Yet Leah signals that they will be going deeper into the imagery in this sermon.)

Exposition

2. Let's start with this first verse, where God is referred to as a shepherd. Now, we're not an agrarian nation anymore. And most of us don't know any sheepherders personally. My daughter had a cute little toy lamb as a baby, a ball of fluff that she would cuddle in her tiny arms as she slept—that's about as close as we've gotten to sheep, aside from petting zoos. But back when this psalm was written, herding sheep was a common profession. Sheep, as you may know, are not the brightest animals on the farm. They have to be led where you want them to go. It is up to the shepherd to find suitable pasture for the sheep to graze. And the shepherd must find water for them. Not just any water, but still water, so that they won't be swept away by currents that are too fast for them.

(The image of the sheep is primary in paragraph 2. You should have underlined the sentence with the image of the "cute little toy lamb" and circled the vibrant words "ball of fluff" and "cuddle.")

3. When we think of this image of water, as Christians, we can't help but think of the baptismal waters. In the still waters of our mothers' wombs, we were created. In the still waters of the font or pool, we were baptized children of God. And this water—when it is protected and kept clean—sustains us all our lives.
4. On a spiritual level, this psalm so beautifully expresses our need for God. I don't know about you, but my personality is Type A, driven and hardworking. So I actually have to be led to places that replenish my spirit. Those places often include green meadows and still waters. By reconnecting with God's Creation, my soul is restored. God knows that and often leads me down those paths.

(Paragraphs 3 and 4 offer a theological commentary on the first two verses of the psalm. Paragraph 3 connects to the sacrament of Baptism, while paragraph 4 makes a connection to ecological theology. Notice, also, the repetition of "still waters" and the different examples used to illustrate this image.)

5. And speaking of paths, this line about being led down right paths for God's namesake echoes a theme we hear in Psalm 1, which talks about staying on the right path and being like the tree planted by the water. Psalm 23 makes reference to this same kind of imagery. Both of these are what Walter Brueggemann called "psalms of orientation"—they orient us to the goodness of God. You might recall the hymn "He Leadeth Me," which has these lyrics: "By waters still, o'er troubled sea, Still 'tis [God's] hand that leadeth me."
6. There is such truth in those words. As the psalmist reminds us, there will be difficult times in life. And this psalm does not shy away from that fact. "Yea, though I walk through the valley of the shadow of death, I will fear no evil. For you are with me, your rod and your staff, they comfort me." What is this rod and staff? Again, this has to do with the shepherd. A shepherd always carries a long stick to beat away any predators that may attack the sheep. And the staff is the crook, a long hook used to reach out and pull the sheep back that are wandering close to danger. The psalmist is saying that just the sight of the rod and the staff are a comfort to him. It says, "God's got my back! God's looking out for me."

(In paragraphs 5 and 6, verses 3 and 4 are discussed. Recall that in Chapter 8, we said that hymns can convey theological truths, which we see in paragraph 5. We might think of this as an "aural image," which can be an effective illustration in a sermon. In paragraph 6, two images are described—the rod and the staff—by painting a word picture of how they are used by shepherds.)

7. Then the imagery for God changes from a shepherd to that of the host of a welcoming household. The psalmist is saying that God has laid out a banquet even with enemies lurking around. She knows that God will keep danger at bay while she feasts at the table.
8. That's often the way I think of Communion. Here we come to the table to partake of the bread and the wine. A whole world of worry awaits us outside these walls. But for this moment we're invited to the banquet of Jesus Christ to feed on the food of forgiveness, restoration, and rejuvenation.
9. This table reminds us how important it is to ensure that all people have access to nutritious food free of chemicals and industrial waste that harms our bodies. The table is where all of our efforts to care for God's Creation are most visible. Have we made sure that the land on which the grapes and wheat grow is healthy, the water clean, the air pure? Are we addressing issues of food distribution, unnecessary waste, and equitable sharing of what God's Creation has produced? All of this can ensure that the table is full and open to all.

(The first part of verse 5 is addressed in paragraph 7 using the imagery of a feast in the midst of "lurking" enemies. Just as the sacrament of Baptism is connected to the psalm earlier in the sermon, here the sacrament of the Communion meal provides both imagery as well as theological commentary. Paragraph 9 reiterates the ecological theology from paragraph 4.)

10. And then the psalmist says that God has anointed his head with oil. I read this one time to a group of teenagers, and they said, "Ew, that's gross. I don't want oil poured on my head." Again, we have to understand the cultural and historical context. In the desert regions of the Middle East, people's hair and skin would

get very dry. So they would pour fragrant oil on themselves to keep the moisture in and smell nice. It's the same as washing your hair with conditioner, or putting aftershave or fragrant lotion on yourself after a bath or shower. Think of it as God putting baby lotion on you, smoothing out the rough spots.

11. How do we smooth out the rough spots for others, letting them know that God is still caring for them? Oil is a healing balm; are we advocating for people who are in need of healing? Are we reaching out to those who are hurting? Our actions for and on behalf of the sick, the suffering, and the dying help to provide assurance that the sacred oil of God's healing is still at work today.

(There is a plethora of vibrant words in paragraph 10: "pour fragrant oil," "washing your hair with conditioner," as well as a salient image, "God putting baby lotion on you, smoothing out the rough spots." The paragraph also encourages listeners to think about the theological implications of this healing oil, that we are called to advocate for others who are in need.)

12. Then we come to the promise of abundance. My cup runs over. Goodness and mercy will follow me all the days of my life. You've heard of the phrase: "being pursued by the hounds of hell." Well, this is just the opposite. The psalmist is saying that she is being pursued by the angels of goodness and mercy. God is so good to her, blessings just overflow in her life.
13. Finally, we come to our journey's end, our heart's desire, our soul's rest—the house of the Lord. There are different ways of translating this. Traditionally, we say, "I shall dwell." But it can also be read as "returning" or "coming home." In any case, it tells us that when all is said and done, we will be with God. We came from God; we will return again to God. And all will be well.
14. Those are comforting words. What we have in this psalm is an intimate reflection on the grace of God: "the restoration of soul, the protection from death, the gifts of abundant and unending life, and the meal in God's presence" as John Eaton describes it.[18] For Christians, it is the psalm of the sacraments, Baptism and Communion. It is the psalm of life and death: the dark valley and the house of the Lord. This psalm touches on every important aspect of our lives. And it is the psalm that each of us should know by heart. Just as we say the Lord's Prayer from memory, so should Psalm 23 be right at the forefront when we are going through both the joys and sorrows of life.

(The exposition part of the sermon concludes by summing up what has been covered so far in the psalm. In the last sentence of paragraph 14, you can see the Central Purpose [This sermon takes listeners on a "guided tour" of Psalm 23 so that, by the end, listeners will experience it as faithful companion for life's journey and want to learn it by heart and teach it to others] make its first appearance.)

Application

15. I'll tell you why I think it's so important to have this psalm memorized. Many years ago when my daughter was a restless baby who would not sleep through the night, my husband took her up to his office on the third floor of our home so I could get some rest. But as he was bringing her back down to her crib, his foot slipped on a step, and they both fell down the stairs. She slipped from his arms and her head hit the wall at the bottom of the steps. Sitting in the emergency room as I held this girl in my arms, my little lamb, I went numb when the doctor told us that she had a fractured skull. We waited for the ambulance to take us to Children's Hospital. With all my seminary training and all the Scripture I had read over the years, all the experience I had with pastoral care, only one phrase would come to my mind: "The Lord is my shepherd."
16. I just kept repeating those words silently to myself. I needed something to cling to, something to get me through that dark valley, if that was indeed where we were headed. And at that point we just didn't know what was ahead. I prayed those words frequently in the days that followed. When they put the neck brace on her, I looked for the shepherd's staff. When she screamed as they did the CAT scans and X-rays, I prayed for the crook to pull her back to calmness. And during the two long nights we spent in her hospital room, I prayed for God's presence as we waited in that dark valley. Psalm 23 shepherded me every step of the way.
17. Thankfully, it turned out that her fracture was not life- or brain-threatening. She was going to be okay. But me and Psalm 23 developed a very close relationship during those days. And I will always be grateful to it for getting me through that very difficult time.

(Paragraphs 15 through 17 present a story to show how Psalm 23 meant something to Leah in a possibly life-threatening situation for her child. Notice how the description of her daughter as "my little lamb" referred back to the toy lamb mentioned earlier in the sermon. Thus, the image works on two levels by both describing her vulnerable daughter and by recalling the biblical imagery. Also, think about whether this story meets the criteria for effectiveness. Does it make sense, flow naturally, and have an emotional connection?)

Conclusion

18. I had that psalm because it was ingrained in my brain from the time I was a young child. I learned it in Sunday School. I heard it at funerals. And I repeated it so many times to parishioners in the churches I have served. When I have visited people with Alzheimer's who have difficulty remembering even their own children or what they had for lunch that day, there are always two Scripture passages that they can repeat—The Lord's Prayer and the Twenty-third Psalm. Even when the rest of their memory has failed, even when their minds are being blanked out by that terrible disease, they still retain those precious Bible passages.
19. We need these words to give shape and meaning to our lives and to frame our experiences within the larger picture of God's loving will for us. Psalm 23, when we learn it by heart, can be the very presence of God shepherding us, restoring us, protecting us, guiding us, and blessing us with abundance. If you have young people in your circle of influence, I encourage you to help them learn and even memorize this psalm. Because it will be one of the greatest gifts you can give them for their lives. Let's start right now, saying it together. *(Begin reciting Psalm 23 with congregation.)*

(Notice how the conclusion recapitulates the Central Claim [God gives us Psalm 23 as a steadfast companion to faith, which becomes stronger as we commit its words to our hearts and minds.] and reinforces the Central Purpose [This sermon takes listeners on a "guided tour" of Psalm 23 so that, by the end, listeners will experience it as faithful companion for life's journey and want to learn it by heart and teach it to others.])

CONCLUDING THOUGHTS

A preacher's attention to language, imagery, and stories is not just for our listeners. It's also for our own preaching souls. Alcántara reminds us that the pastoral imagination enables us to sustain ministry when we are feeling frustrated or hurt by our congregation. "Remember that your listeners are always more than they appear to be. They are children of God right now, and what they will be has not yet been made known."[19] This means "pastors *have* to believe that God is doing much more than is within their capacity to see. Long-term pastoral ministry demands a rich pastoral imagination for the people to whom we minister. Otherwise, disillusionment or discouragement sets in and blurs our ability to see people through the eyes of faith."[20]

In other words, cultivating "theological imagination" makes possible a transformation not just for our congregations, but for us as preachers as well. Remember, you are the first one who will "hear" this sermon—you are preaching God's Word to yourself first. Crafting sermons with illustrations that are salient, resonant, coherent, and creative is a spiritual discipline. It can also be enjoyable and even fun! Like Wisdom co-creating the world with God in Proverbs 8:22-31, we delight God with our creativity. Verse 30 describes Sophia-Wisdom as a "master worker," but it can also be translated as "little child." Just imagine a vivacious and precocious little girl sculpting the mountains, pouring out the rivers, and painting the sky, giggling with exuberant joy! Your sermon preparation can tap into these same inventive and artistic reservoirs of imagination and then share them with your listeners through vibrant words, vivid images, and evocative stories to make the sermon—and their faith—come alive!

KEY POINTS IN THIS CHAPTER

1. Illustrations in sermons help to illuminate the message, bring the Word of God to life, and connect with listeners.
2. A sermon illustration meets the "glory standard" when it does the following: contributes to listeners' understanding of the biblical text or their context; illuminates some aspect of who God is or what God does; supports or makes clear the Central Question, Central Claim, or Central Purpose; and has salience, resonance, and coherence for this sermon.
3. A preacher should use vibrant words and descriptive language in their sermon illustrations that draw on the five senses as well as emotions.
4. Illustrations should utilize metaphors that help listeners expand their understanding of God as well as give concreteness to abstract theological concepts.
5. Images in sermons should be vivid, meaning they should stand out and provide a "hand hold" for the listeners. At the same time, we must be careful not to use images that reinforce or reinscribe harmful stereotypes.
6. Evocative stories can help bring both the Scriptures and the sermon itself to life. Stories can use both vibrant words and vivid images to activate people's "theological imagination" so that they can envision the world of the text, the world as it is now, and the vision of God's Realm we are invited to see.
7. Stories can be used in many different ways in a sermon, but they should always make sense, flow naturally, and have an emotional connection. Remember to exercise caution when using personal stories and be sure to get permission if you are using others' stories that have not been made public.

DISCUSSION QUESTIONS

1. "When Psalm 23 Shepherded Me" is a sermon that Leah has preached in different congregations at different times. This is what's known as an "evergreen" sermon because it has a timelessness that transcends current events and particular locations. While a preacher should never repeat a sermon in the same congregation, it's good to have an evergreen sermon like this on hand in case you are called to fill in for a colleague at the last minute, to give a spur-of-the-moment testimony, or if serving as a guest preacher for different congregations. Talk with your preaching mentor or colleagues about evergreen sermons. Do they have one on hand? Have they ever preached the same sermon more than once? If so, what was the occasion? What criteria would they use for determining whether or not to "recycle" or "upcycle" a sermon? What would they do with the previously preached sermon to refresh and revise it?
2. In paragraph 15 of the sermon on Psalm 23, Leah had considered using more graphic imagery to describe her daughter's fall, such as the sound of her head thudding against the wall and her tiny body lying on the floor. But she decided against this imagery because she felt it might be too intense, get listeners offtrack, and overshadow the message of the sermon. Discuss with your preaching partner, group, or mentor the question about how much detail is too much when it comes to sermon illustrations. How do preachers determine what is just enough to evoke the imagination, and how much is overwhelming or distracting?
3. Some homileticians recommend using illustrations that a congregation can easily relate to and to avoid images or stories that are so far beyond the context of listeners that they can't make a connection. Other teachers of preaching encourage the use of illustrations that expand the congregation's cultural, geographic, socioeconomic, heteronormative, racial, and linguistic horizons. Talk with your preaching partner, group, or mentor about how to balance the use of familiar illustrations with those that stretch our listeners.

FOR FURTHER READING

Jared E. Alcántara. Ch. 6, "Preach Creatively." In *The Practices of Christian Preaching: Essentials for Effective Proclamation.* Grand Rapids, MI: Baker Academic, 2019.
O. Wesley Allen and Carrie La Ferle. *Preaching and the Thirty-Second Commercial: Lessons for Advertising for the Pulpit.* Louisville: Westminster John Knox, 2021.
Mary Catherine Hilkert. *Naming Grace: Preaching and the Sacramental Imagination.* New York: Continuum, 2003.
John S. McClure. *Mashup Religion: Pop Music and Theological Invention.* Waco, TX: Baylor University Press, 2011.
Alyce M. McKenzie. *Making a Scene in the Pulpit: Vivid Preaching for Visual Listeners.* Louisville, KY: Presbyterian, 2018.
Thomas H. Troeger. *Imagining a Sermon.* Nashville: Abingdon Press, 1990.

NOTES

1. Jared E. Alcántara, *The Practices of Christian Preaching: Essentials for Effective Proclamation* (Grand Rapids, MI: Baker Academic, 2019), 165.
2. Kirk Byron Jones, *The Jazz of Preaching: How to Preach with Great Freedom and Joy* (Nashville: Abingdon Press, 2004), 31.
3. Alcántara, 166.
4. Ibid., 168.
5. Thomas H. Troeger and Leonora Tubbs Tisdale, *A Sermon Workbook: Exercises in the Art and Craft of Preaching* (Nashville: Abingdon Press, 2013), 43.
6. Ibid., 89.
7. Ibid.
8. Ibid., 91–92.
9. Emily Askew and O. Wesley Allen, *Beyond Heterosexism in the Pulpit* (Eugene, OR: Cascade Books, 2015), 7.
10. Ibid., 9.
11. HyeRan Kim-Cragg, *Postcolonial Preaching: Creating a Ripple Effect* (Lanham, MD: Lexington Books, 2021), 10.
12. Ibid., 32–33.
13. Ibid., 33.
14. Graham Johnston, *Preaching to a Postmodern World: A Guide to Reaching Twenty-First Century Listeners* (Grand Rapids, MI: Baker Books, 2001), 159.
15. Karyn Wiseman, *I Refuse to Preach a Boring Sermon: Engaging the 21st Century Listener* (Cleveland, OH: Pilgrim Press, 2013), 24.
16. Ibid., 42.
17. Ibid., 31.
18. John Eaton, *The Psalms* (New York: Continuum, 2005), 123.
19. Alcántara, 170.
20. Ibid., 171.

20

Structuring Your Preaching

Basic Sermon Forms

So far, you have learned to build the foundation for a solid sermon. You have studied how to exegete a biblical text and analyze it for its theological content, as well as how to exegete your preaching context. You learned the process for developing the Central Statements—the Central Question, the Central Claim, and the Central Purpose—that provide the engine, direction, and destination for your sermon. And you've been introduced to some exercises for cultivating theological imagination to engage your listeners and make the sermon come alive. Now it's time to think about the means by which your sermon will get where it needs to go, the kind of "vehicle" you need for preaching. In other words, we need to consider what **sermon form** would be effective for preaching a particular message at a particular time for a particular congregation.

If you are new to learning the art and skill of preaching, you may not have thought much about sermon forms. And unless any of your listeners are English majors or rhetoricians, most people in your congregation would have no idea about the sermon's form, just as many people who enjoy music have no concept about the music theory that undergirds what they're listening to. But for those who preach, it is essential to learn about, experiment with, and perfect sermon forms for our craft. As we are learning about sermon forms, you can think of this as the equivalent of lifting the hood of the car in order to understand how it runs (and how to fix it). Or moving from being a simple user of a computer program to being the one who writes the code to make the programs run. Or going beyond simply enjoying the cake to learning how to bake it yourself. When you know how to organize a sermon from beginning to end, you increase the likelihood that both you and those who receive the sermon will have a fulfilling preaching experience because it will be coherent, engaging, easy to follow, and clear enough to inspire faith, hope, and love.

WHAT ARE SERMON FORMS?

In his book *Preaching Words*, John McClure defines *form* as "the overarching shape of a sermon, based upon the arrangement or ordering of the sermons parts."[1] There are myriad forms available to the preacher (see "A Short List of Sermon Forms and How the Central Claim Can Be Used" in Appendix L). Thomas G. Long described nearly twenty different stock forms and designs in *The Witness of Preaching*.[2] Ronald J. Allen included thirty-four different approaches to preaching in the edited volume *Patterns of Preaching: A Sermon Sampler*.[3]

Using a variety of forms over time keeps both the preacher and congregation from falling into boring predictability. Troeger and Tisdale encourage using "a repertoire of methods for organizing sermons so that we do not put ourselves—or our listeners—to sleep. We need a repertoire because different individuals receive, process, and respond in a variety of ways. Using a range of homiletical forms is a way to recognize and honor people's multiple intelligences, the varied ways they learn and gain knowledge."[4] These homileticians and others also note that because the Bible itself uses many different ways to communicate the Word of God, such as poetry, hymns, parables, and letters, so, too, should sermons employ different modes of getting across their message (see Chapter 3, "Using Literary Analysis to Understand the Text").[5]

Because this book is an introduction to preaching, we will not delve into all the different sermon forms that can be used. Instead, we will focus on four that we have found to be the most accessible for early-career preachers. They are: Four Pages, Motion Pictures, Homiletical Plot, and Expository or Puritan Plain Style. What makes these forms easy to use is that they each have a specific structure that can organize the ideas and flow of the sermon. Before examining them, however, we need to learn the difference between **deductive** and **inductive** preaching, because these two types of logic inform many different sermon forms.

DEDUCTIVE AND INDUCTIVE SERMONS

Within the field of rhetoric, preaching is a form of speech that both communicates ideas and persuades listeners. This means that understanding certain principles for constructing an argument can be helpful in crafting sermons. Key among them are the concepts of deductive and inductive logic.

Deductive logic starts by stating the premise of an argument and then backing up the claim with supporting reasons, explanations, and illustrations. A sermon using deductive logic will typically state the major claim near the beginning of the sermon either in the introduction or shortly thereafter. The rest of the sermon will give reasons why this claim is true, building its case with examples and supporting points and often using appeals to one or more poles of the Wesleyan Quadrilateral (Scripture, Tradition, Reason, Experience). The sermon's conclusion reiterates the claim, with which, by the end, listeners are (hopefully) in full agreement based on the case that the preacher has made.

Inductive logic, in contrast, starts by gathering evidence and then arriving at a claim. A sermon using inductive logic may begin with a question, a conundrum, a story, or a series of illustrations that, at first, may not indicate where the preacher and the congregation are going. However, the preacher will be building their case for the claim that will come later in the sermon by connecting the dots so that a picture emerges from these smaller details. In an inductive sermon, the claim usually comes either in the middle or at the end of the sermon. However, for those who follow Fred Craddock's model of inductive "journey" preaching, the claim may not ever be stated outright but rather left for the listener to infer on their own.[6] The sermon's conclusion may end with a question or an enigmatic statement that leaves listeners scratching their heads at first. But oftentimes the clever preacher will have skillfully been leading their listeners to an irrefutable conclusion that hits them with an "aha!" moment of realization. Think of it as Sherlock Holmes trying to solve a mystery—there is a case to solve and clues to follow, but it's not until the very end when the major claim of the sermon is made.

THE CENTRAL CLAIM AND SERMON FORMS

The placement of the Central Claim helps to determine the form of the sermon. For example, if the claim is at the beginning and then you break it down point by point, that would be a deductive sermon. If the sermon begins by taking us on a journey and gives us clues along the way but waits until the end to make its claim, that would be an inductive sermon. The claim can also be somewhere in the middle of the sermon or repeated throughout the sermon as a kind of refrain that guides and holds the sermon together.

In the forms we study for this chapter, we will use examples where the Central Claim is clearly visible or obviously informing what the preacher is trying to say in the sermon. As the saying goes, "Put it where the goats can get it." In other words, when you are preaching—feeding people the Word of God—make sure it is within their reach. Don't make it too difficult to obtain or put up obstacles that frustrate them when they are trying to receive what you are offering them. Of course, this doesn't mean that the sermon has to be pedantic, overly simple, or dull. Just the opposite! When a sermon form is skillfully used and enhanced with images, stories, and illustrations that draw on the senses and make the Word of God come alive, while also delivered with engaging voice and embodiment (which we will cover in Part V), preaching can be one of the most powerful forms of rhetoric people experience.

Let's look at four sermon forms that are basics for any preacher. For each of these forms, we'll refer to the work we have done on Exodus 20:1-6 (see Chapters 15, 16, and 17) to practice using these forms and see them in action.

FOUR PAGES

A sermon form that is usually very accessible and easy to work with for preaching students is the Four Pages form developed by Paul Scott Wilson.[7] Wilson's form is based on the theological dialectic of "law and gospel," or "trouble and grace." In Chapter 5, we used the terms "exigence and response." Wilson's idea was to divide the "trouble" and "grace" into four "pages" (movements, not actual pages) in the sermon highlighting the bad news in the biblical text, the bad news in the world, the good news in the text, and the good news in the world.

"Trouble/the law" is God's judgment on those things that drive us away from God and one another, compel us to neglect or hurt others, and separate us from God's love and the Beloved Community. In short, the law both reflects and is a consequence of human sin, conflict, and brokenness. We find this "trouble" both in the biblical text and in our current time. In a Four Pages sermon, the preacher spends equal time explaining the "trouble in the text" and "trouble in the world" in order to compel the listener to experience the "grace in the text" and "grace in the world."

"Grace/gospel" is God's merciful response to human sin as well as its implications for our lives, our churches, society, and God's Creation. The gospel (literally, "good news") can take the form of forgiveness, hope, healing, restoration, justice for the oppressed, and vision for a new way of living and being. Like trouble, grace also is found both in the Bible and (with the help of the preacher pointing it out) in the world today. Equal time is spent on the grace "pages" of the sermon so that the listeners can encounter and fully comprehend what God has done and is doing to bring about God's Realm.

Keep in mind that there is a bit of flexibility in the order of the Four Pages. A preacher may want to start with naming the trouble in the world first and then note how the biblical text illustrates the same problem. After that, the sermon could move to how God responds to the problem in the text and how God may be responding in the same manner today. Or you may want to start with the trouble in the text and go right to the grace in the text. Then do a parallel move with trouble in the world and corresponding grace today.

A preacher using this form has different options for where the Central Claim might be used. If utilizing a deductive form, the preacher could make their claim at the beginning and then introduce doubt about its veracity by noting the "bad news" in the text or the world that makes us question whether such a claim is true. Then the Central Claim could be reasserted in the section on grace in the text and repeated for grace in the world. Conversely, in an inductive sermon, the Central Claim could be held back until after the trouble in the text and trouble in the world have been established. Using inductive logic, the sections on grace in the text and grace in the world could follow clues that lead to the Central Claim, being sure to assert it clearly and confidently by the end of the sermon. Remember, too, that the Central Claim can either be clearly stated word for word in the sermon or implicitly informing different parts of the sermon but not stated outright.

EXERCISE 1

Using the Four Pages Form for a Sermon on Exodus 20:1-6

1. Review your exegesis notes for Exodus 20:1-6. Write a sentence for the "trouble in the text." What is the exigence, the human sinfulness at work in the background? Why was it necessary for God to give this commandment to have no other gods and not to create graven images?
2. Write a second sentence for the "grace in the text." How is God responding to this sin through the establishment of this commandment? How is it good news that the Israelites are given this command and what does it mean for their life together?

3. Review your notes for creating your Central Question where you exegeted your congregation. Write down a sentence for the "trouble in the world" stating the parallel problems you see in our contemporary situation with idolatry and, specifically, graven images in the form of the national flag in the church sanctuary. What is the human sinfulness exemplified by the presence of the flag in the church that requires the first commandment today?
4. Write a fourth sentence for the "grace in the world." How is God responding to this sin of nationalism and the church's embrace of the flag in the worship space? How is it good news that the flag is *not* necessary in the sanctuary? How might the congregation experience liberation by moving the flag from the worship space?

Now think about how you might structure a sermon around these "four pages." Would you start with trouble in the text or trouble in the world? Or maybe trouble in the text followed by grace in the text? Discuss your ideas for sequencing with your preaching partner and then read Chapter 21 to see one suggestion for how Four Pages might be used for a sermon on Exodus 20:1-6.

MOTION PICTURES

Another form that is useful for constructing a sermon was developed by the homiletician David Buttrick and is known as "motion pictures."[8] Buttrick used the analogy of a photographer or cinematographer framing a succession of images that, ideally, creates a complete experience of understanding. He called each frame a "move" in which the preacher follows a precise sequence to enable listeners to focus on an idea and then move onto the next one. With an introduction and conclusion on either end, there are typically three or four moves that follow this internal sequence as follows (each taking about four minutes):

1. Opening statement that contains the main idea.
2. Development through illustration, clarification, antithesis, or elaboration.
3. Closure with a restatement of the main idea.

You can see that within each move is a deductive sequence, in that the idea is stated very clearly at the beginning, is developed, and then is restated. The key to using this form is to have what we might call a "hinge" that opens and closes each section so that the listener is clued into the sequence of ideas. (Homiletician Alyce McKenzie uses the term "throughline" to describe this technique of using a repeating idea, image, or phrase to give coherence to a sermon. We will learn about this in Chapter 22.) The hinge is usually a phrase that is repeated throughout the sermon at key points of transition, allowing the listener to move in and out of each movement within the sermon. The outline for a sermon using the Motion Pictures form, then, would look like this:

1. Introduction
2. Move 1 (opening statement, development, restatement)
3. Move 2
4. Move 3
5. Move 4 (if needed)
6. Conclusion

A good example of a sermon using the Motion Pictures form is one that Thomas Long preached at Duke University Chapel on May 11, 2011, entitled "Pathways to Belief" based on the resurrection story in John 20:1-20.[9] He begins the sermon recounting a Christian radio call-in show in which a minister asks a troubled woman "Are you a believer?" He proceeds to pressure her into receiving his book with "irrefutable proof" about the resurrection of Christ. Long notes that not all people come to belief in Christ by the same path. He uses the four characters in

John's story of the resurrection (the "other disciple," Peter, Mary, and Thomas) to illustrate those different paths. For each character, he describes how they come to believe and then shares a compelling contemporary story to illustrate that particular path. Each move ends with the hinge, "Some people are like that. But not everybody." He repeats this for three of the moves, signaling that each has come to an end and a new one is starting. After the fourth move, Long gives a short conclusion that ends with a recapitulation of the original question, "Are you a believer?" which, by this point, the congregation is led to the irrefutable answer of Yes! (It's also worth noting that he ends the sermon with the same question with which the sermon began. This is called "bookending," which is a rhetorical technique we'll discuss in Chapter 22.)

A preacher using the Motion Picture form has different options for integrating the Central Claim. For a *deductive* sermon, the claim could be asserted at the beginning and each move could serve as an illustration of the truth of the claim. Or the introduction could introduce a question that leads to a series of moves responding to that question, and in each of those moves, the Central Claim could be used. It could even be used as the hinge for the sermon. In contrast, the Central Claim for an *inductive* sermon using the Motion Picture form would come later. The sermon could introduce a quandary or conundrum to be unraveled. Each move could provide a clue to the answer that would be revealed or at least inferred by the sermon's conclusion. Whatever logic is used, the Motion Pictures form offers a reliable structure for crafting a creative and inspiring sermon.

EXERCISE TWO

Using the Motion Pictures Form for a Sermon on Exodus 20:1-6

1. Review your Central Claim for Exodus 20:1-6. Decide if you would like this to be an inductive sermon (following clues in each move and only revealing the claim at the end) or a deductive sermon (stating the claim at the beginning and using each move to substantiate the claim).
   a. How you decide to use inductive or deductive logic may depend on your congregation and your Central Purpose. If you have people in the congregation who will need to be convinced that it's necessary to have a conversation about the placement of the flag in the sanctuary, induction may be the best strategy. Following each clue and building your case to reach your Central Purpose will feel less heavy-handed and more invitational. On the other hand, if you have already tried a more "soft" approach and it hasn't gained much traction, perhaps a deductive sermon that clearly and repeatedly makes the claim and directly asks for discussion of this issue may be the better route.
2. Consider how you want to begin the sermon. Think about your Central Question. Is there a question you could ask, or an opening illustration to get them thinking, or an image you can describe that captures the essence of the conundrum?
3. Write down three moves that would illustrate the claim you are making in this sermon. What are biblical examples of the claim you are making? What are contemporary examples or illustrations?
4. What is the hinge, refrain, or throughline that could tie these stories together? Think about what these moves all have in common that could give the transitions coherence.
5. Consider how you want to conclude the sermon. Think about your Central Purpose. If your sermon is deductive, how can you restate the Central Claim in a slightly different way that reinforces your argument and invites a response? If inductive, how can you create the "aha" moment so that the listeners are likely to arrive at the response you desire from them?

As you are developing your ideas for the sermon, you can experiment with the order of the moves. Each one should build tension and then release as well as move the listener along without getting too bogged down in each story. Discuss your ideas for sequencing with your preaching partner. Then read Chapter 21 to see an example of the Motion Pictures form for a sermon on Exodus 20:1-6.

HOMILETICAL PLOT

The third form we recommend for preaching students is Eugene Lowry's "Homiletical Plot."[10] This form takes the classic structure of a plot diagram (exposition, conflict, rising action, climax, falling action, resolution) and applies it to a sermon. This is not to say that the sermon should necessarily be a story in and of itself (although that is one form that a sermon can take). Rather, the preacher should work with the same principles that draw people into an engaging story from beginning to end.

For example, think of the way a good story is constructed. There is a beginning that grabs the listener's (or reader's) attention; this is called the *exposition.* Then a *conflict* is introduced that hooks the listener because it presents a problem to be solved, an issue to address, or an existential "itch" that needs a "scratch." But it's not so easily solved, otherwise the story would lack drama and end too quickly. Instead, there is a *complication,* something that puts up obstacles and impinges on an easy solution. We feel tension around this conflict and complication, which makes us yearn for some clue as to how the situation might find resolution. This comes in the form of the *sudden shift,* an "aha" moment where we see a glimmer of hope, a way forward, the key that can help us unlock the mystery. The rest of the story draws out the implications of this shift, this new information, and leads to the story's conclusion.

Lowry works with the premise that sermons should be organized around this same movement of the plot. They should begin by upsetting the equilibrium that sets off a chain of complications until there is a sudden shift, which is the gospel offering a clue as to how the conflict might be resolved. Following this "aha" moment, the rest of the sermon unfolds the ramifications of the gospel by helping the congregation to experience its impact and anticipate a future in light of the gospel's revelation.

Lowry's Homiletical Plot, then, follows this sequence:

1. Conflict ("Uh-oh!")
2. Complication ("Ugh!")
3. Sudden Shift ("Aha!")
4. Experiencing the Gospel ("Whee!")
5. Anticipating the Consequences ("Yeah!")

The Homiletical Plot uses inductive logic. In fact, Lowry insists that revealing the claim at the beginning would strip the sermon of its power and remove the reason for listening in the first place. The sermon's beginning should create imbalance and either generate the conflict in need of resolution or raise the felt need to the level of awareness so that it can be addressed directly. The stages of the sermon carry through the energy of the conflict all the way through to its resolution, allowing for a powerful proclamation of the gospel by the sermon's end.

The Central Statements easily can be layered into the Homiletical Plot form. For example, the Central Question would naturally inform the conflict and complication. The Central Claim is revealed at the sudden shift and developed in experiencing the gospel. The Central Purpose would be apparent in the final two parts, experiencing the gospel and anticipating the consequences, where the preacher would suggest how God's response to the human condition might elicit a response from the listeners.

EXERCISE THREE

Using the Homiletical Plot Form for a Sermon on Exodus 20:1-6

1. Review the Central Question for Exodus 20:1-6 (*What does it mean to worship the God of Israel in a culture that deifies its national identity, and how will the church witness to the God of liberation in this community?).* What would "upset the apple cart" of the status quo so that listeners will be drawn into this question? Think of an example or a story for stage one that would illustrate this question and either disrupt the equilibrium or highlight an existential dilemma for the listeners. For example, you might begin with a

story about the Nazis forcing churches to display the swastika flag during the Third Reich in Germany. How and why was that problematic for clergy and congregations? Or you could begin by setting the stage for the biblical drama in which the Israelites in captivity know they are to worship God, but everywhere they turn, they see carved images of the sun, frogs, and the Nile River, each representing that deity. What are they to do?

2. For stage two, explore the problem or ambiguity in more detail, so that the listener more fully experiences or understands the complication of the dilemma. In what ways do we see national identity deified today in our own country? When the Israelites asked to be released to worship their God, how did Pharaoh respond? Why did he not allow them to worship their God?
3. For stage three, review the Central Claim (*Because the God of Israel commanded believers to have no other gods, our congregation must engage in a serious discussion about the appropriateness of having the American flag, an engraved image of nationalism, within our worship space*). What is the "aha" moment that could offer a clue about the way forward? How does the commandment to worship no other gods and eschew graven images provide the shift that would move the listeners to see this as a resolution to the issue of idolatry?
4. For stage four, explore the meaning of this new God-guided direction for the congregation. Could God be inviting them into a dialogue about the presence of the flag in the worship space? How will this liberation enable them to more fully live into their mission? How might it help them to serve both God and neighbors? How might they experience the intertwined aspects of God's liberation *and* God's expectation for covenantal living through this commandment?
5. For the final stage, cast a vision for what might be possible moving forward. Depending on which of the three Central Purpose statements you chose, this might be a ceremonial relocation of the flag, or an invitation to a forum about the first commandment and its implications for the church, or an interfaith discussion with Jewish and Muslim believers who also strive to follow this same commandment.

As you are developing your ideas for the sermon, think about the role of Experience, Reason, Tradition, and Scripture from the Wesleyan Quadrilateral. Which will be the primary authority for the message you want to convey as you are working through the stages? Discuss your ideas with your preaching partner. Then look at the example in Chapter 21 to see one possibility for a sermon using the Homiletical Plot form for Exodus 20:1-6.

EXPOSITORY (ALSO CALLED PURITAN PLAIN STYLE)

One of the most popular sermon forms is Expository, or verse-by-verse preaching. Some call it exegetical preaching or know it as the Puritan Plain Style. Exposition means to explain something and convey its meaning and purpose. In this form, the preacher moves through a biblical text to make its meaning plain for the listeners. Exegetical skills in the historical-critical method are front and center in this form where the preacher can focus on what the text meant for its original hearers.[11] Sometimes a preacher may focus on just one verse or one word within the passage to do a "deep dive" on what it means. But then the sermon moves to theological analysis to help elucidate the Theological Claims in the text. All of this drives to application—drawing out the implications of the text for the congregation's life and faith.

This form is what many people have in mind when they say they prefer "biblical preaching." They like the preacher to help them understand the deeper meaning of the biblical text and appreciate the more didactic style of this kind of sermon. An Expository sermon asks "What does this Bible passage mean? And why does it matter?" in the most straightforward way. When used skillfully and with engaging illustrations, Expository preaching can be dynamic for the congregation.

However, if preached as a pedantic lecture, verse-by-verse preaching can weary listeners. When delivered as an academic treatise, the sermon can feel like it concentrates too much on intellect and leaves the heart cold. Especially if this is the only form a preacher uses week in and week out, a congregation may find such sermons tedious, mechanical, and predictable. Also, if the preacher fails to keep the big picture in mind and point out the ramifications of the theological message for the listeners, an Expository sermon can feel like it lacks direction and relevance for their lives.

Thus, the Central Statements can be helpful for an Expository sermon. The Central Question can give the preacher a sense of energy while working through the exegesis of the verses in order to connect their importance to the lived experiences of listeners. The Central Claim can enable the sermon to draw out the theological message of the passage and make a definitive statement without getting too caught up in the detailed minutiae of each verse. And the Central Purpose can direct the application of the text to the congregation's everyday life and sense of mission for the church.

In general, the outline of an Expository or Puritan Plain Style sermon looks like this:

1. Introduction
2. Exposition of the biblical text
3. Theological analysis of the text
4. Application of the interpretation of the text
5. Conclusion

The Expository sermon could work with either deductive or inductive logic. In a deductive form, the preacher could begin with the Central Question and immediately state the sermon's Central Claim in the introduction. Then the preacher would move through each verse or each unit of thought in the passage and explain how it supports the Central Claim. In the sermon's conclusion, the preacher would reiterate the Central Claim and summarize what they would have learned in the exposition that verifies the claim. Throughout such a sermon, the preacher can use evocative language, short stories, or illustrations to help flesh out the theological meaning of the text and how it applies today.

Conversely, an Expository sermon using inductive logic could begin with a brief modern-day conundrum and have the Central Question propel them into a journey with the passage. As they move through the biblical text, the preacher and congregation would find clues that might help them discover an answer to the question. The Central Claim might be introduced in the theological analysis section and expounded on in the application. Or the preacher might wait until the conclusion to offer the final "aha" moment of the sermon. This requires a skillful drawing together of the seemingly disparate threads of the text into an inexorable conclusion.

In Chapter 19, you saw an example of an Expository or Puritan Plain Style form with the sermon on Psalm 23. As you may have noticed in that sample, the preacher does not always have to explicitly name every single verse as they're preaching, although that is one way an Expository sermon can be constructed. Instead, a preacher may move through the sections of the passage in a more organic way, weaving theological insights and application throughout.

In the exercise below, you'll try your hand in sketching out a sermon on Exodus 20:1-6 using the Expository/Puritan Plain Style form. In the next chapter, you'll see an example of how Leah uses the form—but with a twist.

EXERCISE FOUR

Using the Expository or Puritan Plain Style Form for a Sermon on Exodus 20:1-6

1. Review your exegesis notes for Exodus 20:1-6, and the Central Question, Central Claim, and Central Purpose you wrote based on your work in previous chapters. Decide if you want to use an inductive or deductive approach to the sermon.
2. For each verse of the passage, use one of the creativity exercises from Chapter 19 for how you might illustrate the ideas, words, or images in the text. For example, do a mind-map of the word "idol" or create a sensory net for each verse to explore the visual, auditory, or emotional aspects of the verse that are evoked for you.

3. As you work on the theological analysis of the passage, consider what this text wants the congregation to believe about God and contrast that with what other gods (particularly the god of nationalism) want them to believe.
4. The way in which you approach the application of the text will depend on how direct you want to be in this sermon and what your Central Purpose is. If you want to make the case that the text is inviting conversation, is there a story you could share of another congregation engaging this topic together? Or, if you are making the claim that the text is convicting us of our sin of nationalism and requires a change in the way we think about the location of the flag, can you paint a picture of what different options might be acceptable?
5. The conclusion of the sermon, again, depends on whether the sermon is deductive or inductive. If you have made your Central Claim at the beginning, you will need to reiterate it at the end and summarize how the biblical text demonstrated the veracity of the claim all along. But if you are preaching an inductive sermon, you might want to end the sermon in a more open-ended way by inviting listeners to grapple with the issue beyond the conclusion of the sermon.

CONCLUSION

Now that you've been introduced to these four sermon forms—Four Pages, Motion Pictures, Homiletical Plot, and Expository/Puritan Plain Style—in the next chapter, we'll show you examples of how each of them can be used to craft a sermon on Exodus 20:1-6. Also, you can find "A Short List of Sermon Forms and How the Central Claim Can Be Used" in Appendix L for other structures you can use in preaching.

KEY POINTS IN THIS CHAPTER

1. The sermon form is the shape and structure of a sermon as determined by the ways in which the parts are arranged and organized. Basic forms covered in this book include Four Pages, Motion Pictures, Homiletical Plot, and Expository or Puritan Plain Style.
2. Preachers can and should vary the sermon forms they use to keep their preaching fresh and avoid boring their listeners.
3. Generally, preaching uses either deductive or inductive logic to organize the flow of thought around the claim of the sermon. Deductive logic starts with a premise, gives reasons why the premise is true, and restates the premise at the end. Inductive logic starts with a question and follows clues that lead to the claim.
4. Deductive sermons begin with the Central Claim (either explicitly or paraphrased). Then throughout the sermon, the preacher gives reasons for why this claim is true throughout the sermon. Then it restates the claim at the end of the sermon.
5. Inductive sermons do not reveal the Central Claim until later in the sermon. The sermon begins by introducing a question, quandary, or a story. While the point may not be immediately obvious, the inductive journey engages the attention of the listeners and draws them toward the Central Claim near the middle or end of the sermon.
6. The placement of the Central Claim helps to determine the form of the sermon. If the Central Claim is at or near the beginning, the sermon is deductive. If it is later or at the end, the sermon is inductive.
7. All sermon forms should be informed in some way by the Central Statements. The Central Question, Central Claim, and Central Purpose will each influence some part of the sermon either directly or indirectly. Likewise, the various elements of the Wesleyan Quadrilateral (Scripture, Tradition, Experience, Reason) can be utilized in any number of ways for these sermon forms.

8. The Four Pages form consists of the following "pages" in some order or another: "trouble in the text," "trouble in the world," "grace in the text," "grace in the world."
9. The Motion Pictures form consists of "moves," each of which has an opening statement with the main idea, development, and restatement of the idea. A typical sequence would be: introduction, move 1, move 2, move 3, move 4, conclusion.
10. The Homiletical Plot form uses an adaptation of the classic structure of a plot diagram for a dramatic story (but is not necessarily a story in and of itself). The sequence is: conflict ("Uh-oh!"); complication ("Ugh!"); sudden shift ("Aha!"); experiencing the Gospel ("Whee!"); anticipating the consequences ("Yeah!").
11. The Expository form (also called Exegetical or Puritan Plain Style) moves the listeners through the biblical text verse by verse, drawing out its theological meaning and showing how it applies to the contemporary context. Care must be taken to avoid sounding "lecturish" in this sermon while being sure to use creative illustrations and evocative language to help the sermon connect head and heart.

DISCUSSION QUESTIONS

1. Practice determining a sermon's form by revisiting the sermon "Jesus, Mother Hen" in Chapter 11. As you read through the sermon, ask yourself whether this sermon uses the form of Four Pages, Motion Pictures, or Homiletical Plot. Here's a clue: look for the "hinge"!
2. Another sermon you can analyze to determine the form is in Chapter 17, "Finding Our Way in the Wilderness of Conspiracy Theories: What Is the 'Straight Path'?" based on Mark 1:1-8. Here's a clue: look for the five stages of "Uh-oh," "Ugh," "Aha," "Whee," and "Yeah."
3. To see an example of a Four Pages sermon form, look at "Composting Our Anger and Grief," based on Luke 13:1-9 in Chapter 26. As you read the text, see if you can determine the order of "trouble" and "grace" in the sermon.
4. Discuss with your preaching mentor what types of sermon forms they prefer. Ask them to share a sermon manuscript with you and see if you can detect its form. (See Appendix L for a list of sermon forms.) How does your preaching mentor determine what form to use? Do they intentionally vary their sermon forms or stick with a few stock sequences?

FOR FURTHER READING

Ronald J Allen. Ch. 6, "Does the Sermon Move in a Way That Is Easy to Follow?" In *Preaching: An Essential Guide.* Nashville: Abingdon Press, 2002.

O. Wesley Allen Jr. *Determining the Form: Structures for Preaching.* In Elements of Preaching Series, edited by O. Wesley Allen Jr. Minneapolis, MN: Fortress Press, 2008.

David Buttrick. *Homiletic: Moves and Structures.* Philadelphia: Fortress Press, 1987.

Fred B. Craddock. *As One without Authority*, third edition. Nashville: Abingdon Press, 1979.

Thomas G. Long. Ch. 5, "The Basic Form of the Sermon" and Ch. 6, "Refining the Form." In *The Witness of Preaching*, third edition. Louisville: Westminster John Knox, 2016.

Eugene Lowry. *The Homiletical Plot, Expanded Edition: The Sermon as Narrative Art Form.* Louisville: Westminster John Knox Press, 2000.

Paul Scott Wilson. *The Four Pages of the Sermon, Revised and Updated: A Guide to Biblical Preaching.* Nashville: Abingdon Press, 2018.

NOTES

1. John S. McClure, *Preaching Words: 144 Key Terms in Homiletics* (Louisville: Westminster John Knox, 2007), 38.

2. Thomas G. Long, Ch. 5, "The Basic Form of the Sermon" and Ch. 6, "Refining the Form," in *The Witness of Preaching*, third edition (Louisville: Westminster John Knox, 2016).

3. Ronald J. Allen, ed., *Patterns of Preaching: A Sermon Sampler* (St. Louis: Chalice Press, 1998).

4. Thomas H. Troeger and Leonora Tubbs Tisdale, *A Sermon Workbook: Exercises in the Art and Craft of Preaching* (Nashville: Abingdon Press, 2013), 71.

5. Paying attention to the genres of the Bible can guide the form of our own preaching. For example, if the biblical text contains a hymn, the sermon could as well. If the text is a letter, the sermon could take that form too. See: Leander E. Keck, *The Bible in the Pulpit: The Renewal of Biblical Preaching* (Nashville: Abingdon Press, 1978); Thomas G. Long, *Preaching and the Literary Forms of the Bible* (Philadelphia: Fortress Press, 1989).

6. See: Fred B. Craddock, *As One without Authority*, third edition (Nashville: Abingdon Press, 1979).

7. Paul Scott Wilson, *The Four Pages of the Sermon, Revised and Updated: A Guide to Biblical Preaching* (Nashville: Abingdon Press, 2018).

8. See: David Buttrick, *Homiletic: Moves and Structures* (Philadelphia: Fortress Press, 1987).

9. Thomas Long, "Pathways to Belief," Duke University Chapel, May 11, 2011, accessed August 1, 2021, https://www.youtube.com/watch?v=wIVEU9oLJbg&t=3516s.

10. Eugene Lowry, *The Homiletical Plot, Expanded Edition: The Sermon as Narrative Art Form* (Louisville: Westminster John Knox Press, 2000).

11. Expository preaching also can be used to illuminate a doctrine, practice, or topic.

21

Examples of Four Sermon Forms

Four Pages, Motion Pictures, Homiletical Plot, and Expository

In the previous chapter, you learned the importance of sermon forms for organizing what you want to preach and how you want to present it. You also learned the difference between inductive and deductive sermons and how each form of logic can be used for the sermon forms we introduced in that chapter: Four Pages, Motion Pictures, Homiletical Plot, and Expository. As we discussed these different forms, we noted how the Central Question, Central Claim, and Central Purpose can both inform and be explicitly integrated into the parts of the sermon's structure. We also gave you exercises to think about how you could apply each form to a sermon about Exodus 20:1-6.

In this chapter, you'll see four examples of those sermon forms in action, and we'll invite you to analyze them for how they use the Wesleyan Quadrilateral—Scripture, Tradition, Reason, and Experience—and where you detect the use of the Exegesis Guide Chart and the Central Statements. The first two examples are not full sermons, but rather sermon trajectories that will give you a sense of how each of the forms can be used. The second two examples are full sermons to allow for more detailed analysis of the forms of Homiletical Plot and Expository.

REVIEW: CENTRAL STATEMENTS FOR EXODUS 20:1-6

Exodus 20:1-6 is the first part of what many call the "Ten Commandments." These verses contain the command to worship only God and eschew graven images of idolatry. Recall from the example in Chapter 15 that our Theological Claim was this:

> *God has claimed the Israelites as God's own and liberated them from slavery, so that the worship of other gods is both unnecessary and blasphemous.*

The context we imagined for this sermon is a church where the American flag is in the chancel area of the sanctuary, clearly visible. The preacher wants to craft a sermon raising questions about what the congregation truly worships and whether the nation's flag in this sacred space is a form of idolatry that needs to be addressed. The preacher knows that some in the congregation may be open to this conversation; however, there are others who would think it unpatriotic and disrespectful to veterans if the flag was removed from the sanctuary. So, after exegeting both the biblical text and the church's context, our Central Question was this:

> *What does it mean to worship the God of Israel in a culture that deifies its national identity, and how will the church witness to the God of liberation in this community?*

This led us to craft the following Central Claim:

Because the God of Israel commanded believers to have no other gods, our congregation must engage in a serious discussion about the appropriateness of having the American flag, an engraved image of nationalism, within our worship space.

When it came time to write the Central Purpose, we drafted three possibilities, each with a different tone, emphasis, and expectation for the congregation:

1. *The Central Purpose of this sermon is to compel the congregation to confront nationalism, name it as idolatry, and worship only the God of liberation.*
2. *This sermon will challenge listeners to question their loyalties to those things that are not of God, including nationalism and the display of the American flag in the church sanctuary, so that we can worship the true God of freedom.*
3. *This sermon initiates a conversation about what it means to worship the God of Israel so that we can speak honestly about fulfilling the commandment not to worship other gods.*

You'll see how each one can inform a sermon form depending on what the preacher wants to accomplish. Each of the sermons below utilizes one of the Central Purpose Statements.

EXAMPLE 1: SERMON STRUCTURE FOR EXODUS 20:1-6 USING FOUR PAGES

Using the work we have done so far on Exodus 20:1-6, we could craft a sermon addressing the idolatry of the American flag in the worship space by following Wilson's Four Pages form. In this sermon, the Central Purpose could be #2: *This sermon will challenge listeners to question their loyalties to those things that are not of God, including nationalism and the display of the American flag in the church sanctuary, so that we can worship the true God of freedom.*

As you read through this sermon sequence, see if you can detect whether it is using inductive or deductive logic. Also notice where you see direct references or at least inferences to the four parts of the Wesleyan Quadrilateral: Scripture, Tradition, Experience, and Reason. And take note of where you see the exegesis, Central Question, Central Claim, and Central Purpose informing this sermon sequence. Note that this is not a full sermon but a description of the sermon trajectory.

FOUR PAGES SERMON TRAJECTORY: "FLAGGING THE FLAG— IDOLATRY AND FREEDOM"

Page One—Trouble in the text

God liberated the Israelites and gave them the command to have no other gods and no other graven images. But we might not realize why this command was necessary. What led to this point on the mountain where Moses received this commandment from God? We have to look at this background on two levels. The story is about when the Israelites were slaves in Egypt, but the original hearers of the story were exiles in the Babylonian Captivity. In the narrative, enslaving the Israelites was made possible by a theological heresy claiming that Pharaoh is a god whom they must obey and worship. This idolatry was symbolized by the graven images of multiple sub-deities such as the sun, frogs, water, insects, and the Nile River, all of which were believed to be under Pharaoh's control.

Page Two—Trouble in the world

Nations today continue to make images that symbolize their omnipotence, ubiquity, and omnipresence—all divine qualities. When a nation's flag is placed anywhere in the world (or even on the moon!), it is making a claim that this nation has sovereignty and control, and that it exercises ultimate power. When that nation's flag is placed in a church, there is a complex array of both subtle and explicit meanings that could be quite problematic. At the very least, it raises questions about the appropriateness of graven imagery in the worship space.

Page Three—Grace in the text

> God revealed the fallacy of Pharaoh's claims to divinity and established that the true God is one of liberation and freedom for the oppressed and enslaved. God did this first through the ten plagues, each of which affected one of the smaller deities of Egypt and showed Pharaoh to be powerless over them. Then God freed the people, and with that freedom came the responsibility to make sure future generations did not make the same mistakes as their Egyptian oppressors. So, God gave them the command to have no other gods and no graven images. The good news is that no other deities are necessary, and they are free from this idolatry that had exploited them.

Page Four—Grace in the world

> God is still sovereign and requires believers to forego any graven images, lest they unknowingly (or knowingly) worship an idol. The church can be free from any symbols of nationalism, any advertising, any images that compete with our loyalties and our worship of the one, true God. This allows us to be truly liberated to serve God and neighbor.

Was this an inductive or deductive sermon? If you said deductive, you are correct. You can tell this is deductive because the Central Claim is stated at the beginning in the first sentence. The congregation is told where they are going in this sermon at the outset and are presented with two situations (trouble in the text, trouble in the world) that illustrate how God responds and what God is doing. The Central Claim then appears again in Page Three, Grace in the text.

But this could have been just as easily designed as an inductive sermon where the preacher could have launched into the "trouble in the text" without introducing the claim in the introduction. The congregation would not know why they are hearing these examples of modern-day idolatry but would be caught up in the drama and the tension leading to the Central Claim. The preacher could have used the two "trouble" pages to build tension around idolatry that breaks only when the Central Claim becomes clear in Page Three and is more fully understood in Page Four for how it applies to their own situation.

You may have noticed that this form tracks well with the Central Statements you have learned in this book. The exegetical work you do for the Scripture passage and your preaching context leads to the Central Question—articulating the trouble, or what we have called the *Occasional Exigence*, in both the biblical text and your preaching context. This part of the sermon would explain the existential realities that are troubling the author of the passage, the original hearers, as well as our contemporary situation. The theological analysis leading to the Central Claim is what enables the preacher to proclaim the grace in the text and in the world. The Central Purpose then draws out the implications of this good news for the listeners and the larger community.

Here's where you should have detected the parts of the Wesleyan Quadrilateral throughout the "pages":

Page One—Scripture (The biblical passage is the source of revelation about what God has done in liberating the Israelites and why God has a problem with other deities and graven images.)

Page Two—Reason (We apply logic to draw a correlation between the idolatry and graven imagery in the nation-state of Egypt with the idolatry of nation-states today, and why this is theologically problematic.)

Page Three—Scripture (Notice the four theological statements in that paragraph pointing out who God is and what God has done by undoing Pharaoh's oppressive reign and freeing the Israelites from slavery.)

Page Four—Reason and Experience (Logic is again applied to the contemporary situation, this time leading to the experience of the church resisting nationalism as a way in which God frees people from oppression and exploitation today.)

EXAMPLE 2: SERMON STRUCTURE FOR EXODUS 20:1-6 USING MOTION PICTURES

For this sermon on Exodus 20:1-6 using the Motion Pictures form, let's imagine a situation where the pastor has had some initial conversations with church members about the appropriateness of the American flag in the worship space but has encountered resistance. Not only have some insisted that removing the flag would be disrespectful of veterans, others have made the argument that the flag symbolizes the freedom for Americans to worship as they wish. As such, they argue, having the flag in the sanctuary is an important reminder of the source of this right. Further, they insist, honor is due the American flag because of the protection the state provides the church, enabling it to be able to exist in the first place. Of course, this rationale overlooks or ignores who truly enables the church—and the state, for that matter—to exist: God. Thus, this kind of thinking is undergirded by bad theology in need of correction. For these individuals who see no competition between the flag and the Christian symbols, believing they can coexist in harmony and symbiosis, the sermon will need a strategic approach to challenge this assumption.

With this in mind, Leah would choose Central Purpose #1: *Compel the congregation to confront nationalism, name it as idolatry, and worship only the God of liberation.* Using the Motion Pictures form, she would begin by talking about a lesson on the Ten Commandments she once taught to Confirmation students where she asked them to discuss the different "gods" we worship. (In the Lutheran denomination where Leah is ordained, teens who were baptized as infants take part in Confirmation classes that culminate in an Affirmation of Baptism ritual.) She would use each of the moves to describe a thought experiment she did with the class where they debated the appropriateness of certain symbols in a worship space.

As you read through this sermon sequence, determine whether it uses inductive or deductive logic and where you see the influence of the Exegesis Guide Chart, as well as the Central Question, Central Claim, and Central Purpose. Also note where you see Scripture, Tradition, Reason, and Experience in the sermon. When it comes to Tradition, you will see that Leah references the Apostle's Creed throughout the sermon. This is because the sermon would be preached in a Lutheran congregation where the credal tradition is foundational to the church's self-understanding and, thus, to the Confirmation students' education.

MOTION PICTURES SERMON TRAJECTORY: "A DOLLAR SIGN, CELL PHONE, AND FLAG WALK INTO A CHURCH"

1. Introduction. Leah describes the scene of the Confirmation students discussing the First Commandment to worship no other gods nor create any images of these idols. She spreads out a myriad of magazines and invites them to cut out pictures symbolizing the "gods" that people worship today. They imagine what it would be like to see these different symbols in the sanctuary. Leah notes the connection to the first article of the Apostle's Creed, "I believe in God the Father Almighty, creator of heaven and earth," and invites them into a thought experiment to substitute some of the images they have identified. In this way, "I believe in ______ the Almighty, creator of heaven and earth" becomes the hinge for the moves.
2. Move one: Someone cut out a picture of a dollar sign. "I believe in Money the Almighty, creator of heaven and earth." They discuss a series of questions: How is money like a god? Does it provide for us? Does it create things? Does it seem to be everywhere? Does it hurt us? Does it care about us? Through a dialectic exchange, the students conclude that a dollar sign in the sanctuary would not be appropriate because it would be idolatry.
3. Move two: Two students cut out pictures of cell phones and the symbol for the internet. "I believe in Internet the Almighty, creator of heaven and earth." With both humor as well as philosophical engagement, the students again work through the series of question. How is cyberspace like a god? Does it provide for us? Does it create things? And so on. Again, the students conclude that the symbol of the internet in the sanctuary would also be idolatry.
4. Move three: One student cut out a picture of the Earth. "I believe in Earth the Almighty, creator of . . ." This one is trickier. Earth is actually mentioned in the first article of the Apostle's Creed. The discussion becomes more somber as the students discuss the need to honor and take care of God's Earth, but that it shouldn't be worshipped in and of itself. (One astute student notes, however, that Gaia was worshipped as a goddess in ancient Greek mythology.) Though they think Earth should not be seen as a symbol of a deity, they suggest that having a picture of the Earth in the worship space would be appropriate for Earth Day.
5. Move four: The last image they discuss is the American flag. "I believe in America the Almighty, creator of heaven and earth." The room gets very quiet. One student points out the obvious, that there *is* a flag in the sanctuary. They go through the questions. How is America like a god? Does it provide for us? Does it create things? Does America seem to be everywhere? Does it hurt certain people? Does it care about us? After much discussion (which mirrors what the adults have been discussing in other forums), the students are divided as to whether the flag should be in the sanctuary.
6. Conclusion. Leah reminds her listeners that in ancient Egypt, Pharaoh forced the Israelites to be subservient to all of the idols and to himself, claiming to be divine. Pharaoh made the same arguments that any country could make about its benevolence, ubiquity, and omnipresence. But his power ultimately relied on violence

and control. We may be divided on whether the flag belongs in the sanctuary, but our creed is clear: "I believe in God the Father Almighty, creator of heaven and earth." And our Scripture is clear: God would not approve of having the flag in the worship space. Our desire to have it there is something we can discuss, but God is unequivocal that idolatry and graven images are unacceptable in church. She would conclude by re-reading Exodus 20:1-6 and let that be the last word of the sermon.

As you can see, the Motion Pictures sermon form allows for a cohesive sequence in preaching. In this sermon, the congregation is compelled to grapple with the issue of nationalism but it happens *vicariously* through listening to the description of the students' discussion (often with chuckles at the silliness of certain images in the worship space). The congregation is a step removed because it is a story about *others'* discussion about the flag in church. This allows them to "fishbowl"[1] the discussion without having to feel like they are debating the pastor or one another on the issue.

Notice, too, the use of the Wesleyan Quadrilateral in this sermon outline. Tradition via the Apostle's Creed is a primary source of authority.[2] But so is Reason as the students engage in thoughtful discussion weighing the pros and cons of certain symbols and what they mean in relationship to theology, thus allowing them to understand something about God. Experience is more nuanced, in that the listeners participate in the tension of a faith community's discernment through listening to the description of the students' discussion. In this way, God's grace is "caught" through the experience of listening in on the conversation, rather than received in a direct way. Scripture makes its strongest appearance at the end of the sermon, which gives it at least equal if not slightly more weight than Tradition.

The Central Question (*What does it mean to worship the God of Israel in a culture that deifies its national identity, and how will the church witness to the God of liberation in this community?*) is never stated word for word. But it can be detected in the introduction and is the energy that powers the sermon. Describing the historical background of the First Commandment at the sermon's conclusion and drawing parallels with our contemporary situation draws on the Exegesis Guide Chart and impresses upon the listeners the Central Claim (*Because the God of Israel commanded believers to have no other gods, our congregation must engage in a serious discussion about the appropriateness of having the American flag, the engraved image of nationalism, within our worship space*). While this claim is not stated explicitly, it is experienced intuitively. Finally, the Motion Pictures form helps to achieve the Central Purpose, because by the time they reach the end of the sermon, the congregation will have been challenged to name nationalism as idolatry and worship only the God of liberation.

Thus, you can see that this sermon used inductive logic because the Central Claim did not make its presence known until the conclusion of the sermon. Leah began with a series of clues in each move building toward her claim at the end. By this point, the congregation is invested in the story, drawn in by the discussion of the youth, and feeling the tension between what they want (flag in the worship space) and what God wants (no graven images). Concluding with a reiteration of the commandment seals the sermon.

EXAMPLE 3: SERMON FOR EXODUS 20:1-6 USING HOMILETICAL PLOT

In this example of a sermon for Exodus 20:1-6, Leah chose Central Purpose #3: *This sermon initiates a conversation about what it means to worship the God of Israel so that we can speak honestly about fulfilling the commandment not to worship other gods.* For this example of the Homiletical Plot form, we've included the full sermon. You'll see that each of the five stages is clearly marked in paragraphs 2, 5, 9, 10, and 11. As you read the sermon, see if you can discern the influence of Scripture, Tradition, Reason, and Experience. Also note where you detect the direct or indirect influence of the Exegesis Guide Chart, Central Question, Central Claim, and Central Purpose.

HOMILETIC PLOT SERMON: "PASTOR TOM, GLADYS, AND A FLAG WITH LEGS"

1. *[Introduction]* Pastor Tom begins his new call at Church of the Savior fresh out of seminary. He is passionate about addressing social issues and is on fire to prove himself as a social justice advocate for the sake of the gospel. On his first day, he strides into the empty sanctuary and sees the US flag right in the front of the

chancel. Pastor Tom knows that having the flag in the sanctuary breaks the First Commandment because it is a form of graven imagery and an idol of nationalism. God gave this command so that the Israelites could be free from their oppressors and not fall prey to idolatry once they were free. Having the US flag right there in the sanctuary just a few feet from the cross makes his blood boil. So without a second thought, he marches it out of the sanctuary and into a closet in the church basement.

2. *[Stage One: Conflict/"Uh-oh!"]* But a few days later, the flag mysteriously appears right back in the sanctuary where it had been before. Grumbling to himself about idolatry, he moves it again to the basement. And again a few days later, it pops up right back in its usual spot. "Hm," Pastor Tom says to himself. "This flag has legs."
3. He doesn't know who keeps moving the flag back into the sanctuary, but he suspects it might be the custodian, Albert. So, he confronts Albert about why he keeps moving the flag back into the sanctuary, explaining to him why it is idolatrous for the flag to be there. The custodian shakes his head, "It wasn't me. But you could ask Gladys, the head of the altar guild. She might know."
4. Gladys is the sweet, unassuming widow who makes sure that the paraments on the altar are clean and correct for every season. She faithfully sets out the Communion elements each week. And she sees to it that there is a glass of water on the pulpit for Pastor Tom every Sunday. One day after the service as she is in the sacristy washing out the chalice, he asks if she knows who might be moving the flag back to the sanctuary after he removes it. He mentions that it is idolatrous for the flag to be there because it breaks the First Commandment.
5. *[Stage Two: Complication/"Ugh"]* Sweet Gladys erupts in tears and anger. "So, *you're* the one who keeps moving the flag! I wondered why all of a sudden the flag grew legs!" She tells him about her husband, who died in the war defending this country. When she sees that flag, it reminds her that her husband is still with her in spirit every Sunday at church. "You have no appreciation for the sacrifice he made for you," she spits before whirling around and walking out of the sacristy.
6. Realizing that he had mishandled the situation, Pastor Tom sends a heartfelt note of apology to Gladys and asks if he can take her out for coffee so that they can clear the air. "I want to hear more about your husband," he writes. Generously, she invites him to her home, where she shows him pictures of Stewart, her beloved. There he is with sparkling eyes in his grade school picture. Here they are on their wedding day. In this one he is posing proudly in his military uniform. Over fresh-squeezed lemonade, Gladys tells Pastor Tom about her husband and why his sacrifice for the country means so much to her.
7. "But enough about me," Gladys says. "Tell me about how you decided to become a pastor." He tells her about his grandparents who brought him to church as a boy and encouraged him as he joined the youth group and went on mission trips. He explained that his grandfather had fought the Nazis in Germany. "He told me about how the Nazis put that hateful swastika flag in churches. 'No flag belongs in a church,' he told me. 'The church is God's house, no matter what country it might be in.' I've always remembered that. And when I went to seminary and learned about why it's so important to honor the First Commandment, I promised myself that I would never allow a flag in a church, no matter where I served. That's why I moved the flag out, Gladys. Not to dishonor your husband, but to honor God."
8. Gladys listened thoughtfully and nodded her head. "It seems we've reached an impasse. I'm not willing to see the flag removed. You're not willing to see the flag stay. What do we do?"
9. *[Stage Three: Sudden Shift/"Aha"]* The pastor thought for a moment, then said, "I'm sure we're not the only ones to have conflicted feelings about this. I wonder if we could have a larger conversation about this with others in the church? Maybe together we can have a dialogue to help us find a way through. Maybe God is using this to invite us into a conversation."
10. *[Stage Four: Experiencing the Gospel/"Whee!"]* So the two of them, Pastor Tom and Gladys, talked with the church council about their dilemma. Together, they came up with the idea to hold a series of forums for people to share what the flag means to them—the good, the bad, and the ugly—as well as what the First Commandment means to them. With Bible studies, personal stories, and deep, honest sharing and listening, the congregation spent several weeks discerning God's will for them regarding this issue. In the end, they agreed to move the flag to the back of the sanctuary so that it was not in the chancel but could still be visible for those who wanted to see it. And rather than bringing the flag front and center for the holidays of Memorial Day and Fourth of July (which had been their custom), they added a special remembrance on All Saints Day for those who died in service of their country.

11. *[Stage Five: Unfolding/"Yeah!"]* What does it mean to worship the God of Israel who commands us not to have graven images? In what ways can we listen to the different ideas and meanings each of us attaches to the flag? How will the church witness to the God of liberation in this church, and in this community? I don't know the answers, but I'm really interested in these questions. I know each of us takes seriously the First Commandment. And I also know there are very strong feelings about having the flag in the sanctuary—both for and against. As with Pastor Tom and Gladys, I believe God is inviting our congregation to a conversation, and I hope you will join us for this. [Invitation to the date and time of the discussion.]
12. The flag has legs, yes. But so does the cross. Both the flag and the cross can move front and center—and they can step aside. They can kneel and they can stand. They can walk towards each other, and they can walk away. God can do powerful things with just one step forward. Let's take that step together. Amen.

The Homiletical Plot sermon form was an ideal vehicle for carrying out the purpose of this sermon, which was to *initiate a conversation about what it means to worship the God of Israel so that we can speak honestly about fulfilling the commandment not to worship other gods*. The sermon modeled the kind of conversation the preacher would hope to have within the congregation. Notice that the pastor in this story was not the "hero." He made some blunders. But guided by compassion and with the grace of forgiveness, Pastor Tom and Gladys were able to try again to listen and learn from each other. They took their dilemma to the church's governing body in the spirit of dialogue, which resulted in an outcome that moved beyond the dichotomous thinking that created the conflict in the first place. Like the previous sermon about the dialogue with the Confirmation students, a congregation would be able to *vicariously* enter into the discussion.

By upsetting the equilibrium with Pastor Tom moving the flag and explaining the complication with Gladys connecting the flag to her husband's memory, the first two stages end with a standoff between the two of them. In terms of the Exegesis Guide Chart and the Wesleyan Quadrilateral, Scripture is obvious in stage one with Pastor Tom using the biblical background for the First Commandment as his rationale for removing the flag. Stage two surfaces the tension of bringing personal experience (Gladys's grief) into conversation with the discernment of the larger church. This happens when Pastor Tom appeals to Tradition through the teaching of his grandfather about the German church's idolatrous display of the Nazi flag. Stage three contains a version of the Central Claim ("Maybe God is using this to invite us into a conversation"), which signals the shift in the conflict. Stages four and five both use Experience and Reason to describe the congregation's deliberation about the issue and inviting the preacher's own congregation to consider the same invitation to dialogue.

The sermon concludes by recapitulating Pastor Tom's words, "The flag has legs," which had been a moment of ironic drama when Gladys said the same thing. At the sermon's end, this image of the flag having legs is juxtaposed with the cross also having legs, and the metaphor frames the invitation to dialogue by inviting them to step forward together. In this way, the sermon comes to its resolution while also leaving open possibilities for future engagement.

EXAMPLE 4: SERMON STRUCTURE FOR EXODUS 20:1-6 USING EXPOSITORY PREACHING

Recall that for the Expository sermon form (also called Exegetical or Puritan Plain Style), the preacher moves through a biblical text to make its meaning plain for the listeners. Some preachers prefer to go verse by verse, while others might focus on an important word in a text and explicate that for the listeners. To avoid the sermon feeling bookish and tediously methodical, the preacher will need to employ some of the creative techniques we outlined in Chapters 18 and 19.

In Chapter 19, you saw a more traditional version of the Puritan Plain Style with the sermon "When Psalm 23 Shepherded Me." In that sermon, the preacher went section by section, explaining each part of the psalm and drawing out its theological implications, followed by a section where the psalm is applied to everyday life (a parent in a hospital with an injured child). But there are other ways to utilize the Expository form. For this sermon on Exodus 20:1-6, a preacher could work through each verse, but with a twist. Before preaching the sermon, the pastor could use a method of engaging the text developed by John S. McClure called "the roundtable pulpit." In this method, the preacher meets with a group of parishioners to study and discuss the passage with the idea that the wisdom and experiences of the members can and should inform the sermon. This collaborative approach is reflected in the sermon by the use of certain rhetorical techniques that enable the whole congregation to experience the participatory and community-building nature of the dialogue. As McClure puts it, such an approach "implies that members of the community of the Word decide on ways to stand *with* and *for* one another by claiming tentative *directions* of thought and action as God's Word."[3]

With this idea that the sermon should represent a diversity of voices both within and beyond the congregation, the Central Purpose for this sermon would be #3: *This sermon initiates a conversation about what it means to worship the God of Israel so that we can speak honestly about fulfilling the commandment not to worship other gods.*

As you read through this hypothetical sermon, try to determine whether it is using inductive or deductive logic. Also be sure to highlight when you see influences of the Exegesis Guide Chart as well as any of the four parts of the Wesleyan Quadrilateral: Scripture, Tradition, Experience, and Reason. Note that for this sermon, the theological analysis is woven throughout the exposition to capture the flow of the group's conversation.

EXPOSITORY SERMON: "THE BIG RED, WHITE, AND BLUE IN THE ROOM"

Introduction

The aroma of freshly brewed coffee filled the room as chairs scraped across the floor and, one by one, we unbundled ourselves from the evening winter's chill. The Bibles waited patiently, evenly spaced around the table. We were gathering for our weekly study of the text in preparation for the sermon I would be preaching today.

But there was a special guest that evening. I had brought the US flag down from the sanctuary and set it at the table. It stood silently at attention, gazing down at the Bible in front of it.

There was good-natured teasing about my inviting this guest to the study. "There you go again, Pastor, being political," said one.

"Well," I responded, "if we welcome the flag into our sanctuary, don't you think we should invite it to our Bible study as well?"

Amidst groans and arched eyebrows, Bibles flipped open to the passage under consideration, Exodus 20:1-6.

Exposition of the biblical text and theological analysis

Before we dove into the text, I gave some historical background about it. Even though this story takes place on Mt. Sinai just after God leads the Israelites out of Egypt, the book of Exodus was actually written about six hundred years later at a time when the Israelites were captives in the land of Babylon. Their sacred temple had been destroyed. Many of their people had been massacred, and the rest of them were now living in exile in this foreign land. They were forced to worship foreign gods and assimilate to the Babylonian culture.

So, I invited our Bible study group, and I invite you, to think about what this passage might have meant to the Israelites during the Babylonian captivity. Why did they need to hear this story about God giving them what we call the Ten Commandments?

Verse 1

As soon as I read verse 1, "Then God spoke all these words," one person jumped right in with a comment.

"Well, that tells you something right there," the person said. "It must have been a big deal just to say that God spoke to them."

We agreed this was an astute theological observation. If God spoke to Moses and gave them these commandments, then they still meant something for the people living in exile.

Verse 2

This led us right into verse 2, "I am the Lord your God, who brought you out of the land of Egypt, out of the house of slavery."

"Isn't it interesting that God describes himself by what he did for them?" one person observed.

"Right," I said. "So why is *this* important for the Israelites living in exile?"

"Because if God did this for them before, God will do it again?" someone suggested.

Heads nodded in agreement.

Verses 3-4

But then we got to the third verse and the sparks started to fly. "I know what you're going to say next, Pastor," one person piped up before we even read verse 3. "That's why you brought this flag down here. You think that the flag is an idol, don't you?"

I held up my hands in surrender. "I do think that," I admitted. "But I'm interested to hear what you all think as well. That's why I invited you here. I want to know your thoughts about this. Because it's been bothering me for a long time that we have the flag in the sanctuary. I've avoided bringing it up directly, but as I read this text, I'm really concerned about it."

"Well, I think you're making too much of it," said one person. "It's just a flag. It's not a god. It's not an idol. We don't worship it."

"Don't we?" asked another. "They say you can tell what people worship by what they spend their money on. And I can tell you our military budget is out of control. We spend more on fighter planes than we do on schools."

"Yeah, well those fighter planes keep us safe," said a third person. "You know my son works on those planes as a mechanic for the Air Force and I'm proud of him and what he's doing for our country. It doesn't bother me at all to have the flag in the sanctuary. It makes me proud."

"But does it make God proud?" asked another person. And we all got very quiet.

"Can you say more about that?" I encouraged.

Verse 5

"It says right here in verse 5 that God is jealous," the person explained. "I mean, I think that it's weird that God would get jealous, because, I mean, it's God, so why should he care?"

"I think that's weird, too," said someone else, pulling up a Bible app on their phone. "It says here in Chapter 34, verse 14, that even God's name is Jealous."

"I guess I'd be jealous, too, if I went to all that trouble to get them out of slavery and they turn right back around and make another god for themselves and worship it," one person said.

At that point, I reminded them about the situation in Egypt. "Remember that Pharaoh was considered a god who was in charge of all the mini-gods of the sun and the river and even the moon. That's why Yahweh sent the plagues—to prove that Pharaoh truly had no power."

"So God was like Toto in the *Wizard of Oz*, pulling back the curtain on Pharaoh," one person suggested, and we all laughed at the image.

"Yes!" I said. "Pharaoh wanted everyone to think he was all-powerful. But in fact, no human entity, no human-fashioned idol can come close to the power of God. Yet, if you can convince people you're the great and powerful Oz, you can get them to obey you, be afraid of you, even kill for you."

"Sounds a lot like our government," a voice murmured.

"Bite your tongue!" said another.

"What? It's true," the person said in defense. "Think about what our country did bringing slaves over here from Africa. Think about what we did to the Native Americans. That's what I think about when I look at the flag sometimes. I know it means a lot of positive things to a lot of people. But I can't get the negative things out of my head either. So I actually don't think that flag belongs in the church."

"Not anywhere?" someone challenged.

"Actually, no," the person replied. "I don't think the flag belongs in the church at all. Not flying over the parking lot. Not here in the fellowship hall. And certainly not in the sanctuary."

"What about in the Scout room?" another person asked.

"Well, maybe that's okay," the defender conceded.

Verse 6

At this point I drew the group back to the text. "What about verse 6, which tells us that God shows steadfast love to the thousandth generation of those who love God and keep God's commandments. What do we make of that?"

Everyone paused for a moment to think. Then one person observed, "There's certainly a much better return on our investment from following the commandments than there is from breaking them."

"Yeah, like a thousand to four," another added. "I like those odds!"

We all chuckled.

Application of the interpretation of the text

Then our conversation turned back to the flag. "Well, Pastor, what do you think our 'guest' has to say about all this? It's been pretty quiet this whole time."

"Well, personally, I think the flag would be hurt if we took it out of the sanctuary. That's where it's always been. It's tradition!" said one.

"More than hurt," said another. "If I was the flag, I would be pretty angry. I'd feel very disrespected if I was removed from the sanctuary. I feel like this whole conversation is unpatriotic."

"But that's the thing," said a third person. "A church sanctuary isn't supposed to be the place where we honor the flag. It's supposed to be the place where we worship God. There are plenty of other places where the flag can and should be displayed and honored. But church shouldn't be one of them."

"I just don't see why we can't have both," was the response. "You can love God and love your country. And I can tell you if that flag gets moved, you're gonna have a big fight on your hands."

"Hold on," I said. "No one's saying we're going to move the flag."

"Yeah, this isn't worth fighting about," someone added.

"Maybe it is," another person countered. "Maybe this *is* something worth fighting about. Well, not fighting, but at least having the discussion like we're having now. I mean, God wants to show us steadfast love. Isn't God's love worth having this discussion?"

Conclusion

At that point the coffee cups were drained and so were we. "This has been a really good and really important discussion," I said to the group. "I'm proud of all of you for engaging this text and being welcoming to our guest."

"So where do we go from here?" one person asked.

"That's a good question," I said. "And it's one that I will pose to the congregation when I preach this sermon."

So: where *do* we go from here? Where does *God* want us to go from here? Do we keep talking? Perhaps expand the conversation? Or do we say, we've talked enough and it's time for action? Do we do something different now? Or, should we not change a thing?

What do we think the Israelites would say to us as they stood at the foot of the mountain looking back over their shoulder to the land that had enslaved them? What do we think the Israelites in captivity would say with the Babylonian flag hung from every home, every government building, every sports stadium, and looming over the spot where their temple once stood?

Better yet, let's ask our guest. [Moving to the flag and addressing it directly]: So tell us: where do we go from here? Where do *you* go from here?

I would encourage us to keep talking and to keep listening—to each other, to the Bible, to the flag, and, most importantly, to God. Amen.

As you read through this example of Expository preaching, were you able to see how the Central Question (*What does it mean to worship the God of Israel in a culture that deifies its national identity, and how will the church witness to the God of liberation in this community?*) provided the current for the flow of the sermon? Beginning at verse 3, the group grapples intuitively with that question. You might have also noticed that the question is never actually answered, which should tell you something about which form of logic this sermon used. If you guessed *inductive*, you would be correct.

The Central Claim (*Because the God of Israel commanded believers to have no other gods, our congregation must engage in a serious discussion about the appropriateness of having the American flag, an engraved image of nationalism, within our worship space*) is implied throughout the sermon, but the conclusion leaves the listeners to answer the question in their own minds. This is a risky move, but in light of the Central Purpose (*This sermon initiates a conversation about what it means to worship the God of Israel so that we can speak honestly about fulfilling the commandment not to worship other gods*), it is an appropriate ending. This is because the Expository form—presented as a roundtable story—organically accomplished the sermon's goal: the conversation was initiated.

In terms of the Wesleyan Quadrilateral, Scripture is not only discussed in the sermon but is the platform for the sermon itself because of the Expository form. Tradition is mentioned by one of the Bible study participants, but in a way that is potentially problematic and leads to pushback from a fellow participant. When the tradition of the church is something that goes against God's commandment, it should rightly be challenged. Experience is also referenced throughout the sermon as those who favor the flag are challenged by others who experience the flag as a symbol of oppression, thus testing the community's practice and assumptions. Reason plays an interesting role in this sermon. In fact, it is the dialogue itself that reveals the Spirit of God moving among the participants as they discuss, debate, and discern the theological implications of the First Commandment for their ecclesiology.

As we noted earlier, this version of the Expository form diverges from the traditional verse-by-verse format. This was intentional in order to draw the listeners into the sermon through a story about the dialogue rather than a dry exegetical exercise or using a "preachy" tone. The preacher still provided the necessary exegetical information, and the sermon sequence proceeded in order through the verses. But by setting the stage with descriptive language (the aroma of coffee, the scrape of the chairs, the Bibles waiting patiently, the flag standing at attention), and by recounting the drama of the discussion, the Expository form becomes a lively narrative instead of a scholarly treatise.

Finally, a word about the ending of the sermon that included the question posed to the flag, "Where do *you* go from here?" There are different schools of thought about whether it is appropriate to end a sermon with a question, which we will discuss in the next chapter (see "Concluding Convincingly" in Chapter 22). Because this was a roundtable sermon that included different perspectives, ending with the question was intentional, in the sense that it allowed the listener to provide their own answer to the question posed to the flag instead of imposing a final, authoritative conclusion. Also, the ending was in keeping with the Central Purpose, which was to initiate a conversation about what it means to worship the God of Israel so that we can speak honestly about fulfilling the commandment not to worship other gods. Ending with a question was a way to rhetorically invite further theological reflection and conversation.

FINAL THOUGHTS

By this point, you should have a good sense of the ways in which different forms shape the structure of the sermon. In fact, the form is not just the vehicle to get you where you want to go with your preaching. Sometimes the form mirrors or even amplifies the content of the sermon and plays an integral part in how the preacher conveys the message and accomplishes the goal of the sermon. You should also have seen the myriad ways a single text can be preached depending on the form that is used. Hopefully, this will encourage you to experiment with different forms rather than stay with the same one week after week.

As you've read through these sermons, you may have noticed the different ways they began, the elements within the middle that helped them stay together, and the way the conclusion brought home the message. This "connective tissue" is also very important to the form and content of the sermon. So in the next chapter, we'll learn these basics of starting, "threading," and ending a sermon.

KEY POINTS IN THIS CHAPTER

1. Sermon forms organize what you want to preach and how you want to present it. They provide a cohesive arrangement or sequence that allows for listeners to track with the preacher as they deliver the sermon.
2. Sermons using inductive logic begin with a question or point of inquiry and follow clues that lead to the Central Claim. Sermons using deductive logic begin with the Central Claim, give reasons why the Central Claim is true, and restate the Central Claim at the end.
3. Sermon forms can be seen as vehicles that are powered by the Central Question, given direction by the Central Claim, and carry out the Central Purpose. The Wesleyan Quadrilateral—Scripture, Tradition, Reason, and Experience—can be used to inform the Central Statements, which, in turn, inform the sermon form.
4. The sermon form is also informed by what a preacher learns from filling out the Exegesis Guide Chart and can provide different options for integrating key insights from the Occasional, Literary, Theological, and/or Contemporary Exigence and Response.
5. Using vibrant words, salient images, and evocative language to create effective sermon illustrations is essential for any sermon form.
6. Sermon forms are not an exact science or formula. Any of the forms can be modified to better serve the preaching of the message.

DISCUSSION QUESTIONS

1. Of the four sermon examples in this chapter ("Flagging the Flag—Idolatry and Freedom" [Four Pages], "A Dollar Sign, Cell Phone, and Flag Walk into a Church" [Motion Pictures], "Pastor Tom, Gladys, and a Flag

with Legs" [Homiletical Plot], "The Big Red, White, and Blue in the Room" [Expository], which one do you think would be the most effective in your congregation and why? Which one would you be hesitant to preach and why?

2. Turn to Appendix L, where there are several more sermon forms listed. If you were to choose one of these forms not covered in this chapter, which sermon form would you like to experiment with for a sermon on Exodus 20:1-6? Briefly sketch out what you might do with the problem-resolution-conclusion form, or the three points form, or one of the others. Would you use an inductive or deductive approach for the sermon?
3. As you saw from the four different sermons, one biblical text can inspire any number of different approaches, images or stories for illustration, and messages for a congregation. This is good to note especially for those who use the *Revised Common Lectionary* in which the same texts come up every three years. Discuss with your preaching mentor or peers how they keep their preaching fresh and revitalized when revisiting a text they have preached before.

FOR FURTHER READING

Ronald J. Allen, ed. *Patterns of Preaching: A Sermon Sampler*. St. Louis: Chalice Press, 1998.
John S. McClure. *The Roundtable Pulpit: Where Leadership & Preaching Meet*. Nashville: Abingdon Press, 1995.

NOTES

1. In a fishbowl exercise, one group of participants engages in a roundtable discussion while a second group encircles the group and observes but does not interact. The observing group listens and later reflects on and shares their observations with the inner group. In the case of this sermon, the congregation is the group of observers and the Confirmation students are the group in the roundtable discussion, albeit only through the pastor's relaying of the story.
2. In a non-credal church, a sermon could reference a church's (or denomination's) statement of faith or mission statement that reinforces the First Commandment. Or the preacher could forego Tradition altogether and simply stay with the First Commandment, thus using Scripture as the primary source of authority for the sermon.
3. John S. McClure, *The Roundtable Pulpit: Where Leadership & Preaching Meet* (Nashville: Abingdon Press, 1995), 24.

22

Starting Strong, Threading Through, and Concluding Convincingly

Beginnings, Transitions, and Endings of Sermons

In the previous two chapters, you learned about sermon forms and how to use deductive or inductive logic to craft the sermon. We introduced four forms that are especially accessible and manageable for early-career preachers: Four Pages, Motion Pictures, Homiletical Plot, and Expository. Then we used these forms to craft four different sermons based on the same biblical text and noted how the Central Question, Central Claim, and Central Purpose can inform the sequence of the sermon forms.

This chapter focuses on how a sermon is constructed from beginning to end and how the preacher can ensure that the congregation can track with them throughout the sermon. You'll learn strategies for starting a sermon, different ways to thread the different parts of the sermon together, and options for concluding the sermon in a way that has an impact and is most effective. As we discuss these techniques, we'll correlate them to ways they can be used with the sermon forms you learned about in the previous chapters.

HOOK THEM, HELP THEM FOLLOW YOU, AND GIVE THEM A REASON TO SAY "AMEN!"

A sermon must begin by "hooking" our listeners. They need a reason to want to begin paying attention to what you have to say. Once they are paying attention, they need a reason to keep listening, and they have to be able to follow the logic of your sermon. Finally, the sermon must end well. The listener needs to feel that it was worth their time and energy to have paid attention to the sermon. Even if it was a challenging or uncomfortable sermon, they at least need to feel that they have come away from the proverbial table having been offered food of substance.

Creating sermons that make sense and are easy to follow is, frankly, one of the biggest hurdles for early-career preachers (and even some seasoned preachers!). There are many reasons why a sermon may lack coherence and a smooth flow. Here are just a few.

- *The preacher may not be clear on exactly why they are preaching.* The preacher may not have discerned what the compelling reason is for tackling this text and putting together this sermon in the first place. This is where the Central Question can be helpful, because it disciplines you to articulate the exigence of the biblical text and your preaching context. Harnessing this energy can help the sermon engage both the preacher's attention and that of their listeners so that the sermon follows through on the inquiry to the very end.

- *The sermon may not be organized well.* The preacher may have many good ideas, but without a logical flow to them, listeners may be left scratching their heads and wondering if they missed something. This is where the Central Claim can be helpful, because it guides the sermon with a clear proclamation about who God is, what God does, and what it means for us today. Keeping the Central Claim always in our minds as we're constructing the sermon can help us to develop a coherent sequence and keep us from following "bunny trails" that lead us away from our main point.
- *The sermon may not have a clear objective.* If a listener comes to the end of the sermon and is left asking, "So what?" it is likely that the preacher did not provide a satisfactory reason for them to have listened. This is where the Central Purpose is needed, because it compels the preacher to articulate what the sermon aims to do and why. When we know the reason for this sermon, we can look at every part and ask, "Is this contributing to the Central Purpose in some way?" If it's not, we can either trim it out or rework it so that it serves the goal of the sermon. A sermon with a strong Central Purpose is more likely to leave the listener with the feeling that an invitation to respond has been offered and that they want to put their faith into action in some way.

Even with a strong and clear set of Central Statements, the preacher needs to know some basic techniques for: 1) how to begin their sermon so that it engages the congregation, 2) how to order the parts of the sermon so that the listeners can track with them, and 3) how to end in a way that results in a hearty "Amen." In the sections that follow, we will give you tactics for beginning strong, techniques for utilizing effective transitions, and options for finishing a sermon in ways that are satisfying, inspiring, and memorable.

BOOKENDS AND THROUGHLINES: TWO DEVICES FOR BEGINNING AND ENDING SERMONS

There is no one way to create a sermon. Some preachers mull a biblical text for days, poring over commentaries until the kernel of an idea begins to form for what they might preach. Others skim a text at first but then engage in deeper conversation about the passage with preaching peers or parishioners, which helps them shape their ideas for the sermon. Still other preachers plan their sermons weeks or even months in advance, sketching out a series with major themes and then praying and percolating on them as they write the sermon for each successive Sunday.

Just as there is no one way to create a sermon, there is also no one way to begin and conclude a sermon. Two preachers may be working on the same text and come up with vastly different approaches and two contrasting ways of starting and ending the sermon. But there are two rhetorical devices that may prove useful for you as you are learning how to write sermons: the **bookend** and the **throughline**. We are introducing these to you early in this chapter because they can provide cohesion for a sermon's beginning, middle, and end.

The Bookend

One technique for beginning and ending the sermon is the bookend, which is where the sermon starts and finishes with two similar things or the same idea, phrase, image, verse of a hymn, or some pointed detail. For example, you might introduce a story at the beginning of the sermon and then come back to it at the end to reinforce the point you are making. Or you could introduce a metaphor for understanding God at the start of the sermon and circle back to it at the conclusion—either to reaffirm or contradict it. Or you could describe a character at the sermon's beginning and come back to that person at the end to draw out implications of the Central Claim for that character.

Bookends can be very satisfying for the listener for several reasons:

- There is a feeling of resolution and closure when the end of the sermon recapitulates what the listener heard at the beginning.
- A bookend can reinforce the Central Claim by reiterating a theological point made at the beginning.
- The bookend allows the listener to make connections between the beginning and ending of the sermon, which, in turn, helps them understand what your intention was and where you were going all along.
- A bookend can provide an "Aha" moment at the end of the sermon if the preacher references something they said at the beginning and shifts it slightly at the end to give it new or enhanced meaning.

EXERCISE

Analyzing Bookends in Sermons

To see examples of bookends, revisit the following sermons: "Climate Migration—How Should the Church Respond?" in Chapter 4, "A House with Many Rooms—The 'Living Stones' of a Seminary" in Chapter 7, and "Jesus, Mother Hen—This Is the God I Want to Worship" in Chapter 11. Consider the following questions as you analyze the beginning and ending of each sermon:

1. What are the images or stories that are introduced at the beginning and recapitulated at the end? Does the sermon reaffirm these images/stories or refute them? How does this bookending serve the main idea of the sermon?
2. How does the bookend reinforce the Central Claim or Central Purpose of the sermon?
3. In what ways does the ending resolve the tension introduced at the beginning of the sermon?

The Throughline

In her book *Novel Preaching*, Alyce McKenzie draws on fiction-writing strategies to help preachers shape their sermons. One technique she suggests for preachers to clarify the flow of their thoughts is something that screenwriters use called a "throughline." The throughline is a term used by screenwriters to refer to the flow of the thought of the movie, or in this case, the sermon. She explains, "The throughline is the plotline that answers the question, 'What happens to the protagonist?' In a sermon, it's called the focus or the theme. It's what the sermon is about, summed up in one sentence. Novelists differ in the way they work, but many say they figure out the last scene of their novel first and then plot the whole novel toward it."[1] We can see in this description of the throughline how the Central Claim can be woven in and through the sermon. And by knowing the Central Purpose, the sermon can be plotted toward it, just as a novelist knows the ending of their story and can build backwards from there.

Where and when the throughline first makes its appearance will depend on whether a preacher is using a deductive or inductive approach. McKenzie explains that the traditional, deductive, three-point sermon states its throughline (its focus) first, while a sermon using inductive logic (moving from the specifics to the general) may have its throughline either in the middle or at the end with everything in the sermon flowing toward it.

A throughline may be invisible to the listener, as when a thread is sewn into a piece of clothing in such a way that it holds the cloth together but is folded into the fabric and tucked away from sight. This is often the case for inductive sermons where listeners are not sure at first where the sermon is going. For instance, in the sermon "Jesus Meets Us in the Wilderness of Grief," whose beginning you read in Chapter 13 and which continued in Chapter 15, the sermon began by giving the list of rulers in Luke 3:1-6 and then recasting the list with contemporary leaders. The listeners were drawn in with the question "Where do you fit into this story?" but the throughline is not obvious at first. As the sermon unfolds around the theme of grief, the throughline of the Central Claim (*Just as the word of God came to John in the wilderness to prepare the way of the Lord, so Jesus still comes to us in the wilderness today, even when the paths are still crooked, the valleys are still deep, and the mountains seem insurmountable*) is like the force of a current moving beneath the surface. Only in the last paragraph does the throughline of the Central Claim become visible. By the end, it's apparent that the Central Claim was there all along, doing its work behind the scenes of the sermon and making its presence known in the last scene.

Or the throughline can be clearly stated early on and intentionally woven into the sermon so that the listener recognizes it when they hear it repeated in strategic places. As an example of a visible throughline, one of our students developed a sermon on Matthew 22:1-14, Jesus's parable of the wedding banquet where a guest is thrown out for not wearing the proper attire. He titled his sermon "The Dress Code Will Be Strictly Enforced" and used that line throughout the sermon. First, he gave examples in society where dress codes are required, and then he explained the meaning of the parable. His use of repetition with the throughline built dramatic tension that culminated at the end of the sermon when he reiterated God's expectation for disciples to put on "robes of righteousness," because "the dress code will be strictly enforced." Even more striking was the way he mirrored his throughline in his presentation by taking off his suit jacket near the end of the sermon and hoisting on his preaching robe, all the while explaining what "robes of righteousness" can look like for his congregation, such as acts of charity, kindness, forgiveness, service, and learning together as a community.[2]

EXERCISE

Analyzing Throughlines in Sermons

To see examples of throughlines, revisit the following sermons: "Climate Migration—How Should the Church Respond?" in Chapter 4, "A House with Many Rooms—The 'Living Stones' of a Seminary" in Chapter 7, "Jesus, Mother Hen—This Is the God I Want to Worship" in Chapter 11, and "When Psalm 23 Shepherded Me" in Chapter 19. Consider the following questions as you analyze the sermons to find the theme, metaphor, image, repeated phrase, or idea that helps to stitch the sermon together.

1. Where do you first notice the throughline? Does it appear at the beginning and get repeated often? Do you detect it in the middle? Or do you notice it closer to the end, realizing that it had been at work on the sermon all along?
2. In what way does the throughline pick up on the Central Question, Central Claim, or Central Purpose?
3. What relationship do you see between the throughline and the sermon form? Do you see it repeated in different parts of the Four Pages? Is it used as a hinge between the different moves in Motion Pictures? Does it regularly appear as an image in the Homiletical Plot? Is it repeated at strategic places of the Expository form?
4. How does the conclusion of the sermon expand on or slightly modify the throughline?

STARTING STRONG: KEYS TO BEGINNING THE SERMON IN AN ENGAGING WAY

In addition to the bookend and throughline options, there are several other ways to begin a sermon. As you read through these, remember that you only have one opportunity to start a sermon and grab the attention of your listeners. When fishing in a lake or stream, the lures that attract are ones that shimmer, wriggle, sparkle, glint, or draw the eye with interesting colors or features that tempt the hungry fish. The fish won't bite if they're not presented with an interesting lure. Similarly, our sermons need to have something that hooks the listeners and offers them a reason to turn their attention to the preacher. This is not to say that a sermon should be gimmicky—far from it. But if Jesus wants us to "fish for people," we'll need to have sermons with attractive lures and strong nets!

Start with a Question

Opening a sermon with a question is a way to hook the listener's interest right out of the gate. An opening question is an ideal device to use in the Homiletical Plot sermon form because it can introduce the dramatic tension that will draw in the listener. It can also be used in Four Pages as a way to introduce either the "trouble in the text" or "trouble in the world." With Motion Pictures, a question can be used in the introduction to set up the frames of the scenes to follow. The Expository form can begin with a question that is answered by going verse by verse through the text and then applying the insights from the Scripture to a contemporary situation.

Questions can identify the exigence you discovered when filling out your Exegesis Guide Chart and invite listeners to ponder it with you. In other words, the opening question can be based on the biblical text. For example, in the sermon "Jesus Meets Us in the Wilderness of Grief" based on Luke 3:1-6, Leah begins with a question that the congregation might be asking themselves upon hearing the lesson read: "When we read this list of names, did it make you wonder: who are these people, and why should we care?" This allowed her to offer insights from her exegesis and apply them to the listeners' contemporary situation.

Or an opening question can draw on the Central Question you developed as you were exegeting your congregation. Perhaps you've observed something going on in the community, or in your congregation's lives, or in the news that needs our attention. In other words, the opening question can be based on the contemporary situation of the congregation. For instance, in the sermon "Finding Our Way in the Wilderness of Conspiracy Theories: What Is the 'Straight Path'?" based on Mark 1:1-8 (in Chapter 17), the opening question is this: "Guess what Tuesday is? It's Safe Harbor Day! What, you've never heard of Safe Harbor Day?" Right away, the listeners' ears perk up because they might have heard this on the news regarding the ongoing election process.

A sermon can also begin with a question that is more philosophical or general. For example, in this same sermon on Mark 1:1-8, the introduction also included these questions, "Who should we believe? Who can we trust?" Leah could have started her sermon by simply asking those questions and then applying it to the situation of the political turmoil at the time. If she had wanted to start the sermon with referencing the biblical text first, those questions also could have been used to introduce the implicit inquiry about John's proclamation and the person of Jesus Christ by the people coming to the Jordan River. Then she could have segued into the contemporary situation by noting that those questions apply in our current political upheaval.

Start with an Illustration

Beginning a sermon with an illustration is an effective option both to get your listeners' attention as well as to introduce a throughline or a bookend. The key is to use descriptive language that engages the senses and draws in the listener so that they are invested in the sermon at the outset. In Chapters 18 and 19, we talked about sermon illustrations in detail. Here, we'll focus on the ways that a story or an illustration can be useful for some of the sermon forms and give examples of each.

An opening story or illustration can be used in Four Pages to bring the "trouble" in the text or world into sharp relief. For example, in Chapter 21, Leah suggested a Four Pages sermon structure for Exodus 20:1-6 (the commandment against idolatry and graven images). She wanted to explain what had happened to the Israelites in Egypt that made the First Commandment necessary. So she could begin with a scene like this:

> *Abiah stands trembling as she watches the barbed whip crack against her father's back, leaving a lightning-shaped slash of red against his skin. He was just one load short of the bricks he was to make for Pharaoh's palace. But how could he have time to make his quota when he had to go out first and gather the straw used to strengthen the bricks?*
>
> *Abiah turns away so she doesn't have to watch. Her eyes sweep across the images carved and painted into the walls: the sun, a frog, squiggly lines representing the Nile River, and many more. All of them are symbols of the deities that supposedly control every aspect of life and nature. She has prayed to all of them for relief for her father, for her family, for her people, for herself, desperately hoping even one of them would show them mercy. Perhaps they do not answer because Pharaoh says he controls them all. Or maybe . . . maybe they are not really gods at all?*

Not only would such a story provide a dramatic opening for the sermon, it would also implicitly introduce the theme of idolatry that the sermon would go on to address. Later, in "trouble in the world," a similar scene could be painted of a young slave girl in the colonial south of the United States watching her father whipped and seeing the Confederate flag waving nearby.

An opening story or illustration can also be useful for a Motion Pictures sermon form. For example, recall the sermon structure for "A Dollar Sign, Cell Phone, and Flag Walk into a Church" based on Exodus 20:1-6. Leah used the lesson with the Confirmation students to illustrate the contemporary struggle with idolatry. To begin the sermon, she could describe watching the students sprawled out on the floor flipping through glossy magazines, scissors in hand, looking for images of modern-day "gods." On a giant poster board are the words "I believe in ______ the Almighty, creator of heaven and earth," and the students affix the images they have cut out, laughing and chattering. Describing this scene would not only draw in the listeners to "overhear" the kids' conversations but would also introduce the "hinge" to be used throughout the sermon.

For the Homiletical Plot sermon "Pastor Tom, Gladys, and a Flag with Legs," in Chapter 21, the introduction in paragraph 1 is fairly straightforward and could use some details to help the listener place themselves in the scene. Instead of just saying, "Pastor Tom begins his new call at Church of the Savior fresh out of seminary. He is passionate about addressing social issues and is on fire to prove himself as a social justice advocate for the sake of the gospel," which is a rather dull reporting of the facts, the sermon could begin by *showing instead of telling*. So a more engaging beginning could look like this:

> *Pastor Tom steps back from his bookshelf and surveys the titles that he has just finished arranging in his new office at Church of the Savior. They are lined up like soldiers at attention, organized into platoons—this shelf for biblical studies; next to that, books on preaching; below that the bulging tomes on theology. His newly framed diploma with his freshly minted Master of Divinity degree is situated majestically on the wall above the shelves. And in the shelf that faces his desk across the room, he has placed his collection of books on social justice, his favorite subject in seminary. He has put them there to remind himself every time he looks up from his desk that he is called to preach and teach God's justice for the sake of the gospel.*

From these details, listeners will know that Pastor Tom is fresh out of seminary and that he is eager to address social issues because the details about the books and his new degree are described with precision instead of being dictated like a report. The sermon could go on to show Pastor Tom marching into the empty sanctuary and seething when he sees the flag, setting up the drama that unfolds throughout the sermon. Note that not all sermons using the Homiletical Plot form need to tell a story. But if a story is used, be sure to engage the listeners with vivid language and pointed details to hook them as the sermon begins.

THINGS TO AVOID OR USE WITH CAUTION WHEN BEGINNING A SERMON

There are some rhetorical devices that are risky when used at the beginning of a sermon, and there are others that are best avoided.

- *The lecture*. There will be times when you will want to teach something to edify your congregation. But don't turn your sermon into a lecture. A sermon that begins by dryly explaining the scholarly works you consulted for your sermon prep will sound like the muted-trombone voice of the teacher in the *Peanuts* cartoons. Remember, the congregation doesn't care how much you know—they want to know how much you care. You need to communicate to them that you care, and that God cares about them, about the church, about the world, and about our future.
- *Long quotes*. Reading a long quote—even from a well-known person—is not an ideal way to begin a sermon. Short quotes that are relevant and are immediately explained can be effective but reading extended quoted material will only bore listeners.
- *The question you never answer*. The caveat to beginning the sermon with a question is that you want to avoid asking a question that you never get around to answering. This does not mean that your sermon needs to be a Q&A session. Nor does it mean that all questions have definitive answers. In fact, many theological conundrums, moral questions, and ethical issues do not have easy answers. But if you as the preacher are going to raise a question, you'll need to find some way to address it, even if all you can say is, "There are no easy answers, but we are assured of the Spirit's presence as we are grappling with this."
- *The story that goes on too long or that never resolves*. Sermons with loose narrative ends are very unsatisfying for listeners. And a sermon that begins with a story that either takes up an inordinate amount of time or leaves an unresolved question in the listeners' minds is equally frustrating. If you start with a contemporary story, a good rule of thumb is to keep it tight and tie it to the biblical text sooner rather than later. And if you tell a story that has a cliff-hanger or open-ended question, be sure to circle back to it before the sermon concludes. Otherwise, your listeners will be distracted by the loose ends and won't be able to focus on your main point.
- *Jokes*. Beginning a sermon with a joke is risky. Often, the joke is only tangentially tied to the biblical text or the main point of the sermon, so it's more of a distraction than a support to the Central Purpose. And, frankly, preachers are not comedians; they often lack the timing and delivery skills to pull off a joke. Also, telling a joke implicitly communicates that neither you nor the listeners need to take the sermon topic seriously. This is not to say that humor can't be used in a sermon—it can! Jesus himself used humor in his teaching, especially when poking fun at hypocrites. But, generally, telling a joke in a sermon is best avoided.

THREADING THROUGH: TECHNIQUES FOR UTILIZING EFFECTIVE TRANSITIONS

When Leah was a kid, her dad would walk with her in the woods and teach her how to identify animal tracks and follow them. Whether on muddy or snowy ground, tracking is easy if the paw prints show the animal was following a well-worn trail, kept to a relatively straight line, and had not been startled or thrown off course. But a tracker could lose the trail if the deer took a leap in an unanticipated direction, or went off into the brush that made the tracks hard to see, or meandered into a stream and obscured the trail altogether. Using this metaphor, a sermon should be easy to track so that listeners are not forced to find where you made leaps in logic, went off into a messy brush pile, or meandered into the stream and lost them.

The four sermon forms we've introduced in this book will help to keep your sermon on track. Four Pages, Motion Pictures, Homiletical Plot, and Expository each have definitive steps in a logical order that will help a congregation track with you as you are moving through the sermon. But there are also rhetorical techniques a preacher can use that either remove barriers or smooth the way so that the listener can follow with ease. We'll cover three in this section: repetition, questions, and what we call "connective tissue." There is also a fourth way to indicate transitions in a sermon that has to do with performative cues, but we will cover that in Part V, "Sermon Delivery and Performance."

Repetition

Our attention perks up when we hear something said once and then repeated. Repetition in speech implicitly communicates that this is content to pay attention to or remember; it indicates that something important is being said. Repetition can also be used in the throughline, as we've already covered. For example, the Motion Pictures form uses repetition for the hinge that moves the sermon from one part to the next, as we saw with the "Mother Hen" sermon in Chapter 11. Repetition is also a key rhetorical technique used in some African American preaching and is often used to build suspense toward a sermonic climax.

Repetition can be used in the Homiletical Plot or the Expository form, where it can build narrative tension or be used as a stepping-stone to move the sermon along. You saw an example of this in Chapter 22's sermon about Pastor Tom and Gladys. The repeated sentence, "This flag has legs," became both a plot point and a way to tie the sermon together at the end.

In Four Pages, repetition can be used to connect the biblical story to the contemporary situation. For instance, in the sermon excerpt above that introduced Abiah watching her father being beaten in Egypt, the scene ends with this line, "Or maybe . . . they are not really gods at all." This line could be repeated after the "bad news in the world" section about modern-day idols. It could be repeated again in "grace in the text" and "grace in the world" to reiterate the point that only God is sovereign and the graven images of Egypt, as well as the flag in our own sanctuary, are not really gods at all.

One caveat to using repetition: there can be too much of a good thing. Repetition overused is, simply, repetitious. This rhetorical device should not be used as a gimmick or a distraction from lack of substance. But when employed strategically and judiciously, repetition can be an effective way to keep listeners with you as you preach.

Questions

Just as the use of a question at the beginning of the sermon can be a good way to hook the listeners, it can also be effective in bringing back someone's attention that may have wandered in the middle. Sometimes, it can be a simple check-in question, such as, "Are you with me so far?" This is especially useful when telling a story. Or a question can be used in explaining a concept, as in, "What does this mean, prepare the way of the Lord, make his paths straight?" Other times, a question can be used to help listeners move from the Central Claim to the Central Purpose by inviting them to concretize what they're hearing, such as asking, "So what might it look like for us to live out God's grace in this situation?"

When using a question, you'll need to decide whether it is one that you want people to actually answer aloud (or in a chat, if the sermon is online), or if it is one that you want them to silently answer in their own mind. This brings up one caveat to using questions: be careful of asking a question for which you might not like the answer, even if asked rhetorically. Before using a question in the sermon, it's wise to ask yourself, "What if they don't answer in the way I would hope?" It may be better, in fact, to simply state your point rather than to ask a question that could derail the point you are trying to make. (We'll share more about questions in the section further on, "Concluding Convincingly.")

Connective Tissue

In the field of anatomy and physiology, connective tissue is what links and supports the different organs and parts of the body, allowing the organism to maintain cohesion. We don't usually think about connective tissue until something goes wrong with it. Anyone who has suffered a torn ligament or tendon, for example, knows how important these connectors are and how painful it can be when they are not functioning properly.

The same can be said of a sermon that lacks "connective tissue." If a sermon flows well and is easy to follow, the connective tissue is barely even noticeable. But if there are the equivalents of torn ligaments in the structure of the sermon, it can be a confusing or uncomfortable experience for listeners. Without certain linguistic cues and signals, a sermon can't maintain cohesion.

In a Four Pages form, connective tissue can enable the preacher to weave between the biblical text and the contemporary situation. For instance, a preacher moving from "trouble in the text" to "trouble in the world" might say, "That's what was happening for the Israelites. Where do we see this kind of idolatry today?" In Motion Pictures and Expository, there are certain words and phrases that can serve as connective tissue between the different moves or the verses of the passage, such as: "and yet," "unless," "in addition," and "however." In both Expository and Homiletical Plot sermons, connective tissue can consist of short summaries of what the sermon has covered so far to remind listeners where they've been. Or, if there is a repeating idea, a phrase could be used such as, "As I said earlier."

Connective tissue is also important for setting up the conclusion of the sermon. Words like, *finally, keep in mind, remember*, and *ultimately* can cue the listener that the sermon is coming to an end. This prepares the congregation to refocus their attention one last time in order to receive the concluding point of the sermon.

WHEN TO USE THE WORD "SO" AND WHEN TO LEAVE IT OUT

The word "so" has become both ubiquitous and overused in everyday conversation over the last decade. This presents a challenge to preachers when they are deciding when to use *so* as connective tissue in a sermon. If used appropriately, it can be a helpful narrative or logistic cue. But if used carelessly, it can sound too casual and colloquial.

So in its original usage was meant to indicate the continuation of a narrative or an indication of a consequence, as in: "So, the solution to the problem was to get a new shovel." Or: "It started to rain so he took an umbrella."

But *so* has evolved (or devolved) into other purposes of late. When used at the beginning of a sentence, it appears to imply that the speaker is about to say something interesting: "So, the other day I was checking my emails and guess who contacted me?" Or it can be used as a conversational prompt or a segue to a different topic.

When considering when and how to use *so* in a sermon, ask yourself if the word truly serves a function or is it merely filler? Certainly, it is not advisable to use *so* as the very first word of the sermon, since there is nothing that has come before the start of the sermon to warrant the use of the word. However, when used correctly, *so* can be useful as connective tissue for linking words, phrases, clauses, or sentences.

CONCLUDING CONVINCINGLY: "LANDING THE PLANE" WHILE GIVING THEM WINGS

You've hooked your listeners, and you've guided them through your sermon with a solid structure and linguistic cues so that it's easy to follow. Now it's time to "bring it home," "land the plane," or whatever euphemism you prefer for concluding the sermon. This is another challenge for some early-career preachers (as well as some seasoned ones!).

So much effort is put into the exegesis, theological analysis, and initial construction of the sermon that the preacher sometimes has little energy left to think about an effective ending to the sermon. But an effective sermon ending should not only leave listeners with a reason to say, "Amen!," it should also give them wings to lift off, inspired to live out the gospel in their lives and in the world.

If you've followed the recommendations in this book so far, coming up with an effective ending should flow naturally from the work you have already done. The Central Question, Central Claim, and Central Purpose should give you all the material you need to create a conclusion that is theologically sound, compelling, and inspiring or motivational. Also, the forms you learned each provide a way to end the sermon so that the gospel is proclaimed clearly and definitively, whether that's with "grace in the world" for Four Pages, the final "move" in Motion Pictures, the "Yeah!" of Homiletical Plot, or the application in Expository.

The end of a sermon is the final opportunity to answer (or at least acknowledge) the Central Question, to draw out the implications of the Central Claim, and inspire the congregation to respond to the Central Purpose. Remember that the ending of the sermon is your last chance to reiterate the Theological Claim of the sermon. We recommend that a sermon not just end with a moralistic platitude or instruction telling the listeners what *they* must do. Rather, use the ending as an opportunity to boldly proclaim who God is, what God does, and what this means for us today. In other words, make a strong theological statement so that listeners will have no doubt that they have heard the Word of God. You can see an example of a final theological statement in the ending of the sermon in Chapter 17, "Finding Our Way in the Wilderness of Conspiracy Theories: What Is the 'Straight Path'?":

> *This is the truth to which John testified. This is what Jesus's ministry, life, death, and resurrection were about. This is who God is, what God does, and what God wants to church to be about. Prepare and make straight the way of the Lord. Seek out the path of truth. Listen to John. Follow Jesus. Amen.*

This ending clearly states that Jesus's ministry was about truth, which is a core characteristic of God and God's people. It also includes a succession of four short sentences with vigorous verbs exhorting listeners to respond.

EXERCISE

Analyzing Two Sermon Endings

At the beginning of this chapter, we gave you two rhetorical devices that can lead to satisfying endings: the bookend and the throughline.

ANALYZING A BOOKEND

A bookend is when a sermon starts and finishes with two similar things or the same idea, phrase, image, or pointed detail.

1. Reread the ending of the sermon "Jesus Meets Us in the Wilderness of Grief" from Chapter 15:
   There are all kinds of important, famous people in that list—but we are in that list, too. And you may be the very person God uses to remind someone that they, too, shall see the salvation of God. . . . The Word of God is still breaking into the wilderness places of our lives, lighting the way with this Divine Love.
2. How does this bookend recapitulate something from the beginning of the sermon?
3. Discuss with a partner how (or if) this feels like a satisfying ending to the sermon. Does it provide closure? Does it provide an answer to the Central Question? Does it reiterate the Central Claim? Does it drive home the Central Purpose and elicit a response?

ANALYZING THE FINAL APPEARANCE OF A THROUGHLINE

The throughline at the end of a sermon can either reemphasize the repeated idea in a final, definitive way or make its grand appearance if it comes at the end of an inductive sermon.

1. Reread the ending of the sermon "Pastor Tom, Gladys, and a Flag with Legs," which used the Homiletical Plot form:
   The flag has legs, yes. But so does the cross. Both the flag and the cross can move front and center and they can step aside. They can kneel and they can stand. They can walk towards each other and they can walk away. God can do powerful things with just one step forward. Let's take that step together. Amen.
2. What is the image or phrase that was repeated in the sermon that makes its final appearance here? How is the image expanded and pushed in a different way for the conclusion?
3. Discuss with a partner, in what way do the last two sentences contain a strong Theological Claim as well as give a final push for putting faith into action?

MISTAKES AND MISSTEPS TO AVOID AT THE END OF A SERMON

- *Not stopping.* One surefire way to blow the ending of your sermon is to keep preaching after you've already stuck the landing. Once the plane has touched down and taxied up to the gate, it needs to stop. So does your sermon. If you've given them the "finally" but continue to make another point, you either need to cut out the afterthought or move your "finally."
- *Introducing a completely different image, idea, or train of thought at the end.* Another fatal flaw for an ending is to throw in a non sequitur. The end of the sermon is not the time to trot out a complex metaphor that needs unpacking, or an extended story that will exhaust the listener, or a completely unrelated theological concept that has nothing to do with what you've already talked about in the sermon. Remember—keep your Central Question, Central Claim, and Central Purpose always before you until the final amen!
- *"If you take nothing else away from this sermon."* Saying this at the end of a sermon is exasperating to a listener. If this was the point you wanted to make, why didn't you say this earlier, or reiterate it during the sermon? If you truly want them to take away a particular point from this sermon, just state it and repeat it if necessary by using the throughline or the bookend.
- *The extended prayer.* Some preachers like to conclude their sermon with a final prayer. This is fine as long as it is brief and to the point. Avoid using a final prayer to re-preach your sermon or recapitulate extensive points you were trying to make in the sermon proper. The prayer at the end of the sermon also should not turn into yet another sermon. Nor should it be used to call on God to make happen whatever you called for in the sermon. Trust that what you preached is enough. As a general rule, use the sermon to preach and use the liturgy for prayers.
- *Avoid "lettuce" in a sermon.* "Let us" do this. "Let us" not do that. When sermons end with "lettuce," we miss the chance to proclaim God's work. In *Let the Whole Church Say Amen,* Laurence Stookey explains why the phrases *may we* and *let us* are anemic in the context of prayer:

> In fact, they are phrases addressed not so much to God as to the congregation. They are words of exhortation, not petition. As such, they tend to convey a "bootstrap" theology: All we have to do to get the answer to our prayers is work harder, think more positively, exert more faith. Taken to the extreme, such verbiage seems to make God unnecessary. "Let *us* do what is called for"; "May *we* work more diligently and be more faithful." And suddenly prayers of petition for divine help evaporate into the thin air of psychological manipulation and good works. God's role becomes unclear and seemingly unnecessary.[3]

The same applies to sermons. Don't turn the ending of your sermon into a call for "bootstrap theology" by using phrases like *may we* and *let us*. First of all, it sounds "preachy." There's a lofty tone to "let us" that implies that the preacher is separate from the flock and paternally directing them from above. Why is this a problem? Because if it's all about us, then we lose the focus on God, Jesus Christ, and the Holy Spirit. The sermon becomes an admonition towards works righteousness instead of proclaiming who God is and what God does. A better conclusion is to state what you already see God, Jesus Christ, or the Holy Spirit doing that casts a vision of God's Realm. Affirm God's character and God's action as you bring the sermon to an end.

THE QUESTION OF ENDING A SERMON WITH A QUESTION

While it is not a hard and fast rule that a sermon should never end with a question, the preacher must be very judicious in determining when a question is appropriate and how it will be used. There are different kinds of questions that can serve different purposes. Let's take them in turn.

- *Rhetorical questions.* Rhetorical questions require no reply, either because the answer is obvious or because the asker already knows the answer they think should be obvious to others. When used effectively, rhetorical questions can be used to call the church to act in accordance with the characteristic of God we have named. However, when used flippantly or coercively, rhetorical questions are not an ideal way to end a sermon. Here's an example: "Jesus instructs us to love our neighbor, so shouldn't we follow his command?" Yes, of course. But such a question can feel manipulative, as if the preacher is taking a patronizing tone. Instead, simply end with a declarative statement that invites listeners into response, such as: "Jesus instructs us to love our neighbor, and this church is living that out with every backpack we give away, every meal we serve, and every hand we hold. Thanks be to God!"
- *Invitational questions.* Invitational questions have a goal of asking the listener to respond in some way. For example, a sermon inviting people to take part in an effort to help resettle a refugee family may end with, "Won't you join us?" The risk with ending with this kind of question is that the listener might not answer in the way you hope. It can feel coercive, and a listener may be answering "No" in their minds, which is not the way you want a sermon to end. A better approach is to issue the invitation as a declarative statement and to give options for response. Such as: "God has given us an opportunity to welcome the stranger in our midst. I hope you'll join us in this effort, whether through donations, coming to meet the family, or simply through your prayers. Together, we can be the open arms of Christ."
- *"Chew on this" or "The ball is in your court" questions.* There are times when a preacher addresses a complex ethical topic with many different perspectives and no clear right or wrong answer. In a case such as this, the intention is to leave the sermon open-ended in the spirit of honoring different viewpoints that might lead to further dialogue. While it may be appropriate to occasionally end with a question, the preacher will need to be aware of the risks. Some listeners may feel frustrated, confused, or disturbed. They expected a solid conclusion, so the open-ended question can leave them unsettled. However, this is not necessarily a bad thing. As Hebrews 4:12-13 tells us, the Word of God is "sharper than any two-edged sword, piercing until it divides soul from spirit, joints from marrow; it is able to judge the thoughts and intentions of the heart. And before God no creature is hidden, but all are naked and laid bare to the eyes of the one to whom we must render an account." While we don't want to end every sermon with this kind of ambiguity, it can be an effective rhetorical technique for challenging listeners to think further and engage God's Word beyond the sermon's end.

Whether or not you decide to end with a question, keep in mind that this is not something you want to do with every sermon. Be selective, intentional, and strategic about when, why, and how you end a sermon with a question. Also, be sure that the question flows naturally from the logic of the sermon and is not simply coming out of the blue without any context. If used thoughtfully and astutely, a question can be an effective *occasional* ending for a sermon.

KEY POINTS IN THIS CHAPTER

1. The four sermon forms introduced in this book—Four Pages, Motion Pictures, Homiletical Plot, and Expository or Puritan Plain Style—each offer structures for sermon beginnings, transitions, and endings.
2. A sermon must "hook" listeners at the beginning, make it easy to follow through the middle, and end effectively.
3. There are many ways to begin a sermon, including starting with a question or starting with a story or illustration.
4. The sermon can use a *bookend,* which is an idea, phrase, image, verse of a hymn, or pointed detail that is introduced at the beginning and recapitulated at the end. This technique can be used to provide resolution, closure, reinforcement of the Central Claim, or an "aha" moment that is satisfying to the listener.
5. The sermon can use a *throughline,* which is an idea, image, phrase, question, metaphor, or refrain that provides focus and flow for the sermon. The throughline can be invisible to the listener yet hold the sermon together, or it can be intentionally apparent throughout the sermon.
6. Different rhetorical devices for smooth transitions include repetition, questions, and different forms of "connective tissue" such as linguistic cues and signals.
7. The conclusion of the sermon should be informed by at least one of the Central Statements by either answering (or at least addressing) the Central Question, reinforcing the Central Claim, or inspiring a response to the Central Purpose. Sermons should end with a strong Theological Claim and not just moralistic platitudes.

DISCUSSION QUESTIONS

1. Ask a seasoned preacher to share with you one of their sermon manuscripts. Analyze the beginning, transitions, and conclusion. What technique did they use to hook their listeners? Where did you see the "connective tissue" holding the sermon together and linking the different parts? How did they construct their ending to make it as compelling or inspirational as possible?
2. As Alyce McKenzie suggests, preachers can learn a great deal from fiction writers that can be applied to sermons. Think of your favorite novel or short story. Do you detect the author's use of the bookend either for certain chapters or for the whole book? In what way do you see the throughline either invisibly holding the story together or visibly showing up as a literary device?
3. Trade sermon manuscripts with a preaching partner for a sermon you have recently preached or are planning to preach. Each of you experiment with rewriting either the beginning or ending of the sermon. Try using one of the techniques suggested in the chapter. How would the sermon be different with this rewrite?

FOR FURTHER READING

Ronald J. Allen. Ch. 6, "Does the Sermon Move in a Way That Is Easy to Follow?" In *Preaching: An Essential Guide.* Nashville: Abingdon Press, 2002.

Thomas Long. Ch. 7, "Beginnings, Connections, and Endings." In *The Witness of Preaching,* third edition. Louisville: Westminster John Knox, 2016.

Alyce McKenzie. *Novel Preaching: Tips from Great Writers on Crafting Creative Sermons.* Louisville: Westminster John Knox, 2010.

NOTES

1. Alyce McKenzie, *Novel Preaching: Tips from Great Writers on Crafting Creative Sermons* (Louisville, KY: Westminster John Knox, 2010), 53.

2. Patrick McKenzie, "The Dress Code Will Be Strictly Enforced," unpublished sermon preached at New Vessels Christian Church, Oklahoma City, Oklahoma, in February 2018. Referenced with permission.

3. Laurence Stookey, *Let the Whole Church Say Amen: A Guide for Those Who Pray in Public* (Nashville: Abingdon Press, 2001), 28.

V

SERMON DELIVERY AND PERFORMANCE

23

Editing, Formatting, and Practicing Your Sermon

In Parts I and II of this book, you learned the basics of interpreting biblical texts and identifying Theological Claims for preaching. In Part III, you learned the steps for preparing a sermon using the Central Question, Central Claim, and Central Purpose. Part IV helped you to activate theological imagination to make your sermons come alive and connect with listeners. You also learned four basic sermon forms and how to start, thread, and end a sermon effectively.

Part V covers the basics of sermon delivery and performance. In this chapter, we will talk about the necessities of editing the sermon, choosing a format for **sermon delivery** (manuscripts, outlines, electronic devices, or note-free), and practicing the sermon. Chapter 24 will discuss preparing the voice and body for preaching and how to handle nervousness. Chapter 25 will consider embodiment, authenticity, and presence in the performance of the sermon as well as special concerns for those preaching in historically marginalized bodies. Chapter 26 will look at the use of space both in and out of the pulpit, including issues around preaching, media, and technology.

TIPS FOR EDITING YOUR SERMON

Now that you've learned the basics for beginnings, transitions, and endings of sermons (see Chapter 22), you'll need to think about the process of editing your sermon once you have a first draft. Here are questions to ask and tips for editing your sermon to ensure that it is as strong as possible and that it makes sense to your listeners.

- *Is there more than one sermon in this sermon?* This is one of the biggest challenges we observe with preachers—having two or three sermons in one. Especially with early-career preachers or those who preach only a few times a year, the temptation is to try to cram too much into one sermon. One way to avoid overcrowding your sermon is to use the Central Statements to keep your focus.
- *Prune, prune, prune!* Imagine the editing process like pruning a bush or a tree. When a sermon is growing in our minds, it may have several branches that all seem to be important. But without pruning, the sermon will never truly take shape and the listener will get tangled in a mess of leafy chaos. Don't be afraid to prune out extraneous ideas, stories, or lines of thought that do not fit the Central Statements for this sermon. You can always keep good ideas in a file for future sermons.
- *If I was hearing this sermon for the first time, could I follow it?* Read your sermon with "beginner's mind." Put aside for a moment all your exegesis and analysis of the text. Pretend you know nothing about this passage, its history, or the topic you're addressing in the sermon. Could you understand what this sermon is trying to say?

- *Will a visitor be able to follow this sermon?* Leah advises her preaching students to preach with the first-time visitor in mind. Put yourself in the shoes of someone who has never even been in a church before as well as someone who has not visited this particular church. Avoid "churchy" jargon, inside jokes, cultural references without explanation, and "insider" language that will leave outsiders feeling excluded. Incidentally, some preachers may argue that their church never gets visitors, so they don't need to follow this advice. However, as more and more churches post sermon videos online (especially after many churches moved to putting worship services online in response to the COVID-19 pandemic), the reality is that you may have more "visitors" watching your sermon than you realize.
- *Read the sermon out loud.* What's in your head when you are typing or using your pen will sound different when you read it aloud. You will catch things that don't make sense, disjointed thoughts, and the places where smooth transitions are lacking.
- *Ask another preacher to read the sermon for you.* A preaching colleague who you trust can give you honest and forthright feedback on whether or not the sermon hangs together or lacks coherence.
- *Ask a friend or family member to listen to you preach a draft of the sermon.* While a fellow preacher can give you feedback on things like your exegesis, theological engagement, and homiletical form, lay listeners can provide much-needed assessments of the basics. Did the sermon grab their attention? Did it make sense and was it easy to follow? Where did they get lost? How did they feel at the end of the sermon? What were they inspired to do as a result? If their reactions don't match your intentions, then you'll need to retool, tweak, or (in some cases) start from scratch.

HOW LONG SHOULD YOUR SERMON BE?

Sermon length is determined by a number of factors, including the length of the worship service, the tradition of the denomination or expectations of the congregation, and what else is happening in the liturgy that day. When preachers were delivering their sermons online during the height of the COVID-19 pandemic, many discovered that listeners began tuning out if the sermon went on too long. Yet, there's a delicate balance between trimming the fat and cutting into the bone of the sermon.

Generally, a substantive sermon needs *at least* ten minutes to be developed and engage the listeners. Many sermons typically last between twelve and twenty minutes. However, some cultures and traditions expect their ministers to preach no less than forty-five minutes. With such a wide range of expectations for sermon length, if you're preaching for the first time in a congregation, ask the church leadership about the typical length of a sermon. And if you're wanting to experiment with a shorter or longer sermon than the congregation is used to, you may need to make adjustments elsewhere in the service to accommodate.

LOST IN TRANSLATION: WHY YOUR CONGREGATION MAY BE MISSING WHAT YOU'RE TRYING TO SAY

There is a scene in the 2003 film *Lost in Translation* where Bill Murray's character, Bob Harris, is trying to understand instructions from a Japanese director for shooting a commercial for a brand of whiskey. The director speaks to Harris in Japanese, and then the translator speaks to him in English. Harris is confused because the director speaks to him passionately and at great length, but the translator's version is comically short. When Harris tries to do what he heard from the translator, the director expresses exasperation, and the process starts over again. The breakdown in communication is both frustrating and laughable. Harris has to guess at what is expected of him, resulting in an exchange that is both awkward and funny, because whatever the director is trying to say is obviously lost in translation.

Sometimes the sermon that we have in our mind and the one that the congregation hears are two different things because something gets lost in translation. You as the preacher know what you're trying to say. It makes sense to you.

Maybe you're even impassioned about it. But if your "translator" (the preached sermon) isn't getting your message across, your listeners will be as puzzled as Bob Harris awkwardly holding his tumbler of fake whiskey.

Alyce McKenzie explains how she helps preaching students think through the construction of their sermons so that listeners can follow what they're doing. "When I edit students' sermons, I write things in the margins . . . like 'Why are you telling me this? Why are you telling me this now? How does this relate to what has gone before?' 'How does it pave the way for what comes next?'"[1] These are questions our listeners unconsciously ask as we preach. As you are putting your sermon together, and especially after you have the first draft of your sermon (and even as you are practicing the sermon out loud), these are good questions to ask yourself as you are reviewing what you've written.

At the same time, the reality is that sometimes preachers do all they can do to make their sermon as clear, engaging, and compelling as possible, but some people are not going to get the message for any number of reasons. They may be tired, distracted, grumpy, or lost in their own thoughts through no fault of the preacher's. Preachers are responsible for the things they can control but cannot be responsible for things happening on the receiving end of the sermon beyond their control. Nevertheless, we may find that the Holy Spirit works in ways to help bridge the distance between preacher and listeners in spite of ourselves!

CHOOSING YOUR SERMON DELIVERY FORMAT: MANUSCRIPTS AND OUTLINES

There are many different formats that can be used for delivering a sermon. Some preachers use a manuscript printed on full sheets of paper. Others use a small note card or half sheets with only an outline or brief notes. Still others use handheld electronic devices, or even a teleprompter. Yet some preachers prefer to preach without any notes at all. There are advantages and downsides to all of these sermon formats, which we'll discuss below.

Full Manuscript

A full manuscript should be written as an oral document to be heard with the ears—not a document to be read only with the eyes. Therefore, you should write the sermon as you would speak it—not as you would write for an academic paper. *Read the manuscript aloud several times* to see if your wording is natural and flows easily. If not, make changes. Also, use a font size large enough to see clearly. In all, using a full manuscript requires great connecting skills and intentional eye contact. Practice, practice, practice!

Tips for Using a Manuscript

- Only print on the top half of the page. That way your eyes and head won't have to drop down to see the words, and you can maintain more consistent eye contact with your listeners.
- Experiment with using serif or non-serif fonts to see what your eye prefers.
- Consider printing your sermon using **sense lines** to make it easier to read. (See "Formatting and Delivering a Sermon Using 'Sense Lines'" below.)
- Do not "flip" the pages of your manuscript. This is a visual distraction. Instead *slide* the pages aside as you move through the sermon.
- Be sure to have page numbers on each sheet of paper so you can put them back in order if they fall or get disorganized. Also, have two copies of the manuscript in case the pulpit copy accidentally gets moved or taken.

Abridged Manuscript

This is a manuscript with several key sections left out so they can be delivered from memory or extemporaneously. For example, you could write just a single word or phrase to remind you of a story or illustration you want to share (e.g., "Jim's Dad" or "Story about trees"). This allows you to tell a key piece of the sermon without being bound to the manuscript. You will need to be intentional about transitioning back and forth between the manuscript and note-free delivery, as well as maintaining eye contact with your listeners. Practice, practice, practice!

Extended Outline

Some preachers start with a full manuscript and then turn the structure of the sermon into a detailed outline. It can be effective for untethering your eyes from the page but will also require some degree of double effort if you work in this fashion. Alternatively, some choose to take notes from their exegesis and then turn their notes into an outline to either be used in the pulpit or from memory without ever writing a full manuscript. One could also use key words for a few sections to move away from the outline. Practice, practice, practice!

Limited Outline

As with the extended outline, the limited outline can be done either from a manuscript or from one's exegetical notes, but this version is more slimmed down. Instead of full thoughts for sections and subsections, the limited outline would have simple words or phrases to remind the preacher of their progression from one section to another. This format can serve as a safety net for those wanting to move to note-free delivery but who fear they might forget the progression of the sermon as they preach it. Transitions are key here—you need to remind yourself where you are going in the sermon and also how you are going to get there. In fact, figuring out your transitions is probably the most important thing you need to do when using a limited outline. (See Chapter 22 for more on transitions.) Practice, practice, practice!

FORMATTING AND DELIVERING A SERMON USING "SENSE LINES"

Sense lines are a way to format text so that the eye can follow it with ease. Traditional prose is printed margin to margin in paragraph from. Sense lines look more like poetry. If your tradition uses a worship book, you may have noticed that many of the communal prayers are written in sense lines to make it easier for the congregation to stay together when reading aloud in unison. Text printed in sense lines uses narrow widths and wider margins, inserting line breaks according to natural pauses and thought units. Each full sentence starts at the left edge with each subsequent thought unit indented and "stacked" underneath.

Sense lines can be helpful for preachers using a manuscript for their sermons. Laurence Hull Stookey explains, "The goal is to provide text of a narrow width so that the eye flows down the page. When the line of type is wider, the eye flows across the page; then sometimes when moving to the next line, the eye gets lost and ends up at the wrong place. . . . The goal is to create a downward stream of vision that follows grammatical structure."[2]

To format your sermon using sense lines, have each full sentence start at the left edge and then create a line break where you would naturally take a breath or pause, such as at a period or semicolon. Indent that next line. Start back at the left margin when moving to the next major idea or move in the sermon. See the example below and note where the line breaks are and how much easier it is to read the text out loud compared to the same text in paragraph form. The sermon "Jesus Sighed: Being Open in Mark 7:24-37" in Chapter 25 is written in sense lines. Below is the first paragraph written in paragraph form; the second is written in sense lines.

Margin-to-margin paragraph form
Jesus sighed. You might have missed it. You might have breezed past it on the way from Tyre to the Decapolis. But pause for a moment on that word in Mark 7:34, *estenazen*. There's a lot going on in that sigh.

Sense lines form
Jesus sighed.
    You might have missed it.
    You might have breezed past it on the way from Tyre to the Decapolis.
        But pause for a moment on that word in Mark 7:34, *estenazen*.
        There's a lot going on in that sigh.

Notice that with sense lines, it's much easier to find where you left off when you are looking up from the page to deliver the sermon. Your eye can always count on starting again from the left-hand side of the page. If you add in some underlines, highlights, or asterisks, you'll make it even easier to deliver the sermon without reading it word for word from the page.

EXERCISE

How to *Not* Read Your Sermon

When using a full manuscript, the preacher may be tempted to look down at the pages and read word for word. When preachers do this, they lose eye contact with their listeners, thus severing a vital link of communication. Also, as Fry Brown observes, the congregation is "left to overhear the sermon instead of being addressed."[1] Here are some exercises that will help you to minimize looking down so that you can maximize eye contact.

Use this paragraph from the sermon "Composting Our Anger and Grief" in Chapter 26 to practice. Notice that it is written in sense lines.

A couple weeks ago, I dug up my garden to prepare for planting.
I grabbed my shovel and hoe and dug into the weeds that had started to take root.
Then I sorted through the compost that was in our bin.
It's a messy, gross job,
but I spread it over the soil and worked it into the garden.
It's hard work breaking up all those clumps of soil.

1. "Gulp" one sentence at a time with your eyes and then say it out loud while looking forward. Do the same thing with the next sentence. Using a manuscript with sense lines will enable you to take "sips" at commas, semicolons, colons, or dashes if the sentence is longer.
2. The temptation will be to look down when you come to the end of a sentence so that you know where you're going next. But this will cause you to lose your audience's eyes, sometimes at key points you're trying to make. Instead, keep eye contact all the way through the end of the sentence and then look down briefly to see what's next and take your next "sip" or "gulp" of words.
3. Bold or highlight "anchor points" in the manuscript to help your eyes easily find where you are going on the page. Using asterisks or colored markers can provide "handholds" for your eyes.
4. If there is a story to tell in the sermon, see if you can memorize just that part of it. Tell the story as naturally as possible, keeping eye contact with your listeners.
5. Try to memorize both the beginning and ending of your sermons. Keeping eye contact as the sermon begins will secure the listeners' attention. Keeping eye contact at the end will reinforce the point you are making and drive it home.

NOTE

1. Teresa L. Fry Brown, *Delivering the Sermon.* In Elements of Preaching Series, edited by O. Wesley Allen Jr. (Minneapolis, MN: Fortress Press, 2008), 67.

SPECIAL CONSIDERATIONS FOR USING HANDHELD ELECTRONIC DEVICES AND TELEPROMPTERS FOR PREACHING

Handheld electronic devices have become increasingly popular as a mode of sermon delivery. There are many positives to using these devices. For one, it is easy to change the font size and screen brightness to allow the text to be more easily seen. Also, having the document on a device avoids the risk of papers fluttering to the floor or accidentally being gathered up by the altar guild before the service.

However, there are also downsides to using electronic devices; they can run out of power, lock up, do an unplanned restart, or glitch in any other number of ways. Thus, it is advisable to print out the sermon as a backup.

Another thing to keep in mind when using an electronic device for preaching is that if you wear glasses, depending on the angle of the screen, the light can reflect off your lenses. This can happen both with live and online preaching. Why is this a problem? Teresa Fry Brown notes that "*oculesics*, or eye contact and usage, helps establish the preacher's credibility and authenticity."[3] So if the light reflects off your glasses, it will obscure the congregation's view of your eyes. So, experiment with the angle both of the screen and your glasses to minimize the reflection and allow the congregation to see your eyes.

There can also be an unintended cultural communication when using a handheld electronic device. If one preaches from a smart phone, it can give the impression that texts are being checked or websites browsed while preaching. Of course, this is (hopefully) not the case. However, the finger-swipe across the screen with eyes turned downward implicitly communicates that a person is in their own cyber-world rather than being fully present in the moment. Consider using a tablet-size device instead, which gives a feeling of more substance and significance.

Finally, a word about teleprompters. As clergy were forced to preach to screens during the first year of the COVID-19 pandemic, some discovered that they could use teleprompters to display their manuscripts. There are both free and low-cost teleprompter apps for phones, tablets, and laptops, as well as dedicated devices often used in more elaborate or sophisticated productions. The advantage of the teleprompter is that it leaves your hands free because it scrolls the text for you, and you can adjust the speed and font size to suit your needs. When the teleprompter is positioned behind the camera, the effect creates the illusion that the preacher is speaking without notes. However, there are challenges to using a teleprompter. We have seen preachers whose eyes are obviously reading the manuscript and who sometimes get flustered when the scrolling goes by too fast or too slow. Also, if you go off-script, it can be difficult to rejoin the scrolling text, and you can get lost. As with any sermon format, practice, practice, practice!

PREACHING WITHOUT NOTES

Preaching without notes does not necessarily mean that no writing happens in the sermon preparation process. Many who preach with no notes still write full manuscripts or extended outlines. They then memorize the sermon or outline so that they can deliver the sermon without something in their hand or on a pulpit. Other preachers will *only* develop the sermon in their minds and avoid paper altogether.

Joseph Webb's book, *Preaching without Notes*, provides both a rationale for delivering sermons without a manuscript as well as a method for doing so.[4] Webb asserts that preaching without script or notes is both exhilarating and memorable both for the preacher and the congregation alike. It maximizes connectedness and participation and reflects an authentic witness that engages the listeners. In each chapter, he walks the reader through a step-by-step, day-by-day process for planning the sermon, creating the outline and sequence, memorizing it through "chunking" (breaking the sermon into several units or "chunks"), and practicing it for delivery.

There are, of course, risks to preaching without notes. One risk is forgetting what you want to say next or losing your place in your train of thought. Here are two methods that Leah has found helpful in remembering the order of a sermon.

1. Find ways to help your *body* memorize want you want to say.
   a. Practicing your sermon while taking a walk is one method to integrate your mind memory and your muscle memory. You can work out your progression of ideas while walking a particular route. Practice saying the sermon to yourself as you walk. When you deliver the sermon, your body movement will help trigger your thought progression.
   b. Use your fingers to help you remember the progression of your sermon. Each move of the sermon could be a certain finger. For example, if you are using Four Pages, the thumb could be "trouble in the text," index finger could be "trouble in the world," middle finger, "good news in the text," fourth finger, "good news in the world." Or a Motion Pictures sermon could have an introduction (thumb), three moves (middle fingers) and conclusion (pinky).

2. Practice preaching the sermon in the space where you will actually deliver it. This works best by preaching away from the pulpit. Move to different places in the chancel area for each part of the sermon. As you practice progressing through the sequence, your muscle memory will help you stay on course. For example, when I move to the left side of the chancel, I'm in section A. When I stand at the center, I'm telling the story about Aunt Jane. And so on. Having the visual cues of your setting will help you remember what you want to say.

Another risk in preaching without notes is getting off track and "wandering." While the preacher sometimes has a sudden inspiration during the preaching moment, such thoughts can also result in meandering down rabbit trails. This is why the Central Claim and Central Purpose are important. If you are preaching without notes and get a sudden flash of something you want to say, make sure that it aligns with one of your Central Statements, otherwise, it may pull you off course. As is the case for preaching with a manuscript or outline, preaching without notes also requires practice, practice, practice!

THE IMPORTANCE OF PRACTICING YOUR SERMON

As you've seen with all the sermon delivery vehicles mentioned above, they each require practice. Ronald J. Allen notes, "A sermon does not truly become a sermon until the preacher steps into the pulpit and speaks it in the presence of the congregation. The ways in which the preacher and congregation engage one another in that moment contribute significantly to the congregation's response to the sermon."[5] He then asks an important question that preachers should consider when practicing their sermons: "How can your voice and body in the act of preaching help the congregation enter the world of the sermon?"[6] Dedicating time for practice will help the preacher experiment with ways to use their voice and body to support and enhance the message they want to convey.

Whether using a manuscript or delivering the sermon without notes, all preachers need to rehearse their sermons before the worship service. For manuscript preachers, be sure to read your text *out loud.* You will catch things with your ears that your eyes may miss. Here are questions to ask yourself as you practice:

- Does the wording flow well? (If not, rearrange your sentences or words.)
- Are the sentences, phrasing, and syntax clear? (If not, rephrase them so that they make sense to read out loud.)
- Do you have run-on sentences or sentences with many phrases set off by commas or semicolons? (If so, break them into separate sentences.)
- Can the sentence or paragraph structure be simplified for easier speaking and understanding? (If so, rewrite them so that they can be understood by your listeners.)
- Are there places where you stumble when you say the words aloud? (If so, simplify the wording.)

For preaching without notes, be sure to rehearse the delivery of your sermon. You might think you have it all in your head, but your brain uses different functions for *thinking through* a sermon compared with *speaking it out loud.* So, you need to give that part of your brain and body time to get comfortable and confident with what you want to say. Here are questions to ask yourself as you practice:

- Am I clear on the different parts of the sermon and their order? (If you keep getting lost, either rearrange the sections, simplify your flow of logic, or give more time to practicing your transitions.)
- What are the key words for my transitions between the sections? (Transition words are those such as: for example, in other words, however, at the same time, meanwhile.)
- Can I use a throughline or a repeated phrase to help me connect the different sections? (See Chapter 22 for more about throughlines.)
- Have I practiced telling the story or describing the illustration I want to share? (Practice using descriptive nouns and adjectives as well as vigorous verbs.)
- Have I practiced the beginning and ending of the sermon? (Remember: hook them and then give them a reason to say "Amen!")

As you are working to integrate your voice and body into the act of preaching, it will be helpful to have a basic understanding of what makes for effective use of vocals and the body. In the next chapters, we'll give an overview of the *spaces* of preaching, including the opportunities and limitations of each.

KEY POINTS IN THIS CHAPTER

1. Editing is a crucial part of the sermon-creation process. Tightening the focus, pruning extraneous material, and writing with a visitor in mind are ways to ensure that the sermon makes sense and accomplishes its purpose.
2. If using notes or a manuscript, preachers can choose from any number of sermon delivery vehicles, including full manuscript, abridged manuscript, extended outline, limited outline, and electronic devices.
3. Preaching without notes requires just as much, if not more, preparation as preaching without a manuscript. But it can be very effective for maintaining eye contact, connecting with the listeners, and making full use of one's hands.
4. Regardless of the method a preacher uses to deliver the sermon, practice is a must.

DISCUSSION QUESTIONS

1. Discuss with your preaching mentor what sermon delivery vehicle(s) they use. Ask if they've experimented with different modes of delivering the sermon. What do they find most helpful? What have they learned that they can recommend to you?
2. Talk with your preaching partner or group about the use of handheld devices in preaching, as well as other technologies such as PowerPoint, teleprompters, or video clips. How can technology serve the preaching moment? And in what ways can it be a distraction?
3. Discuss with your preaching mentor or group how much time they dedicate to practicing their sermon each week. What are the methods they use to practice? Do they go into the sanctuary and practice in that space? Do they practice in their office at home? In the car? On walks? Do they record themselves or ask a friend or family member to watch and critique?

FOR FURTHER READING

Joseph M. Webb. *Preaching Without Notes.* Nashville: Abingdon, 2001.

NOTES

1. Alyce McKenzie, *Novel Preaching: Tips from Great Writers on Crafting Creative Sermons* (Louisville, KY: Westminster John Knox, 2010), 53.
2. Laurence Hull Stookey, *Let the Whole Church Say Amen! A Guide for Those Who Pray in Public* (Nashville: Abingdon Press, 2001), 64.
3. Teresa L. Fry Brown, *Delivering the Sermon*. In Elements of Preaching Series, edited by O. Wesley Allen Jr. (Minneapolis, MN: Fortress Press, 2008), 79.
4. Joseph M. Webb, *Preaching Without Notes* (Nashville: Abingdon Press, 2001).
5. Ronald J. Allen, *Preaching: An Essential Guide* (Nashville: Abingdon Press, 2002), 107.
6. Ibid.

24

Preparing Your Voice and Body for Preaching

As we prepare for delivering a sermon, we must attend to both the verbal and nonverbal aspects of preaching. As Teresa Fry Brown notes, "The content of the sermon may be excellent, the context fully understood, the exegesis may lead biblical scholars to cheer, but a weak delivery can overshadow all the preliminaries."[1] Therefore, we will discuss some fundamentals about communication, sound delivery, and use of the body in this chapter and the two that follow.

Preachers must use their whole body in the preaching act. In her book *And Then, You Act: Making Art in an Unpredictable World*, theatre director Anne Bogart describes what happens when actors craft and articulate each moment on the stage. Her words could just as easily apply to preachers.

> The words are explained to the audience by the condition of the body. This is not an emotional condition, rather it is an expression of the amount of energy that you are trying to access for yourself. Energy is the result of setting up oppositions in the body. Starting with a compression of energy, you hear, compose, and speak all in the same instant. . . . The situation engenders a physical state and from that state, you speak. You articulate. And then you refine the expression as it gushes forth. You multitask and allow expression to burst forth. It is all breath. It is a physical body in search of freedom. This is the essence of articulation.[2]

In this chapter, we'll take some time to focus on the elements that the preacher must multitask to "allow expression to burst forth," as Bogart puts it. We'll begin with sound production and include some exercises for warming up and conditioning the voice. Then we'll look at different aspects of using one's body in delivering the sermon and provide exercises to stretch and warm up the body for preaching as well.

A WORD OF CAUTION WHEN EXERCISING OUR VOICES AND BODIES

As you begin reading and practicing the exercises in this chapter as well as in Appendix M, "Exercises for the Preacher's Voice and Body," please note: exercises using our voices and bodies may be painful for those who have experienced certain kinds of physical trauma and/or triggering for those who have experienced sexual and/or physical abuse. Our bodies and voices can hold and remember trauma even when our conscious minds seem to forget. Thus, these exercises may bring up memories or uncomfortable feelings for some people that should be worked out with a trained counselor. Do not continue with these exercises if you are experiencing physical, emotional, or psychological pain. Seek help from a trusted professional.

VOICE PREPARATION AND SOUND PRODUCTION

In preaching, the word **voice** can be used metaphorically to refer to a preacher's unique way of communicating based on their preaching identity; their tradition, cultural, and denominational context; and their style. Voice also has to do with the right to express oneself openly. Physically, voice is how sound is produced by means of lungs, larynx, vocal cords, and mouth. For this section, we will be talking about voice in the physical sense.

No two voices are alike. Each has an "imprint" that is so unique, computers can use voice recognition software for security access. Jesus used the analogy of sheep recognizing the unique voice of their shepherd to explain why people followed him in John 10:1-18. It is important, then, for preachers to think about, experiment with, and care for their own voice.

In the Bible, the voice is the primary conduit of prayer, lamentation, and instruction. Hagar lifted up her voice to God when she and her son had been put out by Abraham. God heard both her voice and the voice of Ishmael and responded with a blessing "because you have obeyed my voice" (Genesis 21:18). The voice is also the means by which people praise, celebrate, and, yes, preach. Sophia-Wisdom is personified as raising her voice in the public square in Proverbs 1:20. John the Baptizer's voice "crying in the wilderness" preached the message of preparation and repentance at the Jordan River in Mark 1:1-11, and God's voice responded by declaring Jesus beloved. From the Hebrew prophets to Jesus and the apostles in the Christian Scriptures, the voice is what calls people to faith, accountability, justice, forgiveness, healing, and hope.

How do you and others experience your own voice in relation to proclaiming the Word of God? Whether high-pitched or low, soft or resonant, Ron Allen explains the necessity of the voice in conveying the sermon:

> The preacher needs to speak in a full enough *voice* that the congregation can hear the sermon easily. When the congregation has difficulty hearing, they often lose attention quickly. Furthermore, one needs to speak with variety in his or her voice (loud, soft, fast, slow) to help the congregation maintain an interest in the sermon. If one's voice pattern is always the same—even if it is loud—it has a narcotic effect on the listeners.[3]

In this section, we will introduce basic terminology and aspects of speaking and learn how to prepare one's voice for preaching as well as maintain its health for longevity.

Breath

Be sure that your posture supports the full expansion of your diaphragm and lungs. Practice taking full, deep breaths in through the nose and exhaling out through the mouth. This will allow for a full intake of air to vibrate your vocal cords and resonate through the cavities of your throat and head. See the exercises below to help increase your breath capacity.

Volume

If the congregation cannot hear the preacher, then the sermon will be lost. At the same time, if the preacher sounds like they're yelling the whole time, the congregation may become annoyed or simply tune out. Ideally, a preacher should modulate their volume so that their highs are not too overpowering and their lows can still be heard. Don't rev up to the highest gear right out of the gate and remain there. You'll exhaust your listeners and yourself. But don't speak so softly that people must strain to hear you. Here are some other things to keep in mind about volume.

- Even when using a microphone, you will still need to project your voice. Be sure to test the microphone level before the service begins.
- Watch volume drop-offs at the ends of sentences. Many preachers swallow their words when looking down to find their place in the manuscript. Follow through with your volume all the way to the end of the sentence. (See Chapter 23 for tips on how to deliver a sermon well when using a manuscript.)
- The key to being heard when speaking softly is not necessarily to lower the volume, but to speak more slowly, at a lower pitch, and with greater articulation of consonants.
- If a preacher's pitch, loudness, or quality of sound calls more attention to itself than what the preacher is saying, this will need to be addressed by a vocal coach or physician. Sometimes the issue is only temporary, as with a cold or laryngitis. But chronic issues need professional attention.

EXERCISE

Increase Your Breath Capacity

Teresa L. Fry Brown offers many exercises to maintain a healthy preaching voice in her book *Delivering the Sermon.* Here are just a few that we recommend:

1. *Respiration exercise #1*: After taking a deep breath, count slowly, one second per number, in a good loud voice. Repeat until you can count aloud to fifteen slowly on one breath. Work up until you are able to count to twenty or thirty.[1]
2. *Respiration exercise #2*: Sound the vowel /ah/ in a full voice and prolong it in a monotone until you feel like all the breath is exhausted. Time each trial and notice that the more you practice, the longer you can maintain the sound. When taking a breath, place your hand lightly on your abdomen. *Diaphragmatic breathing* means that your stomach should distend when air is taken in. If your shoulders move up (*clavicular breathing*) and your stomach goes in, you are breathing incorrectly and will have minimal airflow.[2]
3. *Volume, intensity, and projection exercise:* Sound the vowel /ah/ in a full voice and prolong it at a normal pitch level. Gradually increase the loudness of the sound /ah/ in a monotone as long as the breath lasts. Make sure you increase the sound gradually, imagining that a person is walking away from you. Try to reach someone standing twenty feet away (about the length from the pulpit to the first pews). If you feel a tickling, cough, or hoarseness, you are overstraining. Stop if this occurs. Next decrease the volume as if the person is walking toward you. Always direct your voice toward the person. Once you master this distance without strain, try thirty or forty feet, and then the full distance from the pulpit to the last pew. Also, vary the exercise by having inflection patterns go up and down as well as monotone /ah-h/.[3]

See Appendix M, "Exercises for the Preacher's Voice and Body," for more exercises for warming up your voice for preaching.

NOTES

1. Teresa L. Fry Brown, *Delivering the Sermon.* In Elements of Preaching Series, edited by O. Wesley Allen Jr. (Minneapolis, MN: Fortress Press, 2008), 39.
2. Ibid.
3. Ibid., 39–40.

Speed, Pacing, Pauses

Many listeners process what they hear more slowly than many preachers speak, so be sure to talk at a rate of speed that allows people to track with you. You can also vary the speed: pick up the pace to match a rise in the energy when needed and slow it down when coming to a point to ponder or emphasize.

Pausing at key points in the sermon is another effective use of the voice. "A pause calls attention to what the preacher has just said. It allows the congregation to ponder or otherwise process the preacher's remarks. It can create a holy moment in which, in the silence, the preacher and congregation feel deeply present to each other and to God," says Allen.[4] Also, as Fry Brown explains:

> The use of a pause in speech is an indication of control and transition. The speaker may use the pause as a means of allowing the listener to catch up, integrate what has been said, or satisfy expectations of the homiletical event. At times preachers are reticent to pause. They feel the need to fill a void, resort to repetitions, or fear waiting even briefly for the communication to be transmitted. The pause, however, indicates the completion of a thought, timing for vocal variety, maintenance of interest, and allowing the listener to reconnect or attend the content of the message.[5]

Schedule "Vocal Sabbaths"

Fry Brown recommends that preachers find a space for voice rest (no talking) before the worship service.[6] It's also a good idea to take a day off from speaking, if possible, to allow the voice to recover from the preaching event. Admittedly, this is very difficult to do, but carving out even half a day for voice-rest can help ensure the health of your vocal cords over the long term. Some preachers also find that going on a silent retreat helps both their voice and their minds to rest from the constant demands of speaking.

AVOID THE "PREACHER VOICE"

Ron Allen observes, "Preachers sometimes speak in a 'pulpit voice' or move in peculiar ways that differ dramatically from the ways that they speak and move at other times. Such differences communicate that preaching is a contrived moment and not real life."[7] Of course, the preacher's volume and gestures need to be bigger than normal conversation. But if it feels as if the preacher is "putting on an act," the sense of authenticity and believability will be negatively affected. There is no need to take on a different persona when stepping into the pulpit. Be your authentic self and trust that God will be able to use your own unique voice to proclaim the gospel.

Also, it's best to avoid a "sing-songy" voice characterized by a recurring cadence. A repetitive rising and falling of voice inflection or rhythm can become tedious for the listener. Instead, follow a more natural cadence and modulate your inflection as you would in a normal speaking voice.

Finally, avoid the "breathy voice" in preaching. Also called a "whispery voice," this is when the speaker allows too much air to escape through the vocal folds. Some preachers will use the breathy-voice-effect when wanting to make a serious point, when making a plea, or to draw attention to a particular idea. Often the whispery voice is done unconsciously, but it has the opposite effect of what the preacher intends. First, the breathy voice is simply more difficult for listeners to hear. Second, the breathy voice can be irritating to listeners and unconsciously undermine the point you are trying to make.

To correct the breathy voice, simply allow less air to pass through your vocal cords. If you're looking for a different way to emphasize a point, try lowering the pitch—while also retaining sufficient volume. This takes some practice. However, through experimentation, the preacher can find ways to use their air, pitch, volume, and even their facial expressions for effect or emphasis instead of the whispery voice.

USING THE BODY: NONVERBAL COMMUNICATION IN PREACHING

Just as the Bible shows us countless examples of people using their voices to convey the Word of God, there are also myriad stories of using their bodies as well. For example, Miriam used dance and a tambourine to express her joy at seeing their captors vanquished by God's hand at the Sea of Reeds (Exodus 15:20-21). Ezekiel acted out the wrongdoings of the people in the time of exile by lying on his left side for 390 days, symbolling the 390 years that Israel had sinned (Ezekiel 4:1-5). And Jesus laid his hands on children in blessing to demonstrate the tender love of God (Matthew 19:13-15).

How do you experience your own body as a conduit of God's word? No matter your size or shape, skin color or hair style, gender or sexual orientation, "The whole self of the preacher brings the sermon to life, and the listeners receive the sermon in their whole selves—mind, hearts, and wills," Allen observes.[8] This means that "Preachers should *move their hands, arms, and the rest of their body*, in ways that enhance the content of the sermon and that are consistent with their personality."[9]

Yet preachers who have not had much experience with or training in public speaking can sometimes be self-conscious about gesturing and uncomfortable with the performative aspects of delivering a sermon. Thus, when first learning to preach, it can be helpful to work with a theatre coach, public speaking instructor, or preaching mentor or small group to experiment with how to use your hands, fingers, arms, feet, and entire body. Even if it feels awkward at first, the more you practice, the less self-conscious and more natural it will feel. (Note: there are special challenges for those who preach in historically marginalized bodies, which we will cover in Chapter 25.)

Posture

Standing upright (not stooped) with your shoulders relaxed and stacked over your hips not only creates a stance that conveys confidence, it allows for the body to be receptive to the energy of the room, while fully breathing in and out. How do you know if your posture is correct? Stand with your back, shoulders, and the back of your head against the wall. Then step away and maintain this posture. If you tend to stoop, this may feel awkward or rigid at first. But if you observe your profile in the mirror, you'll notice how straight and alert your body looks. If you practice good posture over time, it may come to feel more natural.

Facial Expressions

The ways in which we use our eyes, lips, jaw, forehead, tongue, and nose can bring to life the emotional aspects of a sermon. Consider, for example, how you can furrow your brow in anger, wrinkle your nose in disgust, widen your eyes in surprise, purse your mouth in contempt, and scrunch your face in confusion. All of these facial expressions and more can help to convey the feelings of a biblical character, or a question you want to pose, or the joy in the gospel that you want to express. Granted, some preachers may be concerned that the use of facial expressions may be interpreted as being overly emotional, contrived, or too much like "acting." However, when used judiciously, appropriately, and with the intention of bringing God's Word (and your sermon) to life, facial expressions can enhance the sermon and are preferable to a preacher who displays low affect or seems bored by their own sermon.

Arms, Hands, and Fingers

Think of your arms, hands, and fingers as the underlines, boldface, and italics of physical speech. Use your hands selectively for emphasis, but not indiscriminately. Be intentional and thoughtful about the gestures you use. Make notes in your manuscript to remind yourself to use appropriate body language at suitable places in the sermon. For example, if you say you have three points to make, hold up three fingers, with your hand out and away from your body so it can be seen. Or gesture to the communion table if mentioning it in the sermon. You can also use your arms spread wide to indicate inclusiveness or expansiveness. Some preachers even teach their congregations words in sign language to help them grasp the meaning of a text in an embodied way.

What should you do with your hands when you're not using them? Refrain from gripping the pulpit. Instead, rest them on the podium in a way that feels natural. Or keep one hand at your side and one on the pulpit.

Feet and Knees

Whether you stand in a pulpit or preach pulpit-free, it's important to have stability with your feet. Wear shoes that are comfortable and that reduce the risk of tripping or wobbling. When standing, a good way to position your feet is by bringing your dominate foot just slightly forward and away from the instep of the opposite foot. This makes for a steady stance while also allowing your body to lean forward, backward, or side to side without losing your balance. It also makes it easier to take a next step forward.

Also, be conscious of your knees when you preach. Knees have a surprising but often unnoticed impact on public speaking. The knee is a weight-bearing joint that can allow for forward, backward, and rotating movement. But when knees are "locked," it's a sign of tension in the body. Locked knees equate to constricted breath. Here's how you can tell: stand up and take a deep breath with your knees loose. Then lock your knees and try to take a deep breath. Notice the difference? Loosening the knees means releasing tension and tightness, which in turn allows for better breathing and lessened nervousness.

See Appendix M, "Exercises for the Preacher's Voice and Body," for more exercises for warming up your body for preaching.

HOW TO DEAL WITH NERVOUSNESS AND RECOVER FROM MISTAKES OR STUMBLES IN PREACHING

"The truth about ministry . . . is that it is one of the most vulnerable vocations imaginable. It is radical exposure. There is really nowhere to hide."[10] So observes Karoline Lewis, whose words are especially true for preaching.

Standing up in front of people to share your exegesis and interpretation of a biblical text and what it can mean for the congregation is one of the most vulnerable things you will do as a minister. Even experienced preachers can feel some level of nervousness from time to time. But this is actually a good thing! If a preacher doesn't feel some level of "fear and trembling" for the task they are undertaking with preaching, that would be cause for concern. Why? Because there is a great deal at stake in the preaching event for the congregation and their relationship with the preacher, God, one another, and the larger society, as well as God's Creation. The key is to find a way to handle the momentousness of preaching with humility while productively channeling the energy generated in the preaching event.

Nervousness Is Actually Energy!

Speaking of energy, this a way to rethink what is happening when you are feeling "nervous." Recall from Anne Bogart in the earlier quote that actors (and preachers) are accessing and channeling energy. Using theological language, we might say that this is the work of the Holy Spirit activating and stimulating your brain and somatic systems for the task of preaching. Remember that when you are leading worship and preaching, you are on a kind of frontier the entire time. You are in a liminal place between the Divine and the people. This generates a great deal of energy, so it's only natural for you to feel some nervousness.

People experience nervousness in various ways, including sweaty palms, dry mouth, restlessness, racing heartbeat, or butterflies in the stomach. Remember, however, that these physical sensations are all due to the energy that is surrounding you and the congregation in the midst of that sacred space and sacred time of worship. It is energy welling up in the world and through the power of the Holy Spirit that your mind and body are sensing. It's what we *do* with the energy that is important. Because if we don't ground ourselves, then the energy can either backfire, get misdirected, or go into a feedback loop (which can lead to stage fright). Here are a few ways to manage and direct this energy so that you can use it in productive ways.

GROUNDING AND CHANNELING YOUR ENERGY FOR PREACHING

1. Ground yourself in preparation—devote time to reading the Scriptures, working the Central Statements, and crafting the sermon, all the while praying through the process to channel your energy.
2. Ground yourself in practice. As you'll learn in Chapter 25, there's no substitute for practicing your sermon. Don't just practice it in front of a mirror; take a video of yourself and/or preach in front of someone who can give you constructive feedback. The more you practice, the more your body will learn how to channel the energy and feel more comfortable with it, because it knows what's coming.
3. Ground yourself through deep breathing and warm-up exercises. As described in the exercise above and in Appendix M, take deep, slow breaths in through the nose and out through the mouth to center yourself before and during the service. Also, by practicing the vocal and body exercises before the preaching moment, you'll help to harness the energy and channel it into the service of the sermon.
4. Ground yourself in trust of the Spirit's guidance. Remember, God has called you to this preaching vocation. God will equip you with what you need. Learn to trust and channel the Spirit's energy and not see it as a sign of nervousness, but as a clear indication that the Spirit is moving in this place and in you!

If you would like to learn more techniques for dealing with nervousness and how to get out of your own head in order to be fully present in the moment, we recommend either of these two books: *The Inner Game of Tennis* by W. Timothy Gallway or *The Inner Game of Music* by Barry Green with W. Timothy Gallway. They give great tips for how to be fully present instead of caught up with the inner critic that can sometimes derail our performance.

HOW TO CENTER YOURSELF AND THE CONGREGATION BEFORE LAUNCHING INTO THE SERMON

The sermon doesn't begin when you start to speak. It begins in the moments just before you utter the first word. These few seconds before the sermon begins are often charged with energy, so you'll want to make them count and rein in the wild horses of your racing heart. While each preacher needs to find their own way of centering themselves and the congregation before the sermon begins, here are some recommendations:

- Pause. Don't just launch into the sermon. Take a moment to breathe deeply.
- During the pause, let your eyes sweep the congregation. Look at them, these people in your congregation who you love with a pastor's heart. Take them in with your eyes and give them a warm smile. Think to yourself, "You are about to hear the Word of God, blessed ones!"
- Some preachers like to begin with a brief prayer before preaching. For example, some use Psalm 19:14, "May the words of my mouth and the meditations of our hearts be acceptable in your sight, O Lord. Amen." But it is not always necessary to pray before beginning the sermon. Depending on the sermon form you are using, or the context in which you are preaching, you may want to simply begin the sermon with the question or sentence or story that starts the sermon.

No matter how you hover in those brief seconds before the sermon begins, remember that your listeners are rooting for you—they want you to succeed! While there may be a few curmudgeons or stony hearts in the congregation, for the most part, people are on your side and want you to do well with the sermon. Because they, like you, are longing for a divine Word, and they are trusting that you have done the work on their behalf to make sense of the Bible and bring them insights and inspiration that will speak to them in that moment.

RECOVERING FROM MISTAKES OR STUMBLES IN PREACHING

Even the most accomplished preachers and longtime worship leaders can fumble, stutter, lose their place, or go blank from time to time. But keep in mind that the goal is excellence in worship leadership and preaching—not perfection. You *will* make mistakes—you're only human. It's just like playing a musical instrument or playing a sport or any other endeavor that involves a public performance in some way—mistakes will happen, and that's okay. What's more important is how well you recover from mistakes.

If you do stumble over a word or phrase, or lose your place, or trip up in some way, the best thing to do is just pick up and move on. There's no need to apologize. This only draws attention to the error and distracts from what we're here to do—worship God and proclaim God's Word. Also, it's very likely that most people won't even realize you made an error if you just move on. While it may feel uncomfortable to have so many eyes on you, the congregation is not waiting for you to mess up. They will be forgiving if you trip on a word or flub a sentence. So do your best, and be assured that grace abounds!

Above all remember to be gentle with yourself. In the words of François Fénelon, a seventeenth-century French Roman Catholic archbishop: "Do not be discouraged at your faults; bear with yourself in correcting them, as you would with your neighbor. Accustom yourself gradually to carry prayer into all your daily occupations. Speak, move, work in peace, as if you were in prayer."[11]

KEY POINTS IN THIS CHAPTER

1. Effective use of one's voice and body are just as important as the content of the sermon.
2. Preachers need to tend to all elements of the body's sound production, including breath, volume, articulation, speed, pacing, pauses, and resting the voice for long-term health.

3. Preachers need to utilize their bodies in the preaching act, being intentional about the use of their posture, arms, hands, fingers, gestures, feet, and whole body to convey the message of the sermon.
4. Nervousness is natural when preaching. Thinking of it in terms of energy allows the preacher to ground and channel that power in service of the preaching event rather than letting it overwhelm or debilitate them.
5. There are several ways to center yourself and the congregation just before the sermon begins. Use those few seconds wisely.
6. Mistakes will happen when preaching. Move on with the sermon without drawing attention or apologizing. Don't expect perfection; instead, strive for excellence.

DISCUSSION QUESTIONS

1. How do you experience the energy of preaching in your body? What causes you to feel nervous? How do you process that energy and tame your nerves? Talk with your preaching mentor and colleagues about what they have found helpful for overcoming stage fright and grounding their energy.
2. Record yourself practicing a sermon you plan to deliver and listen to it with your preaching partner. How would you describe the timbre of your voice? What could you do to make your words more clear, audible, or distinct?
3. Do you use your hands when you talk? If so, how can you be more intentional with them when preaching? If not, what are ways you can experiment with using your arms, hands, fingers, and gestures when delivering a sermon? Watch experienced preachers and take notes on how they use their hands and bodies.

FOR FURTHER READING

Anne Bogart. *And Then, You Act: Making Art in an Unpredictable World.* New York: Routledge, 2007.

Teresa L. Fry Brown. *Delivering the Sermon.* In Elements of Preaching Series, O. Wesley Allen Jr., series editor. Minneapolis, MN: Fortress Press, 2008.

Jana Childers. *Performing the Word: Preaching as Theatre.* Nashville: Abingdon Press, 1998.

Jana Childers and Clayton J. Schmit. *Performance in Preaching: Bringing the Sermon to Life.* Grand Rapids, MI: Baker Academic, 2009.

Richard Ward. *Speaking of the Holy: The Art of Communication in Preaching.* St. Louis: Chalice, 2001.

NOTES

1. Teresa L. Fry Brown, *Delivering the Sermon.* In Elements of Preaching Series, O. Wesley Allen Jr., series editor (Minneapolis, MN: Fortress Press, 2008), 2.
2. Anne Bogart, *And Then, You Act: Making Art in an Unpredictable World* (New York: Routledge, 2007), 21.
3. Ronald J. Allen, *Preaching: An Essential Guide* (Nashville: Abingdon Press, 2002), 110.
4. Ibid., 111.
5. Brown, 35.
6. Ibid., 34.
7. Allen, 109.
8. Ibid., 107.
9. Ibid.
10. Karoline M. Lewis, *She: Five Keys to Unlock the Power of Women in Ministry* (Nashville: Abingdon Press, 2016), 53–54.
11. François Fénelon, "Keeping a Spirit of Prayer," in *The Complete Fénelon,* Robert J. Edmonson, CJ, and Hal M. Helms, translators (Brewster, MA: Paraclete, 2008), 144.

25

The Performance of Preaching

Embodiment, Authenticity, and Presence

In the previous chapter, we began to think about the basic mechanics for our voices and bodies in preaching. We considered the elements of the body's sound production, including breath, volume, articulation, speed, pacing, pauses, and resting the voice for long-term health. And we thought about how to use our bodies in the preaching act, being intentional about posture, arms, hands, fingers, gestures, and feet to convey the message of the sermon. This chapter will delve deeper into the performative aspects of preaching. We will also reflect on what it means to preach in a body that has been "othered" by society and church tradition, as well as ideas for preaching a sermon that explores issues of gender, sexuality, race, or disability within Scripture and theology. This chapter will also include a sermon example that illustrates some of the performative aspects of preaching discussed in this and the previous chapter.

PREACHING AS PERFORMANCE: EMBODIMENT AND THEOLOGY

In *A Sermon Workbook*, Thomas Troeger and Leonora Tubbs Tisdale explain, "We need always to remember that a congregation sees and hears rather than reads a sermon. . . . Preachers do not just create sermons. They perform sermons."[1]

Is a sermon really a ***performance***? This term may be off-putting to some given that the word *perform* is usually associated with entertainment. But homiletical scholar Richard Ward clarifies that "the term *performance* comes from the old French *par + fournir*, which literally means to 'carry through to completion.' . . . What is it that we do when we speak the sermon we have written in the study? Do we not bring it forth to completion in the act of speaking it?"[2] More than just speaking, in fact, the sermon requires the preacher's whole body for the sermon to be brought to completion. As Ronald Allen states, "the whole self of the preacher brings the sermon to life, and the listeners receive the sermon in their whole selves—minds, hearts, and wills."[3]

The word for bringing one's whole self to the sermon is **embodiment**, which is the use of the physical self in preaching. Teresa Fry Brown explains that "Embodiment is the act of representing something in a bodily or material form. It occurs when someone speaking uses their physical self to transform an abstract, mental idea into a concrete form, shape, or representation in order to assist in establishing its meaning for the audience."[4]

Yet, as we noted in Chapter 24's preparation exercises, our voices and bodies are fraught with vulnerability, and this has profound implications theologically and anthropologically. Just think about some of the theological categories in Appendix D and how they are impacted by embodiment. Consider, for example, what the "Body of Christ" and ecclesiology mean in terms of the very real bodies in a congregation with all of their frailties, injuries, and sensuality. Or the ways in which theological anthropology is shaped by how we regard the shapes, sizes, skin colors, heights, weights, sexual orientations, and physical abilities of human bodies.

Christology is another theological category that has profound implications for preaching. As Karoline Lewis observes,

> When you imagine the doctrine of the incarnation not as a doctrine, per se, but as God's commitment to the inherent vulnerability of humanity, the focus of God's intention for humanity shifts exponentially. That is, an essential component of how we understand ministry in God's church is intimately tied to God's commitment to the entirety of what it means to be human.[5]

Consequently, what it means to be human is inseparable from what it means to be in a human body. "Our bodies are essential to and revealing of who we are," Lewis says. "We express ourselves through our bodies, which communicate what we think and feel as much as our words do. . . . Ministry does not happen solely through speech, but through action, through our bodies acting out our theological commitments."[6] Since preaching is one of, if not the most public act of theology in ministry, we must be attentive to what and how our bodies are communicating.[7]

AUTHENTICITY AND PRESENCE IN PREACHING

When our theological commitments are in alignment with our embodiment in preaching, the result is **authenticity** and a sense of **presence**. Those who listen to our preaching long for leaders who are honest, have integrity, and demonstrate congruence between what they say and how they act. "Authenticity, therefore, is also a matter of ensuring that words and emotions match in such a way that the preacher is actually living inside the words that he or she is speaking," according to John McClure.[8]

When a preacher is authentic in the pulpit, this allows them to be fully present to their own selves, to God's Word, and to the congregation. One of the ways this can happen is through the Theological Claims we articulate in the sermon and, in turn, the Central Question, Central Claim, and Central Purpose that are all integrated not just in our spoken words but also through our embodiment of the sermon. In other words, communicating clearly about who God is and what God does—and what this means for the community—is conveyed through our speech and exemplified in our bodies as we are present with our listeners and the preaching moment. You'll see an example of this congruence between one's words and how they are embodied in the sermon "Jesus Sighed" later in this chapter.

Presence is the state of being attentive, open, centered, and poised in preaching. As Ronald Allen reminds us, "The preacher needs to signal that he or she is attentive to the congregation and is emotionally, intellectually, and physically open to the community. There is no inventory of characteristics to determine presence, but the congregation draws more deeply into the sermon when they sense it."[9]

SUGGESTIONS FOR CULTIVATING PRESENCE IN PREACHING

Indeed, there is no definitive "inventory of characteristics to determine presence" in preaching. However, here are some things a preacher can do to cultivate that state of attentiveness, openness, centeredness, and poise when delivering a sermon:

- *Practice breathing and vocal exercises.* You'll find these exercises in Chapter 24 and Appendix M. Breathing deeply and having confidence in one's voice frees the preacher to be centered and present in the moment by channeling their energy in productive ways.
- *Practice body warm-up exercises.* You'll find these exercises in Appendix M. As you are preparing to preach, and even while you are preaching, try to be aware of where your body is holding tension. Intentionally tighten and then release the muscles in that area to allow your body the freedom of movement and openness it needs to be fully present.
- *Practice the sermon.* The more confident you are in what you are going to preach and how you are going to preach it, the more you can focus on being in the moment without worrying about your content or delivery.
- *Smile!* The act of smiling with one's full face—including the eyes—not only conveys warmth and openness to one's listeners, it also activates positive feelings in the one who smiles and those who receive that smile. Of

course, there are times when smiling isn't suitable, but when appropriate, practice smiling before the sermon begins and at key moments when preaching in order to cultivate a sense of positive presence.

- *Use pauses.* As discussed in Chapter 24, the pause is a powerful tool for centering and recentering both the preacher and the congregation. An intentional pause while looking at the congregation with a certain facial expression or holding a particular gesture, such as an outstretched palm, is an effective way to create a sense of presence in preaching.
- *Engage with eye contact.* Preachers who avoid looking people in the eye when preaching sometimes have more difficulty conveying a sense of presence. Conversely, meeting people's eyes communicates that the preacher is interested in connecting with the listeners. This sense of connection goes a long way in cultivating a sense of both authenticity and presence.
- *Engage in body awareness activities during the week.* Yoga, meditation, contemplative prayer, mindfulness exercises, and physical exercise can all help in connecting the preacher with their own sense of embodiment, their breath, emotions, and self-awareness. All of this, in turn, helps the preacher be present in the moment of the sermon.

EXERCISE

Gauging Presence and Authenticity in Preaching

For this exercise, make a video of yourself preaching to a congregation (even if it is just a few people in a sermon workshop group). As you watch the recording with your preaching partner or group, discuss the following questions:

1. How did I experience this sermon in my body at the beginning? At certain points in the middle? At the end?
2. How did I utilize my body to preach? In what ways did I use my hands, facial expressions, voice, gestures, movement, or other nonverbal communication to convey or support the message of the sermon?
3. Was my embodiment congruent with my words? Was it congruent with my Theological Claims in the sermon? Were there times when my gestures, stance, or vocal tone seemed to be out of sync with what I was saying?
4. At what point(s) in the sermon did I feel myself to be most authentic? Most present? Conversely, were there points where I felt distracted or not as present?
5. Did I notice things that might have distracted listeners from what I was saying? Did I see things like self-touch (adjusting glasses, twirling hair, or checking wristwatch, for example); overuse of filler words such as "so," "um," or "er"; or excessive or repetitive movements (swaying, head twitching, finger tapping)?

The idea is not to erase the unique characteristics of preachers and turn them into bland, boring automatons. One's mannerisms, idiosyncrasies, and even eccentricities can actually enhance the message and become part of one's style. As Brown notes, "Authentic preaching is to be conscious of one's unique preaching presence and use it as fully as possible in proclaiming the gospel."[1] However, if these mannerisms and idiosyncrasies draw attention to the *preacher* rather than the serve the proclamation of the gospel, then the preacher will want to think about how they might modify these habits.

NOTE

1. Teresa L. Fry Brown, *Delivering the Sermon*. In Elements of Preaching Series, O. Wesley Allen Jr., series editor (Minneapolis, MN: Fortress Press, 2008), 60.

PREACHING IN HISTORICALLY MARGINALIZED BODIES

Thus far, we have examined several internal factors that affect the embodiment of preaching. In this section, we discuss some of the external factors that are imposed on a preacher simply by virtue of the fact that they are preaching in a particular body—especially one that society or the church has not historically welcomed into the pulpit. Preachers who are "othered" because of their body's, gender, sexuality, skin color, hair texture, size, or disability are sometimes at a disadvantage when stepping into the preaching space.

For example, even when they're not conscious of it, female preachers are often scrutinized and subjected to a double standard that is different from their male peers. As Karoline Lewis describes:

> We tell ourselves, "I am more than my body," and we are, but only so much self-talk can convince us of that truth. We tell ourselves that our bodies are as unique as the souls that inhabit them. We tell ourselves, "This is the body God has given me." We tell ourselves that we just have to do better about being comfortable in our own skin. But no amount of self-talk can overcome those many moments when, as a woman in ministry, it is your very body that will be rejected—every curve, every angle; your waist, your breasts; your height and your weight. People will notice and comment on every change in your body and any change you make to your body. And your body will likely be connected to your perceived abilities for ministry. One pastor shared that one response in a performance review was, "She excels in every way except that she is overweight."[10]

This kind of prejudice can result in feeling unfairly judged and result in doubting one's call to preach or sense of authority in the pulpit. For women this sense of doubt may be reflected in their voices or demeanors when they preach. As Teresa Fry Brown observes, "For women, issues of authority and call may produce hesitant, weak, or inaudible 'I'm not really here' or 'I'm sorry to bother you,' or 'I'm just a woman' voices."[11]

For Black female preachers, the stakes are even higher. Lisa Thompson notes that "When expectations centered on performances of masculinity determine what is and is not valid preaching, these expectations render Black women as bodies of difference or bodies desired to be unseen in the pulpit (desired invisible). Black women are displaced from the pulpit and their citizenship status within the community is that of outsider."[12] Similar experiences of being an outsider can happen with bodies that are transgender, disabled, or any shape, size, or color that is different from the White, male body that society has inscribed as normative.

Several of Leah's students over the years have expressed feelings of intimidation and hesitancy to be completely themselves because their very bodies remind listeners of truths they'd rather not grapple with—truths about racism, sizeism,[13] sexism, ableism,[14] transphobia, and homophobia,[15] for example.[16] As these preachers step into the pulpit, listeners unconsciously (or consciously) heap on them all of their prejudices, stereotypes, biases, and cultural ascriptions before they even open their mouths to proclaim the Word. At the same time, these minoritized preachers are expected to defy expectations and win over their audience. And if they are judged to fall short, the preacher bears the weight of harmful assumptions, stereotypes, and narratives that the congregation uses to reinforce the implicit (or explicit) message that this person is not worthy to preach. These harmful messages not only limit the individual preacher, but the whole of preaching itself. As Thompson warns:

> When preaching and its hopes are conflated with the presence or absence of a particular body, that body inherently restricts the possibility of preaching. Preaching becomes an unimaginative practice. The fields in which proclamation may occur are now limited, narrowed, and confined. This mirrored illusion of preaching that is perpetuated by communal rigidity closes preaching off from its own possibilities—the free-expression, unlimited, and unrestrained encounter of sacred-in-breaking. The spirit of God that enables preaching through her free will has now been confined to a community's terms and conditions.[17]

Yet, Thompson turns this oppressive reality inside out to reveal the stitching of hopefulness underneath. Speaking from the perspective of Black female preachers, she notes that they can choose to "creatively engage the power postulated by the tradition and its guardians. Their preaching is the tactical expression of their own creativity and ingenuity."[18] In other words, preachers who find themselves "othered" by a congregation because of their bodies can "riff off of the expectations of preaching and its ephemeral scaffolding, for the sake of the hope and ethics preaching espouses—a word from God that fosters life abundant."[19]

In fact, the Bible itself offers many opportunities to go deeper with these questions and uncover the hidden intimidation that wants to suppress the proclamation of the gospel. That process can help preachers to attune themselves to a biblical character or story that longs for voice and embodiment. "Through preaching we are able to help a community fully embrace an otherwise minoritized body in its pulpit space," says Thompson.[20] Further, she says, "As they do this, preaching becomes the means by which synthetic practices of preaching are disrupted in both more hushed and resounding ways; in turn, the community generates new possibilities and means of understanding preaching as its members are able to say, 'This, "too" is preaching.'"[21]

In order to help preachers practice this discipline of embracing minoritized bodies, Leah has designed an exercise called the Five-Minute Embodied Monologue where she challenges the preacher to choose a biblical character very different from them and to imagine what the story is like from their perspective. We encourage you to try this exercise with your preaching partner or group to experiment with aspects of embodiment that challenge your assumptions, your comfort zone, and your biases.

EXERCISE

Five-Minute Embodied Monologue

Present a five-minute monologue on a biblical character chosen from one of the six options below. Challenge yourself to choose a character that is different from you in terms of either gender, disability, race, or ethnicity.

- Hagar in Genesis 21:1-21
- Queen Vashti in Esther 1:10-20
- The man lowered through the roof in Luke 5:17-26
- The woman with a spinal deformity in Luke 13:10-17
- The Gerasene man afflicted with demons in Mark 5:1-20
- The Ethiopian eunuch in Acts 8:26-40

In the monologue, become this character. As you tell your story, consider these questions:

1. What is it like to live in a body that is not accepted by society and/or by those in power?
2. How can I convey the biblical character's social position, health (mental, emotional, and spiritual), gender, sexuality, age, and physical ability in this monologue?
3. Is this character's body betraying them or letting them down in some way?
4. Has this character's body been ridiculed, objectified, or abused?
5. How does this body relate to God/Jesus Christ through body and voice?
6. What does resistance to oppression look like from this body's perspective?
7. How is injustice and/or justice experienced in this body?

For this monologue *show*, don't just *tell*. Use strong descriptive language that evokes sight, smell, sound, texture, and taste. Use your whole body in this monologue—inhabit this character. Tell your story without notes. Experience the freedom to fully engage with your eyes and body without the hindrance of a manuscript.

You are using your whole body for this monologue, so think about how you will use your facial expressions, feet, legs, hips, waist, back, shoulders, arms, hands, and fingers. How will your voice personify this character? What will be the quality of your speech?

If you record this monologue, have the camera positioned so that it will take in the full expanse of your arms when extended, but not so far away that viewers can't see your facial expressions.

As you debrief this monologue with your preaching peers, discuss the following questions:

A. What was the preacher's relationship with their body in this monologue?
B. What changes were evident in the preacher's use of their body between the beginning, middle, and end of the sermon? What did those changes convey about the character or the story?

C. How did the preacher's embodiment of the character resonate with your own sense of embodiment as you watched?
D. In what way did you experience the exigence of the text and the good news of the text through the preacher's embodiment?

After debriefing this monologue with your preaching partner or group, think about how you might develop it into a fuller sermon. For example, you might begin the sermon in character and tell the first part of the story, then move out of character to comment on the story as the preacher, then move back into character, and so on. Or you might preach the entire sermon as the character in the biblical story. Alternatively, you might ask another person to serve as the narrator while you embody the character's story. Or you might preach the sermon informed by your insights from the monologue while retaining your own preaching persona. In the sermon below, "Jesus Sighed," you'll see an example of a sermon informed by insights from this exercise applied to Mark 7:24-37.

SERMON EXAMPLE: "JESUS SIGHED: BEING OPEN IN MARK 7:24-37"

Leah was the guest preacher for Hunter Presbyterian Church in Lexington, Kentucky, when she delivered this sermon on Mark 7:24-37, the Gospel reading assigned in the Revised Common Lectionary *for September 5, 2021. In the notes for each section, you'll see how this sermon illustrates many of the points made in this chapter and Chapter 24 about sermon delivery, voice, and embodiment. You'll also notice that this sermon uses "sense lines" in the formatting, which we explained in Chapter 23. This format worked well in giving cues for when to pause, make gestures, and emphasize certain points in the sermon.*

EXERCISE

Sermon Analysis of "Jesus Sighed"

1. As you read the sermon, underline the sentences that are Theological Claims.
2. Star the sentence that you believe is the Central Claim of the sermon.
3. After you finish reading the sermon, write down what you think was the Central Question and Central Purpose of the sermon.
4. Which one of the sermon forms did you detect Leah using in this sermon—Four Pages, Motion Pictures, Homiletic Plot, or Expository/Puritan Plain Style?
5. At the end of the sermon, you'll see the Central Question, Central Claim, and Central Purpose that Leah wrote down for this sermon. See how yours compare with hers. You'll also see which sermon form she used.

SECTION 1

(Leah was intentional with the use of her voice when saying the word "sigh." She sighed as she initially said the word and went on to demonstrate four different types of sighs. In this section, you can see evidence of her exegesis through the explanation of the word stenadzo *and other places in the Christian Scriptures where the word can be found. Thus, literary*

criticism provides background here. This first section ends with foreshadowing about where the sermon might be headed, giving listeners a reason to "stay tuned" to what's going on with Jesus's sigh.)

Jesus sighed.
You might have missed it.
You might have breezed past it on the way from Tyre to the Decapolis.
But pause for a moment on that word in Mark 7:34, *estanazen.*

Jesus sighed.
It wasn't an exhalation of contentment after a belly-filling meal. *[Demonstrate.]*
Nor was it a breath released through a smile looking out on a sunny valley.
[Demonstrate.]
No, this was a *groaning* kind of sigh. *[Demonstrate.]*

The Greek root word is στενάζω, stenadzo.
It's the same word used to describe the groaning of those waiting for the redemption of their bodies in Romans 8:23.
The same word used for those yearning for heaven in 2 Corinthians Chapter 5.

And in the next chapter of Mark,
it's this same groan Jesus releases in exasperation
when the Pharisees demand a sign from him, testing him.
Not one for a dog-and-pony show, Jesus refuses.
With that sigh he gets back on a boat and leaves.
But with *this* sigh in Chapter 7, he stays.

Jesus sighed, and he healed a man who could neither hear nor speak.
Yet there's more going on in that sigh than you might think.

SECTION 2

(In this section, Leah lowered her volume when saying that Jesus called the woman a dog, then immediately raised her volume, using inflection to indicate disdain. Right after that, her voice, face, and hands reflected the "ouch" upon hearing those harsh words. She also gasped when saying the word "gasp," thus using her voice to reinforce the shocking aspect of the story. Then she used her hands and fingers to denote the shift when the women countered Jesus's words. After a pause to draw out the tension of the moment, she dramatically enacted backhanding. The section ends with a question that draws in the listener—"Do we recognize what is happening here?")

This healing comes after an encounter with the Syrophoenician woman.
She begged Jesus to heal her daughter.
When she first approached him, he refused her and called her a dog.

"Let the children be fed first,
for it is not fair to take the children's food and throw it to the dogs" (Mark 7:27).

Ouch.
No matter how high your Christology,
there's no getting around this low-down insult.
This is an ethnic slur.
It would have made the original hearers of Mark's Gospel gasp.
It makes us gasp, too.

But her response—
the response from this Gentile woman not worthy of his healing—
stops him in his tracks.

"Sir, even the dogs under the table eat the children's crumbs" (Mark 7:28).

The disciples probably gasped. Maybe Jesus gasped, too.

He could have backhanded her for saying that.
This insolent woman. Who does she think she is?
But no. He does not kick her away like a dog.
He recognizes what is happening here.
Do we? Do we recognize what's happening here?

SECTION 3

(In this section, Leah explains the implications of the encounter between Jesus and the Syrophoenician woman. The message countering ethnocentrism and prejudice implicitly conveyed by her to Jesus is intended to be "caught" by the congregation as well. This section also counters misogyny by lifting up the intelligence, wit, and determination of the woman. Leah once again used her voice when describing the sigh of relief. By this point, you should recognize that the sigh is a kind of throughline for the sermon. Toward the end of this section, Leah changed the rate at which she spoke; she sped up when describing Jesus's stress, then slowed down and lowered her volume when speaking in the voice of the woman. In the last part of this section, Leah used her arms outstretched for "the whole world," and used her fingers and hands to point to the parts of her face for "eyes opened," "ears unstopped," and "tongue released.")

Jesus changes his mind.
This foreign woman,
this desperate mother from a people not his own—
she teaches the greatest teacher something that changes his mind.
She teaches him that there is enough for everyone.
That it's okay to move beyond your own clan and share with others.
There is no need to withhold healing or food or miracles
just because someone is from a different tribe than you are.

She is unchosen, begging on her knees.
And yet—
she is clever and witty enough to deescalate the situation and ask for what she needs.

And Jesus's response?
"For saying that, you may go—the demon has left your daughter" (Mark 7:29).

Touché. You got me. You're right. I was wrong.

Wow. Just wow.
Everyone breathes a sigh of relief:
the Syrophoenician woman, the disciples, and Mark's church.
We breathe a sigh of relief, too.

Because this means Jesus is the best kind of healer—
the best kind of teacher:
the kind who listens and learns.
The kind who can admit when he's wrong.

He's the kind of teacher who can be grumpy
and probably needs a nap
because everyone is after him all the time to do something for them
and all he wants is a break.

Get away from me.
You're not even one of my people.
You're no better than a dog.

Oh, but sir, there's more in you than you know.
Even the crumbs of your healing power are enough.
Just touching the hem of your garment
is enough to heal a woman who bleeds.
Just saying a prayer over a few loaves of bread
is enough to feed thousands.

Jesus, there is enough in you to go further than you think.
Your power is not just for your own people. It's for the whole world!

And in that moment, his eyes are opened. His ears are unstopped.
His tongue is released to give *her* the release she needs for her daughter.

SECTION FOUR

(This section begins with a clear transition sentence about the pivot point in Jesus's ministry. This allows Leah to shift to the next part of the story about Jesus healing a Gentile man. Leah's commentary provides historical background to help the congregation understand the juxtaposition of this story with the previous one. Notice the repetition of words and phrases from previous sections that helps to create a sense of recognition for the listener, allowing them to connect the dots within this biblical narrative. Leah made full use of embodiment when describing Jesus healing the man while alluding to the contemporary situation of "social distancing" during the COVID-19 pandemic. The use of the breath returns once again with the word "breathtaking" and the description of the word ephphatha. *Using the rhetorical device of onomatopoeia, she riffed on the meaning and implications of being opened for Jesus, and for the congregation as well. This is the climax of the sermon.)*

This is a pivot point in Jesus's ministry.
Because right after that, he goes to the region of the Decapolis.
Ten cities in Gentile territory.
Did you catch that? He's going out of his comfort zone.
He's pushing beyond his ethnocentrism. He's taking his healing to the Gentiles.

And who is the first person he encounters there?
A man who cannot hear and cannot speak.
He's a Gentile. A man not of Jesus's own people.
"They begged him to lay his hand on him" (Mark 7:32).

Just a touch, Jesus. That's all. You can do it!

This is not a public healing, though.
Jesus takes the man away from the crowd.
Perhaps he's not quite ready for the Gentile gaze,
the scrutiny of a people who would deem him inferior.
Maybe even thought of him and his people as dogs.

But there they are,
the Jewish healer
and the Gentile man who cannot even ask for crumbs from the table.

It's such a fleshy, spitty healing.
No social distancing here.
There is an exchange of bodily fluids.
There is a touching of the tongue. Maybe even tongues?

The intimacy between these two strangers, these two ethnic groups,
these two men, these two humans, is, well,
breathtaking.
And that's when the sigh happens.

You might have missed it.
You might have breezed right past it on the way to "Be opened."
But don't skip that sigh. There's a lot going on in that sigh.
The groaning sigh as Jesus looks up to heaven,
pushed beyond his limits,
nudged by a dogged woman from a people not his own.
"Ephphatha."

The word even sounds like a sigh: Effatha. Effaahhhthaaahhh.
Be opened!

Maybe this word was not just for the man, but for Jesus himself.
Be opened.
Be open to people who are different from you.
Be open to changing your mind.

Jesus sighed with a groan that released his prejudice and his bias.
A groaning sigh that comes from the gut-wrenching realization
that you are touching a man—
exchanging spit with a man—
whose people have conquered your people.
A people whose soldiers will spit on you
and whip you
and nail your wrists and ankles to a cross for these kinds of healings.

It's a groaning sigh released while looking up to heaven,
entrusting his breath
to the One who sent to him a dogged Gentile woman.

The One who breathes through him
to open the ears and release the tongue of this Gentile man.
A man whose earwax is now on his fingers.
Whose spit is now mixed with his own.
For they are, truly, one body.

SECTION 5

(Typical of a story plot, the denouement of the sermon is short and to the point. You should be able to detect the influence of the Central Claim and Central Purpose in this final section. Because they are most evident here at the end, this tells us

that Leah used inductive logic for this sermon, picking up clues along the way that lead to an inevitable conclusion. The sermon ends with a final "breath" of the word ephphatha.)

The external labels fall away.
Language barriers lift. Skin touches.
Their shared humanity heals them both.
Because this is what Jesus has come to do.
Heal the world.
Heal the divisions, the racism, the sexism,
the homophobia, the disabled-phobia, the xenophobia.
Jesus sighed. Don't miss that sigh.
Be opened! Effaahhhthaaahhh . . .

CENTRAL QUESTION, CENTRAL CLAIM, CENTRAL PURPOSE, AND SERMON FORM FOR "JESUS SIGHED"

In the exercise above, we invited you to analyze the sermon in order to find out what you think was the Central Question, Central Claim, and Central Purpose of the sermon, as well as the sermon form. Here is what Leah wrote. How do they compare with your answers?

Central Question. How can we grapple with the juxtaposed stories of healing where Jesus pushes beyond his ethnic origins, and how does this shape our faith in Jesus Christ in our own society divided by "isms" and phobias?

Central Claim. Jesus's healings of the Syrophoenician woman's daughter and the Gentile man in the Decapolis challenge us to be changed, expanded, and pushed beyond our prejudices and biases to embrace the full scope of humanity.

Central Purpose. This sermon creates an experience of tension and release around issues of ethnocentrism, prejudice, bias, and human connection so that listeners will find themselves changed by Jesus's own journey of being opened.

Sermon Form. This sermon utilized the Homiletical Plot form:

1. Conflict ("Uh-oh!")—Jesus sighed; scriptural background for the word *estanazen*; foreshadowing of healing the man who could neither hear nor speak
2. Complication ("Ugh!")—Jesus and the Syrophoenician woman; confrontation informed by ethnic prejudice and discrimination
3. Sudden Shift ("Aha!")—Syrophoenician woman changes Jesus's mind; implications for Jesus's ministry beyond his own people
4. Experiencing the Gospel ("Whee!")—Jesus and the Gentile man in Decapolis; Jesus's sigh "being opened" both for himself and for the man
5. Anticipating the Consequences ("Yeah!")—Labels fall away, barriers lift, connection and healing because of Jesus's sigh

DIFFERING EXEGETICAL PERSPECTIVES ON MARK 7:24-37

Sometimes preachers and biblical scholars do not always agree on how to interpret a biblical text and draw out its implications for a sermon. Such is the case with this example of "Jesus Sighs." Jerry understands the story of the Syrophoenician woman in a way that is different from Leah. He does not think it shows Jesus learning that Gentiles are to be included in the Kingdom. While this has been a popular reading in many church contexts, it is a reading that Gospel scholars have come to find unlikely (including some who previously advocated this view). In the flow of the literary context, Jesus has already shown that he includes Gentiles among those his ministry is to embrace. In Chapters 5-8, Jesus intentionally makes multiple boat trips into predominantly Gentile regions, often performing the same kind of miracle on the Decapolis (Gentile) side as on the Jewish side of the lake. On the first of those trips into the Gentile region, Jesus exorcised a demon from a possessed Gentile and then commissions him to proclaim to those in that region all "the Lord" had done for him (5:19-20). (This is in contrast to Jesus regularly telling Jewish recipients of healings not to tell anyone.) Here Jesus clearly includes Gentiles in his ministry, and the Kingdom includes Gentiles.

In addition, the story of the Syrophoenician woman immediately follows the story in which Mark has Jesus declare that the Jewish traditions that separated Jews and Gentiles should no longer be allowed to separate these groups (7:1-23, esp. v. 19). Further, this story with its talk about bread comes between the feeding of the 5,000 on the Jewish side of the lake and the feeding of the 4,000 on the Gentile side. These aspects of the setting of the story in Tyre (a predominantly Gentile city) makes the interpretation that Mark intends readers to see Jesus learning that Gentiles are included in the Kingdom unconvincing to Jerry.

From Jerry's perspective, a more plausible reading would take into account more aspects of the identity Mark gives this woman. Notably he identifies her as a Greek, rather than a Gentile. This probably intends to identify her as a person of wealth who participated in the privileges of Hellenistic culture. Having her live in Tyre and identifying her as Syrophoenician also identifies her as a person who is among the traditional enemies of Israel. Living in the urban area and being among the more privileged, she is among those who take advantage of the farmers in regions like Galilee—where most of Jesus's ministry has been to this point.

A more intersectional analysis of the way Mark identifies this woman can help us see that issues other than simply being a Gentile are in play here. Other regional, social, and economic issues are more prominent than her identity as a generic Gentile that Jesus has to learn to include. This does not make what Jesus says to her easier to hear nor does it make her less rhetorically skillful. This does mean that we are to seek a meaning for this story that fits better with the chronology of Mark's story and his presentation of Jesus.[22]

In contrast, Leah had a different perspective after consulting with Amy Jill Levine, a highly respected Jewish New Testament scholar at Vanderbilt Divinity School, about this passage. In their conversation, Levine explained, "A model teacher is one who can learn. If Jesus has nothing to learn, and if he is not going to listen to others, then he is not a teacher, he is not in relationship, and he is not human."[23] Levine further noted what Jesus came to realize by the woman's response to his insult: "Jesus realizes that he can yield his own position of authority, his own job description, for the sake of someone who has no authority of her own. This yielding shows he cares about the people. And more—he listens to them. She, on the other hand, demonstrates Jesus's teaching: she persisted, cleverly, without elevating the violence. Everyone wins."[24]

Ultimately, this sermon invited the congregation on a journey into the complexities of Jesus's "fleshy" encounter with people who were in need of healing. The primary theological category of the sermon, then, was Christological in that it implicitly interrogated previously sanitized depictions of Jesus in favor of developing a deeper and more meaningful engagement with his humanity, and thus his role as divine healer and teacher.

CONCLUSION

As you should have noticed, the sermon "Jesus Sighed" was informed by—and spoke to—many aspects of embodiment. *Vulnerability* was an underlying theme of the sermon in that both the Syrophoenician woman and the Gentile man in the Decapolis were at a disadvantage because of their needs for healing. Yet, Jesus was also vulnerable when he decided to move beyond the safe zone of his home context and engage the very people who were oppressing the Jews (and would later crucify him). Leah used this theme of vulnerability to build up different levels of tension and release throughout the sermon and to create a willingness to be open on the part of the congregation.

"Outsider" bodies are the focal point of these stories in Mark Chapter 4. As a White, temporarily able-bodied, cisgender, female preacher, Leah occupies an intersection of race, gender, ability, and sexuality that might be considered a problem for some people or some congregations. Yet she fully entered into the biblical text with her own body to both incarnate as well as transcend socially inscribed divisions.

As you work on developing your own sense of embodiment, presence, and authenticity, you can experiment with different ways to interact with the biblical text and tell the story of who God is, what God does, and what difference it makes for us today. Your own body is an instrument that can give voice to the message of grace as well as corporally portray divine justice, healing, forgiveness, and love.

KEY POINTS IN THIS CHAPTER

1. Preaching is a performance, in the sense that it utilizes the voice and body to convey the message of the sermon.
2. Preachers with a solid sense of presence and authenticity are more likely to invite engagement and cultivate trust on the part of their listeners.
3. There are special considerations and challenges for preaching in historically marginalized bodies. However, preachers dealing with racism, sizeism, sexism, ableism, transphobia, and homophobia because of their own unique embodiment can engage dominant norms through Scripture and theology in order to creatively express God's work in the world.

QUESTIONS FOR DISCUSSION

1. Do you feel comfortable in your own body when preaching? Do you feel self-conscious about some aspects of your physical self? How do you process those feelings?
2. Is there a voice in your head that judges what you do, how you move, what your body looks like, or how your face is received by others? Whose voice do you hear, or what is the quality of the voice that is judging you and making you self-conscious? Discuss with seasoned preachers how they have dealt with self-consciousness around gesturing and spontaneity.
3. Watch a recording of one of your sermons with your preaching partner. Discuss where you felt the sermon in your body at any given moment. Where did it resonate in your body? In your knees? The back of your neck? The pit of your stomach? Somewhere just above the top of your head? Tuning into this energy can enable the preacher to consider how they can harness the energy of preaching and direct it in ways that serve the preaching moment and the proclamation of God's Word.
4. As you read in the section "Differing Exegetical Perspectives on Mark 7:24-37," Jerry and Leah disagreed in their interpretations of the text. What did you make of their differing exegetical conclusions? Discuss with your mentor, preaching partner, or colleagues the tension between different scholarly analyses of Scripture. How can preachers navigate these various interpretations?

FOR FURTHER READING

Teresa L. Fry Brown. *Delivering the Sermon.* In Elements of Preaching Series. O. Wesley Allen Jr., series editor. Minneapolis, MN: Fortress Press, 2008.
Jana Childers. *Performing the Word: Preaching as Theatre.* Nashville: Abingdon Press, 1998.
Karoline M. Lewis. *She: Five Keys to Unlock the Power of Women in Ministry.* Nashville: Abingdon Press, 2016.
Lisa L. Thompson. *Ingenuity: Preaching as an Outsider.* Nashville: Abingdon Press, 2018.
Richard Ward. *Speaking from the Heart: Preaching with Passion.* Nashville: Abingdon Press, 1992.
Richard Ward. *Speaking of the Holy: The Art of Communication in Preaching.* St. Louis: Chalice, 2001.

NOTES

1. Thomas H. Troeger and Leonora Tubbs Tisdale, *A Sermon Workbook: Exercises in the Art and Craft of Preaching* (Nashville: Abingdon Press, 2013), 71.
2. Richard Ward, *Speaking from the Heart: Preaching with Passion* (Nashville: Abingdon Press, 1992), 77.
3. Ronald J. Allen, *Preaching: An Essential Guide* (Nashville: Abingdon Press, 2002), 107.

4. Teresa L. Fry Brown, *Delivering the Sermon*. In Elements of Preaching Series, O. Wesley Allen Jr., series editor (Minneapolis, MN: Fortress Press, 2008), 60.
5. Karoline M. Lewis, *She: Five Keys to Unlock the Power of Women in Ministry* (Nashville: Abingdon Press, 2016), 47.
6. Ibid., 58.
7. Richard Ward, *Speaking of the Holy: The Art of Communication in Preaching* (St. Louis, MO: Chalice, 2001), 38–39.
8. John S. McClure, *Preaching Words: 144 Key Terms in Homiletics* (Louisville, KY: Westminster John Knox Press, 2007), 6.
9. Allen, 108.
10. Lewis, 61.
11. Brown, 33.
12. Lisa L. Thompson, *Ingenuity: Preaching as an Outsider* (Nashville: Abingdon Press, 2018), 18.
13. Sizeism is prejudice or discrimination against bodies because of their size or weight. Two books that can help counter these prejudices are: Linda Bacon, *Health at Every Size: The Surprising Truth about Your Weight* (Dallas, TX: BenBella Books, Inc., 2008), and Linda Bacon and Lucy Aphramor, *Body Respect: What Conventional Health Books Get Wrong, Leave Out, and Just Plain Fail to Understand about Weight* (Dallas, TX: BenBella Books, Inc., 2014).
14. Ableism is prejudice or discrimination against people with disabilities. Homiletician Kathy Black writes on preaching and disabilities in her book, *A Healing Homiletic: Preaching and Disability* (Nashville: Abingdon Press, 1996).
15. See: Emily Askew and O. Wesley Allen, *Beyond Heterosexism in the Pulpit* (Eugene, OR: Cascade Books, 2015).
16. For a collection of essays that address issues around racism, disability, ethnic perspectives, and LGBTQIA+ issues, see Christine Marie Smith, ed., *Preaching Justice: Ethnic and Cultural Perspectives* (Eugene, OR: Wipf & Stock, previously published by Pilgrim Press, 1998).
17. Thompson, 14–15.
18. Ibid., 18.
19. Ibid.
20. Ibid., 12.
21. Ibid., 18.
22. See M. Eugene Boring, *Mark: A Commentary*, New Testament Library (Louisville: Westminster John Knox, 2014), 206–14. And for a review of many options for interpreting this text, including from explicit perspective interpretations, see Warren Carter, *Mark*, Wisdom Commentary (Collegeville: Liturgical Press, 2019), 187–200.
23. Leah D. Schade, "Calling People Dogs: Juxtaposing Jesus and Trump," Patheos, September 9, 2018, accessed March 20, 2022, https://www.patheos.com/blogs/ecopreacher/2018/09/calling-people-dogs-juxtaposing-jesus-and-trump/.
24. Ibid.

26

Exploring the Space of Preaching

On-site and Online Sermons

In the previous chapter, we looked at some of the unique challenges that come with embodiment in preaching. In addition to the factors of one's own body that affect the delivery and reception of the sermon, there are also factors that include the physical or online space for delivering the sermon. In this chapter, we will explore the challenges and opportunities for the spaces of preaching—both in and out of the pulpit as well as with various digital platforms. We will also give an overview of the challenges of delivering a sermon either in real time or as a recording. The chapter will conclude with a sermon example that illustrates some key points about the performative aspects of preaching in Chapters 24, 25, and this chapter.

TO PULPIT OR NOT TO PULPIT?

Throughout this book, we have talked about the pulpit as the space where preaching happens, both metaphorically and physically. Pulpits come in all shapes, sizes, and materials. Some are made from either ornately carved or elegantly designed wood. Others are made of stone, fiberglass, or plastic. Some pulpits elevate the preacher high above the congregation. Others are simple reading desks placed at floor level. In whatever way the pulpit is designed, it can provide physical support for the delivery of a sermon, such as a place to hold a glass of water, cough drops, props, and, of course, the manuscript. Also, a pulpit can provide psychological support, in that it creates a feeling of safety, security, and at-home-ness for the preacher.

Yet the pulpit can also be restrictive, again, both physically and psychologically. Some pulpits are designed for people of a certain height and swallow up shorter preachers or obscure their view of the congregation. Even if using a step stool, the preacher's movement is limited in such a pulpit. Also, if the pulpit can be accessed only through stairs, preachers with mobility issues may find these steps prohibit entrance to the preaching space. Psychologically, some preachers find the pulpit to be too confining or restrictive. Or they may be uncomfortable with the implicit message of a pulpit that elevates them above the people, walls them off from the congregation, or creates a sense of separation in an event that is about connection and communication.

Depending on the architectural design of the church, as well as the receptiveness of the congregation, preaching does not need to be confined to the platform in the sanctuary designated for the sermon. You might experiment with preaching away from the pulpit in order to come into closer proximity to the congregation, to allow fuller use of your body in preaching, or to experience the freedom that can come with being in a more open space. Granted, some preachers (and congregants) may feel uncomfortable with a sermon preached away from the pulpit. But the preacher has the prerogative to try new things, especially when there are sound biblical or theological reasons for doing so. Also, the pulpit is not a zero-sum space. Some preachers use the pulpit on certain occasions (funerals or more solemn services, for example), but preach away from the pulpit on others (weddings, youth Sundays, or for sermons that require movement with the feet or other parts of the body).

Whether preaching in or out of the pulpit, however, remember that there is much that you can do with the space of preaching regardless of the physical container for it. "Space does not have to be descriptive, literal, or representational. Space can be magical and alchemical. Space can be transformative," advises theatre director Anne Bogart.[1] For example, if you look to the left as you describe seeing a tree in the distance, your listeners will be cued to conjure that tree in their mind. If you cradle your arms while talking about Mary holding the Christ child, the congregation may be able to imagine an infant there.

In other words, you can use whatever space you have to activate "theological imagination," which we discussed in Chapters 18 and 19. Use the space of preaching—as well as your own body and voice—to invite the listeners to create their own interpretive space for the sermon. "What ignites thought, association, and imagination?" asks Bogart. "Words can do it. Space can do it. Gesture can do it. Sound can do it. And best of all, it is a combination."[2]

PREACHING, MEDIA, AND TECHNOLOGY: POINTS TO CONSIDER

These principles of sparking theological imagination for the preacher and congregation are not limited to the physical space of the church sanctuary. Many ministers learned new ways to lead liturgy and preach online in the early spring of 2020 when the coronavirus emerged as a pandemic and congregations were forced to put a pause on worship in the physical space of the church. While some congregations had already been live streaming or videotaping their worship services, nearly all preachers and worship leaders were challenged to find new ways to proclaim God's Word and lead worship through electronically-mediated spaces.

This book was written in the midst of the COVID-19 crisis, which kept people away from church buildings and necessitated an online presence for preachers and worship leaders. During this time, the church underwent tremendous changes that will be rippling out for the foreseeable future. The COVID-19 pandemic marked a watershed moment where, from that time on, preachers were challenged to think about how their message will work for both in-person as well as online listeners.

Logistics for Preaching in Digitally Mediated Spaces[3]

Preaching, media, and technology is a vast and ever-changing field of study and practice. In this limited space, we can address this topic only in broad terms. Below we offer general suggestions, recommendations, and points to consider regarding the logistics for preaching within a screen-space.

There are currently three options for preaching online: 1) broadcasting or live streaming, 2) videoconferencing (such as Zoom or similar format), and 3) pre-recording for playback at another time. All three of these platforms have both synchronous and asynchronous aspects to consider. Asynchronous means that online content can be accessed at any time the viewer chooses. **Asynchronous worship** is either pre-recorded, edited together, and made available as a complete video; or it is recorded in real time (either through live stream or videoconferencing) and made available later. Synchronous means that the event is happening in real time. In **synchronous worship**, participants are required to participate at a specific day and time and on a specific link or website in which the content is being offered. Congregations that conduct worship via live stream offer the service in real time and simulcast it over a social media platform such as YouTube, Facebook Live, or the church's website. The service can also be recorded for later viewing, thus adding an asynchronous element.

Live stream and broadcast

The advantage of live streaming a worship service and sermon is that it allows those who cannot attend the service in person to participate in real time from wherever they are, as long as they have internet access. This is especially helpful for those who are physically unable to make their way to church, are home-centered, are traveling, or even moved away. Worshippers near and far can access the service, engage each other in real time through the chat function, and maintain a connection with the church and one another. Live streaming also allows for viewers to hear the music of the liturgy, see the sacred space of the sanctuary, and imagine themselves in the pews or chairs as the service is happening. However, live streaming requires significant financial investment in audiovisual and internet equipment, as well as people who know how to use these technologies and tools, which many congregations simply do not have access to or personnel to cover. As well, parishioners or church buildings with unreliable internet service may experience disruption if the signal is dropped.

Videoconferencing

Videoconferencing applications such as Zoom or Google Meet are another platform for preaching. In this venue, worshippers participate synchronously online by individually signing into a platform that allows everyone to see and hear each other in real time. Videoconferencing allows for a greater level of connection and intimacy since people can interact visually, aurally/orally, and through the chat feature that allows participants to type in their comments. Some preachers have found that they enjoy the opportunity to interact with their listeners during or immediately after the sermon or worship service in this platform. However, there are also challenges, such as the screen size limiting the preacher's range of motion and squeezing the embodied aspects of the sermon into a small, rectangular space. Also, as with live streaming, those using videoconferencing to participate in the worship service may experience interruptions in internet service.

Pre-recording

A third option for preaching online is pre-recording the sermon. There are several advantages to this mode of sermon delivery. For example, the preacher can do several "takes" of the sermon until they get one that is satisfactory. Pre-recording also allows for creativity in terms of location and use of illustrations. For example, in the sermon further on, "Composting Our Anger and Grief," Leah was able to record the sermon while preaching from her garden. Also, with basic video editing software, the sermon can utilize imagery, music, and stills of Scripture passages or other words, creating a multisensory experience. Once the sermon is complete, it can be made available to anyone on the internet, with options to pause the playback, share the link with others, and have access at any time or place. However, pre-recording takes more time than delivering the sermon live and can seem over-produced and less natural than preaching in real time. Pre-recording a sermon also requires planning ahead and precludes the possibility of responding to contemporary events in real time. In addition, some preachers dislike the challenges of recording a sermon, such as preaching apart from the flow of the liturgy, preaching to an empty room, or preaching to a camera. With practice, however, these unique aspects of pre-recording a sermon can become less awkward and more comfortable.

Regardless of what platforms preachers may use, many congregations have realized the importance of investing in quality audiovisual equipment so that viewers can both see and hear the recording as clearly as possible. During the pandemic when the world was in lockdown to curb the spread of the coronavirus, preachers discovered that they could deliver a sermon from virtually any location. Some preached from their church's empty sanctuary. Others preached from their living rooms or other locations within their homes. Still others experimented with preaching from outdoor locations. No matter where the sermon is delivered, however, preachers must consider the literal framing of their sermon within an electronic screen and the recording and playback of the audio. Below are some suggestions for ensuring a high-quality experience for preaching in a digital platform.

CHECKLIST FOR PREACHING IN A DIGITAL PLATFORM

- Make sure the camera is neither too far away nor too close. It should be placed mid-distance so that viewers can see your facial expressions and hand motions.
- The camara should be in a horizontal orientation rather than vertical.
- Position the camera at eye level so that you're neither "preaching down" nor "preaching up" to the viewer.
- The recording of the sermon must have clear audio with ample volume.
- There must be sufficient lighting to be able to see the preacher.
- Remember that the recording of the sermon could be heard by anyone at any time who has no idea about your congregational context. So, be sure to explain "insider information," doctrinal shorthand or code language (see Chapter 8, "Theology and Theological Claims"), cultural or locational references, or recent happenings that a live, in-person local audience would already know, so that these are not lost on those viewing outside the original time and place of the preaching moment.

Hybrid On-site/Online Worship and Preaching

In a lecture for an online workshop on "What's Next in Digital Worship?" hosted by New Brunswick Theological Seminary in 2021, technology and media specialist Jason Moore pointed out the challenges of preaching in a hybrid on-site/online space.[4] In this scenario, some worshippers are live in the sanctuary while some are watching on-screen either live or as a recording. Moore likened this to the difference between reading a book compared with watching the film version of the story. While conventional wisdom holds that the book is usually better than the film, Moore stresses that without the film, far less people would ever engage the story. Similarly, preachers have an opportunity to share the biblical story through online worship and preaching with people who would otherwise never step foot in a church.

With this dual audience in mind, it is important to create worship experiences that will translate to both on-site and online worshippers. It's like a sports event, which can be watched in person or at home: the action on the field is the same, but there are two totally different experiences for the viewers in the stands versus the viewers watching on-screen. Similarly, we must remember that there are two different congregations that need to be engaged. Says Moore, "We don't want *watchers*, we want *worshippers*. We don't want *viewers*, we want *participants*."[5] Below are questions to ask to gauge the effectiveness of the worship experience for both online and on-site congregations.

AUDITING YOUR HYBRID ON-SITE/ONLINE WORSHIP AND PREACHING PRACTICES

For congregations that utilize both in-person and online modes of worship, technology and media specialist Jason Moore suggests putting together a worship team with advocates from both perspectives.[1] Here are questions to ask that can help the team "audit" the worship experiences and preaching for both sets of worshippers:

1. What is the purpose of this aspect of worship and preaching, and does it translate to both audiences?
2. Does this moment belong in both the in-person and online experience?
3. Is there a participatory or interactive way of doing this?
4. Is this part of the service too short or too long for either audience?
5. For in-person, how does this translate on-screen, and do we need an alternative moment? For online, how does this translate on-site, and do we need an alternative moment?
6. Does this need additional contextualization for either audience?
7. How will a first-time worshipper, either in-person or online, receive this?

NOTE

1. Jason Moore, "Both/And: Maximizing Hybrid Worship Experiences for Online and In-Person Audiences," New Brunswick Theological Seminary, March 9, 2021, https://nbts.edu/whats-next-digital-worship/, accessed January 2, 2022.

Hybrid on-site/online worship presents special challenges for the preacher. For instance, we must ask, where should we focus as we preach? If we preach to the camera, we give the impression to the congregation in the sanctuary that they are merely a "studio audience." If we preach to the congregation in the sanctuary, those who watch online may feel as if they are just "overhearing" the sermon. "We want to create worship experiences where no one feels like an afterthought," says Moore.[6] Here are some recommendations for navigating and accommodating these competing demands in hybrid worship and preaching:

- Properly prepare. Think through every aspect of the service and sermon and how it might be experienced by both the in-person and online worshipper.
- Remember that you do not have a captive audience online and that they judge more harshly than an in-person audience. While an in-person audience may tolerate and sit through a boring sermon, the online worshipper will click off if they are not engaged.
- Consolidate the liturgy and sermon. Keep it tight, focused, and engaging.
- If preaching to the in-person congregation, plan intentional moments where you address those viewing at home or elsewhere. If live streaming, invite them to greet one another in the online chat feature, for example. Or simply name that God's Word comes to us no matter where we are—the sanctuary, the kitchen table, a hotel room, even walking in the park.
- Consider creating separate worship services—one for the in-person worshipper and one for the online worshipper. For example, record the in-person service and then create a version that edits out the parts that do not translate well onscreen, such as passing the peace, announcements, collecting the offering, and so on. Offer this "repurposed" worship service later in the day for online worshippers.
- Alternatively, show pictures of congregational actions, people, or church architectural features during times in the worship service that do not translate well for the online worshipper.
- Consider pulling out just the sermon from the worship service and creating a separate video that can be shared online.

USING TECHNOLOGY AND SCREENS FOR PREACHING IN THE WORSHIP SPACE

In the late 1970s and early 1980s, it was rare to see large screens in houses of worship other than mega-churches seating thousands of people. Sound systems, stage lighting, and video projection equipment enabled congregants to experience highly produced worship and to see close-ups of the preacher on massive screens. As the costs of equipment became more affordable in the 1990s and 2000s, more churches began investing in sound equipment, projectors, and screens to enhance the worship service.

Today, it's not unusual to see flat screen video displays mounted in the chancel area of the sanctuary, some of which compete in size and grandeur with the cross and liturgical art in that same space. Some churches use screens to display announcements, show artwork or short videos, and even project the entire written liturgy complete with hymns, prayers, and responsive readings. This not only reduces the need for printed bulletins, it creates a shared experience of everyone looking in the same place, thus enhancing a sense of community. Yet, some churches reject the use of any screens in worship and, in terms of electronic equipment, allow nothing more than sound systems.

There are many advantages to using a video display in preaching. Creating video slides with large words and images can help listeners to grasp ideas quickly. Video displays with stimulating content can grab the attention of listeners and illustrate concepts the preacher is trying to communicate. Such visual enhancements can increase retention, aid those who are visual learners, and add "pizzazz" to a sermon. Also, for preachers in bilingual congregations, sermon notes can be displayed in both languages.

However, there are risks with misusing, overusing, or underusing video displays in preaching. First, technology changes rapidly and can quickly become outdated; this means added costs for updating the equipment on a regular basis. Second, there can be a steep learning curve for understanding how to use the equipment effectively to create quality content for worship. Third, it can be difficult to recruit, train, and retain volunteers to run the equipment. Responsibility for creating audio-visual content may fall to the pastor, who may or may not welcome this added task in their already full schedule. Finally, it is sometimes the case that the audio-visual content generated is inappropriate, incongruous, distracting, difficult to see, or otherwise detrimental to the sermon.

As media and technology become increasingly ubiquitous in Christian worship, preachers will undoubtedly need to put some thought into how they use this equipment in their sermons, if they choose to do so. This is especially the case for the current generation of young worshippers raised as "digital natives" who have come to expect high-quality technology to be part of their worship experience. The challenge is to use technology and audiovisual displays effectively so that the content has a positive and enhancing effect for the sermon and worship. Otherwise, it becomes a distraction or points only to itself rather than serving the larger purpose of giving glory to God.

Granted, all of these questions and considerations about worship and preaching can feel overwhelming. However, if we see this as an opportunity for engaging new audiences with the Word of God, we can see the numerous possibilities for bringing the gospel to people in new and innovative ways. Also, if we help to frame these questions theologically in terms of ecclesiology (what it means to be the church), discipleship (what it means to follow Jesus Christ), ethics (what it means to live out our faith), and worship (what it means to gather in praise of God), we can help our congregations think deeply and robustly about the challenges of worship and preaching in the ever-changing technological landscape of our time.[7]

SERMON: COMPOSTING OUR ANGER AND GRIEF—LUKE 13:1-9

This sermon was preached from Leah's backyard and recorded for an online worship service for Lexington Theological Seminary on June 21, 2021. The service was designed with the seminary's Green Task Force and focused on a theme of caring for God's Creation.

The sermon mentions the names of three people who were murdered in 2020. Those individuals were unarmed, Black, and killed either by police or White vigilantes. The sermon also mentions the "presidential invasion of St. John's Episcopal Church." This is in reference to former president Trump marching unannounced and uninvited to stand holding a Bible in front of the church for a propaganda photograph, the way having been cleared of protestors with tear gas and rubber bullets.

EXERCISE

Analyzing the Sermon "Composting Our Anger and Grief"

1. As you read the sermon, underline the sentences that are Theological Claims. Star the sentence that you believe is the Central Claim of the sermon.
2. After you finish reading the sermon, write down what you think was the Central Question powering the sermon. Also, write down what you think was the Central Purpose of the sermon.
3. Which one of the forms did you detect Leah using in this sermon—Four Pages, Motion Pictures, Homiletical Plot, or Expository/Puritan Plain Style?

At the end of the section, you'll see the Central Question, Central Claim, and Central Purpose that Leah wrote down for this sermon. See how yours compared with hers. You'll also see which sermon form she used.

This sermon was delivered using a manuscript written in sense lines, but the stand holding the papers was off-screen, and Leah had memorized many parts of it to be able to look at the camera when delivering the sermon. You can watch the video at https://www.youtube.com/watch?v=6vbNw9IK0Rw as you follow along with the manuscript below. In the notes for each section, you'll see how this sermon illustrates many of the points made in this chapter and the previous one about sermon delivery, voice, and embodiment.

Paragraph 1

A couple weeks ago, I dug up my garden to prepare for planting.
I grabbed my shovel and hoe and dug into the weeds that had started to take root.
Then I sorted through the compost that was in our bin.
It's a messy, gross job,
but I spread it over the soil and worked it into the garden.
It's hard work breaking up all those clumps of soil.

Paragraph 2
But I'll let you in on a little secret.
For me, digging up the garden is therapy.
We might say that gardening is part of my "anger management program."

[Leah asked her daughter to record this sermon so that the camera could follow her movements in this part of the sermon as she dug up the soil and showed the compost in the bin. They practiced filming the sermon first so that her daughter could see what she would need to do with the camera at different parts of the sermon.]

Paragraph 3
Remember Mr. Rogers' song,
[Singing:]
"What do you do with the mad that you feel,
when you feel so mad you could bite?
When the whole wide world seems oh so wrong,
and nothing you do seems very right?"[8]
Well, this is one of the things I do—I work it all into the dirt.

[One of the things preachers can do with their voices during a sermon is sing a verse of a song, if they feel comfortable doing so. In paragraph 3, Leah sings the first verse of a well-known song by Fred Rogers to illustrate her point about feeling anger.]

Paragraph 4
Last year, I had a lot to be angry about.
I was angry about the murders of George Floyd and Breonna Taylor and Ahmad Arbery.
I was angry about what happened to those who protested the murders.
The police brutality.
The presidential invasion of St. John's Episcopal Church.
The growing wave of White Christian nationalism.
All of that got worked into the garden last year.

Paragraph 5
And I was angry about what was happening with the pandemic.
Certain leaders lying about the virus, downplaying the severity.
All the conspiracy theories and disinformation.
This year, when I worked the shovel and the hoe,
I thought of the millions of people who got sick,
the hundreds of thousands of people who died.
And their families who are in mourning.
It didn't have to be this bad.
Especially in communities of color that have been deliberately under-resourced in health care infrastructure for decades.
All of this got worked into the garden as well.

Paragraph 6
I also have to admit,
my personal anger toward certain people in my life
is somewhere in this garden as well.
My frustration, the mad that I feel, my grief—
all of it is somewhere in this soil.

[Notice Leah's use of her hands during this part of the sermon. In addition to wearing gardening gloves and holding onto the shovel, she uses them to gesture to the garden when she explains about working her anger into the soil.]

Paragraph 7
One of the things I've come to appreciate about Jesus's parables
is the way he uses imagery from his agrarian culture to teach spiritual truths.
Like the parable about the fruitless tree in Luke 13:1-9.
While talking to the crowds,
he gets into a discussion with them about why bad things happen to people.
Apparently, some of them think that misfortune and accidents are a result of sin—
even when it's obvious that sometimes accidents just happen.
Or sometimes people die because of political violence through no fault of their own.
So Jesus tells them this parable about a king who wants to cut down a tree
because it won't bear fruit.

Paragraph 8
The king is judge and jury over this tree and is ready to sentence it to death.
The gardener, however, pleads with him to give it another year.
He tells the king that he'll dig around the soil and work in fertilizer.
Just like I do with my garden.
Just like Jesus's listeners did with their plots of soil and vineyards.

[In paragraphs 7 and 8, Leah uses her hand to gesture a cutting motion about the tree and uses her body to act out pleading. In paragraph 8, she utilizes a pause to signal a shift from the biblical text to the connection to her own garden.]

Paragraph 9
Jesus is like that gardener,
pleading with us to relent from our harsh judgments against people
and writing them off as unworthy.
His parable challenges me, challenges the church,
to rethink our approach to the people and the problems that frustrate us.

Paragraph 10
When I dug through this soil last year,
it occurred to me that some of the things I was angry about
were no longer a problem.
And the same thing happened this year.
Those things don't go away.
All of that anger and grief is still in the soil.
But some of the people who ticked me off have shifted in their approach to me,
because, frankly, I shifted in my approach to them.

[Notice how Leah uses her facial expressions to animate this part of the sermon. When talking about the shift in the people who angered her, she raises her eyebrows. When she admits her own shift, she looks up and away, signifying realization and confession.]

Paragraph 11
So even though all of that anger and grief is in the soil,
this compost is working in ways I'm not always seeing.
It became the fertilizer for the seeds and plants I put into the ground.
This squash plant is absorbing the nutrients from the composting I've worked into the soil over the past few years.
God is transforming that rotting, smelly compost
into food that will sustain me and my family.

Paragraph 12

Also, I used my anger about White Christian nationalism
for the energy to create the Clergy Emergency League in the summer of 2020
to support pastors in their prophetic ministry.[9]
We now have a network of more than 2,500 clergy—a fruitful harvest!

[Leah uses both her hands and her full body to gesture toward the garden, including kneeling down beside a plant, which serves as an illustration for the sermon's message of God transforming anger and grief into something life-giving.]

Paragraph 13

That's what the gardener hopes will happen in this parable,
that we'll see possibility instead of hopelessness.
Of course, we don't know the end of the story.
The parable leaves us with questions.
Will the king listen to the wisdom of the gardener and learn patience?
Will he trust the gardener?
Or will he insist on his own way and order the gardener to chop down the tree?

Paragraph 14

Notice, the tree wasn't dying.
It just wasn't getting the nutrients it needed to produce fruit.
If the king has the tree chopped down,
he'll lose the chance for the fruit to appear.
What a lost opportunity that would be.

[In paragraph 13, Leah uses the hoe in a chopping motion to indicate chopping down the tree. At the end of paragraph 14, notice the use of the pause right before and right after the last sentence to emphasize the significance of her point about the lost opportunity.]

Paragraph 15

Jesus is urging us to reconsider our approach,
our attitude, our mindset.
The gardener is standing there with the shovel and hoe inviting us to dig in,
to do the hard work that can lead to transformation,
to fruitfulness.

Paragraph 16

As I was composting, digging, and turning over the soil,
turning over all these thoughts in my mind,
I remembered a line from the hymn, "Come, Ye Disconsolate":
[Sing:] "Earth has no sorrow that heaven cannot heal."[10]

[The soil takes center stage as Leah positions the shovel, spade side up, to underscore the words "dig in." Then she reenacts the moment of "turning over" both the thoughts in her head and the soil in the garden. This leads to another song, this time a line from a hymn, thus employing the technique of bookending by singing at the beginning and end of the sermon.]

Paragraph 17

I invite you to put your hands in some soil,
to work your anger and grief into the dirt.
I invite you to connect with the Ground of All Being,
the ground that God created.

If you don't have a garden,
maybe you have a small yard
where you can dig into the soil and plant some flowers or vegetables.
Don't have a small yard?
Maybe you have a window
where you can place a pot of soil and plant a few seeds.
If you don't have a place to plant a few seeds,
maybe you can find a nearby park where you put your feet on the ground
and root yourself into the Earth.

Paragraph 18
And there, you can give your anger and your grief over to the soil.
Allow the Gardener to compost the mad that you feel,
your frustration, your deep sadness.
"Earth has no sorrow that heaven cannot heal."
Amen.

[In this last part of the sermon, the camera shows Leah's feet and then her hands illustrating the idea of rooting into the Earth as well as God composting "the mad that you feel." The final paragraph ties together the first song with the hymn, leading to a feeling of completion at the end of the sermon.]

CENTRAL QUESTION, CENTRAL CLAIM, CENTRAL PURPOSE, AND SERMON FORM FOR "COMPOSTING OUR ANGER AND GRIEF"

In the exercise above, we invited you to analyze the sermon in order to find out what you think was the Central Question, Central Claim, and Central Purpose of the sermon, as well as the sermon form. Here is what Leah wrote. How do they compare with your answers?

Central Question. How can we deal with the enormous feelings of anger, frustration, and grief that accompany injustice, and what insights can Jesus's parable about the fruitless tree offer us for processing those emotions?

Central Claim. Jesus, like the gardener in Luke's parable, invites us to "compost" our anger and grief so that God can transform them into fruitfulness.

Central Purpose. This sermon invites the listener to give their anger and grief over to God by connecting with God's Earth and allowing their negative feelings to be used for good.

Sermon Form. This sermon's form was Four Pages with an added conclusion. Paragraphs 1 through 6 were "bad news in the world." Paragraphs 7 through 9 were "bad news in the biblical text." Paragraphs 10 through 12 were "good news in the world." Paragraphs 13 through 15 were "good news in the text." Paragraphs 16 through 18 make up the conclusion.

CONCLUSION

The sermon "Composting Our Anger and Grief" is just one example of utilizing space in a creative way for a prerecorded sermon. You may have noticed the features, noises, and movements of Leah's neighborhood while she was preaching—her neighbor's vehicle parked in the driveway, a dog barking, a person walking along the sidewalk. While these can be distracting, they also added to the authenticity of the sermon being preached in the backyard of a community neighborhood.

Leah could have just as easily preached this same sermon in the sanctuary of a church. She could have brought the hoe and shovel with her and used them as props for the sermon in the same way she did in her yard. While she wouldn't have had the actual compost bin or the plants in the garden, she could have invited the congregation to imagine her backyard and those features by using descriptive words that engaged the senses.

You also may have noticed that Leah made references to "political" issues of that time. Some preachers are hesitant to address or even mention current events in a sermon for fear of getting pushback from their congregations. Leah has written about preaching on contemporary issues in her book *Preaching in the Purple Zone* and will write more about preaching on social issues in a forthcoming book.

KEY POINTS IN THIS CHAPTER

1. Preachers have options for using the pulpit or moving away from the pulpit to deliver their sermons. They must consider the challenges and opportunities of both spaces.
2. When preaching in digitally-mediated spaces, preachers will have to think about the benefits and drawbacks when live streaming, videoconferencing, or pre-recording, as well as dual challenges for hybrid on-site and online worship services.
3. Preachers need to consider the logistics of asynchronous worship, synchronous worship, or a hybrid of both types of worship experiences.
4. While the demands of preaching in online or hybrid settings can be formidable, there are also numerous creative possibilities to use as well. With preparation, practice, and attention to the needs of both in-person and digital worshippers, preachers and worship leaders can design sermons and liturgies that engage both congregations.

QUESTIONS FOR DISCUSSION

1. Talk with your preaching mentor or group about their preference for using the pulpit to preach or delivering the sermon away from the pulpit. Have they ever tried preaching in a different space? What was it like for them? How does their congregation respond when they preach from a different space?
2. Discuss with preaching colleagues how their congregations handle online and/or on-site worship and preaching. What do they find frustrating? What do they find liberating? How do they navigate the technological issues, as well as the need for personnel to work with this aspect of ministry? Share with one another your "best practices" and "tips and tricks" for hybrid worship and preaching.
3. When it comes to preaching in physical and/or online spaces, what are ways in which our bodies and voices either "expand" or "shrink" in any given space? What might be going on both internally and externally that impinges on our volume and timbre, embodiment and presence?

FOR FURTHER READING

Teresa L. Fry Brown. *Delivering the Sermon.* In Elements of Preaching Series. O. Wesley Allen Jr., series editor. Minneapolis, MN: Fortress Press, 2008.

Jana Childers. *Performing the Word: Preaching as Theatre.* Nashville: Abingdon Press, 1998.

NOTES

1. Anne Bogart, *And Then, You Act: Making Art in an Unpredictable World* (New York: Routledge, 2007), 91.
2. Ibid.

3. Thanks to the Rev. Dr. Casey Sigmon, Assistant Professor in Preaching and Worship, and Director of Contextual Education at St. Paul School of Theology, for sharing her lecture, "Preaching, Media, and Technology: Best Practices," Spring 2021.

4. Jason Moore, "Both/And: Maximizing Hybrid Worship Experiences for Online and In-Person Audiences," New Brunswick Theological Seminary, March 9, 2021, accessed January 2, 2022, https://nbts.edu/whats-next-digital-worship/.

5. Ibid.

6. Ibid.

7. See Appendix D, "Theological Categories," for other ways you might be able to frame online worship theologically.

8. "What Do You Do with the Mad That You Feel?" was a song written and sung by PBS personality Fred Rogers in the children's television program *Mister Rogers' Neighborhood.* Rogers recited the song in testimony before the US Senate in 1969, early in the funding process of PBS, during an exchange with Sen. John Pastore. The song first appeared on the program in 1968.

9. https://www.clergyemergencyleague.com/.

10. "Come, Ye Disconsolate," Text: Thomas Moore, 1816, adapt. Thomas Hastings, 1831; Music: Samuel Webbe Sr., 1792. Public domain.

Afterword

Now that you've come to the end of this *Introduction to Preaching*, we hope that you feel equipped to begin on your own path of preaching! You've been introduced to tools for interpreting Scripture. You've learned how to identify and write Theological Claims. And you've practiced using the Central Question, the Central Claim, and the Central Purpose to provide the drive, direction, and destination for your sermons.

You've also experimented with exercises for activating "theological imagination" that spark creativity for writing sermons. And we've given you an overview of different sermon forms to help you structure your preaching as well as how to effectively begin, thread through, and end your sermon. In the last part of the book, we offered you guidance on sermon delivery and performance so that you can think about how to use your voice and body for preaching. Our goal in this preaching textbook has been to give you the tools for creating sermons that connect the Scripture to your listeners' context, connect Theological Claims to their lives, and help them experience the gospel in a way that clearly communicates God's love for them and for the world.

MULTIPLE PATHS OF PREACHING

After learning the method of the Central Question, Central Claim, and Central Purpose, one of our students expressed some frustration. "Sometimes I get the inspiration for a sermon, and I just want to write it out. But having to come up with the Central Statements *first* throws me off. Aren't there different ways to write a sermon?"

The answer is, yes! There are *many* different ways of writing a sermon! As we stated in the Introduction, the Central Question, Central Claim, Central Purpose method is just one way that a preacher can use for sermon preparation; but it is not the *only* path of preaching. You may wake up one morning with a sermon idea after having pondered a biblical passage or a particular theme, topic, or idea as you were falling asleep. If that happens, by all means, capture your thoughts and write them down. When the Spirit gifts you with inspiration, ride that wave! You can then use the Central Statements to ensure that your biblical exegesis is sound, your Theological Claim is appropriate, and your sermon is coherent and easy for the listeners to follow. In other words, while we gave you a step-by-step process, these tools can be used in any order and for any path of preaching.

WORDS OF ENCOURAGEMENT FOR LEARNING HOW TO PREACH

Keep in mind that whenever you're learning something new, it will feel cumbersome and awkward at first. Just like learning how to cook, or learning to play basketball, or learning to play a musical instrument, the process of learning how to preach might feel tedious at first. New cooks break a lot of yolks when learning to flip an egg before they get the hang of it. The basketball feels heavy and unwieldy when first trying to dribble and throw the ball into that tiny hoop. Musicians sometimes grow weary of learning scales and rudiments, much less the mechanics of music theory. But over time, the brain develops solid neural pathways for the new skills and the body develops "muscle memory" so that practicing culinary arts, or a sport, or a musical instrument becomes second nature.

Similarly, there are a lot of "moving parts" in preaching that need to be integrated so that a cohesive, coherent, and compelling sermon can emerge. Consulting biblical commentaries may feel cumbersome at first. Thinking about the theology of a biblical text and a sermon might seem tedious at times. You may grow weary of going through the steps of the Central Question, Central Claim, and Central Purpose. However, the more you practice the method, the easier it will become and the more seamless it will feel. The path of preaching will become well-traversed in your brain, and your "muscle memory" for preaching will come to feel like second nature.

"I SOLEMNLY URGE YOU: PROCLAIM THE MESSAGE." 2 TIM 4:1-2

God needs preachers to raise their voices for proclaiming the Good News of Jesus Christ. This involves aspects of teaching, pastoral care, ethics, calling out injustice, advocating for the vulnerable, and working with our congregations and communities using all of our skills to proclaim and work towards the Realm of God. As you are answering the call to preach, be assured that God is appointing you and lifting you up to do this work in your own unique way, with your own unique gifts, in your own unique context. You are being sent as a powerful and visible sign to the world that God is still at work.

As you are studying the Word of God, grappling with the theological implications of a cross-shaped love that has come into the world, and delivering sermons that proclaim who God is, what God does, and what this means for us today, you will be challenged and blessed. The challenges will mean you will need to be brave and bold, building bridges across divides of culture and race, across chasms of disability and privilege, and across the red-blue divides of politics in order to proclaim God's vision of justice, healing, and peace. The blessings mean that you get to catch a vision—and share that vision in the most compelling way possible—of the Realm of God, which has come near to you, your congregation, your community, and all of Creation.

We pray that this *Introduction to Preaching* will both challenge and bless you in that task.

Appendix A

How to Use Biblical Resources for Exegesis; List of Recommended Commentaries

Biblical commentaries offer interpretations of a given biblical book. Some work on sections of the text, while others give attention to nearly every word. They intend to help readers understand the text, but they can have different emphases and concerns. It is important, then, to think about what purpose you have in mind when you choose commentaries. Our goal is to interpret biblical texts in their original contexts in a way that helps make them relevant today. So the commentaries recommended here will be those that help in that process.

HOW TO JUDGE THE VALUE OF A BIBLE DICTIONARY

Even before turning to commentaries, you may want to read the entry on the biblical book you are studying in a Bible dictionary. As with all kinds of materials, some Bible dictionaries are better than others. Many popular Bible dictionaries fail to take the scholarship of the last hundred years into account. Among the few Bible dictionaries that are good, the following stand out: The *Harper/Collins Bible Dictionary* and the *Mercer Bible Dictionary* are good one-volume Bible dictionaries. The most recent edition of *Eerdmans Dictionary of the Bible* is also quite useful. The best multiple-volume Bible dictionaries are the *New Interpreter's Dictionary of the Bible* and the *Anchor Bible Dictionary*. Other dictionaries that focus on specific parts of the Bible can also be useful (for example, the *Dictionary of Jesus and the Gospels*).

One way to judge the value of a Bible dictionary is to see if the entries are signed. At the end of each entry, you will find the name or initials of the person who wrote that piece. You can then look them up in the front of the book to see who they are and where they teach or what they do. This information helps you evaluate what the person says in their entry; it helps you to know whether they are really experts in the subject they are telling you about in the entry. If a Bible dictionary does not identify the authors of entries in this way, it usually means the entries are not written by experts on the topic, but rather by someone (perhaps on an editorial staff) who may or may not be qualified to speak about the subject. Dictionaries that do not identify the authors of entries are not good sources. Always use Bible dictionaries that identify who wrote each entry.

HOW TO JUDGE THE VALUE OF A BIBLICAL COMMENTARY

There are many commentary series that do not appear in the list below. Some of these may be very good and others less valuable. The list that follows includes series that are found fairly widely. The series that are listed here engage in critical readings of the biblical texts; in other words, readings that employ the kinds of analytical tools that scholars use. To do exegesis (getting to the meaning the original audience would have understood) you should use commentaries that focus on what the biblical books meant in their original setting, rather than using commentaries that give primary attention to what a text tells people to do today. It is important to understand the text in its original context before making any contemporary use of it.

As you begin study of a passage (sometimes called a pericope), you should start with the more accessible commentaries and move to the more technical. The more accessible commentaries will introduce you to the questions, issues, and problems involved with understanding a particular text. But they will usually simply give you the conclusions the author of that particular commentary reaches on the meaning of a particular text or issue. As you move to more detailed commentaries, these will give arguments for the position the author takes on a text or an issue. The more detailed and technical a commentary is, the more it will be engaged with the disputes about the meanings of specific things in your passage. They might engage in a long discussion of the meaning of a word in first-century Greek or a Hebrew word in the wisdom tradition in the fourth century BCE, for example. They also engage larger questions such as whether the categories Paul uses to discuss an issue are from philosophers or from rabbis. Or they might discuss what ideas another author is rejecting. The less technical commentaries will assume answers to these questions without letting you know why they chose that option; they may not even hint that there is a question about the matter. So, the more accessible commentaries are the place to begin, but you will need to move to more detailed commentaries to engage a text in more depth and detail.

COMMENTARIES GROUPED BY LEVEL OF ACCESSIBILITY

Very accessible and brief
Augsburg Commentary on the New Testament (most of these are more than twenty years old)
Westminster Bible Companion

Accessible but more lengthy
Abingdon New Testament Commentaries
Abingdon Old Testament Commentaries
Interpretation
New Cambridge Bible Commentary
Reading the New Testament
The New Testament in Context
New International Biblical Commentary (many, but not all, of these are from fairly conservative writers)

More lengthy and demanding, but still accessible to many readers
New Interpreter's Bible
New Testament Library
Old Testament Library
Sacra Pagina
Berit Olam

More demanding, in the sense that they are longer and expect the reader to know more before beginning to use them
Anchor Bible Commentary
Word Bible Commentary (these are written mostly by conservative authors; in the Old Testament volumes, this sometimes influences some of the critical and interpretive decisions)
New International Commentary on the New Testament
New International Commentary on the Old Testament
Paideia

The following expect you to know Greek or Hebrew and to be ready to enter the conversation about issues at the level of scholars. While you will not be an expert, you may be able to follow the arguments (at least some of them) in these commentaries after you have worked through the less detailed and technical commentaries above.

International Critical Commentary
New International Greek Testament Commentary
Hermeneia

SERIES TO AVOID WHEN DOING EXEGESIS

Most of all the old commentaries that are free online (including, for example, Matthew Henry, Spurgeon, etc.). They are free because they are very old, most more than two hundred years old. They do not reflect the advances in biblical studies from the last two hundred years.

All commentaries by William Barclay. Some of the historical information in these commentaries is wrong, and the exegetical work often does not set the passage in its original setting.

New Testament for Everyone. These are done by a good scholar but are not detailed enough for exegetical work.

Old Testament for Everyone. These are done by a good scholar but are not detailed enough for exegetical work.

(Old) Interpreter's Bible. The "Exposition" is particularly unrelated to the exegesis.

NIV application series. There are multiple types of these, but none focus on the meaning of the text in its original setting.

Tyndale New Testament Commentary. These commentaries are too short to give the reasons for the interpretations they give.

Appendix B

Genres in the Bible Quick Reference Guide

Here is a list of the different types of genre categories in the Bible and the books that fit each genre. Keep in mind that these are general categories that broadly describe the genre of the book. In fact, there can be more than one genre within any given book. Be sure to consult a good Bible dictionary or biblical commentaries when determining the genre of a pericope within a biblical text.

GENRES IN HEBREW SCRIPTURES

Primarily legend and sacred stories
Genesis
Exodus
Numbers
Deuteronomy
Ruth
Esther
Daniel (parts of)

Laws
Leviticus
Deuteronomy (parts of)

Theological narratives/histories
Joshua
Judges
1 and 2 Samuel
1 and 2 Kings
1 and 2 Chronicles
Ezra
Nehemiah

Poetry
Psalms
Song of Solomon

Wisdom literature
Job
Proverbs
Ecclesiastes

Prophetic literature
Isaiah
Jeremiah
Lamentations
Ezekiel
Daniel
Hosea
Joel
Amos
Obadiah
Jonah
Micah
Nahum
Habbakuk
Zephaniah
Haggai
Zechariah
Malachi

Apocalypse
Daniel (parts of)

GENRES IN CHRISTIAN SCRIPTURES

Theological ancient biography
Gospel of Matthew
Gospel of Mark
Gospel of Luke
Gospel of John

Theological narrative/history
Acts of the Apostles

Letters
Romans
1 and 2 Corinthians
Galatians
Ephesians
Philippians
Colossians
1 and 2 Thessalonians
1 and 2 Timothy
Titus
Philemon
Hebrews
James
1 and 2 Peter
1, 2, and 3 John
Jude

Apocalypse
Revelation

Appendix C

Exegesis Guide Chart

Use the chart on the next page to help you organize the information you gather from reading Bible dictionaries and biblical commentaries to determine your interpretation of the biblical text.

For texts that address situations directly, such as the oracles of prophets in the Hebrew Scriptures and Paul's letters in the Christian Scriptures, we recommend starting with the Occasional Exigence and Response to determine what concerns of the community the author is addressing. That leads to the Literary Exigence and Response, where we look at the overall structure of the document and this pericope's place in the flow of the argument.

For genres such as narratives, histories, wisdom literature, poetry, and apocalyptic literature, it's best to start with Literary Exigence and Response to see how the pericope fits into the text as a whole. Then move to Occasional Exigence and Response to determine what historical factors might be informing the author's intent in writing the story or historical narrative, for example.

Theological Exigence is the theological question or issue that the occasional problem or issue raised. As part of this, you must determine the theological category(ies) that best fits this text (see Appendix D). The Theological Response is what the author says that this theological question shows about why the readers should act in a particular way or what they should believe in the face of the issue(s) raised.

Contemporary Exigence seeks creative analogies between the ancient situations the texts addressed and the world that we live in. We think about what kind(s) of present-day issue(s) or situation(s) might be parallel to the Theological Exigence that the passage raises. We are not looking for the very same problem or question, but rather matters in our churches that seem to grow out of the same theological questions and occasional (on the ground, practical) quandaries. Contemporary Response looks to how preachers can draw on the Theological Response (that is shaped by the Occasional and Literary Response) to address those analogous issues in their churches or society. It asks how the understanding of the faith that shaped the specific response in the ancient situation can speak to and shape what the church today does and believes.

Exegesis Guide Chart

	Primary Exigence	Primary Response
Occasional Historically, what's happening "on the ground"? What specific things were going on for believers at the time?		
Literary Within the text itself, what has happened in the flow of the written document that leads to this passage? How does this pericope fit with and function within the rest of the document?		
Theological What is the theological category (see Appendix D)? What is the theological question or issue that the occasional problem or issue raised? What aspect of faith is being addressed? How does the author think the reader should think or act in response to this issue?		
Contemporary What are creative analogies between the ancient situations the texts addressed and the world we live in? What kinds of present-day issues or situations might be parallel to the Theological Exigence that the passage raises?		

Appendix D

Theological Categories

When determining the Theological Exigence and Response in your Exegesis Guide Chart, and when doing a theological analysis of the biblical passage, it's helpful to figure out the category of the text's theological message. Remember that the Theological Exigence is the theological question or issue that the Occasional problem or issue raised. The authors of these texts purposefully frame the issues in particular ways. They tell a story or raise a question about a practice in the way they do so that the readers will see how it relates to some specific aspect of the faith. That is, the author wants the readers to shape their thinking about the issue around a particular belief that the community holds (or should hold). The author may discuss the issue or tell the story so that it points to an aspect of the character or actions of God or so that it relates, for example, to how they understand the community (ecclesiology) or some other theological framework.

Giving attention to the theological category of the text can help us see its broader message rather than falling back onto moralistic advice or general exhortations about being good people. It helps us remember that these texts are doing serious theological work. Here is a list of general theological categories with brief explanations to help you determine what the text is saying about who God is or what God does. These categories can help you shape your Central Question and Central Claim. Knowing the theological category, in turn, will help you determine what this means for those who will engage your sermon, thus developing your Central Purpose. These categories offer brief descriptions of the themes within them but are not meant to be exhaustive. They will simply give you a general idea of what is being considered.

CATEGORIES

Christology

Christology is the category that includes themes related to the person and work of Jesus Christ. Here we find statements about Jesus Christ's two natures as both fully human and fully divine and his role in salvation (which includes ideas about his voluntary self-giving, his suffering, his death, and his resurrection), as well as his ministry in the world of teaching, healing, feeding, and casting out demons.

Discipleship

Talking about discipleship, or following Jesus Christ, is an important way to think about theological/ecclesial ethics. It acknowledges that the church proclaims that the character and will of God is seen most clearly in Jesus Christ but insists that this be done with theological depth and rigor.

Ecclesiology

Ecclesiology is the study of the church as a worshipping community, that is, of those "called out" (*ekklesia)* to be the Body of Christ. Under this category are questions about how the church should comport itself as the Body of Christ internally in relation to other believers and in the world. We ask about how the church situates itself when it is in the world but lives by values of God's Beloved Community, in other words, the church exists at the intersection of the "already" and the "not yet." We also ask about how to understand traditional tasks of the church: *diakonia* (service), *koinonia* (fellowship/community), *didache* (teaching), *kerygma* (proclamation), and *liturgia* (liturgy), as well as the four marks of the church as One, Holy, Catholic (meaning "universal," not Roman Catholic), and Apostolic.

Eschatology

Eschatology is the study of "last things" and includes themes about a final judgment of all people, the end of the world, and the beginning and fullness of the Realm of God. This category includes questions of Christ's second coming as well as themes of heaven and hell and our existence after death.

Ethics, Theological/Ecclesiological

Theological/ecclesiological ethics is the study of how believers live out the faith in the context of both the church community and in relation to all other ethical matters. It frames questions of morality in theological terms (rather than philosophical or political terms). It asks how imitating the character of God and the work of Christ determines what Christians should think about ethical issues and, in turn, how they should act. Here as well are the related issues of ministerial ethics, by which we mean what particular duties, responsibilities, and ethical demands are made of those who lead the church.

Hermeneutics

Hermeneutics is the study of interpretation. How do we come to understand communications and experiences from outside ourselves? Here it refers primarily to how we interpret sources of revelation of God. It asks how we should approach reading Scripture, tradition, what we know about God from empirical observation and philosophical inquiry, as well as from our experiences of God. It asks specifically how we understand biblical texts and materials from church tradition (creeds, etc.) in their original context and how we use what we find to determine what the church should believe and do today. It also asks how those possible sources of revelation are related to one another.

Pneumatology

Pneumatology includes themes about the person and work of the Holy Spirit. In trinitarian formulations, the Spirit is the third "person" of the Trinity. According to the Gospels, the Spirit is actively identified with the conception of Jesus, as having descended on Jesus like a dove at his baptism, and is promised as a "Comforter" to the disciples at the Last Supper. The Spirit is also promised as an inner presence or guide in the lives of all believers and as the giver of gifts to human beings (e.g., 1 Cor).

Revelation

Revelation refers to the various ways God makes God's self known to us. We can talk about two kinds of revelation: general revelation and special revelation. General revelation refers to the ways God is known through observation of the world such as science, philosophy, and the arts. The field of apologetics (arguments made in defense of doctrine and faith) is one way of drawing on general revelation. Special revelation speaks of the ways God is known through explicitly religious means such as Scripture and the church's traditions. Such special revelation may at times be understood to include revelations people believe that they receive from the Spirit.

Sacraments/Ordinances, Theology of

Certain rituals within Christian worship are believed to enable a special connection between God and God's people. These rituals are known as sacraments or ordinances, depending on how believers see the relationship between God's role and people's role in the ritual. The two most common rituals are Baptism and Communion, though some traditions also consider things such as Confession and anointing of the sick to be sacraments. Each of these rituals has a certain function and meaning within Christian worship that congregants believe enables the sacred to enter into the human realm in a particular way.

Soteriology

Soteriology is the study of salvation. It includes some of the themes we named above under the category of Christology and also includes theological anthropology (see below). This includes answers to such questions as: "How does Christ save us?" "What is God's role in our salvation?" "What is our human condition that requires salvation?" and "What does embracing our salvation offer us in the present and in the future?"

Theological Anthropology

Theological anthropology, at its most basic, is the study of what it means to be human through the lens of faith. It is the category under which come themes about what it means to be made in the image of God (*imago Dei*). Along with that come themes about our human nature as sinful, including questions about what it means to talk about "original sin" and the role (if any) we might play in our own salvation. This category also considers questions about whether or not we are capable of knowing God through some human capacity (for instance, reason) or if the ability to know God is given by God as a gift to human beings (epistemology and revelation).

Theology

The word "theology" is both the general term for the entire field under which all the categories listed above fall, and it is also the specific study of God's nature and works. Under this smaller, specific category we find themes of God's character such as just, holy, righteous, and loving. Theology also includes God's role in creating and sustaining the world (creation and providence) and issues about God's nature as always both transcendent and immanent, as well as issues surrounding the role of God in the realities of suffering and evil (theodicy).

Worship, Theology of

A theology of worship is concerned about the relationship between God and God's people when they gather as an assembly to worship God. This category includes things like liturgy (literally, "the work of the people"), patterns of worship ("ordo"), hymnody and music, public prayer, the sacraments/ordinances, and preaching. When thinking theologically about the worship services of the church, we consider how both sacred space and sacred time shape the places people gather for worship as well as the cycles of days, weeks, and the liturgical year.

Appendix E

Worksheet for Choosing Texts and Planning to Preach

(Note: You will not always need to fill out every part of this worksheet for every sermon.)

DATE OF WORSHIP SERVICE ______________________________

THEME OR SPECIAL EVENT ______________________________

First text ______________________________

Psalm ______________________________

Second text ______________________________

Gospel ______________________________

PRIMARY TEXT FOR PREACHING: ______________________________

First Reading, notes:

____

____

____

____

____

____

____

____

Second Reading, notes:

____
____
____
____
____
____
____
____

Third Reading, notes:

____
____
____
____
____
____
____
____

1. What the biblical commentaries and other resources say about the readings that strikes me:

2. Connections between the readings:

3. What puzzle is present in the texts that invites us to question and explore?

WHAT IS HAPPENING THIS WEEK:

in the WORLD (politically, economically, environmentally, etc.)

in the LOCAL COMMUNITY (neighborhood, town, city)

in NATURE (locally or in a larger context)

in MY CHURCH (the life of the congregation)

4. Striking quote from the psalm, hymn of the day, verse, or offertory, collect/opening prayer, or proper preface that helps focus on what I would hope to preach from these texts:

5. What is the relationship of these texts to the Eucharist/Holy Communion and/or Baptism?

6. What is God/Jesus Christ/Holy Spirit doing by means of these texts?

7. Three possible images or stories to use in the sermon:

8. CENTRAL QUESTION (primary driver for the sermon):

9. CENTRAL CLAIM (primary assertion for this sermon):

10. CENTRAL PURPOSE (what I want this sermon to do, what this sermon will accomplish):

Appendix F

Grammar Refresher for Determining Theological Claims

Welcome to a short review of grammar to help you determine Theological Claims! We are going to go through some basics because you will need to be able to identify parts of sentences (such as subject, verb, and object) to recognize Theological Claims in Scripture and sermons. If some of this is familiar or seems boring, great! It means you will be a star at recognizing and writing Theological Claims.

NOUNS, PRONOUNS, VERBS, PREPOSITIONAL PHRASES

We are going to start with the building blocks of sentences: nouns, pronouns, verbs, and prepositional phrases.

- Nouns are simply the names of people or things: Emily, the cat, Daniel, the lion's den.
- Pronouns are used in place of nouns: I, you, we, she/he/it, they.
- Verbs are actions (run, jump, create, think) or states of being (is, are, have).
- Remember that a preposition is a word that sits before a noun or a pronoun and modifies or acts on it. Prepositions are words like in, from, to, at, toward, around, about, across, and so on that usually are followed by nouns or pronouns, for example, "in the wilderness" and "at the foot of the cross."

So, nouns and verbs and prepositional phrases become the standard parts of a sentence. Simple sentences can be built from just nouns and verbs: "Jesus wept." "I ate." An important grammatical term is the *subject*. The subject of the sentence is what or who is doing an action. In the sentence "Jesus wept," Jesus is the subject. "Wept" is the action.

DIRECT OBJECTS AND INDIRECT OBJECTS

Most sentences include objects. An object is a thing or person that is receiving the action of the verb: "Jesus wept" with an object becomes—Jesus wept *tears of sadness. Tears of sadness* are what Jesus wept. "I ate" plus an object becomes "I ate *a plate of spaghetti*." Spaghetti tells you what I ate—the object of the verb. These examples are direct objects—they are directly affected by the verb.

There are also indirect objects which usually occur in sentences that also have direct objects. These are nouns or pronouns that are not the direct recipient of the verb but usually receive the direct object. So, for instance, in the sentence "Moses brought them the stone tablets," the word "them" is an indirect object. Could we say, "Moses brought the stone tablets"? Yes, and "stone tablets" in this sentence is the direct object—it is what Moses brought. When you add "them," you add an indirect object—"they" received the stone tablets that Moses brought.

Sometimes direct objects are prepositional phrases. Let's take the "Jesus wept" example. "Jesus wept *in the garden*" is a sentence in which the object is a prepositional phrase. It takes the whole phrase to serve as the object because it makes no sense to say, "Jesus wept *the garden*" or "Jesus wept *in*." The preposition "in" plus a noun "the garden" make up the whole object of the sentence.

SUBJECTS, VERBS, AND COMMANDS

All sentences need subjects (which are nouns and pronouns) and verbs and usually objects, but some forms of sentences, namely commands, can be tricky. In these sentences, the subject of the sentence is hidden. Let's look at an example: "Seek God's face." The noun phrase here is God's face, but is God's face doing the seeking? No. God's face here is what is *being sought*, so it is actually the direct object. The subject of this sentence that is hidden is "You." You, me, and all believers are being told to seek God's face. Many commands have an implied "You" before the verb. "Stop in the name of love!" is really "You should stop in the name of love." "Fear God" is really "You must fear God."

If you see a command in Scripture or in a sermon, the implied subject is usually the reader or hearer of the command. There are also commands in which the implied subject is God, for example, "Do not turn your face from me." Here the speaker is pleading "God, do not turn your face from me." In both cases, the subject is hidden, and you need to stop and ask yourself *who* or *what* is the subject of the sentence.

USING GRAMMAR TO ANALYZE CLAIMS

You are going to learn how to identify and also write Theological Claims as the foundation for sermons. Theological Claims have as the subject God, Jesus Christ, or the Holy Spirit. Here are some examples.

- "God's face shone upon them."
- "God delivered the Israelites from the nations."
- "In the beginning, God created the heavens and the earth."
- "Jesus Christ sits at the right hand of God."
- "The Holy Spirit comes to us in the fire of Pentecost."

There are also anthropological claims. These claims have us—human beings—as the subject. So commands with the implied "You" at the beginning are anthropological claims—are about what we humans should do. Even if God or Jesus *speaks* the command, the subject is still us and is thus anthropological and not theological. Take this example: "Be still and know that I am God." Is God the subject of the sentence? No, we are. God is telling us what to do, but we are the subjects. Just because God/Jesus Christ/the Holy Spirit says something does not automatically make any of them the subject of a sentence. Thus, not every sentence in which God speaks is a Theological Claim. So, be careful with sentences that are statements from God.

Let's look at an example of a Theological Claim that has God doing the speaking: "I am the Lord your God." Compare that with the one above: "Be still and know that I am God." Both are said by God but in only the first one is God the subject of the sentence. You are always looking to figure out what the *subject* of the sentence is.

Finally, there are ecclesiological claims. These have the church as the subject and not God/Jesus Christ/the Holy Spirit. Here is an example: "The church is the body of Christ." While there are claims about the identity of the people of God in the Hebrew Bible, only in the Christian Scriptures is the term *ekklesia* used. Therefore, for our purposes, ecclesiological claims are found only in the Christian Scriptures since the church did not come into existence until the time of Christ and beyond.

USING GRAMMAR TO DISTINGUISH BETWEEN EXPLICIT AND IMPLICIT THEOLOGICAL CLAIMS

In Chapter 8, we identify two kinds of Theological Claims: explicit and implicit. The word "explicit" means clearly and obviously. An explicit claim is stated plainly and directly. There is no doubt about what the subject of the sentence is doing. Here is an explicit Theological Claim: "In the beginning, God created the heavens and the earth." Here is another one: "The work of the Holy Spirit is to transform our lives and to conform us to Christ, to perfect us."

In contrast, the word "implicit" means something is suggested or alluded to but not said outright. Here is an implicit Theological Claim: "We hear the story of the world's creation in Genesis, conceived from the great unfathomable depths of God's love." This is an anthropological claim. But what is being *implied* here about God? The implication is that God creates out of great love. This is an anthropological claim (about us) with an implied Theological Claim (What God does).

Here is another anthropological claim with an implied Theological Claim: "But we are wonderful creatures of the living God and we have been encouraged and helped to stand up time and again." What is the subject? "We," so it is an anthropological claim. What is the implied Theological Claim? "God creates us and helps us stand time and again."

So, as you are analyzing scriptural passages and then writing and analyzing sermons, remember that you are always searching for the *subject* of a sentence, which will tell you if the sentence is about God/Jesus Christ/the Holy Spirit and thus a Theological Claim; or about human beings, in which case it is an anthropological claim; or about the church, in which case it is an ecclesiological claim. Every sermon you write needs to a have an explicit Theological Claim somewhere in it that will tell the listeners who God is or what God does.

Appendix G

Names and Metaphors for God, Jesus Christ, and the Holy Spirit from the Bible[1]

A

ABBA (Romans 8:15)
ADVOCATE (1 John 2:1)
ALMIGHTY (Genesis 17:1)
ALL IN ALL (Colossians 3:11)
ALPHA (Revelation 22:13)
AMEN (Revelation 3:14)
ANCIENT OF DAYS (Daniel 7:9)
APOSTLE (Hebrews 3:1)
AUTHOR OF ETERNAL SALVATION (Hebrews 5:9)
AUTHOR OF OUR FAITH (Hebrews 12:2)
AUTHOR OF PEACE (1 Corinthians 14:33)
AVENGER (1 Thessalonians 4:6)

B

BEGINNING (Revelation 21:6)
BISHOP OF SOULS (1 Peter 2:25)
BLESSED & HOLY RULER (1 Timothy 6:15)
BREAD OF GOD (John 6:33)
BREAD OF LIFE (John 6:35)
BREATH OF LIFE (Genesis 2:7, Revelation 11:11)
BRIDEGROOM (Isaiah 62:5)
BRIGHT MORNING STAR (Revelation 22:16)
BUCKLER (2 Samuel 22:31, Psalm 18:2, Psalm 18:30, Proverbs 2:7)

C

CAPTAIN OF SALVATION (Hebrews 2:10)
CARPENTER (Mark 6:3)
CHIEF SHEPHERD (1 Peter 5:4)
CHRIST (Matthew 22:42)

CHRIST OF GOD (Luke 9:20)
CHRIST THE LORD (Luke 2:11)
CHRIST, SON OF LIVING GOD (Matthew 16:16)
COMFORTER (John 14:26)
CONSOLATION OF ISRAEL (Luke 2:25)
CONSUMING FIRE (Deuteronomy 4:24, Hebrews 12:29)
CORNERSTONE (Ephesians 2:20)
CREATOR (1 Peter 4:19)
CROWN OF BEAUTY (Isaiah 28:5)

D

DAYSPRING (Luke 1:78)
DELIVERER (Romans 11:26)
DIADEM OF BEAUTY (Isaiah 28:5)
DOOR (John 10:7)
DWELLING PLACE (Psalm 90:1)

E

EAGLE (Deuteronomy 32:11)
EMMANUEL (Matthew 1:23)
END (Revelation 21:6)
ETERNAL GOD (Deuteronomy 33:27)
ETERNAL LIFE (1 John 5:20)
ETERNAL SPIRIT (Hebrews 9:14)
EVERLASTING GOD (Genesis 21:33)
EXCELLENT (Psalm 148:13)

F

FAITHFUL & TRUE (Revelation 19:11)
FAITHFUL WITNESS (Revelation 1:5)
FATHER (Matthew 6:9)
FIRSTBORN (Romans 8:29, Revelation 1:5, Colossians 1:15)
FIRSTFRUITS (1 Corinthians 15:20-23)
FORTRESS (Jeremiah 16:19)
FOUNDATION (1 Corinthians 3:11)
FOUNTAIN OF LIVING WATERS (Jeremiah 2:13)
FRIEND (Matthew 11:19)

G

GENTLE WHISPER (1 Kings 19:12)
GIFT OF GOD (John 4:10)
GLORY OF THE LORD (Isaiah 40:5)
GOD (Genesis 1:1)

GOD ALMIGHTY (Genesis 17:1)
GOD OF THE WHOLE EARTH (Isaiah 54:5)
GOD OVER ALL (Romans 9:5)
GOD WHO SEES ME (Genesis 16:13)
GOODNESS (Psalm 144:2)
GOOD SHEPHERD (John 10:11)
GOVERNOR (Psalm 22:28)
GREAT HIGH PRIEST (Hebrews 4:14)
GREAT SHEPHERD (Hebrews 13:20)
GUIDE (Psalm 48:14)

H

HEAD OF THE BODY (Colossians 1:18)
HEAD OF THE CHURCH (Ephesians 5:23)
HEIR OF ALL THINGS (Hebrews 1:2)
HIDING PLACE (Psalm 32:7)
HIGHEST (Luke 1:76)
HIGH PRIEST (Hebrews 3:1)
HIGH PRIEST FOREVER (Hebrews 6:20)
HOLY GHOST (John 14:26)
HOLY ONE (Acts 2:27)
HOLY ONE OF ISRAEL (Isaiah 49:7)
HOLY SPIRIT (John 15:26)
HOPE (Titus 2:13)
HORN OF SALVATION (Luke 1:69)
HUSBAND (Isaiah 54:5, Jeremiah 31:32, Hosea 2:16)

I

I AM (Exodus 3:14, John 8:58)
IMAGE OF GOD (2 Corinthians 4:4)
IMAGE OF HIS PERSON (Hebrews 1:3)
INTERCESSOR (Romans 8:26,27,#34, Hebrews 7:25)

J

JAH (Psalm 68:4)
JEALOUS (Exodus 34:14)
JEHOVAH (Psalm 83:18)
JESUS CHRIST OUR LORD (Romans 6:23)
JUDGE (Isaiah 33:22, Acts 10:42)
JUST ONE (Acts 22:14)

K

KEEPER (Psalm 121:5)
KING (Revelation 15:3)

KING ETERNAL (1 Timothy 1:17)
KING OF GLORY (Psalm 24:10)
KING OF KINGS (1 Timothy 6:15)
KING OF SAINTS (Revelation 15:3)

L

LAMB OF GOD (John 1:29)
LAST ADAM (1 Corinthians 15:45)
LIFE (John 14:6)
LIGHT OF THE WORLD (John 8:12)
LILY OF THE VALLEYS (Song of Solomon 2:1)
LION OF THE TRIBE OF JUDAH (Revelation 5:5)
LIVING GOD (Daniel 6:20)
LIVING STONE (1 Peter 2:4)
LIVING WATER (John 4:10)
LORD (John 13:13)
LORD GOD ALMIGHTY (Revelation 15:3)
LORD GOD OF HOSTS (Jeremiah 15:16)
LORD JESUS CHRIST (1 Corinthians 15:57)
LORD OF ALL (Acts 10:36)
LORD OF GLORY (1 Corinthians 2:8)
LORD OF HARVEST (Matthew 9:38)
LORD OF HOSTS (Haggai 1:5)
LORD OF LORDS (1 Timothy 6:15)
LORD OUR RIGHTEOUSNESS (Jeremiah 23:6)
LOVE (1 John 4:8)
LOVING KINDNESS (Psalm 144:2)

M

MAKER (Job 35:10, Psalm 95:6)
MAJESTY ON HIGH (Hebrews 1:3)
MASTER (Luke 5:5)
MEDIATOR (1 Timothy 2:5)
MERCIFUL GOD (Jeremiah 3:12)
MESSIAH (John 4:25)
MIDWIFE (Psalm 22:9, Psalm 71:6, Isaiah 66:9)
MIGHTY GOD (Isaiah 9:6)
MIGHTY ONE (Isaiah 60:16)
MOST UPRIGHT (Isaiah 26:7)
MOTHER (see FEMALE IMAGES further on)

O

OFFSPRING OF DAVID (Revelation 22:16)
OMEGA (Revelation 22:13)
ONLY BEGOTTEN SON (John 1:18)
OUR PASSOVER LAMB (1 Corinthians 5:7)
OUR PEACE (Ephesians 2:14)

P

PHYSICIAN (Luke 4:23)
PORTION (Psalm 73:26, Psalm 119:57)
POTENTATE (1 Timothy 6:15)
POTTER (Isaiah 64:8)
POWER OF GOD (1 Corinthians 1:24)
PRINCE OF LIFE (Acts 3:15)
PROPHET (Acts 3:22)
PROPHET OF THE HIGHEST (Luke 1:76)
PROPITIATION (1 John 2:2, 1 John 4:10)

Q

QUICKENING SPIRIT (1 Corinthians 15:45)

R

RABBONI (TEACHER) (John 20:16)
RADIANCE OF GOD'S GLORY (Hebrews 1:3)
REDEEMER (Job 19:25)
REFUGE (Jeremiah 16:19)
RESURRECTION (John 11:25)
REWARDER (Hebrews 11:6)
RIGHTEOUS ONE (1 John 2:1)
ROCK (1 Corinthians 10:4)
ROOT OF DAVID (Revelation 22:16)
ROSE OF SHARON (Song of Solomon 2:1)
RULER OF GOD'S CREATION (Revelation 3:14)
RULER OVER KINGS OF EARTH (Revelation 1:5)

S

SAVIOR (Luke 2:11)
SCEPTRE (Numbers 24:17)
SEED (Genesis 3:15)
SHADE (Psalm 121:5)
SHEPHERD OF OUR SOULS (1 Peter 2:25)
SHIELD (Genesis 15:1)
SHILOH (Genesis 49:10)
SONG (Exodus 15:2, Isaiah 12:2)
SON OF DAVID (Matthew 1:1)
SON OF GOD (Matthew 27:54)
SON OF MAN (Matthew 8:20)
SON OF THE MOST HIGH (Luke 1:32)
SOURCE (Hebrews 5:9)
SPIRIT (John 4:24)
SPIRIT OF ADOPTION (Romans 8:15)
SPIRIT OF GOD (Genesis 1:2)
SPIRIT OF TRUTH (John 14:17,15:26,16:13)

STRENGTH (Jeremiah 16:19)
STONE (1 Peter 2:8)
STONE OF ISRAEL (Genesis 49:24)
STRONGHOLD (Nahum 1:7)
STRONG TOWER (Proverbs 18:10)

T

TEACHER (John 13:13)
TEMPLE (Revelation 21:22)
THE ONE (Psalm 144:2,10)
TRUE LIGHT (John 1:9)
TRUE WITNESS (Revelation 3:14)
TRUTH (John 14:6)

V

VINE (John 15:5)

W

WALL OF FIRE (Zechariah 2:5)
WAY (John 14:6)
WIND (Genesis 1:1)
WISDOM OF GOD (1 Corinthians 1:24)
WORD (John 1:1)
WORD OF GOD (Revelation 19:13)
WOMAN (see FEMALE IMAGES below)

Y

YAH (Isaiah 12:2, Psalm 68:4)

FEMALE IMAGES FOR GOD[2] IN THE BIBLE[3] (LISTED IN CANONICAL ORDER)

Women and men created in God's image
"Humankind was created as God's reflection: in the divine image God created them; female and male, God made them." Genesis 1:27

God described as a mother eagle
"Like the eagle that stirs up its nest, and hovers over its young, God spreads wings to catch you, and carries you on pinions." Deuteronomy 32:11-12

God who gives birth
"You deserted the Rock who gave you life; you forgot the God who bore you." Deuteronomy 32:18

God as a midwife
"Yet you drew me out of the womb; you nestled me in my mother's bosom; you cradled me in your lap from my birth; from my mother's womb you have been my God." Psalm 22:9-10 (see also Psalm 71:6)

God's wisdom as a woman
"Doesn't Wisdom call? Doesn't understanding raise her voice? On the hills along the road, at the crossroads, she takes her stand; beside city gates of the town, at the gates themselves, she cries out." Proverbs 8:1-3

God as a woman in labor
"For a long time I held my peace, restrained myself and held myself in check. But now I groan as if giving birth, gasping and panting." Isaiah 42:14

God compared to a nursing mother
"Can a woman forget her baby at the breast, or fail to cherish the child of her womb? Yet, even if these forget, I will never forget you." Isaiah 49:15

God as a comforting mother
"As nursling, you will be carried in her arms, and fondled in her lap; as a mother comforts her child, so will I comfort you; in Jerusalem you will find your comfort." Isaiah 66:12-13

God described as a mother bear
"Like a bear robbed of her cubs, I will attack them and tear them asunder." Hosea 13:8

Jesus as a mother hen
"Oh, Jerusalem, Jerusalem—you murder the prophets, and you stone those sent to you! Oh, how often have I yearned to gather you together, like a hen gathering her chicks under her wings!" Matthew 23:37 (see also Luke 13:34)

God as a woman baking bread
"And again Jesus said, 'To what should I compare the kingdom of God? It is like yeast that a woman took and mixed in with three measures of flour until all of it was leavened.'" Luke 13:20-21 (NRSV)

God as a woman looking for her lost coin
"Or what woman having ten silver coins, if she loses one of them, does not light a lamp, sweep the house, and search carefully until she finds it? When she has found it, she calls together her friends and neighbors saying, 'Rejoice with me, for I have found the coin that I had lost.' Just so, I tell you, there is joy in the presence of the angels of God over one sinner who repents." Luke 15:8-10 (NRSV)

NOTES

1. Thanks to Rev. Pamela Pettyjohn, who curated this list and gave us permission to share it here.
2. See also Gail Ramshaw, *God Beyond Gender: Feminist Christian God-Language* (Minneapolis, MN: Fortress, 1995).
3. Bible quotations for this section are from *The Inclusive Bible: The First Egalitarian Translation*, a Sheed & Ward Book (Lanham, MD: Rowman & Littlefield, 2007), unless otherwise noted.

Appendix H

Central Question Worksheet

(See Chapters 12 and 13 for full instructions and examples.)

The Central Question is the compelling inquiry for the sermon.

- In *one* sentence, it asks the question that is at the heart of the biblical exegesis and one's preaching context.
- This question captures the "existential oomph" for why you are crafting this sermon.

Informing the Central Question is the basic inquiry: "Why does this matter?" In other words, why did the biblical writer think it was important to put stylus to parchment and write these words? Similarly, why should anyone today care about this text? And why should your listeners want to listen to you preach about it?

STEPS FOR WRITING THE CENTRAL QUESTION

1. *List the questions the text/author is asking.* Based on your consultation with biblical commentaries and your Exegesis Guide Chart, write down three questions that you hear the biblical author or community asking that articulates what was happening in the world behind the text that makes this passage necessary. What was happening in the faith community that this passage addressed? What was on the hearts and minds of the author and/or listeners that necessitated this passage?

   a.

   b.

   c.

2. *Answer the Five Questions for Exegeting a Preaching Context.*
   - What is happening in the world or society that is on people's minds (or that they need to pay attention to)?
   - What is happening in the local community?
   - What is happening in the congregation as a whole?
   - What are individual congregation members dealing with?
   - What are the political, cultural, and social dynamics that shape our hearing and interpreting of the text today?

3. *List the questions the congregation or community are asking.* Based on your answers to the Five Questions, write down three questions that you or your congregation are asking (explicitly or implicitly). Circle the one that seems most compelling. This may change as you work on your sermon, but it's a place to start.

   a.

   b.

   c.

4. *Write three possible Central Questions.* Write down three sentences that connect the biblical and contextual questions in a coherent and compelling way. Circle the one that seems to capture the most energy for your preaching about this passage at this time for these people. This is the Central Question for the sermon.

   a.

   b.

   c.

After prayerful consideration, circle the one that you have chosen to inform the Central Claim and Central Purpose. Remember: The Central Question gives us the compelling drive for the sermon. The Central Question is the "engine" of your sermon. It is what drives you to preach about this text at this time for this congregation. It contains the intellectual, emotional, and spiritual energy of the sermon.

Appendix I

Central Claim Worksheet

(See Chapters 14 and 15 for full instructions and examples.)

The Central Claim is the primary assertion of the sermon—in *one* sentence. Think of it as distilling the message down to a one-sentence sermon.

The Central Claim is informed by two things:

1) the Theological Claim that you derived from exegeting the Scripture passage and
2) the Central Question that you derived from exegeting the biblical text and your preaching context.

Together, the Theological Claim and Central Question are connected so that you can make a singular Central Claim that conveys both the message of the biblical passage and its implication for your preaching context.

Theological Claim: ______________________________

+

Central Question: ______________________________

=

CENTRAL CLAIM: ______________________________

Remember:

1) The Central Claim needs to mention God, Jesus Christ, and/or the Holy Spirit and say something substantive about their nature, character, or actions.
   If there is no mention of who God is or what God does, this means there is no theological content.
2) The Central Claim needs to make an explicit connection between the content of the biblical text and the preaching context.
   - If there is no biblical connection in the statement, this means that there is no scriptural basis for the claim.
   - At the same time, if there is no connection to the preaching context, then the sermon will be too abstract.
   - We might think of the Central Claim as the answer to the Central Question. Because the Central Question contains the compelling inquiry about the Bible and one's context, the Central Claim needs to make an assertion that responds to this question.
3) The Central Claim is not a statement about the theme of the sermon. Nor is it a lengthy excurses describing the sermon. It's also not a sermon title. The Central Claim should convey both the message of the biblical passage and its implication for your preaching context.

Appendix J

Central Purpose Worksheet

(See Chapters 16 and 17 for full instructions and examples.)

The Central Purpose is the primary goal of the sermon—stated in *one* sentence. In the Central Purpose you will succinctly state what you want this sermon to do or accomplish in and for the listeners.

The Central Purpose is informed by two things:

1) the Central Question that you derived from exegeting the text and your preaching context
2) the Central Claim (derived from the Theological Claim and the Central Question) that contains the primary assertion of the sermon

Together, the Central Question and the Central Claim inform the Central Purpose so that you can state in one sentence what the sermon aims to do and why.

Central Question: ______________________________

+

Central Claim: ______________________________

=

CENTRAL PURPOSE: ______________________________

SENTENCE FORMATS FOR THE CENTRAL PURPOSE

The Central Purpose of this sermon is to [VERB] [OBJECT] so that [VERB] [OBJECT].

Or

This sermon will [VERB] [OBJECT] in order to [VERB] [OBJECT].

You can also use the present tense:

This sermon [PRESENT TENSE VERB] [OBJECT] resulting in [NOUNS].

QUESTIONS TO HELP YOU CRAFT THE CENTRAL PURPOSE

- Who is your intended audience for this sermon? What is important to them and for them in terms of this biblical passage?
- If the Central Claim was an answer to the Central Question, what is your intention for your listeners upon hearing that answer? What do you want them to do or how would you hope they would respond? What would you like to see changed in their lives, in the congregation, in the community, or in God's Creation?
- How do you want the listeners to feel by the end of this sermon?
- What is the aim of the sermon? What might be indicators that your listeners are heading in the right direction toward that goal?

QUESTIONS FOR DEVELOPING THE "SO THAT" OF THE CENTRAL PURPOSE

The Central Purpose states what the sermon will accomplish and, just as importantly, why, or what might result. In other words, the Central Purpose needs a "so that."

- Why does your congregation need to hear this sermon about this text at this particular time?
- Who will care that this sermon has been preached? What difference will this sermon make in the lives of your listeners, the church as a whole, those who are vulnerable, God's Creation, or the community?
- Why does the Central Claim matter? How do you hope your listeners will respond to the Central Claim?
- How do you envision things being different as a result of this sermon?

VIGOROUS VERBS TO USE IN A CENTRAL PURPOSE

accompany
advocate
beckon
build
challenge
comfort
compel
create
direct
disrupt
encounter
encourage
establish
guide
initiate
inspire
instruct
invite
lead
model
open
persuade
prepare
proclaim
reconcile
reshape
restore
reveal
strengthen
support
surprise
teach
transform
unite
urge

ANEMIC VERBS TO AVOID

clarify
communicate
convey
explain
express
help people understand that
make the case that
reflect on
share
suggest
tell

Appendix K

Creativity Exercises Quick Reference Guide

EXERCISE 1: LECTIO WITH A BIBLICAL TEXT

Things you'll need:

- A Bible open to the passage you've chosen for the basis of your sermon.
- A notebook and pen or pencil.
- (Optional) A recording device, such as a voice recording app on your phone.

1. Begin with centering prayer asking for the Spirit to open your heart and mind to receive the Word of God.
2. Have someone read the text out loud and simply listen.
3. Sit in contemplative silence for sixty seconds. Take deep cleansing breaths.
4. Have someone else read the text (perhaps from a different translation) and record it for future listening. Notice one word that jumps out for you. Write down that word.
5. Sit in contemplative silence for sixty seconds. Take deep cleansing breaths.
6. Have a third person read the text and each person write down their questions, observations, "gaps," and "splinters."
7. Sit in contemplative silence for sixty seconds. Take deep cleansing breaths.
8. Share and discuss what has come up for you that might guide your Central Question.
9. Conclude with prayer thanking God for the insights, wisdom, and questions that have been shared through this reading.

EXERCISE 2: MIND-MAPPING

Things you'll need:

- Bible open to the passage you've chosen for the basis of your sermon.
- Large piece of paper and pen/pencil. Also works with large notepad on an easel or dry erase board for large groups.

1. Begin with centering prayer, then read the text out loud. Choose one word you think is central to the text (either a concept or a thing/person/place/verb).

2. Write down the word in the center of the page.
3. Without discussion or judgment, write down all the words that come to your mind about the center word. Don't stop to assess what you've written—that comes later. Simply write other words and phrases all over the paper surrounding that word.
4. Circle five things that resonate for you.
5. In a "wheel-and-spokes" fashion, draw lines connecting those five words with one another and how they relate to the center word.
6. Think about or discuss with others how these ideas might inform the Central Question, Central Claim, or Central Purpose.

EXERCISE 3: WRITING OFF THE PAGE

Things you'll need:

- Bible open to the passage you've chosen for the basis of your sermon.
- Journal or piece of paper and pen/pencil.
- Timer.

1. Begin with centering prayer and then read the text. Underline one word, phrase, or image that calls to you.
2. Set your timer for five minutes.
3. Write the word, sentence, or image at the top of the page and then start the timer.
4. Using stream of consciousness, write down your thoughts about the word without stopping for five minutes. Even if it's gibberish, just keep writing and don't stop until the five minutes are up.
5. Go back through and underline the ideas that seem salient or resonant for you.
6. Think about or discuss with others how these ideas might inform the Central Question, Central Claim, or Central Purpose.

EXERCISE 4: SENSORY NET

Things you'll need:

- Pen/pencil.
- One piece of paper oriented vertically. Make six columns with the following headings:
  a. I see . . .
  b. I taste . . .
  c. I smell . . .
  d. I touch . . .
  e. I hear . . .
  f. I feel . . .
- An audio recording of the biblical text you will use for the basis of your sermon.

1. Begin with centering prayer. Then, using a recording app on your phone, record yourself (or someone else) reading the biblical text *slowly*. (Alternatively, you can use one of the many audio recordings of the Bible available on the internet or in an audiobook.)
2. Listen to a recording of the text and write down the sights, tastes, smells, textures, sounds, and emotions that come to you as you listen.
3. Think about (or discuss with a group) how you might use this sensory information to inform your Central Question, Central Claim, or Central Purpose.
4. Begin jotting notes for how you might use what you've collected in this Sensory Net to create evocative images and illustrations for your sermon and to connect head and heart in your preaching.

EXERCISE 5: PREACHING OFF THE PAGE

Things you'll need:

- Bible open to the passage you've chosen for the basis of your sermon. Do not read it silently ahead of time because that will defeat the purpose of the exercise.
- Timer.
- Recording device such as a video camera or audio recording app. You don't want to lose what nifty idea might come to you in this exercise!

1. Begin with centering prayer and then set your timer for three minutes.
2. Hit the "record" button.
3. Read the text out loud.
4. Pause for thirty seconds to breathe, calm your mind, and gather your thoughts.
   a. Ideas and questions to get you started:
      i. Does this passage remind you of a story?
      ii. Can you talk about an image or a word in the text and what it brings up for you?
      iii. What were you taught or what did you think about this passage growing up? What do you think about it now?
      iv. Who does this passage remind you of?
      v. When was a time you faced something like this in your life?
      vi. How does this passage make you feel?
      vii. What are the sights, smells, sounds, textures, and tastes that come to you as you read this passage?
5. Begin the timer.
6. If in a group, be sure to look at the people in the room. If alone, look in the camera or pretend that you're looking at a group of people, talking to them.
7. Remember that you don't have to have a complete "sermon." Your conclusion of this impromptu speech might be that you have hit upon the question you want to address in the rest of the sermon or that you see a clue about what your Central Claim might be for this sermon.
8. When the timer stops, finish your sentence and stop the recorder.
9. Watch the recording and think about or discuss with others how these ideas might inform the Central Question, Central Claim, or Central Purpose.

EXERCISE 6: "PLAY-DOH-ING" WITH THE BIBLE

Things you'll need:

- Bible open to the passage you've chosen for the basis of your sermon.
- Containers of Play-Doh or modelling clay.
- Dry erase board (for larger groups).

1. Choose one container of Play-Doh and then begin with centering prayer.
2. One person reads the Scripture passage out loud—slowly, so that people have time to knead the dough and allow their fingers and hands to work. Repeat the reading if people need more time to finish.
3. As the passage is read, work the dough into an image or something that represents how you feel when you hear the words read. It can be something concrete or more abstract, like a design.
4. A second person reads the Scripture passage. This time, everyone walks around and looks at the different sculptures as they listen to the text.
5. Reflect on the sculptures. Each person shares one word about what they saw expressed in others' sculptures. Write these on the board.
6. Circle the words in one color that have a negative connotation. Circle the words in a different color that have a positive connotation. (Dotted-line circles for uncertain connotations.)

7. Invite each person to share why they sculpted what they did.
8. Discuss—where are the "heart" places of this passage? What are the "pain points"? Where is hope or growth? Where is the struggle? Where is God?
9. Discuss how these ideas might be worked into your Central Question, Central Claim, or Central Purpose.

EXERCISE 7: GROUP-SCULPTING THE SCRIPTURE

(Note that sculpting exercises even of the Bible can elicit strong emotions. The Bible has words, images, and stories that could have a powerful impact on people, so be pastorally prepared.)

Things you'll need:

- Bible open to the passage you've chosen for the basis of your sermon.
- At least three to five participants—one to serve as the "sculptor" and the others as the participants in the sculpture. This can be done with fellow preachers or with youth and/or adults in one's congregation.
- A few chairs to serve as props or to enable sitting.

1. Begin with centering prayer and then read the passage out loud.
2. Invite the sculptor to place participants in positions that they feel represent some aspect or aspects of the text (and/or the historical situation, if some exegesis has been done).
3. After freezing in the position for a minute, invite the sculptor to explain their choices for placement.
4. Ask each participant to share how it felt to be in their posed position.
5. Discuss the experience and how the insights might inform the Central Question, Central Claim, or Central Purpose.

EXERCISE 8: IMPROV WITH THE BIBLICAL TEXT

Things you'll need:

- Bible open to the passage you've chosen for the basis of your sermon.
- At least four participants—one to serve as reader and the others to do the improv. This can be done with fellow preachers or with youth and/or adults in one's congregation.

1. Begin with centering prayer and then choose a narrator and assign parts in the story to the participants.
   a. Don't overlook the silent characters in the story when assigning parts. This includes the other-than-human characters as well. For example, in Jesus's parable about the birds of the air and the flowers of the field, assign someone each of those roles so that God's Creation can be represented as well. This can result in perspectives and insights coming to light that are often overlooked from an anthropocentric reading. (See the "Ecological Readings" section in Chapter 4, "Using Explicit Perspectives to Understand the Text.")
2. In the first round, have the narrator read the story out loud, slowly and with dramatic inflection. Participants act out what they hear but *without talking*.
3. Discuss the experience.
4. In the second round, have participants switch roles. Have them act out the story without words *and* without the Scripture being read.
5. Discuss the experience. Notice what things people remembered and carried with them from the first improvisation. What new aspects were added this time, and what things changed?
6. In round three, have participants switch roles again. The narrator reads the story out loud, but this time participants act out the story and are allowed to speak—even to the narrator if they wish!
7. Discuss the experience. What differences did they notice between acting without words compared with being allowed to speak? What insights from the exercise might inform the Central Question, Central Claim, and Central Purpose?

Appendix L

A Short List of Sermon Forms and How the Central Claim Can Be Used

In Chapters 20 and 21, we provide an in-depth look at four sermon forms for preaching—Four Pages, Motion Pictures, Homiletical Plot, and Expository/Puritan Plain Style. There are many more forms, and, if so desired, a preacher could preach a different sermon form or design almost every Sunday of the year. The following page shows just a sampling of sermon forms that can spark ideas for devising a sermon.

In the chart, you'll see the name of the form, a short description, and suggestions for where in the sermon the Central Claim would be most visible or exert itself most strongly. See Chapter 20 for a full description of how the Central Claim can be used with Four Pages, Motion Pictures, Homiletical Plot, and Expository/Puritan Plain Style.

Sermon Form	Description	Possible Location(s) of Central Claim
Expository (also called exegetical or Puritan Plain Style)	Introduction, verse-by-verse explanations of the text, theological interpretation, contemporary application, conclusion	Beginning (if deductive), middle (throughline), end (if inductive)
Four Pages (Wilson)	Trouble in the text, trouble in the world, grace in the text, grace in the world	Grace in the text, grace in the world
Journey (Craddock)	Following the preacher through the process of discovery	Conclusion, or not at all (only inferred, left up to the listener)
Motion Pictures (Buttrick)	Introduction, 3–4 moves (with connecting "hinge"), conclusion	Beginning (if deductive), middle (throughline), end (if inductive)
Homiletical Plot (Lowry)	Following the plot form of a story: Oops, Ugh, Aha, Whee, Yeah	Beginning (if deductive), middle (throughline), end (if inductive)
Problem—resolution—conclusion	Pastoral, societal, or theological concern—biblical or theological response—ramifications	Resolution and/or conclusion
Sermon—dialogue—sermon (Schade)	Two sermons that bookend a community dialogue about a social issue. Sermon #1 is the Prophetic Invitation to Dialogue. Sermon #2 is the Communal Prophetic Proclamation.	Prophetic Invitation to Dialogue: middle and conclusion (emphasizing that God invites us to dialogue and engage the issue); Communal Prophetic Proclamation: middle and/or conclusion (inductive, following the journey of the group's dialogue)
Sermon exploring or explaining a doctrine	Teaching about and illustrating theological and ecclesial concepts	Beginning (if deductive), middle (throughline), conclusion (if inductive)
Sermon structured around a Christian practice	Examining the multifaceted aspects of some part of worship, faith formation, service, etc.	Beginning (if deductive), middle (throughline), conclusion (if inductive)
Sermon structured around an image	Exploring different meanings of biblical or contemporary image	Beginning (if deductive), middle (throughline), conclusion (if inductive)
Thesis—antithesis—synthesis	Argument, counterargument, deeper truth	Synthesis (conclusion)
Three points	Introduction, three points with illustrations, conclusion	Beginning, middle, and conclusion (deductive)

Appendix M

Exercises for the Preacher's Voice and Body

Just as a musician or athlete needs to warm up before a performance, so, too, do preachers need to prepare their voices before the worship service begins. Here are basic breath, vocal, and body warm-ups that any preacher can do that take just minutes. These can be done at home or in the car on the way to church.

Remember: exercises using our voices and bodies may be painful for those who have experienced certain kinds of physical trauma and/or triggering for those who have experienced sexual and/or physical abuse. Our bodies and voices can hold and remember trauma even when our conscious minds seem to forget. Thus, these exercises may bring up memories or uncomfortable feelings for some people that should be worked out with a trained counselor. Do not continue with these exercises if you are experiencing physical, emotional, or psychological pain. Seek help from a trusted professional.

EXERCISES FOR INCREASING BREATH CAPACITY[1]

1. *Respiration exercise #1*: After taking a deep breath, count slowly, one second per number, in a good, loud voice. Repeat until you can count aloud to fifteen slowly on one breath. Work up until you are able to count to twenty or thirty.
2. *Respiration exercise #2*: Sound the vowel /ah/ in a full voice and prolong it in a monotone until you feel like all the breath is exhausted. Time each trial and notice that the more you practice, the longer you can maintain the sound. When taking a breath, place your hand lightly on your abdomen. *Diaphragmatic breathing* means that your stomach should distend when air is taken in. If your shoulders move up (*clavicular breathing*) and your stomach goes in, you are breathing incorrectly and will have minimal airflow.
3. *Volume, intensity, and projection exercise:* Sound the vowel /ah/ in a full voice and prolong it at a normal pitch level. Gradually increase the loudness of the sound /ah/ in a monotone as long as the breath lasts. Increase and then decrease the sound gradually without overstraining. Also, vary the exercise by having inflection patterns go up and down as well as monotone /ah-h/.

BASIC VOCAL WARM-UP[2]

- Face rub. Massage your face, paying particular attention to your jaw and the back of your head where your head meets your spine. Do this for 20 to 30 seconds.

- Pretend chewing gum. Pretend like you are chewing a humongous wad of gum for 20 to 30 seconds. Really give your jaw and mouth a workout; smack that gum like a kid in middle school.
- Blow. Blow through your lips, adding sound behind it and moving up and down your pitch register. In other words, make your voice go really high and really low, over the course of 20 to 30 seconds.
- Tongue slobber. The tongue is a muscle and needs warmed up as well! Stick out your tongue and move the tip of it up, down, and side to side in clear, intentional movements. Do this 5 to 10 times and then make 5 circles with the tip of the tongue and 5 more reversing direction.
- Vocal exercise #1:
  - Say Ma-ma-ma-ma-maaaaa, making sure your jaw goes up and down, and ending with a long clear tone. Repeat 5 to 10 times.
- Vocal exercise #2:
  - Say Pa-Pee-Pa-Pay-Pa-Paw-Pa-Paper, with two clear objectives: 1) make sure every single P is clear and distinct and 2) get your jaw really going up and down, trying for clear vowel sounds; when you can do it clearly, slowly increase your speed.
  - Say Ba-Bee-Ba-Bay-Ba-Baw-Ba-Baber, meeting the same two objectives.
  - Say Ta-Tee-Ta-Tay-Ta-Taw-Ta-Tater, meeting the same two objectives. Make sure your Ts are clean (no ssss should escape).
  - Say Da-Dee-Da-Day-Da-Daw-Da-Dader, meeting the same two objectives.
  - Say Ka-Kee-Ka-Kay-Ka-Kaw-Ka-Kaker, meeting the same two objectives. This will require more work on your jaw, and you won't be able to go as fast.
  - Say Ga-Gee-Ga-Gay-Ga-Gaw-Ga-Gager, meeting the same two objectives. This will require more work on your jaw, and you won't be able to go as fast.
- Vocal exercise #3:
  - Say "A critical cricket critic." Start slowly and put particular emphasis on having clear T and K sounds.
- Face rub. End with another nice face rub, giving thanks to God for all the parts of your body that enable you to preach with full voice.

BASIC PHYSICAL WARM-UP[3]

Warming up and stretching the body before preaching gets the blood flowing, releases tension, and puts the preacher in touch with their own physicality. Below is a basic physical warm-up that any preacher can do that takes just minutes. It can be done at home or in your office before the worship service begins. *Note: Everyone's body has different capacities. You may feel some discomfort as you're "waking up" the different parts of the body, but you should not feel pain when doing these exercises. If you do, stop and modify the exercise.*

- Shake it out. Shake your body all over to loosen everything up and get the blood flowing.
- Neck rolls. *Gently* roll your neck from side to side, do not go all the way around, as it puts undue strain on the neck. Repeat 5 to 10 times.
- Shoulder rolls. With your arms at your side, make big circles with your shoulders going backwards 5 times, and then reverse direction for 5 more.
- Shoulder stretch. Straighten one arm in front of you, and then use your other arm to gently pull it across your body to stretch the back of your shoulder for 5 to 10 seconds. Repeat with your other arm. Then massage each shoulder with the opposite hand, feeling the tension release.
- Triceps stretch. Bend your elbow and point it towards the sky with your arm behind your head. Pull gently on your elbow to stretch the triceps for 5 to 10 seconds and then repeat on the other side.
- Wrist stretch. Hold your arm out in front of you with straight elbows. With your other hand, gently grab the fingers and pull down and back to stretch the tendons in the forearm. Then flip your hand to the other side and pull down and back gently. Repeat with your other hand. Then with both hands extended, rotate your wrists in circles for 5 to 10 seconds.
- Waist stretch. Holding your hands together in front of you, gently swing your torso to the left and right to loosen your lower back, 5 times on each side. Then switch your hips back and forth, like doing "the bump" dance.

- Back stretch. Bending at the waist, let yourself hang down, making sure your neck and shoulders are loose and relaxed. Take a few deep breaths while hanging with your hands on your lower back, seeking to feel the outward pressure of your breath from your diaphragm (indicating a nice supported deep breath!). Slowly stand back up, stacking each vertebra on top of the other. Don't rush as you feel each vertebra settle into place, ending with your head stacked over your shoulders.
- Side stretch. Stretch one arm over your head tilting towards the opposite side to feel a stretch from the arm all the way down your side. Hold for 5 to 10 seconds and then repeat on the other side.
- Leg stretch. Using something for balance if you need it, bend one leg behind you, gently grabbing it to feel a stretch on the front of your leg for 5 to 10 seconds, and then repeat with the other leg.
- Knee loosening. Begin by consciously tightening the knee and muscles in the leg. Then release the tension and gently move the knees back and forth, then side to side. Repeat this 2 to 3 times.
- Ankle stretch. Lift one foot a few inches off the ground in front of you and then alternate pointing and flexing your foot 5 to 10 times, and then making 2 to 3 circles in the air with your toes to loosen the ankle. Repeat on the other side.
- Shake it out. One last whole-body wiggle to show that everything is loose and ready for preaching!

NOTES

1. Teresa L. Fry Brown, *Delivering the Sermon.* In Elements of Preaching Series, O. Wesley Allen Jr., series editor (Minneapolis, MN: Fortress Press, 2008), 39–40.
2. Thanks to Dr. Peter Civetta, actor and theatre studies instructor at Northwestern University, for this exercise.
3. Thanks to Dr. Peter Civetta, actor and theatre studies instructor at Northwestern University, for this exercise.

Appendix N

Tips and Advice for Guest Preachers and Supply Preachers

Serving as a guest preacher or supply preacher for a congregation carries unique challenges and responsibilities that are different from those of a settled pastor. Whether you're a seminarian asked to fill in for a pastor's vacation Sunday, or you're invited to preach for a particular occasion or on a certain topic, or you've been asked to preach for a local retirement home, you won't have the kind of knowledge of the congregation that a settled pastor has. For example, you won't know what individual congregants are dealing with. And it's likely you won't have more than a cursory understanding of what is happening in the local community or the congregation as a whole. So what are ways you can make use of the Five Questions for Exegeting a Preaching Context (see Chapter 12) when preparing your Central Question and crafting a sermon for a congregation you don't know?

ADAPTING THE FIVE QUESTIONS FOR EXEGETING A PREACHING CONTEXT WHEN YOU'RE UNFAMILIAR WITH THE CONTEXT

Below are the Five Questions for Exegeting a Preaching Context and how they can be adapted if you are a guest preacher or supply preacher. We also include some cautions and best practices in these situations.

1. *What is happening in the world or society that is on people's minds (or that they need to pay attention to)?* Supply preachers or guest preachers have an opportunity to address contemporary issues that a settled pastor might be hesitant to address. In fact, a guest preacher may be asked specifically to preach about a topic so that the congregation can hear a different voice or perspective.

   Caution: Try not to leave a "mess" for the settled pastor to clean up in your wake. If you push too hard with a prophetic word or intentionally trip some "land mines," the person who gets the backlash may be the settled pastor after you're gone.

   Best practice: If possible, talk with the settled pastor ahead of time to get a sense of what they are hoping you will address—and what may be best to avoid—in the sermon. If talking with the pastor is not possible, it's best to err on the side of caution and avoid unnecessarily controversial topics.

2. *What is happening in the local community?* If you have the opportunity, talk with the settled pastor to find out if there are issues going on in the local community that you should be aware of. What things are people talking about? Are there local conflicts, for example, that are affecting the congregation? Are there celebrations or

points of pride that you can point to or lift up? If it's not possible to talk with the settled pastor, other people you can ask are the church administrator, the worship leader/musician, or the head of the governing board. You can also do an internet search to read the local newspaper and learn more about the context in which you'll be preaching.

Caution: While it's good to be aware of local issues, the same caution regarding global or societal issues applies here as well. Unless you are truly up to speed on an issue, it's best not to weigh in on a local controversy, especially if you're an outsider to the community.

Best practice: Draw on the local character and flavor of the community in a positive way if you're going to reference the local area in a sermon. Again, an internet search on the local community can tell you a great deal, but not everything. As they are practicing hospitality toward you by inviting you to preach, honor that with graciousness and respect.

3. *What is happening in the congregation as a whole?* Again, talk with the settled pastor about the congregation. What will you be walking into on that Sunday morning? If you can't ask the settled pastor, ask the church administrator, or whoever invited you to preach. You can also check out the church's website and Facebook page as well as the newsletter to get a sense of the congregation, what's important to them, and what's on the horizon for their ministry.

   Caution: Ask where the "sunburn" is. In other words, what are sensitive areas or topics for a congregation that should be avoided or handled with care? Especially if you hope to be invited back in the future, the first time preaching to a church generally should be done with care so that you can establish trust and begin to build a positive relationship.

   Best practice: One way to find out what's important to the congregation is to ask what they're studying in adult Sunday School classes or forums. What are they reading in book club? What service activities or mission trips are the youth planning or what have they recently completed? You can also ask the settled pastor for a copy of the sermon they will have preached just prior to your coming so that you can tie in points they made the previous week or highlight a theme they addressed if it's appropriate to do so in your own sermon.

4. *What are individual congregation members dealing with?* This question will likely be the most difficult for a guest preacher or supply preacher to assess. Since you have no pastoral relationship with the members, you haven't established the trust or the connections to be able to know what individuals are dealing with.

   Caution: The settled pastor and the congregation certainly know the "quirky" folks in their midst and make accommodations, but they may come as a surprise to you. Or there may be some individuals who have disabilities that will need special accommodations. So, you can ask if there is anyone with special needs or concerns that you should be aware of as you are leading worship and preaching that morning.

   Best practice: There are some questions you can ask the settled pastor or whoever hired you to preach so that you can get an idea of the people you might encounter and what's on their minds. You can ask: who am I likely to see on Sunday morning? What am I likely to notice? Will I see children or teens? Have there been any recent deaths that have affected the congregation? Any recent celebrations or moments of joy that can be highlighted? If appropriate, it may be possible to reference them in a general way in the sermon.

5. *What are the political, cultural, and social dynamics that shape our hearing and interpretation of the text today?* As with question 1, this question can also be emotionally charged and could result in backlash if a guest preacher or supply preacher hasn't handled these issues with care. One way to gauge what you can say—and how you can say it—is to ask the settled pastor if there are any political, cultural, or social dynamics within the church that you should be aware of as you're crafting your sermon.

   Caution: Sometimes the settled pastor does not know their congregation as well as you might think. For example, Leah was once invited to supply preach for a congregation and was assured that they would be open to hearing a sermon that addressed contemporary issues. However, it turned out that there were some in the church who took offense at the mere mention of certain topics, which resulted in blowback both for Leah and for the settled pastor. Sometimes the guest preacher can be a lightning rod for unresolved issues and feelings that the congregation has not processed in a healthy way.

Best practice: Avoid "trigger words" that might unnecessarily cause a hostile reaction. For example, talking about politicians by name in a sermon is usually best avoided. Also, as Leah has discovered in her research, certain "buzz words" such as *capitalism, climate change*, and *guns* can cause a knee-jerk reaction for some listeners. For guest preachers and supply preachers, it may be better to address more general biblical themes such as grace, forgiveness, or prayer and to use stories and illustrations that are more neutral so as to avoid being unnecessarily provocative. This doesn't mean you have to deliver a milquetoast sermon. It simply means being strategic about what you say and how you say it.

Glossary

Anemic verbs: actions words that are vague, weak, or flaccid; examples include words such as *explain, share, tell,* which are about mere intellectual knowledge rather than compelling action; both Central Purpose statements and sermons should avoid the use of anemic verbs; see also Vigorous verbs (Ch. 16, Appendix J)

Anthropological claims: sentences that make claims about who human beings are as creations of God and, as such, what they are to believe or do; distinguished from Theological Claims (about God) and ecclesiological claims (about the church); anthropological claims have human beings as the subject of the sentence; commands are "hidden" anthropological claims (Ch. 9, Appendix F)

Argument: a series of reasons, facts, or statements that make a case for a point of view or particular claim; in Scripture or a sermon, an argument is not meant in the sense of disagreement but in terms of persuading through making points to convince the reader or listener (Ch. 3)

Asynchronous worship: an online worship service that is either pre-recorded, edited together, and made available as a complete video, or is recorded in real time (either through live stream or videoconferencing) and made available for later viewing; see also, Synchronous worship (Ch. 26)

Authenticity: the quality of a preacher that is characterized by congruence between what they say and how they act; when a preacher is authentic in the pulpit, this allows them to be fully present to their own selves, to God's Word, and to the congregation; see also Presence (Ch. 25)

Bookend: a technique for beginning and ending a sermon wherein the same idea, phrase, image, verse of a hymn, metaphor, character, or story is included at both the start and finish of the sermon (Ch. 22)

Central Claim: the main point of the sermon that should mean something for the congregation, the community, and/or God's Creation; the primary assertion of the sermon—in *one* sentence that states the message of the sermon; the Central Claim conveys both the message of the biblical passage and its implication for one's preaching context; the Central Claim is formed from the Central Question and the Theological Claim of the biblical passage; the Central Claim needs to mention God, Jesus Christ, and/or the Holy Spirit and say something substantive about their nature, character, or actions, and it needs to make an explicit connection between the content of the biblical text and the preaching context (Chs. 14–15, Appendix I)

Central Purpose: a statement that articulates where you want the sermon—and the congregation—to arrive and why you want them to be there (the "so that"); the Central Purpose is the primary goal of the sermon—stated in *one* sentence; the Central Purpose succinctly states what you want the sermon to do or accomplish in and for the listeners as well as the reason for, or outcome of, this intention; the Central Purpose is made up of: 1) the Central Question that you derived from exegeting the text and your preaching context and 2) the Central Claim, which contains the primary assertion of the sermon (Chs. 16–17, Appendix J)

Central Question: the compelling inquiry for the sermon; in *one* sentence, it asks the question that is at the heart of one's biblical exegesis of a passage and one's preaching context; informing the Central Question is the basic inquiry: "Why does this matter?"; the Central Question is like the "engine" of the sermon, providing the intellectual, emotional, and spiritual energy (Chs. 12 and 13, Appendix H)

Claim: an assertion that one posits as true, accurate, and genuine; a claim says something about the ontological nature of the subject, its being, its essence; claims are to be distinguished from observations, descriptions, opinions, and facts; see also Theological Claim, Anthropological claim, Ecclesiological claim, Central Claim (Ch. 8)

Coherence: in preaching, the quality of a sermon in which the parts hold together and are in alignment with one's exegesis and Theological Claims as well as with the Central Question, Central Claim, and Central Purpose (Ch. 18)

Contemporary Exigence and Response: in biblical studies, Contemporary Exigence seeks creative analogies between the ancient situations the texts addressed and the world that we live in; Contemporary Response looks to how preachers can draw on the Theological Response in the biblical text to address those analogous issues in their churches or society (Ch. 5)

Context: the environment or setting; in biblical exegesis, determining context means considering the historical factors that give rise to, or are addressed by, the scriptural passage; in preaching, context means that the sermon is crafted for a particular time and a particular congregation and takes into consideration the interrelatedness of individual, communal, and societal issues, as well as with God's Creation (Ch. 12)

Deductive sermon: preaching that is structured according to deductive logic wherein the claim is made at or near the beginning of the sermon; in contrast with inductive sermons, deductive sermons make a claim and back it up with evidence instead of gathering evidence and building toward a claim; see also Inductive sermons (Ch. 20)

Ecclesiological claim: a sentence that makes a claim about the growth or nature of the church as the body of Christ; while the church has learned much from the Hebrew Bible about what it means to be a people of God, we are using the term "ecclesiology" to refer to the Christian church; distinguished from anthropological claims (about humans) and Theological Claims (about God) (Ch. 9)

Eisegesis: imposing the reader's own meaning on the text instead of drawing out the meaning from the text on its own terms; imposing an interpretation that is driven by an ideological agenda or bias; the opposite of eisegesis is *exegesis* (Ch. 2)

Embodiment: the use of the physical self in preaching; the act of bringing one's body into the event of the sermon in order to perform and concretize one's proclamation (Chs. 25, 26)

Exegesis: the process of determining what the biblical text meant in its original context, or what the specific instruction was, what the underlying theological support for the instruction is, and what that meant for the original recipients; involves discerning the presenting issue and what cultural, political, and religious matters gave rise to the text; the opposite of exegesis is *eisegesis* (Chs. 1, 2, 3)

Exigence: a condition that needs to be addressed or demands attention; in biblical studies, exigence is the need, desire, condition, or concern that led the author to write about what a particular text contains; in sermon preparation, the preacher will consider the exigence of individuals, the congregation, the community, society, or Creation when bringing the biblical text into conversation with their context (Chs. 5, 12)

Genre: in the Bible, a genre is a type of writing with socially agreed-upon conventions developed over time, such as letters, histories, biographies, or apocalyptic; an important step to understanding a biblical text is determining what type of genre it is (Chs. 1, 2, 3)

"Glory standard": in crafting a sermon, a means by which to evaluate the appropriateness of a sermon illustration using the following criteria: 1) contributes to an understanding of the biblical text or the context of the listeners, 2) illuminates some aspect of who God is or what God does, and 3) supports or makes clear the Central Question, Central Claim, or Central Purpose (Ch. 19)

Hermeneutics: the study of interpretation; in biblical studies, hermeneutics is the study of how we determine the meaning of a text; also refers to the lens through which we interpret a text, for example, historical critical, feminist, womanist, and so on (Ch. 1)

Historical-critical method: a process of interpreting the meaning of a biblical passage that investigates the origins of the text in order to understand what was happening at the time it was written so that readers can take the text on its own terms; this method is distinct from reader-response or perspective-explicit interpretations (Chs. 2, 3)

Homiletics: the study and art of preaching; the word comes from the term "homily," which is a short sermon; those who study and teach preaching are called "homileticians" (Introduction)

Illustration: in preaching, an illustration is a word, image, or story that illuminates and makes clear the biblical text and the theological concepts the preacher wants to convey; illustrations in sermons help to illuminate the message, bring the Word of God to life, and connect with listeners; sermon illustrations should meet the "glory standard": that which gives glory to God or illustrates something about who God is or what God does; see also "Glory standard" (Ch. 18)

Image: a picture, either tangible or in one's mind, that is the likeness or representation of something; in preaching, images are word pictures that help listeners conceive of the character and nature of God, the stories of God's people, and the vision of how we are called to live in the world in light of our faith (Ch. 19)

Imagination: the capacity to form concepts or images in one's mind that are not immediately present; this mental faculty enables us to create pictures in our minds, solve problems, create art, music, poetry, and, for preachers, engaging sermons; see also Theological imagination (Ch. 18)

Inductive sermons: preaching that is structured according to inductive logic wherein the claim is not immediately evident but is placed later in the sermon; in contrast with deductive sermons, inductive sermons gather evidence and build toward a claim, rather than making a claim at the beginning and backing it up with evidence; see also Deductive sermons (Ch. 20)

Intersectionality: the ways in which multiple kinds of identities intersect, impinge upon, complexify, and co-inform one another; differing kinds of privilege and disadvantage are complicated by the ways in which things such as race, ethnicity, gender, sexuality, disability, country of origin, economic status, and language are interrelated (Ch. 4)

Lectio divina: literally, "divine reading"; a method of engaging Scripture through prayer and meditation (Ch. 18)

Lectionary: a collection of selected readings from the Bible; examples include the *Revised Common Lectionary*, the *Narrative Lectionary*, the *Season of Creation*, the *African American Lectionary*, the *Women's Lectionary*, and several fourth-year lectionaries (Ch. 6)

Literalism: interpreting the Bible literally rather than using historical-critical methods, literary criticism, or metaphorical understandings of the text; note that even those who claim to read the Bible literally are still using an interpretive method and do not actually read the entire Bible literally; note also that even mainline preachers choose to interpret some texts literally (Ch. 1)

Literary analysis: a way to interpret Scripture by examining the types, forms, and structures of the text; includes genre criticism, form criticism, tradition criticism, source criticism, redaction criticism, rhetorical criticism, and narrative criticism (Chs. 2, 3)

Literary Exigence and Response: in biblical studies, Literary Exigence asks what has happened in the flow of the written document that leads to the discussion in the passage under consideration; Literary Response addresses the matter that the Literary Exigence raises (Ch. 5)

Metaphor: a figure of speech in which two (or more) words are put together in a tension of similarity and dissimilarity, for example, war is a chess game (war both is and is not like a game of chess); analogies between words stress the similarity of the words, while metaphors preserve a tension; biblical metaphors often lose that tension when we use them exclusively, such as, God the Father; the Bible is filled with metaphors that attempt to say something about the ultimately inexpressible nature of God; all language to describe God is metaphorical and not intended to be literal descriptions of God (Ch. 8)

Occasional Exigence and Response: in biblical studies, Occasional Exigence is the specific historical things that were going on for believers at that time that are being addressed; what is happening "on the ground" for the community that leads the author to take up the topic in the passage; the Occasional Response is how the author reacts to that exigence and what they recommend readers do or believe (Ch. 5)

Performance: in preaching, performance is the act of speaking and embodying the sermon; effective sermon performance involves a congruence between theology, expression, the use of the body, authenticity, and presence (Ch. 25)

Pericope: a set of verses from a book of the Bible that forms one coherent unit or thought; literally means "cutting around"; a pericope is a reading used for preaching or worship; a group of pericopes for any given Sunday make up a lectionary; see also Lectionary (Chs. 2, 5, 6)

Perspective-explicit interpretations: ways of reading the Bible that recognize, highlight, and take advantage of the observations and reactions that come when readers listen from various social locations, identities, ideologies, and hermeneutical lenses; some examples include Latin American Liberation, Feminist, African American, Womanist, Mujerista, Post-colonial, Asian American, Queer, Ecological, and Disability readings (Ch. 4)

Preaching: the proclamation of the good news of salvation in Jesus Christ; *preach* comes from the Latin word *praedicare*, which means to speak in front of or to announce; to preach means to deliver a sermon (Introduction)

Presence: in preaching, the state of being attentive, open, centered, and poised (Ch. 25)

Resonance: in preaching, a sermon illustration that activates the listeners' hearts and minds, enabling an experience of theological imagination and reverberating with authenticity; see also Salience (Ch. 18)

Salience: in preaching, a sermon illustration that grabs the listeners' attention, speaks to the heart, helps create understanding through theological imagination, or elucidates a biblical story or teaching; see also Resonance (Ch. 18)

Sense lines: a type of manuscript arrangement that formats the text with narrow widths and wider margins, inserting line breaks according to natural pauses and thought units instead of margin-to-margin formatting of the traditional paragraph; resembling poetry, each full sentence starts at the left edge with each subsequent thought unit indented and "stacked" underneath; sense lines allow the eye to follow a downward stream of vision to help the reader know how to phrase each thought unit as well as when to pause (Ch. 23)

Sermon: a religious address or exhortation; the written or oral event of preaching; based on the Latin word *sermo*, which means speech or conversation; a sermon links together the four sources of authority for preaching: Scripture, Tradition, Experience, and Reason, what are commonly known as the Wesleyan Quadrilateral; a sermon needs to say something about who God is, what God does, and what this means for believers, a congregation, a community, society, and God's Creation (Introduction)

Sermon delivery format: the layout of the sermon for delivery, whether full manuscript, extended or brief outline, note cards or half sheets, electronic handheld device, teleprompter, or without notes (Ch. 23)

Sermon form: the shape and structure of a sermon as determined by the ways in which the parts are arranged and organized; basic forms covered in this book include Four Pages, Motion Pictures, Homiletical Plot, and Expository or Puritan Plain Style (Ch. 20, Appendix L)

Symbol: physical objects or visual representations that take on meaning beyond their immediate properties and point to something beyond themselves (Ch. 19)

Synchronous worship: an online worship service where participants are required to participate at a specific day and time and on a specific link or website in which the content is being offered; congregations that conduct worship via live stream offer the service in real time and simulcast it over a social media platform or on the church's website; synchronous worship services can also be recorded for later viewing, thus adding an asynchronous element; see also Asynchronous worship (Ch. 26)

Systemic sin: the values and practices that manifest in the economic, social, and political systems of the world that violate the will of God; examples include racism, patriarchy, and heteronormativity, each of which oppress vulnerable or historically marginalized peoples (Ch. 4)

Theological Claims: assertions about the nature of God (including Jesus Christ and the Holy Spirit) and God's work in the world; Theological Claims in sermons will name God (or Jesus Christ or the Holy Spirit) as the subject of the sentence and then name an attribute or action of God in the predicate of the sentence; distinguished from anthropological claims (about humans) and ecclesiological claims (about the church) (Chs. 8, 9)

Explicit Theological Claim: a sentence that clearly names the nature or actions of God, Jesus, or the Holy Spirit; in an explicit Theological Claim, God, Jesus Christ, or the Holy Spirit is the subject of the sentence; an explicit Theological Claim is plainly expressed and direct; distinguished from implicit Theological Claims (Ch. 9)

Implicit Theological Claim: a sentence that suggests something about God, Jesus Christ, or the Holy Spirit but has as its primary focus a different subject for the sentence; implicit Theological Claims usually are derived from either *anthropological* or *ecclesiological* claims; implicit claims are indirect so the Theological Claim must be inferred (Ch. 9)

Theological Exigence and Response: in biblical studies, the Theological Exigence is the theological question or issue that the Occasional problem or issue raised; the Theological Response is what the author says that this theological framing shows about why the readers should act in a particular way or what they should believe in the face of the issue(s) raised (Ch. 5)

Theological imagination: the capacity to be inspired and guided by God's mysterious Spirit, which gives us the capability to envision God's Realm and how we might be partners in co-creating it (Chs. 8, 18)

Theology: the study of God; "God talk"; the word can stand for the whole field of theology and its subdisciplines or refer to a specific doctrine that considers the nature and actions of God (Ch. 8, Appendix D)

Throughline: a writing technique that refers to the flow of the plotline; applied to sermons, the throughline is the focus or theme that helps stitch the sermon together; throughlines can work behind the scenes or be noticeable within the sermon itself (Ch. 22)

Vigorous verbs: action words that are energetic, robust, and dynamic; examples include words such as *inspire, surprise,* and *transform;* the Central Purpose statement, as well as the sermon, should use vigorous verbs; see also Anemic verbs (Ch. 16, Appendix J)

Voice: a) sound produced by means of lungs, larynx, vocal cords, and mouth; in preaching, the voice requires preparation and care to ensure quality of sound production; b) metaphorically, voice is the preacher's unique way of communicating based on their preaching identity; their tradition, cultural, and denominational context; and their style; c) the right to express oneself openly (Ch. 24)

Wesleyan Quadrilateral: a method of determining how God reveals Godself through four sources—Scripture, Tradition, Reason, and Experience; a means by which to describe four sources of authority for theology and doctrine; though derived from the work of John Wesley, this was not a method he invented per se (Chs. 1, 8)

Bibliography

Alcántara, Jared E. *The Practices of Christian Preaching: Essentials for Effective Proclamation*. Grand Rapids, MI: Baker Academic, 2019.

Allen Jr., O. Wesley. *Determining the Form: Structures for Preaching*. In Elements of Preaching Series. O. Wesley Allen, ed. Minneapolis, MN: Fortress Press, 2008.

Allen Jr., O. Wesley, and Carrie La Ferle. *Preaching and the Thirty-Second Commercial: Lessons from Advertising for the Pulpit*. Louisville, KY: Westminster John Knox, 2021.

Allen, Ronald J., ed. *Preaching the Manifold Grace of God, Volume 1: Theologies of Preaching in Historical Theological Families*. Eugene, OR: Cascade, 2022.

———. *Preaching the Manifold Grace of God, Volume 2: Theologies of Preaching in the Early Twenty-First Century*. Eugene, OR: Cascade, 2022.

———. *Preaching the Topical Sermon*. Louisville, KY: Westminster John Knox Press, 1992.

———. *Patterns of Preaching: A Sermon Sampler*. St. Louis, MO: Chalice, 1998.

———. *Preaching: An Essential Guide*. Nashville: Abingdon Press, 2002.

Allen, Ronald J., and O. Wesley Allen Jr. *The Sermon without End: A Conversational Approach to Preaching*. Nashville: Abingdon Press, 2015.

Allen, Ronald J., John S. McClure, and O. Wesley Allen Jr., eds. *Under the Oak Tree: The Church as Community of Conversation in a Conflicted and Pluralistic World*. Eugene, OR: Cascade, 2013.

Andrews, Dale P. *Practical Theology for Black Churches: Bridging Black Theology and African American Folk Religion*. Louisville, KY: Westminster John Knox, 2002.

Askew, Emily, and O. Wesley Allen Jr. *Beyond Heterosexism in the Pulpit*. Eugene, OR: Cascade, 2015.

Black, Kathy. *A Healing Homiletic: Preaching and Disability*. Nashville: Abingdon Press, 1996.

Bogart, Anne. *And Then, You Act: Making Art in an Unpredictable World*. New York: Routledge, 2007.

Bonhoeffer, Dietrich. *The Cost of Discipleship*. New York: Touchstone, 1995 (previously published: New York: Macmillan, 1959).

Boring, M. Eugene. *Mark: A Commentary*. New Testament Library. Louisville: Westminster John Knox, 2014.

Bradshaw, Paul. *New Westminster Dictionary of Liturgy and Worship*. Louisville: Westminster John Knox, 2002.

Brown, Sally A., and Luke A. Powery. *Ways of the Word: Learning to Preach for Your Time and Place*. Minneapolis, MN: Fortress Press, 2016.

Brown, Teresa L. Fry. *Delivering the Sermon*. In Elements of Preaching Series. O. Wesley Allen Jr., ed. Minneapolis, MN: Fortress Press, 2008.

Buttrick, David. *Homiletic: Moves and Structures*. Philadelphia: Fortress Press, 1987.

Carter, Warren. *Mark*. Wisdom Commentary. Collegeville, MN: Liturgical Press, 2019.

Childers, Jana. *Performing the Word: Preaching as Theatre*. Nashville: Abingdon Press, 1998.

Childers, Jana, and Clayton J. Schmit. *Performance in Preaching: Bringing the Sermon to Life.* Grand Rapids, MI: Baker Academic, 2009.

Clader, Linda L. *Voicing the Vision: Imagination and Prophetic Preaching.* Harrisburg, PA: Morehouse, 2003.

Cone, James. *A Black Theology of Liberation.* Maryknoll: Orbis, 1986.

Craddock, Fred B. *As One without Authority*, third edition. Nashville: Abingdon Press, 1979.

Cressman, Lisa. *Backstory Preaching: Integrating Life, Spirituality, and Craft.* Collegeville, MN: Liturgical, 2018.

———. *The Gospel People Don't Want to Hear: Preaching Challenging Messages.* Minneapolis, MN: Fortress Press, 2020.

Eaton, John. *The Psalms.* New York: Continuum, 2005.

Gafney, Wilda C. *A Women's Lectionary for the Whole Church.* New York: Church Publishing, 2021.

Gibson, Scott M. *Preaching for Special Services.* Grand Rapids, MI: Baker Books, 2001.

Gilbert, Kenyatta. *The Journey and Promise of African American Preaching.* Minneapolis, MN: Fortress Press, 2011.

Helsel, Carolyn. *Anxious to Talk about It: Helping White Christians Talk Faithfully about Racism.* St. Louis, MO: Chalice, 2017.

———. *Preaching about Racism: A Guide for Faith Leaders.* St. Louis, MO: Chalice Press, 2018.

Hilkert, Mary Catherine. *Naming Grace: Preaching and the Sacramental Imagination.* New York: Continuum, 2003.

Johnston, Graham. *Preaching to a Postmodern World: A Guide to Reaching Twenty-First Century Listeners.* Grand Rapids, MI: Baker Books, 2001.

Jones, Kirk Byron. *The Jazz of Preaching: How to Preach with Great Freedom and Joy.* Nashville: Abingdon Press, 2004.

Jones, Robert P. *White Too Long: The Legacy of White Supremacy in American Christianity.* New York: Simon & Shuster, 2020.

Keck, Leander E. *The Bible in the Pulpit: The Renewal of Biblical Preaching.* Nashville: Abingdon Press, 1978.

Kim, Eunjoo Mary. *Christian Preaching and Worship in Multicultural Contexts: A Practical Theological Approach.* Collegeville, MN: Liturgical, 2017.

Kim-Cragg, HyeRan. *Postcolonial Preaching: Creating a Ripple Effect.* Lanham, MD: Lexington Books, 2021.

LaRue, Cleophus J. *The Heart of Black Preaching.* Louisville, KY: Westminster John Knox, 2000.

Lewis, Karoline M. *A Lay Preacher's Guide: How to Craft a Faithful Sermon.* Minneapolis, MN: Fortress Press, 2020.

———. *She: Five Keys to Unlock the Power of Women in Ministry.* Nashville: Abingdon Press, 2016.

Long, Thomas. *The Witness of Preaching*, third edition. Louisville, KY: Westminster John Knox, 2016.

———. *Accompany Them with Singing: The Christian Funeral.* Louisville, KY: Westminster John Knox, 2009.

———. *Preaching and the Literary Forms of the Bible.* Philadelphia: Fortress Press, 1989.

Lord, Jennifer L. *Finding Language and Imagery.* In Elements of Preaching Series, edited by O. Wesley Allen Jr. Minneapolis, MN: Fortress Press, 2010.

Lowry, Eugene. *The Homiletical Plot, Expanded Edition: The Sermon as Narrative Art Form.* Louisville, KY: Westminster John Knox, 2000.

McClure, John S. *The Roundtable Pulpit: Where Leadership and Preaching Meet.* Nashville: Abingdon Press, 1995.

———. *Other-Wise Preaching: A Postmodern Ethic for Homiletics.* St. Louis, MO: Chalice Press, 2001.

———. *Preaching Words: 144 Key Terms in Homiletics.* Louisville, KY: Westminster John Knox, 2007.

———. *Mashup Religion: Pop Music and Theological Invention.* Waco, TX: Baylor University, 2011.

McFague, Sallie. *Metaphorical Theology: Models of God in Religious Language.* Philadelphia: Fortress Press, 1982.

———. *The Body of God: An Ecological Theology.* Minneapolis, MN: Fortress Press, 1993.

McKenzie, Alyce M. *Novel Preaching: Tips from Great Writers on Crafting Creative Sermons.* Louisville, KY: Westminster John Knox, 2010.

———. *Making a Scene in the Pulpit: Vivid Preaching for Visual Listeners.* Louisville, KY: Presbyterian, 2018.

McMickle, Marvin A. *Shaping the Claim: Moving from Text to Sermon.* In Elements of Preaching Series. O. Wesley Allen Jr., editor. Minneapolis, MN: Fortress Press, 2008.

Mitchell, Henry H. *Black Preaching: The Recovery of a Powerful Art.* Nashville: Abingdon Press, 1990.

Myers, Jacob D. *Stand-Up Preaching: Homiletical Insights from Contemporary Comedians.* Eugene, OR: Cascade Books, 2022.

Rose, Lucy Atkinson. *Sharing the Word: Preaching in the Roundtable Church.* Louisville, KY: Westminster John Knox, 1997.

Schade, Leah D. *Creation-Crisis Preaching: Ecology, Theology, and the Pulpit.* St. Louis, MO: Chalice Press, 2015.

———. *Preaching in the Purple Zone: Ministry in the Red-Blue Divide.* Lanham, MD: Rowman & Littlefield, 2019.

Schade, Leah D., and Jerry L. Sumney. *Apocalypse When? Interpreting and Preaching Apocalyptic Texts.* Eugene, OR: Cascade, 2020.

Schmitz, Barbara G. *The Life of Christ and the Death of a Loved One: Crafting the Funeral Sermon.* Lima, OH: CSS Publishing Company, 1995.

Sheppard, Phillis-Isabella, Dawn Ottoni-Wilhelm, and Ronald J. Allen, editors. *Preaching Prophetic Care: Building Bridges to Justice, Essays in Honor of Dale P. Andrews.* Eugene, OR: Pickwick Publications, Wipf & Stock, 2018.

Smith, Christine M., ed. *Preaching Justice: Ethnic and Cultural Perspectives.* Eugene, OR: Wipf and Stock, 1998.

Snider, Phil, ed. *Preaching as Resistance: Voices of Hope, Justice, & Solidarity.* St. Louis, MO: Chalice, 2018.

Stookey, Laurence Hull. *Let the Whole Church Say Amen! A Guide for Those Who Pray in Public.* Nashville: Abingdon Press, 2001.

Sumney, Jerry L. *The Bible: An Introduction*, third edition. Minneapolis, MN: Fortress Press, 2021.

———. *The Politics of Faith: The Bible, Government, and Public Policy.* Minneapolis, MN: Fortress Press, 2020.
Thomas, Frank A. *How to Preach a Dangerous Sermon.* Nashville: Abingdon Press, 2018.
———. *Surviving a Dangerous Sermon.* Nashville: Abingdon Press, 2020.
———. *The God of the Dangerous Sermon.* Nashville: Abingdon Press, 2021.
Thompson, Lisa L. *Ingenuity: Preaching as an Outsider.* Nashville: Abingdon Press, 2018.
Tisdale, Leonora Tubbs. *Preaching as Local Theology and Folk Art.* Minneapolis, MN: Fortress Press, 1997.
———. *Prophetic Preaching: A Pastoral Approach.* Louisville, KY: Westminster John Knox, 2010.
Troeger, Thomas H. *Imagining a Sermon.* Nashville: Abingdon Press, 1990.
Troeger, Thomas H., and Leonora Tubbs Tisdale. *A Sermon Workbook: Exercises in the Art and Craft of Preaching.* Nashville: Abingdon Press, 2013.
Voelz, Richard W. *Preaching to Teach: Inspire People to Think and Act.* Nashville: Abingdon Press, 2019.
Ward, Richard. *Speaking from the Heart: Preaching with Passion.* Nashville: Abingdon Press, 1992.
———. *Speaking of the Holy: The Art of Communication in Preaching.* St. Louis, MO: Chalice, 2001.
Webb, Joseph M. *Preaching Without Notes.* Nashville: Abingdon Press, 2001.
White, James F. *Introduction to Worship,* third edition. Nashville: Abingdon Press, 2001.
Wilson, Paul Scott. *The Practice of Preaching,* revised edition. Nashville: Abingdon Press, 2007.
———. *Setting Words on Fire: Putting God in the Center of the Sermon.* Nashville: Abingdon Press, 2008.
———. *The Four Pages of the Sermon, Revised and Updated: A Guide to Biblical Preaching.* Nashville: Abingdon Press, 2018.
Wilson, Paul Scott, ed. *New Interpreter's Handbook of Preaching.* Nashville: Abingdon Press, 2008.
Wiseman, Karyn L. *I Refuse to Preach a Boring Sermon! Engaging the 21st Century Listener.* Cleveland, OH: Pilgrim Press, 2013.
Yang, Sunggu A. *Arts and Preaching: An Aesthetic Homiletic for the Twenty-first Century.* Eugene, OR: Cascade Books, 2021.

Scriptural Index

HEBREW SCRIPTURES (OLD TESTAMENT)

CHRISTIAN SCRIPTURES (NEW TESTAMENT)

Topical Index

Note: Terms in glossary and/or Theological Categories (Appendix D) are in bold along with page number of definition.

About the Authors

Leah D. Schade is Associate Professor of Preaching and Worship at Lexington Theological Seminary in Lexington, Kentucky. An ordained Lutheran minister (ELCA) for more than twenty years, Leah earned both her MDiv and PhD degrees from the Lutheran Theological Seminary at Philadelphia (now United Lutheran Seminary). She has pastored congregations in suburban, urban, and rural contexts. Her book *Preaching in the Purple Zone: Ministry in the Red-Blue Divide* (Rowman & Littlefield, 2019) explores how clergy and congregations can address controversial social issues using nonpartisan, biblically centered approaches and deliberative dialogue. She is also the author of *Creation-Crisis Preaching: Ecology, Theology, and the Pulpit* (2015), as well as *For the Beauty of the Earth*, a Creation-centered Lenten devotional (2019). She is co-editor and author with Margaret Bullitt-Jonas of *Rooted and Rising: Voices of Courage in a Time of Climate Crisis* (Rowman & Littlefield, 2019) and co-author with Jerry Sumney of *Apocalypse When? A Guide to Interpreting and Preaching Apocalyptic Texts* (2020). She is also the EcoPreacher blogger for Patheos. She has been a featured speaker for the Festival of Homiletics, leads workshops and retreats, and keynotes events throughout the country. She was the director of a Wabash grant exploring the use of deliberative dialogue in congregations and theological education and is part of a research exchange with the Kettering Foundation studying the role of religious organizations in democratic community building. Dr. Schade also conducts longitudinal research about ministry, preaching, and social issues and has surveyed nearly three thousand clergy and a thousand laity since 2017. She was elected to serve as the President of the Academy of Homiletics in 2024.

Jerry L. Sumney is Professor of Biblical Studies at Lexington Theological Seminary. He specializes in the historical-critical method of biblical interpretation and has written more than ten books on the Bible and New Testament texts. He is a member of the Society of Biblical Literature and is past president for the Southeastern Region of the Society. He was elected to membership in the Studiorum Novi Testamenti Societas (SNTS) in 2005. His books include: *The Bible: An Introduction* (2010; third edition, 2021); *The Politics of Faith: The Bible, Government, and Public Policy* (2020); *Steward of God's Mysteries: Paul and Early Church Tradition* (2017); *Paul: Apostle and Fellow Traveler* (2014); *Colossians; A Commentary*, New Testament Library Series (2008); *Philippians, A Handbook for Second-Year Greek Students* (2007); *Servants of Satan, False Brothers, and Other Pauline Opponents* (1999); *Preaching Apocalyptic Texts* (co-authored with Larry Paul Jones; 1999), and *Identifying Paul's Opponents* (1990). He is editor of *Reading Paul's Letter to Romans* (2012); *The Order of the Ministry; Equipping the Saints* (2002), co-editor of *Theology and Ethics in Paul and His Interpreters* (1996) and *Paul and Pathos* (2001), and senior New Testament editor for *Oxford Encyclopedia of Bible and Theology* (2015). He also has written more than forty articles in journals and books and contributed entries to the *New Interpreter's Dictionary of the Bible*, the *Dictionary of the Later New Testament and Its Developments*, and the *Dictionary of Scripture and Ethics*. Jerry has presented papers at regional, national, and international academic conferences. He has also led numerous workshops for elders and deacons as well as Bible study workshops and series, including in the Lay School of Theology at Lexington Theological Seminary and for the school for licensed ministers sponsored by the Kentucky region of the Christian Church. He is the regular teacher of an adult Sunday School class in his home church.

Emily Askew is Professor Emeritus of Theology at Lexington Theological Seminary. She earned her Bachelor of Arts degree in Philosophy from Smith College in 1983, graduating cum laude. She received her Master of Arts degree from the University of Northern Iowa in 1991 with a specialty in Mental Health Counseling. After working as a mental health professional for several years, Dr. Askew was captivated by the theological dimensions of the human experience and returned to school, receiving her PhD in theology from Vanderbilt University in 2004. As a Fulbright scholar, in the summer of 2006, she studied the challenges of Muslim immigration in France and Germany. A member of the LGBTQI community, she co-authored, with O. Wesley Allen, *Beyond Heterosexism in the Pulpit* (2014) to help preachers to learn to be more inclusive of LGBTQIA+ people in preaching and teaching in the church. She also writes on issues of immigration, and her courses include an immersion experience on the US/Mexico border in Tucson/Sonora. She also teaches courses on theology and domestic violence, African American and womanist theologies, and Queer theology.

Made in the USA
Columbia, SC
19 April 2024